Running Microsoft® Internet Information Server

Matt Powell
Leonid Braginski

Microsoft

PUBLISHED BY
Microsoft Press
A Division of Microsoft Corporation
One Microsoft Way
Redmond, Washington 98052-6399

Library of Congress Cataloging-in-Publication Data
Powell, Matthew.
Running Microsoft Internet Information Server / Matthew Powell, Leonid Braginski.
p. cm.
Includes index.
ISBN 1-57231-585-7
1. Internet (Computer network)--Computer programs. 2. Microsoft Internet information server. 3. Web servers. I. Braginski, Leonid. II. Title.
TK5105.875.I57P695 1998
005.7'13769--dc21 98-22764
CIP

Printed and bound in the United States of America.

4 5 6 7 8 9 QMQM 3 2 1 0 9

Distributed in Canada by Penguin Books Canada Limited.

A CIP catalogue record for this book is available from the British Library.

Microsoft Press books are available through booksellers and distributors worldwide. For further information about international editions, contact your local Microsoft Corporation office or contact Microsoft Press International directly at fax (425) 936-7329. Visit our Web site at mspress.microsoft.com.

Acquisitions Editor: David Clark
Project Editor: Barbara Moreland
Technical Editor: Robert Lyon

To Cindy, who had to work at least as hard as I did running our home while I was writing this book.

— MP

To my aunt and uncle, Lisa and Isaac, who believed in me from the very start. To my mom and dad, Marina and Alexander, sister Zina, and grandpa for forever keeping me in their hearts.

— LB

xiii *Acknowledgments*
xv *Introduction*

Contents

1 **Part One Installing, Configuring, and Using Internet Information Server**

3 **Chapter 1 What Is Internet Information Server?**

4 The HTML File Server
4 CGI Applications
4 ISAPI: Making Internet Server Business Solutions Viable
5 Active Server Pages
6 Internet Information Server 4.0
6 The Future of IIS

9 **Chapter 2 Network Overview**

9 Basic Truths About Networking
11 Client/Server Architecture
12 The Network Layered Approach
15 Seven Layers in the ISO/OSI Model
18 Web Browser and Web Server Architecture
24 Sample Network Configurations

29 **Chapter 3 Exploring the Network Environment**

30 Computer Naming and Address Schemes
37 Network Communication Basics
40 Machine Names and Name Resolution
47 Configuring the Network
52 Getting Connected

■ 55 **Chapter 4**
Web Server Configuration

55 Setup

57 The IIS Hierarchy

59 Configuration Options

■ 89 **Chapter 5**
The Metabase

89 The Metabase Hierarchy

92 Objects in the Metabase Hierarchy

93 Metabase Entries

94 Metabase Properties

96 Manipulating the Metabase

100 Writing Your Own Applications

■ 109 **Chapter 6**
Logging and Monitoring Tools

109 Log Files

122 The Windows NT Event Log

125 Performance Monitor

139 Simple Network Management Protocol

■ 145 **Chapter 7**
Index Server

146 Setting Up Index Server

149 Inside Index Server

155 Query Language

157 Customizing Index Server

177 Administering Index Server

■ 185 **Chapter 8**
Server Add-Ons

185 Site Server Express

204 FrontPage Server Extensions

211 **Chapter 9**
The FTP Server

211 Basic Concepts
213 Installing FTP Server
214 Configuration Options
232 Managing the FTP Server Programmatically

237 **Chapter 10**
News Server

238 Installing the NNTP Service
240 Managing the NNTP Service
256 Managing the NNTP Service Programmatically

259 **Chapter 11**
Mail Server

259 The Internet Mail System
262 IIS Mail Solution: CDO for NTS
266 Installing SMTP
271 Setting Default Domain Properties
285 Creating a Domain

289 **Chapter 12**
Windows NT Security and IIS

289 Security Descriptors and Access Tokens
291 Impersonation
295 Privileges
296 The Big Picture
298 Securing the Desktop
299 Windows NT Services
306 Security and IIS
310 User Authentication and Impersonation
316 Other Mechanisms for Controlling Access
317 An Overview of Security Logic
318 Auditing
321 The FTP Service

■ 323 **Chapter 13**
Secure Communications with SSL

323 Encryption

335 Secure Socket Layer

339 Setting Up IIS for Secure Web Communication

■ 349 **Chapter 14**
Certificate Server

352 Installing Certificate Server

356 Managing Certificate Server

365 Programming and Scripting Interfaces

374 Coordinating Front-End and Back-End Interfaces

■ 379 **Chapter 15**
Advanced Services

379 Microsoft Transaction Server

397 Microsoft Message Queue Server

▲▲▲ 417 **PART TWO**
THE MICROSOFT INTERNET APPLICATION SERVER

■ 419 **Chapter 16**
IIS and Application Architecture

419 Three-Tiered Client/Server Architecture

423 IIS Architecture

424 Script Files

433 Authentication and Impersonation

437 ISAPI Filters

■ 439 **Chapter 17**
ASP Basics

439 Introduction to ASP
442 Manipulating ASP Pages
450 Application, Session, and Page Scopes
455 ASP Built-In Objects
465 Installable Components for ASP
473 Other Components Available from ASP
475 Writing Your Own Components
484 Script Debugging

■ 487 **Chapter 18**
Transactional ASP

487 Transactions
489 The *ObjectContext* Object
492 ASP Transaction Basics
497 Transactions Using ADO from ASP
500 Transacting Components Called from ASP
510 Transactional C/C++ Components

■ 513 **Chapter 19**
Using Microsoft Message Queue Server

514 Messages
520 Transactional Messaging

■ 525 **Chapter 20**
Web Server Applications

525 Common Gateway Interface
536 Internet Server Application Programming Interface

■ 565 **Chapter 21**
ISAPI Filters, Extensions, and Custom Script Interpreters

565 ISAPI Filters
582 Custom Script Interpreters

597 **PART THREE UNDER THE COVERS OF INTERNET INFORMATION SERVER**

599 **Chapter 22 The Hypertext Markup Language (HTML)**

599 Architecture: How Browsers Interpret HTML

611 Client Scripting

615 Objects

617 Dynamic HTML

621 **Chapter 23 The Hypertext Transfer Protocol (HTTP)**

621 An Overview of HTTP

627 HTTP Requests

633 HTTP Responses

640 HTTP Protocol Details

649 **Chapter 24 The File Transfer Protocol (FTP)**

650 FTP Implementation

651 FTP Connection Management

658 FTP in Action: Using the FTP Client

662 More Action: Using the Telnet Client

665 Data Representation

669 **Chapter 25 The Network News Transfer Protocol (NNTP)**

669 Internet News Delivery Systems

675 NNTP Overview

■ 691 **Chapter 26 The Simple Mail Transfer Protocol (SMTP)**

691 SMTP Overview

692 SMTP Implementation

696 Supported Commands

697 Extended SMTP

700 Creating a Mail Transaction

707 Index

Acknowledgments

Although there are only two names on the front cover of this book, we would like to thank the dozens of individuals who contributed directly or indirectly to making our idea a reality. In particular we would like to thank Nick Evans for help and insight on Chapters 7 and 18 and Mike Meserve for his contribution to Chapter 20. Special thanks go out to Barbara Moreland and Lisa Theobold for all the work they performed in managing this project and for their expert abilities at whip cracking. We would also like to thank Robert Lyon for his exceptional feedback and constant responsiveness in editing this book, testing the samples, and coordinating the accompanying CD. Jennifer Harris did a superb job of turning our efforts at writing into coherent, well organized prose. And a sincere thank you goes to the other members of the Microsoft Press team: Elizabeth Hansford, Paula Gorelick, Jack Beaudry, Pamela Buitrago, and Thom Viertler. Thanks also go out to Steve Roeder, who enlightened us on the underpinnings of such items as Event Sinks, and to Don Crouch for his early help and hard work providing the graphical know-how for a sample application that has long since been eliminated from the content of this book—oh well.

On a more personal note, Matt would like to thank those who have stepped up to the plate to cover the various nonwork projects he has let slide during the writing of this book. And finally, Leon wants to extend his personal thanks to the developers of spellcheck and to Matt for his help in putting "a", "an," and "the" in their correct places.

INTRODUCTION

Welcome to *Running Internet Information Server*, a look at one of the most exciting products available today. This book covers it all. It gives you the ins and outs of getting your server installed and running, explains how Microsoft Internet Information Server (IIS) works, shows you what's going on "under the covers" of the product, demonstrates how the many features of IIS can work for you, and tells you how to take full advantage of the capabilities of IIS and of Microsoft Windows.

Running Internet Information Server was written to be useful for a wide audience, from the novice who is setting up his or her first Web server to an experienced application developer who is looking for a way to release all the platform capabilities IIS provides. If this is the first Web server you have installed, we want to help you make that first installation a success. We want you to understand what you are doing at each step, and we want to open your eyes to what is actually possible with a product like IIS. Whether you want to share a few HTML pages with your coworkers on your local network or build a mission critical, client/server solution on your corporate intranet, if you're setting up business on the Web, you will benefit from this book.

We intend for this book to be a thorough and logical resource when read from cover to cover. But we also want it to be an easy-to-use reference for specific questions you might have and to provide you with a good one or two chapter overview of aspects of IIS that your current project might require you to know.

Running Internet Information Server is divided into three sections:

Part I	Installing, Configuring, and Using Internet Information Server
Part II	The Microsoft Internet Application Server
Part III	Under the Covers of Internet Information Server

Part I walks you through the variety of components that make up IIS, explaining how to configure and use each one. In Part II, you will get into the specifics of writing applications. Finally, Part III looks behind the scenes at the protocols supported by IIS: HTML, HTTP, FTP, NNTP, and SMTP.

If you are setting up IIS, you will want to focus on the first section in the book, but you might also want to skip to Chapter 23 to get a thorough understanding of the

HTTP protocol so that you can take full advantage of the options you are configuring on your server. Are you setting up the News Server that comes with IIS? You should definitely read Chapter 10 for all the details about how the News Server works, and you might also want to skip to Chapter 25 to review the NNTP protocol that the News Server uses. Maybe you just want to get a better feel for what IIS is and how it works. In addition to reading the explanations of the protocols in the last section, you might want to read Chapter 16, which covers in detail exactly what IIS does and the platform it provides to its users.

We would also like to encourage you to use this book as a resource for taking you and your Web site to a higher level. If you have written only a few HTML pages, read Chapter 22 to learn how to add some scripting capabilities to your content. If you have a little experience with JavaScript or VBScript that executes on the client's browser, it's easy to go the next step and write some server side script using Active Server Pages; that's covered in Chapter 17. Maybe you have dabbled in server side scripting and have written a fair amount of dynamic content. You might be ready to take the next step toward writing a real Web application that takes advantage of services such as Microsoft Transaction Server or Microsoft Message Queue Server. Chapters 18 and 19 show you how nicely these services meld with the middle-tier environment that IIS provides. Perhaps you want to get the unprecedented performance and the low level control available for Web applications by writing your own ISAPI extension, or maybe you want to get inside IIS and manipulate how it works by writing your own ISAPI filter or script map. Chapters 20 and 21 tell you how.

Much of the knowledge that went into *Running Internet Information Server* came from our work on the Internet Server team in Microsoft's Developer Support organization. This position has given us a unique insight into IIS. We worked with the product team from the product's early stages, learning the new technologies from the source, providing feedback, asking questions and reviewing the documentation, and learning firsthand why the product is designed the way it is, what its capabilities are, and how it is intended to be used. Just as important to our understanding of IIS is the fact that, as part of the support organization, we work with customers who are using IIS every day. We hear their success stories and listen to their questions. Customer input is an invaluable resource that is reflected throughout this book.

The line between the product user and the application developer has never been as blurred as it is with today's Internet-related products. We encourage you to take advantage of this opportunity to develop your own skills, enhance your Web presence, and explore new technologies. Go ahead—take full advantage of the possibilities provided by Internet Information Server.

Part One

Installing, Configuring, and Using Internet Information Server

CHAPTER 1

What Is Internet Information Server?

The title of this chapter poses a question that we were asked quite often during the course of writing this book. Usually the question was raised by friends and relatives who have little to do with computers. Sometimes it was raised by individuals who work with computers but have limited their use to word processing and spreadsheet manipulation. But even some of the most computer-savvy users don't understand what Internet Information Server (IIS) really is, and that's why we're writing this book. This chapter offers a broad picture of IIS and sets the stage for details discussed in the rest of the book.

One way of answering the question is simply to say that IIS is a Web server. For those who are familiar with browsing the Internet, this is a relatively easy idea to grasp. Web servers in their basic form are the holders of Hypertext Markup Language (HTML) files that we can download with our browsers. But there is much more to IIS than its ability to download HTML files. Internet Information Server is the next extension of the Microsoft Windows operating system platform and provides myriad system services for Windows-based applications. Not only is Internet Information Server the best Web server on the market for downloading HTML files, but it also provides the most features and system integration for business applications.

Obviously, you want to get the most out of any software you purchase. With the release of IIS, Microsoft is raising its expectations regarding where Internet technology is headed. In the competitive environment of building Web sites, providing Internet services, and creating Internet and intranet business solutions, those who take advantage of available technology will have a significant advantage over competition that ignores the state of the art. Your business's bottom line might well be at stake, and riding the wave of readily available Internet server technologies is the wisest and easiest solution for making the most of the Internet's ever-increasing capabilities. A look at how Internet servers have evolved should give you a better understanding of how and why this is true, and it should help you understand Microsoft's vision for IIS.

The HTML File Server

Early Web servers had a single task: to send simple HTML files to client browsers. Although there are many good reasons for putting HTML files on a server, the power of client/server computing is certainly not being realized by providing one more mechanism for downloading files from a server. Having HTML content on a server might work well for displaying scanned photos of your dog, but the number of business solutions that can be built on HTML is pretty limited. If you happen to have a company Internet site today that uses strictly HTML, you have some catching up to do.

CGI Applications

The first Internet server applications used the Common Gateway Interface (CGI). CGI is a mechanism that launches an executable file on the server to service a client browser's request. With CGI, the server can generate customized output in response to a client request, and customization is something that simple HTML files do not support. But CGI applications require launching a new process for each request sent to the server. Allocating memory and loading an executable file into memory are relatively lengthy processes for a server. Therefore, if a server receives a large number of requests, it can easily get bogged down in performing the overhead tasks associated with creating a large number of processes and it can spend too little time actually executing the CGI code.

Glossary

process *A running program. On Windows, each process runs in its own memory space.*

ISAPI: Making Internet Server Business Solutions Viable

ISAPI is Microsoft's answer to the limitations of CGI. Application program interfaces (APIs) are sets of external routines used by a program, and they are nothing new. But ISAPI is a relatively new specification that takes Internet server solutions to new heights. Like CGI, ISAPI extensions provide a means for executing code on the server, but ISAPI provides a number of efficiencies lost in CGI. ISAPI extensions are dynamic link libraries (DLLs) instead of executables, so they can be loaded once and the same version of the DLL code can be called again and again. In the same way, a pool of worker threads can be created to handle requests, but as soon as one request is finished, the same thread can be used over again. With ISAPI, it's not necessary to create a new thread (or process) for each request. With

ISAPI and IIS, Microsoft made Web applications a much more viable platform for business applications.

Glossary

dynamic link library *A library of functions that can be loaded and unloaded as needed by an application.*

executable *A file that can be executed to run a program. An executable has the .EXE extension.*

thread *A logical execution unit. A process can have more than one thread running simultaneously.*

worker threads *Usually a pool of threads waiting to handle client requests. Any thread in a pool of worker threads should be able to handle any request.*

Active Server Pages

With IIS version 3.0, Active Server Pages (ASP) were included for the first time. ASP brought the first Microsoft Visual Basic scripting engine to Internet server development, which made Web server application development the easiest it had ever been. With ASP, 30 million developers of Visual Basic programs were given an environment in which they could immediately be productive. And despite the interpreted nature of ASP script, it was still significantly faster than running CGI code.

However, the power of ASP does not rest in how easy it makes server-side development; ASP is powerful because it is the most flexible hosting mechanism for launching custom server controls. Using ASP technology, a business that has already written code to perform its business functions can simply call its components from ASP over the Internet or via an intranet. This allows the business's client/server application to take advantage of all the benefits HTML provides but still execute code that could have been written originally for a Visual Basic front-end application.

As Internet servers offer more and more business application capabilities, businesses are demanding more of the common features required for their client/server applications. When doing business online, you need to be sure that the people with whom you communicate are really who they say they are and that your communications are secure. For that you need a means of authentication and solid security. To better process dynamic applications that require repeated interactions between the client and server to process a single task, you need a way to keep the channel of communication open—a means of preserving what is referred to as *user state* between Hypertext Transfer Protocol (HTTP) requests. These are some of the issues addressed by features of IIS 4.0.

Internet Information Server 4.0

With Internet Information Server 4.0, Microsoft has taken the next step in making the Internet server the platform of choice for business applications. Transaction concepts that had previously been limited to mainframes and high-powered databases are now easily available to the ASP programmer. IIS not only makes transaction concepts like commits and aborts extremely easy to implement, but the IIS server itself is actually built right on top of Microsoft Transaction Server (MTS). The request/response nature of HTTP communication fits the transactional paradigm extremely well, so IIS uses the abilities of MTS to efficiently pull together and manage Web server components to provide unparalleled Web server performance. Another leap forward is the integration of Microsoft Message Queue Server into IIS so that processing tasks can be queued and then submitted together as a "batch" type of execution. If you had to develop both message queuing and transactional processing on your own, they could potentially take months or years to complete. With IIS, these features are provided and can easily be taken advantage of in your Internet and intranet applications.

Glossary

Microsoft Transaction Server *The Microsoft service that provides transactional support of components—mainly database transaction support, but also transactional resources as well as packages of components.*

Microsoft Message Queue Server *The Microsoft service that provides a mechanism for the delayed processing of certain tasks. The tasks are added to a queue and can then be pulled out of the queue when desired.*

The Future of IIS

As IIS has evolved, it has provided more and more seamless integration with Microsoft Windows NT system components. Whether through the use of low-level file transfer mechanisms, integration with Windows NT security, or intrinsic access to transaction and message queuing resources, IIS is becoming a more integral part of the Windows NT operating system. And Microsoft has already announced plans to take this integration to the next step.

Microsoft's Component Object Model (COM) specifications are a major factor in this evolution. COM specifies the way external software components can be used with existing programs. With the advent of COM+ (the enhanced Component Object Model), Distributed COM (which allows COM components to communicate across networks) will run over Internet-based resources such as HTTP and Secure Sockets Layer (SSL), which are implemented by IIS.

Ultimately, IIS will be considered another protocol on which system services will be able to run. IIS completes the transformation of Internet servers from simple applications that sit on top of the operating system to system service providers that are used for key operating system capabilities.

Part I will discuss some concepts and details about computer networks, Internets, and intranets. You will examine details of setting up and configuring your TCP/IP environment, installing and configuring IIS, and a number of other services and features that are available to you. The second part of this book will focus on the powerful application environment IIS has become and will discuss how you can take advantage of it. Finally, the book will take a step back to study the details of the underlying protocols and specifications that allow the Web environment to work for you.

CHAPTER 2

Network Overview

A very bright, young professional, who had recently completed his master's degree in computer science, was well versed in network theory and applied the concepts in his daily work. One day he spent 45 minutes composing an e-mail message about the conceptual limitations regarding how many MACs (media access controllers), also known as network cards, can be plugged into a single network server. Unfortunately, his erudite essay was written in response to a person who asked, "How many Macs can attach to a single server?" To most of us in the computer business, "Macs" is obviously short for Apple Macintosh computers, and this was in fact the intended meaning of the original question's composer. Thus, the response ended up only providing ammunition for some good-natured ribbing by the young man's peers. Suffice it to say, what is often considered obvious to one person might mean something completely different to another.

It might be a good idea for us to take heed of this lesson in misinterpretation and lay down some fundamental definitions and ideas to establish a common background with which to discuss the other concepts in this book.

Basic Truths About Networking

The administrator of a local network for a small group of investors found that a number of them were not particularly impressed with what he thought was a pretty nice setup. One day he asked one of them what she thought a network was. Her response was something like this: "It's a bunch of computers all hooked together in some complicated mess that's slow and always going down."

Although the administrator scoffed at the technical ignorance of such a reply, we think that simple comment held quite a bit of insight. In fact, we can use it to point out some of the basic truths about networking.

Networks Are Multiuser

"It's a bunch of computers all hooked together..."

Although the intricacies of how a computer talks to itself can make for quite an interesting study, when this book mentions *computer networks,* it refers to two or more computers that are communicating with one another. A "bunch of computers" usually implies that a bunch of people are using those computers. As is the inclination of most groups of human beings, the various individuals on a network tend to have different goals, tasks, and priorities. These differences can lead to some interesting network challenges, particularly when the goals of two users conflict.

Networks Are Complicated

"...in some complicated mess..."

Whenever two or more wires are involved, you know you've got something pretty complicated on your hands. Networks can, in fact, be very complex, and they have been the topic of countless books even before the recent Internet rave. By breaking down the discussion into some basic concepts and then building on those concepts early on, the mysterious complexity should start to make a little sense to you.

Networks Are Slow

"...that's slow..."

We've all experienced some network anomaly that has caused one or more of our computers to seemingly crawl in response to our keystrokes and mouse clicks. Yes, networks can sometimes slow down your computer, but when we say, "Networks are slow," we are referring to the fact that it can take seconds or minutes before a response to a request is received. This might not be long in geological time, but in computer time it seems like centuries. How these delays are handled has a lot to do with how computer networks function.

Networks Are Unreliable

"...and always going down."

A manager of end-users did a survey in which one of the questions asked was, "How reliable do you think your LAN is?" The network administrator was appalled by the responses, since the LAN was her pride and joy. Those ignorant users had no idea of the millions of bytes of successful reads and writes they were making every hour. One file a week got lost or corrupted—and they called that unreliable?

Our ideas of reliability might vary with our relationship to the network, but yes, any way you slice it, networks are unreliable. Even if you haven't lost a file in five years, network packets are lost every millisecond of every day and often for good reasons. The fact that network packets are quite frequently lost explains why networks are said to be unreliable. The job of the underlying network layers is to hide this unreliability from users so that they don't have to worry about whether the files they just saved on their server will actually be there tomorrow.

Glossary

network packets *The discrete blocks of data sent across a physical medium and managed by the data link layer.*

network layers *System services that provide network functionality to higher-level network layers and applications above them.*

Client/Server Architecture

Before getting into network architecture details, we should discuss one fundamental of computer science—the client/server paradigm. Client/server reflects the fact that access to a system's resources usually entails two separate entities. The first entity is the client, which makes the request to access the system resource. The second entity is the server, which is activated only when a client request is received. The server manages direct access to the resource and then returns the results to the client. Although this model is particularly well suited for describing computer network requests, it is also the model used for handling resource requests within a single computer. For instance, when you want to save a file, you request that the operating system write it to disk. The operating system performs this service for you, and the task is accomplished. You, as the client, requested that the file be saved, while the operating system, as the server, was sitting idly waiting for your request. When it received the request, it immediately kicked into action and performed the task at hand. It finally delivered a response saying that the requested action had been accomplished. The action of any server is triggered by the requests of its clients.

This model works particularly well for describing networks, since the server might be an entire machine that is waiting for requests from clients. When a request comes in, the server quickly attends to the request and sends a response. In the case of a database server, an application on a client machine sends a request that contains an SQL query. When the database server receives the query, it provides the services by running through its database and finding all the corresponding records. When it has found all the records, it transmits their contents across the network in the form of a response to the original request.

It's also important to note that, although database servers are probably the most common client/server scenario that comes to mind, any sort of network request and response falls into this realm. In terms of the topic of this book, Microsoft Internet Information Server is software that acts as a bona fide server system, responding to client requests made by various Web browsers that run on client machines on the network.

The Network Layered Approach

To dilute the complexity of network architecture, a "divide and conquer" approach has been designed to make it easier to write applications that can take advantage of network capabilities. A layered architecture ensures that a programmer can design a network application whose higher levels can depend on lower levels to provide services that can be built on and used, without the designer or user having knowledge of the details of the lower level's implementation. It allows layers to communicate with peer layers on other machines as if they were communicating directly with one another, despite the fact that the conversation is being routed down through the lower network layers. In addition, a layer's ability to provide network services is made possible by the fact that a peer service provider must be present on the remote machine with which it is communicating. This remote service provider must be able to understand the commands and the responses necessary for communicating with its peer. Figure 2.1 illustrates how a layered architecture fits together.

The rectangles in Figure 2.1 represent the network service providers on two separate machines. A layer and its peer have a virtual conversation to provide requests and responses to one another in a language they both understand. In networking terms, this language is referred to as the *protocol*. In actuality, two peer services have no physical means to communicate with each other except through the services provided by the next lowest layer. This reliance on the next lowest layer continues until communication travels to the very bottom level, at which point there is a physical connection between the remote computer's peer service, often in the form of a wire of some sort.

For layers to take advantage of the services provided to them by their immediate subordinate layers, a well-defined mechanism must be in place for submitting service requests. The mechanism is the *interfaces* that are provided by the subordinate layer and used by the immediately higher layer. Thus, a request such as "Give me the file RUMORS.DAT" cannot be given directly to the peer service on a second machine; instead, it is handed to the next lowest service layer on the same machine through a well-known interface. As a request is passed down from layer to layer, each service encapsulates the received request by adding information and passing it down to the next layer. This continues until the request is passed to the lowest layer, which sends the encapsulated request to the second machine. On the second machine, the lowest layer receives the request and then propagates the data up to the layer immediately above it. This propagation continues until finally the peer service to the original requester receives the data that was originally destined for it. The peer service sends the response back by passing the response data back down through the layers below it, back to the first machine, which then propagates the data back up to the original service. The result is the U-shaped data flow shown in Figure 2.1.

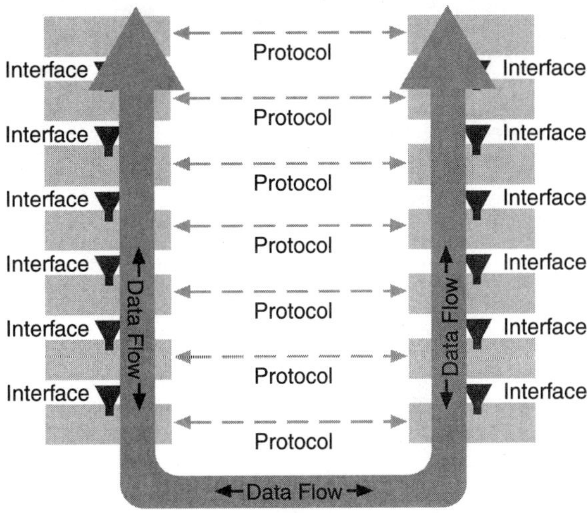

FIGURE 2.1

A network's layered architecture.

Every request submitted by a layer to an interface has two parts: the data destined for the peer layer on the other machine and the control information that must be provided to the subordinate layer for it to know what is supposed to be done with the data. To illustrate this point, you can think of a marketing analyst, JoeBob, who needs to know the results of a survey performed by one of his fellow analysts, SueAnn. The request will be made to JoeBob's peer service, in this case SueAnn, who happens to sit in an office down the hall. JoeBob and SueAnn share a common protocol, the English language. So when JoeBob builds his request, the actual data that he wants to send to his peer service is the sentence, "What are the results of the survey?" Before JoeBob passes this data to the interface below him, namely an interoffice mail drop, he adds the control information required to deliver the request where he wants it to go. In this case, JoeBob fills out SueAnn's name in the destination field, puts his own name in the origination field (so that the results won't be sent to the wrong person), and finally fills in the date in a third field. With the construction of the entire request completed, containing the final data and control information, JoeBob hands off the request through the interoffice mail drop interface that happens to be located next to his desk. JoeBob is relying on the services of the interoffice mail layer to hand the data intact to his peer service down the hall. Later that day, SueAnn receives the request, first looking at the control information displayed on the outside of the interoffice envelope and then reading the data. SueAnn jots down a response, "Survey shows that 72 out of 100 people prefer hot dogs to Spam." She then fills out the control information for her response by putting JoeBob's name in the destination field on the envelope, her own name in the origination field, and the date in the date field. She drops the envelope into the interoffice mail slot by her desk.

This illustration also shows how the actual data destined for the peer service doesn't travel alone to the remote location. JoeBob's written request was packaged in an interoffice envelope that also made the journey down the hall. Had the destination been some location across town, the envelope might have been thrown in a bin marked, "Cross-Town Office," and the bin along with the interoffice envelope and the original message would have made the trip. In this case, the higher interoffice mail layer is relying on the cross-town delivery layer to get its data to its peer at the other office. The data is now the interoffice envelope plus the original request for the survey results. Marking the bin "Cross-Town Office" is the control information required by the delivery service to get the data where it needs to go.

With computer network service layers, our requests take the form of buffers of data. These buffers are passed to an interface along with the control information to the subordinate layer that will use the control information to build its own data so that its peer service will know what to do with what it receives. The result is that our original data actually includes additional data, maybe an extra header and potentially a trailer. This encapsulated data is now passed down to the next layer for transmission along with some more control information. Multiple layers can add multiple headers and trailers to a piece of data; these additions are then stripped out by the corresponding peer services on the remote machine. It is also possible that one of the lower layers might decide that the data passed to it is too long and so breaks the passed data into several shorter pieces. This layer would then add its own headers and trailers to each of the shorter pieces so that when its peer service on the remote machine receives all the small pieces of data, it knows to put them back together in the right order before passing them up to the next layer. Note that although the headers and trailers of the different layered services might be closely associated with the control information passed to each of them from the next higher layer, the control information itself is not part of the data that gets sent across the network. It is up to the layers to interpret the control information and build their own data headers and trailers from it.

Glossary

buffer *A block of memory used to temporarily store data.*

Seven Layers in the ISO/OSI Model

So far, this discussion has been rather nebulous since it hasn't covered the actual functionality of the different network service layers or how many of these service layers exist. Fortunately, the International Organization for Standardization (ISO) has defined the number and function of computer network services in its Open Systems Interconnection (OSI) reference model. Although this model is seldom used in the real world, it provides a clear frame of reference because within the model each layer is relatively restricted to a single functionality. This allows programmers to better understand the specific network service areas and then map these functionalities to the real-world implementations to make it clear which components are doing what in the larger scheme of things.

The OSI model has divided networking into seven layers, as shown in Figure 2.2. We will use these layers to describe the services provided by the different components involved while using IIS.

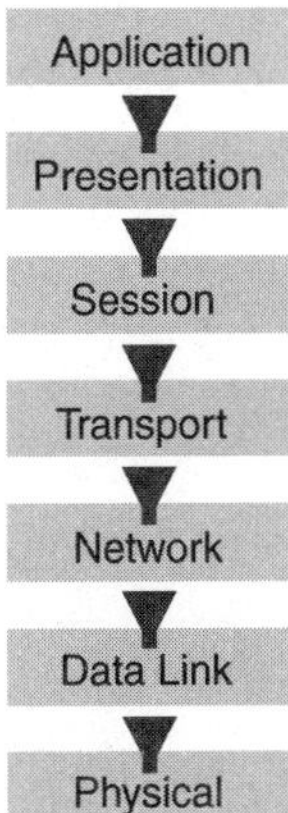

FIGURE 2.2

The OSI model's seven layers.

The Physical Layer

The physical layer is the actual medium, which is capable of carrying data, that is connecting two or more computers. This layer can take the form of one or more copper wires, or it could be radio wave signals, or it could even be a fiber optics system. Normally, the physical layer is the Ethernet or Token Ring lines that make up the corporate network or the phone lines to which a modem connects when dialing into an Internet access provider or another server. The network card in a machine, or the modem on a serial port, handles the task of converting the electronic pulses on the physical medium to the 1s and 0s that a computer is capable of holding in memory. The medium, its electronic characteristics, and a standardized means for transmitting bits on the medium all fall into the definition of the physical layer.

The Data Link Layer

The other day, we were listening to the stereo at home when we were rather surprised to hear the conversation of two construction workers suddenly blare from the speakers. Their radio transmissions were being picked up by the turntable, and the results were now echoing from the speakers. The moral of this story is that when a computer attempts to make an electronic transmission in order to send a 1 bit to another computer on the network, that bit could very well be a 0 bit by the time it gets to its destination because of electronic interference of many kinds. It is the responsibility of the data link layer to account for and correct any transmission errors that might occur. Also, since little functionality is provided by sending a bit at a time across the network, the data link layer supplies the notion of data frames that are sent between machines. It is the responsibility of the data link layer to recognize frame boundaries as well as handle duplicate frames and frame acknowledgments. Getting the data frames to the intended machine(s) is also part of the data link layer's responsibility, so physical addressing schemes are implemented at this level.

Glossary

frame *A discrete block of data sent across a physical medium and managed by the data link layer. On Ethernet networks, frames have a maximum size of 1500 bytes.*

The Network Layer

It used to be that most people's exposure to computer networks was to a small LAN at the office. This became more complicated when groups of departments realized that by connecting their LANs together, they could easily share information among departments. Pretty soon entire companies were wired, and now the trend is that they are all wired to the Internet on one global network. To lessen the complexity and strain on these large networks, *subnets* come into play. A subnet is much like that initial LAN, in which everyone was on the same physical segment of wire. The subnet is connected to other subnets via *routers,* which allow communications between subnets. But routers send transmissions only to the specific subnet destinations for which they are intended. Resolving subnet destinations and dealing with network bottlenecks and congestion fall into the responsibilities of the network layer.

The Transport Layer

Most networks, like Ethernet and Token Ring, have physical size limits of only a few thousand bytes on their data streams. However, much of the data that needs to be sent across networks is much larger than this. The transport layer is responsible for breaking these large pieces of data into sizes digestible by the underlying layers. It is also at the transport layer that different kinds of network delivery might be made available. For instance, you might want to have a one-to-one connection with a single machine, or you might want to send a one-to-many multicast or broadcast. You might want guaranteed delivery of your data, or you might want to avoid the overhead of guarantees and acknowledgments. It is also at the transport layer that a single machine-to-machine connection can be multiplexed to allow multiple channels of communication among two or more network applications communicating between the same two machines.

The Session Layer

The terms *session* and *connection* are understandably used often with network communications and can mean different things to different people. For the most part, the concept of both terms is the same—that is, a reliable channel between a specific network application on one machine and its peer network application on another machine. Communication management via this channel is the functionality that falls to the session layer. Sometimes connections are half-duplex (one direction) or full-duplex (bidirectional). Managing the synchronization of who can talk at any given time or setting up the characteristics of sessions whether they be half-duplex or full-duplex is the responsibility of the session layer.

The Presentation Layer

If you've ever communicated over a network from your PC to a mainframe computer, you might have run into a situation in which text strings on the mainframe were normally stored in EBCDIC, while text on your PC was normally assumed to be ASCII. The presentation layer provides for a mechanism to use some sort of standardized network representation for text strings or other data and convert it to the host's intrinsic format when it is received by the application. This layer concerns itself with formatting data for displaying and printing. If a string was sent to your PC in EBCDIC, a presentation layer service could convert the string to ASCII for you. A presentation layer service can also include encoding data for privacy or compressing data to minimize network resource utilization.

Glossary

EBCDIC *External Binary Coded Decimal for Interchange Code. Developed by IBM, EBCDIC is a way to represent alpha characters in numeric form.*

ASCII *American Standard Code for Information Interchange. An industry for standardizing data transmission across different hardware and software.*

The Application Layer

The presentation layer is concerned with converting incoming data types to the corresponding data type of the PC, but the application layer is concerned with converting application-defined types to types supported by the specific application that is currently running. For example, your network browser might support displaying images only in a Microsoft Windows BMP format. An application layer service might be used when data is received in JPEG or GIF format to convert those types of images to BMPs. The difference between application layer conversions and the kind done by the presentation layer is that the presentation layer is making conversions specific to the CPU of the host machine, while application layer conversions are specific only to the application involved. Other services that are placed in the application layer include file transfer, e-mail messaging, and directory manipulation.

Web Browser and Web Server Architecture

Now that the groundwork has been laid for all the theoretical network services that can be provided, let's take a look at Microsoft IIS and see how it matches up to the conceptual model. First we'll examine the basic service layers that are involved. Figure 2.3 shows the four service layers of components. IIS relies on the services provided by the TCP/IP driver, which in turn might rely on a network interface card (NIC) driver (Token Ring or Ethernet) or a serial driver. The drivers use the services of either the network card or the modem on the serial line, both of which provide the direct interface to the physical connection between the client and the server. Although this figure has been simplified, it gives a general feel for the main layered services involved. Figure 2.3 also shows that a number of peer layer to peer layer protocols are being used as well as interfaces between layers. The next sections look at the specific layers' functionalities and map them back to the services provided in the seven layers of the OSI model.

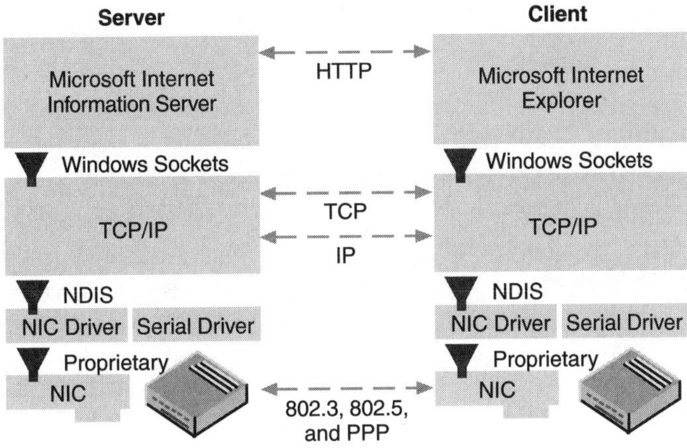

FIGURE 2.3

Server and client architecture showing four service layers.

Ethernet and Token Ring

Ethernet and Token Ring are probably the most popular computer network topologies available today. Both provide the physical medium that connects machines as well as a certain amount of low-level functionality. You have probably already guessed that these are examples of services that reside in the physical layer in the OSI model. But Ethernet and Token Ring also provide services that allow for the transmission of data frames back and forth between workstations, which means that they provide data link layer services as well.

In fact, Token Ring networks can include what is called *source routing* capabilities. Routing between subnets falls to the network layer, so the lowest layer in the four-layer model could potentially include services from three of the seven OSI layers involved. But just like many theoretical models, real-world examples can't always be pigeonholed into the theoretical options you have provided.

Ethernet is defined by the Institute of Electrical and Electronics Engineers (IEEE) 802.3 standard and is known as a Carrier Sense Multiple Access with Collision Detection (CSMA/CD) network. The idea behind CSMA/CD is simply that any node can start sending data anytime it needs to. A collision occurs when two or more machines attempt to send data at the same time. With collision detection, the machines that sent data at the same time will realize by the time they've finished sending that a collision has occurred; they then will hold off for differing periods of time to try to avoid another collision and will attempt to send again.

The physical wire layout of the Ethernet is typically a single backbone wire to which all machines are connected. The backbone wire needs to be properly terminated so that no echoes occur from the end of the wire. The 10BaseT network is becoming more and more popular, and although its physical wire layout might appear different from that of the single backbone wire, in reality the two are the same. The hubs that appear to create a central star-type of layout are actually connecting the two wires of each star to make one long wire backbone that is properly terminated on each end.

Token Ring was defined by the IEEE 802.5 standard, although IBM added source routing capabilities to its Token Ring network, which enhanced the standard. Token Ring is a token-passing bus topology, which basically means that a token is passed between all the machines on the ring. If your machine has the token, it is allowed to send data frames. If your machine doesn't have the token, it must wait until the token propagates around the ring before it can send anything.

Glossary

token *An entity passed from machine to machine on a Token Ring network that determines who is allowed to send frames on the network. Only the machine that holds the token is allowed to send data on the network.*

Serial Connection

The other common type of physical connection to a network these days is the Internet access provider, a dial-up system that connects users' machines to a network. Fundamentally, this is treated like an Ethernet connection, but a little more is going on in this case.

First of all, when you call in to an Internet access provider, such as Microsoft Network, you must initially take some specific actions, such as dial your modem and then walk through an authentication scheme. Both of these actions involve higher layer services than the physical and data link layers describe, since some password encryption (which falls under the presentation layer) and modem-specific setup communications (which fall under the application layer) can occur. But once the phone number has been dialed and the connection has been successfully made, things look much like they do with Ethernet or Token Ring except that data transmission occurs much slower. Just as with Ethernet and Token Ring, a protocol, called the Point-to-Point Protocol (PPP), provides a means for reliable data frame transmission.

All three low-level means (Ethernet, Token Ring, and dial-up) provide the medium for physical connection and the transmission of bits (physical layer services) as well as reliable data frame transmission (data link layer services). Thus, two of the seven layers in the OSI model are covered.

Although there is an obvious physical separation between a network card and a network card's software driver, there is little functional difference between the services provided by the card and the services provided by the driver. How much processing is done by the card's own physical processor and how much is done by the driver is a gray area. In the end, the network card driver's main role is to convert network card communication into a common interface that with Microsoft Windows is the Network Driver Interface Specification (NDIS) interface. By providing a common interface to the layers above them, network card drivers allow their services to be accessed easily without requiring any specific knowledge of the particular card or cards that might be in use. Serial-line communication has been made transparent as well because a conversion driver has provided an NDIS interface to the serial line, despite there being no network card involved at all.

TCP/IP

The TCP/IP family of protocols is the most common provider of network, transport, and session layer services on the Internet. However, much to the surprise of quite a few users of the Internet, Transmission Control Protocol (TCP) and Internet Protocol (IP) are not required to communicate over the Internet. That said, quite a few Internet-standard higher level protocols and applications do require TCP/IP as the transport. Because Web browsers and servers are among those applications that require this family of protocols, discussions throughout this book will assume that the network protocol involved is TCP/IP.

Notice in Figure 2.3 that, in the larger TCP/IP boxes, two protocol arrows represent peer-to-peer communication. The same TCP/IP driver can support more than one protocol at work. In fact, the TCP/IP driver is supporting more than just the two protocols when it establishes network communications between two machines; however, the main functionality is in fact provided by IP and, in the case of Web servers, TCP. Hence the name TCP/IP seems like a good choice for the larger driver. Let's look separately at IP, at another TCP/IP family protocol called UDP, and then at the specifics of TCP.

Internet Protocol

The Internet Protocol is the part of TCP/IP that allows communications to be routed through a series of subnets in order to reach the destination machine on the other side. IP also provides the transport layer capability of breaking up data into sizes that can be sent because of the constraints of the underlying physical medium. The routing functionality of IP is placed squarely in the network layer of the OSI model. IP achieves its routing capability by abstracting a machine's *physical address* (a universally unique address that is embedded in the network card by the manufacturer) and associating it with an *IP address*.

An IP address is a 4-byte value that is broken into two parts: a network identifier and a host identifier. These addresses are assigned in such a fashion that every machine on a network must have a unique IP address. Machines that are on the same physical subnet will have the same network identifier, but each will have a different host identifier. Thus, if you have my machine's IP address, your machine will be able to determine whether my machine is on the same subnet as yours. If it is, you can send me packets directly. If it's not, you will send packets to me through a router, which along with other routers has the ability to track down the location of the physical subnet to which my network identifier refers. (For more on routers, see Chapter 3.)

Assigning unique IP addresses to every machine on the network might not be too difficult if you have a small network with a few subnets, but as you might expect, making sure every computer on the Internet has a unique IP address is a monumental task. That is why when a network administrator connects a network to the Internet, it is important that the administrator receives network identifiers from a central authority. In fact, whenever you dial into an Internet access provider via your modem, you are functionally adding your own little network to the Internet. Your Internet access provider has its own network identifier that it assigns to your machine, along with a host identifier, so that your ID will be unique and you will be able to communicate with all the other IP addresses on the Internet.

User Datagram Protocol

A number of the TCP/IP family of protocols rely on the services of IP. The main two are User Diagram Protocol (UDP) and TCP. UDP corresponds with the transport layer of the OSI model and provides connectionless communication capabilities. This means that no handshaking mechanism establishes a guaranteed delivery virtual circuit between the two sides of a UDP conversation. In fact, *broadcasts* (sent messages that are intended to be received by every machine on the network) are performed using UDP since there is no efficient way to provide guaranteed delivery when you are sending to potentially thousands of machines. UDP can be used to send packets to specific machines; however, an application that uses UDP will need to realize that some packets can be lost and will have to come up with its own method for dealing with this. The benefit of UDP is the potential for performance gains, since the overhead of acknowledging received data on a guaranteed connection can slow down communications, particularly when a large number of small pieces of data need to be sent.

Transmission Control Protocol

TCP also corresponds to the transport layer of the OSI model, but in contrast to UDP, TCP is a connection-oriented protocol, which means that data receipt is acknowledged and thus delivery is guaranteed. Packets can still be lost, but TCP will resend the data if it doesn't receive a timely acknowledgment. Although waiting for acknowledgments might seem a little time intensive, sliding window algorithms, piggyback acknowledgments, and other methods have provided some extensive efficiencies such that when transferring a large amount of data, little difference in performance would be noticed between UDP and TCP communications. Another feature of TCP is that it provides acknowledgment mechanisms that give it synchronization capabilities that fall under the session layer's realm in the OSI model.

TCP is a *byte-mode protocol*, as opposed to a *message-mode protocol*. This means that if you do a single send of 25,000 bytes of data from one side of the connection, the other side will not necessarily receive 25,000 bytes when it does a single receive. It might receive less than 25,000 bytes, in which case it would need to do more receives until it gets all the data. It might also receive more than 25,000 bytes if you happened to do another send shortly after the first one. In other words, with TCP, message boundaries are not preserved. Message-mode protocols, on the other hand, do preserve message boundaries so that if you send 25,000 bytes, you will receive 25,000 bytes. Using a byte-mode protocol like TCP can sometimes create a challenge when you are attempting to determine when all the data that is going to be sent has been received on the other side of a connection. This issue will be covered further in Chapter 23, which discusses the HTTP content-length header.

Hypertext Transfer Protocol

Anyone who has ever heard or used a reference to a Web page is familiar with the leading "HTTP" of a URL, such as *http://www.microsoft.com*. However, a large number of users of HTTP URLs do not realize that HTTP stands for Hypertext Transfer Protocol, and even more do not understand the OSI model presentation and application layer services provided by HTTP.

When you hear about HTTP, the first thing that should pop into your head is that the "P" stands for "Protocol." After our discussions of the layered network architecture, this should ring a familiar bell: peer-to-peer virtual communication that occurs between components at the same level on different machines. Figure 2.3 on page 19 makes this point a little more obviously, and it shows that the peers involved at this level are IIS and the client's Web browser, which in our illustration is Microsoft Internet Explorer. IIS relies on the connection-oriented, guaranteed delivery services of TCP to receive its HTTP requests and send its responses. Ultimately, HTTP provides a standard and efficient means to transfer a variety of data, but the most popular data that HTTP transports is that for Hypertext Markup Language (HTML) files.

HTTP is highly extendable, which enables it to provide more and new capabilities. One such capability is user authentication. Although the current HTTP 1.1

specification provides only an easily interpreted user name and password, HTTP has provided the means to extend this functionality so that encryption schemes and public-key and private-key security mechanisms can be used instead. In this fashion, HTTP provides presentation layer functionality from the OSI model.

HTTP can also be considered to provide application layer services, since it allows applications to request such objects as image files in the specific formats understood by the particular application. For example, suppose that you know how to display a Windows .BMP file, but you don't know how to display a .JPEG file. When your application builds the HTTP request, you can request that the response be sent only in Windows BMP format. Figure 2.4 illustrates the relationships among the four layered services used by Microsoft IIS and the seven layers of the OSI model.

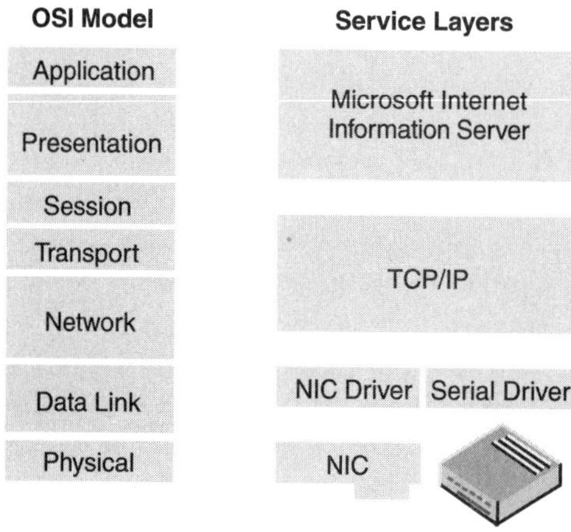

FIGURE 2.4

Mapping the layered architecture used by IIS with the layered architecture of the OSI model.

Sample Network Configurations

This section takes a closer look at some actual network configurations that might involve Microsoft IIS and tracks the course of information from an initial Web request to receipt of the final Web response.

Simple Token Ring Configuration

Here's a basic scenario in which the client machine and server machine are on the same network segment, as illustrated in Figure 2.5. This figure demonstrates a scenario for a Token Ring network, but the fundamentals are the same for Ethernet.

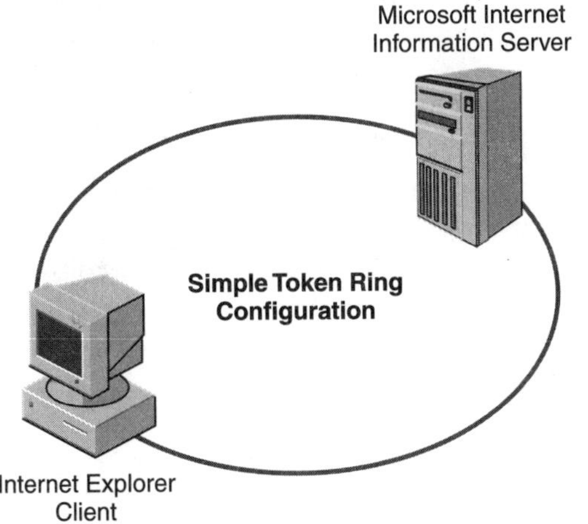

FIGURE 2.5

A scenario in which IIS is on the same physical network as the browser accessing it.

First the user at the client machine makes the request to read an HTML page off the IIS server from his or her Internet Explorer client. Internet Explorer reads the URL from the typed request, constructs the HTTP request associated with the URL, and then makes a request through Windows Sockets (Winsock) to open a TCP connection to the IIS server. (If you look back at Figure 2.3 you'll see that Winsock is the TCP/IP interface under Windows.) The TCP/IP protocol driver resolves the IIS host name to an IP address, which it recognizes is located on the same subnet. It therefore passes an "establish TCP connection" request through NDIS to the Token Ring driver and tells the driver to send the request to the Token Ring card that is attached to the server. The server's Token Ring card receives the packet, recognizes it as a TCP/IP packet, and passes it to the TCP/IP driver through NDIS on the server machine. The server's TCP/IP driver receives the request, sees that it is using a port being used by IIS, and tells IIS that a TCP connection is being requested through Winsock. The IIS server responds positively to accept the connection, which is passed down to TCP/IP, sent out through the Token Ring driver on the server, received by the Token Ring driver on the client, and passed up to the TCP/IP driver on the client. Eventually, notification is given to Internet Explorer that the connection request succeeded.

Internet Explorer then takes the HTTP request it built from the initial URL and sends it through the TCP connection that it has established. The request marches its way down through the layers, across the network, and up the server layers, where it is received by IIS. IIS finds the requested HTML file, encapsulates it in an HTTP response, and sends it back down the chain. The IIS server also closes the TCP connection at this time. On the client machine, the HTTP response is received on the TCP connection. The client sees that the response is indicating success and therefore goes about the process of displaying the contents of the HTML data received. When it finishes reading all the data, it receives an indication that the server has closed the connection and thus knows there is no more HTML data to read.

Dial-Up Connection to IIS

The following is a common scenario: a user at home is reading an HTML page off IIS running on the Internet, as illustrated in Figure 2.6. We won't track all the details we went through in the first example, but let's check out some key differences between the two.

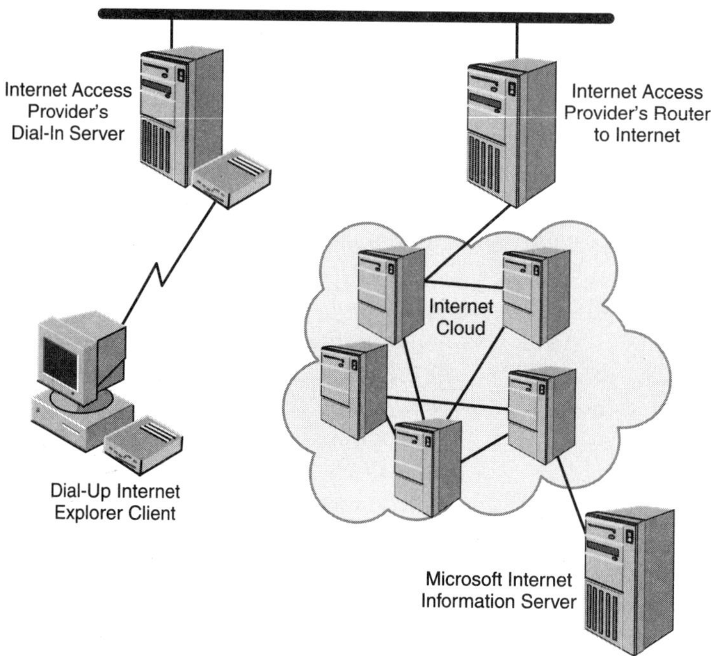

FIGURE 2.6

A connection over a dial-up Internet client to an IIS connected directly to the Internet.

First of all, when Internet Explorer sends the request to establish the TCP connection with the IIS server, the phone connection to the Internet access provider might not even be established. The TCP/IP driver triggers the remote network access drivers to dial the phone number, make the connection, and provide any authentication required by the Internet access provider for the phone connection. Then it notifies TCP/IP that the line is ready for business.

The TCP/IP driver realizes that the IP address it needs to reach is not on the same subnet, so it sends the "establish TCP connection" request to the Internet access provider's router that is connected to the Internet. This and all further communications travel first through the Internet access provider's dial-in server, which serves as a bridge to pass the requests transparently to the Ethernet backbone to which it is attached. The router that receives the client's request looks up in its routing tables that this subnet can be reached through another router and forwards the request. The Internet can be thought of as a giant network cloud filled with an intricate web of connected routers, all capable of forwarding requests through the proper channels to get them to the proper subnet. The cloud analogy is effective because it is as if we are blinded to the route taken to reach our intended Internet host—just as though the route was enveloped in a blinding fog bank. We do know that eventually our request reaches the proper subnet, where it is received by the IIS server in question. A response is sent back through the routed cloud to the Internet access provider's Ethernet, where it is transparently forwarded over the phone line to the client. The client and server then continue their communication via this routed connection that has been established until the response has been completely received.

Routed Ethernet Configuration—Proxy to Internet

The third sample configuration, illustrated in Figure 2.7, shows a routed intranet in which the client machine might be accessing IIS servers on the corporate network as well as on the Internet. For the client to get to the Internet, however, some sort of routed path must be available. But this also means that anyone on the Internet could potentially use the same path to access information on the company's corporate intranet network. Obviously, this scenario should be avoided if any sensitive data is shared on the corporate network. The solution is to use an HTTP proxy, such as Microsoft Internet Proxy Server, to provide a firewall that will allow requests to go out to the Internet but won't allow requests from the Internet to come in.

When the client makes a request, it can propagate in the normal fashion to servers on the inside of the firewall. However, to request data from a server on the Internet, the client must be configured to use the proxy, which becomes the server to which

Glossary

HTTP proxy *A Web server configured to receive HTTP requests presumably from an internal network that forwards the requests to Web servers on the Internet. The proxy provides a level of security by allowing requests to leave a corporate network but not allowing requests to enter the same network from the outside.*

firewall *Any of a number of mechanisms that restrict access from one network to the resources of another.*

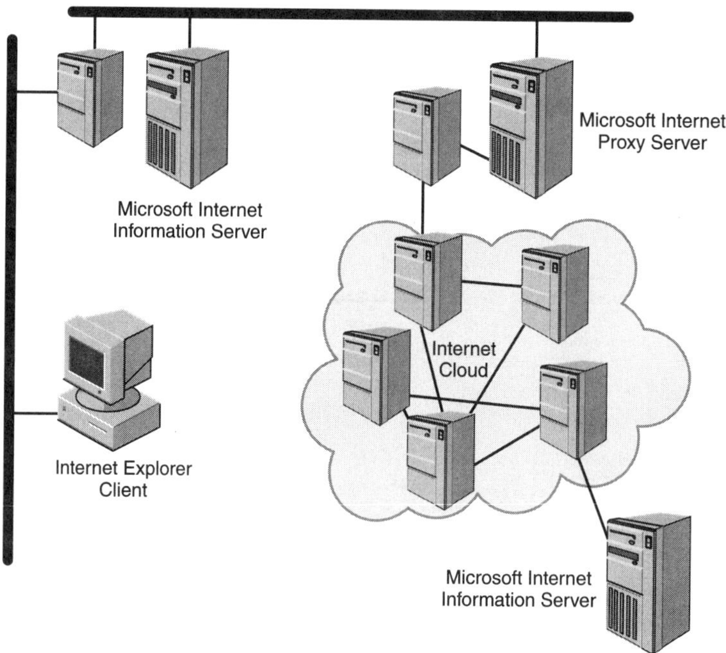

FIGURE 2.7

Using an HTTP proxy to allow access between a corporate network and the Internet.

the client makes its TCP connection and then sends its HTTP request. The proxy server receives the HTTP request, almost as though it is the actual Web server; but before it sends a response back to the client, it establishes its own TCP connection to the IIS server on the Internet and creates an HTTP request that mirrors the original client. Because the IIS server on the Internet can't really tell the difference between the proxy's request and any other request, it sends the HTTP response directly back to the proxy. Now the proxy takes the HTTP response and forwards it via the connection to the client, which is able to display the HTML as if it were directly connected to the Internet. Any request made from a machine on the Internet would have to be routed through the proxy server, but the proxy server is servicing only requests that it receives from its Ethernet card attached to the corporate network. It ignores any connection requests that are received from its connection to the Internet.

Now you've looked at a number of different network configurations, analyzed the theory behind the various protocols involved, and even learned a little about the OSI networking model. With this theory behind you, in the next chapter you will find some of the concrete details involved in getting your TCP/IP network set up and configured so that clients can connect to your server.

CHAPTER 3

Exploring the Network Environment

In this chapter you will move from the theoretical principles of Chapter 2 to more practical information about about networks and how to prepare them for running Internet Information Server. You'll examine the tasks involved in setting up the following operations:

- **Using an intranet with a connection to the Internet** A corporate-wide network of computers that use the same tools as the Internet (that means browsers and TCP/IP protocols) is known as an intranet. Connecting an intranet to the Internet is optional, but it's often desirable. Under this configuration, a company might use IIS as its primary mechanism for information exchange among different departments within the organization. An employee's desktop computer will not be directly connected to the Internet. However, the company can still provide a connection between the intranet and the Internet to allow the user to access the Web using an HTTP proxy. (Proxies will be discussed in Chapter 23.)
- **Connection through an Internet Service Provider (ISP)** An ISP is a company that has a direct connection to the Internet (via a connection to the backbone, as discussed in Chapter 2). The ISP provides Internet access services to clients at the subscribing company, who connect via modem. The ISP might also host Web pages for its dial-up customers. Both MSN and America Online are ISPs.

These tasks are not trivial, and a certain amount of groundwork must be laid before we can proceed. We will begin with some basic assumptions concerning portions of your network that are already set up:

- All computers are wired into a local area network (LAN).
- The TCP/IP protocol is installed, and machines on the corporate network can communicate with each other.

- For the ISP business, incoming phone lines have been established for incoming calls.
- ISP clients dial in via Point-to-Point Protocol (PPP) or Serial Line Internet Protocol (SLIP) and become full-fledged Internet-reachable machines.
- Computers running different operating systems (such as Microsoft Windows 95 or Microsoft Windows NT Workstation) might be connected to the network; however, this chapter deals only with machines running Windows NT Server 4.0.

Computer Naming and Address Schemes

Before we go any further into the details of configuring your LAN, you need to learn about computer naming schemes. As you know from reading Chapter 2, each computer connects to the network with a unique numeric identifier called the media access control (MAC) address. The MAC address (or network adapter address) is a 48-bit number that uniquely identifies your computer's network card. Every network card manufacturer is assigned the first 24 bits of this number by the IEEE so that no two network cards in the world have the same MAC address. MAC addresses are long and extremely hard to work with—imagine the hassles of having to use URLs that are 48 digits long. To resolve this and for other important reasons related to TCP/IP network architecture, the Internet Protocol (IP) operates with a different addressing scheme called IP addresses.

IP Address Resolution

The TCP/IP family of protocols supports Address Resolution Protocol (ARP) and Reverse Address Resolution Protocol (RARP), which are responsible for IP-to-MAC address translation and MAC-to-IP address translation. ARP is a simple protocol. When an IP address needs to be resolved to a MAC address, the computer sends a broadcast to the local network with the request to determine who owns the specified IP address. The machine with the matching IP address replies with its MAC address, allowing the first computer to make the IP address/MAC address association. For performance reasons, the TCP/IP stack *caches* recently resolved IP/MAC pairs. You can view the contents of the ARP cache while using Windows NT and Windows 95 by running the ARP.EXE utility (discussed later in this chapter). Reverse address lookups are performed by diskless workstations and other types of machines that don't know their own IP addresses when they start up. In these instances, when a machine boots, it sends a broadcast with its MAC address that it obtained from the network card. An RARP server on the network, listening for these requests, sends back a reply that contains the IP address it associates with the original machine's MAC address.

Glossary

cache *Temporary storage for frequently used data. The cache is allocated and managed by the application. Instead of performing the repetitive task of obtaining data again and again (like sending an ARP broadcast), the application looks in the cache to determine whether the data (such as an IP address) is already there.*

Subnets

Before going any further with the specifics of IP addressing, let's take a closer look at subnets. Even on the same LAN, not all computers can be connected to the same physical network cable. For instance, if you are on a corporatewide network that spans multiple buildings on multiple floors, the maximum Ethernet segment length will be quickly surpassed. In such cases, it is a good idea to divide one network into multiple physical segments.

The logical term for a segment is *subnet.* Subnets reduce unnecessary network traffic by limiting the reach of transmitted *datagrams*. Sometimes machines need to send out *broadcasts* to an entire network. It would be nice if this broadcast could be limited to the segment of the network that has computers with a reason to receive the broadcast.

Glossary

datagram *A packet of information containing data and routing information that is independently transmitted over the network. A letter sent through ordinary mail is similar to the datagram: it has routing information (the address on the envelope) and data (a letter and photo inside the envelope). When a datagram is sent to all machines on the network at the same time, it is called a broadcast.*

If this doesn't seem like a big deal to you, consider the Internet itself. The Internet is the ultimate wide area network (WAN), consisting of multiple subnets (actually physical subnetworks). For example, one subnet (the networked computers on the Microsoft campus) is connected to another subnet (all CalState University computers), which is connected to another subnet (the networked computers at the New York Public Library) through each subnet's respective connection to the Internet. Even though the term "subnet" is used loosely here, you can see that it is not possible to connect all machines to the same physical wire without incurring a horrendous cost in network bandwidth. That said, it's obvious that two pieces of information are required to uniquely identify a computer on an IP network.

- The address of the network—the subnet address
- The address of the computer on the subnet—the host address

The subnet address and the host address are analogous to geographical coordinates. If longitude and latitude are known, a place can be located on a map.

Decoding IP Addresses

An IP address is a 32-bit number that consists of four groups of 8 bits (where each 8-bit group equals a unit of data called an *octet*). This type of number can be used to represent almost 2^{32} (roughly 4 billion) different machines. (However, the actual number of available IP addresses is less than 2^{32} because some addresses, such as local network addresses and broadcast addresses, are reserved.) For now the 32-bit number meets the global need for IP addresses. With the current growth of the Internet, however, available addresses are being assigned very quickly.

There are five classes of IP addresses. The three major classes are A, B, and C; class D is reserved for multicasting (sending data to multiple computers at the same time); class E is currently reserved for future use. The IP address's class defines how many bits in the address represent the network; the remaining bits of the IP address then represent the host address. To make IP addresses easier to read, they are in *dotted decimal notation*, which looks like this: 192.168.1.1. The dotted decimal number is calculated by translating each group of 8 bits from binary to decimal notation. The IP address is derived from a combination of the subnet address and the host address on the subnet. To get the host portion of the address, the IP address is binary AND'ed with the *network mask*. The network mask is specific to the subnet, and it helps to factor out the host portion of an address.

> **Glossary**
>
> **network mask** *A binary number that leaves only the network portion of an address (that is, it zeroes out the host ID portion) when binary AND'ed with the IP address. The network mask is represented in dotted decimal notation, similar to the IP address itself.*

Figure 3.1 shows a class C address in its binary representation. Network hardware (such as routers and bridges) looks at the first 3 bytes to determine what class it is dealing with. The first 3 bits (*110*) identify the address as class C. Class C addresses use the first 24 bits (or 3 bytes) for the network address, leaving the remaining 8 bits (1 byte) for the host address, as shown in the figure.

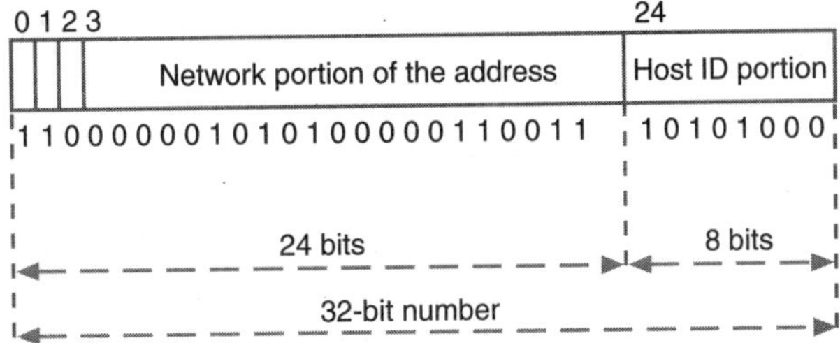

FIGURE 3.1

A binary class C address.

A class C address allows for 2^8, or 256, available hosts. Actually, there will be only 254 valid hosts, since host addresses with all 0s and host addresses with all 1s are not allowed. The host address with all 1s (255 for class C, such as 192.168.51.255) refers to the network broadcast address. The host address made of all 0s refers to the network itself (such as 192.168.51.0 for class C).

◆ Finding the IDs of a Network Address

There is no better way to learn than by solving problems. Assume that we have a network address of 192.168.51.168. What is the host ID, and what is the network ID? You can use a scientific calculator to convert decimal to binary (or you can cheat and look at Figure 3.1):

1. Convert 192 to binary: 11000000.
2. The given IP address is class C because it starts with *110.*
3. In a class C address, only the last 8 bits represent the host ID; therefore binary AND'ing of the IP address with 11111111 11111111 11111111 0000000 will zero out the host ID portion, effectively leaving only the subnet address. The long number with 1s and 0s looks like 255.255.255.0 in dotted decimal notation and represents the subnet mask for the class C address.
4. Do a binary AND of 255.255.255.0 and 192.168.51.168. The result is the network ID 192.168.51.0.
5. The host ID is the rest of the number: 168.

This is a very simple example—once you determined that this is a class C address, no AND is really needed. This algorithm is used by computers for determining host and network IDs for routing.

Unique Identification

Because IP addresses uniquely identify a single machine across the entire network, you will face many network troubles if more than one machine has the same address. If you are building an intranet solution in which your network is not connected to the Internet, you can choose virtually any valid set of IP addresses for your machines. However, the Internet Architecture Board (IAB), after issuing a Request For Comments (RFC 1918), recommends using the following blocks of IP addresses for private intranets:

10.0.0.0–10.255.255.255

172.16.0.0–172.31.255.255

192.168.0.0–192.168.255.255

Figures 3.2 and 3.3 demonstrate that this chapter uses numbers within the recommended ranges for isolated intranets. However, these ranges do not make sense when the intranet has a direct connection to the Internet. If an enterprise decides to build an internal TCP/IP–based intranet, any assignments falling within the ranges can be used without coordinating their use with any Internet authority, and the numbers need to be unique only throughout the enterprise's network. To ensure the numbers' availability for intranet usage, the Internet Address Numbering Authority (IANA) will never assign them to any subnets connected to the Internet. One of the benefits of using numbers within these ranges is that you can enjoy all the features of an IP-based network without actually registering it with any authority. However, if in the future you want to connect such an intranet to the Internet, you must first apply for a valid range of addresses and reissue new addresses for each host.

If your network is directly connected to the Internet, the situation is very different from that described above. In this case, the IP addresses of every machine on your network must be universally unique (just as they'd be for a private LAN, but on a bigger scale). How is this enforced? When your operation sets up a connection to the Internet via a service provider (whether yours is a family-owned business or a major corporate carrier), you will be granted your own blocks of IP addresses from a central authority—the Internet Information Center (InterNIC). By applying appropriate subnet masks, you can create multiple subnetworks within your given ranges.

InterNIC issues only the network portion of an address, and it is up to the particular business or corporation to assign specific host addresses within the given network. By submitting an appropriate application, your organization can obtain addresses directly from InterNIC (see *http://www.inetnic.net*). Having a valid IP address is enough to start advertising your machine as a server (when it is physically connected to the Internet, of course). If, for example, your server is configured to be 206.155.0.1, you can create a URL that refers to your server: *http://206.155.0.1* is a perfectly valid and acceptable form for a URL.

With all this said, it's easy to see how handy IP addresses can be. But as is true with any seemingly good concept, there is a drawback. Consider the following example. A corporation has hundreds of computers, including laptops that require frequent switching from one physical subnet to another. Moving a machine from one network to another requires a change in the IP address of the host as well as other IP configuration parameters. (Remember that an IP address contains the network address.) System administrators need to have a handle on each IP address, plus they need to assign new addresses to machines that are moved from one network to another, and this is not a trivial task. In the old days, this monitoring was often done with the help of Microsoft Excel spreadsheets that kept track of IP addresses and machine name mappings. Each time a machine was moved or a new one was added, the system administrator would have to change the master list manually. But even using Excel's advanced capabilities, this was far from being a high-tech solution.

Another troubling scenario arose if the network included diskless workstations. When such a machine booted up, it needed to know its IP configuration. Calling the system administrator each time to ask him or her to enter the name and IP address was never an acceptable solution. A computer smart enough to determine its own configuration was needed. Today, these problems have been resolved by the Dynamic Host Configuration Protocol (DHCP).

The Dynamic Host Configuration Protocol

DHCP is not a Microsoft proprietary protocol. It is based on RFC 1541, "Dynamic Host Configuration Protocol." DHCP evolved from a protocol known as Boot Protocol (BOOTP). (Their relationship is described in RFC 1534, "Interoperation Between DHC and BOOTP.")

BOOTP is used by diskless UNIX-based workstations to allow them to determine their own vital configuration parameters. Parameters such as IP addresses, subnet masks, and default gateways are sent from the server to the workstation. Following the specifications drawn by the Internet Engineering Task Force (IETF), Microsoft has implemented DHCP functionality in its network protocol stack. Today many vendors other than Microsoft also support DHCP. The idea behind DHCP is similar to that of BOOTP. The typical client/server architecture enables centralized IP address management. The Microsoft DHCP server runs on a Windows NT server and keeps a database of valid IP addresses for a specific subnet. The database also contains information on subnet masks, name resolution servers (more about this later in this chapter), and all the other important TCP/IP parameters needed for a client to function properly. Administrators can also configure DHCP to provide optional parameters such as print server addresses. A client machine that is configured to use DHCP, as shown in Figure 3.2, sends a network broadcast to discover a local DHCP server.

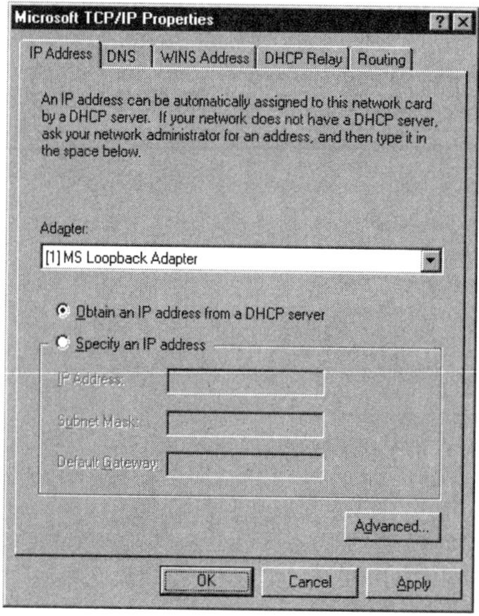

FIGURE 3.2

Configuring a client to use DHCP instead of static IP.

In reply, the server sends the client's IP address, subnet mask, and any preconfigured optional parameters to the client. The need for administrators to statically assign an address to the client has been removed. The DHCP server machine is now the ultimate authority on the network and behaves as a smart IP manager. Note that the DHCP server itself must have a static IP address (since it can't really ask itself to assign one).

Another highlight of the DHCP architecture is that it allows you to move machines between physical networks without any TCP/IP reconfigurations. This is a perfect solution for laptop clients and for ISPs. When clients dial into an ISP network, they are assigned a dynamic address that will be reused after a predefined time. A DHCP server can have a range of network addresses (called a *pool*) that it will use to assign addresses to its clients. It is possible to enter individual IP addresses and to exclude subranges of addresses from the main range. This ability can come in handy for some machines for which you might have static IP addresses.

Only temporary IP address are given to DHCP clients—they are *leased*—and it is possible for you to configure a time interval when IP addresses need to be released, as shown in Figure 3.3. A DHCP client can also release a given IP address and renew it (that is, request a new address). In Windows 95, this can be done through a graphic utility called WINIPCFG.EXE. In Windows NT, the command-line utility IPCONFIG.EXE does the same thing. Using a DHCP server can make IP management a breeze. With the Windows NT network architecture, the system administrator can manage DHCP from virtually any Windows NT server on the network.

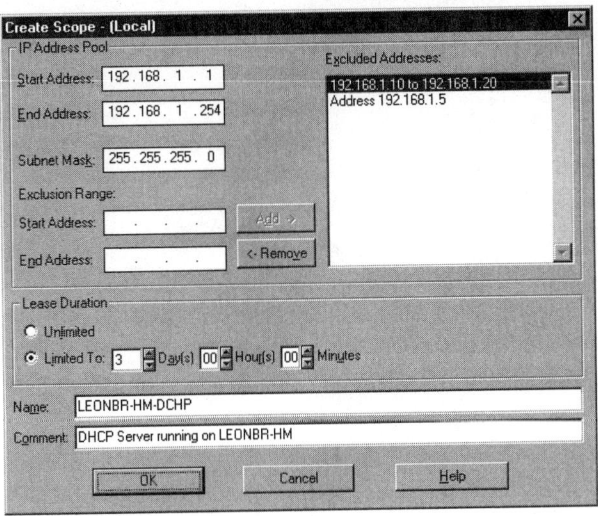

FIGURE 3.3

The DHCP server scope configuration showing the Lease Duration as Limited To 3 Days.

Network Communication Basics

Now you know all about subnets, addresses, and other nifty details. But do you know how subnets and different networks communicate with each other? When machine A wants to establish a connection to machine B on a different network, the network traffic needs to be routed properly—through routers and gateways.

Routers and Gateways

Let's take a look at a scenario in which a corporation has two different subnets, as shown in Figure 3.4. One subnet's address is 192.168.1.0 and the other is 192.168.10.0. These are class C addresses. Notice that the host ID of 0 refers to the network itself.

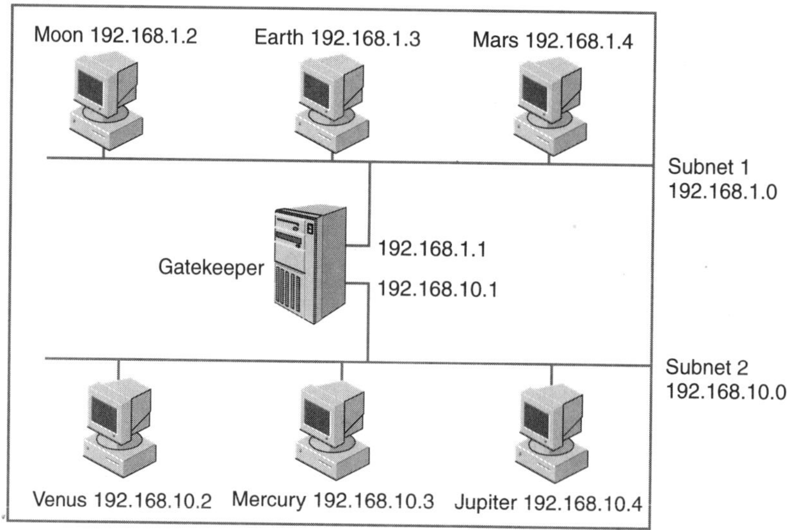

FIGURE 3.4

Network routing showing two different subnets.

Assume that the machine named Venus wants to send a network packet to the machine named Moon. These two machines are not directly connected—that is, they do not share the same physical medium. This is not a problem so long as both subnets are connected to each other via a special network device called a *router*. Usually the router is a hardware device that has two network cards—each card connected to a separate network—and the device is running software that can route network packets from one network card to the other. In Figure 3.4, a machine called Gatekeeper serves as the router between the two subnetworks.

To provide an alternative to using a dedicated hardware router, Windows NT server contains a Network Service that enables a Windows NT–based machine to act as a router (when, of course, it has two network cards). A computer with more than one network card is called a *multihomed host*. Note that a Windows NT server with two network cards is not automatically a router; it must be configured to route network traffic between two network cards to be considered a router. Figure 3.5 shows the Routing page in the TCP/IP Properties window, which is accessible from the Network Control Panel. You can enable the routing capabilities of Windows NT from this page.

When a multihomed machine wants to send a packet, it must decide which network card to use. Each computer has a *routing table*, which tells the machine where to send a specific network packet. If a destination is not reachable directly on the network—for instance if Venus wants to send a packet to Moon—the Venus machine will pass the network packet to its default gateway. Venus's gateway knows how to route traffic to other subnets. The route to the default gateway is called the *default route*. If the Venus machine doesn't know what to do with the packet, it simply sends the packet to its default route and hopes that the gateway knows what to do next.

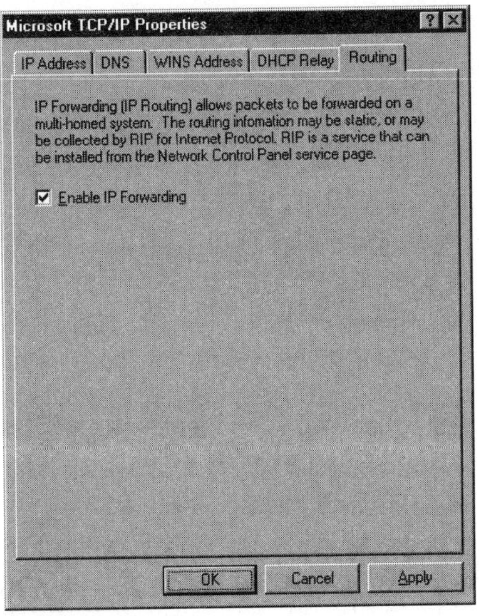

FIGURE 3.5

Enabling Windows NT server routing capabilities in the TCP/IP Properties window.

A host on the network has two types of routing tables: a *dynamic routing table,* which configures itself automatically, and a *static routing table,* which is configured manually by using the ROUTE.EXE utility (discussed later in this chapter). Assume that in this example the routing table will have an entry that tells the Venus computer, "Any network packet destined for anything other than network 192.168.10.0 should be given to my default gateway 192.168.10.1." The default gateway's IP address is either statically configured by the administrator or arrives via DHCP at boot time. Dynamic routing tables can change on the fly. If something fails down the road, routers supporting only static routes will have a hard time recovering because they cannot update routing tables without intervention by the system administrator. A router supporting dynamic routing, on the other hand, is a much smarter (and more expensive) device. It is capable of learning new and more efficient routes dynamically via the Routing Information Protocol (RIP). Routers also use plenty of other network tricks that have been designed to speed routing and to change routes on the fly in case of network hardware failure.

If we consider the case of a network that has a connection to the Internet, the idea behind routing is exactly the same as that described above. Figure 3.6 shows how it would look schematically. Assuming we have a Token Ring network for this case, Gatekeeper is a multihomed computer that is routing network traffic between a Token Ring network and the Internet. Note that a network card connected to the Internet must have a valid IP address, shown as A.B.C.D in the figure.

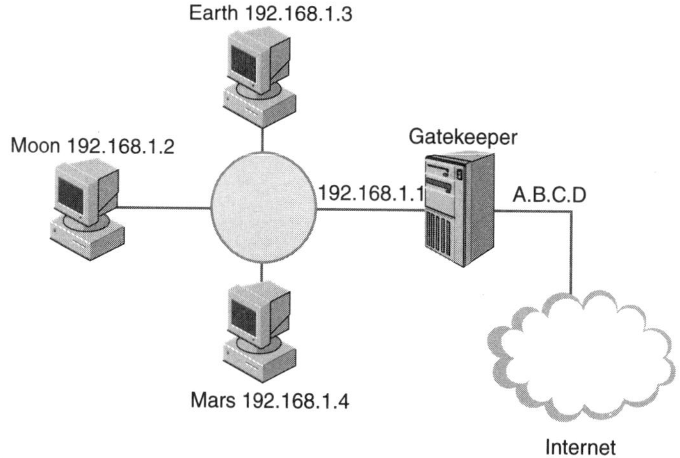

FIGURE 3.6

A Token Ring network connected to the Internet.

Machine Names and Name Resolution

So far, we haven't talked about human-readable machine names. Wouldn't it be nice to refer to your own server as *http://www.yourcompanyname.com*? It beats referring to your computer by its IP address. TCP/IP and Internet domain names to the rescue!

People have a hard time remembering computers by their IP addresses. Such groups of numbers just don't make much sense to our nondigital minds. The TCP/IP family of protocols not only lets you associate an IP address with a particular machine, but TCP/IP also allows machines to have friendly, easy-to-remember names as well. Just as with the IP addressing scheme, the name of a TCP/IP machine must be unique on the network (or at least within a specific domain).

NOTE

Notice how Internet addressing has evolved from the very lowest physical layer with MAC addresses to the higher network layer with IP addresses—and finally all the way to the presentation layer with TCP/IP names.

Consider an intranet—a self-contained network. As long as all the computers on the intranet have different names, there is no risk of name collisions. But how do you ensure name uniqueness across the Internet? *Internet domain names* provide the solution. But before diving into the subject of Internet domains, you should understand that domain names are completely optional; if some ISP does not have a registered domain, it is still reachable by its IP address alone. Be aware, however, that some sophisticated servers will deny connections to clients if reverse name lookup (mapping from an IP address to a friendly name) cannot be performed.

Static Mapping and HOSTS Files

If your network is a small intranet or a simple LAN with a reasonable number of machines, a domain structure is not necessary. Each IP address simply statically maps to one or more simple names. One name will normally map to only one IP address at any one time. Static mapping of addresses to names is easy and can be accomplished by keeping this information in a text file called HOSTS on every computer running TCP/IP on the network. In Windows NT, the HOSTS file resides in the %SystemRoot%\System32\drivers\etc directory. HOSTS files are text files that use the following format:

```
# This is a comment.

102.54.94.97     rhino.acme.com          # source server
38.25.63.10      x.acme.com              # x client host

127.0.0.1        localhost               # This is a required line.
```

The HOSTS file is a simple mapping of IP addresses to machine names, and as you can see from the comment in the preceding code, that last line is required.

According to the TCP/IP specification, each host has a so-called *loopback address*. This address denotes the internal host's address. Sending data to this IP address does not generate network traffic because the data never reaches the network card. So using this address for testing is ideal. In later chapters, you will see how extensively *localhost* is used.

One major drawback of the HOSTS filename resolution mechanism is that each computer needs to have identical information in its HOSTS file. If a host machine's name or address changes, the HOSTS file on each machine needs to be updated to include that change. Also, when an intranet includes many machines, the size of the HOSTS files can quickly become unmanageable. HOSTS files are also not a practical solution for ISPs. Dynamic IP address assignments for dial-in clients will always dictate constantly changing name-address pairs. Trying to keep track of all this with HOSTS files would be a very tough job, and there is a better solution for host-to-IP address resolution. In fact, a number of name resolution schemes are available. The next section discusses these schemes.

Name Resolution Schemes

One mechanism for handling dynamic addresses and machine names is the Windows Internet Names Service (WINS). Before TCP/IP became popular, Windows-based networks relied on a different network protocol: the NetBIOS Frames Protocol (NBF). Computers on an NBF network have unique names and addresses, just as those on a TCP/IP network do. (NBF uses MAC addresses.) The NBF protocol has one major drawback, however: it is not routable. Thus, the Jupiter machine on subnet 2 from the previous example (Figure 3.4) wouldn't be able to communicate with the Moon machine on subnet 1.

To compensate for the routing deficiency of NBF, a NetBIOS-compatible protocol was developed to run on top of TCP/IP. NetBIOS over TCP/IP resolved names by sending broadcasts. If, for example, Jupiter wants to send a packet to Mercury (both computers being on the same subnet, as shown in Figure 3.4) and needs to resolve Mercury's MAC address, the following scenario occurs:

1. Jupiter sends a name resolution broadcast to the entire network with the request to resolve the name Mercury.
2. Mercury replies with its address.
3. Jupiter sends the packet to the specified IP address.

But this procedure would not work if Jupiter wanted to send the packet to Moon. Because routers usually don't route broadcast packets and Moon is on a different subnet, Jupiter's name resolution queries will never reach the machine named Moon. Machines separated by gateways or routers will not be able to resolve each other's names. To solve this problem, the LMHOSTS file was introduced. The LMHOSTS file serves a similar purpose as the HOSTS file on a straight TCP/IP network—mapping IP addresses to names. In this example, we are mapping IP addresses to NetBIOS names. The format of the LMHOSTS files allows not only static IP-to-NetBIOS name mappings but also the inclusion of other LMHOSTS files located on different machines. However, NetBIOS name resolution via static files suffers from all the same problems that HOSTS files have—the size of the file grows with the size of the network, and keeping all the LMHOSTS files up to date can be a nightmare.

WINS

To correct these problems, Microsoft introduced WINS name resolution. WINS is proprietary to Microsoft and will work only in the Windows network environment. It can be installed on any Windows NT server. The idea behind WINS is somewhat similar to that of DHCP. A centralized server maintains a database of IP address and machine name pairs. When a computer starts, it registers its name with the WINS server. If such a name already exists on the LAN, an error will occur and the operation will fail. When a machine wants to connect to another peer on the network, it sends a name query to its WINS server. The address of the WINS server is configured in the TCP/IP settings, as shown in Figure 3.7, or it is supplied via DHCP at boot time. In reply to name inquiries, the WINS server sends an IP address to the requestor.

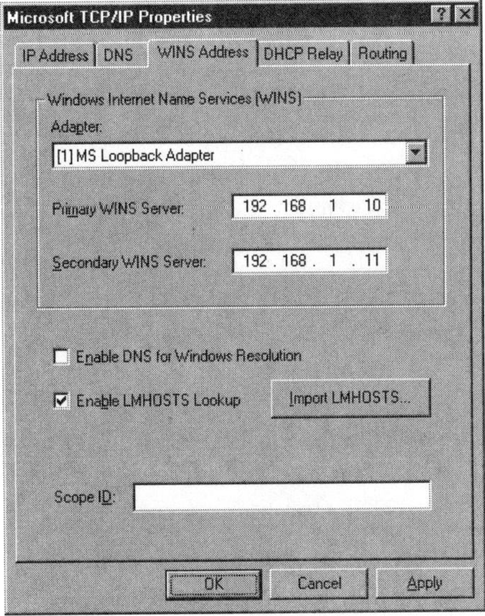

FIGURE 3.7

The WINS Address page in the TCP/IP Properties window, with the Enable LMHOSTS Lookup checkbox selected. (WINS servers 192.168.1.10 and 192.168.1.11 are not shown in Figure 3.4.)

In the spirit of Windows NT networking, a system administrator can access a WINS server from any Windows NT–based machine on the network. WINS seems like a fine solution, but it is not a network standard solution as DNS is.

DNS

WINS is a solution to resolve names, but there is still the question of how to resolve friendly host names used by people to IP addresses used by computers. Indeed, many thousands of machines access the Internet; there has to be a way to organize them. The solution to this problem is the Domain Name System (DNS). (Note that these domains have nothing in common with Windows NT domains.)

DNS has existed for almost 20 years. The first DNS software was known as BIND (Berkeley Internet Name Daemon) and ran on UNIX systems. Today DNS runs on a number of platforms, including Windows NT server. The general idea of DNS is straightforward. A network is divided into logical units known as *zones* and *domains*. A zone is the lowest administration unit of the DNS name space. A name server can spawn multiple zones, and each zone has a primary DNS server with a database of static IP addresses. The same zone can have redundant secondary DNS servers to provide fault tolerance. If one of the DNS servers is down, the secondary DNS server will service name resolution requests, providing redundancy and fault tolerance. Primary and secondary servers keep their databases in sync by transferring zone information at predefined periods of time (or when the primary server database changes). The database is maintained in the form of ASCII text files in a special format. These files contain special records that describe host information (IP addresses and names) and the address of the authoritative contact for the specific domain. Quite a few different types of DNS records exist. Each type serves its own purpose. For instance, Mail Exchanger (MX) records contain information for processing electronic mail sent to this Internet domain. HINFO records hold information about hardware, such as CPU type.

When a client wants to determine the address of a particular host, it needs to send a name resolution query to a DNS server. The DNS server then sends a reply. Because of its static database structure, DNS works only with static addresses. DHCP would not be a welcome addition to a DNS-enabled network.

Even though DNS is straightforward, let's take a look at what happens behind the scenes to resolve a name like *www.microsoft.com* to its real IP address. The Internet has a well-defined domain structure similar to that shown in Figure 3.8. In the figure, you can see that *ee* (which stands for electrical engineering) and *cc* (which stands for computer science) are subdomains of the *csun.edu* domain, which in turn is a subdomain of *.edu*. And *huey.ee.csun.edu* represents a specific machine in the *ee.csun.edu* subdomain. Along with specific machines in the subdomains, *csun.edu* can also have individual machines. Machine *www.csun.edu* is a member of the *csun.edu* domain.

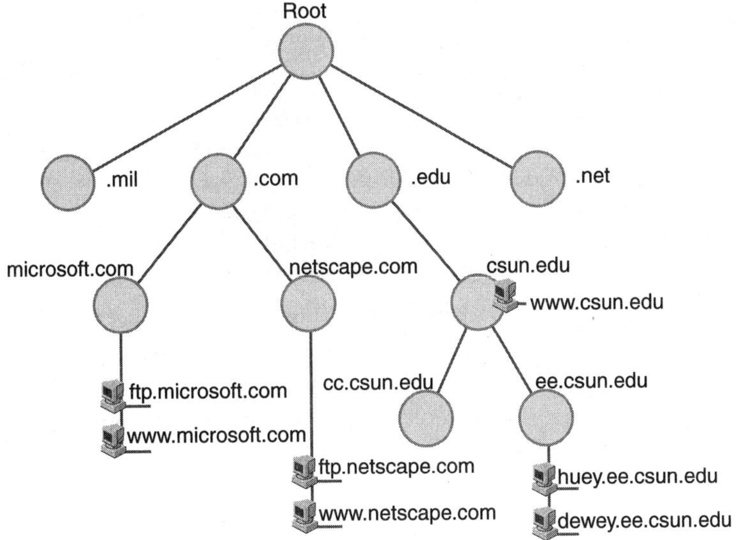

FIGURE 3.8

The Internet Domain Name System.

Any company can request a domain name (such as *microsoft.com*). InterNIC manages issuance and registration of these domain names. Historically, domain names use the following conventions:

- *.com* for commercial organizations (*www.microsoft.com*)
- *.mil* for military (*www.navy.mil*)
- *.edu* for nonprofit educational institutions (*www.csun.edu*)
- *.org* for nonprofit organizations (*www.pbs.org*)
- *.net* for network providers (*www.uunet.net)*
- *.gov* for government organizations (*www.whitehouse.gov*)
- two-letter abbreviation for foreign countries (Russia, for example: *www.ru*)

NOTE

Because of the huge growth of Internet domains in recent years, geographical domain structures are becoming popular. For example, if we were to get a domain in our hometown, it would be something like seattle.wa.us.

Each domain requires a DNS server that knows how to contact the authoritative name server for all of its specific subdomains. So the root server knows who the contact is for *.org, .com, .edu,* and so on. The DNS server for the *.com* domain knows who is the authoritative contact for the *microsoft.com* domain. The authoritative contact for *microsoft.com* has a database that contains each computer in the *microsoft.com* domain and can resolve names such as *www.microsoft.com* to its IP address.

In this example, let's assume that *www.csun.edu* wants to resolve the name for *www.microsoft.com.* The entire DNS works in the following fashion:

1. *www.csun.edu* sends a name resolution request to the DSN server for *csun.edu.domain.*
2. The DNS server for *csun.edu* does not know about *microsoft.com;* therefore, it looks up the address of the authoritative contact for the *.edu* domain and sends this information to *www.csun.edu.*
3. *www.csun.edu* sends a request for the name resolution to the *.edu* domain's DNS server. The DNS server for *.edu* still can't resolve the name for the machines in the *.com* domain. The address of the root server (shown as Root in Figure 3.8) is sent back to *www.csun.edu* instead.
4. *www.csun.edu* sends a request to resolve *www.microsoft.com* to the root server.
5. The root server looks up the address of the authoritative contact for the *microsoft.com* domain and sends it to *www.csun.edu.*
6. Since *www.csun.edu* now knows which machine keeps the database of all addresses for *microsoft.com,* it can send a query directly to this server.
7. *www.csun.edu* sends a request to Microsoft's authoritative contact (*microsoft.com*'s DNS server) and receives the IP address for the *www* machine, which is in the *microsoft.com* domain.

NOTE

The scenario above describes the work of the iterative DNS server. When an iterative server can't resolve a name, it sends a name of another server that might be able to do so. Recursive servers do all the work themselves: when a name can't be resolved, the server contacts the next server itself. Instead of sending an address of the authoritative server to the client, the recursive server eventually returns a final result—the IP address for the queried name. Regardless of the internal representation, the final result is always the same: the name is resolved to the IP address. The client's request for name resolution may specify the type of handling preferred: recursive or iterative. Most of the DNS servers now are implemented as recursive servers.

Microsoft has added a special value to its DNS server. It now works with WINS. This feature allows resolving the leftmost portion of the Fully Qualified Domain Name (FQDM) via WINs as a NetBIOS name when the TCP/IP name does not exist. Thus, if a DNS server receives a query for *foo.foozbar.com* and the machine and computer with the TCP/IP name *foo* does not exist, the DNS server can send a request to a WINS server to resolve *foo* as a NetBIOS name. In reality, the process of resolving names is much more complex because extensive caching and zone-transfer algorithms are involved. The objective is to make a query as efficient as possible and to avoid getting outdated information. Efficiency is generally achieved by caching information from root servers. Accuracy is achieved by propagating updated database files in the form of zone transfers from domains to their root servers.

Configuring the Network

Now that you know all about computer names and addresses, name resolution, and routing, you can put it all together. Look at the simple networking configuration shown in Figure 3.9.

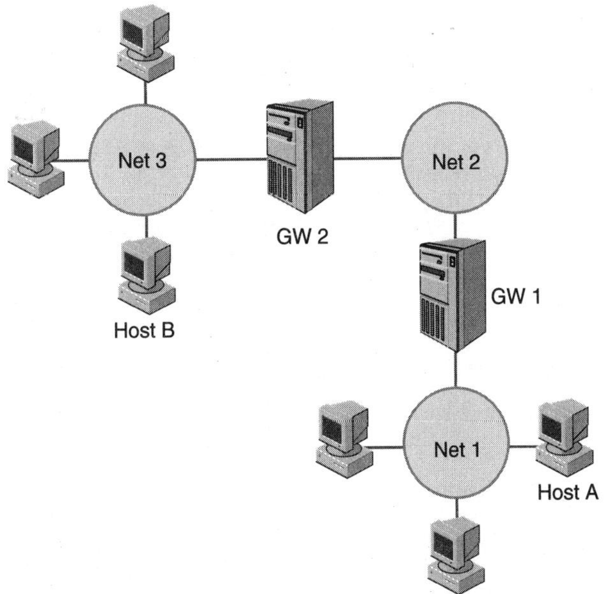

FIGURE 3.9

A simple network configuration.

Let's say we have three networks—Net 1, Net 2, and Net 3—that are connected via two gateways—GW 1 and GW 2. Host A on Net 1 tries to send a network message to Host B on Net 3. The following sequence of steps will occur.

1. Host A obtains the IP address of Host B (via the HOSTS file or DNS).
2. Host A looks at its routing table. Since it does not have a direct route to Host B's network, it gets the IP address of its own default gateway for Net 1.
3. Now Host A knows the IP address of its default gateway. It looks in its ARP cache for GW 1 to get its physical (MAC) address. If there is no entry in the cache, Host A sends the ARP broadcast and waits for a response.
4. As soon as Host A gets the physical address for GW 1, it sends the packet.
5. GW 1 gets the packet and looks for the IP address of the next hop. (*Hops* are the intermediate passes through gateways and routers.) If there is a static route in the GW 1 routing table for Net 3 with GW 2 as the entry (assume this is the case), it uses GW 2 as the next hop. If there is no static route entry for GW 2, GW 1 will use its default route, which is preset by the system administrator.
6. Given the IP address for GW 2, GW 1 determines GW 2's MAC address (ARP cache or ARP broadcast again).
7. As soon as GW 1 determines GW 2's MAC address, it sends the packet.
8. Host B is on the same network as GW 2, so GW 2 just hands the packet to Host B without any other routing hops. (Of course, another ARP might be involved to resolve Host B's IP address to a MAC address.)

Not too difficult, right? Once the network is set up and routing is properly configured, this process is very smooth indeed. But what do you do if something isn't working right? Is there a way to determine and isolate network problems? The answer is yes to both questions. Both Windows 95 and Windows NT are installed with a variety of network utilities. On Windows NT they are HOSTNAME, ARP, PING, TRACERT, ROUTE, and NSLOOKUP.

HOSTNAME.EXE

This utility is the simplest one. It prints the TCP/IP host name.

ARP.EXE

We have talked about the ARP cache. This utility allows you to view the ARP cache and modify it if needed. If you want to create an IP-to-MAC association, ARP.EXE is your tool. Here's how ARP.EXE's output looks:

```
D:\TEMP>arp -a

Interface: 157.54.165.146 on Interface 2
  Internet Address      Physical Address      Type
  157.54.160.1          08-00-02-06-83-41     dynamic
  157.54.165.43         00-aa-00-60-d6-e6     dynamic

D:\TEMP>
```

PING.EXE

PING.EXE is one of the most useful of all tools. It simply tests to determine if the remote machine is reachable. Suppose you type *http://www.doesnotexist.com* in your browser and get an error. The first thing you need to do is check to see whether machine *www.doesnotexist.com* exists. PING.EXE's output looks like this:

```
D:\>ping www.netscape.com

Pinging www81.netscape.com [198.95.251.36] with 32 bytes of data:

Reply from 198.95.251.36: bytes=32 time=261ms TTL=246
Reply from 198.95.251.36: bytes=32 time=190ms TTL=246
Reply from 198.95.251.36: bytes=32 time=170ms TTL=246
Reply from 198.95.251.36: bytes=32 time=240ms TTL=246
```

Note that even though we have specified *www.netscape.com* on the command line of the output, *www81.netscape.com* is "pinged." This occurs because of so-called round-robin DNS. The idea is that one well-known server such as *www.netscape.com* can be resolved to many other servers with different names. In this case, a "smart" DNS server finds the server with the lowest load and resolves requests to its IP address.

TRACERT.EXE

PING.EXE can determine only whether a destination is reachable. But what about when multiple intermediate machines and routers are involved? We basically are depending on a chain of network routes—and every separate link can fail. TRACERT.EXE can help to pinpoint precisely which link failed. Here is its output:

```
D:\>tracert www.microsoft.com

Tracing route to www.microsoft.com [207.68.137.56]
        over a maximum of 30 hops:

  1   220 ms   171 ms   170 ms  Max4.Seattle.WA.MS.UU.NET [207.76.5.10]
  2   201 ms   170 ms   160 ms  Ar1.Seattle.WA.MS.UU.NET [207.76.5.3]
```

(continued)

```
  3   290 ms   190 ms   251 ms  Fddi0-0.GW2.SEA1.Alter.Net [137.39.33.44]
  4     *      301 ms   190 ms  ms3-gw.customer.ALTER.NET [137.39.136.162]
  5   190 ms   180 ms   180 ms  207.68.145.46
  6   211 ms   170 ms   180 ms  www.microsoft.com [207.68.137.56]

Trace complete.
```

This output shows all the intermediate hops that occur between our computer and the *www.microsoft.com* machine. If any single link fails, we could not connect to Microsoft's Web server. Tracing would show exactly where the failure occurred.

ROUTE.EXE

This utility allows you to directly manipulate your machine's routing tables. Not only can you see the current routing table, but you can also add or delete routes directly. It is easy to render a machine unusable on a network by improperly configuring its routing tables, so be careful. (We suggest that you leave the use of this utility for your system administrator or TCP/IP routing expert.) Following is the routing table for our machine:

```
D:\WINNT\system32>route print

Active Routes:

  Network Address          Netmask  Gateway Address        Interface  Metric
          0.0.0.0          0.0.0.0      206.155.0.1      206.155.0.1       2
          0.0.0.0          0.0.0.0    153.34.36.136    153.34.36.136       1
        127.0.0.0        255.0.0.0        127.0.0.1        127.0.0.1       1
      153.34.0.0      255.255.0.0    153.34.36.136    153.34.36.136       1
    153.34.36.136  255.255.255.255        127.0.0.1        127.0.0.1       1
      206.155.0.0    255.255.255.0      206.155.0.1      206.155.0.1       2
      206.155.0.1  255.255.255.255        127.0.0.1        127.0.0.1       1
    206.155.0.255  255.255.255.255      206.155.0.1      206.155.0.1       1
        224.0.0.0        224.0.0.0    153.34.36.136    153.34.36.136       1
        224.0.0.0        224.0.0.0      206.155.0.1      206.155.0.1       1
  255.255.255.255  255.255.255.255      206.155.0.1      206.155.0.1       1
```

NSLOOKUP.EXE

If you are configuring DNS servers and you are not sure whether you have set them up correctly, this is your tool. NSLOOKUP.EXE is an interactive program that allows you to choose various DNS servers and interrogate their data in the form of various DNS records. (Recall the MS and HINFO records earlier.) The output of NSLOOKUP.EXE can be as detailed or as brief as you want. In the sample that follows, we have used the detailed view. (The output has been slightly edited to conserve space. The boldface lines represent user input.)

```
D:\WINNT>nslookup
. . .
> server 204.255.246.17
Default Server:  [204.255.246.17]
Address:  204.255.246.17

> www.msn.com
Server:  [204.255.246.17]
Address:  204.255.246.17
www.msn.com     canonical name = msn.com
msn.com nameserver = dns1.moswest.msn.net
. . .
msn.com nameserver = dns6.moswest.msn.net

> set type=all
> directnet.com
Server:  [204.255.246.17]
Address:  204.255.246.17
. . .
Non-authoritative answer:
directnet.com   nameserver = NS2.directnet.com
directnet.com   nameserver = NS.directnet.com
directnet.com
        primary name server = NS.directnet.com
        responsible mail addr = sysadm.directnet.com
        serial  = 960612
        refresh = 10800 (3 hours)
        retry   = 3600 (1 hour)
        expire  = 3600000 (41 days 16 hours)
        default TTL = 86400 (1 day)

directnet.com   nameserver = NS2.directnet.com
directnet.com   nameserver = NS.directnet.com
NS2.directnet.com       internet address = 204.177.0.5
NS.directnet.com        internet address = 204.177.0.2
>
```

This output certainly deserves some explanation. The first step we performed was to choose a DNS server. NSLOOKUP.EXE will use your default DNS server, if it is available. We then entered *www.msn.com.* NSLOOKUP showed the list of DNS servers for the *msn.com* domain. To maximize reliability, there are many redundant DNS servers containing *msn.com* records. The next step was to set the records type to *all,* which generates much more detail about a particular domain. By default, not all records are shown.

Then we see the results after querying the *directnet.com* domain. The *directnet.com* domain is serviced by two name servers: NS2 and NS. NS is the primary name server. We also can see information about zone transfers, such as the refresh rate, expiration, and time to live (TTL). Once you configure your own DNS server, you will see how helpful NSLOOKUP.EXE is for testing.

Getting Connected

This chapter has presented much of what you need to know about preparing, configuring, and troubleshooting your network before installing Internet Information Server. It described the core TCP/IP principles and looked at some sample installations. The details of your network configuration might vary, depending on what purpose your network will serve: whether yours is an ISP or a corporate network connected to the Internet.

As shown in Figure 3.6, we often symbolize the Internet with a cloud to represent the fact that we can't see what actually happens behind the scenes, and frankly it doesn't matter. The important fact is that if a piece of data is sent from a machine on one side of the Internet to a machine on the other side of the Internet, the data will reach the other side through some unknown series of events (unknown unless you are using the TRACERT utility).

Our real interface to the Internet is usually an ordinary jack in the wall. For high-speed lines, the jack looks like a standard telephone connection, except the plug is a little wider. This jack can provide a high-speed digital network connection, such as a T1 line, from your friendly network-provided company. (AT&T and MCI are two of the biggest carriers.) A T1 line has a bandwidth of 1.536 Mbps (megabits per second). In comparison, a standard Ethernet network has a maximum bandwidth of 10 Mbps. If you want to pay the big bucks, you can get a T3 line that has a bandwidth of 44.736 Mbps. Depending on your network requirements, slower, faster, and more and less expensive options are available to meet your needs. A schematic of a high-speed link is shown in Figure 3.10.

You will need three major hardware devices to service the digital circuit on your end. From the wall jack, the high-speed digital circuit connection leads to a repeater. The repeater is then connected to the data service unit/channel service unit, which is in turn connected to a network router. As mentioned previously, Windows NT server can be configured to act as your router. But be aware that Windows NT uses software for routing, which can be slow for dedicated high-speed lines. Dedicated network routers (hardware) are usually much more suitable for such purposes.

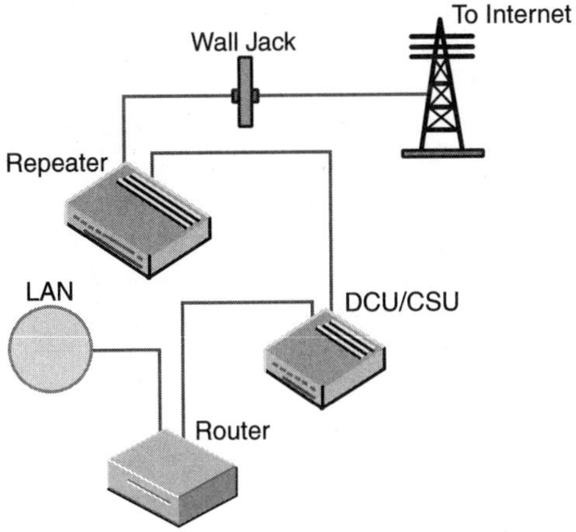

FIGURE 3.10

A high-speed Internet connection.

Once the network is configured and connected to the Internet, you should consider the details for your different purposes. An ISP acts as an Internet access reseller, so to speak. The ISP will have many incoming phone lines and special dial-up servers. This setup enables many users to dial in and be connected to the Internet for the duration of their call.

As we said, Windows NT server comes with special software that acts as a dial-in server. The *remote access service* (RAS) runs on a Windows NT–based machine with potentially a pool of modems. It uses special network protocols such as PPP to make client machines with modems pretend that they are full-fledged Internet hosts with their own IP address. But if we make the assumption that our ISP company has many clients who regularly dial-in for a short time (hours, not days), we need to devise a solution that can accommodate this scenario.

DHCP with a short lease duration (a few hours) is the perfect solution for dynamic address assignment. Most likely, dial-in clients will not be using NetBIOS, so WINS as a name resolution mechanism is probably not a good idea. On the other hand, a dial-up client will need to be able to easily resolve Internet names such as *www.microsoft.com* to IP addresses. Setting up one or more DNS servers on the network and configuring DHCP to supply the DNS server's address to the clients when they connect is a perfect solution. Since clients do not really need to have static names, using DNS with the dynamic addresses assigned by DHCP works fine.

We should also consider another scenario: a large corporate intranet. In the case of the corporate network, unique computer names are essential. It also would be a good idea to continue using dynamic IP addresses with DHCP for ease of administration. Dynamically assigned IP addresses and permanent names for computers make WINS the best name resolution mechanism. You can still use DNS, however, since it integrates with WINS for Internet domain name resolution. Remote dialing into your corporate network is a valuable addition to this configuration, since some employees will likely work from home. Unlike a large ISP, however, you probably don't need to provide dial-in capabilities for hundreds of users at the same time.

Now that you understand some of the requirements for a TCP/IP network, it's time to move on to Chapter 4, which explores the options available when you install Internet Information Server.

CHAPTER 4

Web Server Configuration

The heart of Microsoft Internet Information Server (IIS) is the World Wide Web publishing service. In Chapter 12 you will learn about services in detail. For now, it is enough to know that a *service* is a special program that runs in the background and performs certain tasks. The IIS Web server not only receives HTTP requests but also activates other components such as Active Server Pages. The Web Publishing Service, for example, handles Web browser requests by sending requested Web pages back to the browsers. This chapter takes a quick look at how the Web server is installed and discusses the many configuration options available in this environment.

Setup

At the beginning of the installation process, the IIS Setup provides both minimal and typical installation options, in addition to a custom option. Minimal installation is designed to conserve your hard drive space—only bare necessities are installed. Typical installation adds some optional components such as Microsoft Script Debugger as well as extended documentation. The Custom installation option lets you choose installation options from a list of all available components.

If you are interested in running only WWW service and have limited hard disk space, the Minimal installation option might be the best one. With the Minimal installation option, Setup creates different directories during installation, including the \InetPub directory that will hold much of your published information. Two subdirectories included in \InetPub are \scripts, which is usually reserved for ISAPI, CGI, and ASP, and \wwwroot, which is the default home directory for the Web site. You'll learn much more about ASP applications in Chapter 17 and about ISAPI and CGI applications in Chapter 20.

NOTE

Throughout this book, whenever a particular component is discussed, we will point out which installation option you need to choose to install it.

The Typical installation adds additional components, directories, and documentation to your hard drive, but the basic directory structure stays the same.

If you choose the Custom installation option, you will be presented a list of choices during IIS installation. Figure 4.1 shows the Microsoft Windows NT 4.0 Option Pack Setup window when the Custom installation option is selected.

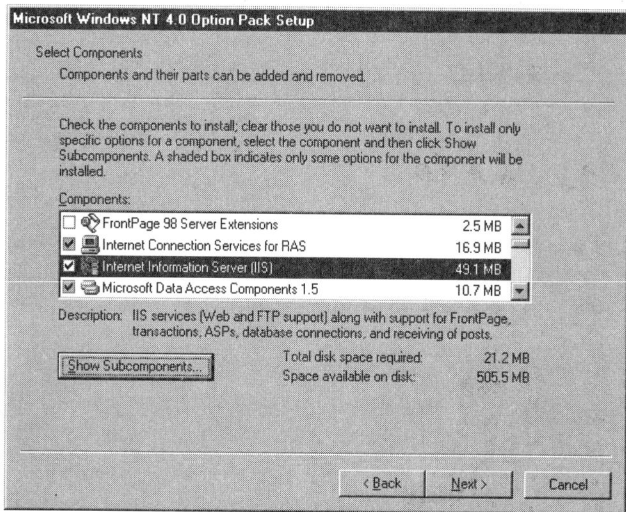

FIGURE 4.1

The components of the Windows NT Option Pack with the Internet Information Server (IIS) component selected.

After the user selects a component to install and clicks the Show Subcomponents button, the dialog box shown in Figure 4.2 appears, listing the specific subcomponents for the component selected (in this case, IIS). Most of the subcomponents listed in this dialog box represent additional services that run alongside IIS. These services will be discussed in later chapters.

NOTE

The only optional subcomponent directly related to the Web Publishing Service (WWW service) is the installation of the HTML version of the Internet Service Manager. The HTML Internet Service Manager (which we will call HTML-based administration pages) allows you to administer your WWW service from any browser (subject to secure authentication).

In Figure 4.2, the HTML Internet Service Manager subcomponent is checked so that it will be installed.

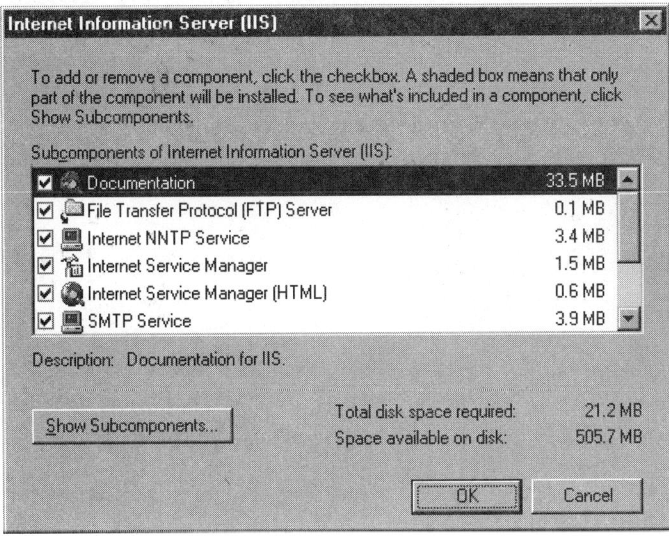

FIGURE 4.2

The subcomponents of Internet Information Server.

The IIS Hierarchy

Before you explore the configuration options available under IIS, you need to understand a few concepts, including the hierarchy of the following IIS configurable units: the Web server, Web sites, home directories, virtual directories, and applications. The Web server, the top level of our hierarchy, can contain multiple Web sites on a single machine. A Web site is usually considered the equivalent of a single host machine running a Web server. However, using IIS, multiple Web sites can be located on a single machine.

Web Sites

If you choose to install the optional HTML Internet Service Manager (which we will call HTML-based administration pages), two Web sites will automatically be created on your machine: the default site and the administration Web site. Most standard

HTTP requests are handled at the default site. The administration site is waiting to accept connections from browsers on a nonstandard TCP (Transmission Control Protocol) port (other than 80). The sole purpose of the administration site is to provide remote administration capabilities over HTTP protocol. Therefore, it is configured as an entity in itself.

As noted earlier, IIS allows you to have multiple sites on one machine. That means you can create other sites that listen on different ports or use other IP addresses or even sites that just use a different host name. For example, a single machine could have a site created for the host name *www.cmpny.com* and another site created for *www.cmpny2.com.*

Web sites can contain many virtual directories and applications. Each individual site can have its own distinct properties, such as directory structure, default documents, scripts, and so on. For example, even though both *http://www.cmpny.com* and *http://www.cmpny2.com* are located on the same physical machine, the two sites could be completely different. By locating different sites on the same machine, you can access many virtual computers for the cost and maintainability of one physical machine.

The Home Directory

Each site on a machine must have one and only one home directory. The home directory is the site's default location on the server and contains the default page shown in the browser when the server is accessed without being asked for a specific Web page. Assume that the browser specifies a URL such as *http://www.microsoft.com*. Because no specific Web page is requested in this URL, the Web server finds a default document in the home directory (DEFAULT.HTM, for example) and sends it to the browser. You cannot change or delete a site's home directory, although it is possible to configure a site's home directory as a different physical directory on another computer on the same network. (You will learn how to do this later in this chapter.)

The Virtual Directory

The IIS Web server does not make just any directory available to client browsers—obviously, there would be grave security concerns if a client were able to roam around your server's hard drives. So when you want to make the contents of a certain directory available via your Web site, you need to configure this directory either as a home directory or as a virtual directory for the site. Because you can have only one home directory per site, all other locations must be created as virtual directories.

Virtual directory names do not have to be the same as the physical directory names that they publish. For example, rather than have your client browsers use the entire path d:\InetPub\Support\Drivers\NtDrivers\Instructions, you can use an alias such as /NtDrvInst to refer to the lengthy physical directory name. Once the virtual directory is created, it can be accessed via the URL *http://machine/NtDrvInst.* A virtual directory usually contains a number of files and possibly subdirectories, and it has common properties that apply to all files residing within it. However, it is possible to override the common settings for individual files in a file's Properties window. Also, if you have subdirectories within the physical location of a virtual directory, you can configure common options for that particular subdirectory that override the virtual directory's options. And if you want to go the next step, any files within the subdirectory can override the common subdirectory options. All of these overrides are accomplished using the properties settings for the specific file or directory in question. Thus, IIS provides endless possibilities for configuration options in terms of inheritance and granularity.

Application

Files within a virtual directory don't have to be grouped together for any logical reason. The virtual directory is merely a common place to store files, much as physical directories do on your hard drive. With the general paradigm shift to Internet applications, the Web server needs to have another component to describe applications other than just a common file location. IIS uses another logical unit called an application. An application is a logical unit that potentially spawns several different virtual directories that can contain scripts, pictures, HTML files, and other files. All files and directories within an application are logically connected with each other—they are all considered part of the same application, such as an online shopping catalog, for example. You might find that the idea of grouping individual files all used for a single activity under the umbrella of "application" to be an obvious one. Technically, however, this is an important concept because all scripts and ISAPI extensions of one application share the same memory space. This means that it is possible to pass a pointer to a common memory location from one component of an application to another, thereby sharing data between them.

Configuration Options

Now it's time to get to work setting and changing server configuration options. This chapter assumes you are working with the Microsoft Management Console interface for configuring IIS. Administration tasks can also be performed by using the HTML-based administration pages. As you remember from earlier in the chapter, the HTML-based administration pages are an optional IIS component. To use the administration pages, you need access to an Administration Web site by specifying this URL: *http://localhost/iisadmin.* Using the HTML-based administration pages, you can create your own scripts and applications to perform management tasks. (This will be discussed in later chapters.)

As shown in the Management Console in Figure 4.3, the server has two different Web sites: the Default Web Site and the Administration Web Site. The default Web site includes three applications: IISSAMPLES, IISADMIN, and IISHELP. The default site also includes two virtual directories: SCRIPTS and IISADMPWD. Notice that the icon that represents an application looks like a little package (we will talk more about packages once we start talking about Microsoft Transaction Server), and the icon for a virtual directory looks like a folder with a little globe in the corner. Also notice that the icon associated with the Web sites is different from the one next to the Default FTP site. Icons always provide a visual clue for users.

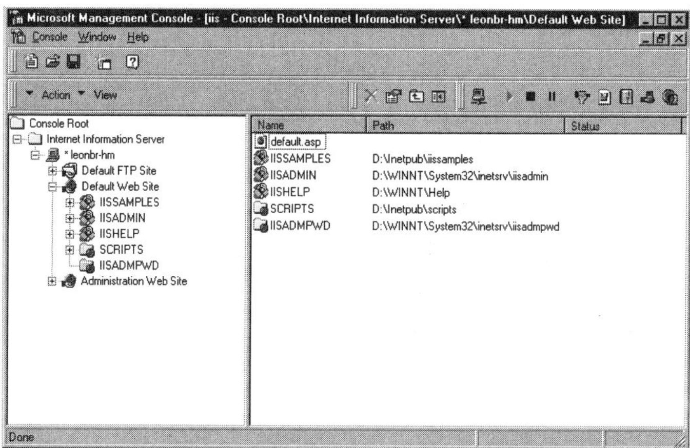

FIGURE 4.3

The Microsoft Management Console.

As mentioned earlier, IIS uses a hierarchical architecture. Web site objects are located one level below computer objects (indicated by the little computer icon labeled *leonbr-hm* in Figure 4.3). Virtual directories reside a level below each site. Objects on the lower levels inherit configuration parameters from the objects above, so, for example, setting values once for a computer object property makes all lower level objects inherit the same property value. This property inheritance can save a lot of time and memory storage space.

Because of property inheritance, the configuration property pages for the IIS master properties look similar to the configuration property pages for individual Web sites. If you right-click on the computer icon labeled *leonbr-hm* and choose Properties from the pop-up menu, the Properties dialog appears, as shown in Figure 4.4.

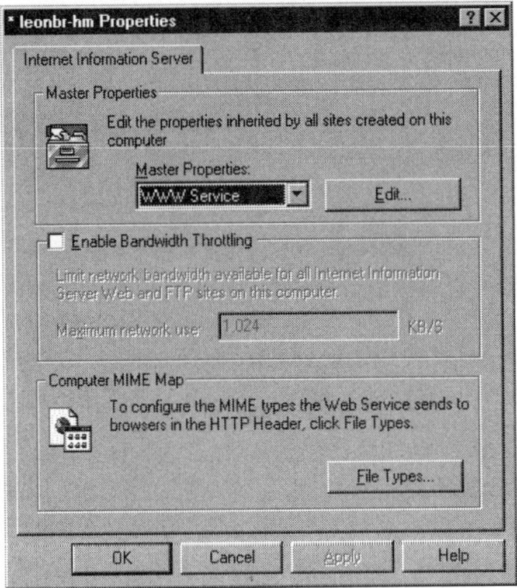

FIGURE 4.4

The Properties dialog box for the master computer named **leonbr-hm.**

NOTE

Right-clicking on the computer icon also makes available the Backup/Restore Configuration option. If you choose this option, you can create a backup of the entire current configuration (WWW and FTP server settings, virtual directories, and so on). You can use this backup copy to restore configuration settings if necessary.

Master Properties Window and Default Web Site Properties Window

From the Master Properties list box in the Properties window, choose WWW Service and then click Edit to see the WWW Service Master Properties For Leonbr-hm window, shown in Figure 4.5.

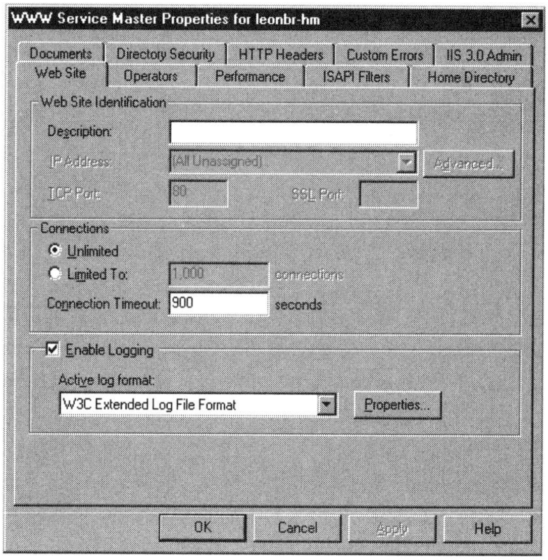

FIGURE 4.5

The WWW Service Master Properties window.

This window provides access to 10 different tabbed pages full of configurable property options. Similarly, if you look at the Properties window for the Default Web Site (see Figure 4.6), you will find all but one of the same tabbed pages.

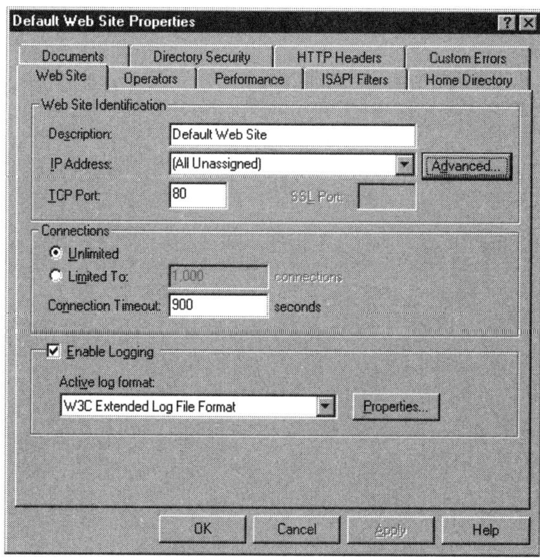

FIGURE 4.6

The Default Web Site Properties window.

Some property pages are available only at particular levels in the Management Console hierarchy, and the IIS 3.0 Admin page is not available at the Web Site level.

NOTE

To see the individual configuration site settings shown in Figure 4.6 for yourself, go to the Management Console window, right-click on the Default Web Site option, and choose Properties from the pop-up menu.

The next section explains the IIS 3.0 Admin page that is accessible from the Master Properties window. Then the rest of this chapter is devoted to all the tabbed pages available in the Default Web Site Properties window.

The IIS 3.0 Admin Page

This page, shown in Figure 4.7, allows you to control compatibility with IIS versions 3.0 and earlier. Version 3.0, like 4.0, shipped with an administration tool that allowed connections to remote servers. Older versions of IIS did not support multiple sites, so an old version's administration tool does not know how to handle multiple sites on a single machine. It is still possible to manage IIS 4.0 with the tool shipped with versions 3.0 and earlier, but only one site can be managed per machine. This page indicates which site it will be. (A similar option for FTP services will be discussed in Chapter 9.)

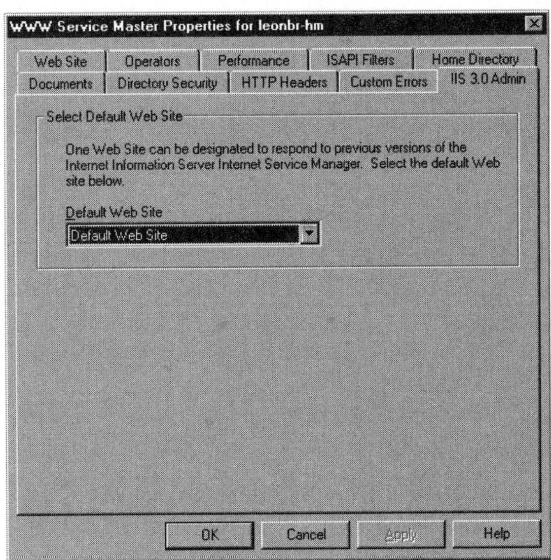

FIGURE 4.7

The IIS 3.0 Admin page.

The Web Site Page

As shown in Figure 4.6, you can use the Web Site properties page to change a description of the site as well as to change the default port (port 80) to a different port. If you change the port from the default, however, your clients will need to know the new port number to include in the site's URL. For example, if you change the port to 4000, the URL might look something like this: *http://machine_name:4000/default.htm.* Why would someone change the default port number? One reason the site administrator would do this is to make the site available only to users who know the port number assigned to that site, thus limiting the site to a specific group of users.

To associate more than one address or a different port to the same Web site, you can click the Advanced button on the right of the IP Address text box in the Default Web Site Properties window. This brings up the Advanced Multiple Web Site Configuration dialog box shown in Figure 4.8.

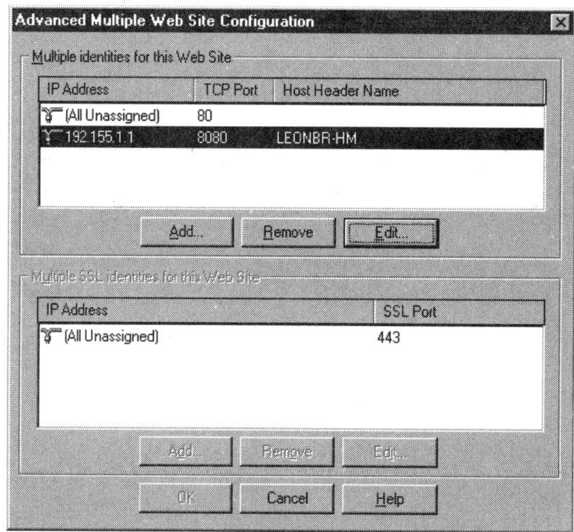

FIGURE 4.8

Using the Advanced Multiple Web Site Configuration dialog box to associate more than one IP address and port with the server.

Because it is possible to assign more than one computer name to the same IP address (by adding entries to your DNS server or by editing your TCP/IP HOSTS file), the server needs to have a unique identifier for each different site. Clients compatible with HTTP version 1.1, such as Microsoft Internet Explorer 4.0, support the Host header that helps differentiate requests to multiple computer names.

Headers are a way for a server and browser to exchange auxiliary information. (Chapter 22 will cover headers in more detail.)

For instance, suppose you have two host names, *machine1.domain.com* and *machine2.domain.com*, which both resolve to the same IP address, *123.123.123.123*. The server administrator will probably want to use different sites for each machine name. Because both names will eventually be resolved to the same IP address (*123.123.123.123*), the browser needs to pass information about what host name was specified in the requested URL. That is precisely what the Host header does. It reflects the target host of the request. So a request to *http://machine1.domain.com* will have this Host header:

```
Host: machine1.domain.com
```

After the request has arrived at the server, the Host header is examined and the correct Web site is determined. If for some reason the requested site is not available or the Host header is missing, the default page from the default site is sent.

Other configuration options accessible from the Default Web Site Properties window include restrictions on the number of simultaneous connections allowed to the server and the connection timeout period for idle sessions. By default, IIS uses HTTP version 1.1. This version of HTTP has a provision that allows connections to stay open (that is, to not close the underlying socket) even after the request has been completed, which can greatly improve performance if you are making multiple requests to the same server. When no requests occur after the specified timeout, the server closes the socket associated with that session.

Glossary

socket *Communication endpoint used in low-level network protocols (such as TCP/IP). Clients and servers use sockets to exchange information remotely.*

You can also specify options for logging server activity on the Web Site property page. (You can read about logging options in detail in Chapter 6.)

The Operators Page

The Operators property page shown in Figure 4.9 is fairly simple. Individual users or groups listed here as operators have the right to administer the Web site. Administration can occur either through the Management Console, the HTML-based administration pages, or the management programming interfaces. This page simply displays the users and groups that have operator privileges to write changes to the metabase, where configuration information is stored.

Glossary

metabase *A special storage area used by IIS to store its configuration settings.*

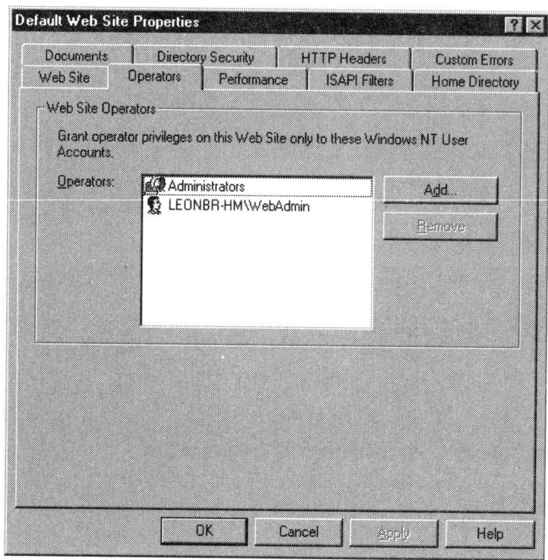

FIGURE 4.9

The Operators page in the Default Web Site Properties window.

The Performance Page

The Performance page, shown in Figure 4.10, allows you to optimize performance of the server based on the number of anticipated requests per day. This has the effect of determining how much memory IIS will reserve for caching request information. If your server receives a high number of requests, more of the server's memory will be used by IIS's cache. In the case of fewer requests, setting this option too high will waste memory by saving unnecessary cache space.

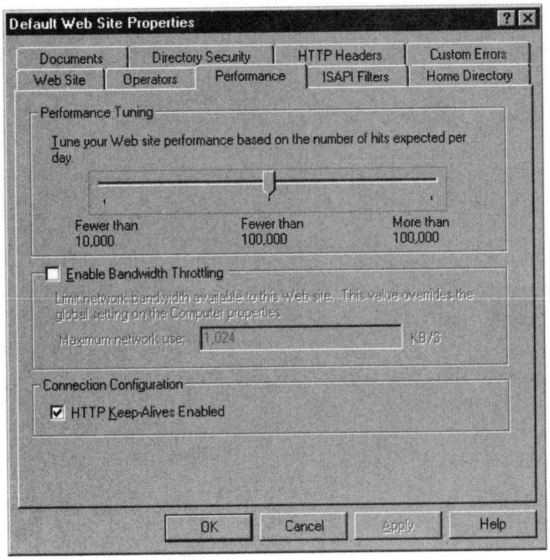

FIGURE 4.10

The Performance page in the Default Web Site Properties window.

The Enable Bandwidth Throttling option allows you to limit the network bandwidth used by this specific site. Site bandwidth settings take precedence over the master WWW settings.

In the Connection Configuration section there is an option to enable or disable HTTP Keep-Alives. Remember our note on keeping sockets open to improve efficiency? Checking this box (the default) indicates that Keep-Alives are enabled.

The ISAPI Filters Page

The ISAPI Filters page is shown in Figure 4.11. ISAPI filters are covered in detail in Chapter 21, but for now you can think of them as special DLLs that are loaded by the server and are notified at particular points for each request received by the site. This page shows ISAPI filters listed for this particular site (namely, SmartRedir or the Smart Redirector filter). In general the Web server might have global ISAPI filters that are installed through the Master Properties window. Global ISAPI filters receive notifications for all Web sites on the machine. Even though Figure 4.11 does not list global scope ISAPI filters, they still affect all sites because of the inheritance architecture of IIS objects.

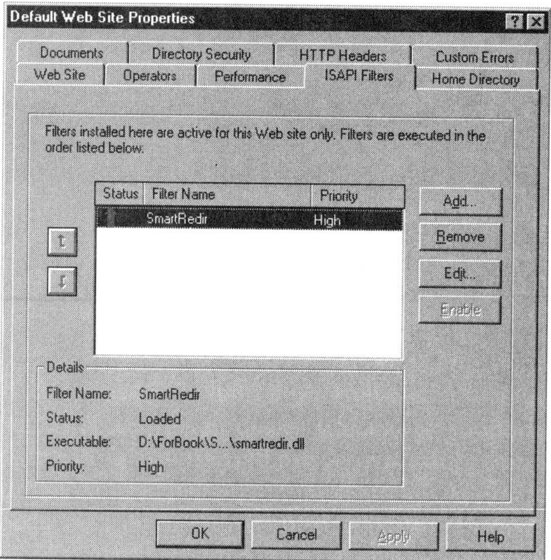

FIGURE 4.11

The ISAPI Filters page in the Default Web Site Properties window.

After a filter has been loaded by the server, the internal filter properties are shown on the property page. The filter listed on this page controls which browsers are allowed to access certain directories. We will look into this filter in greater detail in Chapter 21.

If more than one filter were loaded, you could arrange for them to be called in a specific order to allow incoming requests to be handled by multiple filters in that order. The ISAPI Filters page also shows you at a glance the specific priorities for any loaded filters. This can be a handy feature when you're trying to track down ISAPI filter problems.

The Home Directory Page

The Home Directory page is shown in Figure 4.12. This page contains items similar to those you would see for any virtual directory.

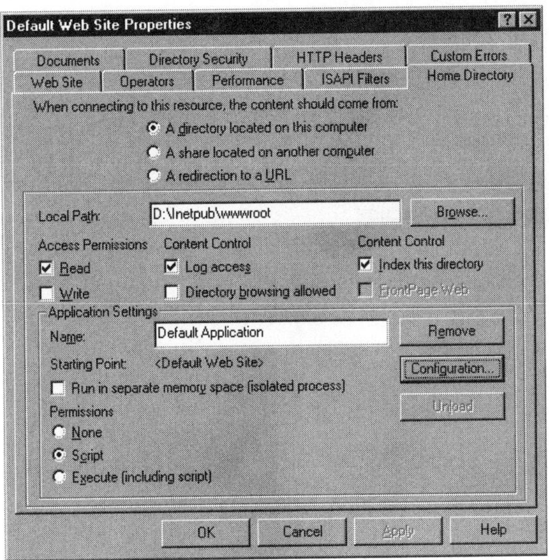

FIGURE 4.12

The Home Directory page in the Default Web Site Properties window.

Share location You can change many Web site options from this page, including the physical location where the Web content is stored. In the simplest scenario, the home directory resides on the local machine, as shown in Figure 4.12. It is possible, however, to make IIS serve content from other machines on the network. In that case, the machine that contains the data does not necessarily have to run IIS. The machine is addressed via the UNC (Uniform Naming Convention) in this way: *server**share*. Because the IIS process itself runs under the Local System account, the account is known only to the local machine and cannot connect to remote shares on the network. (The mysteries of the Local System account—that is, the account built into the Windows NT operating system—will be explained in Chapter 12.) IIS avoids this problem by prompting for the user name and password that are necessary to connect to a remote machine. To enable this feature, from the Home Directory page choose A Share Located On Another Computer. When you do this, the Connect As button will appear. Click it to enter the credentials (user name and password) required to connect to the remote share.

Glossary

Local System account *An account built into the Windows NT operating system. This account is used internally by Windows NT to run system services, such as the IIS Web Publishing Service.*

URL redirection IIS can not only serve content from a remote machine, it can also initiate redirection. For instance, assume the server is configured to provide content for a virtual directory from the /my_org_content directory. But for some reason this directory needs to be changed. This could be necessary because of changes in the drive's partitions or in NTFS permissions, directory structure changes, the directory might need to be renamed, or some other reason. You could create new virtual directories with a new name and create links to the new location. This will, of course, affect bookmarks made earlier to the original location. Instead of allowing the browser to report a "URL Not Found" error to the user, you can configure the server to send a new location to the browser when a request is made for the original location. This is called a *server redirect*. IIS sends a special HTTP status code to the browser with the new URL; if the browser supports redirection, it sends a request to the new URL. When you select the option labeled A Redirection To A URL, the Home Directory page changes to look like the one shown in Figure 4.13.

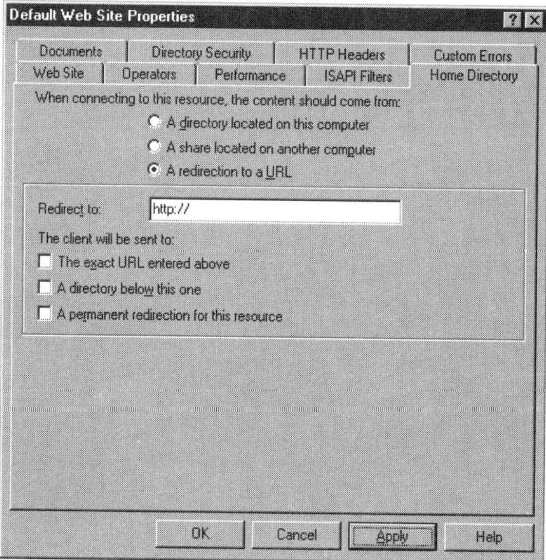

FIGURE 4.13

The Home Directory page in the Default Web Site Properties window when Redirection is selected.

You can choose from three different redirection options, as shown in the lower half of the Home Directory page. By checking The Exact URL Entered Above, you can redirect all requests made to any element in the virtual directory to a single file. For example, if you have a virtual directory named /my_org_content, a request to *http://myserver/my_org_content* or to any file in this directory (such as *http://myserver/my_org_content/myfile.htm*) could be mapped to a single HTML file, such as *MyExplanations.htm*. This option can be helpful when the content of the original directory is not available and you want to explain why. The Redirect To text box contains the URL of the explanation file that will be returned to the client.

The next check box in this section, A Directory Below This One, forces redirection to a child directory. For example, entering *mysubdir* as a redirect target for a virtual directory named /support will force all requests to *http://myserver/support* to be redirected to *http://myserver/support/mysubdir*.

When server redirection occurs, IIS sends a "302 Temporary Redirect" HTTP status code to the client along with the new location. Checking the last option, A Permanent Redirection For This Resource, forces the server to return a "301 Permanent Redirect" HTTP status code to the client. Upon getting the 301 code, a smart browser can even update saved bookmarks.

Server variables and wildcards If you think that IIS's redirection is limited to simple redirection from place to place, you should know that its real power comes from the ability to handle server variables and wildcards. Server redirection variables are special characters inserted in the "Redirect to:" URL. These variables allow you to transfer part of the original URL to the new location. The following table shows the redirection variables and how they are used.

Variable	Function	Example
$S	Passes the matched suffix of the original URL to the target URL	For *http://server/dir/doit.bat*. *$S* represents */doit.bat*. If the suffix does not exist (*http://server/dir*), *$S* is blank.
$P	Passes parameters from the original URL	For *http://server/dir/doit.bat?P1=1*, *$P* represents *P1=1*.
$Q	The same as *$P*, but with the question mark	For *http://server/dir/doit.bat?P1=1*, *$Q* represents *?P1=1*.
$V	Deletes the server name from the original request	For *http://server/dir/doit.bat?P1=1*, *$V* represents */dir/doit.bat*.

Here's an example to help illustrate how server variables work. Suppose that we have configured all requests to the virtual directory /support to be redirected to the exact URL */target$S*$P*$Q*$V*. Notice here that requests are being redirected to the virtual directory/target along with all server variables, which are separated by asterisks to allow an easy match of the resulting substitutions with corresponding parameters. As soon as we enter *http:// server/support/doit.bat?Param1=1* in the address line of the browser, IIS redirects the request to the following location: *http://server/target/doit.bat*Param1=1*?Param1=1*/support/doit.bat*

In the above sample URL, *$S* is matched with */doit.bat*. As you can see "/" is included. Therefore, we don't need to precede *$S* in the target URL (*/target$S*$P*$Q*$V*) with "/". The *$P* is substituted with *Param1=1* and *$Q* with *?Param1=1*. The last variable, *$V*, has generated the */support/doit.bat* string by omitting the server name.

Server variables are powerful (and difficult to use), but wildcards are even more powerful. Wildcards allow you to match any number of characters in the original URL to a pattern in the destination URL. The asterisk (*) wildcard character denotes the portion of the URL that can take any combination of characters. There are, however, some rules to follow when you're using wildcards. You must make sure that The Exact URL Entered Above option is checked in the Home Directory page. Also, the target URL must start with the wildcard character (*), and different pairs of wildcards must be separated with a semicolon.

For example, to redirect all requests for **.ASP* files to *my_new_default.asp* and all requests for **.bat* files to *all_in_one.bat*, type this for the "Redirect to" URL: **;*.asp;/my_new_default.asp;*.bat;/all_in_one.bat*. You can get the matched wildcard part by using the special variables *$0* through *$9*. Now all **.asp* requests are redirected to the *my_new_default.asp* file. What would happen if a browser sent a request for the *my_new_default.asp* file itself? If you don't let IIS know that this file is an exception to the virtual directory redirection order, an infinite loop can occur. By using the exclamation mark (!) as a redirect URL for the *my_new_default.asp* file, you let IIS know that this file is an exception to the redirection. The "!" needs to be entered as a redirection target for *my_new_default.asp* file. To do this, right-click on the individual file (*my_new_default.asp*) and set its individual redirection property. This is one of those times when the ability to set properties for a specific file comes in handy.

Access permissions Setting and controlling access permissions is an important part of running IIS. When redirection is not selected, the Home Directory page allows you to control read and write permissions for a directory. Read permission is self-explanatory—when you grant permission to read, anyone requesting that file is allowed to read it. Write permission, however, is a little more complex. HTTP version 1.1 provides a *PUT* method that allows files, such as HTML documents, to be uploaded directly to the Web server. Checking the Write access permission will allow browsers to upload documents and files to this virtual directory. This right is also essential to allow posting files with the File Upload control, which is discussed in Chapter 8. If the actual directory is located on an NTFS volume, IIS will also check the NTFS permissions before reading or writing, and the most restrictive permissions will take precedence. (NTFS is covered in Chapter 12.)

Content control The four Content Control options—Log Access, Directory Browsing Allowed, Index This Directory, and FrontPage Web—are found near the middle of the Home Directory page when redirection is not selected.

IIS can generate entries in the log file whenever particular resources are accessed. You can enable or disable this for particular sites, virtual directories, directories, or individual files by checking the Log Access check box. IIS allows you complete control over resource logging capabilities.

Another feature of IIS is its ability to perform directory browsing. If a directory contains no default document (usually DEFAULT.HTM or DEFAULT.ASP) and the browser does not specify an exact filename, the server can send back an HTML-formatted directory listing. It will look similar to what your browser displays when it accesses an FTP server. Because looking at the raw directory structure of the server can be somewhat revealing to the user, you should exercise caution before allowing directory browsing. Directory browsing is disabled by default.

Microsoft Index Server is an integral part of IIS, and you can enable its power by checking the Index This Directory check box. Chapter 7 will take an in-depth look at Index Server, but here you need to know that Index Server provides a search engine for finding content on your server. It performs this feat by indexing the specified contents on the server and keeping the results in a local database of keywords and properties. This allows users to query Index Server for any combination of words to see a list of links to specific files that match the search criterion. A background process in Index Server monitors changes in virtual directories and updates the index database accordingly. If the Index This Directory option is not checked, Index Server will neither create nor update the database with information about the contents in this directory.

If the FrontPage server extensions are installed, checking the FrontPage Web check box makes this directory available for access by FrontPage server extensions. When checked, this option allows a user with the appropriate permissions to edit the contents of this directory using the FrontPage HTML editor.

Application settings As mentioned earlier, an application is a logical unit that can tie together many different subdirectories and individual files into one logical piece. ISAPI extensions, ASP scripts, and server-side components all share a single object context and memory space that is configured from the home directory or virtual directory level. If you want, you can convert a virtual directory to an application. Figure 4.12 on page 69 shows a virtual directory that has already been converted to an application named Default Application.

In the bottom section of the Home Directory page, a Create button will appear where the Remove button is located (in the figure) if the virtual directory is not an application. To create an application, click the Create button and enter an application name in the Name text box. After you do this, the icon in the Management Console will change from a folder (that is, a directory) to a package (that is, an application).

Application configuration Many configuration options are specific to particular applications. Clicking the Configuration button in the Home Directory page opens the Application Configuration window, which accesses all of the applications. Remember that properties are inheritable, so all options for a higher-level application (such as the default Web page) are inherited by lower-level applications.

The App Mappings page in the Application Configuration window, shown in Figure 4.14, allows you to map specific file extensions to ISAPI extension DLLs that will be executed when requests for files with those extensions are received. For instance, the .ASP file extension is mapped to the ISAPI extension ASP.DLL. Thus, when a request is received in this application for a filename with an .ASP extension, ASP.DLL is called to handle the request. You can modify the application mappings (with potentially disastrous results), or you can create application mappings for your own files. You can even add to the extensions handled by existing applications. For example, you might have some ASP files with the extension .FOO. You can use this page to add a mapping to associate the .FOO extension with ASP.DLL.

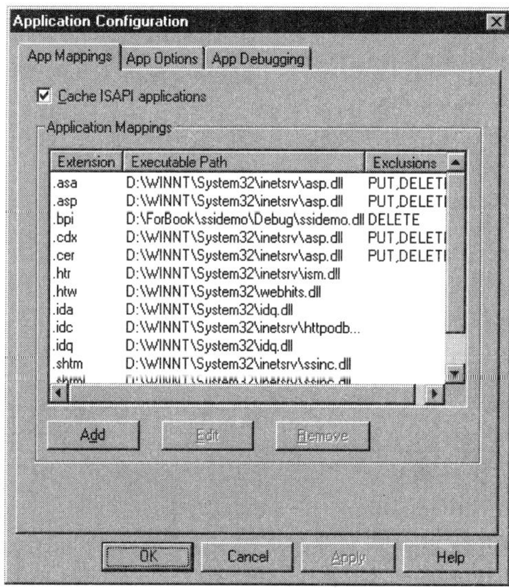

FIGURE 4.14

The App Mappings page in the Application Configuration window.

NOTE

In Chapter 21 you will learn that you can write your own DLL to allow custom processing of specific file types. For example, we wrote a sample ISAPI extension DLL named SSIDEMO.DLL that handles files with the .BPI extension. (BPI stands for "Braginski Powell Include"—pretty creative, eh?) The application mapping replaces all tags (such as AUTHOR_NAME*) in *.BPI files with a predefined value from a registered dictionary file. The dictionary file contains associations such as* AUTHOR_NAME equals "Leon Braginski". *The result is that files with the .BPI extension can contain templates, instead of real text, that will be sent to the browser as a perfect HTML with the tags appropriately replaced.*

You can click the Add button in the App Mappings tab to open the dialog box shown in Figure 4.15 to add *.BPI files to IIS's extension mappings. In this dialog box, you enter the name of the executable or DLL that will be processing the designated file types. In this case, the path to SSIDEMO.DLL is listed, with specifications that it handle files with the .BPI extension.

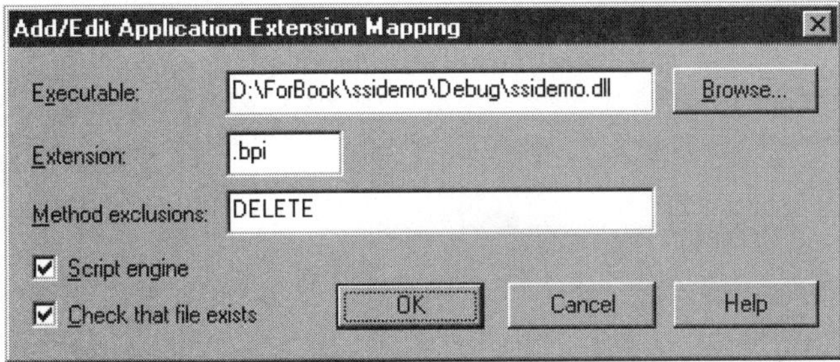

FIGURE 4.15

The Add/Edit Application Extension Mapping dialog box.

You can avoid invoking SSIDEMO.DLL even when a request is made for a *.BPI document by creating a list of exclusion methods. Exclusion methods are the HTTP verbs or methods for which you do not want IIS to execute your extension. More than one method can be entered, and each must be separated by commas. SSIDEMO.DLL is a simple extension and can't handle the DELETE HTTP verb; therefore, DELETE has been added to the exclusions list in the dialog box.

There are two more important check boxes in this dialog box: Script Engine and Check That File Exists. Normally, an EXE or a DLL can be invoked only from a virtual directory that has execute permissions. Because of this, .BPI files would normally need to be located in a directory that has execute permissions. But this problem can be avoided by checking the Script Engine option, which makes file invocation possible from any directory, even without execute permissions. The second option allows you to check for the existence of a script file before invoking an application to process it. This option lets you take advantage of IIS's ability to generate errors for files that do not exist. It will also catch situations in which the client does not have permissions to read a given file.

Back at the top of the App Mappings property page is another configuration option: Cache ISAPI Applications. One of the performance enhancements that ISAPI applications have over CGI applications is that ISAPI applications can be loaded into memory once and reused to handle subsequent requests. This avoids the overhead of having to reload an application into memory repeatedly. Keeping an ISAPI extension loaded in memory does pose a problem, however, particularly when it is in its development stage. If the DLL is cached in memory, newer versions of the DLL cannot be copied over the old one because it is considered to be "in use." Removing the checkmark from this option allows IIS to immediately unload the DLL once a request is finished. Of course unchecking this option can seriously affect the performance of IIS and ISAPI extensions, but it can be a useful tool for development.

The next page in the Application Configuration window, App Options, is shown in Figure 4.16. This page deals mainly with the configuration of ASP applications. In Chapter 17, these configuration concepts are discussed in detail, so the following is simply a quick description of each.

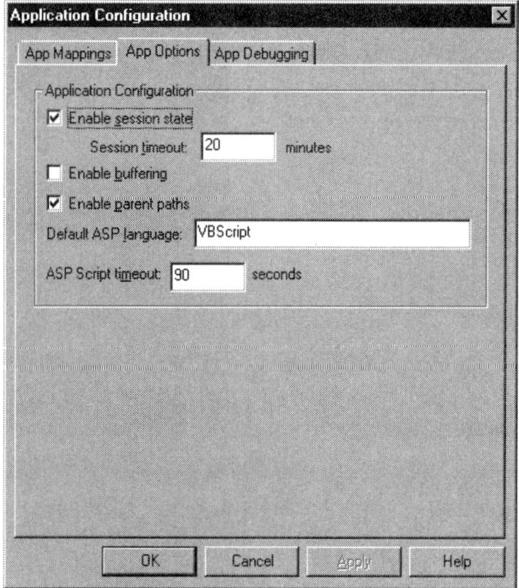

FIGURE 4.16

The App Options tab in the Application Configuration window.

For each user who accesses an ASP page, the server can create a session object. Session objects allow a user to be identified across multiple page requests and provide a means for preserving information across those requests. Because using ASP session objects requires some overhead, and because ASP requires the use of HTTP cookies to preserve state across requests, developers might want to avoid using session objects. The Enable Session State check box lets you turn on and off the underlying support for session objects for the particular application. If sessions are enabled, the time-out value equals the length of time a user's session object will be held in memory without receiving subsequent requests before it is destroyed.

Checking the Enable Buffering check box tells ASP to collect the entire script's response before sending it to the client. Otherwise, the server sends the script output immediately to the client as it interprets the script. An advantage to enabling buffering allows a script to set HTTP headers anywhere within a script since the HTTP headers won't be sent until the entire script has finished executing. If buffering is not enabled, all HTTP header manipulation must take place before a single byte has been sent in the response body.

Checking the Enable Parent Paths option allows scripts to access files in parent directories using the double-dot (..) notation (for instance something like ..*scripts\fdisk_server_drive.asp*). If you enable parent directories, you should not set execute permission on them because it can provide a means for a script to execute an unauthorized program.

ASP scripts can use any number of script languages, although IIS installs with support for only VBScript and JScript. You can, however, write your own script interpreter or get a third-party product (such as REXX or Perl). If a default ASP language is indicated in the Default ASP Language box, any script in an ASP file is considered to be written in that language unless otherwise specified. Specific ASP files can override this option by including the *<%@ LANGUAGE %>* directive inside the ASP file.

You can also specify an ASP script timeout value in the appropriate box, which will cancel the execution of any ASP scripts that have not completed by the specified time. When the timeout period has expired, the running script is terminated and an event is written to the Windows NT event log. This can help avoid problems with script files that have infinite loops or that are perpetually blocked waiting for a troublesome server component. However, too short a timeout specification can create a problem if legitimate scripts take a long time to execute. You can make the timeout indefinite by setting this value to *–1*.

Finally, the App Debugging page of the application Configuration window, shown in Figure 4.17, allows you to configure various ASP debugging options. If script debugging is allowed, upon encountering an error ASP starts a debugger that helps find the problem. Client debugging is not implemented at this point and is reserved for future use.

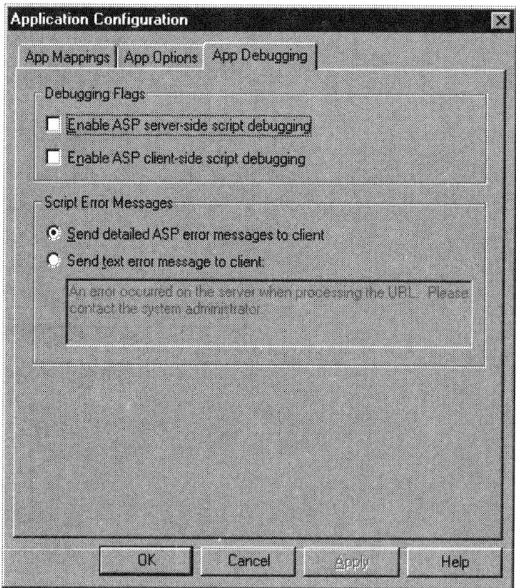

FIGURE 4.17

The App Debugging page in the Application Configuration window.

The Script Error Messages options allow you to send either a specific ASP error that points out the details of the error in the ASP script or a simple static error message. Getting details of script errors is useful when you are developing an application for the Web, but you might not want to expose the details of your ASP code to users who access your Internet site. Therefore, you can choose the Send Text Error Message To Client option to return the specified text for all script errors encountered by this application.

Other options on the home directory page Take another look at Figure 4.12 on page 69. The parameters in the Application Settings area affect how IIS handles scripts and ISAPI extensions. The Run In Separate Memory Space option forces IIS to load all components of the application in a memory space separate from the IIS process. Normally, ISAPI extensions are loaded in the main IIS process space. A poorly written or malicious ISAPI extension could crash the entire Web server (even though IIS tries to prevent this by using such programming techniques as exception handling). When applications run in their own processes, the risk of server instability is reduced.

Precise control of which applications can and cannot be executed is an integral part of server security. You can achieve such control by setting up correct execution permissions. If you select None in the Permissions section at the bottom of the Home Directory page, no code will be able to run in this application (or in the virtual directory, depending on which property pages are opened).

NOTE

The Home Directory page for a Web site (or the Virtual Directory page for lower level entities) looks very similar for virtual directories and for applications. Remember that you can convert any virtual directory to an application. Virtual directories that are not applications disable the Configuration button as well as the Run In Separate Memory Space check box.

Furthermore, script files such as ASP or IDC files are not simple static files but are executed by script maps. For script files to run properly, IIS needs to invoke a server-side script interpreter, such as the SSIDEMO.DLL interpreter that was configured earlier in the chapter for *.BPI files. Choosing the Script option when installing this interpreter indicates that only Script-level access permissions are required for these files to run. But how about executables such as CGI and ISAPI applications? These applications are considered the most serious risks to server security, so to permit executable files to run, you must choose the Execute option. This option will also allow scripts to run.

The Documents Page

Figure 4.18 shows the Documents property page in the Default Web Site Properties window. With the exception of the title bar, this page looks the same whether it is accessed for Web sites or for virtual directories.

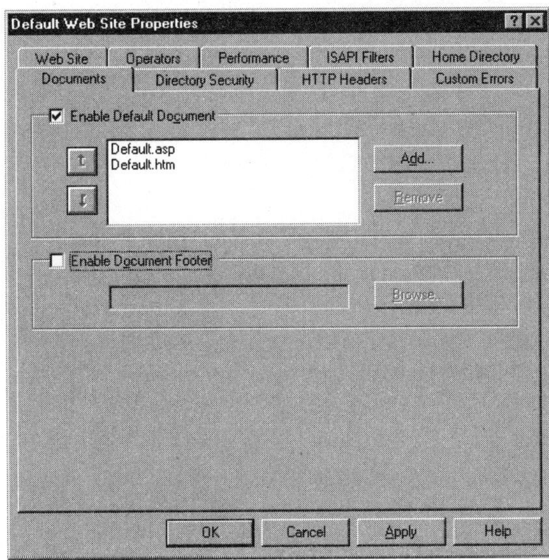

FIGURE 4.18

The Documents page in the Default Web Site Properties window.

As mentioned earlier, when a client sends a request to the server without specifying a filename (for example, *http://www.microsoft.com*), the server sends a default document to the client. Once you check the Enable Default Document check box, you can use the Add button to configure multiple default documents so that IIS will search for each specified document in the list until it locates one.

One of IIS's new features is its ability to add a footer file to all your responses by placing a check mark next to Enable Document Footer and specifying the filename. For example, if you have bunch of pages and want to add the same copyright statement to the end of each one, you can create a little HTML file with the indicated statement and use this document as a footer. By doing this, you can avoid the tedious job of typing the same sentence at the end of each file. Notice that the footer file is not a full-blown HTML document with typical HTML tags. It is simply a piece of HTML that is appended to normal responses.

The Directory Security Page

The Directory Security page in the Default Web Site Properties window, shown in Figure 4.19, is a gateway to many specific options related to IIS security.

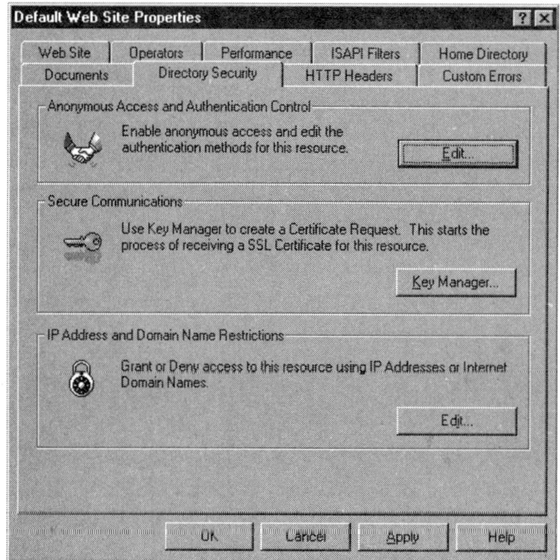

FIGURE 4.19

The Directory Security page in the Default Web Site Properties window.

Before you jump into the mysteries of IIS security, consider some basic security concepts. Under Windows NT, every process must run in the context of a specific user account. A user can log on to a network via either a local account or a domain account if the machine participates in a domain structure. IIS is a Windows NT service that runs as the Local System account. Each machine has its own unique Local System account with virtually unlimited rights on that machine. However, since the credentials differ for each machine's Local System account, trying to access other machines on a network using the Local System account for one particular machine will result in an access deny error. That is why, when we specified a virtual directory located on a UNC share, we had to enter a valid username and password on the target machine.

Because of the broad scope of permissions available on a local machine for the Local System account, running scripts, ISAPI DLLs, and CGI executables under this account could cause a potential security disaster. To prevent this, IIS creates a local account with limited rights. This account is usually named IUSR_*machine_name* (*machine_name* is replaced with the name of your computer) and services each anonymous connection from a browser.

For example, say a browser requests a file named SECURE.HTM from IIS. The server tries to access the specified file by impersonating the IUSR_*machine_name* account. If, however, the IUSR_*machine_name* account doesn't have permissions to read the SECURE.HTM file, IIS will send a specific HTTP error to the client. In response to the error, the browser will ask for a username and password and submit the newly acquired credentials to the server. The low-level details for HTTP authentication are discussed in Chapter 22, but for now assume that the server has the user's credentials and will impersonate this account to try to access SECURE.HTM. Assuming the account has the appropriate privileges, the file will successfully be sent to the client.

Anonymous access and authentication control A number of different schemes govern how the username and password provided by the client's browser is authenticated by the server. IIS has built-in support for two such schemes: Basic Authentication, in which credentials are Base 64 encoded and transmitted in clear text; and NTLM (NT LAN Manager), which is a secure challenge/response authentication scheme that can be used only by Windows-based machines. NTLM is a more complex scheme: the password is never actually transmitted over the network, and credentials are verified by the valid encryption and decryption of an initial challenge.

Glossary

Base 64 encoding *A special encoding scheme in which all characters use the Base 64 numbering system. Just as computers use the binary numbering system (only two digits exist: 0 and 1), a Base 64 system uses 64 different characters.*

challenge/response authentication *A special method of securely verifying a username and password without actually transmitting the information over the network.*

NOTE

For NTLM authentication, if the client and server participate in a domain-based security scheme, a browser might not even ask the user to enter his or her name and password. In this instance, the credentials of the currently logged-on user are utilized to perform the authentication.

IIS can be configured to use any combination of NTLM, Basic, and Anonymous authentications. If you click the Edit button in the Anonymous Access section of the Directory Security page, the Authentication Methods dialog shown in Figure 4.20 appears. From this dialog box, you can edit parameters for anonymous access and authentication control.

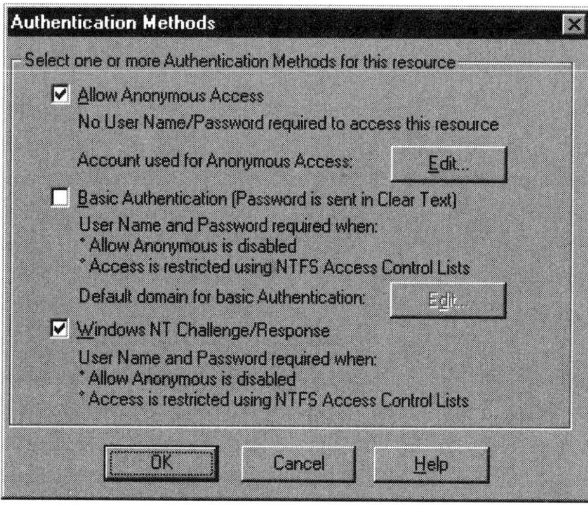

FIGURE 4.20

Configuring authentication schemes in the Authentication Methods dialog box.

If both the Basic Authentication and Windows NT Challenge/Response options are checked in the Authentication Methods dialog box, it is up to the client's browser to decide which type to use. When the Allow Anonymous Access option is checked, requests are executed in the IUSR_*machine_name* context.

This account can also be changed to some other username if required. For instance, you can specify an account in your domain if you want to allow anonymous requests to access resources across the network. To avoid password confusion (the password in the Windows NT security database must match the password specified in the Management Console), you can tell IIS to synchronize password changes between the two storage locations.

When basic authentication is used and certain resources do not allow anonymous access, the client's browser prompts the user to enter credentials. Most users will tend not to enter their names in the Windows NT domain form of "domain/user." By using the Edit button next to the Basic Authentication option, you can configure the basic authentication scheme to use a specified domain, even if the user does not enter one. When a domain structure does not exist or when you want to use only accounts on your local machine, the default domain for basic authentication should be your server machine's name.

Secure communications The Secure Communications section of the Directory Security page allows you to manage Secure Certificates. Secure Certificates are the part of IIS Setup that enables data encryption. (Secure communications are discussed in Chapter 13.).

IP address and domain name restrictions Figure 4.21 shows the IP Address and Domain Name Restrictions dialog box that appears when you click the associated Edit button on the Directory Security page.

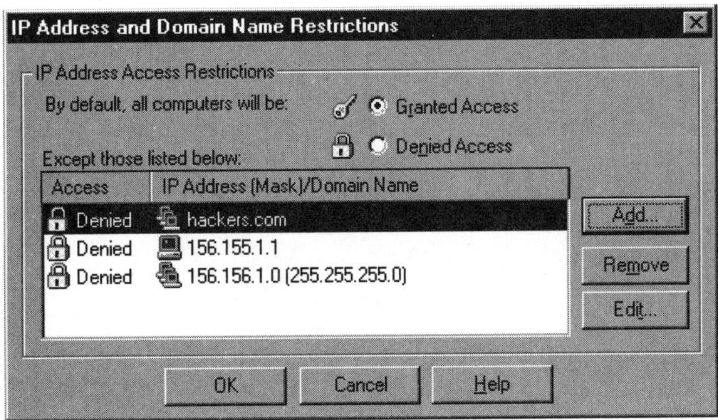

FIGURE 4.21

Setting restrictions in the IP Address And Domain Name Restrictions dialog box.

In this dialog box, you can set up powerful protection against hackers and other unfriendly users. You can deny (or allow) connections from specific IP addresses or ranges of addresses. In fact, you can even filter connections based on a DNS domain name. The dialog box in the figure shows that nobody in the *hackers.com* domain will be allowed to connect to this Web site. Access is also denied to connections from host 156.155.1.1 and from any host located on the 156.156.1 class B subnet. (Recall the subnet discussion in Chapter 3.)

NOTE

If domain-based filtering is turned on, the server must perform a potentially lengthy reverse DNS lookup for each request. On a busy server, this can slow down performance considerably.

The HTTP Headers property page in the Default Web Site Properties window shown in Figure 4.22 allows you to set content expiration, custom headers, content rating, and MIME mapping for HTTP headers. Chapter 21 discusses HTTP headers in detail, but for now you can consider them a way to send auxiliary information with your responses. For example, the Expires header allows you to indicate how long the data in your response will be valid. You can configure IIS to send such a header by enabling content expiration, as shown in Figure 4.22.

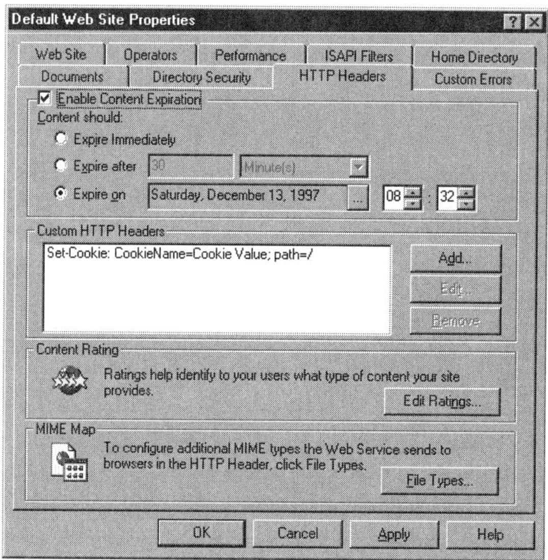

FIGURE 4.22

The HTTP Headers property page in the Default Web Site Properties window.

The header that results from the configuration in the figure is shown here:

```
Expires: Sat, 13 Dec 1997 15:32:09 GMT
```

Notice how IIS is smart enough to convert local Pacific time 8:32 (in the 24-hour system) to Greenwich mean time (GMT). It is also possible to add custom HTTP headers, although not all browsers react to custom headers in a manner that's visible to the user. In the figure, an HTTP Cookie header was added in the

Custom HTTP Headers section. To verify proper reception of our custom header, we configured our browser to warn us upon receiving cookies. Figure 4.23 shows that our browser did in fact receive our cookie just as it was configured.

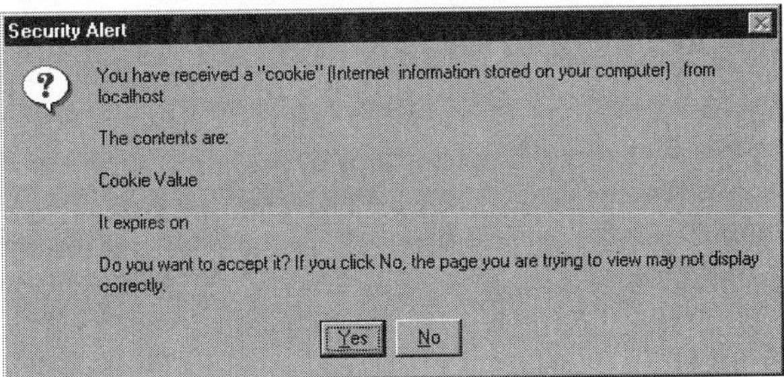

FIGURE 4.23

The browser receiving a cookie and throwing a dialog box with the warning.

The third section of the HTTP Headers page is Content Rating, a feature supported by some newer browsers. The content rating idea is similar to a motion picture rating that indicates whether the content is appropriate for certain groups of viewers. The Ratings page of the Content Ratings dialog box shown in Figure 4.24 appears when you click Edit Ratings.

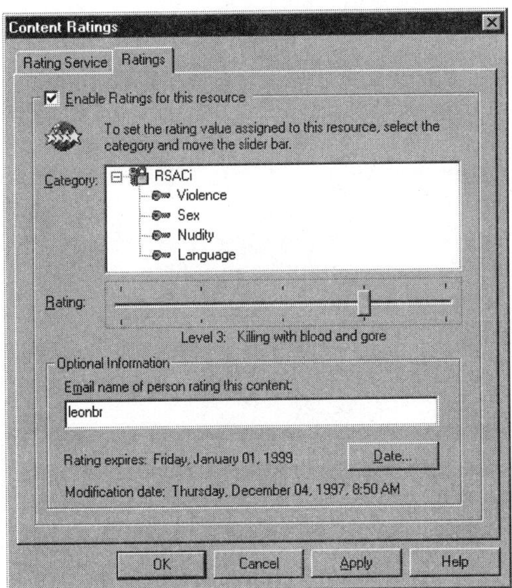

FIGURE 4.24

The Content Ratings configuration dialog box.

Using the configuration shown in the figure, the server sends a specific header to the browser:

```
PICS-Label: (PICS-1.0 "http://www.rsac.org/
ratingsv01.html" l by "leonbr" on "1997.12.04T08:39-
0800" exp "1999.01.01T12:00-0800" r (v 3 s 1 n 1 l 1))
```

Notice again that IIS uses GMT. The browser then interprets the above header to determine whether the content of the site is suitable for viewing by the current user. Pages are rated by their content. The PICS-Label HTTP header above states that this content was rated by leonbr on December 4, 1997. It will expire on January 1, 1999. The available ratings are as follows:

- Violence: Level 3
- Sex: Level 1
- Nudity: Level 1
- Language: Level 1

The browser can be configured to deny access to pages in which ratings exceed preconfigured limits. PICS ratings help guard against kids surfing inappropriate sites. The Rating Service page in the Content Ratings dialog box has links to resources on how to rate Web content. It also allows you to register with the Recreational Software Advisory Council.

Whenever a server sends data to a client, it must indicate what type of data it is sending. Information about the content type helps the browser determine how to handle it. (For instance, it might have to start a helper application.) Information about the type of data being sent from the server to the client is located in an HTTP Content-Type header. The server has a database (which is actually stored in the metabase) of associations of file extensions and their corresponding MIME types. When a request for a specific file is processed, the server finds the correct type based on the file's extension and sends the response with the appropriate Content-Type header. Clicking the File Types button in the MIME Map section at the bottom of the HTTP Headers page in the Default Web Sites Properties window (Figure 4.22) opens the dialog box shown in Figure 4.25. Here you can enter custom data types for any file extension.

The Custom Errors Page

Last but not least is the Custom Errors property page, shown in Figure 4.26.

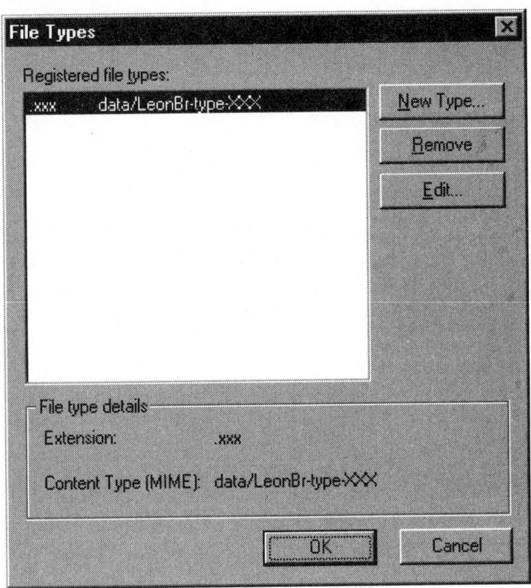

FIGURE 4.25

The File Types dialog box.

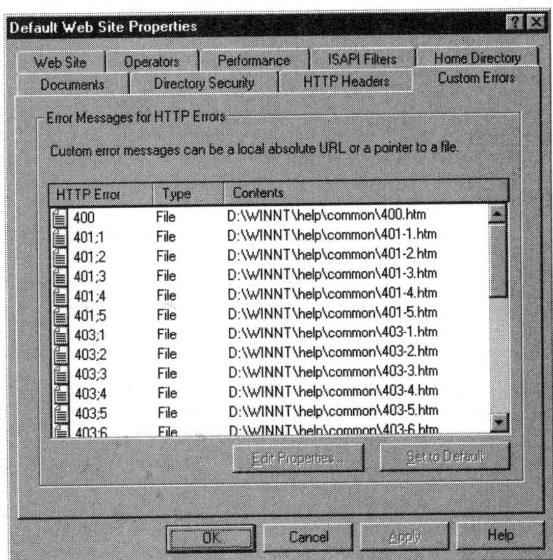

FIGURE 4.26

Configuring URLs for custom error messages in the Custom Errors page.

IIS's flexibility in reporting errors is one of its best features. Normally, IIS replies to a client's request with the HTTP status code of "200 OK" and data such as HTML text. When an error occurs, for example if a resource could not be found, the server sends an appropriate HTTP status code and possibly a brief error message to the browser. The browser displays the text of the message to help the user determine what went wrong.

From this page, you can configure the location from which the message text associated with the error should come. There are three potential sources:

- The default error message, which can be very short, such as "HTTP/1.1 404 Object Not Found."
- A file with the error message as HTML text. You can create a file with explanations of what went wrong and what needs to be done to fix it. (For instance, for "Object Not Found" errors, you might tell the user to correct the URL and try again.)
- A URL that will provide error information. This can be an HTML file, an ISAPI extension, or even an ASP script that will generate extended error information to aid in troubleshooting. Note that the URL must be on the local machine. If the URL is an executable script, such as an ISAPI extension, you need to make sure that when the DLL terminates, it preserves the HTTP status code that it was called for (and does not change it to "200 OK").

IIS comes with a set of preconfigured HTML pages for many errors, as shown in Figure 4.26. If you configure your error messages to be generated somewhere else but decide later that you want to go back to the IIS default files, you can simply click the Set To Default button.

This chapter has covered all the configuration options available via the administration user interface. Now that you understand how all the components work together, you should be able to configure almost any option on your server that you want. All the configuration information for IIS is stored in the metabase. Changing metabase values affects the behavior of IIS, just as if you were manipulating the Management Console. Chapter 5 covers the metabase, its layout, and how you can programmatically access it for managing IIS.

CHAPTER 5

The Metabase

The configuration process for operating system resources has lived an interesting life. In the days of MS-DOS, we configured our operating systems by editing the CONFIG.SYS and AUTOEXEC.BAT files. Any application that ran on top of MS-DOS had its own mechanisms for storing configuration information. With the advent of 16-bit Microsoft Windows came a series of text files, called .INI files, that were opened in Notepad (or some other ASCII text editor) to change options. These .INI files allowed us a new way to store operating system and application information. Operating system information was stored in SYSTEM.INI, whereas application-specific information was stored in WIN.INI or in another .INI file.

Starting with the release of Microsoft Windows NT and continuing with Microsoft Windows 95, .INI files were replaced by the Windows registry. The beauty of the registry is that it can contain information in both textual format and binary format. So if a system component or an application needs to store an element, such as a graphic to be used for its icon, the actual image data can be stored in the registry. The registry's hierarchical tree structure was another major advance. But with the increasing complexity of operating systems and the large amount of information needing to be stored in the registry, it became apparent that the registry structure was not going to make sorting through all the information significantly easier. For IIS, a more sophisticated registry was required, one that could configure options at different levels at once and had quicker information retrieval capabilities.

First of all, the ability to configure many IIS configuration options at different levels made it clear that some sort of hierarchical structure was needed. Second, the kind of performance necessary for expedient responses to HTTP requests would require that configuration information be read considerably faster than it was read in the current registry. Therefore, Microsoft Internet Information Server 4.0 brings you the metabase.

The Metabase Hierarchy

The metabase is a binary file that's similar to the registry—with a few differences. The metabase file is kept in the IIS System directory. By default, this directory, called METABASE.BIN, is located on your hard drive at %SystemRoot%\system32\inetsrv. The metabase uses a hierarchically structured system that is similar to the registry and, like the registry, it can hold binary data as well as textual data. Unlike the registry, though, the metabase uses the idea of *inheritance*, which means that if you set a value in one of the keys, that same value can be inherited by all of the subkeys for that key. This concept is illustrated in Figure 5.1.

Glossary

key *A node in the metabase hierarchy that represents an object, such as a virtual directory. Keys contain properties that hold configuration information for the object. Keys can also contain other keys (often called "subkeys"); for example, a virtual directory might contain a subdirectory.*

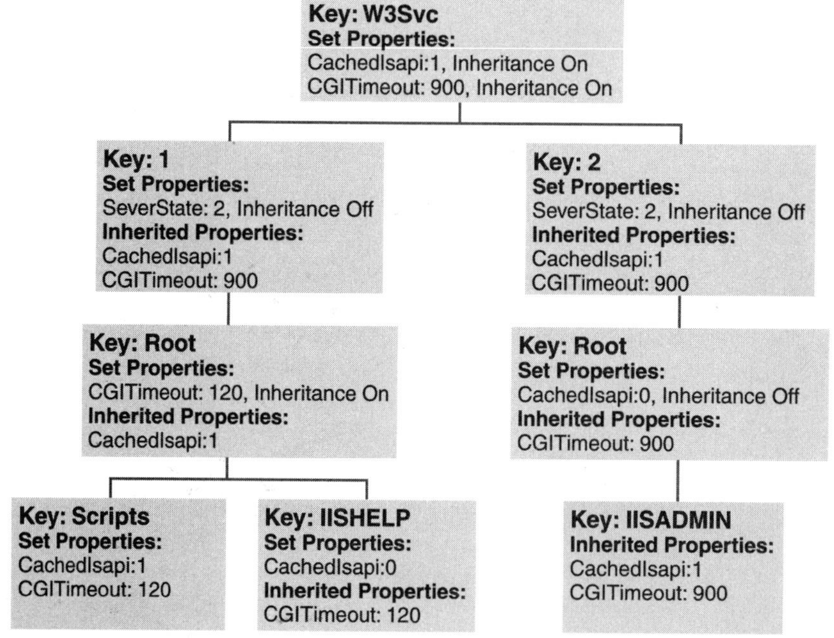

FIGURE 5.1

The metabase hierarchy allows properties to be inherited from a key to its subkeys.

In this figure, two properties are being set at the highest node, */W3Svc*. The property *CachedIsapi* is set to a value of 1 (indicating *TRUE*), and the property *CGITimeout* is set to 900 (indicating that CGI applications have 900 seconds to complete execution before they are timed out). Both of these properties are flagged as having inheritance turned on, which means that if a subkey doesn't explicitly set these properties, the subkey will inherit these property values. In the figure, you can see that at /W3Svc/2/Root/IISADMIN (in the lower right corner), the value for these two properties has been inherited all the way down the line. Note that at an intermediate key, /W3Svc/2/Root, the value of *CachedIsapi* has been overridden with a value of 0 (indicating *FALSE*). However, this value has been flagged as not inherited (Inheritance Off), so at the lower level of /W3Svc/2/Root/IISADMIN, the original inherited value still takes precedence.

On the left side of the figure's tree at the /W3Svc/1/Root level, the value for *CGITimeout* has been overridden with a value of 120. In this case, the overridden value is flagged with inheritance turned on, so all lower level subkeys have inherited this new value as well. Notice that the property *ServerState* set at both the /W3Svc/1 and /W3Svc/2 levels is flagged with inheritance turned off. Because it is neither explicitly set nor flagged as inherited, the *ServerState* property does not exist functionally for the lower-level subkeys. (This setting makes sense, since you can start, stop, or pause only Web sites and not specific virtual directories.)

Inheritance serves two important functions for your metabase implementations. First, it provides an easy way to flag an entire branch of your hierarchy with a specific property value. Second, setting a property value for an entire branch takes only a single entry in the metabase. This means that the metabase file is smaller and therefore faster to read. If you tried to keep the same sort of information in the registry, you would have to set a property for each key in the hierarchy, which would quickly cause its size to get out of hand.

Unlike those in the registry, properties in the metabase are not stored by their names. Instead, each property has an associated numeric identifier that is used in the actual metabase records (as explained later in this chapter). This identifier is important for performance, since with the metabase, property records are scanned via numeric comparisons rather than string comparisons, resulting in a significantly speedier configuration database.

Along with IIS's quick and functional configuration database, one more piece rounds out its status as the ultimate configuration mechanism. That piece is a programming interface that allows developers to take advantage of all the metabase features. With IIS 4.0, developers can add IIS configuration capabilities to their Web application setup programs, build metabase configuration features into their administration applets, enhance the existing administration utilities, and even use the metabase to store their applications' custom configuration information. How this is done will be discussed later in this chapter.

Objects in the Metabase Hierarchy

You already know that the metabase uses a hierarchical structure. Chapter 4 looked at this hierarchy in the discussion of how configuration properties set at a Web site will also affect the various virtual directories located beneath that site. Thus, you can safely assume that the higher-level Web site object has virtual directories located at some level below it. Figure 5.2 shows the various Web site objects and where they are located in the metabase hierarchy.

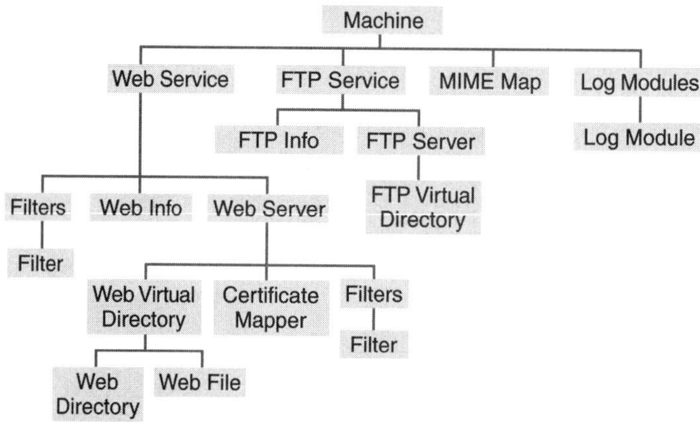

FIGURE 5.2

Web site objects in a metabase hierarchy.

In this figure, for the sake of simplicity, the machine is shown as the root of the hierarchy. The figure provides a good representation of the information that is stored in a machine's metabase file, but you can also use metabase objects across the network on many different machines. In that case, your system would have its root one level higher than indicated in Figure 5.2, with a potentially large number of Machine objects located below that root.

As Figure 5.2 shows, below the root Machine object are the various service objects, along with objects that contain information used machinewide. For instance, the MIME Map object contains a list of file extensions along with their associated MIME types. Similarly, the Log Modules object contains the different types of supported logging mechanisms. Both of these are examples of information that is not specific to a single service, so they sit directly below the Machine object.

One more important branch of information is located under the Machine object, but it isn't exposed as a separate object. That branch is called the *schema*. The schema contains information or rules about what sorts of properties apply to the different types of objects, and it maps numeric property IDs to their friendly names and data types. Utilities such as METAEDIT (which we will look at shortly) use the schema to validate what properties are being set on an object and to ensure that a property is of the correct data type. For example, you wouldn't want to set the *Path* property of a virtual directory object to a numeric value when it actually needs to hold a string, such as c:\inetpub\scripts.

The Web Service and FTP Service objects have a number of similar child objects. Each service has an Info object that contains generic information for the service, such as installed logging options. The Server objects also live under the Service objects. IIS allows multiple copies of these Server objects, or *virtual servers,* to exist (such as the Default Web site and the Administration Web Site that we looked at in the previous chapter). Below the Server objects are Virtual Directory objects, and, in the case of the Web Server objects, Directory and File objects are located below the Virtual Directories. The Web Server also branches into Filter objects, which are simply ISAPI filter DLLs that receive notifications for certain request events. The parent Filters object (note the ending *s*) contains the load order of the filters while the underlying Filter objects (with no *s*) contain the properties for the specific filters. Filters can live at the service level or at the server level. Filters at the service level are called *global filters,* since they receive notifications for requests to all servers on the machine.

Finally, below a Web Server object there can be a Certificate Mapper object. The Certificate Mapper object maps client certificates used for SSL (Secure Sockets Layer) connections to accounts on a Windows NT–based machine. This object provides a means for the server to take advantage of the powerful authentication capabilities that SSL provides.

Although Figure 5.2 shows only the Web and FTP services located below the Machine object, a hierarchy could include a number of other services, such as the SMTP Service and the NNTP Service.

Metabase Entries

Metabase entries are similar to—but not identical to—registry entries. Metabase entries contain data that define metabase properties. Metabase entries can contain binary data, a double-word value, a character string, or a series of character strings, just as registry entries can. Another metabase data type, an *expanded string,* contains environment variable references, such as %PATH%, that would be replaced with the value stored in that environmental variable upon actual usage.

Metabase entries contain *attribute flags*. One type of attribute flag for metabase entries indicates inheritance, which was discussed earlier in this chapter. Other flags indicate whether the data should be stored and transported securely and whether a record should be written to permanent storage. The entries can even contain a flag that indicates that a given value is simply a memory reference to a larger piece of information.

Entries also contain a *user type*, which basically indicates what type of object uses this property. IIS has four user type values: Server, File, WAM (Web Application Management) object, and Application. Entries that are flagged with the Server user type contain information that corresponds to the server. A File user type indicates that a file, directory, or virtual directory uses it. The WAM user type indicates that the WAM object is using the property when it is managing the resources for a particular application. The Application user type is used for Active Server Pages (ASP) application properties that will apply to the ASP engine itself.

Metabase Properties

Earlier in this chapter, you learned that properties are indicated with numeric IDs instead of textual names. For this identification scheme to work properly, each property must have a unique ID. Ranges of numeric IDs have been assigned to specific components to make the identification process more efficient. If you are storing your own information in the metabase, you will probably want to avoid using the ID values in these ranges. The following table shows the ID ranges with their corresponding IIS components.

Metabase ID Range	Owning IIS Component
1000–1999	General server
2000–2999	HTTP server
3000–3999	Virtual directories
4000–4999	Logging
5000–5499	FTP server
5500–5999	SSL
6000–6999	File and Directory Properties
7000–7499	ASP
7500–7999	WAM
0x8000–0x8FFF	Microsoft FrontPage
0x9000–0x9FFF	SMTP server
0xA000–0xAFFF	POP3 server
0xB000–0xBFFF	NNTP service
0xC000–0xCFFF	IMAP Mail server
0xD000–0xDFFF	General Microsoft Commercial Internet System IDs

Not all metabase property IDs are made public because they might hold private information for IIS or other applications. But by using the range list, you can at least find out to which component the property ID belongs. Following are some metabase properties that you can access by using a utility called MDUTIL, which you can run at a command console to manipulate the metabase. You can find MDUTIL on the Windows NT Option Pack CD.

```
C:\>MDUTIL ENUM /W3Svc/1/root
  AccessPerm                    : [IF]     (DWORD)  0x201={Read Script}
  AppIsolated                   : [IW]     (DWORD)  0x0={0}
  Win32Error                    : [IS]     (DWORD)  0x0={0}
  6039                          : [IF]     (DWORD)  0x1={1}
  VrPath                        : [IF]     (STRING) "C:\Inetpub\wwwroot"
  KeyType                       : [S]      (STRING) "IIsWebVirtualDir"
  AppRoot                       : [IF]     (STRING) "/LM/W3SVC/1/ROOT/"
```

This example uses MDUTIL to enumerate the properties of the /W3Svc/1/Root metabase path. These properties correspond to the root directory of the sample default Web site. MDUTIL is displaying only properties that have been specifically set; those properties that have been neither set nor inherited are not displayed. The left-hand column consists of the friendly name that MDUTIL uses to refer to the property IDs for each record. Notice that the fourth row does not have its ID mapped to a friendly name because MDUTIL is doing the mapping itself and is not relying on the schema values for this ID. Unfortunately, MDUTIL does not have a friendly name for a number of well-known property IDs. You can get a complete listing of the properties MDUTIL recognizes and the names it uses for the properties by running "MDUTIL –help."

The second column of the MDUTIL output indicates the flags and the user types associated with each property. The *AccessPerm* property, for instance, is inheritable with a File user type, indicated by *[IF]* in the output. The third column of the output describes what kind of data is stored in each of these metabase records. Finally, MDUTIL displays the data for the record itself in the fourth column.

As noted in the output above, MDUTIL doesn't recognize the property ID 6039. Although you might not recognize this ID either, you can be sure it is a property of a File or Directory because it falls in the 6000 through 6999 range (as shown in the preceding table). If MDUTIL were a little more powerful, it would be able to determine that 6039 represents the *ContentIndexed* property. The output above shows that *ContentIndexed* has a value of 1, which means that the content of this virtual directory is indexed using Microsoft's Index Server. (For more about Index Server, see Chapter 7.)

Manipulating the Metabase

MDUTIL is a powerful application in many ways. It will not only let you display various parts of the metabase, but it will also let you set metabase properties. For instance, if you wanted to change the access permissions for the sample default site's root directory, you could use the following command line to set execute permissions on the directory as well. (The values for the different metabase flags can be found in the file IISCNFG.H, which is part of the Microsoft Platform SDK.)

```
C:\>MDUTIL SET W3SVC/1/ROOT/AccessPerm 0x205
AccessPerm          : [IF]    (DWORD)  0x205={Read Execute Script}
```

WARNING!

You must be very careful while directly manipulating data in the metabase. Setting a property to an invalid value could have disastrous effects on your system. In addition, many properties are interlinked so that one improper value could have a propagating effect on other configuration properties. You must be sure of what you are doing when you start manipulating metabase values!

Making changes in the metabase can drastically affect your system configuration, and if you administer a Web server, you are manipulating the metabase all the time. Lucky for you, however, the IIS administration tools will validate values, and they have all been thoroughly tested.

Many metabase administrative tasks take place from the Management Console. For the next example, we have created a virtual root named NewVRoot that has been configured with read permissions. The example looks at the metabase with another tool that is considerably easier to use than MDUTIL—a utility called the Metabase Editor or MetaEdit. The Metabase Editor (METAEDIT.EXE) is available through the IIS Resource Kit, and it's similar to the Registry Editor that is used to manipulate the registry. As a command line utility, MDUTIL can be convenient for creating batch files with multiple commands, but other than that, MetaEdit is probably the better tool to use.

Figure 5.3 shows the Metabase Editor with properties of the virtual directory NewVRoot displayed. The properties for the virtual directory appear in the right-hand pane. Note that only five properties are listed for this virtual directory. The *KeyType* property indicates that this is a Virtual Directory object. The *Win32Error* property indicates that no errors have been experienced in the use of this virtual directory at this time. *Path* tells you that the physical directory associated with this virtual root is c:\inetpub\newvroot. The *DirBrowseFlags* property is a bitmask that indicates a series of attributes regarding how this virtual root is presented when a specific file within it is requested.

Glossary

bitmask *Usually a 32-bit value in which every bit can represent whether a flag is turned on or off.*

NOTE

If you convert the DirBrowseFlags *value to hexidecimal, determining the specific flags is a little easier. As it turns out, the value 0x4000001E (107371854 in decimal) is the default combination of flags, which indicates that a default file will be displayed for this virtual directory. If directory browsing were allowed, you would see the date, time, size, and extension of the files in a directory listing.*

Finally, the *AccessFlags* property is actually the same property that MDUTIL called *AccessPerm*. Here, the data value *1* indicates that only read privileges have been granted to this virtual directory. Following is a list of the main flags defined for the AccessFlags bitmask:

```
Read Access          0x00000001
Write Access         0x00000002
Execute Access       0x00000004
Script Access        0x00000200
```

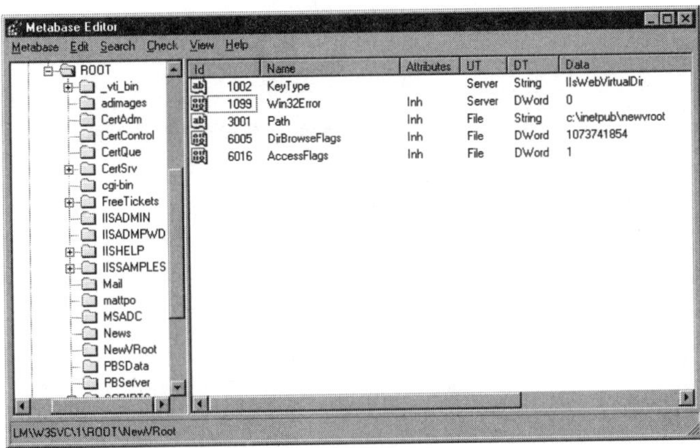

FIGURE 5.3

Virtual root properties shown by the Metabase Editor.

If you open the Management Console and access the properties of your new virtual root by right-clicking on the virtual root and selecting Properties from the menu, a dialog box will appear, similar to the one shown in Figure 5.4. From there you can convert the virtual directory to an application by clicking on the Create button in the Application Settings section. Figure 5.4 shows the result when the application is created and Execute permission is enabled.

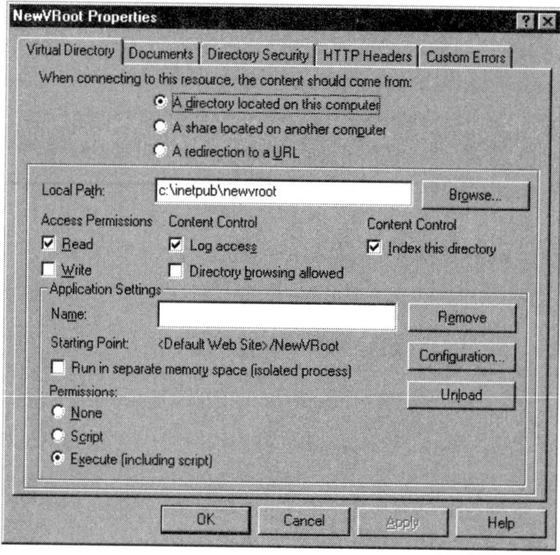

FIGURE 5.4

The NewVRoot Properties window.

Converting the virtual directory to an application will also create additional entries in the metabase. Figure 5.5 shows the Metabase Editor with the additional set of properties.

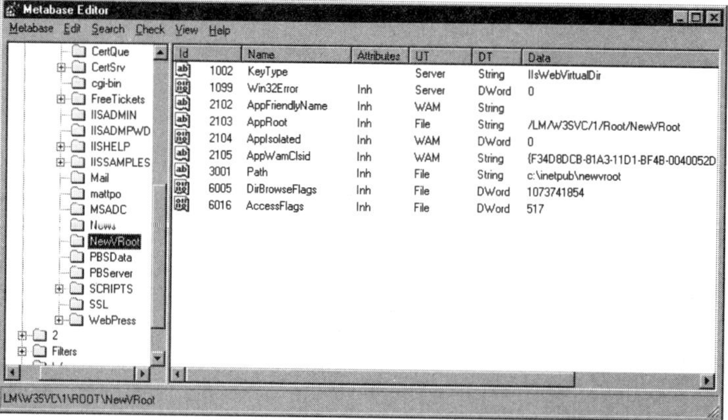

FIGURE 5.5

The virtual root properties in the Metabase Editor after converting the root to an application.

Four new properties have been created, all prefixed with *App*—a good indication of what you did in the Management Console. Because you didn't indicate a name for the application, no name appears in the data column for *AppFriendlyName*, as shown in the figure. And because you did not check the Run In Separate Memory Space option in the NewVRoot Properties page, *AppIsolated* displays a value of 0 to indicate that it is turned off. The *AppRoot* property indicates the path in the metabase at which your application properties live, and *AppWamClsid* is the globally unique identifier (or GUID) that represents the class of the WAM object that corresponds to the new application. You can also see in Figure 5.5 that the *AccessFlags* value was changed to 517 (or hex 0x205), which indicates read, execute, and script permissions.

Glossary

class *A definition of the interfaces and data stored in an object.*

Just as you changed property values in the Management Console and noticed the differences in MetaEdit, you can also change values in MetaEdit to see changes in the Management Console. For example, if you double-click on the *AppFriendlyName* property in MetaEdit, the Edit Metabase Data dialog box appears, as shown in Figure 5.6, allowing you to change a number of characteristics of the *AppFriendlyName* property, including its value.

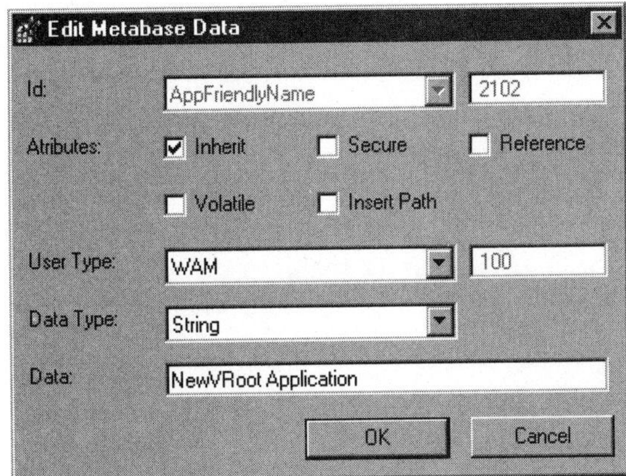

FIGURE 5.6

The Edit Metabase Data dialog box.

Back at the NewVRoot Properties window in the Management Console, you can see the results of the changes you made in the Edit Metabase Data dialog box. Figure 5.7 shows the properties window for the application, with the new application name displayed in the Name text box.

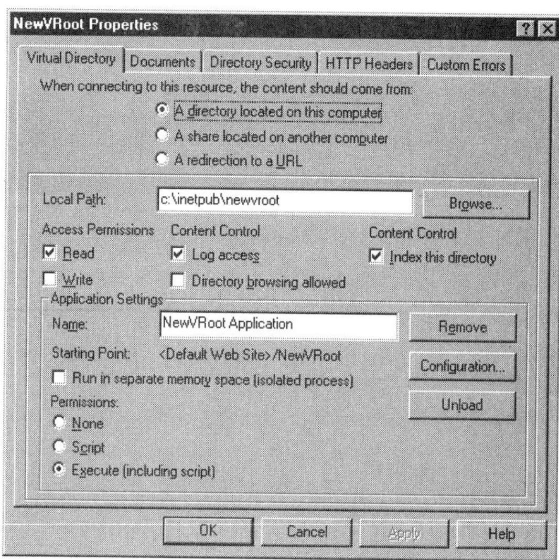

FIGURE 5.7

The NewVRoot Properties window showing results of editing the AppFriendlyName *property.*

WARNING!

Just as you edited the application's friendly name using the Metabase Editor, you might also be tempted to edit the AppIsolated *property to have the application run in its own memory space. Don't do this! When you flag an application in the Management Console to run in its own memory space, not only is the* AppIsolated *property set to* TRUE*, but a number of Microsoft Transaction Server options must be manipulated. You should not set the* AppIsolated *property directly. Instead, you can configure an application to run isolated in your own script or program by using the* AppCreate *method of the* IIsWebVirtualDir *administration object. A number of metabase properties have these types of dependencies, and you should consult the online documentation for details on specific properties.*

Writing Your Own Applications

As mentioned earlier in this chapter, one of the advantages of the metabase is provided by its programmatic interface. You can write your own scripts and applications to perform the same configuration tasks that you can perform from the Management Console. In addition, you can write scripts to perform a number of tasks that you can't easily perform through other standard interfaces. This section looks at the different ways applications can interact with the metabase.

IIS Admin Objects

The IIS Admin Objects provide what is called an Automation interface into the metabase. Because they support Automation, the Admin Objects can be used easily from scripts. The following short piece of scripting code takes advantage of the *IIsComputer* object to backup the metabase.

```
Dim BackupName, BackupVersion, BackupFlags, ComputerObject

BackupName = "ScriptBackup"
BackupVersion = &HFFFFFFFF      'Use MD_BACKUP_FORCE_BACKUP value
BackupFlags = 1                 'Use MD_BACKUP_OVERWRITE value

Set ComputerObject = GetObject("IIS://Localhost")

ComputerObject.Backup BackupName, BackupVersion, BackupFlags
```

This script can be executed in an ASP file, or it can be saved by itself in a VBScript (Microsoft Visual Basic Scripting Edition) file. When you type a script filename with the extension .VBS (or .JS for JScript) at the command prompt, the operating system will launch the Microsoft Windows Scripting Host (which is available with the Microsoft Windows NT 4.0 Option Pack) and execute the script directly. The Windows Scripting Host itself is quite transparent, so the result is that it looks as though the script is running on its own.

The preceding sample script allows you to perform a metabase backup. After declaring some variables and setting some values, the script creates an instance of the *IIS://Localhost* object. This is accomplished with the *GetObject* function, which is supported inherently by VBScript. In this case, *GetObject* is being used in an unusual fashion. Instead of passing the function the name of an object, the script passes it something that looks like a strange URL—but what's actually passed is called an *Active Directory Services Interface* (ADSI) name.

ADSI provides a generic means for accessing objects in hierarchical name spaces. The hierarchical nature of the metabase makes for a good fit with the ADSI model, and IIS has created a name space provider for ADSI that interfaces with the metabase IIS Admin Objects. So when the parameter *IIS://Localhost* is passed to *GetObject*, the *IIS:* portion of the parameter indicates the name space provider that ADSI should use to get the object. The portion that follows *Localhost* is the path within the namespace—in this case, the root object of the metabase hierarchy. Recall Figure 5.2, which showed the relationship between objects in the metabase. In that figure, the object shown at the root was the computer. The parameter *IIS://Localhost* asks for the root object in the metabase name space, which is our machine's computer object. In the IIS Admin Objects reference section of the IIS online help, this *Localhost* object is referred to as the *IIsComputer* object.

Glossary

name space *The logical group of names of a certain type. ADSI requires a Name Space Provider to associate the names in a name space to the proper object. In the case of the metabase, names take the form: IIS://computername/key/subkey/propertyname.*

After obtaining a reference to the *IIsComputer* object for the machine, the script calls the *Backup* method of that object. The *Backup* method is quite useful in that it creates a backup copy of the binary metabase file. If your metabase file gets corrupted—if you happen to mess it up by playing with MetaEdit too much or you mistakenly delete your default Web site, for example—you can get all your configuration information back *if* you have backed up your metabase file. The preceding script does exactly that.

All the objects described in this chapter are accessible via the IIS Admin Objects and the metabase name space. Many of the objects have methods that perform specific tasks, such as the *Backup* method provided by the *IIsComputer* object. For example, the *IIsWebVirtualDir* object has an *AppCreate* method that can be used to create a Web application in a virtual directory. This method provides a benefit, because it is pretty much impossible to create an application properly by simply adding property values with MetaEdit or with any other metabase editor. When you create an application, not only do you have to set up a number of properties in the metabase, but you also need to register a new WAM object with Microsoft Transaction Server. Doing all of this correctly could be difficult, but the *AppCreate* method makes it very easy.

Other IIS Admin Objects methods allow you to stop, start, and pause the Web and FTP services. And you can perform a number of other tasks with applications in addition to creating them, such as unloading them from memory, deleting them, and getting their current status. You can also use some of the Admin Objects methods for different objects to restore the metabase from a backup and to create client certificate mappings (more on this in Chapter 13).

IIS Admin Objects are useful and necessary even if you are interested only in setting property values for objects. For example, if you wanted to change the physical path associated with a virtual directory, you could do this with the following script:

```
Dim VirtualDirObject

Set VirtualDirObject = _
    GetObject("IIS://Localhost/W3Svc/1/Root/NewVRoot")
VirtualDirObject.Put "Path", "c:\inetpub\newdir"
VirtualDirObject.SetInfo      'Save the change
```

This sample script passes a considerably deeper path to *GetObject* than was passed in the previous sample script. Here the script opens the new virtual directory object using the appropriate path in the metabase name space. The *Put* method is a generic ADSI method that can set properties for any ADSI object, and the *Path* property is set to the new value *c:\inetpub\newdir*. After the *Put* line has executed, only a local copy of the virtual directory's properties is changed. If you wanted to change other properties for the virtual directory at the same time, you could do so by using other calls to the *Put* method to change their values as well. But again, any data changed via the *Put* method is changed only in a temporary image of the object's property values.

If you do not want to save your changes, you can simply end the code at this point. However, if you want to save your changes, you need to call the ADSI *SetInfo* method. *SetInfo* will write the current image to the actual object properties, and the changes will finally be saved. Thus, when you call the *SetInfo* method in the sample script, the new value for the *Path* property will actually be written to the metabase.

◆ Calling IIS Admin Objects from ASP Scripts

Only users specified as Web site operators in the Management Console have permission to make changes to the metabase. By default, the list of operators contains only the administrators group. If you are an administrator for your machine, executing scripts using the Windows Scripting Host at the command prompt is a straightforward way of avoiding any security problems. However, if you are attempting to use the IIS Admin Objects from your ASP script, avoiding security problems can be a bit tricky. You should follow two main rules:

- Do not configure your application to run in its own process space.
- Do not use anonymous authentication when accessing your script files.

If you do not heed the first rule, IIS will return a "Server Application Error" message. Noncompliance with the second rule will cause ASP to generate an "Invalid Syntax" error.

The IIS Admin Base Object

So far, this chapter has looked only at scripting samples to manipulate a metabase. But you can also access the metabase from applications written in C or C++. You can use the IIS Admin Objects from your C/C++ applications, but IIS also provides the IIS Admin Base Object, a low-level interface that is more conducive to

C/C++ applications. The following C++ application shows how you would change your virtual directory's path property using the IIS Admin Base Object.

```
#define INITGUID

#include <windows.h>
#include <iadmw.h>
#include <iiscnfg.h>

void main()
{
    IMSAdminBase *pIABase;

    CoInitialize(NULL);
    HRESULT hRes = CoCreateInstance(CLSID_MSAdminBase,
                                    NULL,
                                    CLSCTX_ALL,
                                    IID_IMSAdminBase,
                                    (void**)&pIABase);

    METADATA_HANDLE metaHandle;
    pIABase->OpenKey(METADATA_MASTER_ROOT_HANDLE,
                     L"/",
                     METADATA_PERMISSION_WRITE,
                     5000,
                     &metaHandle);

    WCHAR path[] = L"c:\\inetpub\\newdir";
    METADATA_RECORD MDRecord = {MD_VR_PATH,       // Path ID
                                METADATA_INHERIT, // Is inherited
                                IIS_MD_UT_FILE,   // User Type
                                STRING_METADATA,  // Data Type
                                sizeof(path),     // Size of data
                                (UCHAR*)path,     // Data (our string)
                                0};               // reserved

    pIABase->SetData(metaHandle,
                     L"/LM/W3Svc/1/Root/NewVRoot",
                     &MDRecord);

    pIABase->CloseKey(metaHandle);
}
```

Since this code uses a Component Object Model (COM) interface, the first thing to do is to call *CoInitialize.* The next step is to get an interface pointer to the IIS Admin Base Object by calling *CoCreateInstance.* After the interface pointer is obtained, you can open a handle to the key in question. You should be aware that the Admin Base

Object supports only Unicode strings, which is why the string variables in the preceding script are defined as WCHAR arrays and why the constant string definitions are preceded with the Unicode indicating *L*.

The IIS Admin Base Object will allow multiple handles to a key to be open at the same time only if they all are opened with read-only access. Therefore, when the *OpenKey* method is called, a timeout value must be specified. Since the code is requesting write access to this key, *OpenKey* will wait until all other handles have been closed and it can gain access. If access cannot be gained within the timeout period, *OpenKey* fails with a return code of *ERROR_PATH_BUSY*.

The *METADATA_RECORD* structure contains the property information that you want to set. Note that the *METADATA_RECORD* structure does not take the property name; instead it requires the numeric property ID. You can't see the numeric value in this code excerpt, but the property identifier *MD_VR_PATH* is defined as 3001 in the file IISCNFG.H specified in the beginning of the code. You fill out the structure with the appropriate data and flags and then add a call to *SetData*. When *SetData* is called, you must also pass the Unicode path to the object in the metabase. You can use *LM* to indicate the local machine when building your metabase path.

Finally, to save the changes you have made, you must call the *CloseKey* method of the IIS Admin Base Object class. After *CloseKey* has been called, other open requests for the key can be processed.

Unlike the IIS Admin Objects, which were used in the sample scripts in the previous section, the IIS Admin Base Object does not provide methods to perform complex tasks such as creating an application. If you want to perform these functions from your C/C++ applications, you need to use the *IDispatch* interface of the Admin Objects to call the particular methods.

Metabase Event Sinks

So far, when this chapter has discussed applications using the metabase, the access has occurred in the context of manipulating the IIS configuration. But the metabase can also be used to store an application's configuration data. Creating your own keys and setting your own properties are done in the same manner as manipulating properties using the IIS Admin Base Object. However, if your application is dependent on the information stored in the metabase, you might want to receive notifications when any of your properties have been changed—for example, when your administration application has changed some of your configuration parameters.

IIS provides for this kind of functionality through the use of an *event sink*. Event sinks enable IIS to call your application when any of the metabase data has changed. You create an event sink by building a COM component that supports the *IMSAdminBaseSink* interface. You then use the standard COM connection point mechanism to register the sink with an instance of the IIS Admin Base Object. The Active Template Library (ATL) provided with Microsoft Visual C++ 5.0 makes this task relatively easy.

Event sinks can also be used for other purposes. The next application uses event sinks to create an alarm facility that will display a pop-up window every time a change occurs in the metabase. This feature is useful if you want to track exactly when and where your configuration information is changing. To do this, you first create a COM component that implements the *IMSAdminBaseSink* interface. The class definitions look like this:

```
class CAdminSink :
    public IAdminSink,
    public IMSAdminBaseSink,
    public CComObjectRoot,
    public CComCoClass<CAdminSink,&CLSID_AdminSink>
{
public:
    CAdminSink() {}
BEGIN_COM_MAP(CAdminSink)
    COM_INTERFACE_ENTRY(IAdminSink)
    COM_INTERFACE_ENTRY(IMSAdminBaseSink)
END_COM_MAP()

DECLARE_REGISTRY_RESOURCEID(IDR_AdminSink)

// IAdminSink
public:
    DWORD m_ThreadID;
    STDMETHOD(ShutdownNotify)(void);
    STDMETHOD(SinkNotify)(DWORD dwMDNumElements, MD_CHANGE_OBJECT
        pcoChangeList[]);
};
```

ATL handles most of the declarations by pulling the class and interface definitions out of the include files. Only the two methods that are part of the *IMSAdminBaseSink* notification—the *ShutdownNotify* method and the *SinkNotify* method—must be defined. The implementation of these two methods is fairly straightforward. The *ShutdownNotify* event is used to post a WM_QUIT message to the message loop and effectively end the application. For the *SinkNotify* event, the affected metabase paths are displayed in a dialog box. Note that if you run this application, you might see many notification dialogs since metabase property values are changing all the time on a busy server.

After the class has been created and the event methods have been implemented, the event sink must be registered with an instance of an IIS Admin Base Object. Here is the code:

```
CComObject<CAdminSink>* pDriver;
IMSAdminBase* pM;

CoCreateInstance(CLSID_MSAdminBase,
                 NULL,
                 CLSCTX_ALL,
                 IID_IMSAdminBase,
                 (void**)&pM);

CComObject<CAdminSink>::CreateInstance(&pDriver);
pDriver->m_ThreadID = GetCurrentThreadId();
DWORD dwAdvise = 0;
hRes = AtlAdvise(pM,
                 pDriver->GetUnknown(),
                 IID_IMSAdminBaseSink,
                 &dwAdvise);

MSG msg;
while (GetMessage(&msg, 0, 0, 0))
    DispatchMessage(&msg);

AtlUnadvise(pM, IID_IMSAdminBaseSink, dwAdvise);

pM->Release();
```

To register an event sink, first create an instance of the *IMSAdminBase* object using the *CoCreateInstance* call. Then, with the *CreateInstance* method of the *CComObject* template, create an instance of the sink object. At this point, the *GetCurrentThreadId* is used to identify the current thread ID so that a WM_QUIT message can be posted back to this thread's message loop when the *ShutdownNotify* event is returned. Then the *AtlAdvise* function registers the sink. (Normally, the registration process would entail getting an interface pointer to the *IConnectionPointContainer* interface, finding the appropriate *IConnectionPoint* interface that supports the appropriate event notifications, and then passing an interface pointer to the object's *IMSAdminBaseSink* interface using the *IConnectionPoint::Advise* method. Lucky for us, ATL does all this in a single call.)

Once *AtlAdvise* returns, notifications can begin, so the message loop is started and will continue until the WM_QUIT message is received. Once this message is received, it turns off the event sink and releases the IIS Admin Base Object instance that was created earlier.

For simplicity's sake, this metabase monitor simply displays change notifications in a dialog box. Without much effort, you could write the change notifications to a file and effectively create a metabase log. IIS even includes an IISADMIN extension that allows you to set up the logging server to load and unload when the metabase service is started and stopped. Details for writing an IISADMIN extension can be found in the Programmer's Reference section of the online documentation. See the section entitled "Custom Extensions Interface" under "IIS Administration."

In this chapter, you've seen how much you can do with the metabase. You can write your own applications that take advantage of the metabase; you can programmatically configure IIS through the metabase; you can use the various tools to view and monitor the metabase; or you can simply use IIS, which is built on top of the metabase. With its hierarchical architecture and great performance, the metabase is certainly one of the features that makes IIS such a powerful tool.

Now that we have learned how to configure the different options of IIS and how IIS uses the metabase to store this information, we are going to look at the other side of Web server administration: logging and monitoring. We have seen how to setup and configure our server; now we need to know how to make it run smoothly.

CHAPTER 6

Logging and Monitoring Tools

Setting up and configuring Microsoft Internet Information Server is only the beginning. Now you need to learn how to monitor IIS performance and identify trouble spots and errors. A number of tools are available to help you accomplish this task.

Monitoring the performance of IIS will help you to identify possible bottlenecks before they become critical. IIS has an excellent logging facility, and in this chapter you'll learn how to use it to interpret and identify possible problems. IIS also logs almost all system-level errors to the Microsoft Windows NT event log. But server logs are not the only monitoring options available. IIS performance can also be monitored in real-time via Windows NT Performance Monitor.

Performance Monitor can save current activity to log files, which can be examined at any time. In addition, in the true spirit of Windows NT networking, Performance Monitor can be used remotely from any Windows NT–based machine. Performance Monitor is also capable of sending special alerts or running a custom executable when certain conditions arise. For instance, you might monitor when the number of incoming connections exceeds a predefined threshold. Performance Monitor is not a panacea, however. If a company uses a mixed networking environment with Windows NT and UNIX-based machines, the organization might want to monitor IIS from a UNIX machine as well as via Performance Monitor. This task is almost trivial with the Simple Network Management Protocol (SNMP), which will also be discussed in this chapter.

Log Files

A server can either create logs in the form of ASCII files or log its activity to any ODBC-compliant database. IIS allows information to be collected from all of the core services—WWW, FTP, SMTP, and NNTP—to either a local file or an ODBC-compliant database. Logging options are configured separately for each service; for the WWW service you would go to the Default Web Site Properties window (discussed in Chapter 4), as shown in Figure 6.1. Actually, IIS allows even finer control over logging than just turning it on or off for a service. After logging is turned on for a service, you can enable it or disable it for individual virtual directories.

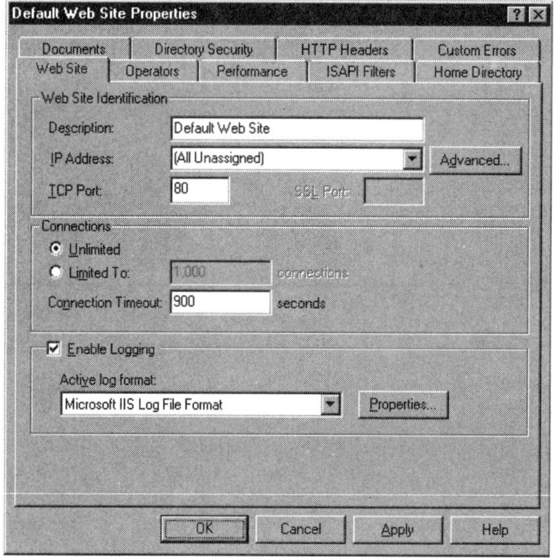

FIGURE 6.1

The Web Site page of the Web Site Properties window with Enable Logging selected.

You can check Enable Logging at the bottom section of the page, and once you choose the desired log format, you can manipulate precise configuration settings (such as log rotation frequency) by clicking the Properties button. This opens the Microsoft Logging Properties dialog box shown in Figure 6.2.

As described in the next sections, many different log formats are possible in IIS. The appearance of the Logging Properties dialog box can vary, depending on the log format you choose. The log format and configuration options are identical for the WWW, FTP, SMTP, and NNTP services, but of course the information logged is different for each service. The focus of this chapter will be on the WWW and FTP logs.

Log Formats and Naming Conventions

IIS natively supports four types of logging. The first three create ASCII log files, and the fourth writes entries to an ODBC database. The four types are:

- Microsoft IIS Log File Format
- NCSA Common Log File Format (National Center for Supercomputing Applications, not available for FTP activity logging)
- W3C Extended Log File Format
- ODBC Logging

The FTP service does not support NCSA logging. The Microsoft IIS Log File Format and W3C Extended Log File Format are chosen by Microsoft to log server activity. The NCSA Common Log File Format was developed by NCSA (authors of Mosaic) and the first World Wide Web servers.

No matter which logging option you choose, however, all log files are created with unique names that indicate the date and log format. Default logs are created in subdirectories according to the service and the site in the %SystemRoot%\system32\LogFiles directory, and they cannot be created on a network share.

Here's how the log directory structure looks on our machine:

```
Directory of D:\WINNT\system32\LogFiles

12/11/97  08:15a        <DIR>          .
12/11/97  08:15a        <DIR>          ..
12/11/97  07:14a        <DIR>          MSFTPSVC1
12/09/97  08:29p        <DIR>          NNTPSVC1
12/11/97  08:15a        <DIR>          SMTPSVC1
12/11/97  06:45a        <DIR>          W3SVC1
```

The number that follows the filename (MSFTPSVC*1*, for example) represents the instance of the service. Because we did not create any additional FTP or WWW sites on our machine, each service has only one instance.

NOTE

The IIS process runs as a Local System Account service on Windows NT. This account has virtually unlimited privileges on the local machine but is not known on the network. To use a network share from a service, you must specify a valid user name and password on the target machine. IIS does not allow you to create log files on a different machine, even though you can create virtual directories on networked resources.

Log naming conventions are shown in the following list. The first few characters in a filename represent its log format, followed by a few digits that represent the date or simply a log number if the log is not created according to a date. (The following placeholder codes are used below: *nn* means sequential numbers, *dd* means day, *mm* means month, *yy* means year, and *ww* means week.)

- *in* (or inetsrv): Microsoft IIS Log Format
- *nc* (or ncsa): NCSA Common Log File Format
- *ex* (or extend): W3C Extended Log File Format
- *nn*: for log files created according to their size

- *yymmdd*: for daily logs
- *yymmww*: for weekly logs
- *yymm*: for monthly logs

ASCII Log Files

When the IIS, NCSA, or W3C Extended formats are used, information is logged to the local file in ASCII form. Of these three choices, only the W3C format allows you to specify what information the log will contain. If you use the first two formats, you cannot choose what information goes to the log file.

You can create new log files daily, weekly, or monthly. Or if necessary, you can direct IIS to create a new log when a log reaches a maximum size (or the log can just keep the same information forever). If you click the Properties button in the Default Web Site Properties window, shown in Figure 6-1, the Microsoft Logging Properties dialog box appears, as shown in Figure 6-2.

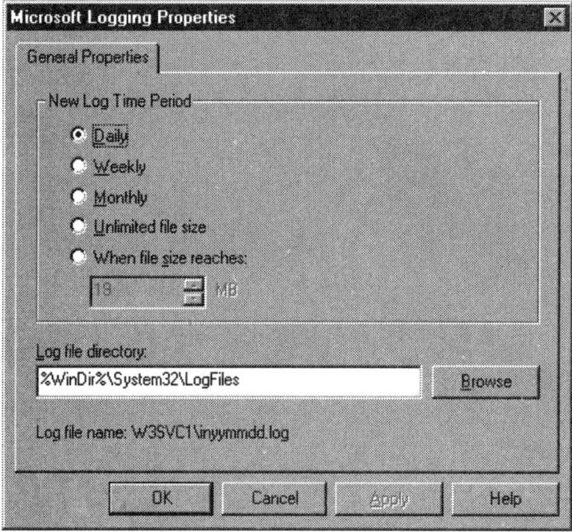

FIGURE 6.2

The Logging Properties dialog box that shows the log name, location, and frequency.

Figure 6.2 shows the log filename format: *inyymmdd.log*. In this log filename, *in* represents the Microsoft IIS Log Format, as described previously. For example, if today were December 10, 1998, this log file would look like this: in981210.log. When the information is logged in W3C Extended Format, the user can configure the type of information that can be logged. With this format, the Logging Properties dialog box includes an extra page, the Extended Properties page shown in Figure 6.3, that allows the user to select information that will be logged.

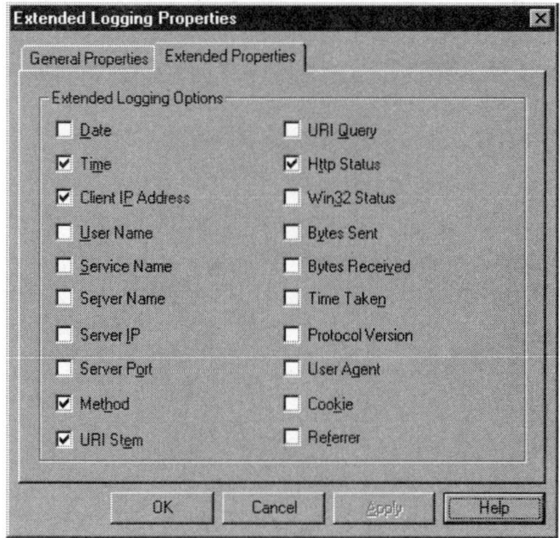

FIGURE 6.3

The Extended Properties page that appears when W3C Extended Log File Format is used.

ODBC Logging

Even though IIS has some powerful tools to analyze ASCII log files, you still might want IIS to log your server's activity to an ODBC-compliant database instead. All you have to do is select the ODBC Logging option in the Default Web Site Properties window, click the Properties button, and provide the information required in the ODBC Properties page of the ODBC Logging Properties dialog box, as shown in Figure 6.4. Then you enter a system Data Source Name (DSN), a table name, and the user name and password that will be used to access the database.

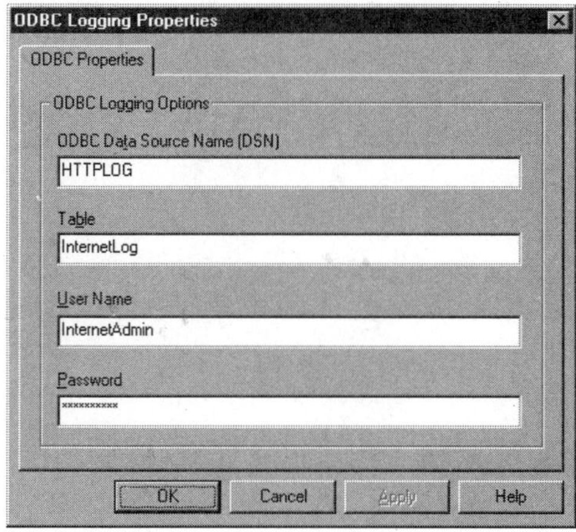

FIGURE 6.4

The ODBC Properties page of the ODBC Logging Properties dialog box.

Setting up a Microsoft SQL Server database or any ODBC-compliant database as a logging backend is a two-step procedure. First you create a table in the database with the fields shown in the table below. Second you create a system DSN in the ODBC Control Panel. The ODBC data source should be configured as a system DSN because regular DSNs are not accessible to services. To set up a system DSN, open the ODBC applet in the Control Panel to display the ODBC Data Source Administrator. Select the System DSN tab, and click Add. Select the correct driver for your database (such as SQL Server), and click Finish. At this point, you will need to enter the name for the DSN, specify the database, and choose other settings.

Field Name	SQL Data Type	Explanations
ClientHost	*varchar(255)*	Client machine's IP address.
Username	*varchar(255)*	User name of the client. If the page is not password protected, this will always be the anonymous user name.
LogTime	*datetime*	Date and time that log entry was created.
Service	*varchar(255)*	Name of the service. Can be WWW, FTP, or some other name.
Machine	*varchar(255)*	Server machine name.
Serverip	*varchar(50)*	Server IP address.
Processingtime	*int*	Time spent on request processing, in milliseconds.
Bytesrecvd	*int*	Number of bytes received.
Bytessent	*int*	Number of bytes sent.
Servicestatus	*int*	Service status, such as *200*.
Win32status	*int*	Windows NT status code; 0 would normally indicate success.
Operation	*varchar(255)*	Type of the operation or command. For example *USER* for FTP service or *GET* for WWW.
Target	*varchar(255)*	Target of the operation—*/DEFAULT.HTM* for example.
Parameters	*varchar(255)*	Any parameters to the above operation. Can be either name/value pairs for invoking CGI or an ISAPI extension. Will be a user name for the FTP command *USER*.

IIS comes with a special LOGTEMP.SQL file in the IIS server directory (normally %SystemRoot%\system32\inetsrv). This file contains an SQL query that automatically creates an INETLOG table with the correct fields. Once you choose to use a database for logging, the server will create a new record for every request. This might not be a good idea for a busy server, however, because it slows down the server and does not scale well under a high level of stress. Logging to the database takes much more time than just appending one line to a text file. And whether you are using ASCII files or ODBC databases as the logging destination, the data being logged is exactly the same.

Interpreting IIS Logs

Log files contain a wealth of information about past IIS actions. They not only indicate the success or failure of certain operations (client's GET requests, for example), but they also provide information needed to resolve problems. In the next sections you will learn how to utilize log files to collect information about IIS performance.

WWW Logs in IIS Log File Format

The output below shows an IIS log's data. (Notice that some lines are wrapped because of the book's limited page width and line numbers have been added to simplify explanations. Genuine log files don't have line wrapping or line numbers.)

```
Line 1: 192.155.1.1, -, 12/11/97, 6:45:59, W3SVC, LEONBR-HM,
    192.155.1.1, 621, 419, 72, 304, 0, GET, /Default.htm, -,
Line 2: 192.155.1.1, -, 12/11/97, 6:46:16, W3SVC, LEONBR-HM,
    192.155.1.1, 230, 399, 2327, 200, 0, GET, /scripts/sheaddump.dll,
    Param1=Foo&Param2=Bar,
Line 3: 192.155.1.1, -, 12/11/97, 6:47:03, W3SVC, LEONBR-HM,
    192.155.1.1, 50, 383, 191, 500, 126, GET,
    /scripts/does_not_exist.dll, -,
Line 4: 192.155.1.1, LEONBR-HM\leonbr, 12/11/97, 7:01:48, W3SVC1,
    LEONBR-HM, 192.155.1.1, 65354, 494, 2730, 200, 0, GET,
    /secure.htm, -,
```

In the data above, each field ends with a comma. A hyphen (-) acts as a placeholder for parameters that are not valid for a particular request. The entries appear in the following order:

```
client's IP address, username, date, time, service used, server's
    name, server's IP address, processing time, bytes received, bytes
    sent, service status code, Win32 error code, name of the
    operation, target or object of the operation, parameters passed
```

Now you can assume the role of a Log Detective to determine whether you can re-create events by examining the log file, line by line.

Line 1 shows that on December 11, 1997, at 6:45:59 a.m., the client from IP address 192.155.1.1 connected to the Web service running on the machine named *leonbr-hm*. The IP address of *leonbr-hm* is 192.155.1.1 (which happens to be the same machine as the client in this case). The client requested DEFAULT.HTM via the HTTP method GET. It took the server 621 milliseconds to process this request. The server received 419 bytes and sent 72 bytes. The server operation responded to the request with HTTP status code 304, which is defined as a "Not Modified" reply to the request with the *if-modified-since* header in the HTTP specification. In other words, the client had DEFAULT.HTM in its cache, and because the server had the same (that is, the unmodified) version of DEFAULT.HTM, the server did not send the entire document again. Notice that the server sent only 72 bytes of information. This process is more efficient than sending the whole file, which is usually much bigger than 72 bytes. This entire operation finished with 0 as the Win32 error code. The 0 error code indicates that the operation completed successfully.

Line 2 is similar to Line 1, with a few differences. The target or object here is /scripts/sheaddump.dll. This means the client has requested that the server execute the ISAPI extension SHEADDUMP.DLL, which is located at virtual root /scripts. The client has passed the following parameters to the DLL: *Param1=Fooz* and *Param2=Bar*.

Line 3 shows the invocation of a strange DLL called DOES_NOT_EXIST.DLL. This request was generated to illustrate a situation in which a DLL does not exist on the server. Indeed, the GET operation has failed with HTTP status code 500 ("Internal Server Error"). Look at the Win32 error code. It is set to 126 ("Specified module could not be found"). All Win32 errors are defined in the WINERROR.H header file, which is included with the Microsoft Platform Software Development Kit (SDK) and is also included with Microsoft Visual C++. Most likely, when the server tried to call the *LoadLibrary* API to load the nonexistent DLL, the call failed because the DLL could not be found. It looks like you just located a problem with your installation: the DLL file DOES_NOT_EXIST.DLL is not at the specified location.

Note that all these HTTP requests came from an anonymous user—that is, the client never prompted the user for a name and password. In this case, the user name variable is blank and the hyphen placeholder is shown instead. Line 4, however, shows that SECURE.HTM was accessed by the LEONBR-HM\leonbr user because we configured our NTFS file permissions for SECURE.HTM not to allow anonymous access.

FTP Logs in IIS Log File Format

Now take a look at the FTP logs to see what they have to say:

```
Line 1: 192.155.1.1, anonymous, 3/22/97, 6:33:24, MSFTPSVC, LEONBR-HM,
    192.155.1.1., 0, 16, 0, 0, 0, [1]USER, anonymous, -,
Line 2: 192.155.1.1, IE40user@, 3/22/97, 6:33:24, MSFTPSVC, LEONBR-HM,
    192.155.1.1., 10, 16, 0, 0, 0, [1]PASS, IE40user@, -,
Line 3: 192.155.1.1, leonbr, 3/22/97, 6:34:49, MSFTPSVC, LEONBR-HM,
    192.155.1.1., 0, 13, 0, 0, 0, [2]USER, leonbr, -,
Line 4: 192.155.1.1, leonbr, 3/22/97, 6:34:50, MSFTPSVC, LEONBR-HM,
    192.155.1.1., 50, 7, 0, 0, 0, [2]PASS, -, -,
Line 5: 192.155.1.1, leonbr, 3/22/97, 6:34:57, MSFTPSVC, LEONBR-HM,
    192.155.1.1., 0, 35, 0, 0, 0, [2]QUIT, -, -,
Line 6: 192.155.1.1, IE40user@, 3/22/97, 6:35:11, MSFTPSVC, LEONBR-HM,
    192.155.1.1., 107234, 0, 0, 0, 64, [1]closed, -, -,
```

The preceding lines were generated by the FTP service. Once again, here's how you can trace the FTP server activity. In this example, the FTP server is configured to allow anonymous connections. At 6:33 a.m., an anonymous connection occurred (Line 1)—the user name is anonymous. The server requested that the client provide a password, and the client supplied IE40user@ (Line 2). Most likely, the client accessed the FTP server via Microsoft Internet Explorer. Internet Explorer has built-in client FTP functionality to support anonymous connections.

NOTE

Internet Explorer is not able to prompt a user for a name and password to access an FTP server by using credentials other than anonymous. You can, however, specify credentials on the URL in this way: ftp://User:Password@hostname.

One minute later, at 6:34 a.m., another user connected to the server (Line 3). The user's name was leonbr. When the server requested a password, I simply pressed Enter. Line 4 shows a hyphen placeholder for the password. Because it's impossible to specify the user name and password from Internet Explorer (other than as part of the URL), it is probably safe to assume that this request came from a full-fledged FTP client. (In fact, I typed *FTP* at the command prompt.) After I logged in as user leonbr, I did not do anything but enter *quit* to log out. This step is reflected on Line 5, in which the user leonbr issues the QUIT command. Compare this request to the logout shown on Line 6, which corresponds to the first user who was using Internet Explorer. Because Internet Explorer is unable to explicitly issue an FTP QUIT command, this FTP connection is just lingering inactive for awhile (even after IE is closed). After 107,234 milliseconds (almost 2 minutes) of inactivity, I have disconnected the lingering connection from the FTP User Sessions dialog box, which is accessible from the FTP Site property page. If I did not force a disconnection, the server would disconnect the inactive user (you would also see a close line in the log), but this would happen after the default connection timeout, which is much more than 2 minutes.

As you can see, the server logs can reveal much about what has occurred on a server. After you know how to read the log data, finding and fixing invalid links and other errors is easy. If you see the HTTP status code 404 ("Not Found") anywhere in the log, you know that the target of the operation could not be found and did not exist. You can then determine whether hot links on any of your other Web pages are trying to send the user to this nonexistent location.

NCSA Common Log File Format

So far, you've learned about the standard IIS log format. Following is a log in another supported format, NCSA. (Again, the line numbers are not part of the log but were added for reference.)

```
Line 1: 192.155.1.1 - - [11/Dec/1997:16:44:22 -0800]
    "GET /scripts/does_not_exist.dll HTTP/1.0" 500 191
Line 2: 192.155.1.1 - - [11/Dec/1997:16:48:13 -0800]
    "GET /samples/Default.htm HTTP/1.0" 200 4273
Line 3: 192.155.1.1 - - [11/Dec/1997:16:50:00 -0800]
    "GET /scripts/sheaddump.dll?Param1=Hello HTTP/1.0" 200 2324
Line 4: 192.155.1.1 - LeonBr [11/Dec/1997:16:41:23 -0800]
    "GET /samples/Protected.htm HTTP/1.0" 200 4273
```

As you can see, not as much information is shown by NCSA as by the standard log format. The NCSA format uses this syntax:

```
Client_IP_address - User_Name [Date:Time -TimeZone] "Method Object
    HTTP_version" HTTP_StatusCode BytesSent
```

In Line 1, a client from 192.155.1.1 has connected on December 11, 1997, at 4:44 p.m. (The time zone is –8 hours from Greenwich Mean Time.) Here the client requested that the server invoke a server extension DLL (DOES_NOT_EXIST.DLL) via the HTTP method GET. This request completed with HTTP status code 500 ("Internal Server Error") and generated 191 bytes of outgoing traffic. "Internal Server Error" can indicate many different problems, but the NCSA log does not provide enough information to help you figure out what went wrong.

Lines 2 and 3 show that a few minutes later the same client used the HTTP GET method to request a default file and then requested that the server invoke a different server extension DLL (SHEADDUMP.DLL). Both requests completed with HTTP status code 200, indicating success. Line 4 shows a request from user LeonBr to return the /samples/Protected.htm file. Because we configured the server to deny anonymous users from accessing this file, the user had to supply a name

(LeonBr in this case) and password to gain access. Once again, you can see that the NCSA log shows considerably less information than the standard IIS log.

NOTE

You might be wondering why anyone would want to use the NCSA log format. Since the NCSA format is a standardized one, some third-party log analyzers might be available that can interpret the NCSA logs. But before you start looking for these programs, remember that IIS comes with a very powerful log analyzing tool: Site Server Express. See Chapter 8 for more information about this tool.

W3C Extended Log File Format

So far, this chapter has covered ODBC logging, the IIS log format, and the NCSA log format. Unlike the W3C Extended log format, none of these other formats allows you to choose what information the server writes to the log. You'll recall that with the W3C Extended log format, you can choose the log fields you want from the Extended Logging Properties dialog box. (See Figure 6.3.) The available fields within this dialog box are summarized in the table below. Because all the same fields are not used for all services, some fields will obviously not apply to some services, so their logs will show a hyphen placeholder rather than a value. (For instance, cookie fields are not necessary for a mail server, so even if you add this field to the log, it will not be available for e-mail activity.)

All Available Fields for W3C Extended Log Format

Field	Appears As	Description
Date	*date*	The date on which the activity occurred.
Time	*time*	The time the activity occurred.
Client IP Address	*c-ip*	The IP address of the client that accessed your server.
User Name	*cs-username*	The name of the user who accessed your server.
Service Name	*s-sitename*	The Internet service that was running on the client computer.
Server Name	*s-computername*	The name of the server on which the log entry was generated.
Server IP	*s-ip*	The IP address of the server on which the log entry was generated.
Server Port	*s-port*	The port number to which the client is connected.
Method	*cs-method*	The action the client was trying to perform (for example, a GET command).

(continued)

continued

Field	Appears As	Description
URI Stem	*cs-uri-stem*	The resource accessed; for example, an HTML page, a CGI program, or a script.
URI Query	*cs-uri-query*	The query, if any, the client was trying to perform; that is, one or more search strings for which the client was seeking a match.
Http Status	*sc-status*	The status of the action, in HTTP terms.
Win32 Status	*sc-win32-status*	The status of the action, in terms used by Windows NT.
Bytes Sent	*cs-bytes*	The number of bytes sent by the server.
Bytes Received	*sc-bytes*	The number of bytes received by the server.
Time Taken	*time-taken*	The length of time the action took.
Protocol Version	*cs-version*	The protocol (HTTP, FTP) version used by the client. For HTTP, this will be either HTTP 1.0 or HTTP 1.1.
User Agent	*cs(User-Agent)*	The browser used on the client.
Cookie	*cs(Cookie)*	The content of the cookie sent or received, if any.
Referrer	*cs(Referer)*	The site at which the user clicked on a link that brought the user to this site.

Here's an e-mail service log:

```
#Software: Microsoft Internet Information Server 4.0
#Version: 1.0
#Date: 1997-12-11 16:42:53
#Fields: date time c-ip s-sitename cs-method cs-uri-stem sc-status
    sc-win32-status cs-version
1997-12-11 16:42:53 192.155.1.1 SMTPSVC1 MAIL FROM - 250 0
    SMTP+Version:+5.5.1774.114.11
1997-12-11 16:42:53 192.155.1.1 SMTPSVC1 RCPT TO - 250 0
    SMTP+Version:+5.5.1774.114.11
1997-12-11 16:42:53 192.155.1.1 SMTPSVC1 DATA - 250 0
    SMTP+Version:+5.5.1774.114.11
1997-12-11 16:42:53 192.155.1.1 SMTPSVC1 QUIT - 0 991
    SMTP+Version:+5.5.1774.114.11
```

Notice that the *cs-method* field for the SMTP protocol represents commands. SMTP commands serve the same purpose as HTTP verbs. (The details of the SMTP protocol are discussed in Chapter 26.)

The Conversion Log Utility

IIS ships with a utility called CONVLOG.EXE that can be found in the default installation directory %SystemRoot%\system32. CONVLOG.EXE takes the log file in any format generated by the server and converts it to NCSA format. This might not seem too important, but the converter can also perform a few more helpful tasks. The converter can change the format of the date, it can convert the GMT offset time in NCSA logs to local time, and it can replace IP addresses with their respective host names. Offsetting the time zone and changing the date format allows one-shot conversion of log files from one country's style to another. (For example, if you set the GMT offset to +3 hours and change the date to *dd.mm.yy* format, the log file will appear just as if it were generated in Moscow.) You can run CONVLOG.EXE from the command prompt to see a screen full of help about how to use it.

Custom Logging Modules

Since IIS has so many logging options available, you might think that most people's logging needs would already be met. But IIS also provides the ultimate level of logging flexibility—the ability to perform your own custom logging.

It is possible to get the log information that IIS uses via the IInetLogInformation COM interface. The server makes the IInetLogInformation interface available to custom logging modules when a logging event occurs. Applications can access logging information via this interface.

Logging modules are the components that perform logging. NCSA, W3C, and other log formats discussed earlier are made possible because of IIS's logging modules. These modules are standardized COM objects, and you can create your own custom logging modules.

A particular custom logging module might perform some task that is not performed by default—for example, it might send logging information over the network to a centralized logging server. Your custom module must expose the ILogPlugin interface and then be registered with the server. The server calls certain methods from the custom module when information is ready to be logged. To use a centralized logging server, for example, you would need to implement some sort of network communications code in the module to ship the event information over the network.

The Windows NT Event Log

Server logs are not the only tools available to the Webmaster. The IIS process also logs its activity to the Windows NT system log. Windows NT's event service receives various event notifications from applications and system components and logs them to system-wide logs. This event service log is a good place to search for IIS errors and warnings.

Windows NT also has a utility that allows you to view system logs, the Event Viewer. This utility can be found in the Administrative Tools group on your Start menu, but you can also launch it from the Event Viewer button in the Management Console. Event Viewer allows you not only to view logs from the local machine but to connect and review logs from virtually any other Windows NT–based machine, as long as you are logged on to the particular machine with an account that has administrative rights.

Using Event Viewer, you can view these Windows NT operating system logs:

- **System log** Windows NT system component messages are stored here.
- **Application log** Windows NT applications log their messages here.
- **Security log** System security activity, such as a security audit, is stored here.

Every event log entry includes the name of the source associated with it (such as W3SVC) and the type of event:

- Error
- Warning
- Information
- Success Audit and Failure Audit (used only in security log)

NOTE

ISAPI extensions don't get loaded directly by the W3SVC service. They are loaded by the Web Application Manager (WAM) component. WAM appears as a source of information in the logs.

Figure 6.5 shows the system log for a Windows NT machine running IIS. An error is included in the system configuration code, and the log in the figure indicates this.

Event Viewer - System Log on \\LEONBR-HM

Log View Options Help

Date	Time	Source	Category	Event	User	Computer
12/11/97	8:19:43 PM	MSFTPSVC	None	100	N/A	LEONBR-HM
12/11/97	8:18:53 PM	WAM	None	205	N/A	LEONBR-HM
12/11/97	8:17:51 PM	W3SVC	None	14	N/A	LEONBR-HM
12/11/97	7:55:49 PM	NNTPSVC	None	93	N/A	LEONBR-HM
12/11/97	7:55:43 PM	NNTPSVC	None	94	N/A	LEONBR-HM
12/11/97	7:55:25 PM	SMTPSVC	None	525	N/A	LEONBR-HM
12/11/97	7:55:24 PM	SMTPSVC	None	554	N/A	LEONBR-HM
12/11/97	7:55:24 PM	SMTPSVC	None	423	N/A	LEONBR-HM
12/11/97	7:55:22 PM	SMTPSVC	None	534	N/A	LEONBR-HM

FIGURE 6.5

The system log showing a warning for the FTP service, errors for WAM and the WWW service, and information messages for SMTP services.

As you can see in the figure, a few error and warning events were generated by the various components of IIS. By double-clicking on the specific event, you can view more detailed information that can help you determine what went wrong. In the figure, the log has been sorted in reverse chronological sequence, so the most recent event is at the top. To view the first error that occurred, you find the entry with a red stop sign that is farthest down on the list, and then double-click on the entry to see the Event Detail dialog box shown in Figure 6.6.

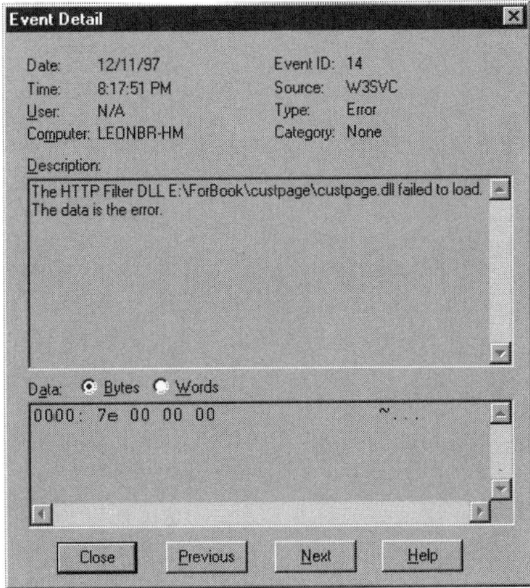

FIGURE 6.6

The Event Detail dialog box showing the W3SVC error.

The problem is clearly stated. The error description tells you that the HTTP Filter DLL could not be loaded. The hexadecimal data in the bottom text box is the error code, which has a value of 0x7E. You can convert this value to decimal, to get 126, and then look up the corresponding Win32 error code. As it turns out, error value 126 means "The specified module could not be found." (Notice that IIS still starts and runs without having loaded this filter.)

Figure 6.7 shows the details of the second error in this event log.

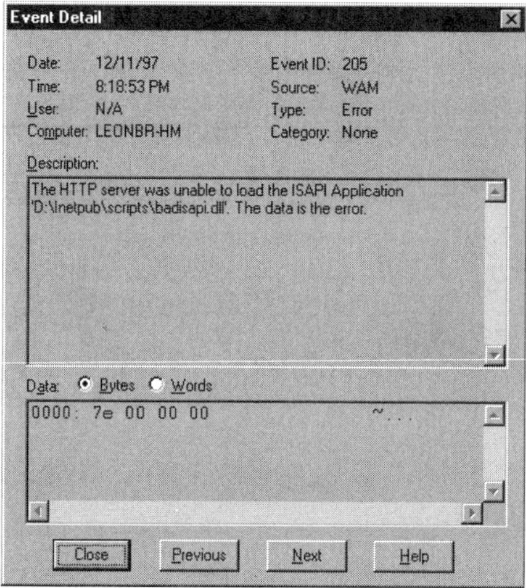

FIGURE 6.7

The Event Detail dialog box displaying an error caused by the invocation of a nonexistent ISAPI extension.

According to this dialog box, a user has tried to invoke an ISAPI extension DLL that does not exist. This problem is even more apparent considering that the name of the requested DLL is BADISAPI.DLL. (Note that ISAPI DLLs are not loaded directly by the IIS service. They are loaded by the Web Application Manager; that's why the source is indicated as WAM instead of as W3SVC.)

The last message description, shown in Figure 6.8, was generated by the FTP service. This is not an error, but a warning.

Looks like somebody tried to log on with a user account called "BadUser." Since an account with such a name does not exist on this machine, the FTP service has denied access to this account and created the appropriate entry in the event log.

Not all events are logged in the system log. Active Server Pages (ASP) and Content Index (CI) Services are considered applications; therefore, their messages are logged to the application log. Figure 6.9 shows a few events generated by ASP and CI. These messages offer information about starting and stopping ASP and updating the index database.

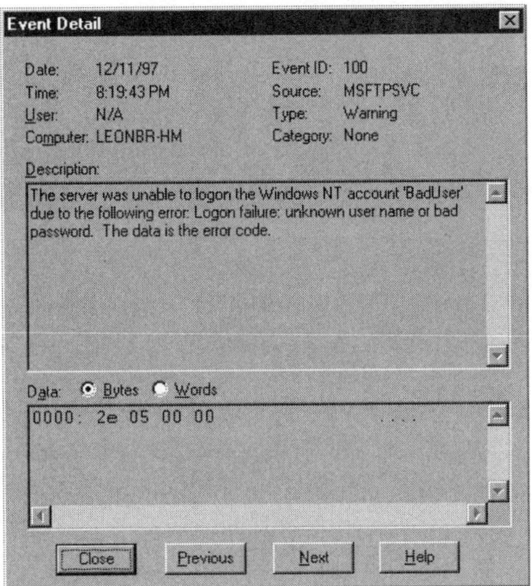

FIGURE 6.8

The Event Detail dialog box displaying a warning caused by a user who tried to log on with an invalid user name or password.

Event Viewer - Application Log on \\LEONBR-HM

Log View Options Help

Date	Time	Source	Category	Event	User	Computer
12/12/97	12:03:06 AM	Ci	CI Service	4103	N/A	LEONBR-HM
12/11/97	8:17:44 PM	Active Server Page	None	4	N/A	LEONBR-HM
12/11/97	8:17:41 PM	Active Server Page	None	4	N/A	LEONBR-HM

FIGURE 6.9

Some of the information messages in the application log.

Performance Monitor

The next tool in the administrator's arsenal is Performance Monitor, a utility included with Windows NT that allows you to monitor performance of an application in real time. Performance Monitor can be found in the Administration Tools group on the Start menu, or it can be launched from the Performance Manager toolbar button on the Management Console or by executing *PERFMON.EXE* from a command prompt. Applications and system components that want to provide information for viewing with Performance Monitor can log such information in special objects called *performance counters*. Although an application might not expose counters, IIS exposes quite of few for each service (Web, FTP, SMTP, and so on) as well as for Active Server Pages and for IIS in general.

In its simplest mode, Performance Monitor allows you to choose any exposed performance counters for a selected object and add them to a chart. To choose these counters, select the Add To Chart option from the Edit menu to display the Add To Chart dialog box shown in Figure 6.10. (For an example of how Performance Monitor can chart selected performance counters, see Figure 6.11 on page 135.)

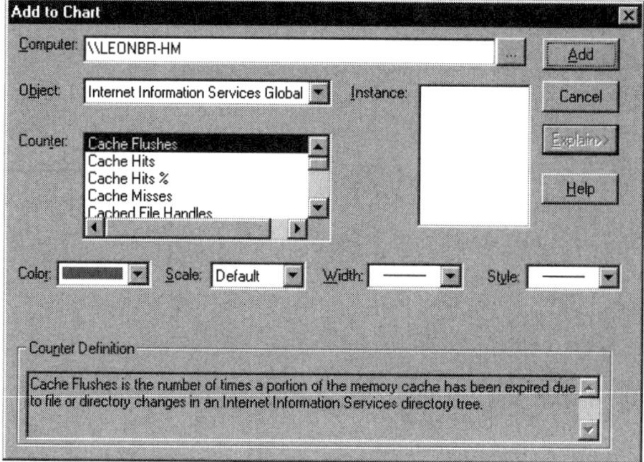

FIGURE 6.10

Adding various performance counters to a real-time chart using Performance Monitor.

Because the range of possible counter values is immense, charts can be plotted at various scale levels. For easy viewing, counters can be shown in a variety of colors with different line styles. Performance Monitor allows monitoring of any NT computer that is reachable over the network, but you do need administrative rights to access remote machines. Each chart can get updated with a frequency that you define. Back in the Performance Monitor window you can select Chart from the Options menu to bring up the Chart Options dialog box. From there you can set the Interval for a Periodic Update, or you can select Manual Update.

These are some of the most important objects relevant to IIS:

- Internet Information Services Global Information
- Web Service
- FTP Service
- Active Server Pages
- SMTP Server

The next sections cover some of the objects and the information they can provide. (Other objects, such as the Content Index object and the NNTP Server object, are also available in the dialog box. To find out more about these objects, check the IIS online documentation.)

Internet Information Services Global Object

The Internet Information Services Global object contains counters that can help you monitor caching and other global characteristics of the IIS services. Caching plays an important role in IIS performance. IIS employs complex algorithms to optimize access to the most frequently used files and extension DLLs and even to perform directory listings. The cache is located in memory that is shared among the IIS services, allowing each to access the data. When a server detects a change in the content of a directory or file, it flushes the corresponding cached information. Flushing also occurs when an object has not been accessed for a long time. The counters shown in the table below monitor IIS internal caching.

Caching Counters

Counter	Description
Cache Flushes	The number of times since service startup that cache has been flushed.
Cache Hits	The number of times since service startup that a file open, directory listing, or service specific object request was found in the cache. A high number indicates efficient cache utilization.
Cache Hits %	The ratio of cache hits to total requests. The higher the number, the better.
Cache Misses	The number of times since service startup that a file open, directory listing, or service specific object request was not found in the cache. A low number means that IIS is using the cache effectively.
Cached File Handles	The number of open file handles cached by all of the IIS services.
Directory Listings	The number of cached directory listings cached by all of the IIS services.
Objects	The number of objects cached by all of the IIS services. The objects include file handle tracking objects, directory listing objects, and service specific objects.

IIS allows you to limit network utilization to a specific amount. For example, imagine that you just set up and advertised a new Internet site. Imagine also that this site is very popular and gets an unexpectedly high number of hits. Such high network traffic can dramatically affect LAN performance or the performance of any other applications or servers running on the same network. It can create performance problems if your server is receiving requests over a low-bandwidth link, such as a 56-KB line. If this line is shared with other servers, they might not be able to function properly because your server is taking up all the throughput of the line. To fix such a situation, you should limit your server's bandwidth to minimize network impact. The server employs an advanced bandwidth throttling scheme to delay or reject requests so that the server does not exceed its preset bandwidth limitation. (Note that bandwidth throttling applies only to static HTML pages.) The counters shown in the following table can be used to monitor bandwidth throttling.

Bandwidth Counters

Counter	Description
Current Blocked Async I/O Requests	The current number of requests that are temporarily blocked by the bandwidth throttle setting. Blocked requests are held in a buffer and then unblocked if more bandwidth becomes available, unless a time-out limit is reached.
Measured Async I/O Bandwidth Usage	The number of bytes received and sent by your Web server, averaged over one minute. This is a measure of the total amount of user traffic on your server.
Total Allowed Async I/O Requests	The number of user requests allowed by the Web and FTP services since service startup. When you throttle bandwidth, the number of allowed user requests will be restricted.
Total Blocked Async I/O Requests	The total number of requests that have been temporarily blocked by the bandwidth throttle setting since service startup. Blocked requests are held in a buffer and then unblocked if more bandwidth becomes available, unless a timeout limit is reached.
Total Rejected Async I/O Requests	The total number of user requests rejected (because of bandwidth settings) since service startup. When a request is rejected, it is not held in a buffer, unlike a blocked request.

The Web Service Object

The Web Service object has multiple counters that reflect all the vital information about the HTTP service process. These counters monitor the amount of data transmitted and the use of HTTP methods, server load, and user logons. In the Add To Chart dialog box, Performance Monitor usually shows at least two instances for the Web Service: the Administration Web Site and the Default Web Site. If other sites exist, they will be visible in the Instance list box. You can get more information about all the available counters by clicking the Explain button in Performance Monitor.

The counters can be organized into a few groups. The table below shows the group of counters that reflect the number of transmitted bytes and files.

Data Transmission Counters

Counter	Description
Bytes Received/sec	Rate at which data bytes are received by the Web service.
Bytes Sent/sec	Rate at which data bytes are sent by the Web service.
Bytes Total/sec	Rate of total bytes/sec transferred by the Web service (sum of Bytes Sent/sec and Bytes Received/sec).
Files Received/sec	Rate of files received by (uploaded to) the Web service since the service started.
Files Sent/sec	Rate of files sent by (downloaded from) the Web service since the service started.
Files/sec	Rate of files transferred by the server since the Web service started.
Total Files Received	The total number of files received by the Web service since the service started.
Total Files Sent	The total number of files sent by the Web service since the service started.
Total Files Transferred	The total number of files transferred by the Web service since the service started (sum of Total Files Sent and Total Files Received).

The HTTP server receives various types of requests: GET, POST, HEAD, and so on. The following table shows all the counters used to monitor these types of requests. Notice that you can keep track of the total, current, and maximum values of specific counters.

Request Counters

Counter	Description
CGI Requests/sec	The rate of CGI requests that are simultaneously processed by the Web service. CGI requests are custom gateway executables (.EXE files) the administrator can install to add forms processing or other dynamic data sources. CGI requests spawn a process on the server that can be a large drain on server resources.
Current CGI Requests	Current number of CGI requests simultaneously being processed by the service.
Current ISAPI Extension Requests	Current ISAPI extension requests simultaneously being processed by the service. ISAPI Extension Requests are custom gateway DLLs that the administrator can install to add forms processing or other dynamic data sources.
Delete Requests/sec	The rate of HTTP requests using the DELETE method.
Get Requests/sec	The rate of HTTP requests using the GET method. GET requests are generally used for basic file retrievals or image maps, although they can also be used with forms.
Head Requests/sec	The rate of HTTP requests using the HEAD method. HEAD requests generally indicate that a client is querying the state of a document to determine whether it needs to be refreshed.
ISAPI Extension Requests/sec	The rate of ISAPI Extension requests that are simultaneously being processed by the Web service.
Maximum CGI Requests	The largest number of CGI requests simultaneously processed by the service since service startup.
Maximum ISAPI Extension Requests	Largest number of ISAPI extension requests simultaneously processed by the service since service startup.
Not Found Errors/sec	The rate of errors due to requests that couldn't be satisfied by the server because the requested document could not be found. These are generally reported to the client with HTTP error code 404.
Other Request Methods/sec	The rate of HTTP requests that do not use the GET, POST, PUT, DELETE, TRACE, or HEAD methods. These can include LINK or other methods supported by gateway applications.
Post Requests/sec	The rate of HTTP requests using the POST method; generally used for forms or gateway requests.
Put Requests/sec	The rate of HTTP requests using the PUT method.
Total CGI Requests	The total number of Common Gateway Interface (CGI) requests executed since service startup.

Counter	Description
Total Delete Requests	The number of HTTP requests using the DELETE method.
Total Get Requests	The total number of HTTP GET requests received by the service.
Total Head Requests	The total number of HTTP HEAD requests received by the service.
Total ISAPI Extension Requests	The total number of HTTP ISAPI extension requests received by the service.
Total Method Requests	The total number of HTTP GET, POST, PUT, DELETE, TRACE, HEAD, and other method requests.
Total Method Requests/sec	The rate of HTTP requests using GET, POST, PUT, DELETE, TRACE, or HEAD methods.
Total Not Found Errors	The number of requests that could not be satisfied by the Web service because the requested document could not be found; typically reported to the client as HTTP 404 error code.
Total Other Request Methods	The number of HTTP requests that are not GET, POST, PUT, DELETE, TRACE, or HEAD methods.
Total Post Requests	The number of HTTP requests using the POST method.
Total Put Requests	The number of HTTP requests using the PUT method.
Total Trace Requests	The number of HTTP requests using the TRACE method.

Connection counters—listed in the table below—are the best indicators of a server's load. You can see the server's load at a glance by looking at the number of connections per second.

Connection Counters

Counter	Description
Connection Attempts/sec	The rate at which connections using the Web service are being attempted. The count is the average for all Web sites combined, regardless of what you choose for Instance.
Current Connections	The current number of connections established with the Web service (sum of anonymous and nonanonymous users). The count is the current total for all Web sites combined, regardless of what you choose for Instance.

(continued)

continued

Counter	Description
Maximum Connections	The largest number of simultaneous connections established with the Web service since service startup. The count is the maximum for all Web sites combined, regardless of what you choose for Instance.
Total Connection Attempts	The total number of connections to the Web service that have been attempted since service startup. The count is the total for all Web sites combined, regardless of what you choose for Instance.*

* *This number does not include connection attempts that failed at the TCP (transport) or IP (network) layer. To monitor all connection attempts, use the Connection counters on the TCP performance object. To monitor currently active connections, use Anonymous Users/sec (the rate users are making anonymous connections using the Web Service object).*

IIS supports anonymous and non-anonymous connections. The HTTP service process runs under the Local System account. Every time a new anonymous request arrives, IIS impersonates an anonymous user account to handle the given request. The anonymous user account is created by IIS at installation and by default is named IUSR_*computername*. This user has limited rights on the system and is a member of the Guests user group only. Some HTML documents or entire directories can deny access to the anonymous user. (That is, the IUSR_*computername* account might not have rights to access HTML files in a particular directory.) You can set up such access denial by configuring file and directory permissions on an NTFS partition or by installing a special filter that performs custom authentication. In each case, the Internet client will ask the user to provide credentials in the form of a user name and password. (Chapter 23 describes in detail how a browser and server interact to pass user and password information.)

Credentials are passed to the HTTP server, which then impersonates the user that made the request. The HTTP server uses the LogonUser API to do the logon; however, the function can fail if the client supplied an invalid user name or password. In the case of a successful logon, IIS will consider the new user as a non-anonymous user and will increment the Total NonAnonymous Users counter. The Logon Attempts counter is incremented for all successful and unsuccessful logons including the anonymous user logon that takes place for anonymous requests. This and all other user-related counters are listed in the following table.

User Logon Counters

Counter	Description
Anonymous Users/sec	The rate at which users are making anonymous connections using the Web service. If a client request for an anonymous connection is rejected and the client responds with valid authenticating data, the connection is counted as non-anonymous.
Current Anonymous Users	The number of users who currently have an anonymous connection using the Web service.
Current NonAnonymous Users	The number of users who currently have a non-anonymous connection using the Web service.
Logon Attempts/sec	The rate at which logon attempts are being made to the Web service.
Maximum Anonymous Users	The maximum number of users who established concurrent anonymous connections using the Web service (since service startup).
Maximum NonAnonymous Users	The maximum number of users who established concurrent non-anonymous connections using the Web service (since service startup).
NonAnonymous Users/sec	The rate at which non-anonymous users are connecting to the Web service. If a client request for an anonymous connection is rejected and the client responds with valid authenticating data, the connection is counted as non-anonymous.
Total Anonymous Users	The total number of users who established an anonymous connection with the Web service (since service startup).
Total Logon Attempts	The total number of successful logons to the Web service since the service started; does not include failed logon attempts. To calculate failed attempts (where clients were able to connect but not log on), subtract Logon Attempts from Connection Attempts.
Total NonAnonymous Users	The total number of users who established a non-anonymous connection with the Web service (since service startup).

Only one counter indicates error information: the Not Found Errors counter. This counter indicates the number of requests that could not be satisfied by the server because the requested document could not be found. These errors are generally reported as an HTTP 404 error code to the client.

FTP Service, ASP, and Other Objects

The FTP service, which operates in a manner somewhat similar to the Web service, accepts either anonymous or non-anonymous connections. A user who successfully logs on can download or upload files. So it is logical that any counters that deal with information transfer would be useful for monitoring FTP server activity. In fact, the counters for FTP service are also similar to the Web service counters.

Performance Monitor includes a wealth of information about Active Server Pages. ASP itself is implemented as an ISAPI extension that allows the processing of server-side scripts. Instead of requesting a static HTML document that is ready to be rendered by the browser, the client requests a script written in a programming language such as VBScript or JavaScript. ASP, on the server side, loads this script and processes it before sending the client the completed (or interpreted) page.

ASP uses cookies to implement user sessions. A session starts as soon as the first ASP page of the application is loaded, and it lasts until a timeout for the application has elapsed or until the script explicitly aborts the session. A session allows an application to preserve some variables (called *session variables*) while the user jumps to different pages of the same application. Because HTTP is stateless in nature, ASP employs HTTP cookies to preserve session state.

Performance Monitor can show you information about the ASP script engine. Counters can be divided into the following groups: ASP Errors, Request counters, Session counters, Transaction counters, and counters reflecting internal information about the ASP script engine (cache, memory, and so on). Depending on the needs of your enterprise, you should explore other counters for services such as mail (SMTP) or news (NNTP).

Simple Chart Reading

Because so many counters are available, you might be wondering what is the best way to choose the most appropriate ones. It might be difficult to add all of them to the performance chart at the same time. Even if you could do so, the chart probably would become unreadable. A good idea, then, is to choose some key counters from different services to get a good performance picture of the server at a glance.

NOTE

Even when varied line styles and different colors are used to represent counters on the chart, having many counters on the same chart makes it very messy. Here is a tip. Highlight the desired counter in the lower portion of the window, and press Backspace or Ctrl-H. The selected line on the chart will be highlighted as a thick white line for easy reading. To deselect the line, press Backspace or Ctrl-H one more time.

Figure 6.11 shows PERFMON.EXE in chart mode, with only a few counters added to the chart. In the figure, Performance Monitor uses line graph mode, which shows you history information; Performance Monitor can also use bar graphs.

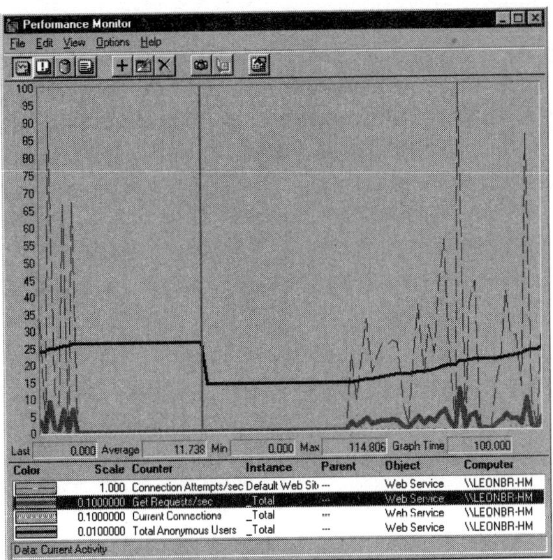

FIGURE 6.11

A Performance Monitor line graph, showing counters for a busy server.

As you can see in the figure, this is a busy server. At its peak, the server has experienced more than 114 connections per second. Now look at the Total Anonymous Users count. You can see that, since server startup, more than 2500 anonymous users have logged on. (Don't forget to use the scale.) It appears that the server has experienced a large number of hits in a relatively short time. (In this figure, the high load level was achieved by the simulation of simultaneous multiple requests from many clients using a stress application.) Of course, you might want to add more or different counters from those the figure uses to monitor your server effectively.

Sending Alerts

Performance Monitor can perform other functions besides showing a real-time chart. It can also trigger a special alert when something goes wrong. You can see which alerts have been triggered by selecting Alert from the View menu. If no alerts have been set, the Alert Log area of the window will be empty.

Suppose, for example, that you want to set up an alert so that the Webmaster or system administrator is notified every time your Web server receives more than 50 anonymous connections per second. The simplest thing to do would be to configure Performance Monitor to send a network message to a specified machine. To do this, you must first configure the network alert option. On the Options menu, click Alerts to see the Alert Options dialog box shown in Figure 6.12.

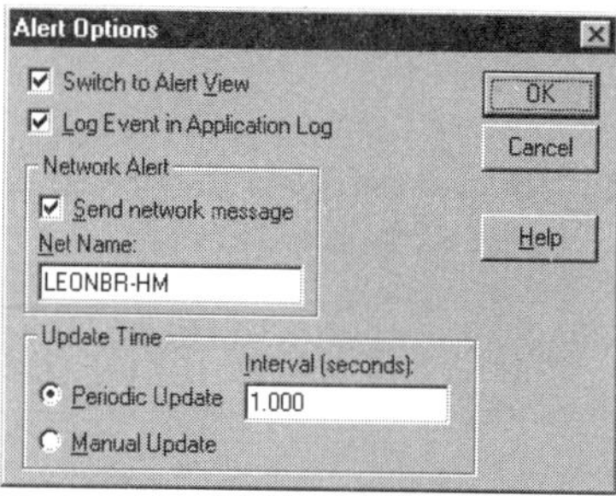

FIGURE 6.12

The Alert Options dialog box configured to send a network message alert.

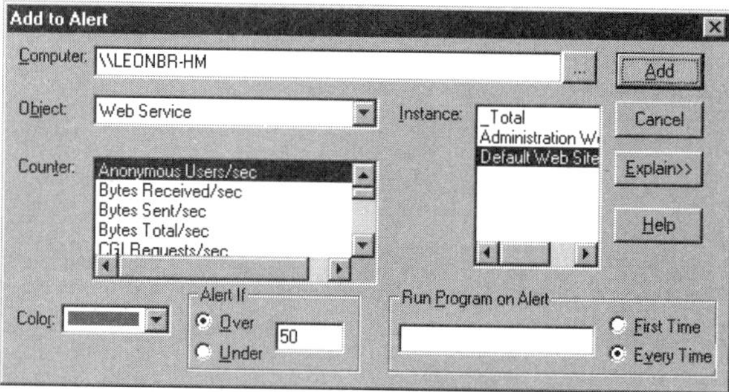

FIGURE 6.13

Adding information to the Add To Alert dialog box to set the alert to be triggered when the anonymous connections exceed 50 per second.

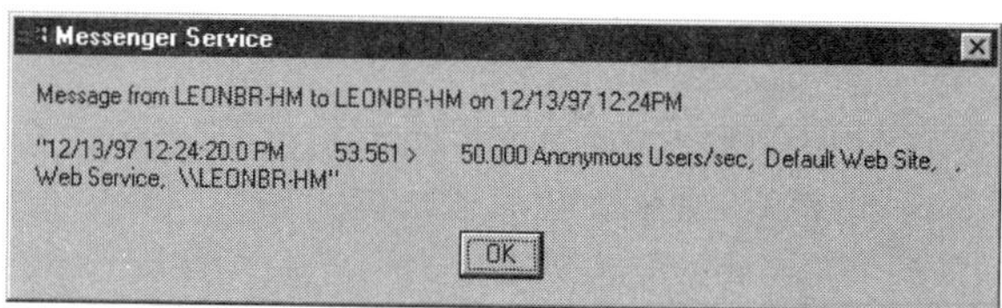

FIGURE 6.14

The pop-up message received when more than 50 anonymous connections per second are encountered at the server.

Next you add an alert for your specific performance counter by selecting Add To Alert from the Edit menu, which displays the Add To Alert dialog box (shown in Figure 6.13).

After you have completed these two steps, the machine named LEONBR-HM (in this example) will display the pop-up message shown in Figure 6.14 whenever the number of anonymous connections exceeds 50 per second. The message shown in the figure is a little cryptic, but you can clearly see that the average number of 53.561 users per second is more than the threshold of 50.

In this example, you've sent the alert to the server machine, but you can configure the alert to be sent to any machine on your network. To receive these alert messages, the machine receiving the pop-up message must be running the messenger service. You can start the service from the command line by typing *net start messenger*.

It is also possible to configure more complex actions on alert. For example, you can have Performance Monitor run custom programs when certain alerts are triggered. These custom programs can perform useful functions, such as reformatting your Windows NT hard drive when the load gets too high—just kidding, of course. But you might want to run a program that sends e-mail or even sends pager notification to a system administrator or a Webmaster. Since it is possible to configure Performance Monitor to handle multiple alarms, each alarm can have a different color. Figure 6.15 shows how an alarm looks in alert view.

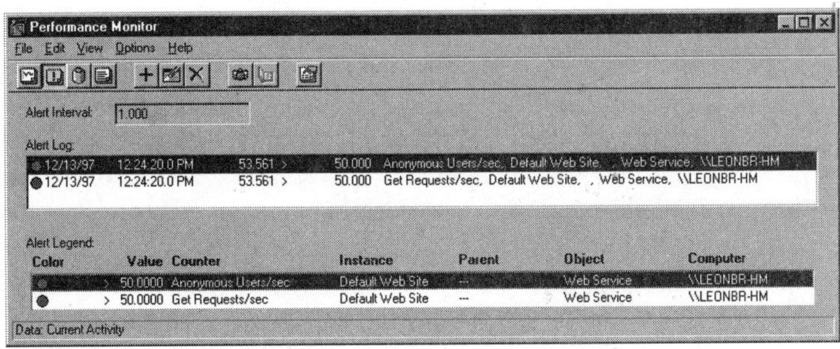

FIGURE 6.15

Alert view showing multiple simultaneous alarms.

Viewing Reports

Performance Monitor's report view shows the exact values for the selected counters at any given time. If you are monitoring multiple machines simultaneously, report view can display information about all of them at one time. Figure 6.16 shows how this looks for a single server. The number 6 in the right corner of the status bar at the bottom of the window indicates that 6 alerts are outstanding.

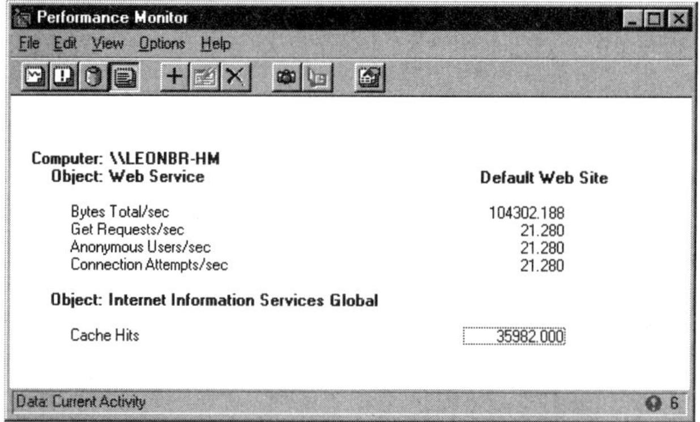

FIGURE 6.16

The report view of Performance Monitor showing selected counters.

Logging Activity to a File

Performance Monitor can also log all current activity to a file that you can use later to get information about the counters, rather than using real-time data. This logging capability is a handy feature for accessing more information because the standard line graph for real-time data shows only information that occurred during the last 100 seconds.

For example, suppose that you want to monitor your server over the weekend. If you prefer to spend your weekends climbing mountains instead of staring at your computer monitor, you can configure Performance Monitor to keep watch and save the data for you to see when you return. Simply switch Performance Monitor to log view (shown in Figure 6.17), add the needed objects, open or create a log file, and then begin logging. You should be aware that these log files can be very large. To see how much information is reasonable to store in the log, you can create a log that will track data for a short time, such as 5 minutes, and then estimate the size of the log for longer durations.

When in Log view, selecting Log from the Option menu brings up the Log Options dialog box that includes buttons to start logging, stop logging, and save a log. When you are ready to look over the past activity in the log, you can choose the Data From option from the Options menu and type in the name of the log file (such as *d:\temp\temp.log*). At this point, you can switch to whatever view you want (chart view or alert view, for example) and add counters from the objects you want to monitor. Only the objects you selected when the log was created will appear in the log. If you choose the Time Window option from the Edit menu, the Input Log File Timeframe dialog box is displayed. This dialog box allows you to specify how much of the logged information you want to display by letting you set the start time and end time.

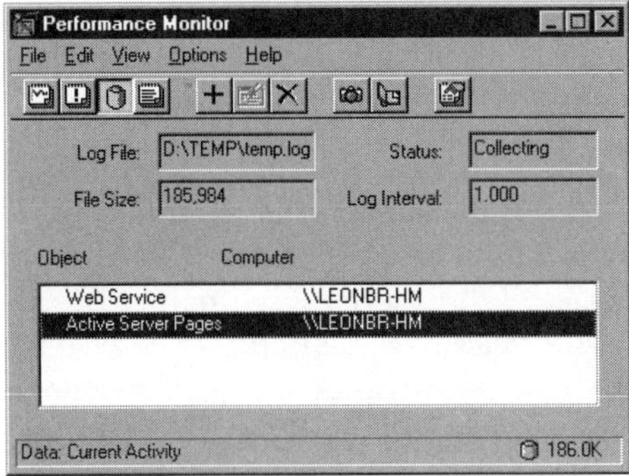

FIGURE 6.17

Performance Monitor capturing current activity to the d:\temp\temp.log file.

Simple Network Management Protocol

All the information covered so far in this chapter deals with monitoring performance from either the local Windows NT server or from a remote Windows NT machine. But you might find it convenient to monitor performance of your Windows NT–based Web server from any platform, such as from a UNIX machine. Or perhaps you use a centralized network management software package, such as SunNet Manager or HP OpenView, and you want to add IIS to the list of manageable objects on the network. You can do this by using the Simple Network Management Protocol (SNMP).

SNMP was developed to manage various network devices on different operating systems. Its purpose is to collect performance data and system parameters from remote network nodes using a centralized management console. It also allows an administrator to modify a remote system's network parameters (such as routing tables). Remote systems can also send alarms to the Management Console, if necessary. Such alarms are called *traps* in SNMP jargon. A trap can be sent by a remote peer in response to some event, such as when the number of requests exceeds a preset threshold or when an elevated temperature in the server's computer room makes the room unsafe. Not all remotely managed machines support traps, though. As you will see shortly, IIS does not issue traps.

To communicate with an SNMP management application, IIS must include a special component called an *SNMP Agent*. On Windows NT, the agent is a DLL that "knows" how to get data from the component it was designed to monitor (such as requests/sec for the HTTP server) and assign it to a counter similar to Performance Monitor. A counter in SNMP is identified using an *Object Identifier* (OID). An OID is a series of numbers that are usually written like this: *1.3.6.1.2.1.6.13.1.1*. Each OID is responsible for particular pieces of information. In their numeric form, OIDs are difficult to memorize and address by humans. It might be handy if a solution existed to map these strange numbers uniformly to something more meaningful. But keep in mind that SNMP Agents can deal with OIDs only and not with their human-friendly representations.

OIDs are mapped to more human-readable strings in special *Management Information Base* (MIB) files. MIBs are text files written in a special form to structurally define all the manageable objects and OIDs defined by them. MIB files can have nested structures, and one file might need to depend on other MIB files that contain common definitions. Some base MIBs are defined as RFCs. Others are distributed by the manufacturer of the system or software. The OID example used earlier (1.3.6.1.2.1.6.13.1.1) is taken from RFC 1213. This document defines human readable strings and their corresponding OIDs used in the second (and current) version of Management Information Base (MIB-II). The sample OID used earlier is mapped to *tcpConnState*. In other words, by using this OID, an SNMP management application can send a request to the remote system's agent to get the status of a TCP connection. MIB files are made of simple ASCII text, but they need to be compiled using a special MIB compiler to convert them to a binary format. Whereas the MIB files are common for all systems, the binary format, as well as the MIB compiler, is proprietary for each system and platform. The binary form of the MIB is stored on the Management Console computer. It is used to convert human-readable objects (such as *tcpConnState*) to their corresponding OID forms, so management software can send requests to the remote machines and get values for a requested OID. Figure 6.18 puts everything together in an architectural overview.

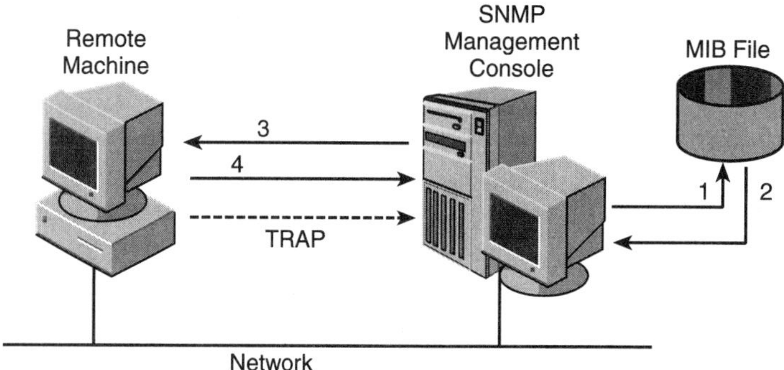

FIGURE 6.18

The SNMP architecture overview.

Following are the steps performed by the SNMP management application. Assume that the SNMP manager wants to get the value for the currentConnections counter on a remote machine.

1. The management application asks the SNMP management library for the OID that corresponds to the human-friendly name currentConnections.
2. The SNMP Management library returns the OID for the needed parameter that it found in the binary MIB file.
3. The management application sends the request to the remote machine to get a value for the specified OID.
4. The SNMP agent on the remote machine receives the request, gets the value of the OID, and sends it back to the management application.

Traps are handled a little differently than counters. SNMP agents send traps to preconfigured hosts whenever certain events occur. Because IIS does not support traps, they will not be discussed further here.

Keeping the architectural overview in mind, take a look at how IIS supports SNMP. IIS installs with SNMP extension agents that are individually responsible for retrieving data for their various services. The SNMP objects are pretty much the same as the objects described in the Performance Monitor section of this chapter. IIS does not allow you to set parameters via SNMP nor to configure IIS to send SNMP traps. The IIS machine should of course have the SNMP service installed and running. This service can be installed by opening the Network Control Panel applet, clicking the Services tab, and then clicking the Add button to add the SNMP service in the dialog box that appears.

The Platform SDK contains a simple SNMP management application called SNMPUTIL.EXE. This is a command line utility, and it is not easy to use. In the next section, you will use an application that we created, which uses the SNMP management APIs.

First you must set up IIS to use SNMP. Two agent DLLs—located in the %SystemRoot%\system32\inetsrv directory—install with IIS: FTPMIB.DLL, the FTP SNMP agent, and HTTPMIB.DLL, the HTTP SNMP agent. Two other agents are included with Windows NT and manage Windows NT, general TCP/IP, and Microsoft network (Microsoft LAN Manager) parameters: INETMIB1.DLL, the MIB II extension agent DLL, and LMMIB2.DLL, the LAN Manager MIB 2 extension agent DLL. These agents are loaded by the SNMP service (SNMP.EXE in the %SystemRoot%\system32 directory) on the IIS machine.

As explained earlier, FTPMIB.DLL and HTTPMIB.DLL collect information directly from IIS and make it available to the SNMP management application. If the core SNMP service is going to be able to load and use the extension agent DLLs, they must be added in a special registry location. If you have installed IIS on a Windows NT–based machine with the SNMP Service also installed, IIS installation automatically configures the registry for you. If your Windows NT–based machine does not have the SNMP service installed before you installed IIS, you need to do one of the following:

- Install SNMP and then install IIS.
- Configure the registry so that SNMP will load the agent DLLs properly.

Because reinstalling IIS might not be a fun thing to do, you can run the application called SNMPCONFIG.EXE on the CD-ROM included with this book. It will locate the IIS agent DLLs, change the registry as needed, and restart the SNMP service so that you can monitor your IIS information.

◆ SNMP Extension DLLs and the Windows NT Registry

You need to make a few registry settings before the SNMP service can load the extension agent DLL. Use the REGEDT32.EXE program that comes with Windows NT to add this information. The SNMP configuration is found at *HKEY_LOCAL_MACHINE\SYSTEM\CurrentControlSet\Services\SNMP\Parameters*.

You also need to add another entry under the *ExtensionAgents* key. (You will see some references to existing extension agents that you can use as examples.) Simply provide a pointer to another registry entry that contains the physical path (in Pathname registry key) at which the DLL can be found. Notice that the key name and values are case sensitive, so you must make sure that they match. In case the SNMP service fails to start after you modify the registry, look in the system log for errors. You can also type *Net Help Start SNMP* at the command prompt to see how to configure error logging of the SNMP agent.

If you are still curious about SNMP configuration, then look for the SNMP.TXT file in the \MSSDK \BIN\WINNT directory of Platform SDK.

Now your IIS server machine should be properly configured to allow it to be managed by an SNMP application. Where do you go from here? You'll need to configure the machine that will be running the management application. If you have applications that support SNMP management, such as HP OpenView or SunNet Manager, refer to those products' documentation to learn how to install their MIBs. You can also use the SNMPMAN.EXE sample on the CD included in this book. It's an easy and inexpensive way to explore SNMP and the information that SNMP makes available to you.

As mentioned previously, management applications need access to the binary form of MIB files. In Windows NT, this file is MIB.BIN and is located in the %SystemRoot%\system32 directory included with Windows NT. MIB.BIN is the database of all OIDs and their mappings to friendly names. Since you already have the MIB.BIN file, you won't need the Microsoft MIB compiler. At this point, you are ready to run the SNMP management application shown in Figure 6.19.

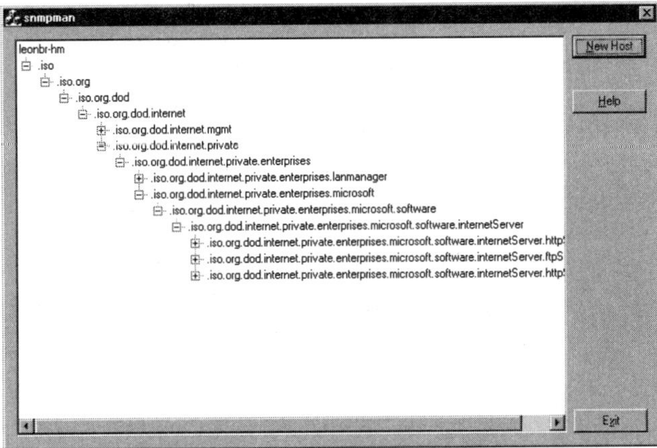

FIGURE 6.19

A custom application, SNMPMAN.EXE, that uses Windows SNMP APIs and shows a hierarchical view of the IIS objects.

◆ Building the MIB Database

Should you ever need to build an MIB.BIN file that supports IIS MIBs, you must have the following *.MIB files. (Remember that these are text files, and they need to be compiled with the MIB Compiler.)

- FTP.MIB, the FTP MIB
- HTTP.MIB, the HTTP MIB
- INETSRV.MIB, the Internet Server Global MIB
- MIB_II.MIB, the required MIB II for TCP/IP, from RFC 1213
- SMI.MIB, the required base MIB for the Windows NT system
- WINS.MIB, the WINS MIB

All these MIB files, can be found on the Windows NT Server 4.0 Resource Kit CD-ROM (COMMON\NETDIAG). Microsoft MIB compiler (MIBCC.EXE) is located in the Platform SDK (\mssdk\bin\winnt\i386). Because some MIB files include other files, you need to compile all of them in the correct sequence. The following will generate MIB.BIN:

```
C:> mibcc smi.mib mib_ii.mib wins.mib inetsrv.mib http.mib ftp.mib
```

The MIB files included with the Platform SDK are different from the ones included with the NT Server Resource Kit. If you use the MIB files included with the Resource Kit to compile MIB.BIN successfully, you will need to uncomment the following two lines in WINS.MIB:

```
--      microsoft       OBJECT IDENTIFIER ::= { enterprises 311 }
--      software        OBJECT IDENTIFIER ::= { microsoft 1 }
```

You uncomment them by removing the -- at the beginning of the lines.

Now you know how to generate and read IIS logs, how to monitor server performance using Performance Monitor, and how to monitor your server using the SNMP protocol. In the next chapter, you will examine some of the other services you can add to IIS, starting with Index Server.

CHAPTER 7

Index Server

Index Server 2.0 is the latest version of the search engine integrated with Microsoft Internet Information Server 4.0 and the Microsoft Windows NT Server 4.0 operating system. Index Server enables you to use any Web browser to perform full text searching of HTML, text, and Microsoft Office documents, including Microsoft Word, Microsoft Excel, and Microsoft PowerPoint documents. This powerful search feature of Index Server means that you don't need to convert all your document contents to HTML. Simply place your documents out on the Web server, and Index Server can do all the work for you, returning detailed summaries and hyperlinks to the actual documents.

Index Server first appeared with IIS 3.0. The latest version includes many exciting new features that leverage the advanced functionality of IIS 4.0, including the following:

- Support for querying from Active Server Pages (ASP)
- Support for querying in structured query language (SQL)
- Improved administration using the Microsoft Management Console
- Internet mail searching
- Improved robustness in the property cache
- Improved response time
- Multiple scopes
- Content filters for Microsoft Office 97

Among the most interesting of these new features are the new ways that you can customize Index Server to create your own search forms and result reports. Not only can you still use the HTM/IDQ/HTX technique from the previous version, but now you can also leverage the full power of both ASP and SQL. With the power of ASP, you can even use Index Server to create your own document management system. In this chapter, you'll find an entire section dedicated to techniques for customizing Index Server using HTM/IDQ/HTX, ASP, and SQL.

Setting Up Index Server

In this section, we'll review the installation and configuration of Index Server. We'll start with some resource requirements, review the recommended configuration, and then look at the installation process and see what files and folders are created on your machine.

Resource Requirements

The Index Server program files by themselves require 3 MB to 12 MB of disk space, depending on the number of languages installed. Another requirement is that the amount of free disk space be at least 40 percent of the size of the *corpus*.

Glossary

corpus *The collection of documents being indexed.*

Recommended Configuration

When planning the optimum hardware configuration for an Index Server installation, you should consider the following questions:

- What is the size of the corpus?
- How many documents are in the corpus?
- What is the maximum rate of search requests arriving at the server?
- What kind of queries (simple or complex) are being executed?
- Are any other applications running on the Web server?

The first four questions relate directly to Index Server, but the fifth question is important as well. If you are running custom ASP applications and other server-side applications such as SQL Server and Microsoft Transaction Server (MTS), you'll need to include capacity for these items in your hardware requirements.

The recommended amount of memory required by Index Server for various numbers of documents is shown here.

NUMBER OF DOCUMENTS	MINIMUM MEMORY	RECOMMENDED MEMORY
Fewer than 100,000	32 MB	32 MB
100,000–250,000	32 MB	64 MB–128 MB
250,000–500,000	64 MB	128 MB–256 MB
Over 500,000	128 MB	256 MB or more

Installation

Index Server is an optional component of the Windows NT 4.0 Option Pack installation. Figure 7.1 shows the Components list box for a custom installation of the Option Pack with the Index Server component selected.

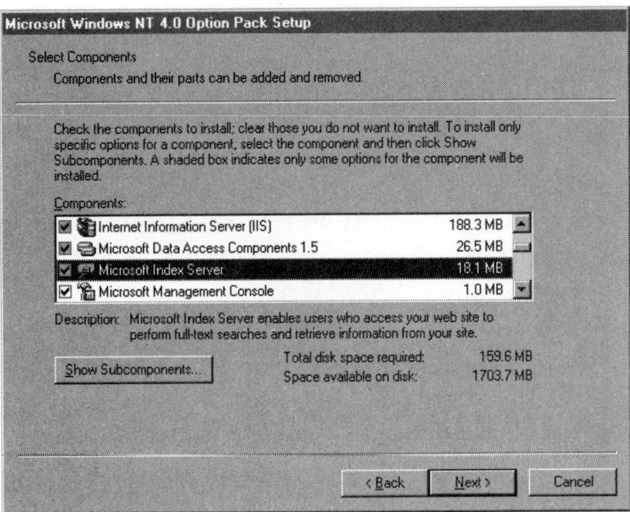

FIGURE 7.1

Windows NT 4.0 Option Pack Setup window, showing Index Server selected in the Components list box.

Once you have selected the Index Server component and proceeded with the installation, you will be presented with an Index Server dialog box. This dialog box prompts you for the directory to store the Index Server catalogs, which by default is C:\Inetpub. A *catalog* is the highest-level unit of organization in Index Server. Each catalog is a completely self-contained unit, consisting of an index and cached properties for one or more *scopes*.

Glossary

catalog *A group of files that contains the Index Server information about the contents of the corpus, including the index itself.*

scope *The breadth of an Index Server query. Scope can be specified by directory paths or by virtual directories on your Web server.*

During installation, a directory named Catalog.wci will be created under the C:\inetpub directory. The Catalog.wci directory stores all the catalogs that Index Server uses to operate. The following files are copied to your computer as well:

- Sample HTML and scripts files are copied to /iissamples/issamples (typically C:\inetpub\iissamples\issamples).
- Administration files are copied to /iisadmin/isadmin (typically C:\winnt\system32\inetsrv\iisadmin\isadmin).
- Documentation files are copied to /iishelp/ix (typically C:\winnt\help\ix).

In addition to these files, the installation creates a new registry key named *ContentIndex* and adds a service named Content Index as a Windows NT service that is started automatically. The registry key created is:

```
HKEY_LOCAL_MACHINE
\SYSTEM
 \CurrentControlSet
  \Control
   \ContentIndex
```

To edit the settings in this registry key, choose the Run command from the Start menu on the taskbar and then enter *regedt32* to start the registry editor. Figure 7.2 shows the *ContentIndex* key within the registry editor. Unless otherwise noted, all the configurable registry values mentioned in this chapter are located in this key.

Once the installation is complete, you should see the following menu items within the Microsoft Index Server program group, which is accessible from the Start menu on the taskbar:

- Index Server Manager
- Index Server Manager (HTML)
- Index Server Sample Query Form

To access the Microsoft Index Server program group, choose Programs from the Start menu on the taskbar and then choose Windows NT 4.0 Option Pack.

The Index Server Manager is the administrative interface for Index Server; it runs within the Microsoft Management Console. A Web-based administrative interface is also available via the Index Server Manager (HTML) menu item. We'll look at these two interfaces in detail in the section "Administering Index Server" later in this chapter. The Index Server Sample Query Form is a Web page that demonstrates several techniques for working with Index Server. These techniques are discussed in the section "Customizing Index Server" later in this chapter.

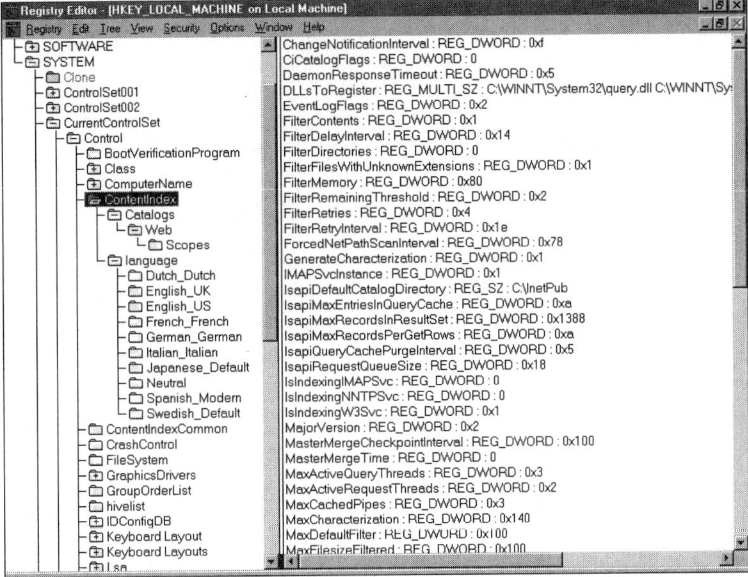

FIGURE 7.2

Registry Editor, showing the **ContentIndex** *key and some of the associated parameters that affect the behavior of Index Server.*

Inside Index Server

Index Server divides the task of creating indexes into three major steps: scanning, filtering, and indexing. During these three steps, numerous processes take place and numerous storage structures are used. The storage structures include both memory storage and physical storage on the hard disk. First we'll take a look at these processes and structures to gain an understanding of how Index Server operates; this knowledge will help you administer and troubleshoot Index Server.

Scanning

Scanning, the first process that Index Server performs on your data, is basically an inventorying process in which Index Server determines the virtual directories (and their corresponding physical directories) to be indexed. By default, all virtual directories are indexed. If you don't want to index a particular virtual directory, use the Management Console to open the Properties window for the directory and then uncheck the Index This Directory check box.

Of the three types of scanning available in Index Server, two are performed automatically: the *full scan* and the *incremental scan*. You can also conduct a *manual scan* of a virtual directory from within the Index Server Manager. (The steps to perform a manual scan are outlined in the section "Administering Index Server.") The result of the scanning process is a list of documents to be filtered and then indexed.

In a full scan, all documents in the directory are scanned and added to the list of documents to be filtered. A full scan is performed the first time a directory is added to the list of indexed documents and is also conducted as part of any recovery from a serious error.

In an incremental scan, Index Server searches only for documents that have been modified since the last time they were filtered. Whenever it is started up, Index Server performs an incremental scan on all the indexed directories, which enables Index Server to catch any files that were modified while it was not running.

NOTE

If your documents are stored on a computer running Windows NT, Index Server is automatically notified of any changes. If your documents are on a computer running Microsoft Windows 95 or Novell NetWare, Index Server will perform periodic scans of the share. You can use the registry setting ForcedNetPathScanInterval *to control the frequency of these scans. See the section "Administering Index Server" for more details about the various registry settings for Index Server.*

Filtering

In the filtering step, Index Server takes the list of documents to be filtered (the output from the scanning process) and applies content filters to the data. The content filters break the data into words (keys) and create *word lists*.

Index Server runs a child process named CiDaemon that is used for filtering the documents. The filtering is carried out in a three-part process that involves a filter dynamic link library (DLL), a word-breaker DLL, and a noise words file. All filtering is performed as a background activity.

Filter DLL

A *filter DLL* is a special-purpose DLL designed to understand the format of one or more document types and to extract the text and properties from the document. Index Server contains preinstalled filter DLLs that can index the following types of files:

- HTML version 3.0 or earlier
- Microsoft Word
- Microsoft Excel
- Microsoft PowerPoint
- Plain text
- Binary files

An interesting aspect of the HTML filter is that you can prevent the filtering of an HTML document by placing the following META tag in the document:

```
<meta name="robots" content="noindex">
```

Index Server also uses two other filters named the NULL filter and the Default filter. The NULL filter is used when a registered binary file is encountered. The NULL filter retrieves only the system properties, such as the filename, last write time, file size, and so on. The Default filter is used to filter documents with unknown extensions when the registry setting *FilterFilesWithUnknownExtensions* is set to *1*. The Default filter retrieves both the system properties and the data inside the file. Since it doesn't know anything about the file's format, it simply reads the file as a series of characters. If the registry setting *FilterFilesWithUnknownExtensions* is set to *0*, only the NULL filter is used.

By default, Index Server filters only files and not directories. If you want to filter directories, you can use Index Server to filter their system properties by setting the registry parameter *FilterDirectories* to *1*.

Index Server's filtering capability can be extended by adding third-party filter DLLs such as the Portable Document Format (PDF) filter DLL from Adobe. In fact, you can even write your own filter DLL to support the indexing of specific types of files. Filter DLLs are simply ActiveX components that support the *IFilter* interface, which is documented in the Microsoft Platform SDK.

If a file is corrupted, the filter DLL might not be able to process it correctly. In this case, an event is written to the Windows NT Event Log. You can also view a list of files that could not be filtered by selecting Unfiltered Documents on the Index Server Manager (HTML) Web page, as shown in Figure 7.3. (We will look at the Index Server Manager in detail in the section "Administering Index Server.")

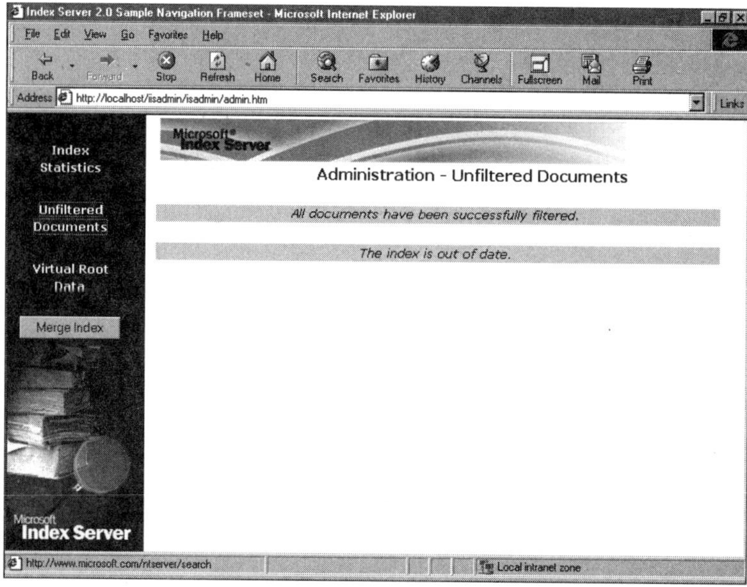

FIGURE 7.3

The Index Server Manager (HTML) Web page, showing a list of unfiltered documents.

If a file cannot be filtered because it is in use, Index Server will retry the operation up to a certain maximum number of attempts. This value is stored in the registry values *FilterRetries.*

The *CiDaemon* process is capable of generating a summary (also called a *characterization* or an *abstract*) for each document. If the registry key *GenerateCharacterization* is set to *1,* the characterization will be generated automatically. By default, Index Server takes the first 320 characters of a document and copies that block of text for the summary. The maximum number of characters in the generated characterization is controlled by the registry value *MaxCharacterization.*

Word-Breaker DLL

The *word-breaker DLL* provides a simple but important function in the overall filtering process: it parses the text and textual properties returned by the filter DLLs into discrete words. This word breaking is a language-dependent process used to create the raw word list from which the index will be built.

Noise Words

Noise words, also known as *stop words,* are those words that are not considered significant for searching. (Some examples are "and," "or," "but," and "if.") They are stored in text files in the *%SystemRoot%*\system32 directory. The default noise word file included with Index Server is named NOISE.DAT. The names of the noise word files for each specific language are stored under the following registry key:

```
HKEY_LOCAL_MACHINE
\SYSTEM
 \CurrentControlSet
  \Control
   \ContentIndex
    \Language
     \<language>
      \NoiseFile
       \<noise filename>
```

You can edit these noise word files using Notepad or any other text editor, and you can add or remove noise words from the file as required. Be careful about removing too many noise words—doing so will increase the size of your indexes.

Indexing

In indexing, which is the third and final step in index creation, Index Server moves the word lists that were created by the content filters to more permanent storage structures. First the word lists are moved to a *shadow index,* and then they are moved to a *master index*. Whereas word lists are actually in-memory indexes, the shadow and master indexes are persistent indexes because they are stored on disk. The process of moving data from one storage structure and combining it with another is called *merging*. There are three kinds of merges: *shadow merge, master merge,* and *annealing merge*. In this section, we'll look at these indexes and merge types.

NOTE

Many processes and storage structures are transparent to the end-user performing a document search. These elements represent the internals of the Index Server engine and are of interest mainly to administrators.

Word Lists

Word lists are temporary storage structures used during the indexing process. They can be created very quickly because they are in-memory indexes and contain data for only a small number of documents. When the number of word lists exceeds a preset maximum, the word lists are merged into the persistent shadow index.

Shadow Index

A shadow index is a persistent index that is created by merging word lists and possibly other shadow indexes via a shadow merge. Shadow indexes simply serve as intermediate indexes as data is propagated to the master index. They provide a means of querying the information they hold while the potentially lengthy process of merging the data with the master index takes place. Multiple shadow indexes can exist in a catalog.

Master Index

A master index is a persistent index that is created by combining all of the shadow indexes and the previous master index, if one exists. A master index is created via a master merge and is highly compressed. In the ideal situation, the master index will be the only index present, allowing Index Server to efficiently retrieve information from a single source.

Shadow Merge

In a shadow merge, multiple word lists, and even shadow indexes, are combined into a single shadow index. The advantage of a shadow merge is that it frees up resources such as memory (tied up by the word lists) and moves the data into persistent storage. A shadow merge can be triggered by any of the following events:

- Number of word lists exceeds the MaxWordLists registry value.
- Combined size of word lists exceeds the MinSizeMergeWordlists registry value.
- Preparation for a master merge.
- Preparation for an annealing merge.

Master Merge

In a master merge, all of the shadow indexes and the previous master index, if one exists, are combined to create a master index. At the end of the master merge, all the other indexes are deleted so that only the master index remains. A master merge is fully recoverable; if errors occur during the merge, it will restart where it left off.

A master merge can be triggered by any of the following events:

- Nightly maintenance master merge.
- Number of changed documents since the last master merge exceeds the *MaxFreshCount* registry value.
- Disk space on the catalog drive is less than the MinDiskFreeForceMerge registry value, and shadow index space exceeds the *MaxShadowFreeForceMerge* registry value.
- Total disk space occupied by the shadow indexes exceeds the *MaxShadowIndexSize* registry value.
- An administrator forces the master merge from the Index Server Manager (HTML) page.

Annealing Merge

An annealing merge is a type of shadow merge that occurs to minimize the number of persistent indexes in a catalog, which helps to make querying more efficient. When an annealing merge is performed, two or more shadow indexes are combined. Annealing merges are triggered when the system is idle for a certain length of time and the total number of persistent indexes exceeds the *MaxIdealIndexes* registry parameter. The length of time is based on the registry parameters *MinMergeIdleTime* and *MaxMergeInterval*.

Query Language

Index Server provides a rich query language that you can take advantage of when formulating your search queries. Users often enter single words into query forms and search through the resulting output for the documents they are interested in. By exploiting the full power of the Index Server query language, now you can refine your queries and extract just the contents you are looking for. This capability saves time and lets you perform more elaborate searches to query your data in a variety of ways.

Boolean Operators

You can use the Boolean operators AND, OR, and NOT (&, |, and ! in shorthand) to create a more precise query. For example, you would enter *visual and interdev* to search for pages containing the words "visual" and "interdev." The same idea applies to the OR and NOT operators. You can string together several of these Boolean operators to form a more complex query—for example, *visual and interdev or basic*—but when you do so, there is a question about the order of precedence in the query. The AND operator takes higher precedence than OR, so the preceding example would be evaluated as follows: *(visual and interdev) or basic*. This order of precedence is probably not what was intended in the original query. To override the default precedence, enter your own parentheses.

If you want to search for a phrase that contains an operator keyword that you don't want Index Server to treat as an operator, simply enclose the phrase in quotation marks—for example, *"Querying and Indexing"*. The quotation marks tell Index Server to search for the exact phrase.

NOTE

When the browser locale is set to German, French, Spanish, Dutch, Swedish, or Italian, you can take advantage of localized keywords in addition to the English keywords AND, OR and NOT—for example, if your site serves French-speaking clients, you can also use the French keywords ET, OU, and SANS.

Proximity Operators

The keyword NEAR (~ in shorthand) is a proximity operator that can be used to search for terms that are located close together within the same page. For example, entering *excel near project* would search for pages with the word "excel" near the word "project."

The NEAR proximity operator is similar to the AND Boolean operator. An important and distinct feature of the NEAR operator is that it will rank documents according to the proximity of the two search words—the closer the two search words, the higher the ranking. If the two search words are more than 50 words apart, the page is assigned a rank of *0*.

Wildcard Operators

The wildcard operators * and ** can be used to help you find pages that contain words similar to a given word. The * operator is used to search for words that contain the same prefix. For example, entering *int** would find words beginning with the letters "int," such as "interdev," "Internet," and "intranet." The ** operator is used to find words containing the same stem word. For example, entering *fly*** would find words such as "flying," "flown," "flew," and so on.

Free-Text Queries

Free-text queries let you enter any set of words or phrases, and even complete sentences. Index Server will extract the nouns and noun phrases and issue a query using those terms. For example, the question "How do I print in Microsoft Excel?" will return pages that mention printing and Excel. To indicate a free-text query to Index Server, prefix the phrase with *$contents*. If you are using the Sample ASP Search Form or the Sample HTM/IDQ/HTX Search Form (both of which are described later in this chapter), simply check the Use Free-Text Query check box. Behind the scenes, the *$contents* prefix will be added for you.

Vector Space Queries

Vector space queries let you enter a list of words or phrases to search for and give them a specific number to indicate their weight. The weight can be specified by enclosing it in square brackets. For example, *"vector space"[400], queries[100]* would search for the phrase "vector space" and the word "queries," with greater weight being given to the phrase "vector space."

Property Value Queries

Property value queries provide another powerful way to search Web page contents. These queries enable you to search basic file properties such as filename and file size and ActiveX properties such as title, subject, author, keywords, and comments. Of course, ActiveX properties will be found only in files that have been created by applications that support this capability, such as Word, Excel, and PowerPoint.

You can issue property value queries in two ways: using relational property queries and using regular expression property queries. Relational property queries consist of the @ character, a property name, a relational operator (=, >, <, >=, <=, or !=), and a property value. For example, to find all files larger than one million bytes , you would issue the query *@size > 1000000*. Regular expression property queries consist of the # character, a property name, and a regular expression. For example, to find all Word (.DOC) files, you would issue the query *#filename *.doc*

Customizing Index Server

Index Server lets you write your own custom code to search for contents within the corpus, enabling you to create highly customized Web applications that are tailored to your needs and to the needs of your end-users. The three basic techniques for customizing Index Server— HTM/IDQ/HTX, ASP, and SQL—are discussed in this section.

We'll start with a look at the sample files included with Index Server; these files are accessible from the Index Server Sample Query Form, shown in Figure 7.4. To get to this page, choose the Microsoft Index Server program group from the Windows NT 4.0 Option Pack and then choose Index Server Sample Query Form. You'll see several samples listed on the left-hand side of the browser window. These samples provide excellent examples of how to set up query forms, control the search, and format the results.

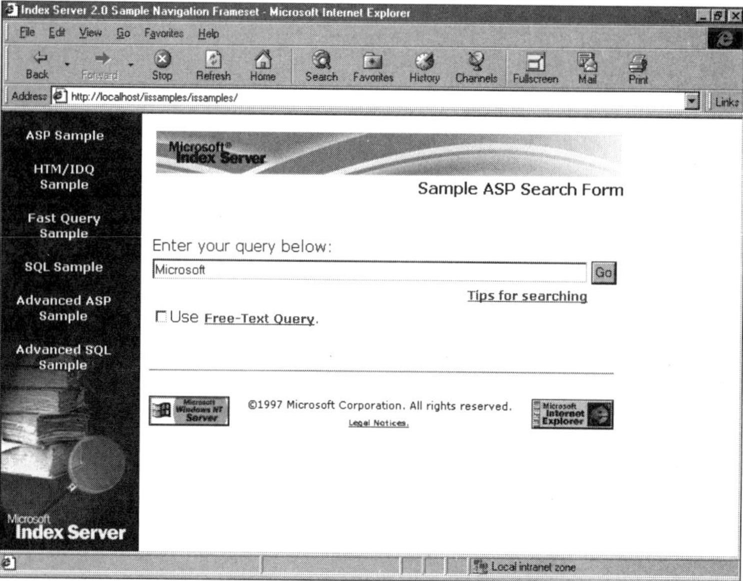

FIGURE 7.4

The opening page of the Index Server Sample Query Form.

HTM/IDQ/HTX

The HTM/IDQ/HTX technique consists of using three separate files for the various operations that need to take place: the HTML file is used to create the query form, the IDQ file is used to process the search, and the HTX file is used to format the results. Prior to IIS 4.0 and Index Server 2.0, this technique was the only way users were able to customize Index Server. Because it performs so well, this is still a good option. To access the Sample HTM/IDQ/HTX Search Form, shown in Figure 7.5, choose HTM/IDQ Sample from the list on the left in the Index Server Sample Query Form.

The files used in this sample are QUERY.HTM, QUERY.IDQ, and QUERY.HTX. By default, they are found in the C:\inetpub\iissamples\issamples folder.

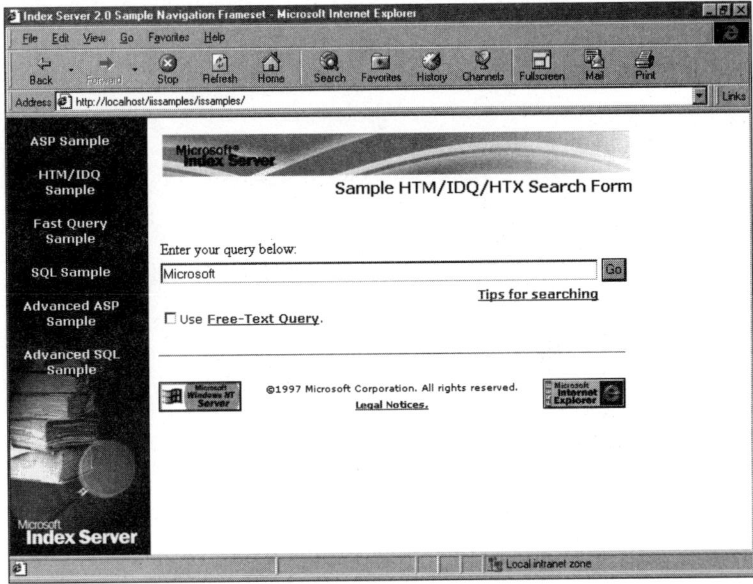

FIGURE 7.5

The Sample HTM/IDQ/HTX Search Form.

The *QUERY.HTM* file

The source code for the QUERY.HTM file is shown here:

```
<!DOCTYPE HTML PUBLIC "-//IETF//DTD HTML 3.0//EN" "html.dtd">
<HTML>
<HEAD>
<!--
    *****       INSTRUCTIONS FOR CUSTOMIZING THIS FORM      *****
    To customize this form, look for remarks in the file beginning
    with 5 stars ("*****"). These lines contain instructions for
    easily customizing the most common query form elements.
-->
<LINK REL=STYLESHEET HREF="is2style.css" TYPE="text/css">
<TITLE>Index Server 2.0 Sample HTM/IDQ/HTX Search Form</TITLE>
<META NAME="DESCRIPTION"
    CONTENT="Sample query form for Microsoft Index Server">
<META NAME="AUTHOR"      CONTENT="Index Server Team">
<META NAME="KEYWORDS"    CONTENT="query, content, hit">
<META NAME="SUBJECT"     CONTENT="sample form">
<META NAME="MS.CATEGORY" CONTENT="Internet">
<META NAME="MS.LOCALE"   CONTENT="EN-US">
```

(continued)

```
<META HTTP-EQUIV="Content-Type" CONTENT="text/html;
    charset=Windows-1252">
</HEAD>

<!--
    ***** To change the form's background pattern, simply save your
    background pattern using the name IS2BKGND.GIF in the same
    directory as this form. *****
-->
<BODY background="is2bkgnd.gif">
<TABLE>
    <TR><TD><A href="http://www.microsoft.com/ntserver/search"
        target="_top">
    <!-- ***** To change the form's logo, simply save your logo
        using the name IS2LOGO.GIF in the same directory as this
        form. -->
    <IMG SRC ="is2logo.gif" VALIGN=MIDDLE ALIGN=LEFT  border=0>
    </A></TD></TR>
    <TR><TD ALIGN="RIGHT"><H3>
    <!-- ***** The following line of text is displayed next to the
        form logo. -->
    Sample HTM/IDQ/HTX Search Form
    </H3></TD></TD></TR>
    </TR>
</TABLE>

<FORM ACTION="query.idq" METHOD="GET">
    <TABLE WIDTH=500>
        <TR>
        <td>Enter your query below:</td>
        </TR>
        <TR>
        <TD><INPUT TYPE="TEXT" NAME="CiRestriction" SIZE="65"
            MAXLENGTH="100" VALUE=""></TD>
        <TD><INPUT TYPE="SUBMIT" VALUE="Go"></TD>
        </TR>
        <TR>
        <TD ALIGN="RIGHT">
        <A HREF="ixtiphlp.htm">Tips for searching</A></TD>
        </TR>
        <TR>
        <TD>
        <P><INPUT NAME="FreeText" TYPE=CHECKBOX>
        Use <a href="ixtiphlp.htm#FreeTextQueries">
            Free-Text Query</a>.
        </TD>
        </TR>
    </TABLE>
```

```
    <!--
        The CiScope parameter allows you to control which documents
        are searched. To search the entire document set, use a value of
        "/", which corresponds to the root of your Web virtual
        namespace. To search a subset of your documents, set the
        value equal to the virtual directory you want to search.
    -->
    <INPUT TYPE="HIDDEN" NAME="CiScope" VALUE="/">
    <INPUT TYPE="HIDDEN" NAME="CiMaxRecordsPerPage" VALUE="10">
    <INPUT TYPE="HIDDEN" NAME="TemplateName" VALUE="query">
    <INPUT TYPE="HIDDEN" NAME="CiSort" VALUE="rank[d]">
    <INPUT TYPE="HIDDEN" NAME="HTMLQueryForm" VALUE="query.htm">
</FORM>

<!-- STANDARD MICROSOFT FOOTER FOR QUERY PAGES -->
<hr width=500 align=left>
<p>
<table border="0" cellpadding="0" cellspacing="0" width="500">
    <tr>
    <!-- IIS GIF -->
    <td>
    <a href="http://www.microsoft.com/iis"><img src="nts_iis.GIF"
        alt="Learn more about Internet Information Server!"
        width="88" height="31" border="0"></a>
    </td>

    <!-- Microsoft Legal Info -->
    <td align=center>
    <font size="1" face="Verdana, Arial, Helvetica">
    ©1997 Microsoft Corporation. All rights reserved.<br></font>
    <a href="http://www.microsoft.com/misc/cpyright.htm">
    <font size="1" face="Verdana, Arial, Helvetica">
    Legal Notices.</font></a>
    </td>

    <!-- Best with IE GIF -->
    <td align=right>
    <a href="http://www.microsoft.com/ie"><img src="IE.GIF"
        alt="Download Internet Explorer!" width="88" height="31"
        border="0"></a>
    </td>
    </tr>
</table>

<!-- END STANDARD MICROSOFT FOOTER FOR QUERY PAGES -->
</BODY>
</HTML>
```

This source code is fairly straightforward HTML. Of primary interest is the FORM tag code block, which calls QUERY.IDQ when the query form is submitted (that is, when the user clicks the Go button). When this event occurs, several form variables are passed along to QUERY.IDQ. The *CiRestriction* variable contains the text typed into the Enter Your Query Below input field, which defines the terms to search for. Notice also the several hidden fields: *CiScope*, *CiMaxRecordsPerPage*, *TemplateName*, *CiSort*, and *HTMLQueryForm*. These fields are query parameters that define the scope of the search, the sort order, and so on.

The QUERY.IDQ file

The Internet data query (.IDQ) file defines query parameters such as the scope of the search, any search restrictions, and query result sets. The source code for the QUERY.IDQ file is shown here:

```
#
# This is the query file for the QUERY.HTM query form.
#

[Names]

#
# To use custom HTML properties in your queries, remove the remark
# character from the following line:
# htmlcolor( DBTYPE_WSTR|DBTYPE_BYREF) =
      d1b5d3f0-c0b3-11cf-9a92-00a0c908dbf1 mycolor

# Then replace "htmlcolor" and "mycolor" with your custom property
# names. Your HTML pages must contain <META> tags, as in the example
# below:
#
#     <META NAME="MYCOLOR" CONTENT="red green blue">
#
# You can then post queries such as "@htmlcolor green" in your query
# forms. To display your custom property in the query
# results, you must configure the Index Server property cache to
# cache your custom property using the Administration tool.
#
# For more information, please refer to the product documentation.
#

[Query]

# The CiCatalog variable must point to where the catalog (index)
# files are stored on your system. You will probably have to change
# this value. If this value is not specified, a default value is
# read from the registry form:
```

```
# HKEY_LOCAL_MACHINE\System\CurrentControlSet\Control\ContentIndex\
#     IsapiDefaultCatalogDirectory

# CiCatalog=d:\      <= COMMENTED OUT - default registry value used

# These are the columns that are referenced in the .HTX files
# when formatting output for each hit.

CiColumns=filename,size,rank,characterization,vpath,DocTitle,write

# Do a recursive search (i.e. all directories under CiScope).
# The opposite is SHALLOW.

CiFlags=DEEP

# The CiRestriction is the query. Here, it's just passed in from the
# form in the .HTM file.

CiRestriction=%if FreeText eq on% $contents "%CiRestriction%" %else%
    %CiRestriction% %endif%

# Don't allow more than 300 total hits in the result set. It can be
# expensive for the server to allow this value to get too large.

CiMaxRecordsInResultSet=300

# Display CiMaxRecordsPerPage hits on each page of output.

CiMaxRecordsPerPage=%CiMaxRecordsPerPage%

# CiScope is the directory (virtual or real) under which results are
# returned. If a file matches the query but is not in a directory
# beneath CiScope, it is not returned in the result set.
# A scope of / means all hits matching the query are returned.

CiScope=%CiScope%

# This is the .HTX file to use for formatting the results of the
# query.

CiTemplate=/iissamples/issamples/%TemplateName%.htx

# This is the list of property names to use in sorting the results.
# Append [a] or [d] to the property name to specify ascending or
# descending sort order. Separate keys in multiple-key sorts with
# commas. For example, to sort on file write date in ascending order
```

(continued)

```
# and then on file size in descending order, use
# CiSort=write[a],filesize[d].

CiSort=%CiSort%

# Setting CiForceUseCi to true means the index is assumed to be
# up to date, so queries that might otherwise force a walk of the
# directory structure (find files older than X) will instead use
# the index and run more quickly. Of course, this means the
# results might miss files that match the query.

CiForceUseCi=true

# The Web browser sends its locale via the HTTP_ACCEPT_LANGUAGE
# parameter. Setting CiLocale allows the Webmaster to override the
# locale sent from the browser. Refer to the Index Server
# documentation for the list of ISO 639:1988 language codes and ISO
# 3166 country codes.
#
#CiLocale=En-US            <== Specified by the Webmaster
#CiLocale=%CiLocale%       <== Sent from the HTML page
#CiLocale=                 <== Value used from the Web browser
```

As you can see from this source code, the .IDQ file provides a powerful way to control the query. Plenty of documentation is included within the file showing you how to customize the IDQ file. The two main sections within the file, the names section and the query section, are indicated by the [Names] and [Query] tags. The names section is optional and does not need to be supplied for standard queries. It defines nonstandard column names that can be referred to in a query. The columns refer to properties stored in the property cache, standard file system properties, or ActiveX properties that have been created in document files. The ActiveX properties in document files can be created by using *IPropertyStorage* or by setting the Microsoft Office summary and custom properties. The query section of the .IDQ file specifies parameters that will be used in the query. This section can refer to form variables and can include conditional expressions to set a variable to alternative values.

The QUERY.HTX file

Index Server uses the .HTX file mainly to format the results of a query. The major portion of our sample file, QUERY.HTX, is shown here:

```
<%begindetail%>
<table border=0>
    <tr class="RecordTitle">
    <td align="right" valign="top" class="RecordTitle"
        style="background-color:white;">
    <%CiCurrentRecordNumber%>.
    </td>
```

```
<td><b class="RecordTitle">
<%if DocTitle isempty%>
<a href="<%EscapeURL vpath%>" class="RecordTitle">
    <%filename%></a>
<%else%>
<a href="<%EscapeURL vpath%>" class="RecordTitle">
    <%DocTitle%></a>
<%endif%>
</b></td>
</tr>

<tr>
<td></td>
<td>
<b><i>Abstract:  </i></b><%characterization%>
</td>
</tr>

<tr>
<td></td>
<td>
<i class="RecordStats"><a href="<%EscapeURL vpath%>"
    class="RecordStats" style="color:blue;">
    http://<%server_name%><%vpath%></a>
<br>
<%if size eq ""%>
    (size and time unknown)
<%else%>
    size <%size%> bytes - <%write%> GMT
<%endif%>
</i>
</td>
</tr>

<tr>
<td></td>
<td>
<a href="oop/qsumrhit.htw?CiWebHitsFile=<%escapeURL vpath%>
    &CiRestriction=<%escapeURL CiRestriction%>
    &CiQueryFile=/iissamples/issamples/query.idq
    &CiBeginHilite=<%escapeURL <b class=Hit>%>
    &CiEndHilite=<%escapeURL </b>%>
    &CiUserParam3=../<%escapeURL HTMLQueryForm%>">
    <IMG src="hilight.gif" align=middle alt="Highlight matching
        terms in document using Summary mode."> Summary
</a>
```

(continued)

```
        <a href="oop/qfullhit.htw?CiWebHitsFile=<%escapeURL vpath%>
            &CiRestriction=<%escapeURL CiRestriction%>
            &CiQueryFile=/iissamples/issamples/query.idq
            &CiBeginHilite=<%escapeURL <b class=Hit>%>
            &CiEndHilite=<%escapeURL </b>%>
            &CiUserParam3=../<%escapeURL HTMLQueryForm%>
            &CiHiliteType=Full">
            <IMG src="hilight.gif" align=middle alt="Highlight matching
                terms in document."> Full
        </a>
        </td>
        </tr>
    </table>
    <br>
    <%enddetail%>
```

The <%begindetail%> and <%enddetail%> tags surround the section of the HTML extension file into which the results of the search will be merged. The section will be interpreted once for each record matching the query on the page, similar to a loop structure over the result set. Figure 7.6 shows the Search Results page after a search on the word "Microsoft."

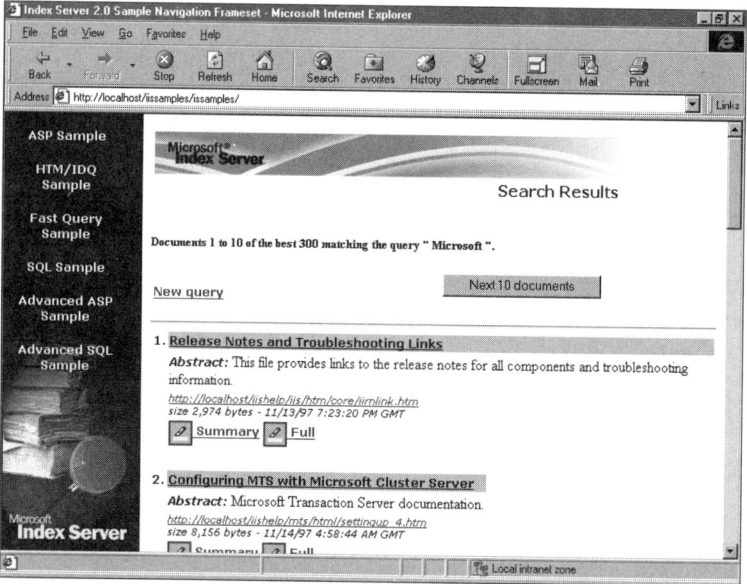

FIGURE 7.6

The Search Results page, showing the results of a search on the word "Microsoft."

The <%begindetail%> and <%enddetail%> section contains the code that displays the document title, document abstract, filename, file size, last modification date, and the hyperlinks to the condensed and full versions of the hit highlighted pages. The hit highlighted pages are discussed in the section "Hit Highlighting" later in this chapter.

You can view the remainder of the code in the QUERY.HTX file available by default on your machine in the C:\inetpub\iissamples\issamples directory. The rest of the code is concerned mainly with navigational items such as the Previous and Next buttons, the total number of pages, and so on.

Active Server Pages

To display the Sample ASP Search Form, shown in Figure 7.4 on page 158, select ASP Sample from the left-hand side of the Index Server Sample Query Form. Active Server Pages (ASP) are interesting because they can be self-posting, which means that you can encapsulate the functionality that takes three files in the HTM/IDQ/HTX method into a single ASP file. The sample ASP file that comes with Index Server, QUERY.ASP, consists of a single input field in which you enter the search string. The entire file is several hundred lines of code, so we'll look at only the main parts of it here.

This section of code within QUERY.ASP creates the Sample ASP Search Form:

```
<%
' Set initial conditions.
    NewQuery = FALSE
    UseSavedQuery = FALSE
    SearchString = ""

    QueryForm = Request.ServerVariables("PATH_INFO")

' Did the user click a Submit button to execute the form?
' If so, get the form variables.
    if Request.ServerVariables("REQUEST_METHOD") = "POST" then
        SearchString = Request.Form("SearchString")
        FreeText = Request.Form("FreeText")
        ' NOTE: This will be true only if the button is actually
        ' clicked.
        if Request.Form("Action") = "Go" then
            NewQuery = TRUE
            RankBase=1000
        end if
    end if
```

(continued)

```
    if Request.ServerVariables("REQUEST_METHOD") = "GET" then
        SearchString = Request.QueryString("qu")
        FreeText = Request.QueryString("FreeText")
        FormScope = Request.QueryString("sc")
        RankBase = Request.QueryString("RankBase")
        if Request.QueryString("pg") <> "" then
            NextPageNumber = Request.QueryString("pg")
            NewQuery = FALSE
            UseSavedQuery = TRUE
        else
            NewQuery = SearchString <> ""
        end if
    end if
%>
</HEAD>
<BODY <%=FormBG%>>
<TABLE>
    <TR><TD><A HREF="http://www.microsoft.com/ntserver/search"
        target="_top"><IMG SRC ="<%=FormLogo%>" VALIGN=MIDDLE
        ALIGN=LEFT border=0></a></TD></TR>
    <TR><TD ALIGN="RIGHT"><H3>Sample ASP Search Form</H3></TD></TR>
</TABLE>
<p>
<FORM ACTION="<%=QueryForm%>" METHOD=POST>
    <TABLE WIDTH=500>
    <TR><TD>Enter your query below:</TD></TR>
    <TR><TD><INPUT TYPE="TEXT" NAME="SearchString" SIZE="65"
        MAXLENGTH="100" VALUE="<%=SearchString%>"></TD>
    <TD><INPUT TYPE="SUBMIT" NAME="Action" VALUE="Go"></TD></TR>
    <TR><TD ALIGN="RIGHT">
        <A HREF="ixtiphlp.htm">Tips for searching</A>
    </TD></TR>
    <TR></TR>
    <TR><TD><INPUT NAME="FreeText" TYPE=CHECKBOX
    <% if FreeText = "on" then Response.Write(" CHECKED")end if %>
    >Use <a href="ixtiphlp.htm#FreeTextQueries">Free-Text Query</a>.
    </TD></TR>
    </TABLE>
</FORM>
<BR>
```

The HTML FORM tag is used to capture input from the end-user. The form stores the input search string in a VBScript variable named *SearchString*. Because the form is self-posting, you can see in the code how this *SearchString* variable is captured using either *Request.Form("SearchString")* or *Request.QueryString("qu")*. The actual name of this ASP file is captured using *Request.ServerVariables("PATH_INFO")*.

Next the QUERY.ASP file uses the *SearchString* value it has captured to control and execute the ASP search. The relevant source code is shown here:

```
<%
if NewQuery then
    set Session("Query") = nothing
    set Session("Recordset") = nothing
    NextRecordNumber = 1

' Remove any leading and ending quotes from SearchString.

    SrchStrLen = len(SearchString)

    if left(SearchString, 1) = chr(34) then
        SrchStrLen = SrchStrLen-1
        SearchString = right(SearchString, SrchStrLen)
    end if

    if right(SearchString, 1) = chr(34) then
        SrchStrLen = SrchStrLen-1
        SearchString = left(SearchString, SrchStrLen)
    end if

    if FreeText = "on" then
        CompSearch = "$contents " & chr(34) & SearchString & chr(34)
    else
        CompSearch = SearchString
    end if

    set Q = Server.CreateObject("ixsso.Query")
    set util = Server.CreateObject("ixsso.Util")

    Q.Query = CompSearch
    Q.SortBy = "rank[d]"
    Q.Columns = "DocTitle, vpath, filename, size, write, " & _
        "characterization, rank"
    Q.MaxRecords = 300

    if FormScope <> "/" then
        util.AddScopeToQuery Q, FormScope, "deep"
    end if

    if SiteLocale<>"" then
        Q.LocaleID = util.ISOToLocaleID(SiteLocale)
    end if
```

(continued)

```
        set RS = Q.CreateRecordSet("nonsequential")

        RS.PageSize = PageSize
        ActiveQuery = TRUE

    elseif UseSavedQuery then
        if IsObject( Session("Query") ) And _
            IsObject( Session("RecordSet") ) then
            set Q = Session("Query")
            set RS = Session("RecordSet")

            if RS.RecordCount <> -1 and NextPageNumber <> -1 then
                RS.AbsolutePage = NextPageNumber
                NextRecordNumber = RS.AbsolutePosition
            end if

            ActiveQuery = TRUE
        else
            Response.Write "ERROR - No saved query"
        end if
    end if
    %>
```

This code makes use of two objects: the *Query* object and the *Utility* object. *Query* and *Utility* are server-side objects that are specific to Index Server. They present various properties and methods so that you can set query parameters and execute the query, producing a recordset for iterating over the results. The *Query* and *Utility* objects are instantiated by using the *Server.CreateObject* syntax. Next the *Query* object properties, such as *Query, SortBy,* and *Columns,* are defined. Another important area is where the *CreateRecordSet* method of the *Query* object is invoked to execute the query and create an ActiveX Data Objects (ADO) recordset for navigating through the query results. ADO is a technology for easily adding data access to applications and Web pages. Notice also that the query and recordset can be cached in session variables for reuse on another page. This capability will prove useful when you display the next page of results for queries that return multiple pages of information.

The last section of the QUERY.ASP file formats the resulting output and displays all the documents that matched the search string. Figure 7.7 shows the results of a search for the word "Microsoft."

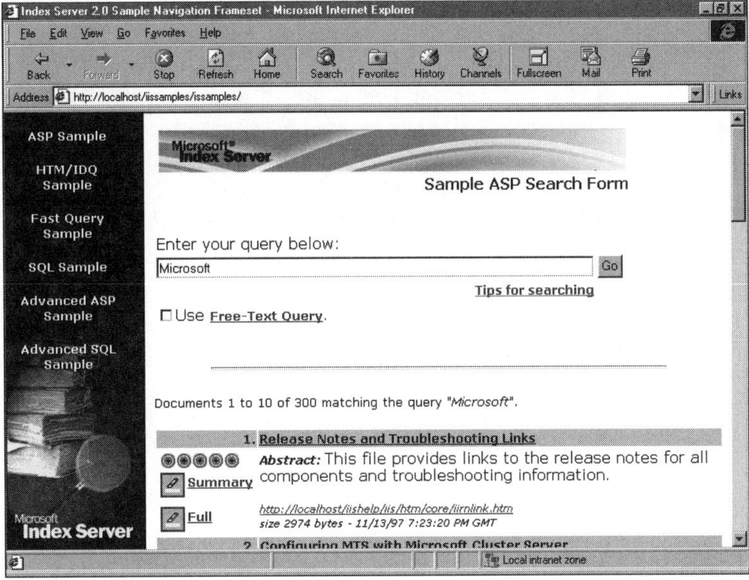

FIGURE 7.7

The Sample ASP Search Form, showing the results of a search for the word "Microsoft."

The following QUERY.ASP code extract is responsible for formatting the output as shown in Figure 7.7.

```
<%
if ActiveQuery then
    if not RS.EOF then
%>
<p>
<HR WIDTH=80% ALIGN=center SIZE=3>
<p>
<%
    LastRecordOnPage = NextRecordNumber + RS.PageSize - 1
    CurrentPage = RS.AbsolutePage
    if RS.RecordCount <> -1 AND _
        RS.RecordCount < LastRecordOnPage then
        LastRecordOnPage = RS.RecordCount
    end if

    Response.Write "Documents " & NextRecordNumber & " to " & _
        LastRecordOnPage
```

(continued)

```
    if RS.RecordCount <> -1 then
        Response.Write " of " & RS.RecordCount
    end if
    Response.Write " matching the query " & chr(34) & "<I>"
    Response.Write SearchString & "</I>" & chr(34) & ".<P>"
%>

<% if Not RS.EOF and NextRecordNumber <= LastRecordOnPage then%>
    <table border=0>
    <colgroup width=105>
<% end if %>

<% Do While Not RS.EOF and NextRecordNumber <= LastRecordOnPage

    ' This is the detail portion for Title, Abstract, URL, Size, and
    ' Modification Date.

    ' If there is a title, display it; otherwise, display the
    ' filename.
%>
    <p>

<% ' Graphically indicate rank of document.
    if NextRecordNumber = 1 then
        RankBase=RS("rank")
    end if

    if RankBase>1000 then
        RankBase=1000
    elseif RankBase<1 then
        RankBase=1
    end if

    NormRank = RS("rank")/RankBase

    if NormRank > 0.80 then
        stars = "rankbtn5.gif"
    elseif NormRank > 0.60 then
        stars = "rankbtn4.gif"
    elseif NormRank > 0.40 then
        stars = "rankbtn3.gif"
    elseif NormRank >.20 then
        stars = "rankbtn2.gif"
    else stars = "rankbtn1.gif"
    end if
%>
```

```
    <tr class="RecordTitle">
    <td align="right" valign=top class="RecordTitle">
    <%= NextRecordNumber%>.
    </td>
    <td><b class="RecordTitle">
    <%if VarType(RS("DocTitle")) = 1 or RS("DocTitle") = "" then%>
        <a href="<%=RS("vpath")%>" class="RecordTitle">
        <%= Server.HTMLEncode( RS("filename") )%></a>
    <%else%>
        <a href="<%=RS("vpath")%>" class="RecordTitle">
        <%= Server.HTMLEncode(RS("DocTitle"))%></a>
    <%end if%>
    </b></td>
    </tr>

    <tr>
    <td valign=top align=left>
    <IMG SRC="<%=stars%>">
    <br>
<%
    ' Construct the URL for hit highlighting.
    WebHitsQuery = "CiWebHitsFile=" & Server.URLEncode( RS("vpath") )
    WebHitsQuery = WebHitsQuery & "&CiRestriction=" & _
        Server.URLEncode( Q.Query )
    WebHitsQuery = WebHitsQuery & "&CiBeginHilite=" & _
        Server.URLEncode( "<strong class=Hit>" )
    WebHitsQuery = WebHitsQuery & "&CiEndHilite=" & _
        Server.URLEncode( "</strong>" )
    WebHitsQuery = WebHitsQuery & "&CiUserParam3=" & QueryForm
    ' WebHitsQuery = WebHitsQuery & "&CiLocale=" & Q.LocaleID
 %>
    <a href="oop/qsumrhit.htw?<%= WebHitsQuery %>">
    <IMG src="hilight.gif" align=left alt=
        "Highlight matching terms in document using Summary mode.">
    Summary</a>
    <br>
    <a href="oop/qfullhit.htw?<%= WebHitsQuery %>&CiHiliteType=Full">
    <IMG src="hilight.gif" align=left alt=
        "Highlight matching terms in document."> Full</a>
    </td>
    <td valign=top>
    <%if VarType(RS("characterization")) = 8 and _
        RS("characterization") <> "" then%>
        <b><i>Abstract:  </I></b>
        <%= Server.HTMLEncode(RS("characterization"))%>
    <%end if%>
```

(continued)

```
        <p>
        <i class="RecordStats"><a href="<%=RS("vpath")%>"
        class="RecordStats" style="color:blue;">
        http://<%=Request("server_name")%><%=RS("vpath")%></a>
        <br><%if RS("size") = "" then%>(size and time unknown)<%else%>
            size <%=RS("size")%> bytes - <%=RS("write")%> GMT
        <%end if%></i>
        </td>
        </tr>
        <tr>
        </tr>
<%
        RS.MoveNext
        NextRecordNumber = NextRecordNumber+1
Loop
%>
</table>
```

In this code extract, a While loop is used to navigate through the recordset and display the details portion of the page. The details include the title, abstract, URL, size, and modification date for the documents that matched the query.

Five images are used to graphically display the ranking of the document. These images are named RANKBTN#.GIF, where # is a value between 1 and 5.

A quick way to customize the ASP code to meet your needs is to start with the QUERY.ASP file and alter the text and graphics on the page. You can also make changes to the nature of the search that is performed. For example, you can easily modify the form's logo, background color, background pattern, search scope, number of returned query results per page, locale, and so on.

Hit Highlighting

Another interesting feature shown in the preceding QUERY.ASP code extract is *hit highlighting*. Hit highlighting provides a way to indicate precisely where any hits (words used in the search query) occurred within a document. The hit highlighting feature generates an HTML page containing a list of *hits*, with those words making up the hit highlighted (by default, shown in red and in italics).

Two types of hit highlighting can be displayed: *condensed* and *full*. With condensed hit highlighting, each hit is displayed together with some of the text that surrounds it in the document. With full hit highlighting, the entire text of that document is displayed. Figure 7.8 shows the Sample Condensed Hit Highlighting Form, and Figure 7.9 shows the Sample Full Hit Highlighting Form.

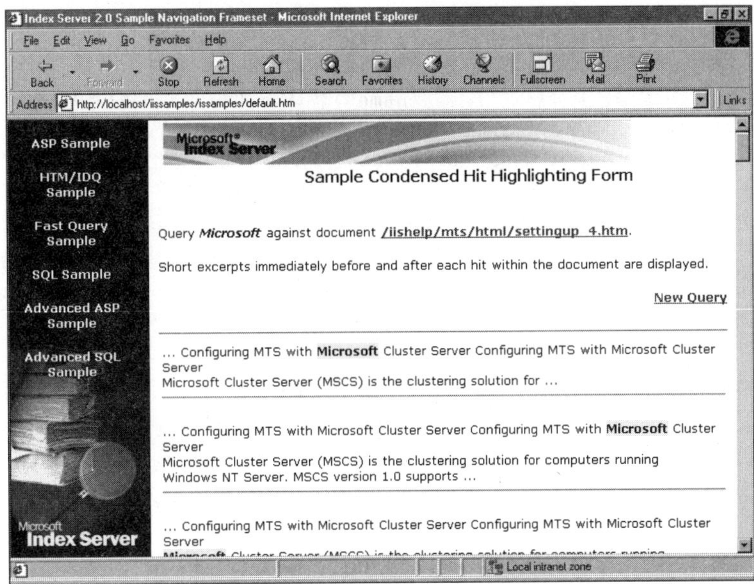

FIGURE 7.8

Sample Condensed Hit Highlighting Form.

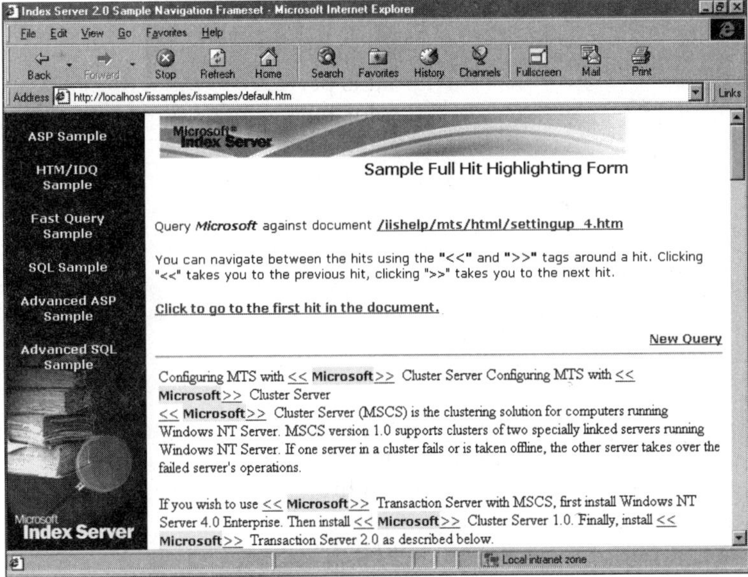

FIGURE 7.9

Sample Full Hit Highlighting Form.

With the release of Index Server 2.0, the Common Gateway Interface (CGI) application WEBHITS.EXE has become the Internet Server API (ISAPI) application WEBHITS.DLL. You invoke the hit highlighting (WEBHITS.DLL) application by making an HTTP request to a URL that references an .HTW template file and passing various *Webhits* parameters. If necessary, this loads the WEBHITS.DLL, which uses the parameters and the .HTW file to create a page that has the hits highlighted. (Recall the reference to the files QSUMRHIT.HTW and QFULLHIT.HTX in the preceding QUERY.ASP code extract.) These .HTW template files are stored by default in the /iissamples/issamples/oop folder and are the template pages for the hit highlighting.

Structured Query Language

The third technique for performing searches on your indexed file system is to use Structured Query Language (SQL). In your .ASP files, you can use SQL extensions to form the query, ADO to retrieve the data, and a scripting language such as VBScript to display the data.

To access the Sample SQL-Based Search Form shown in Figure 7.10, select SQL Sample from the left-hand side of the Index Server Sample Query Form. This page lets you build a SQL query to search the documents indexed by Index Server. The files associated with this sample are SQLQHIT.HTM and SQLQHIT.ASP and are located on your server in the C:\inetpub\iissamples\issamples directory.

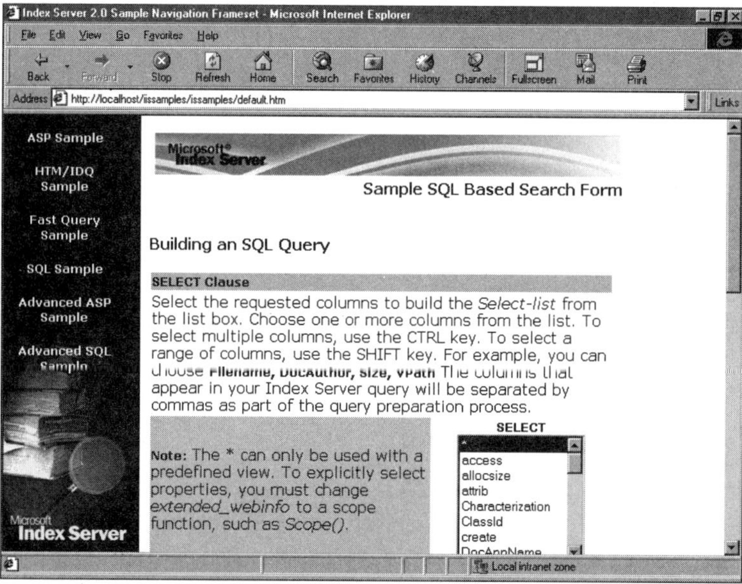

FIGURE 7.10

The Sample SQL-Based Search Form.

When you are working with SQL syntax, the fact that Index Server can function as an OLE Database (OLE DB) provider leads to some interesting possibilities. You can take the results of an Index Server query and use them in a subsequent query against a different OLE DB provider, such as the Open Database Connectivity (ODBC) provider. For example, you can search for all the travel reports in a given directory and then submit a query against SQL Server to find the current travel budget for each trip report author.

The following code sample shows the VBScript code needed to generate an ADO *Recordset* object from Index Server:

```
Set rstMain = Server.CreateObject("ADODB.Recordset")
RstMain.Open "SELECT DocAuthor, DocTitle, FileName
    FROM SCOPE() WHERE size>50000", "PROVIDER=MSIDXS;"
```

As an alternative, if you want to perform several queries or if you want to have more control over the underlying connection properties, you can create a *Connection* object, as shown here:

```
Set Conn = Server.CreateObject ("ADODB.Connection")
Conn.ConnectionString = "provider=msidxs;"
Conn.Open
```

If you choose to create a *Connection* object, you can create a *Command* object, associate it with the active connection, set the *CommandText* property of your *Command* object to your SQL content query string, and create the associated *Recordset* object to retrieve the results of your query.

Once you have obtained the resulting data in the *Recordset* object, you can display the results much like we did earlier in the ASP example. You simply use a While loop to navigate through the data until you reach the end-of-file marker for the *Recordset* object.

Administering Index Server

In the preceding section, we looked at Index Server from the point of view of the developer and the end-user—that is, we learned how to develop and use query forms, control the search, and display the results. In this section, we'll take a look at the product from another point of view—that of the administrator.

As an administrator, you'll want to be sure that Index Server is always operating at the optimal level for your end-users. You'll also want to be able to perform basic administrative functions such as controlling indexing, scanning, and logging; configuring security; controlling catalogs; and perhaps even indexing remote computers. In this section, we'll take a quick look at each of these tasks.

Index Server is designed to minimize administrative requirements. By default, every virtual directory is indexed, but indexing can be controlled on an individual virtual directory basis. Performance statistics can be retrieved by using either the Performance Monitor or the HTML administration pages.

You can administer Index Server in two ways: via the Management Console or via the HTML administration pages. Both of these administrative interfaces are accessible from the Microsoft Index Server program group. You can also add the Index Server snap-in to the default IIS console by choosing the Add/Remove Snap-in option from the Console menu in the Management Console. Select the Add button from the dialog box to get a list of items that you can add to your Management Console. Index Server is one of the items in this list. If you select it and click OK, you will have the Index Server folder added to your standard Management Console display.

The Management Console administrative interface

Figure 7.11 shows the administrative interface available via the Management Console. From this interface, you can see various catalog properties, including the location of the catalog, its total size, the number of documents, and the number of persistent indexes. Figure 7.11 shows a catalog named Web that contains 4940 documents.

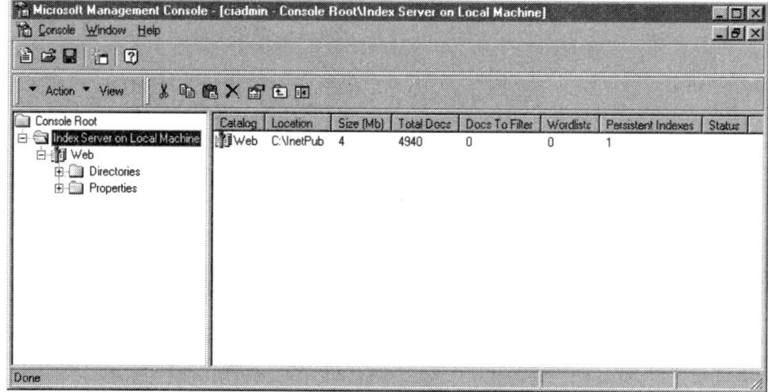

FIGURE 7.11

Index Server Manager showing the Web catalog.

You can perform many administrative operations from the Management Console, including the following:

- Start and stop Index Server
- Edit Index Server properties

- Edit catalog properties
- Add or delete catalogs
- Add or delete directories
- Force a merge on a catalog
- Force a rescan on a directory

To add a new directory to the catalog, select the Directories folder, choose the New command from the Action menu, and choose Directory. You can then enter the physical path to the directory you want to add to the catalog. When you add a directory, Index Server will include all documents in the directory in its indexing process. You should also verify that you have created a virtual directory for this physical path using the Management Console and that the Index This Directory check box is checked in the directory's Properties window.

You typically perform a rescan of the directory after you have made global changes such as adding or removing a filter DLL or adding a new word breaker. To initiate a rescan, you simply select the virtual directory to scan and then choose Rescan from the Action menu. To force a merge, select the catalog from the Management Console and then choose Merge from the Action menu. To start and stop Index Server, select the top-level Index Server folder within the Management Console and then choose Start or Stop from the Action menu as appropriate.

The HTML administrative interface

Figure 7.12 shows the HTML administration pages for Index Server, which is displayed by choosing the Index Server Manager (HTML) option in the Microsoft Index Server program group.

The Index Statistics page is divided into two sections: Cache Statistics and Index Statistics. These statistics let you quickly determine the current state of Index Server and whether any queries are currently being processed. A status message at the bottom of the page informs you of the current state. In this example, you see the typical message "All filtering is complete. Index is up to date." During a merge, you might see a message such as "Master merge in progress. *n*% complete." If you click the Refresh button, you'll see the percent complete value change as the merge progresses. You can initiate a merge by clicking the Merge Index button on the left-hand side of the page. You might want to perform a merge if the index statistics indicate more than one persistent index or multiple word lists.

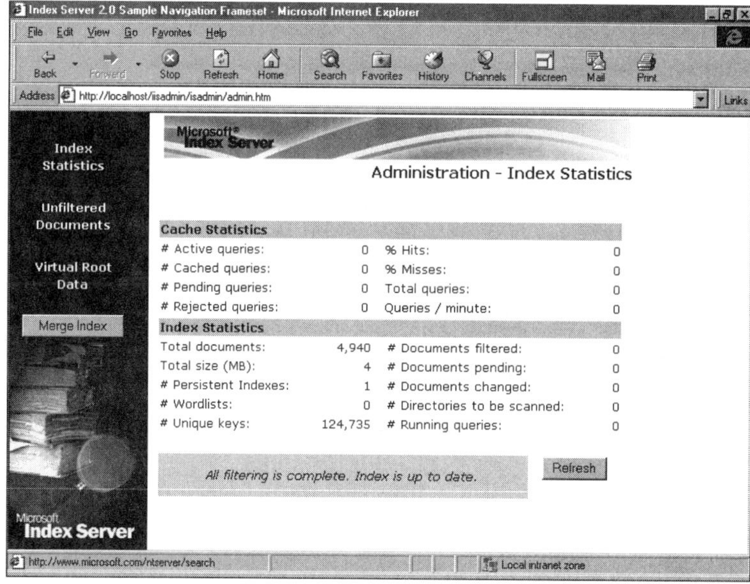

FIGURE 7.12

Index Server Manager (HTML) showing the Index Statistics page.

In addition to the total number of documents in the corpus and the total size of the indexes, the Index Statistics section tells you the total number of several other elements. The # of Unique Keys item tells you the number of unique words that are represented in the indexes. The # of Running Queries in the Cache Statistics section tells you how many concurrent queries are being processed by the server; if you are actively querying the server, this number could change.

The Virtual Root Data page, shown in Figure 7.13, displays a list of all the virtual roots present in your catalog. It can be displayed by clicking the Virtual Root Data hyperlink on the left-hand side of the screen.

If you select the Unfiltered Documents hyperlink from the left-hand side of the HTML administration page, you can view files that are corrupted or files that could not be filtered because of problems in the filter DLL.

NOTE

In addition to using the two administrative interfaces outlined here, you can create and execute your own administrative request pages by writing IDA files. These files are similar to queries, except the parameters are stored in an .IDA file instead of an .IDQ file, and they cause administrative tasks to be performed.

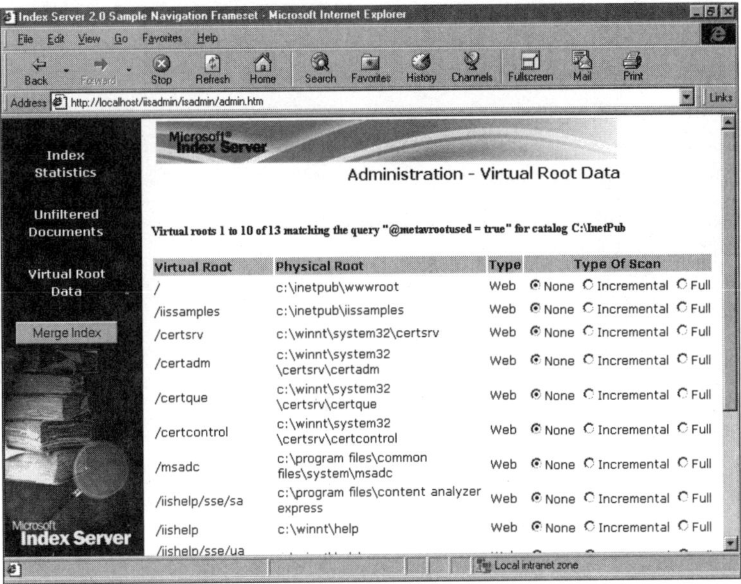

FIGURE 7.13

Index Server Manager (HTML) showing the Virtual Root Data page.

Query logging

One final note about basic administration. Queries are logged using the standard IIS logging mechanism described in detail in Chapter 6, "Logging and Monitoring Tools." Query logs have filenames in the form IN*YYMMDD*.LOG—for example, IN980205.LOG, and by default, are written to the *%SystemRoot%*\system32\LogFiles\W3SVC1 folder. The logging does not record the actual search string, but it does record the Web page that was requested and the Internet Protocol address of the requesting client.

Security

When securing your Index Server contents, you'll want to secure both the actual documents within the corpus and the catalog directory.

When documents are filtered by Index Server, any access controls on the documents are kept in the catalog and checked against client permissions when a query is processed. The resulting output from the query shows only those documents to which the user has access. There will be no indication that any of the other documents exist. From a security standpoint, this mechanism is much more efficient than actually showing the hyperlinks to the protected documents (and then denying access when the user clicks on the hyperlinks), which would compromise the name and location of the protected documents.

When Index Server is first installed, the catalog is set up with an Access Control List (ACL) that allows only system administrators and system services to access it. This ACL prevents unauthorized users from seeing the contents of the catalog either directly or indirectly as the result of a query. The catalog is in binary format, but it is still possible to read the catalog's contents and determine some of the information from the indexed documents, so securing access to the catalog is important.

All administrative operations on Index Server are controlled by the ACL on the following registry key:

```
HKEY_LOCAL_MACHINE
 \System
  \CurrentControlSet
   \Control
    \ContentIndex
```

You can set the permissions on this registry key by opening the registry editor (*regedt32*), selecting the *ContentIndex* key, and then choosing Permissions from the Security menu.

Catalogs

So far we have looked only at scenarios in which there is a single catalog on a server. Index Server allows you to have multiple catalogs on the same machine. By having two or more smaller catalogs, queries do not have to span as much data and tasks are performed faster. Unfortunately, queries cannot span catalogs. If you break your contents into separate catalogs, queries in one catalog will not search the contents in another catalog.

The Management Console provides a way for you to work with catalogs. To add a new catalog, select the top-level Index Server folder within the Management Console, choose New from the Action menu, and then choose Catalog. You can then enter the catalog name and location in the Add Catalog dialog box.

Before you can add a new catalog, you must stop Index Server, and after you create a new catalog, you must restart Index Server to bring the new catalog online. But before you bring the catalog online, you might want to add directories and modify catalog properties. To access the catalog properties, select the catalog in the Management Console, and choose Properties from the Action menu to display the Catalog Properties window. On the Location page, you can view the name, location, and size of the catalog. On the Web page, you can choose whether to track virtual roots or to track messages from the NNTP service. On the Generation page, you can specify whether you want to filter files with unknown extensions and you can control whether summaries are generated for files found in a search and returned on the Results page.

As you can see in the Management Console, each catalog has a directories folder and a properties folder. As we saw earlier, the directories folder is where you can view and modify the directories that are included in the catalog. The properties folder lists all the properties that are indexed within the catalog as well as those properties that are cached. By caching certain properties, you can reduce the time it takes to retrieve values that are frequently queried.

Indexing Remote Computers

Index Server can index across machine, domain, and operating system boundaries. For example, you can set up Index Server to index multiple Web servers, which is especially useful in a corporate intranet environment. This is done by simply sharing a folder on the remote volume and creating a virtual directory on the indexing server. You can also set up Index Server to index documents in other Windows NT domains—if the other domains trust the domain in which Index Server resides.

NOTE

All of these examples can be a bit complicated to configure initially. For more information, consult the Index Server documentation in the Windows NT 4.0 Option Pack under the Administration topic.

As we've seen, Index Server is a complex product. Microsoft has done an excellent job of hiding this complexity from us so that we can easily customize and administer it. To customize Index Server, you can use one of the existing Index Server sample query forms as a template. To administer Index Server, use the Index Server Manager within the Management Console or the Web-based version of Index Server Manager. All in all, Index Server adds some invaluable features to your IIS configuration. Next we are going to look at some other services that provide important, additional benefits to our base IIS installation.

CHAPTER 8

Server Add-Ons

Internet Information Server is more than just an application that allows you to deliver HTML pages to remote clients and create FTP sites. It's a full range of tools that enable the Webmaster to analyze the contents of a server, monitor and detect how many hits a server receives, and even create fancy usage reports. IIS also includes components that enable Web servers to accept uploaded files from a client via HTTP. Without the use of this prebuilt component, you would need to write a heavy-duty ASP script or ISAPI extension DLL for the server to accept such files. (Of course, if your users need to upload files to the server, they can use FTP. This technique involves another application, FTP Client, and is not as convenient as simply dragging the file to the HTML page shown in the browser.) Two major IIS components provide the extra functionality described above: Site Server Express, which is a scaled-down version of Microsoft Site Server, and FrontPage 98 Server Administrator. A third component, Microsoft Posting Acceptor, is actually a subcomponent of Site Server Express. This chapter will describe the two major components in detail.

Site Server Express

Site Server Express incorporates report and analysis tools as well as the Microsoft Posting Acceptor component. These tools help manage content and analyze usage. This section takes a look at them one-by-one.

First, when installing Site Server Express, choose the Custom installation option. Then choose Site Server Express from the list of items that appears in the Microsoft Windows NT 4.0 Option Pack Setup window. Then click Show Subcomponents to display the Site Server Express window shown in Figure 8.1. Notice that the first two subcomponents support analysis functions and the second two relate to publishing and file upload features.

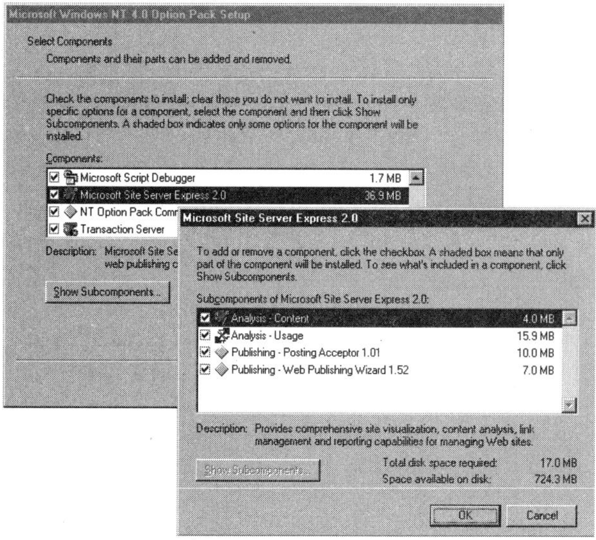

FIGURE 8.1

The Site Server Express window, showing a list of subcomponents.

The Content Analyzer

The Content Analyzer tool allows a Web site developer to represent a site visually. This tool is available to you only if you select the Analysis - Content subcomponent (see Figure 8.1) when installing Site Server Express. The cornerstone of Content Analyzer is the *WebMap*, which visually represents the entire Web site. In the WebMap, all hyperlinks to other pages are clearly shown to ease site management and repair (of a broken link, for example).

When you start the Content Analyzer, you must first connect to a valid URL. You do this by choosing New from the File menu and Map From URL in the submenu in the Content Analyzer window. This example uses the virtual directory that contains the HTML-based help for the Windows NT Option Pack. The URL for this site is *http://localhost/iishelp*. After the connection is established, the Content Analyzer starts exploring the Web site. It examines each file, image, and any other resource included in the site to create the WebMap. Depending on the number of files on the site, this process can take a long time. (On our machine, it took more than five minutes to explore the IIS Help files.) If you find yourself waiting too long to explore an unexpectedly intricate site, you can stop the Content Analyzer at any time by clicking Cancel in the Creating Map dialog box.

After the Content Analyzer has completed the exploration stage, it saves all the site's data in a special file. By default, this file is named *domain*.WMP and is located on your hard disk at \Program Files\Content Analyzer Express\Reports.

The Content Analyzer also generates HTML statistics of the selected site (shown in Figure 8.2), which are stored in the *domain*_SUMMARY.HTML file in the same directory as the WMP file. Notice that the HTML report contains a link to the WMP file, named WebMap For Localhost. (For this example, because we have connected to our local machine, our domain is named *localhost*. If we connect to a machine named *www.microsoft.com*, however, our machine will create a file named MICROSOFT_SUMMARY.HTML.)

The full version of Microsoft Site Server Express creates several reports in addition to the summary report. These additional reports are not available with the Express version. The Site Server Express summary report does, however, provide a link at the top of the browser window (not shown in Figure 8.2) that explains how you can upgrade to the complete version of Site Server.

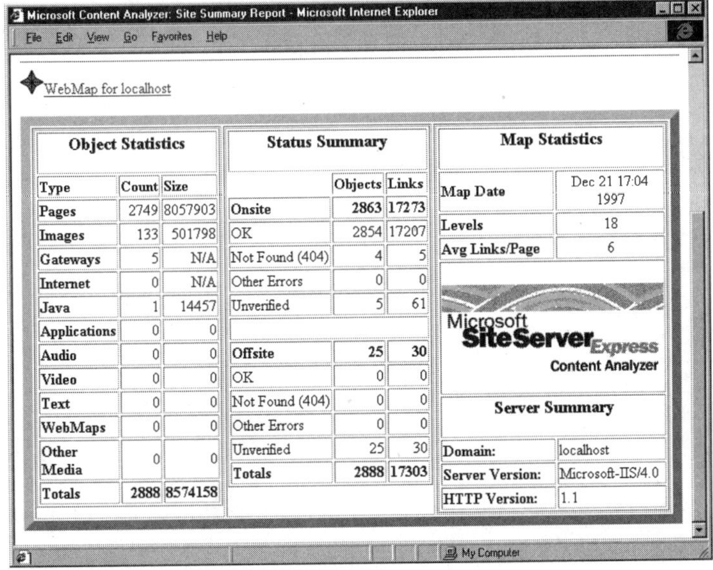

Microsoft Content Analyzer: Site Summary Report - Microsoft Internet Explorer

File Edit View Go Favorites Help

WebMap for localhost

Object Statistics

Type	Count	Size
Pages	2749	8057903
Images	133	501798
Gateways	5	N/A
Internet	0	N/A
Java	1	14457
Applications	0	0
Audio	0	0
Video	0	0
Text	0	0
WebMaps	0	0
Other Media	0	0
Totals	2888	8574158

Status Summary

	Objects	Links
Onsite	2863	17273
OK	2854	17207
Not Found (404)	4	5
Other Errors	0	0
Unverified	5	61
Offsite	25	30
OK	0	0
Not Found (404)	0	0
Other Errors	0	0
Unverified	25	30
Totals	2888	17303

Map Statistics

Map Date	Dec 21 17:04 1997
Levels	18
Avg Links/Page	6

Microsoft SiteServer Express Content Analyzer

Server Summary

Domain:	localhost
Server Version:	Microsoft-IIS/4.0
HTTP Version:	1.1

My Computer

FIGURE 8.2

The summary report created by the Content Analyzer after scanning the Web site.

The Content Analyzer provides two distinct views of the site: a tree view on the left and a cyberbolic view on the right, as shown in Figure 8.3. The tree view is hierarchical. The home page is shown as the root and the individual pages and other resources are represented as the leaves. The cyberbolic view accentuates the web-like structure of the site. All links between objects (such as Web pages) are shown graphically in different colors. By default, black represents the main route—a main hyperlink from one page to another. Because there can be more than one way to move from one page to another, pages accessible by alternative routes are shown in green. Blue indicates an object residing on a different server—that is, an external link. Red indicates a resource that is unavailable—that is, a broken link.

NOTE

To view the alternative routes, you must select the Show Alternate Routes option in the Display Options dialog box, accessed from the View menu.

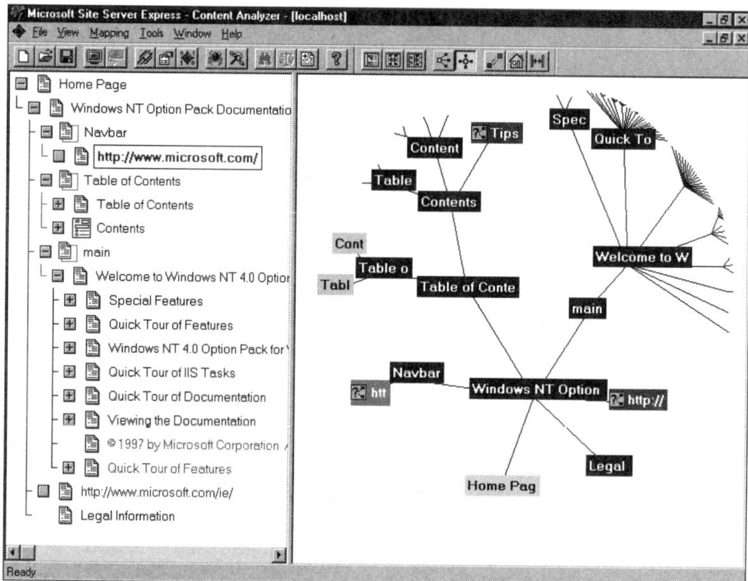

FIGURE 8.3

The Content Analyzer, displaying the tree view on the left and the cyberbolic view on the right for the* http://localhost/iishelp *site.

You can "surf" using either the tree view or the cyberbolic view to explore the set of interconnected documents in as much depth as you want. With the full-featured version of the Content Analyzer, you can export a tree view of the site to an HTML file by choosing Export from the File menu in the Content Analyzer window. (This option is disabled in the Express version.) Doing so creates an interactive HTML-based table of contents to a site in a snap. The Express version of Site Server does not offer this feature.

A little earlier in this section, you saw how the Content Analyzer can save a summary report to an HTML document. Site Server Express can only generate and save the summary HTML report, but the full version can generate many different reports. With the full version of Site Server, it's possible for you to create reports that show all incoming and outgoing links, different media types (Java scripts, .AVI files, and so on), broken links, and many other types of information. However, within Site Server Express, by choosing the Quick Search option from the Tools menu in the Content Analyzer window, you can choose from a variety of different searches that can be performed on your site. Figure 8.4 shows the results of a search for all documents in which load size is over 32 KB in our example IIS HTML–based documentation. You can perform the search and print the results with Site Server Express, but if you want to export the results to HTML, you must use the full version of Site Server. If you aren't satisfied with the predefined reports, the full version of the Content Analyzer allows you to create a custom search and then export it to an HTML file.

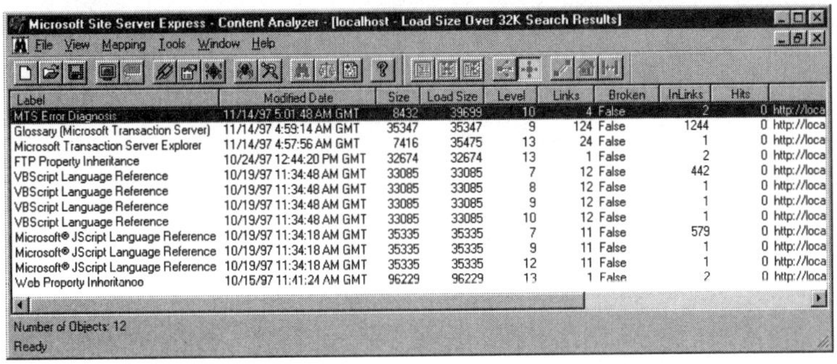

FIGURE 8.4

Search results, showing statistics for all documents larger than 32 KB. The results are shown in a separate child window, which we have maximized.

By choosing Display Options from the View menu, you can display as much or as little detail as you want. (For example, you can filter the site by the various object types—HTML files, images, and so on.) Publishing the results creates a single file that contains only selected information in the compressed form for easy mailing or copying to diskette. However, this feature is not available in Site Server Express. In Express, the Publish item on the File menu is permanently disabled.

You should now have a feel for what the Content Analyzer tool in Site Server Express can do. If you want the functionality provided by many of the grayed-out menu options, you should acquire and install the full version of Site Server.

Usage Import and Report Writer

The Usage Import and Report Writer tools are aimed at a common objective: to generate a wealth of statistical information about IIS, especially about the Web Publishing Service (WWW service) and the FTP server. These tools are available to you only if you select the Analysis - Usage subcomponent (Figure 8.1) when installing Microsoft Site Server Express.

Following is a bird's-eye view of these tools. Their purpose is actually quite simple. Every time the WWW service or FTP server processes a request, it creates a new entry in the log files. (Log files are discussed in detail in Chapter 6.) The Usage Import application takes logs generated by IIS and converts them to a relational database—a Microsoft Access file. This .MDB file provides an efficient place to store and manipulate the logged data. Report Writer is a fancy front end for this database. Report Writer takes parameters either directly from the user or from predefined templates and uses them to query the database created with the Usage Import tool. The Site Server Express version of Report Writer does not allow you to create reports from scratch, although it does provide about two dozen report templates from which you can choose. (Note that there is nothing stopping a programmer from using various tools, such as Microsoft Visual Basic or Access, to create reports from the .MDB file directly.) Figure 8.5 illustrates the relationship among the IIS log files, the Usage Import tool, and Report Writer.

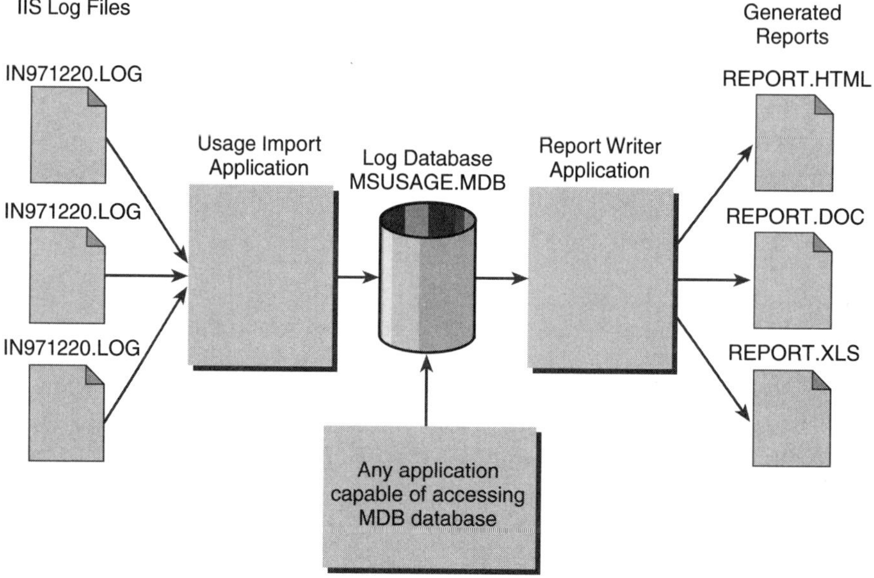

FIGURE 8.5

The relationships among the IIS logs, the Usage Import tool, and Report Writer.

The installation program creates a default MSUSAGE.MDB database that initially does not contain information from your IIS logs. Once you run Usage Import, the database will be populated with real data. The original version (with no data in it) of MSUSAGE.MDB is always available in its compressed form, known as TEMPLATE.ZIP in the \Program Files\UA Express directory.

The Usage Import Application

As you just learned, data from the log files needs to be inserted into the database. The Usage Import application can help you accomplish this task. However, Usage Import does not just blindly transfer the log records to the database. It employs statistical data analysis to present data, such as session duration and the number of user visits. Usage Import is flexible enough to understand different log formats, and it can even read logs generated by different servers.

Along with bare-bones necessities, Usage Import offers some helpful features. As part of the data import process, the log conversion tool can resolve IP addresses to names, get HTML titles for each page in the server hierarchy, and even get an organization name for each domain. This information lets Webmasters keep track of organizations and domains that access their servers. Many other import options are also available. For example, you can configure Usage Import to ignore all requests from "spider" or "crawler" types of browser applications. *Spiders* are software programs that, once configured, work unattended as they retrieve Web content and save it to a user's machine. The user can then access the retrieved content at a later time.

Now you can launch Usage Import to generate some reports. When Usage Import is run the first time, no configured sites from which to create logs exist. To add a new server and its logs, choose Server Manager from the File menu. You must choose the log format and identify the site that will be the subject of your reports. Our example continues using the site *http://localhost/iishelp*. In the Server Manager, you must specify a domain for your Web server. Because we don't have a domain for *localhost*, we entered *localhost* as the domain.

The next step is to enter a full path for the log files in the Usage Import window. In this example, we clicked Browse in the Log File Manager window that appears inside the Usage Import window and highlighted all the log files for our Web Publishing Service. Now you are ready to import all the logs into a database. Before you click the big green arrow (Go) on the Usage Import window's toolbar, verify that the log format in the Usage Import window matches the format of the actual log files. (Note that the Go arrow is grayed out in Figure 8.6 because the Server Manager child window is currently active.) You can determine or set the log format by right-clicking on the My Local Machine item in the Server Manager child window and choosing Edit from the pop-up menu. Once the stage is set, it might take a little while for all the log files to be processed.

Figure 8.6 shows how the Usage Import window looks when Server Manager (the top child window) and Log File Manager (the bottom child window) are filled with information, such as server names and log files.

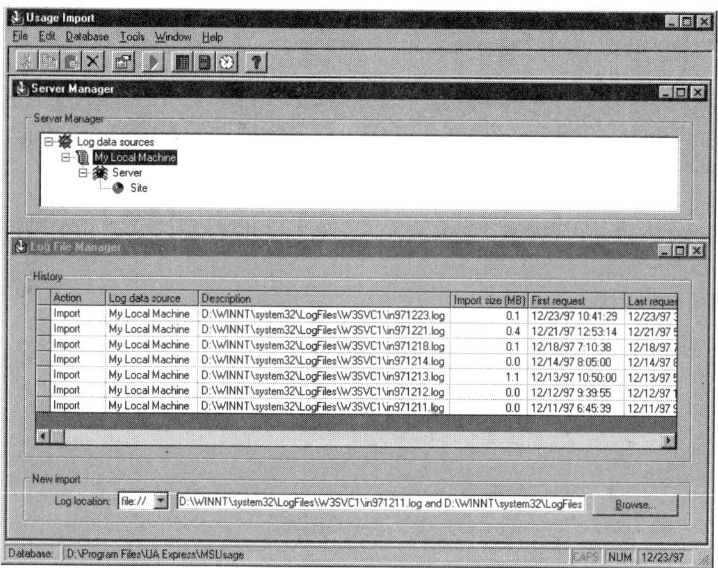

FIGURE 8.6

The Server Manager and Log File Manager shown in the Usage Import window.

After processing is complete, the Usage Import Statistics dialog box showing processing status appears, similar to that shown in Figure 8.7.

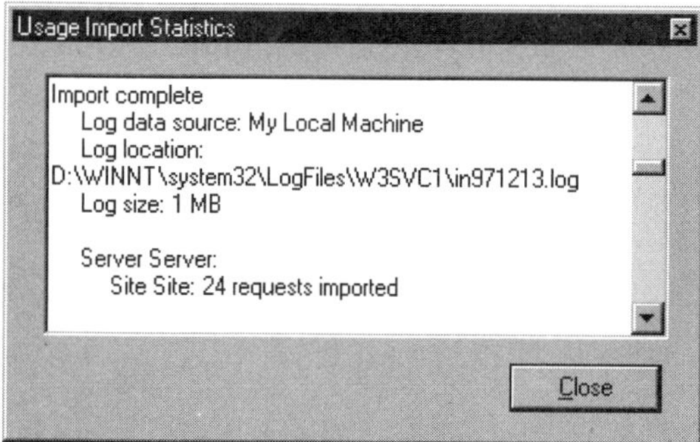

FIGURE 8.7

The Usage Import Statistics dialog box, showing each file and its conversion status.

As mentioned, a number of options can add great value to the information stored in the server logs. All the available options are listed in the Tools menu of the Usage Import window. (One such helpful addition to the Usage Import tool is the scheduler. The scheduler allows you to create jobs in which each task can consist of multiple tasks, as discussed in the section "Scheduling and Task Automation" later in this chapter.) You can also select from among quite a few global options to control application behavior by choosing Options from the Tools menu. Figure 8.8 shows the Usage Import Options dialog box, in which you can view some of the configuration options for Usage Import. Now that you have imported data, you can create a report with Report Writer.

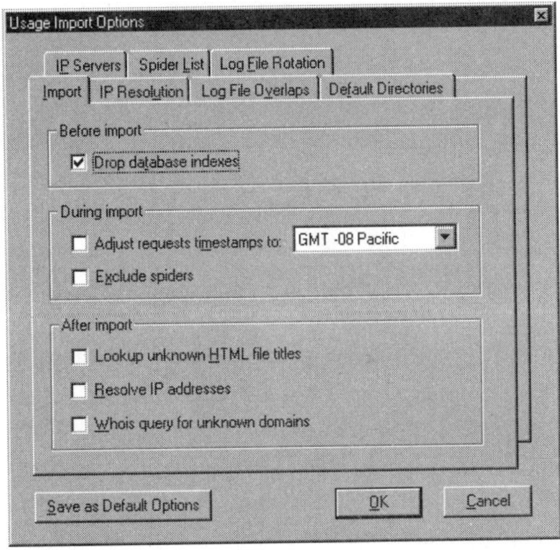

FIGURE 8.8

The Usage Import Options dialog box, showing configurable options for the Usage Import tool.

The Report Writer Application

Report Writer is a fairly straightforward tool. The application takes the raw statistical data from the database and creates a report based on a predefined specification. The full version of the tool can create a report specification from scratch, but the Site Server Express version can create reports based on only one of the templates in its catalog. About two dozen different templates are available in the catalog, so even reports created with the scaled-down version of the tool are informative and helpful.

Data in the database can be represented as a series of objects, such as visits, requests, users, and so on. Each object has unique properties. For example, information about a single request includes the date, time, hour, and other properties. The report itself—that is, what you will see as nicely formatted HTML or in a Microsoft

Excel spreadsheet—can be described as a *presentation object*. The presentation object also has properties, such as fonts, layouts, and formatting. These properties are basically simple attributes that describe the look of the generated report. You can control what goes to the report as raw data and how the report looks by assigning filters to each specific property (or you can leave each property set at its default). So, for example, you can filter all requests shown in the final report according to the time of day or day of the week on which they were made.

When Report Writer starts, you can choose which report you want to use. Figure 8.9 shows the Report Writer dialog box, in which you can use a predefined report from the catalog, create a report from scratch, or continue to work with a previous report of your own creation. (The From Scratch option is disabled in the Site Server Express version of Report Writer.)

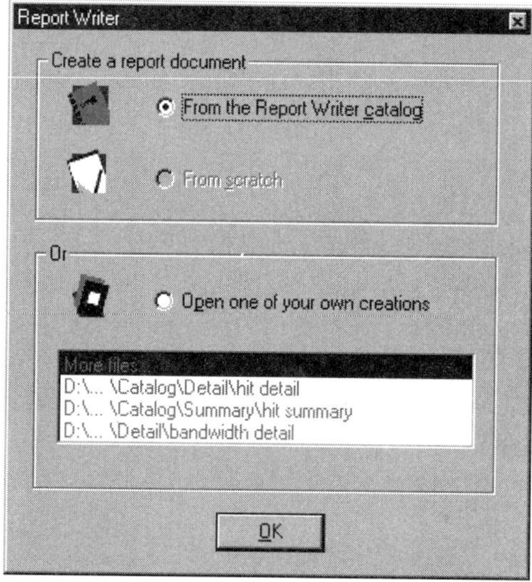

FIGURE 8.9

The Report Writer dialog box, in which you can choose the reports you want to use.

Report Writer templates are organized in the form of a catalog, shown in Figure 8.10. You can select from among the detail or summary reports and see a description in the lower portion of the dialog box.

A report can include one or more graphs, tables, or charts. Once you select Open Report Definition from the File menu and select a report, the content window opens inside the main Report Writer window. Figure 8.11 shows the results of selecting the Request Detail report and maximizing the content window. This window exposes the various attributes (size and dimensions) of the report and each of its elements. By changing the attributes in this window, you can change the appearance of the report.

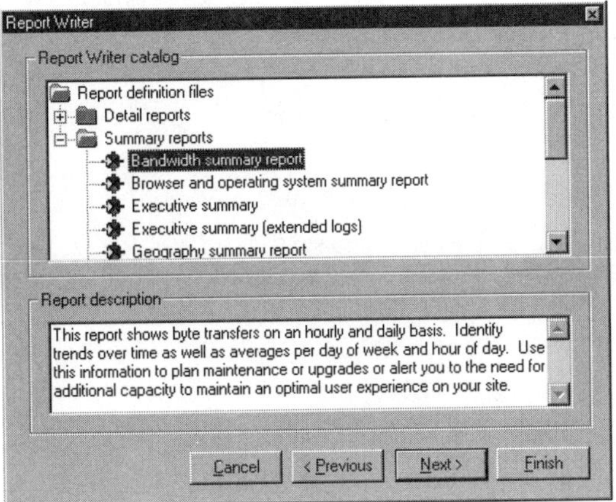

FIGURE 8.10

The Report Writer catalog, which contains a variety of summary and detail reports.

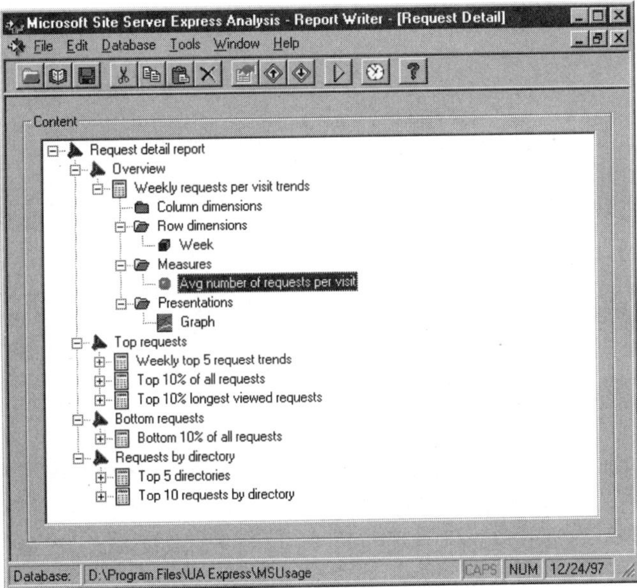

FIGURE 8.11

The Report Writer window, which can be used to change the appearance of a report.

After you have set all the properties, it's time to generate the report. Report Writer can generate a report as a Microsoft Word document, an Excel spreadsheet, or an HTML file. In this example, we chose to create a report that reflects the number of requests made to our server, and we wanted it to be in HTML form. Because our server is not really a production machine, the report does not show thousands of requests. Figure 8.12 shows a portion of this report.

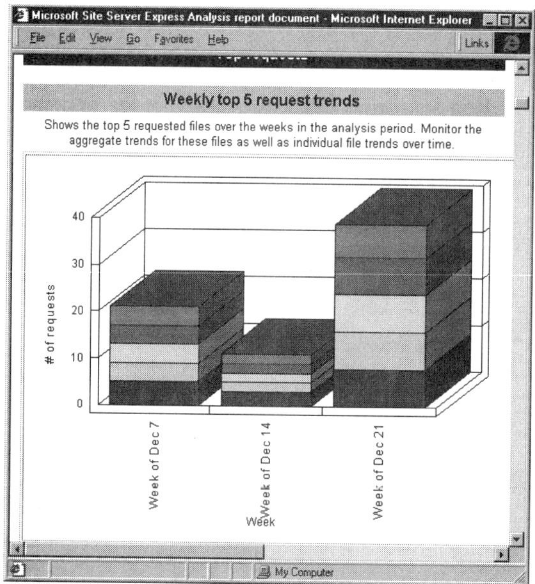

FIGURE 8.12

Part of a report generated by Report Writer.

Scheduling and Task Automation

Because both the Usage Import tool and Report Writer accept various command-line parameters, it's possible to create a batch file that can automate the importing of log data to the database and the generation of reports. The scheduler component of Site Server Express creates batch files (simple MS-DOS .BAT files) that are based on the tasks and jobs they are created to perform. For each job, a new batch file is created in \Program Files\UA Express\Schedule. A job can consist of such tasks as updating the database from log files using Usage Import or creating an HTML file using Report Writer. The full version of Site Server is capable of running these types of .BAT files in unattended mode.

In fact, you don't even need to use the built-in scheduler to automate such tasks. Microsoft Windows NT includes a scheduler service that you can start by typing *net start scheduler* at the command prompt. Once the scheduler is running, you can schedule various tasks by using the *at* command. (Type *at /?* at the command prompt to get help.) If you learn the command-line options for Report Writer and Usage Import, you can create your own batch files and submit them as tasks to the Windows NT scheduler.

◆ Command-Line Parameters

To learn about the command-line parameters for Usage Import, type *import.exe -help* at the command prompt.

To learn about parameters for Report Writer, type *analysis.exe -help* at the command prompt.

To learn more about the Windows NT scheduler service, type either *net help start schedule* or *at /?* at the command prompt.

By now you should have a solid idea of how Usage Import and Report Writer work together. Although this chapter hasn't covered every available capability, you should have a good understanding of both tools' core functionality, and you should be able to learn about other features without much problem. The following section takes a look at the next piece of Site Server Express—the Posting Acceptor.

The Publishing Subcomponents

The last two subcomponents installed with Site Server Express are the Posting Acceptor and the Web Publishing Wizard, as shown earlier in Figure 8.1. These tools do not deal with server statistics or usage analysis. Instead, the Posting Acceptor enables IIS to accept files posted to the server via the Web Publishing Wizard (on the client machines) or from other client applications. Consider the following example. To attract more customers, an ISP enables users to have their own Web pages by hosting those pages for them. When users develop their own pages at home, they need to be able to transfer those files to the server. One way of accomplishing this would be for the ISP to run an FTP server and configure it so that the default directory for each user's incoming FTP files is the user's Web home directory. Once a user develops pages, he or she can start the FTP client and upload the files to the specific Web directory. This solution is perfect for experienced users who understand and use FTP. Because neither Windows NT nor Windows 95 includes an intuitive Windows-based FTP client, users will need to know how to operate the command-line-based FTP client. Unfortunately, this isn't a very seamless solution, particularly when you consider that many Web users are not familiar with how to use command-line applications. We doubt that an ISP would gain much popularity with this kind of publishing solution. But it would be nice if users could use their Web browser to accomplish this task—after all, why involve another protocol like FTP when users simply want to publish their Web pages?

A far more elegant solution for publishing pages via HTTP does exist and is described in RFC 1867. This document describes how any type of data (such as binary .EXE files, text HTML files, and so on) can be encapsulated in the HTTP packets and transferred to the server via an HTTP POST command. Using a solution that is based on an RFC means that there is industry-wide acceptance for the solution. If your posting component on the server works according to the RFC, it can receive data posted by any RFC-complaint client (for instance, it will even work with Netscape's browser on a UNIX-based platform). After the data reaches the server, all you have to do is save it in a file. As usual, you can do this in several ways. For example, you can write a server-side solution using Perl scripts, CGI applications, or ISAPI extensions to parse the incoming data and save it in different files. But since this kind of solution is rather complex, you might find it easier to use the Microsoft Posting Acceptor.

The Posting Acceptor is a very flexible ISAPI extension that not only processes files transferred by the client but also provides certain value-added services, such as the ability to work with HTTP-based RFC 1867 and also with the Microsoft WebPost Application Programming Interfaces (APIs). The WebPost APIs allow programmers to write applications that provide seamless file transferring capabilities from client to host computers. The Web Publishing Wizard installed with IIS and the Microsoft File Upload Control make use of these APIs, so there is no need for you to write any code. If you want your applications to provide you with the ability to publish pages to the Web server, they can use the Web Publishing Wizard, shown in Figure 8.13.

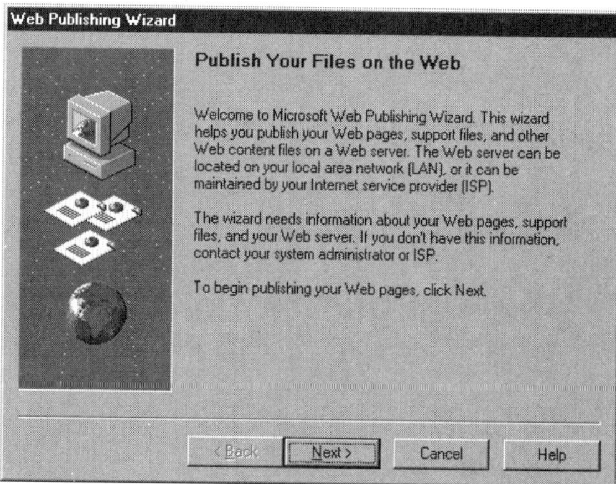

FIGURE 8.13

The Web Publishing Wizard, which automates the tasks of uploading files to the Web server.

Web Publishing Wizard, the Microsoft File Upload Control, and WebPost internals

The WebPost APIs and Web Publishing Wizard SDK are part of the Internet Client SDK (also known as the Internet Explorer Authoring Kit), which is considered a client-side technology. You can start the Web Publishing Wizard programmatically by calling the *WpPost* API function.

All the posting functionality—that is, the code that performs the actual transfer of data from the client to the server—is encapsulated in a WebPost service provider. WebPost functions such as *WpPost* and software such as the File Upload Control or the Web Publishing Wizard all use the provider's services to perform the actual transfer. The posting providers are implemented as COM servers and can employ different transfer mechanisms. Several posting providers are included with the Web Publishing Wizard. One provider implements posting via HTTP (using the RFC 1867 standard we just mentioned); another uses FTP (in which case, the client is ultimately using a simple FTP *put* command to send the content to the specified FTP server). It is possible to write a custom post provider. Companies such as CompuServe and America Online may develop proprietary providers to aid users in uploading their personal home pages on the commercial system.

To further simplify the content upload process, the WebPost API (and of course the File Upload Control and the Web Publishing Wizard, both of which use WebPost internally) retrieves upload parameters from the server rather than asking the user to provide this information. These parameters are different for each protocol. If the HTTP posting provider is used, only the target URL (which indicates where the file should go) and the posting URL (the server script that actually accepts the posted data) are needed. For the FTP posting provider, the client software needs to know the FTP server name, the user name and password to log on to the FTP server, and the target directory. To avoid having the Web Publishing Wizard prompt the user for this data, the relevant information is put in the Post Information file stored in the Web server's home directory. By default, this file is named POSTINFO.HTML and created by the Webmaster in the server's home directory. You can change the name and location of the POSTINFO.HTML file to whatever you please. If you do so, the following META tag must be added to the default HTML document.

```
<META name="postinfo" content="/scripts/postinfo.asp">
```

This tag changes the name and location of the default Post Information file to postinfo.asp in the /scripts virtual root. The WebPost applications first obtain the contents of the Post Information file and then use this data to perform the transfer.

When a file is posted to the Posting Acceptor (that is, to an ISAPI extension), not only are the contents of the file sent to the server, but also the target URL is sent. Conceptually, the target URL is where the file can be accessed after it has been posted. The Posting Acceptor ISAPI extension needs to determine the physical location that corresponds to the URL. This might seem like a fairly straightforward task, but it gets more complicated if you have a group of servers, called a *Web farm,* that represents a single host. For instance, *www.microsoft.com* looks like a single host, but in fact a whole cluster of servers responds to requests for this site. All these servers have the same contents, so each can handle the same requests. Now suppose you wanted to post a file to *www.microsoft.com*. In this case, you would need to post the file to every machine in your cluster. Suddenly, determining where you want a posted file to be copied is not so straightforward. And in fact, the way to handle this sort of situation is to post the file to a staging server and then use Content Replication Services (CRS) from Microsoft Commercial Internet Services (MCIS) or use Microsoft Site Server to copy the files from the staging server to all the servers in the *www.microsoft.com* cluster.

So how does the Posting Acceptor handle this kind of situation? The Posting Acceptor queries the *mapping modules* to determine the physical location to which the file needs to be copied. The mapping modules look at the target URL passed to them by the Posting Acceptor ISAPI extension and decide whether they know the physical location for that URL. If one mapping module does not know the physical location, the next mapping module is queried. The last mapping module, the File System mapping module (built into the Posting Acceptor ISAPI DLL), is the default and determines physical location based on the physical path of the virtual roots configured for IIS. If you were to use the Posting Acceptor without installing CRS, the CRS mapping module wouldn't be used; only the File System mapping module would be used. Therefore, files are posted based on the physical location of your virtual roots. Mapping modules are COM servers that support the *IMapper* interface. The *IMapper* interface has a single function, *GetLocation*, that is called by the Posting Acceptor ISAPI extension. The mapping modules that will be queried are those registered under the *HKLM\Software\Microsoft\WebPost\Acceptors\CPSHost\Mappers* key in the registry.

Figure 8.14 diagrams the entire Posting Acceptor operation. RFC 1867 file uploads are handled directly by the Posting Acceptor ISAPI extension, CPSHOST.DLL. The target URL is passed to each of the registered mapping modules, so it can be resolved to a physical disk location. Uploads from the Web Publishing Wizard and the File Upload Control are handled a little differently. First the WebPost APIs (hidden under the hood of the Web Publishing Wizard or File Upload Control) get a hold of the POSTINFO.HTML file in the server's home directory. If the HTTP posting provider is used, CPSHOST.DLL will be used to accept RFC 1867 POST requests and save the posted data in a file. If the FTP provider is used, the WebPost APIs will establish an FTP connection to the server specified in the POSTINFO.HTML file. No matter how you look at it, the file will end up saved in the server's file system.

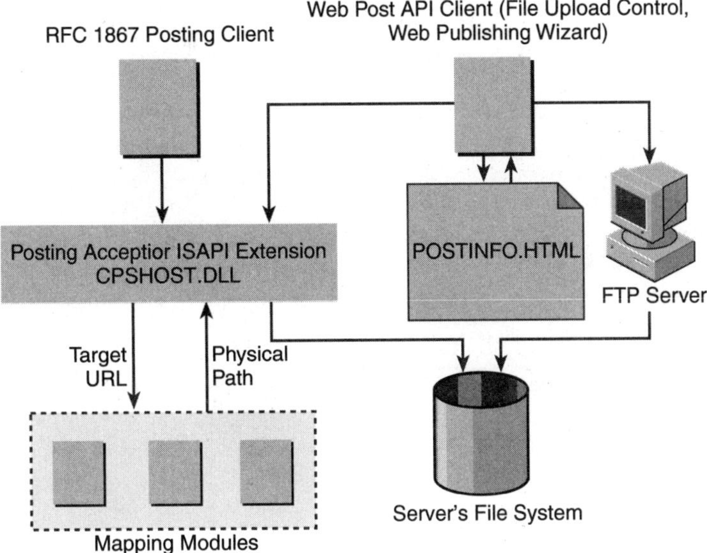

FIGURE 8.14

The Posting Acceptor operation.

The client can actually post data without the help of the Web Publishing Wizard or the File Upload Control. Posting can be accomplished using any browser that understands the *type="file"* HTML tag. (Netscape or Microsoft Internet Explorer 4.0 will work.) The following code (UPLDSMPL.ASP) shows a simple file upload page (using ASP script):

```
<% Response.Buffer = TRUE %>
<% if (Len(Request.ServerVariables("LOGON_USER")) = 0 ) then %>
    <% Response.Status = "401 Unauthorized" %>
    <HTML><BODY><B>Error: Access is denied.</B><P></BODY></HTML>
<% else %>
<html>
<body>
<center><h2>File Upload</h2></center>
<form enctype="multipart/form-data"
action="http://<%= Request.ServerVariables("SERVER_NAME")%>
    /scripts/cpshost.dll?PUBLISH"
method=POST>
File to process: <input name="my_file" type="file"><br>
Destination URL: <input name="TargetURL"><br>
<input type="submit" value="Upload">
</form>
</body>
</html>
<% end if %>
```

Figure 8.15 shows this page as rendered by the browser. For the *type="file"* input control, the browser displays an edit box in which the user enters a filename. Clicking the Browse button displays the standard Open File dialog box.

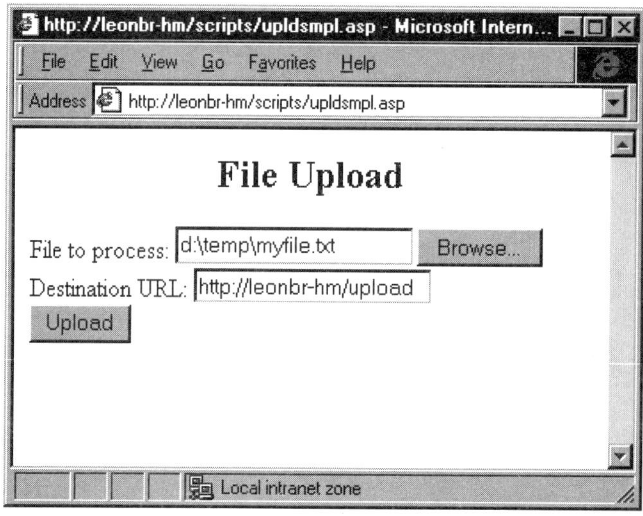

FIGURE 8.15

A typical File Upload page as rendered by the browser from the sample ASP code.

Although the ASP file shown in the preceding code looks simple, it demonstrates some important concepts. The Posting Acceptor *does not* accept files from anonymous users by default. Thus, the script checks to make sure that the *LOGON_USER* server variable is not empty. If it is empty, it causes a *401 Unauthorized* response to be sent that in turn causes the browser to display a dialog box to authenticate the identity of the user. You can allow the Posting Acceptor to accept files from anonymous users by creating an *AllowAnonymous REG_DWORD* registry key in the *HKEY_LOCAL_MACHINE\Software\Microsoft\Webpost\Acceptors\CPSHost* location and setting it to *1*. The action property of the form object that transfers our file is *http://leonbr-hm/scripts/cpshost.dll?PUBLISH*. CPSHOST.DLL is the Posting Acceptor ISAPI extension. The target URL is where the file should be saved. When we enter *http://leonbr-hm/upload*, IIS itself will map this URL to the local file system location: *d:\inetpub\wwwroot\upload*. Because the target URL can be controlled from the Web page (using the Destination - URL edit box), entering a valid URL on the server causes the file to be stored in the selected location. But don't forget to ensure that the upload directory has "write" permission, or the upload will not be accepted; to do this, use the upload directory's Properties window in the Management Console. (See Chapter 4 for details on configuring directories.)

When our simple ASP script is used to upload one or more files to the target location, very little feedback is provided to the user. The Posting Acceptor comes with a sample upload file, UPLOADN.ASP, that is somewhat more complex. It allows the user to transfer multiple files at the same time, and it displays statistics via another ASP page when the upload is finished. When you install Site Server Express, by default the UPLOADN.ASP is located in the \inetpub\scripts directory. The cool part of the HTML approach to uploading files is that it will work on any platform for any browser that can handle file uploads; unfortunately, the same cannot be said for the File Upload Control.

The File Upload Control enables only users on a Windows platform to drag and drop files onto the control on the Web page. The sample script UPLOADX.ASP in the \inetpub\scripts directory shows how to use the File Upload Control. The following HTML refers to the control by its globally unique identifier (GUID) in the <OBJECT> tag:

```
<OBJECT
    classid="clsid:886E7BF0-C867-11CF-B1AE-00AA00A3F2C3"
    id=IFlUpl1
    width=100
    height-100
    align=textmiddle
    color=blue
    codebase=http://<%= Request.ServerVariables("SERVER_NAME")
%>/FlUpl.cab#Version=6,1,27,0
>
</OBJECT>
```

The page containing the File Upload Control (accessible via *http://leonbr-hm/scripts/uploadx.asp* URL) has a little picture of a computer on it. This picture is itself a control; the user can simply drag and drop files onto this control. To change the control's properties, right-click on it. You can change only the local directory, however; the target URL (the *TargetURL* property) cannot be changed by the user. The target URL comes from the Post Information file (POSTINFO.ASP file in the \inetpub\scripts directory, for example).

The drag-and-drop capabilities provided by the File Upload Control are a nice added feature for Windows clients and an improvement over the simple *input="file"* tag. Ultimately, we would like to provide both kinds of file upload, depending on what kind of client is connecting to our server. The Microsoft sample ASP script installed with the Posting Acceptor does just that. When the browser sends a request to the default download script *http://leonbr-hm/scripts/upload.asp*, the script determines the browser type. For Internet Explorer, the client will be redirected to a page that uses the File Upload Control (*UPLOADX.ASP*). Any other browser is redirected to the download page that does not have the control (*UPLOADN.ASP*).

FrontPage Server Extensions

When we started looking at the Posting Acceptor, we used the example of a user who has the ability to develop Web content and then publish it to the ISP server via the Posting Acceptor. This arrangement was fine if the Web developer's entire site consisted of a small number of pages and a handful of image files. But what happens when we take the site to the next level? This new site might consist of hundreds of HTML files and just as many pictures, and to top it all off, these HTML files will probably need to be placed in different subdirectories (making the management of hyperlinks just that much more confusing). Developing such a site and then transferring it to a server is far from being a straightforward procedure. We need a new tool for this kind of job. Microsoft provides a complete solution for this task in the form of FrontPage or Microsoft Visual InterDev. Both of these tools enable the user to easily develop an entire Web site without physically sitting in front of the server machine. You could build and manage your Web site from your home machine and simply connect to the server via a modem. To do this, your server must support Microsoft FrontPage 98 Server Extensions, which are included with IIS.

NOTE

Microsoft Visual InterDev, a tool similar to FrontPage, is also a comprehensive tool for software developers that enables the publishing and deployment of Web applications.

FrontPage Server Extensions are included with the Typical or Custom installation of the Microsoft Windows NT Option Pack, as shown in Figure 8.16. After FrontPage Server Extensions are installed and configured, the developer can use Visual InterDev or FrontPage Explorer to connect remotely to a server to design and deploy new sites and individual pages.

FrontPage itself is a tool that greatly simplifies Web site development. FrontPage features WYSIWYG HTML editing capabilities, a set of powerful wizards that simplify adding ActiveX controls to pages and provide a bunch of other goodies. FrontPage Explorer can show entire Web sites in different views. For instance, you can display the site as a set of directories or as a graphic with a weblike structure. In a way, FrontPage is similar to Content Analyzer, except that FrontPage allows interactive editing rather than passive information gathering. Figure 8.17 shows the FrontPage hyperlink view of the default Web on our computer.

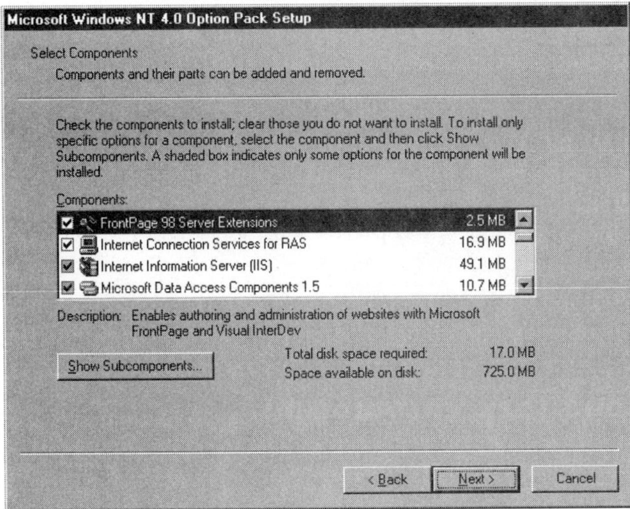

FIGURE 8.16

The Windows NT Option Pack Setup window, showing the FrontPage 98 Server Extensions option available with the Custom installation.

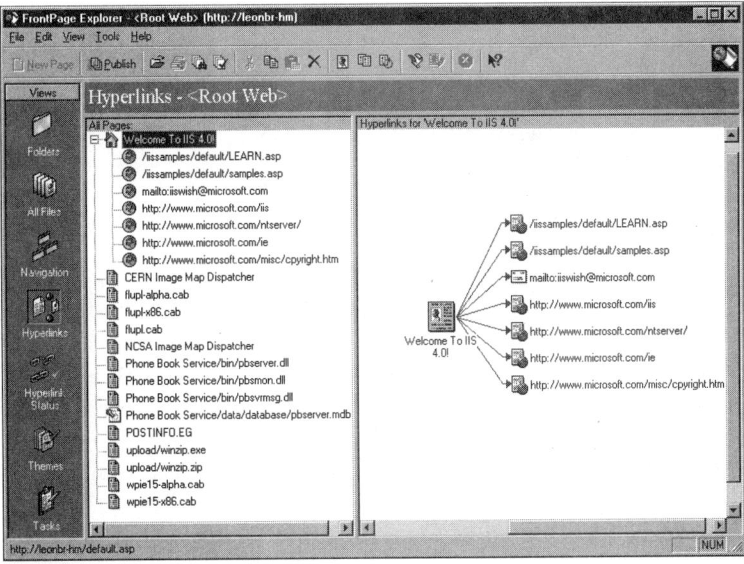

FIGURE 8.17

FrontPage Explorer in hyperlink view.

The main entity used by FrontPage is the *FrontPage Web*. A FrontPage Web is similar to the "application" discussed in Chapter 4. It is a logical unit containing HTML files, scripts, and all other logically connected entities (on a corporate Web site, for example). FrontPage Explorer can enumerate all the Webs on a specific server, so you can pick the one you want to work with. With FrontPage, you can create an entire Web from ground zero and publish it on a remote server. Figure 8.18 shows the Open FrontPage Web dialog box, reflecting multiple Webs on the server LEONBR-HM.

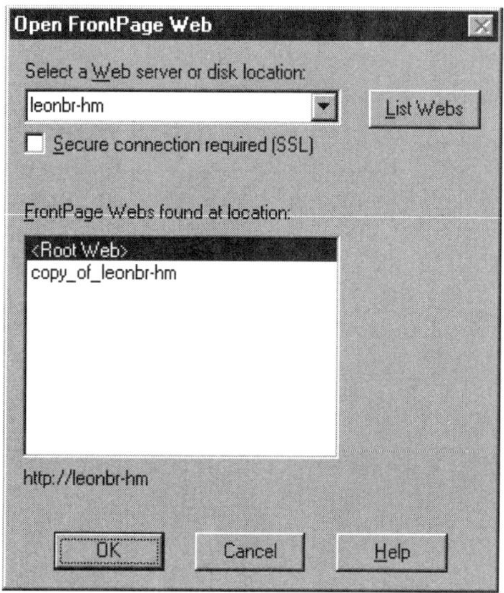

FIGURE 8.18

Two FrontPage Webs on the server LEONBR-HM.

Why are we bothering to talk about FrontPage? After all, FrontPage is an end-user client tool and as such wouldn't appear to be relevant to the server side of Web content creation. The answer is simple: the client-side utility we are all familiar with would not be possible without a special server-side component. FrontPage Server Extensions is the set of CGI scripts that interact with the FrontPage front end. FrontPage uses CGI scripts because they are supported not only on IIS but on other servers as well. FrontPage Editor is a graphic HTML editor that simplifies the development of ASP, HTML, and even Internet Database Connector (IDC) files, and it can insert FrontPage components on a page. A FrontPage component could be a simple hit counter or a much more complex scheduled image that is displayed on the page based on a specified time schedule. All the component functionality is implemented in FrontPage Server Extensions, which are in turn administered by the FrontPage Server Administrator.

The FrontPage Server Administrator

The FrontPage Server Administrator is installed with IIS. The server components do not require the entire FrontPage application—only server-side scripts are needed. Server components are also used by other applications, such as Visual InterDev. The FrontPage Server Administrator application, shown in Figure 8.19, is located in the Internet Information Server group of the Windows NT Option Pack.

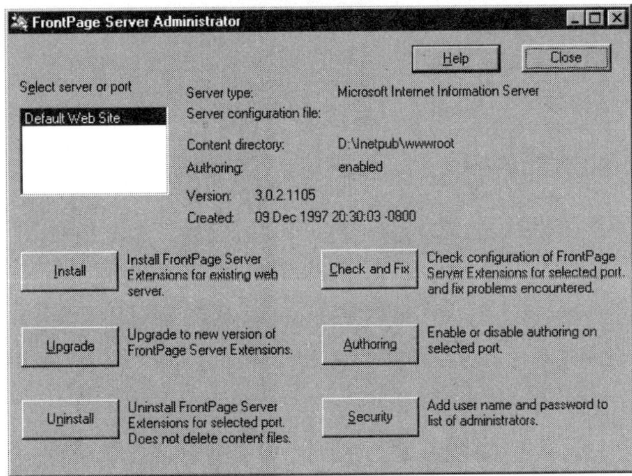

FIGURE 8.19

FrontPage Server Administrator.

FrontPage Server Administrator is fairly straightforward. Let's start by looking at the Install option. If a Web server hosts more than one site, each site must have a server extension installed. Click the Install button, and then choose the correct server type. The dialog box shown in Figure 8.20 will appear.

As you can see, my installation of IIS includes two sites: the Default Web Site and the LeonBr Test Site. Clicking OK at this point will install FrontPage Extensions on that site, since that is the only site selected. The Upgrade and Uninstall options in the FrontPage Server Administrator dialog window (Figure 8.19) are self-explanatory.

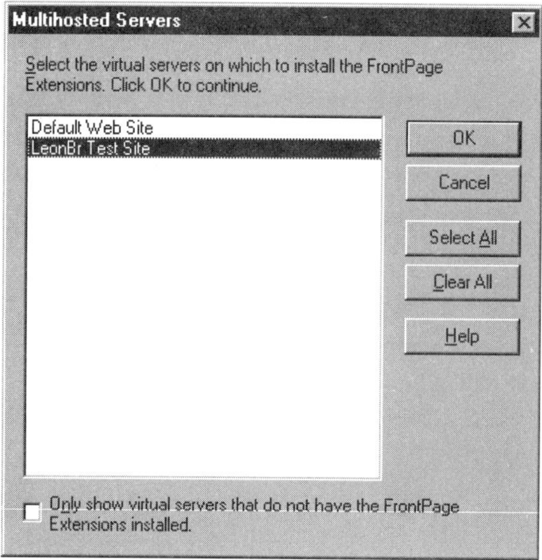

FIGURE 8.20

Installing extensions for a site.

FrontPage Server Extensions consist of many different scripts. You might notice some funny-looking directories (most of them start with an underscore) in your site's home directory after you install FrontPage Server Extensions. These directories are created by the FrontPage Server Extensions installation routine and should not be modified or deleted. If by mistake some of the directories or files get deleted, however, you can use the Check And Fix option as your safety net. There is no need to reinstall the entire set of FrontPage Server Extensions from the Windows NT Option Pack; Check And Fix will go over the FrontPage Server Extensions and fix any problems it finds. If for some reason you want to disable authoring ability for a specific site even when FrontPage Server Extensions are installed, you can do so by clicking the Authoring button. If authoring is disabled, FrontPage will not be able to connect to the specified site; instead, it will display the error message shown in Figure 8.21.

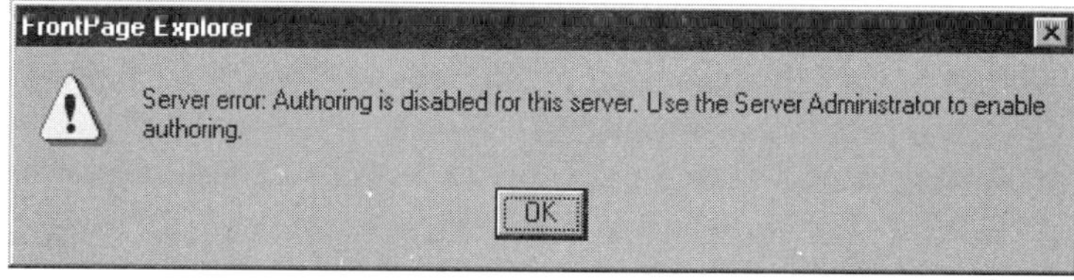

FIGURE 8.21

Error message displayed by FrontPage Explorer when you try to connect to a site for which authoring is disabled.

Even when authoring is enabled, only designated users can edit the site. Clicking the Security button displays the Administrator Name And Password dialog box, as shown in Figure 8.22. The name of the account that you enter will be added to the list of people who can edit this site.

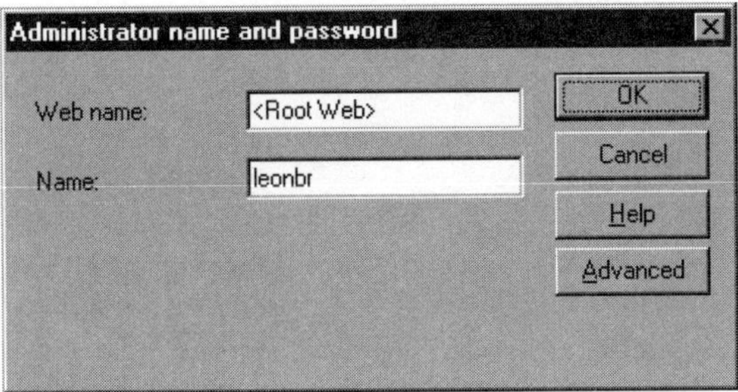

FIGURE 8.22

The Administrator Name And Password dialog box.

To tighten security restrictions for the server even further, you can enter an IP address (or use the wildcard character * to specify a range of addresses) from which authoring is allowed. The IP Address dialog box is accessed by clicking the Advanced button in the Security dialog box.

In this chapter, you have learned how to analyze information, create reports, and publish Web server content. You now know how to configure IIS to accept posting files as well as how to use FrontPage. Where do we go from here? Straight to other services and protocols: the FTP server, NNTP service, and some other good stuff.

CHAPTER 9

The FTP Server

In this chapter, we will learn about the File Transfer Protocol (FTP) server. For now, we'll concentrate on how to set up and manage the FTP server, which can be installed as a part of the Internet Information Server. (We will examine protocol specifics in Chapter 24.)

FTP servers provide a perfect solution to the problem of making many different files available to many different users. FTP client software is available on most hardware and software platforms. File and sample libraries as well as document repositories are ideal FTP server content. FTP is easy to use and almost every computer user has at some time logged on to a public FTP site such as *ftp.microsoft.com* to get a driver update or a code sample. IIS is flexible, supports multiple FTP sites on a single server (similar to virtual Web servers), and provides other functionality necessary for setting up a full-featured FTP solution.

Basic Concepts

Before we get started installing and configuring the FTP server, let's go over some basic terminology. As mentioned, IIS can run multiple FTP sites. This handy feature allows a single physical machine to host multiple FTP servers. Each server can have a unique directory structure and can host different files. Hosting multiple FTP servers provides a perfect solution for an ISP that needs to provide FTP sites for multiple customers (such as *ftp.MyISP.com* for all the ISP users and *ftp.cmpny.com* for one of its business customers) using only one physical machine. You can create multiple sites by having more than one IP address associated with your machine. To configure multiple IP addresses, double-click on Network in the Control Panel, select TCP/IP Protocol on the Protocols page, and then click on Properties. When the Microsoft TCP/IP Properties dialog box appears, click on Advanced to display the Advanced IP Addressing dialog box. Figure 9.1 shows multiple addresses being assigned to a single network adapter.

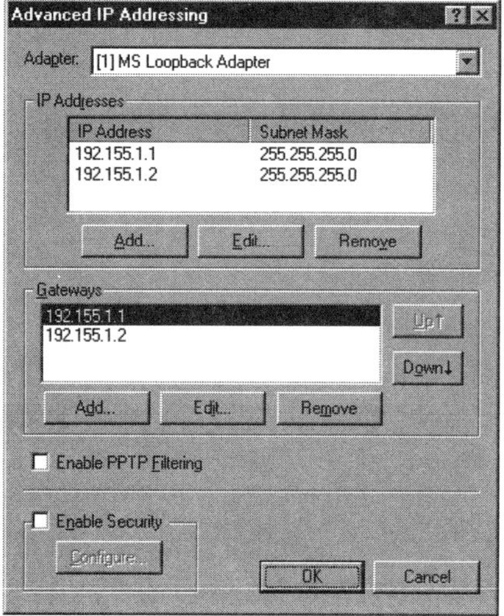

FIGURE 9.1

The Advanced IP Addressing dialog box.

At this point, two IP addresses can be used to connect to the same machine. Multiple IP addresses make it seem to users that they are connecting to different physical machines. As we learned in Chapter 3, typing *ftp://192.155.1.1* or *ftp://192.155.1.2* is not very user friendly. In order to specify *ftp://ftp.MyISP.com* and *ftp://ftp.cmpny.com,* you will need to configure either your domain name server or HOSTS file to resolve each Fully Qualified Domain Name (FQDM) to the corresponding address.

Once you create different FTP sites for Cmpny Corp and for all your ISP's users, you will have a home directory for each site, so that once users have connected to the server, they are located in a home directory assigned to the particular site. Having this home directory prevents users from roaming all over your hard disk by changing directories in the FTP client software. The user cannot gain access to a directory hierarchy above the home directory. If you want to allow users to access either another drive or even another computer from the home directory, you can create an FTP virtual directory. Think of a virtual directory as a link to another location. Such a directory might be a link to a location with a user-friendly name such as Uploads or to a full directory structure unavailable directly from the home directory (for example, *d:\SecureLocation\Uploads*). You can also create a link to a remote machine. One interesting feature of virtual directories is that they are invisible to the FTP client software when there is no physical directory on the server's file system with a matching name. For all other practical purposes, a virtual directory looks like any ordinary directory that you might access using the LS or DIR command. We will talk more about virtual directories later in this chapter.

Installing FTP Server

The FTP server is installed by default with either the Typical or Minimal installation option of the Microsoft Windows NT 4.0 Option Pack. With the Custom installation option, the FTP server is included as one of the Internet Information Server components and is checked by default. (Using the Custom option, however, enables you to turn off installation of the FTP server.) The default settings are shown in Figure 9.2.

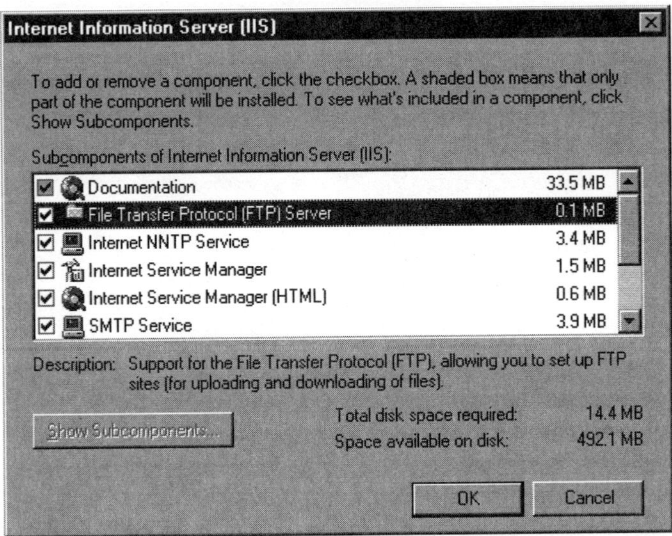

FIGURE 9.2

The default settings for IIS, showing the FTP server as a subcomponent.

As with any socket-based server, only one application can be bound to a specific port. (By default, FTP uses port 21.) This means that only one FTP server can be installed on a system at a time (unless other instances of the FTP server software are using a port other than the default). But what if you have already installed the FTP service that comes with the Windows NT server? The IIS installation will take care of this problem for you by uninstalling the old FTP server and installing the IIS version of FTP. You will be prompted for the default FTP home directory, at which time you can simply accept the default, *%SystemDrive%\InetPub\ftproot*, or you can specify a directory of your choosing. And that's it! Your FTP server is now installed.

Configuration Options

Let's look into the details of IIS configuration. You can create sites and virtual directories as well as manipulate the properties of the FTP server in the following three ways:

- Using the Microsoft Management Console as a management tool
- Using the HTML-based administration pages available to any Web browser
- Programmatically by manipulating values in the Metabase

In Chapter 4, we introduced the idea of using the Management Console and the HTML-based administration pages to configure the Web server options; the same concepts apply here for configuring the FTP server options. Remember that in order to manage IIS using a Web browser, you must install the Internet Service Manager (HTML) subcomponent with the Custom installation option, as shown in Figure 9.2.

In Chapter 5, you learned about the Metabase, in which all the configuration information for IIS is stored, and you were introduced to IIS Admin Objects and IIS Admin Base Objects. You can use these same objects to manipulate the Metabase to configure the FTP server options directly. Setting different values for Metabase properties and calling different Metabase object methods (for example, *Start* and *Stop*) can change an FTP server's configuration programmatically. We will revisit this topic in more detail at the end of this chapter.

Figure 9.3 shows the Management Console with the default configuration for the FTP server running on a machine named *leonbr-hm*.

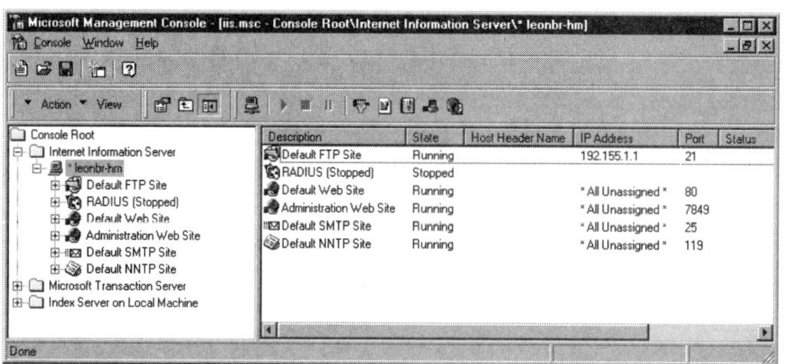

FIGURE 9.3

The default configuration as it appears in the Management Console.

As you can see, the Console window shows a single default FTP site. We are going to create a second FTP site, this one for an imaginary entity named the Cmpny Corporation. Our server has only one network interface card, but two IP addresses are associated with this network card. Here is the output from the IPCONFIG.EXE command-line utility, included with Windows NT:

```
Ethernet adapter ENet161:

        IP Address. . . . . . . . . : 192.155.1.2
        Subnet Mask . . . . . . . . : 255.255.255.0
        IP Address. . . . . . . . . : 192.155.1.1
        Subnet Mask . . . . . . . . : 255.255.255.0
        Default Gateway . . . . . . : 192.155.1.2
```

We will configure the Cmpny Corporation's FTP server in such a way that it will accept only connections targeted to *192.155.1.2*. Connections made to *192.155.1.1* should still go to the default Web site. We must either configure the domain name server to resolve *leonbr-hm* to one address and another name (in this case, *cmpny*) to the other address or modify the HOSTS file. On our machine, we have modified the HOSTS file to resolve *leonbr-hm* to *192.155.1.1* and *cmpny* to *192.155.1.2*, as shown here:

```
127.0.0.1       localhost
192.155.1.1     leonbr-hm
192.155.1.2     cmpny
```

Creating a New Site

You can create a new site by highlighting the Default FTP Site in the Management Console window, right-clicking the mouse, and choosing Site from the New menu to launch the New FTP Site Wizard. You can do the same thing through the HTML-based administration pages by accessing the URL *http://localhost:7849/iisadmin*. Notice that port 7849 is used to connect to the IIS Administration Web site. The port value on your machine probably will be different. You should use the value listed in the Management Console, as shown in Figure 9.3.

NOTE

Omitting the port number in the URL (http://localhost/iisadmin) *causes the HTML-based administration pages to display and to manage configuration options only for the Default Web Site.*

Because we are administering the local machine, we can specify *localhost* as the server name. To create a new FTP site using the HTML-based administration pages, highlight the machine name in the right frame and choose FTP in the first list box of the left frame. Then click New and follow the prompts. Figure 9.4 illustrates these steps using Microsoft Internet Explorer.

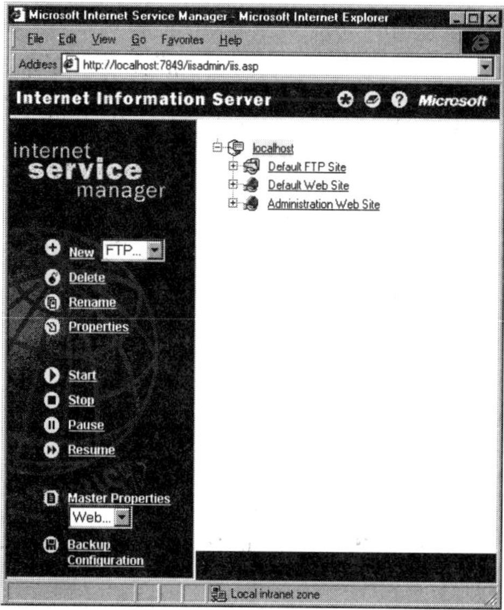

FIGURE 9.4

HTML-based administration pages.

Although the HTML-based interface looks different than it does in the Management Console window, the same information about our new FTP site is entered in both places. For the sake of brevity, here we will look only at how to enter this information using the Management Console interface to launch the wizard. The first screen of the New FTP Site Wizard prompts you for the FTP Site Description, as shown in Figure 9.5.

The next step is to enter the IP address that will be used by the site, along with the TCP port. In our case, the IP address will be *192.155.1.2* and the port will be 21, as shown in Figure 9.6.

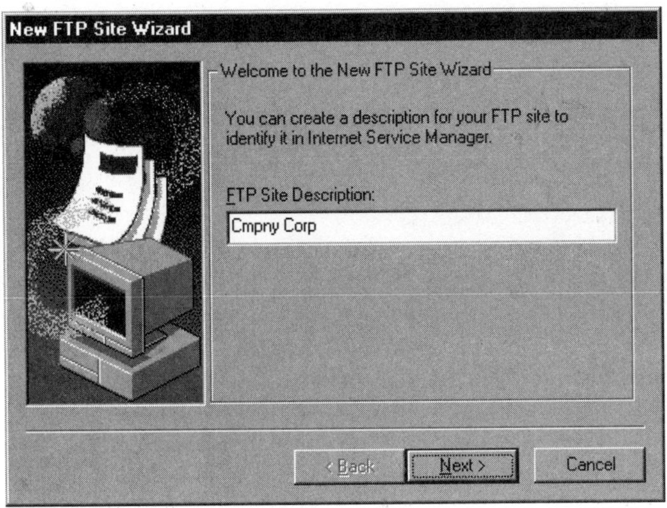

FIGURE 9.5

Entering the FTP Site Description.

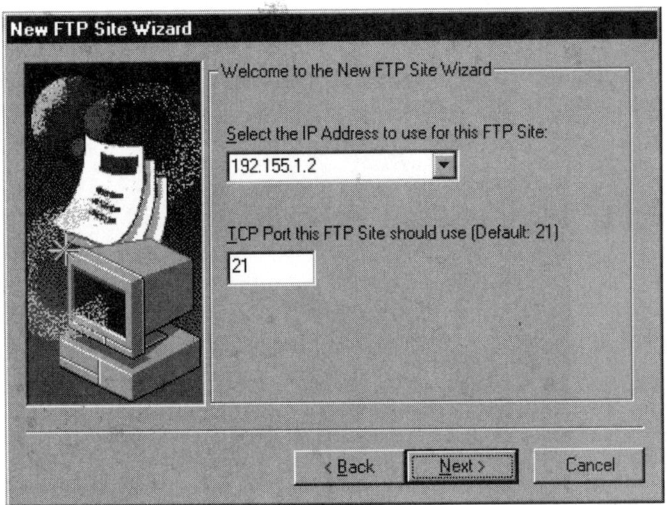

FIGURE 9.6

Entering the site's IP address and TCP port.

Now we need to enter the physical path for the home directory, as shown in Figure 9.7. The home directory will become, by default, the initial working directory on the remote machine for all FTP clients connecting to our machine using IP address *192.155.1.2*.

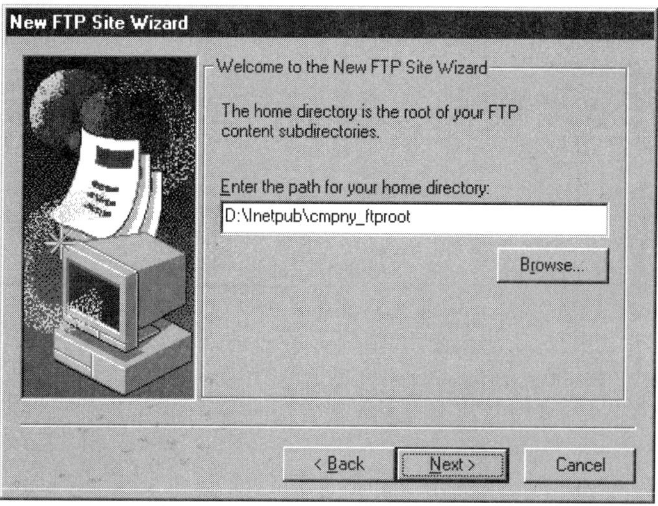

FIGURE 9.7

Entering the default directory.

At this point, we're almost done. Setting up the access permissions on the default home directory is the final step, as shown in Figure 9.8.

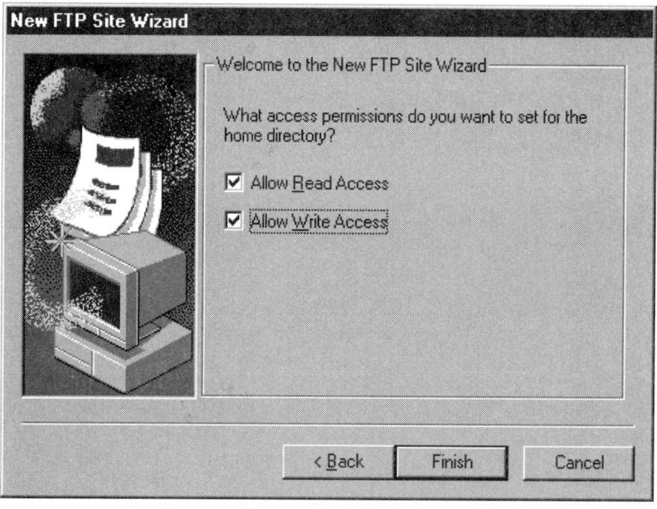

FIGURE 9.8

Specifying access permissions.

Creating a Virtual Directory

Earlier in this chapter, we talked about creating a virtual directory that would allow clients to access a directory on the server machine that would otherwise be inaccessible from the FTP home directory. Let's see how this is done using the HTML-based administration pages. (As always, these steps could be performed just as easily using the Management Console.) First we'll create a virtual directory named Uploads for the Cmpny Corporation FTP site. Figure 9.9 shows the initial HTML-based administration pages.

FIGURE 9.9

HTML-based administration pages for creating a virtual directory.

Highlight the Cmpny Corporation FTP site in the right frame, and then choose FTP from the topmost list in the left frame. Click New to display the dialog box shown in Figure 9.10.

FIGURE 9.10

Entering a virtual directory name.

The directory name is the only piece of information needed to create a virtual directory via the HTML-based interface. When the Management Console window is used, the Virtual Directory Wizard (similar to New FTP Site Wizard) also prompts you for a local path and directory access permissions.

The FTP Properties Window

To complete the configuration using the HTML-based administration pages, highlight Uploads virtual directory, which should now be visible just below Cmpny Corp site in the right frame, and then click Properties in the left frame. The FTP Properties window, shown in Figure 9.11, lets you configure local directory and access permissions in one step. Clicking Save applies the FTP server configuration settings. As you can see, here we configured *d:\SecureLocation\Uploads* as A Directory Located On The Server You Are Configuring. The other option lets you configure a virtual directory as A Directory Located On A Different Server. If a directory is accessible in File Manager or Windows NT Explorer (with the Map Network Drive option), it can be used in the FTP Properties window. To specify a remote directory, you need to know its Uniform Naming Convention (UNC) name (for example, \\server\share), a user name (for example, DOMAIN\User—if a Windows NT domain structure is used), and a password. Remember that the user name and password are for either a local user on the target system or a domain user who has permission to access the target machine.

That's it. We've created a new site—Cmpny Corp—and a virtual directory—Uploads. The Management Console displays our configuration changes, as shown in Figure 9.12.

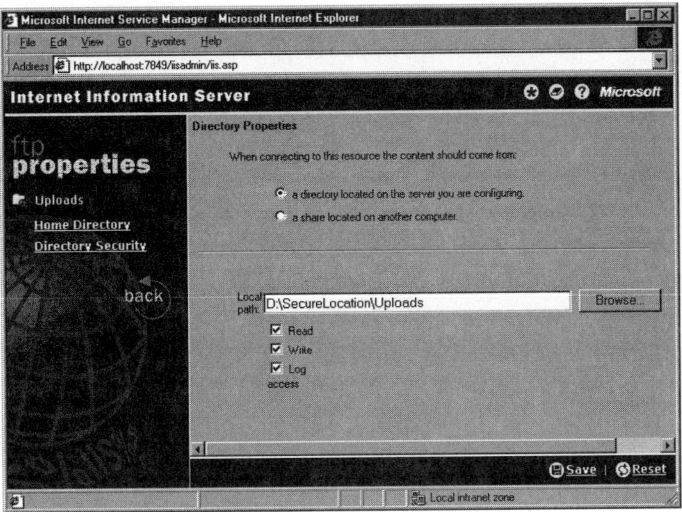

FIGURE 9.11

HTML-based administration pages for specifying FTP Properties.

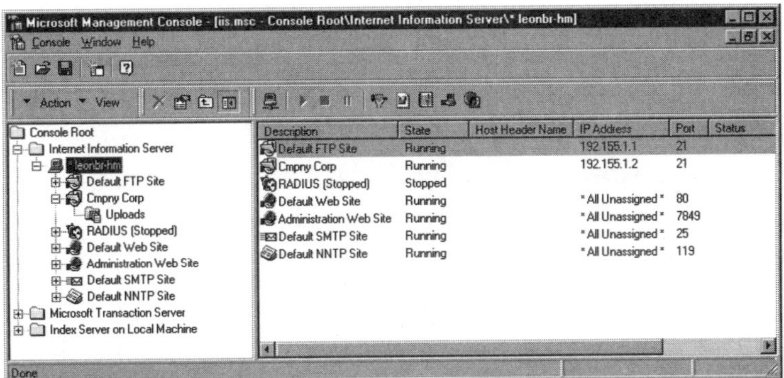

FIGURE 9.12

The final Management Console view.

Properties and inheritance

Now let's take a look at modifying the FTP properties and customizing your FTP server to suit your preferences. FTP properties are *inheritable*, which means that properties set on a higher-level entry are inherited by lower-level entries. All configuration changes made by selecting Master Properties: FTP Service on the Internet Information Server page of the *leonbr-hm* Properties window will propagate to the default FTP site and to the Cmpny Corp site. To get to the Master Properties Window, right-click on the machine name in the left pane of the Management Console window and select Properties. Figure 9.13 shows the resulting Properties dialog box.

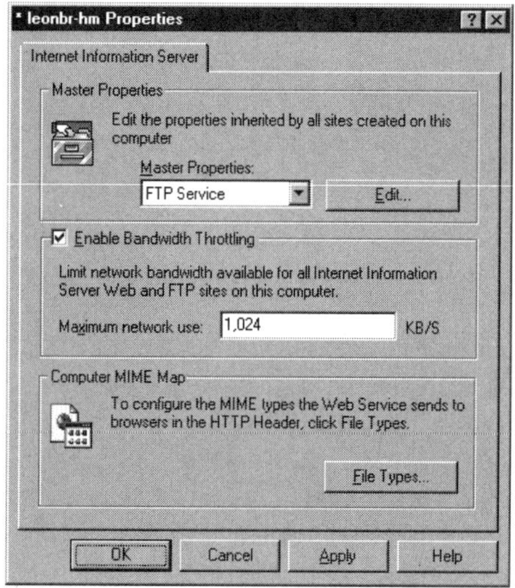

FIGURE 9.13

The Master Properties dialog box for the **leonbr-hm** *machine.*

To view the global FTP properties, choose FTP Service from the Master Properties drop-down list and click Edit to display the FTP Service Master Properties dialog box, shown in Figure 9.14.

To demonstrate the inheritance properties of IIS, let's change the Description for the FTP site to "test" at the Master level, as shown in Figure 9.14. Keep in mind that each lower-level site (such as the default FTP and Cmpny Corp sites) already has its own description.

Changing the Description of the site in Master Properties generates a warning by displaying the Inheritance Overrides dialog box, shown in Figure 9.15.

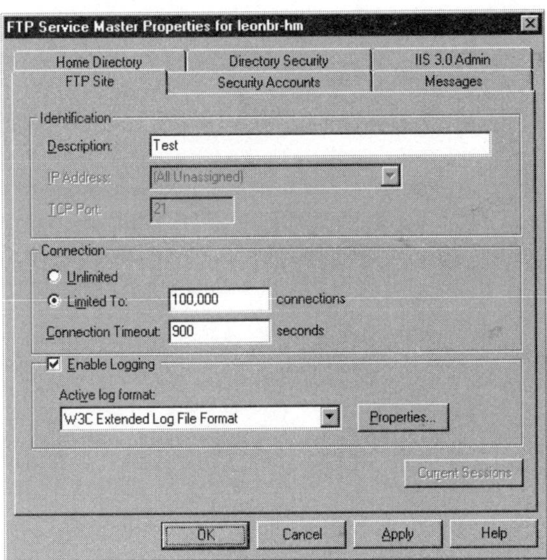

FIGURE 9.14

Changing the FTP site description.

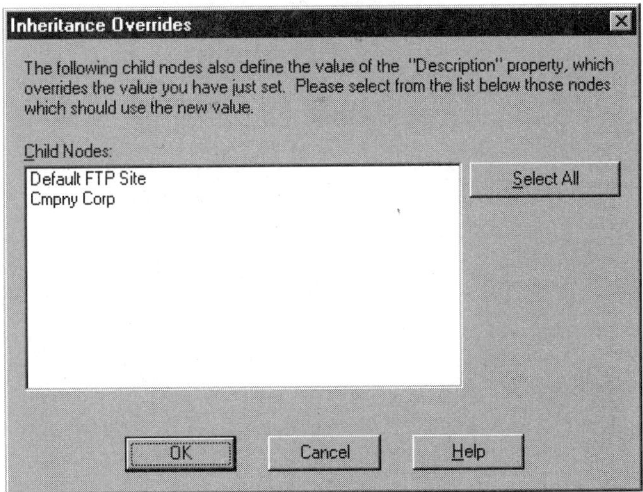

FIGURE 9.15

The Inheritance Overrides dialog box.

This warning indicates that setting the global FTP description to Test would change the descriptions of the lower-level sites. The administrator has to decide whether this description is acceptable and, if so, for what sites.

The FTP Site page

To examine the Default FTP Site page of the Properties window, start by right-clicking on the Default FTP Site option in the Management Console window and then choosing Properties. Figure 9.16 shows the resulting dialog box.

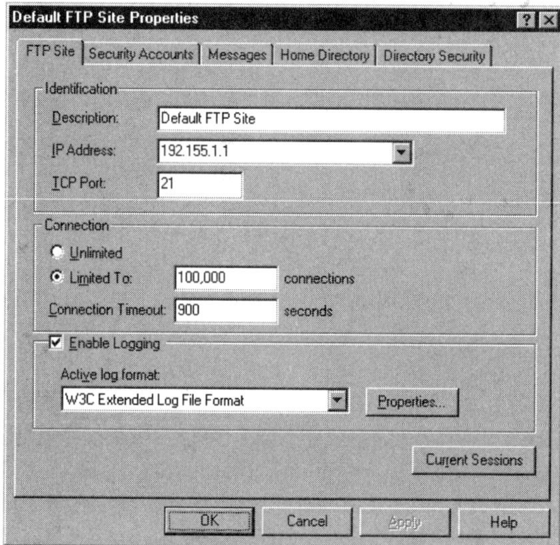

FIGURE 9.16

The FTP Site page of the Default FTP Site Properties window.

From this page, we can change the FTP site's description, change the IP address to any of the addresses associated with the server machine, and change the TCP port value. Changing the port value from the default FTP port, *21* (also called the well-known port), can cause problems. FTP clients and browsers will have to specify the new port either on the URL line, as in *ftp://leonbr-hm:XX*, or the in the client FTP software. The FTP Site page also enables you to specify the maximum number of FTP client connections; this value defaults to *100,000* at any one time. We can also configure our site to disconnect users who are inactive for a specified period of time; the default value is 900 seconds. The FTP server can also log all incoming connections and client commands. The FTP Site page lets you specify the kind of logging you want to perform and the log rotation frequency. The different types of logging were discussed in detail in Chapter 6.

One nice feature of the FTP Site page is the capability to display all the active FTP sessions. Click Current Sessions to view a list of all the users currently logged on, as shown in Figure 9.17. Valid Windows NT accounts will be displayed here, and anonymous logons will be identified by their passwords (traditionally, the user's e-mail address). Anonymous connections are denoted by a large red question mark to the left of the user name. From the FTP User Sessions dialog box, you can also disconnect any or all of the current sessions.

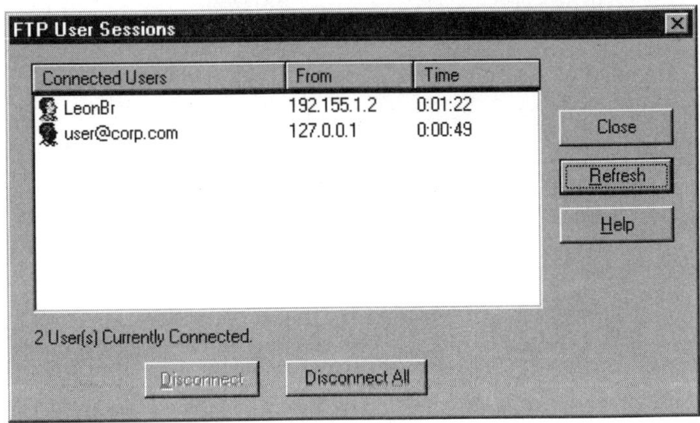

FIGURE 9.17

The FTP User Sessions dialog box.

The Security Accounts page

Let's take a look at the Security Accounts page of the Default FTP Site Properties window, shown in Figure 9.18.

The Security Accounts page controls two kinds of accounts: accounts for users who log on to the FTP site and accounts for users who can administer the FTP site. When IIS is installed on a system, a new user name is created in the form IUSR_*computername*. (In our example, this name is IUSR_*leonbr-hm*.) Because every task on a Windows NT system must run in the context of a *valid* Windows NT user, all anonymous connections for either FTP or HTTP are mapped to the IUSR_*computername* user account. In other words, when an anonymous user logs on, Windows NT impersonates the IUSR_*computername* account in order to control access to the machine's resources (that is, to the files or directories on the FTP server).

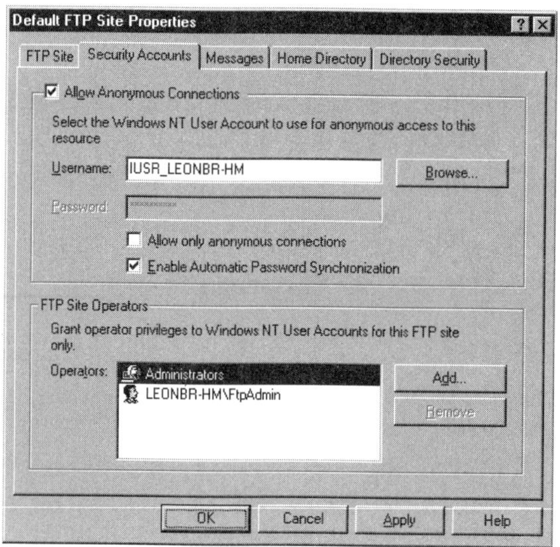

FIGURE 9.18

The Security Accounts page.

The Security Accounts page lets you modify the account configured for anonymous connections (for example, if you want to use a Windows NT domain account instead of a local one). Be sure, however, that the account has been assigned the Log On Locally privilege. Assigning the Log On Locally privilege is done from the Windows NT User Manager For Domains application, included with Windows NT and located in the Administration group. In order to impersonate this account, IIS must know not only the user name but also the password. If you are changing the anonymous user account, you will need to provide the appropriate password for that account. If you check the Enable Automatic Password Synchronization check box and later change the password on this page, IIS will automatically change the password in the Windows NT accounts database. You can configure the FTP server to allow anonymous connections, not allow anonymous connections, or allow only anonymous connections by checking the appropriate boxes. Unchecking the Allow Anonymous Connections check box means that only valid Windows NT users can access our FTP server. When a valid Windows NT user account logs on, the FTP server will impersonate that account instead of the anonymous account when it is accessing the various files and directories.

Be aware that FTP is not a secure protocol; when users supply a user name and password, the information travels in unencrypted form from the FTP client to the server. This security hole could be serious since software like Network Monitor can be used to read the user name and password directly from the packets on the network wire. If you uncheck the Allow Anonymous Connections check box, the Management Console will display a warning describing the potential security problem. It is up to you to balance the trade-offs of individually restricted FTP access with the risk of account credentials being stolen.

By default, the FTP server is set up so that the Windows NT Administrators group has the ability to manage each FTP site. You can add individual users (either local users or users from a domain) to this list. Figure 9.18 shows that an account named *FtpAdmin* has been added to the FTP Site Operators list.

The Messages page

Figure 9.19 shows the Messages page, where FTP server messages are set. Users will see these messages when they log onto the site, when they log off the site, and when the maximum number of connections has been reached and additional client connections are denied. You can enter any message text you want. Here we've inserted a few empty lines before and after the *Welcome to the LEONBR-HM default FTP site!* so that it will be easier to read the message when it is displayed by the FTP client software. Inserting empty lines before and after text is done by pressing the Enter key. You won't see any empty lines after the message in the Figure 9.19 even though they are present.

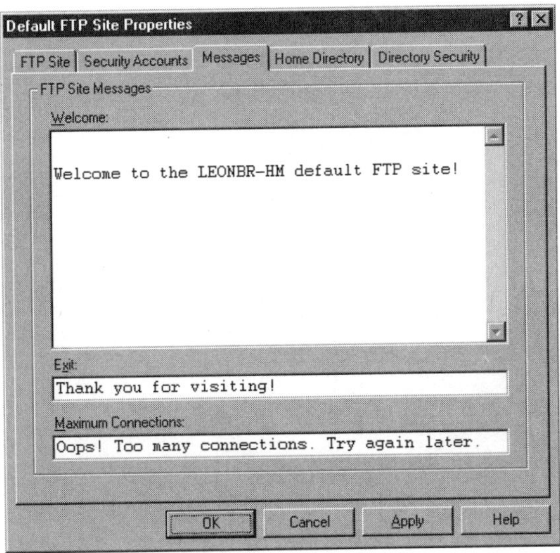

FIGURE 9.19

The Messages page.

The Home Directory page

The Home Directory page, shown in Figure 9.20, contains settings that are similar to the virtual directory configurations (shown in Figure 9.11). As you can see, it is possible to configure your home directory to map to either a local directory or a network share. Directory access permissions are also controlled here. Note that the Log Access check box is checked by default. When logging is set up for this site, checking this box indicates that the server should create a log entry when the client accesses files and directories below this directory.

Setting directory access permission is a bit more complicated than checking permissions check boxes on the Home Directory page. You need to be aware of one other aspect of directory access permissions. When the home directory (or virtual directory) for an FTP site is located on an NTFS partition, the most restrictive security permissions take precedence. For instance, imagine that the d:\inetpub\ftproot directory is located on an NTFS drive. Anonymous users can log on to the server and thus can access all resources in the security context of the IUSR_*computername* account. If the logged-on user tries to access a file whose permissions explicitly deny access to the IUSR_*computername* account, the FTP client will return an access denied error. Thus, you can generically allow anonymous access for an entire directory but still have very precise control over access to individual files and subdirectories. When multiple permissions are applied (via the FTP Property window and NTFS), the most restrictive access is honored.

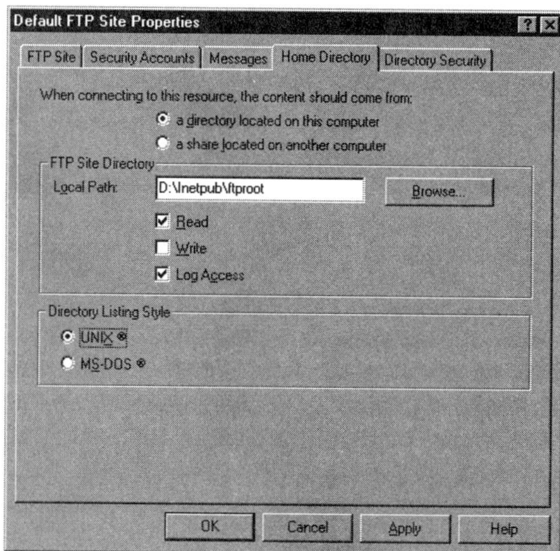

FIGURE 9.20

The Home Directory page.

The Home Directory page also enables the administrator to control how FTP directories are displayed. In the Directory Listing Style section, you can choose traditional UNIX style or you can specify an MS-DOS–style directory listing.

The Directory Security page

Last in the Default FTP Site Properties window is the Directory Security page, shown in Figure 9.21.

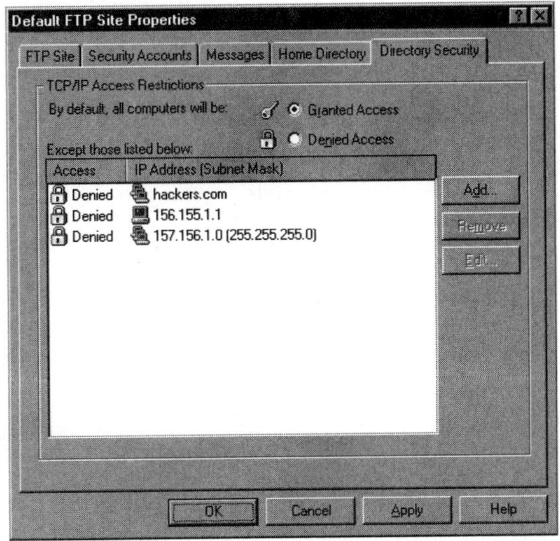

FIGURE 9.21

The Directory Security page.

On the Directory Security page you can set up the most powerful protection against hackers and other unfriendly users. Here you can deny (or allow) connections from specific IP addresses or ranges of addresses. In fact, you can filter connections based on a DNS domain name. In our example, nobody from *hackers.com* will be allowed to connect to our FTP site. Be aware that if domain-based filtering is turned on, the server must perform a potentially lengthy reverse DNS lookup. On a busy FTP server, this process could slow down FTP server performance considerably.

Testing the Configuration

So let's take our server for a spin! The following transcript shows the FTP session with the *leonbr-hm* machine. Here we access the Default FTP Site that we configured on this machine. (The FTP client connects to the *leonbr-hm* machine name that resolved to *192.155.1.1.*)

```
ftp> open LEONBR-HM
Connected to leonbr-hm.
220 leonbr-hm Microsoft FTP Service (Version 4.0).
User (leonbr-hm:(none)): leonbr
331 Password required for leonbr.
Password:
230-
230-
230-Welcome to the LEONBR-HM default FTP site!
230-
230-
230 User leonbr logged in.
ftp> dir
200 PORT command successful.
150 Opening ASCII mode data connection for /bin/ls.
09-16-97  06:53PM                  680 index.txt
09-16-97  06:53PM                  680 readme.txt
09-20-97  11:24AM                   43 welcome.txt
226 Transfer complete.
153 bytes received in 0.01 seconds (15.30 Kbytes/sec)
ftp> quit
221 Thank you for visiting!
```

We connected to *leonbr-hm* machine as the user *leonbr* and supplied the required password. Once a connection was established, we issued a *dir* command to view a directory. This FTP server is configured to send MS-DOS directory listings. Upon disconnecting, we see a polite good-bye message. It looks like everything for our default FTP site is working fine.

Now let's take a look at our test Cmpny Corp site, which is hosted on the same physical machine as the Default FTP Site. Don't forget that our Cmpny Corp site has a virtual directory named Uploads. Here is the FTP session listing:

```
ftp> open cmpny
Connected to cmpny.
220 leonbr-hm Microsoft FTP Service (Version 4.0).
User (cmpny:(none)): anonymous
331 Anonymous access allowed, send identity (e-mail name) as password.
Password:
230-
230-
230-Welcome to Cmpny Corporation FTP server.
230-Server is virtually maintained on LEONBR-HM machine.
230-
230-
230 Anonymous user logged in.
ftp> dir
```

```
200 PORT command successful.
150 Opening ASCII mode data connection for /bin/ls.
-rwxrwxrwx   1 owner    group          43 Sep 20 11:24 Welcome Cmpny.txt
-rwxrwxrwx   1 owner    group         680 Sep 16 18:53 Cmpny File 1.txt
-rwxrwxrwx   1 owner    group         680 Sep 16 18:53 Cmpny File 2.txt
226 Transfer complete.
226 bytes received in 0.00 seconds (226000.00 Kbytes/sec)
ftp> cd Uploads
250 CWD command successful.
ftp> dir
200 PORT command successful.
150 Opening ASCII mode data connection for /bin/ls.
09-25-97  11:14PM                      7 Upload 1.txt
226 Transfer complete.
53 bytes received in 0.00 seconds (53000.00 Kbytes/sec)
ftp> quit
221 Thank you for using Cmpny Corporation products.
```

This FTP session listing seems much more interesting. First we connected as an anonymous user to the virtual FTP site assigned to the *cmpny* host name. Upon connecting, we again issued a *dir* command. This time, the server displays the list of files and subdirectories in UNIX format. Did you notice that something is missing? The virtual directory Uploads is not displayed by the *dir* command. Remember that virtual directories are hidden and cannot be viewed using the *dir* or *ls* commands. However, you still can use the *cd* command to change to a virtual directory, but only if you happen to know the directory name. This facility enables you to create hidden directories, which can be very handy in certain situations. For instance, a corporate FTP site does not want to allow just any user to write files on their server. Creating a hidden directory with write permissions is one way to solve this problem. Only the users who know the hidden directory name can upload files to the site. If you want to create a directory that *ls* or *dir* will display, simply create a subdirectory of the FTP home directory. For example, if we create the Uploads directory under the physical FTP root directory (i.e., D:\InetPub\cmpny_ftproot \Uploads), we get the result shown in the following listing. (The FTP client command, *cd Uploads,* still takes the user to D:\SecureLocation\Uploads instead of D:\InetPub\cmpny_ftproot\Uploads.)

```
ftp> dir
200 PORT command successful.
150 Opening ASCII mode data connection for /bin/ls.
09-25-97  11:23PM       <DIR>          Uploads
09-20-97  11:24AM                   43 Welcome Cmpny.txt
09-16-97  06:53PM                  680 Cmpny File 1.txt
09-16-97  06:53PM                  680 Cmpny File 2.txt
226 Transfer complete.
214 bytes received in 0.01 seconds (21.40 Kbytes/sec)
```

Managing the FTP Server Programmatically

Finally, let's take a look at how we can manage our FTP server site programmatically. You can use IIS Admin Objects and IIS Admin Base Objects to programmatically access the Metabase, where all the FTP configuration information is stored. By changing these Metabase values, we can affect how our server behaves.

IIS Admin Objects

IIS Admin Objects are designed to be used by script-like languages that support accessing COM objects via an automation interface such as the COM *IDispatch* interface. IIS Admin Objects use Active Directory Service Interface (ADSI) notation to access various hierarchical locations of the Metabase. The Metabase structure hierarchy closely resembles the IIS installation—that is, it has structures to reflect multiple sites and virtual directories. The following table shows the FTP-related objects and how to address them in ADSI notation.

Object Name	ADSI Path
IIsFtpServer	IIS://*computername*/MSFTPSVC/*n*, where *n* is the index of the site
IIsFtpService	IIS://*computername*/MSFTPSVC
IIsFtpVirtualDir	IIS://*computername*/MSFTPSVC/*n*/Root, where *n* is the site ID and Root is a virtual directory; IIS://*computername*/MSFTPSVC/*n*/Root/*vdirName* for a specific virtual directory

The *IIsFtpServer* object supports the following methods: *Start*, *Pause*, *Continue*, and *Stop*. These methods let you to start or stop an FTP site from a script written in a language such as Visual Basic or VBScript. Here's an example of a script that stops the second FTP site on our server:

```
Dim ServerObj
' Stop the second FTP site (Cmpny Corporation FTP Site).
Set ServerObj = GetObject("IIS://LocalHost/MSFTPSVC/2")
ServerObj.Stop
```

We discussed the Metabase and how to set various properties using IIS Admin Objects in greater detail in Chapter 5.

NOTE

The Windows NT Options Pack ships with many scripts that demonstrate how to manipulate the Metabase and other aspects of IIS programmatically via IIS Admin Objects. These scripts are located in %SystemRoot%\system32\inetsrv\adminsamples *by default and are written in VBScript. They can be run directly from the command prompt using the Windows Scripting Host component (installed with either the Typical or Custom installation option). The following scripts control FTP sites: CONTFTP.VBS, PAUSEFTP.VBS, STARTFTP.VBS, STOPFTP.VBS.*

To get more help, run the desired script without parameters.

IIS Admin Base Object

Another component used for IIS management is the IIS Admin Base Object. Unlike IIS Admin Objects, the IIS Admin Base Object does not support OLE automation because it doesn't expose the *IDispatch* interface, which means that you have to be a C/C++ programmer to use it. Script-like languages cannot use this object. The IIS Admin Base Object can be used in C/C++ applications by accessing the *IMSAdminBase* interface. The *IMSAdminBase* interface provides a simple means to access and change Metabase properties.

Using the Admin Base Object is much more complex than using Admin Objects. Why then would you want to use it? The answer to this quandary is flexibility and speed. Using the Admin Base Object does not involve accessing methods exposed by objects via the *IDispatch* interface, making it a faster and more efficient technique. You will, however, need to write significantly more code than just a *ServerObj.Stop* line in Visual Basic or VBScript. The following source code, named FTPADMIN, demonstrates what's involved in writing a utility that can start, stop, and pause any FTP site by using IIS Admin Base Object:

```
#define UNICODE
#define INITGUID
#include <windows.h>
#include <stdio.h>
#include <iiscnfg.h>
#include <iadmw.h>
#include <stdlib.h>

int main (int argc, char** argv)
{
    IMSAdminBase *pIABase;
    TCHAR szMetaPath [128];
    METADATA_HANDLE mh;
```

(continued)

```
METADATA_RECORD mr = {0};
DWORD dwCommand;

if (argc != 3)
{
    printf ("Usage: %s site command\n",argv[0]);
    printf ("Commands: \n\tstop\n\tstart\n\tpause\n");
    return 0;
}
mr.dwMDIdentifier = MD_SERVER_COMMAND;
mr.dwMDAttributes = METADATA_NO_ATTRIBUTES;
mr.dwMDUserType = IIS_MD_UT_SERVER;
mr.dwMDDataType = DWORD_METADATA;
mr.dwMDDataLen = sizeof (DWORD_METADATA);

if ( !stricmp ("stop", argv[2]))
    dwCommand = MD_SERVER_COMMAND_STOP;
else if (!stricmp ("start", argv[2]))
    dwCommand = MD_SERVER_COMMAND_START;
else if (!stricmp ("pause", argv[2]))
    dwCommand = MD_SERVER_COMMAND_PAUSE;
else
{
    printf ("Unknown command\n");
    return 0;
}

CoInitialize(NULL);

HRESULT hRes = CoCreateInstance(CLSID_MSAdminBase,
                                NULL,
                                CLSCTX_ALL,
                                IID_IMSAdminBase,
                                (void**)&pIABase);

if (FAILED(hRes))
{
    printf ("CoCreateInstance(IID_IMSAdminBase) failed"
             "with error 0x%X\n", hRes);
    return 0;
}

wsprintf (szMetaPath, L"/LM/MSFTPSVC/%d", atoi (argv[1]) );
printf ("Opening handle %S\n", szMetaPath);
```

```
    hRes = pIABase->OpenKey(METADATA_MASTER_ROOT_HANDLE,
                            szMetaPath,
                            METADATA_PERMISSION_WRITE,
                            5000,
                            &mh);

    if (FAILED(hRes))
    {
        printf("OpenKey failed with error 0x%X\n", hRes);
        return 0;
    }

    mr.pbMDData = (unsigned char*) &dwCommand;
    // Send command to the server.
    // Real application must check current server state
    // via MD_SERVER_STATE property.
    hRes = pIABase->SetData(mh, NULL, &mr);
    if (FAILED(hRes))
    {
        printf ("SetData  failed with error 0x%X\n", hRes);
        pIABase->CloseKey (mh);
        return 0;
    }

    // Successful setting of MD_SERVER_COMMAND does not mean
    // that server changed state successfully.
    // Real applications should check server state via MD_WIN32_ERROR.

    printf ("Command completed successfully.\n");
    CoUninitialize();
    return 1;
}
```

As you can see, that's quite a bit of code just to control FTP sites compared to the few lines needed in Visual Basic. Here's how the utility can be used to stop and start the Default FTP Site:

```
D:\>ftpadmin 1 stop
Opening handle /LM/MSFTPSVC/1
Command completed successfully
D:\>ftpadmin 1 start
Opening handle /LM/MSFTPSVC/1
Command completed successfully
```

NOTE

This utility can be easily modified to control the Web Publishing Service. To do so, simply change /LM/MSFTPSVC to /LM/W3SVC.

In this chapter, we've seen how to configure and run the FTP server. We also examined three configuration tools: the Management Console, the HTML-based administration pages, and accessing the server's properties programmatically. Next on our to-do list is a discussion of the NNTP server; this is the topic of Chapter 10.

CHAPTER 10

News Server

Microsoft Internet Information Server is a complete Internet tool designed to support a variety of Internet protocols and services. The Network News Transfer Protocol (NNTP) and the Microsoft news server that implements it (also referred to as the NNTP service), are an integral part of IIS. News servers provide an industry-wide standard means of creating a collaborative environment. This environment enables you to create bulletin boards and similar areas in which people can engage in online discussions about various topics. Microsoft's NNTP service is robust enough to support thousands of users connecting and accessing news at the same time.

The NNTP service is implemented based on the Internet-standard NNTP. NNTP not only allows users to access bulletin boards, it also enables IIS to communicate with other news servers on the Internet in order to supply a *news feed*. Chapter 25 outlines in detail how different news servers communicate with each other (in Internet jargon, they provide a news feed) to exchange news articles (often referred to as messages).

An Internet news system is organized in the form of thousands of articles on various topics. To introduce order to this set of articles, messages are combined by topic into *newsgroups*. The heart of an individual news server, such as IIS, is the list of newsgroups and the database of news articles residing on the server. As soon as a newsgroup is created, the user can connect to the news server and start posting messages. The NNTP service keeps track of when posted articles were created and when they should be deleted, and it uses expiration policies to enforce an article's lifetime. By creating more than one expiration policy, you can establish different rules for different newsgroups.

For example, on our IIS server, we have created a few newsgroups dedicated to the different aspects of producing this book. The newsgroup *leonbr.book.artwork* contains messages regarding the artwork used in this book; *leonbr.book.publishing* contains information about and discussions on publishing issues in general. This newsgroup structure facilitates collaboration between the book's coauthors, the publisher, and other people involved in the book's production.

Each news server knows how long to save an article in a newsgroup, based on the specified expiration policies. This means that the news administrator can set rules governing the lifetime of a news article. Once an article has expired, the news server deletes it. Setting a reasonable lifetime for articles prevents the news server from becoming clogged with old news.

An NNTP server can also be a welcome addition to a corporate intranet as a valuable information exchange tool. Individual departments might want to keep each other posted about current projects, exchange ideas, and solicit comments from all employees. Different news servers can communicate with one another; in this way, news articles posted on one corporate server with a connection to the Internet can be read by users on the other side of the world. Chapter 25 explains the magic of news transfer and the limitations of the news server included with the Microsoft Windows NT 4.0 Option Pack in terms of its receiving capabilities. But before you can enjoy all the benefits of an NNTP server, you need to learn how to install and configure it.

Installing the NNTP Service

We'll start our discussion with the installation of the NNTP service. Neither the Minimal nor the Typical installation option of the Microsoft Windows NT 4.0 Option Pack installs the NNTP service. To install it, you must choose the Custom installation option.

NOTE

Of course, if you do choose the Minimal or Typical installation option, NNTP service can be added later. To do so, start the Windows NT Option Pack Setup program again and choose Add/Remove Components.

Next, select Internet Information Server from the Components list and click the Show Subcomponents button. In the Internet Information Service dialog box, select Internet NNTP Service from the list box and click the Show Subcomponents button to display the Internet NNTP dialog box. This procedure is shown in Figure 10.1. Notice that the Internet NNTP service list box contains two subcomponents: NNTP Service and NNTP Service Documentation. Don't forget to select NNTP Service Documentation; you might need it in the future. Last, click OK to move on.

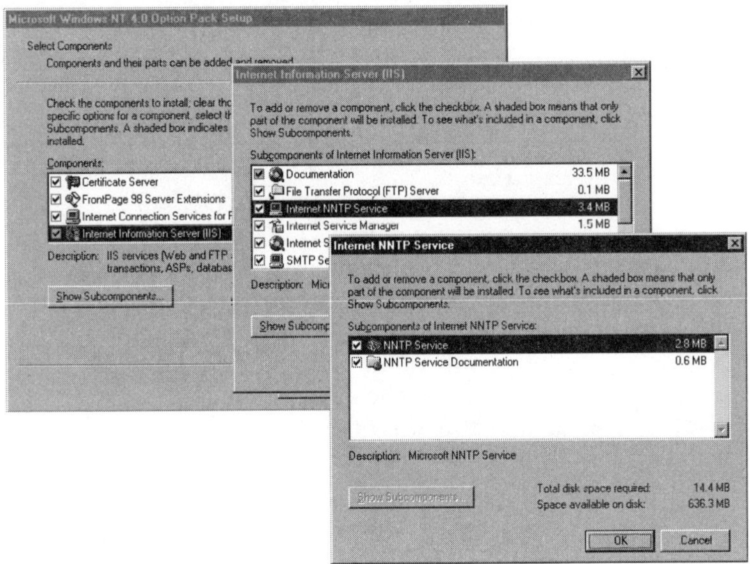

FIGURE 10.1

Using the Windows NT 4.0 Option Pack Setup to install NNTP service.

Directory Structure

The NNTP service installation routine creates two separate directory structures. One directory structure begins at the \InetPub\News location. All directories under this point contain scripts and supporting files for the HTML-based administration pages. The second directory structure begins at the \InetPub\nntpfile location. These directories contain information pertaining to the news database. As soon as the NNTP service is installed, new files are created directly under \InetPub\nntpfile. These files are used exclusively by the NNTP service to perform tasks such as maintaining an internal *hash table* for news articles and indexing files with auxiliary article information. The files contain enough information to enable the server to rebuild a corrupted news database (not that this database is likely to become corrupted).

Glossary

hash table *Special data structure used to organize large amounts of data (such as a news database) when different data items (such as individual articles) must be quickly accessed. Each data item has an identifier (such as an article ID) that is used to locate the entire item (such as the text of the article). The news server uses the hash table to convert an identifier or a key, meaningful to the user, to a value for the location of the corresponding element in the tablelike structure.*

Usually, the administrator does not need to access directories or files in \InetPub\nntpfile directly. One directory deserves special attention, however: \InetPub\nntpfile\root. Every time a newsgroup is created, the NNTP service will create a new directory for this group in the root directory. Several groups are created automatically, immediately following installation: *control.cancel*, *control.newgroup*, *control.rmgroup*, and *microsoft.public.ins*. In addition, on our NNTP service, we have created three more groups: *leonbr.book.artwork*, *leonbr.book.publishing*, and *leonbr.running.iis*. Figure 10.2 shows the directory structure created by NNTP service to accommodate all of these groups. Other news servers will create unique directory structures, depending on their newsgroups, but all will follow a similar hierarchical structure.

```
D:\WINNT\System32\cmd.exe

D:\Inetpub\nntpfile>tree root
Directory PATH listing
Volume serial number is 0012FC94 6C83:F753
D:\INETPUB\NNTPFILE\ROOT
├───control
│   ├───cancel
│   ├───newgroup
│   └───rmgroup
├───leonbr
│   ├───book
│   │   ├───artwork
│   │   └───publishing
│   └───running
│       └───iis
├───microsoft
│   └───public
│       └───ins
├───_SLAVEGROUP
└───_temp.files_

D:\Inetpub\nntpfile>
```

FIGURE 10.2

Directory structure created by NNTP service to accommodate newly created groups.

Managing the NNTP Service

Once the NNTP service is installed, you need to configure it to suit your needs. Compared to the Web server or FTP server, NNTP service doesn't provide much in the way of configuration options. The most important aspect of NNTP service configuration is the creation of newsgroups.

As with any component of IIS, NNTP service can be managed using more than one tool. The Microsoft Management Console with the news server snap-in enables you to manage the news server installed on your local computer as well as connect to any server on the local area network. Using the HTML-based administration pages, you can manage news servers over the Internet; you don't need any special software other than a Web browser. The HTML-based administration pages are accessible via *http://computername/news/admin* or from your Start menu. Under Programs, select Windows NT 4.0 Option Pack, Microsoft Internet Information Server, and Microsoft NNTP Service; you will see the NNTP Service Manager (HTML) entry there.

NOTE

By default, the Web server denies access to this URL to all IP addresses other than the loopback 127.0.0.1 address (that is, the loopback from the browser on the local machine). If you intend to manage your news server via a Web browser, go to the Default Web Site in the Management Console, locate the News virtual directory, display the Directory Security page of the News Properties window, and modify the list of acceptable IP addresses.

Whether you are using the Management Console or the HTML-based administration pages, keep in mind that only authorized users can manage the NNTP service. In the "Security Accounts" section later in this chapter, we'll learn how to modify the list of users.

As you've seen in previous chapters, management tasks can be accomplished using either the Management Console or the HTML-based administration pages. For simplicity's sake, the discussions in this chapter will focus on using the Management Console to perform all management tasks. Unlike the more complex Web Publishing service, the NNTP service operates a limited set of logical objects: news site, newsgroup, expiration policy, and current session. The NNTP service supports only one site on the physical machine (unlike the WWW and FTP servers, which allow you to have multiple sites on the same machine).

NOTE

Microsoft Site Server and its predecessor, Microsoft Commercial Internet Server (MCIS), support multiple news sites for a single machine.

The Management Console, shown in Figure 10.3, displays the Default NNTP Site, expiration policies, directories, and current sessions objects. A list of newsgroups maintained by NNTP service isn't visible in the Management Console window, but it is accessible via the Default NNTP Site Properties window.

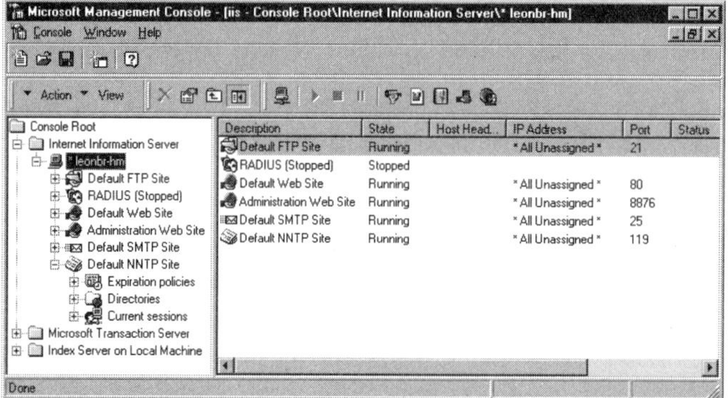

FIGURE 10.3

NNTP service in the Management Console, showing the Default NNTP Site, expiration policies, directories, and current session's objects.

Default NNTP Site Properties

All the configuration settings for the NNTP service are accessible from the Default NNTP Site Properties window, shown in Figure 10.4. To open this window, right-click on the Default NNTP Site in the Management Console window and select Properties.

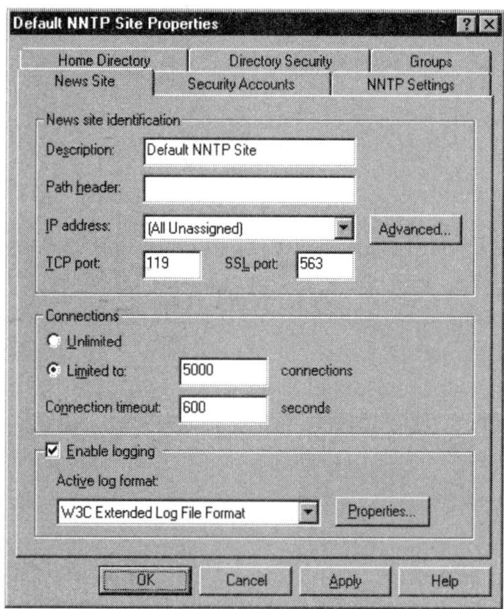

FIGURE 10.4

The Default NNTP Site Properties window, showing the News Site page.

News Site

The News Site page of the Default NNTP Site Properties window, shown in Figure 10.4, lets you change the news site identification information, connections, and logging properties. The Description entered here will be displayed in the Management Console next to the news server icon. The Path Header describes how a news article is identified as it passes from server to server. Individual news articles are formatted much like e-mail messages—headers are followed by a message body. The message headers identify exactly how the news article appeared on the server along with other helpful information. News servers intercommunicate to propagate news articles among all the news servers on a network. Every time a message hops from one news server to another, that news server's name is added to the path header. For example, because our IIS server is the machine *leonbr-hm*, by default the path header for news posted to (or transferred from) this machine will contain the leonbr-hm string. The path header can be changed by typing an alternative string in the Path Header field. But why would someone want to change the news server's identity? Imagine a server that floods hundreds of newsgroups with unsolicited offers like "Make $1,000 a day!" In this case, the administrator wants to keep the real server name hidden. (If the concept of transferring news from server to server is not yet clear to you, Chapter 25 will explain all the details of how NNTP works.)

By default, the NNTP service uses TCP port 119 for unencrypted communications and port 563 for Secure Sockets Layer (SSL)–encrypted connections. These ports are known to all news clients; therefore, users don't need to explicitly specify ports. IIS allows you to change the default ports, but if you do so, you will need to be sure that connecting users know what ports they should be using.

Similar to the Web and FTP servers, the NNTP service can run on a machine with more than one network card (or with more than one IP address assigned to the same card). The default IP Address setting, (All Unassigned), accepts connections destined to all configured IP addresses. You can change this setting simply by choosing another option from this list box. Clicking the Advanced button displays the Advanced Multiple News Site Configuration dialog box, shown in Figure 10.5, which gives you access to even more interesting features. Using this dialog box, the administrator can specify pairs of IP addresses and ports. In this example, we have selected a different port number for each IP address used by our computer—the NNTP service is configured to accept unsecured connections on port 1019 for IP address 192.155.1.1 and on port 1515 for IP address 192.155.1.2.

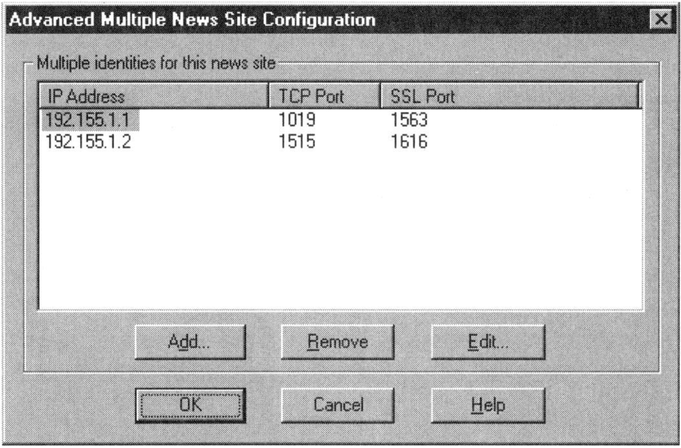

FIGURE 10.5

The Advanced Multiple News Site Configuration dialog box.

The Connections area of the News Site page lets you specify the number of connections the NNTP service will accept—you can either allow an unlimited number of connections or specify an upper limit. The Connections Timeout option specifies a time limit after which inactive clients will be disconnected. In this example, Connections Timeout is set to 600 seconds, meaning that clients connecting to this server will be disconnected after 10 minutes of inactivity.

Like any component of IIS, the NNTP service can generate extensive activity logs. These log files contain detailed information about connecting clients, issued commands, and the completion status of commands. The NNTP service supports the same variety of log settings and formats as the Web and FTP servers. The first step in generating logs is to check the Enable Logging check box on the News Site page. The second step is to log permissions on individual directories in which the news contents are stored; to do this, we need to learn how to set directory properties.

Home Directory

Similar to the Web Publishing service and the FTP server, the NNTP service has a root directory and virtual directories. The function of these directories in the NNTP service is somewhat different, however. The NNTP service uses the root directory and virtual directories to store articles. As we saw in Figure 10.2 on page 240, the directory structure mimics the newsgroups hosted by the news server. The name of a specific newsgroup can be obtained by traversing the directory tree—for example, leonbr to book to artwork leads to *leonbr.book.artwork*. By default, IIS creates an initial, or home, directory tree in the \InetPub\nntpfile\root directory. It is possible, however, to spread directories representing newsgroups across multiple hard drives, multiple directories, or even multiple computers (in which case, the directory hierarchy would appear somewhere other than under \InetPub\nntpfile\root). Such an act might be necessitated by a lack of hard drive space in the home directory location; it is accomplished by creating a virtual directory.

To create a virtual directory, right-click on the Default NNTP Site in the Management Console window and choose Virtual Directory from the New menu. IIS prompts you for two important pieces of information: the newsgroups that should be hosted in this virtual directory and the physical location of the directory. For example, suppose we have created a virtual directory to host the "security" news hierarchy. For this directory's physical location, we have specified d:\InetPub\security. From this point on, for each new group under security (*security.hacking*, *security.protection*, and so on), IIS creates a new subdirectory under d:\InetPub\security, *not* under its default home directory location d:\InetPub\nntpfile\root. To see a list of virtual directories, click on the Directories folder in the Management Console window.

Both the home and virtual directories can be located on the local machine or on another computer. The properties for the Home Directory are controlled through the Home Directory page of the Default NNTP Site Properties window, as shown in Figure 10.6. The properties for virtual directories, however, are controlled through the Virtual Directory page of the Properties window for the virtual directory d:\InetPub\security, as shown in Figure 10.7. As you can see, these two pages are almost identical.

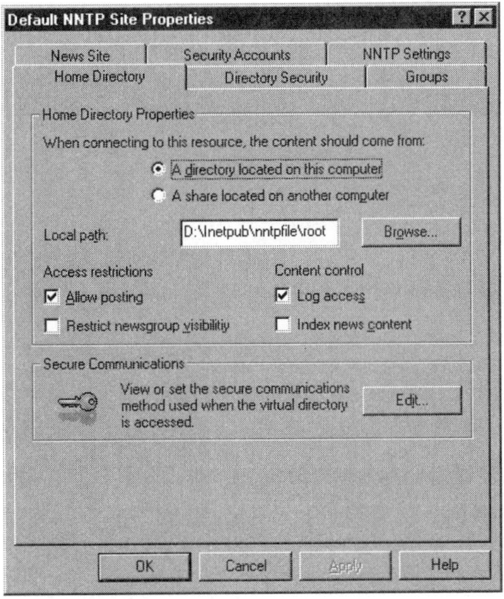

FIGURE 10.6

The Home Directory page of the Default NNTP Site Properties window.

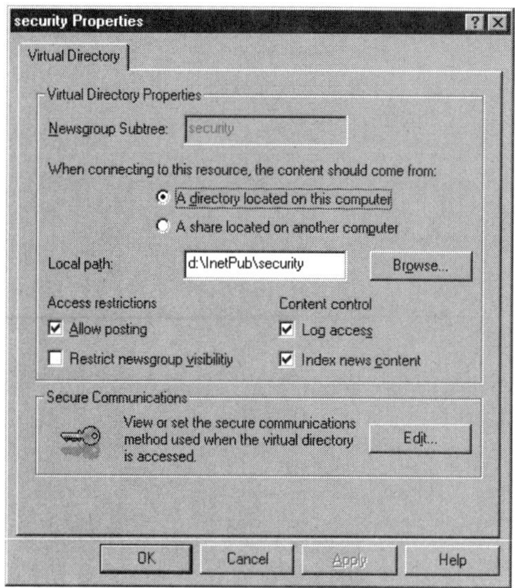

FIGURE 10.7

The Virtual Directory page of the Security Properties window.

The directory path is specified in the Local Path edit box. If you check the A Share Located On Another Computer option, the Browse button becomes a Connect As button and Local Path changes to Network Directory. The Network Directory path is specified by using its Uniform Naming Convention location (for example, \\computername\share) and valid user credentials (user name and user password) that are entered in the Network Directory Security Credentials dialog box, which is displayed when you click the Connect As button.

The Access Restrictions and Content Control check boxes affect the user's ability to post articles in the specified directory (actually in all newsgroups hosted under the specified directory). Restricting the newsgroup visibility causes news clients to not show newsgroups when the client does not supply a user name and password and the server does not allow anonymous connections. When logging is enabled, checking the Log Access check box forces the server to create a log entry for the client connection. Microsoft Index Server will index the contents of all news messages when Index News Content is checked.

Under normal circumstances, NNTP is not a secure protocol. Client and server exchange all information over the network in clear text, which may pose a security problem if the newsgroups contain sensitive information. Clicking the Edit button in the Secure Communications area displays the dialog box shown in Figure 10.8, in which the system administrator can specify only secure connections to the directory.

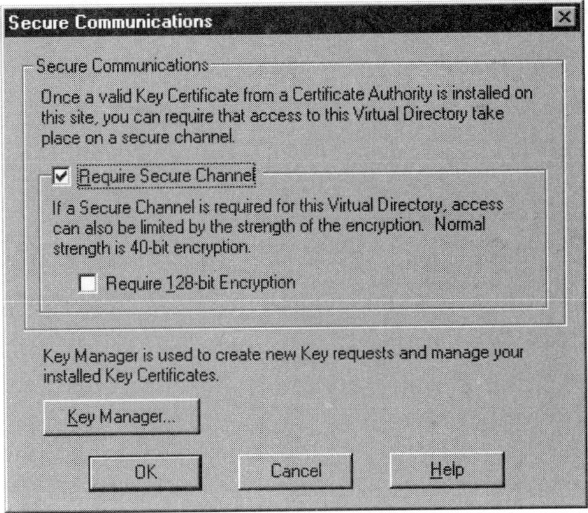

FIGURE 10.8

The Secure Communications dialog box.

Directory Security

The name of the Directory Security page is somewhat unclear. This page lets you configure security parameters for the entire news site, not just for the individual directories. The Directory Security page, shown in Figure 10.9, has only two buttons (both labeled Edit): one controls anonymous access and authentication methods, the other controls restrictions on client connections.

By default, connecting clients (such as Microsoft Outlook Express) don't have to provide a user name or password to connect to the NNTP server; the news server would work just fine for a public news site where anybody is welcome to connect and read the news. But if NNTP server is used to host private newsgroups only, it might be desirable to require the user to enter his or her name and password. The NNTP service is capable not only of restricting anonymous access but also of supporting various *authentication schemes*—methods used to transfer credentials from the client to the server. Clicking the Edit button in the Password Authentication Method area allows the administrator to disable anonymous access to the server. If anonymous access is disabled, one of the authentication schemes must be enabled.

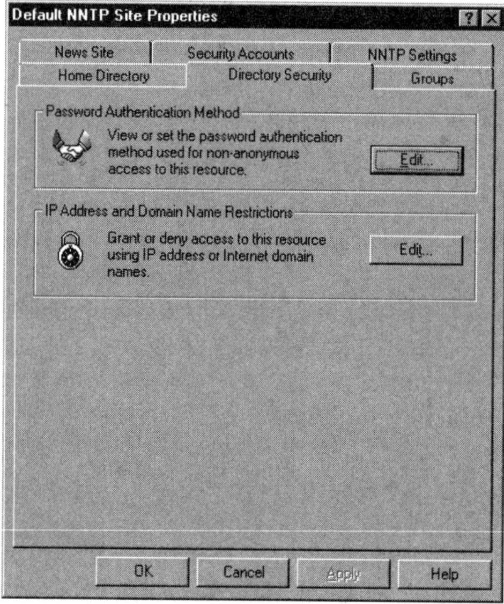

FIGURE 10.9

The Directory Security page.

Like the Web server, the NNTP service supports basic authentication (in which the user name and password are transferred as clear text), the NT Lan Manager (NTLM) authentication scheme (in which the user password never travels over the network), and client certificate–based authentication (in which a client is uniquely identified over an encrypted connection by a client certificate). Unlike the HTTP protocol, NNTP does not allow the news client and server to negotiate authenticated schemes and user credentials on the fly. This means that if the server does not allow anonymous connections and it supports the basic authentication scheme, the news client must be configured to provide a user name and password in clear text as soon as it attempts to perform any actions on the server.

Implementing access control based on a user's credentials is a powerful security feature. Like the other components of IIS, the NNTP service can restrict access based on the client IP address or domain name. To set these restrictions, click the Edit button in the IP Address And Domain Name Restrictions area. The corresponding dialog box is essentially the same as its Web Publishing service and FTP server counterparts, so we won't show it again here.

NNTP Settings

The NNTP Settings page, shown in Figure 10.10, is where the general server parameters are set. If posting is allowed (Allow Client Posting is checked), the news administrator can limit the size of a single article by using the Limit Post Size option and limit the total size of all posted articles across an established connection by using the Limit Connection Size option. When setting these limits, don't forget to take into account file attachments. Articles might contain attachments such as JPEG files or EXE files. Attachments are encoded, so every character in a binary file could be represented by a printable character and included in the text of the news article. Including binary files in the article text might dramatically increase the article's size.

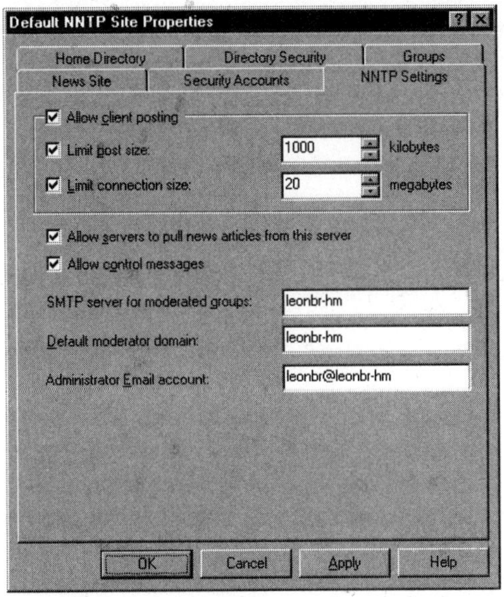

FIGURE 10.10

The NNTP Settings page.

You might have noticed that we have seen two places in which we can choose the Allow Post option: on the Home Directory or Virtual Directory page and on the NNTP Settings page. You can also control posting in the properties windows of individual newsgroups. Configuring posting capability in three locations enables precise news server control. The Allow Post option on the NNTP Settings page has the broadest effect; the Allow Posting option on the Visual and Home Directory pages affects only newsgroups hosted in the specified path; and setting posting permission in the properties windows of individual newsgroups is the most granular technique.

As mentioned, news servers can transfer news messages from one server to another. The NNTP service is capable of providing a news feed to other servers, but it can't accept contents from them. (This is a limitation of the news server included with the Windows NT Option Pack.) The Allow Servers To Pull News Articles From This Server check box controls NNTP service's ability to provide a news feed. If this check box is unchecked, other news servers won't be able to get the latest news from IIS.

When news servers exchange their contents, they can also send each other news articles that have a special Control header or a *CMSG* string in their Subject line. Such news articles can also be posted directly by the news client. These messages are called *control messages;* they usually reside in a special newsgroup hierarchy (such as *control.cancel*, *control.addgroup*, and so on). Control messages are used to ask the server to perform some administrative task, such as creating newsgroups, deleting existing groups, or deleting certain messages. Control messages are transferred just like any other message; the message's author does not need to have any administration rights to your server. In a way, anyone who knows NNTP well enough (as you will, after reading Chapter 25) can create control messages and force the server to manipulate groups and messages. This capability might not be desirable or secure for some servers. Unchecking the Allow Control Messages check box is one technique for defending your news server against control messages.

If posting is allowed for specific newsgroups, a client can post any article it wants to (limited only by the article's size). Again, this might not be desirable for all groups. For example, suppose we have a *support.isapidev.programming* newsgroup dedicated to ISAPI development. Before anyone posts an article, we'd like to have an ISAPI programmer review the article thoroughly for technical accuracy. (We don't want to post incorrect information.) This task can be accomplished by making *support.isapidev.programming* a *moderated newsgroup*. Articles posted to moderated newsgroups don't show up on the server automatically. Instead, the news server forwards them to a specified e-mail address. The e-mail recipient—in this case, an ISAPI programmer—reviews each article and then decides whether to post it or delete it. This process ensures that only approved content goes out the door (which might be a perfect solution for a censored group such as *corporate.public.relationship*).

The SMTP Server For Moderated Groups option on the NNTP Settings page configures the mail server used by NNTP service to connect and send e-mail notifications regarding new postings. The Default Moderator Domain option specifies the domain to which e-mail should be sent. For example, our computer doesn't use a domain name structure and is running the SMTP server. To send e-mail to anyone on this machine, we would use user@leonbr-hm, where *leonbr-hm* is the domain. If this machine were a member of the *corp.com* domain and smtp.corp.com were a mail server, the default domain would be *corp.com*. If a new message is posted in the moderated newsgroup and for some reason can't be delivered to the moderator, the server generates a non-delivery report—(just a fancily formatted error message) and sends it to the news server administrator's e-mail account.

NOTE

By default, the e-mail from a news server does not have a From header (the From field appears blank). For non-delivery reports to be sent to the administrator, you need to force the server to add a From header. To do so, create a MailFromHeader *DWORD registry entry and set it to* 1 *in the following registry location:* HKEY_LOCAL_MACHINE\SYSTEM\CurrentControlSet\Services\NntpSvc\Parameters.

Groups

Maintaining current newsgroups and creating new groups is what the NNTP service is all about. Figure 10.11 shows the Groups page, which enables the administrator to create a new group, change the properties of an existing group, or delete a group.

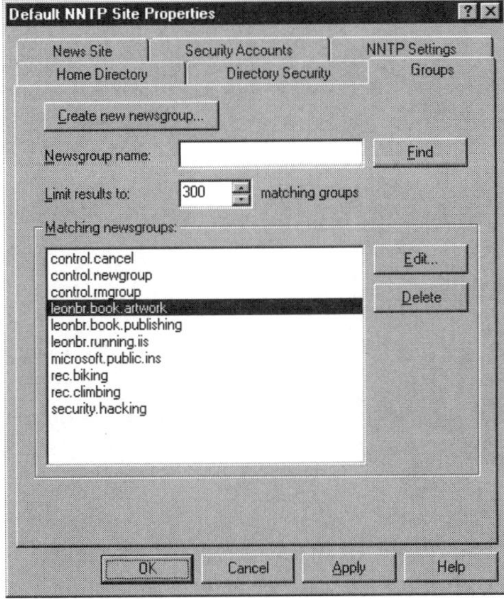

FIGURE 10.11

The Groups page.

Changing a property of an existing newsgroup by clicking the Edit button or creating a new group by clicking the Create New Newsgroup button displays the Newsgroup Properties window, shown in Figure 10.12.

FIGURE 10.12

The Newsgroup Properties window.

As you can see here, newsgroups are identified by name and description. Some news browsing software also provides the newsgroup's nickname, or *prettyname*. The prettyname may even contain foreign language characters (in Unicode). You can also create newsgroups that are read only, meaning that clients won't be able to post messages to this group.

As mentioned, the Newsgroup Properties window is the third place in which you can control posting permission. If the newsgroup is moderated, the server needs to know where to send the new posting e-mail notifications. If the Moderated By Default Newsgroup Moderator option is checked, the server automatically creates an e-mail address in the form *group@default_domain*, where *group* is the name of the current group and *default_domain* is the moderator's domain as configured on the NNTP Settings page. If for some reason you want one address to be used for all moderated groups, enter this address in the Moderated By edit box. As you might have noticed, nowhere in this dialog box is the physical path of the newsgroup specified. The news server itself decides where to host newsgroups based on its virtual directories or its default home directory location.

Newsgroup moderation comes in handy when you are processing control messages. By default, the server has three control groups in which control messages can be posted: *control.cancel*, *control.newgroup*, and *control.rmgroup*. If control messages are not disabled on the NNTP Settings page, they are posted in these groups. By changing the properties of these groups and making them moderated, the administrator is able to examine control messages before they affect the server. If a control message is approved, the moderator can let it through; otherwise, the moderator can delete the message. Making control groups moderated allows better message handling than just banning them.

Security Accounts

In the course of this discussion of the Default NNTP Site Properties window, we have passed freely from one property page to another. Not just any user on a Windows NT system can do this, however—only recognized news site operators are allowed to make these modifications. A list of the users allowed to administer the NNTP service can be created on the Security Accounts page, shown in Figure 10.13. This list of authorized users applies to the HTML-based administration pages as well.

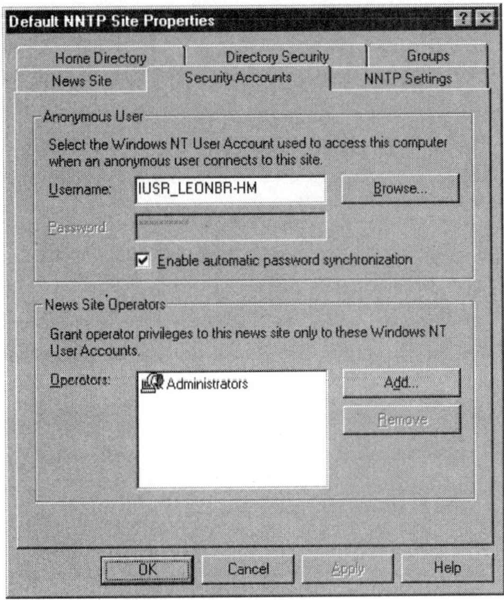

FIGURE 10.13

The Security Accounts page.

Like the Web Publishing Service, the NNTP service runs as the Local System account and impersonates the anonymous user for all nonauthenticated incoming connections. The server accesses news articles in the context of the IUSR_*computername* user—the default anonymous Internet user for the system. To avoid confusing the password IIS remembers for IUSR_*computername* and the actual password in the user database for the IUSR_*computername* account, check the Enable Automatic Password Synchronization check box.

Expiration Policies

As we've seen, expiration policies contain the rules that define the lifetimes of news articles. To view existing expiration policies, click the Expiration Policies icon in the Management Console. To create a new expiration policy, right-click on Default

NNTP Site and choose Expiration Policy from the New menu to open the New Expiration Policy Wizard. This wizard needs the following information for each expiration policy it creates:

- The policy name.
- The newsgroups affected: all groups or selected groups only. If the policy will apply to selected groups only, the names of those groups must be entered. The wildcard character * can be used to denote "any."
- Expiration conditions: the total size of the newsgroup, the age of the article, or both.

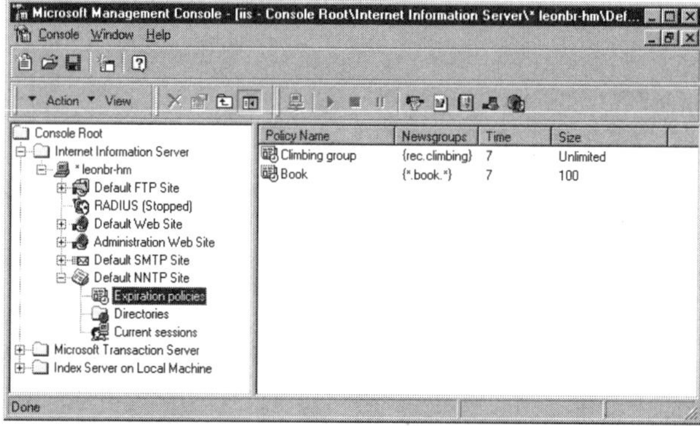

FIGURE 10.14

A list of expiration policies, as displayed in the Management Console.

A list of expiration policies can be viewed in the Management Console, as shown in Figure 10.14. This example list shows the expiration policy Book, which affects all *.book.* groups. Articles are deleted when their total size exceeds 100 MB or when they are more than seven days old.

NOTE

The expiration functions of NNTP service are controlled by the following registry entries in HKEY_LOCAL_MACHINE\SYSTEM\CurrentControlSet\Services\NntpSvc\Parameters*:*

- NewsCrawlerTime *(REG_DWORD, default 30 minutes) defines how often the server should search for expired articles as specified by the expiration policies.*
- NumExpireThreads *(REG_DWORD, default 4) defines how many threads are used by the server to search for expired messages.*

Current Sessions

Monitoring server performance is an important administrative task. Several tools are available that can show past and present server status. Performance counters accessible from the Windows NT Performance Monitor utility and the NNTP server logs can provide a wealth of information about the server. The Perfmon utility and logging are discussed in Chapter 6.

The Management Console can also display a list of currently connected users. To view this list, click on Current Sessions, as shown in Figure 10.15. This example shows two connected users: *leonbr* and *joeb*. If the server allows anonymous connections, the user name would be replaced by a computer icon.

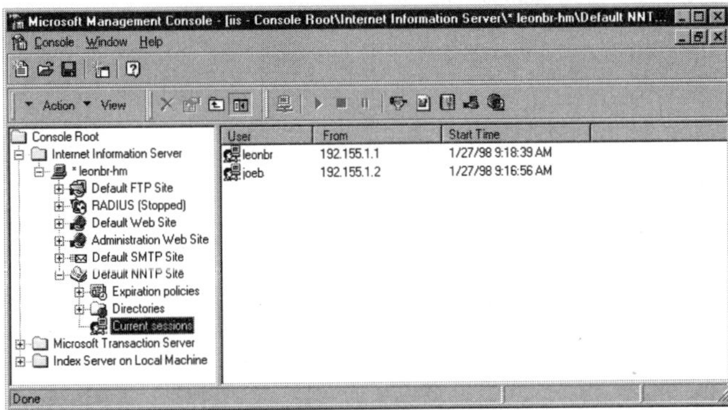

FIGURE 10.15

The list of currently connected users.

Corruption Recovery

The NNTP service is capable of hosting gigabytes of news. News articles are stored as relatively small text files. The news server uses auxiliary files to help organize potentially thousands of independent files in a searchable data structure. Even when articles are accidentally moved or deleted, the index and hash files still contain references to them and their original physical location. Moving groups to different directories without rebuilding the index file can cause the server to "forget" that it still has articles and not just empty newsgroups. To recover from such a situation, the NNTP service provides a Rebuild option. To rebuild a server, you must first stop the NNTP service, either by selecting the Default NNTP Site and clicking the Stop button on the Management Console toolbar or by right-clicking on the site and selecting Stop. Once the service has been stopped, you can rebuild by right-clicking on the site and choosing Rebuild Server from the Task menu. Figure 10-16 shows the resulting Rebuild News Server dialog box.

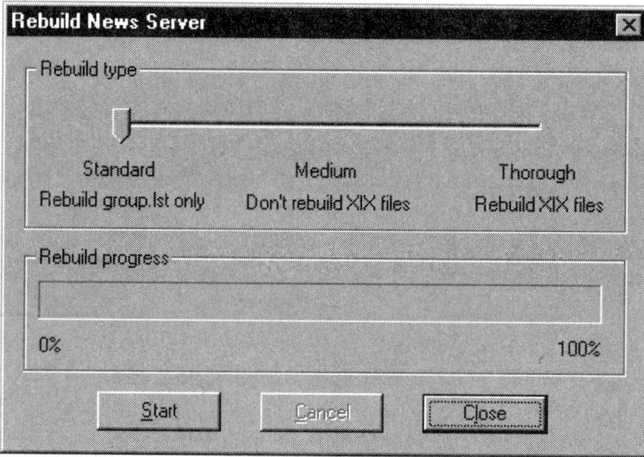

FIGURE 10.16

The Rebuild News Server dialog box.

This dialog box provides three rebuild options: Standard, Medium, and Thorough. The Standard option is the fastest; it rebuilds only the hash table file (GROUP.LST). The Medium option rebuilds files that are perceived to be faulty. The Thorough option rebuilds all files; it is the most time-consuming option. Once a server is rebuilt, you can restart the NNTP site by using the Start button on the toolbar of the Management Console.

Managing the NNTP Service Programmatically

In addition to using the Management Console or HTML-based administration pages, the NNTP service can be managed from the command line or via a custom application. The NNTP service includes a few scripts written in VBScript that can be run from the command line.

NOTE

These scripts will run only with the Windows Scripting Host (WSH) installed. WSH is installed using the Typical or Custom installation option. WSH allows script files to be run directly from the Windows NT command line. See the Windows NT 4.0 Option Pack documentation for more details about WSH.

These scripts are located in the IIS system directory (by default, %SystemRoot%\system32\inetsrv) and support a wide variety of tasks, including the following:

- Changing expiration polices (REXPIRE.VBS).
- Changing groups (RGROUP.VBS)—allows for the creation, deletion, and modification of group properties.
- Session manipulation (RSESS.VBS).
- Server manipulation (RSERVER.VBS)—allows the changing of site parameters. Note that even though this script has the ability to create a new NNTP site, it will not work on the news server included with the Windows NT Option Pack. This version allows only one Default NNTP Site.

Like the other services installed with the Windows NT Option Pack, the NNTP service can be managed programmatically. The IIS Admin Objects interface can be used from scripting languages (like the .VBS applications listed above), or the IIS Admin Base Objects interface can be used directly from applications written in C/C++. In Chapter 9, in which we discussed the FTP server, we saw two programming samples: IIS Admin Objects and IIS Admin Base Object. With minimal modifications, the same samples would work for the news server. To make them manage the NNTP service, simply change all references to MSFTPSVC to NNTPSVC, and use *1* as the site identifier (*1* denotes the Default NNTP Site). Remember that changing MSFTPSVC in scripts to W3SVC converts the scripts to the WWW service management tool.

So far, we have covered three major components of IIS: the Web Publishing Service, the FTP service, and the NNTP service. Last but not least, we will focus our attention on the SMTP server, the topic of the next chapter.

CHAPTER 11

Mail Server

Electronic mail, or e-mail, is the key communication system for a company wanting a powerful collaborative environment. IIS provides an industry standard e-mail solution using the Simple Mail Transport Protocol (SMTP) component to transmit and deliver Internet mail. In this chapter, we'll look at how to configure your e-mail system by using the SMTP component of IIS. SMTP is discussed in greater detail in Chapter 26.

The Internet Mail System

The general idea behind an Internet mail system is simple. One user sends an e-mail message to another user at a specific address—for example, to *Jane@microsoft.com.* The receiving user, Jane, uses an e-mail client to read the message. But the actual process of mail delivery is rather complex. The component of IIS that makes it all work is SMTP.

Sending E-Mail

The mail delivery process starts when a client such as Microsoft Outlook Express sends a message to an SMTP server. A client knows only one server, so all messages originating on the local client, regardless of their final destinations, go to the same server. The local SMTP server is then responsible for figuring out what to do with the message, which is just an ASCII file with a bunch of special text headers. Think of these headers as the address information you'd find on a standard mail envelope.

If the destination domain of the e-mail message is a local domain for the server (for example, the e-mail is sent to *Joe@domain.com* and the SMTP server is *smtp.domain.com*), the ASCII message is stored on that server. Otherwise the message is forwarded to another appropriate server.

All SMTP servers on a network can communicate with one another via the same "language," and as you might have guessed by now, this common language is the SMTP protocol. But how does that initial server decide where to pass the message? It performs a Domain Name System (DNS) lookup for the domain. An example scenario will clarify how this works.

Suppose we start Microsoft Outlook and send a message to *Joe@cmpny.com*. Because *cmpny.com* is not a local domain for our SMTP server, our server performs a DNS lookup for the domain. The SMTP server is especially interested in the DNS Mail Exchanger (MX) record, which is the IP address (or name) of the SMTP server that is servicing all incoming mail for the *cmpny.com* domain. Once the IP address is located, our SMTP server knows where to connect. The message travels from our Outlook Outbox to the local SMTP server, which in turn passes the message along to the e-mail server for *cmpny.com*.

Now we know how a user sends an e-mail message, but we still don't know how the user reads an e-mail message. We'll look at that in the next section.

Delivering E-Mail and the POP3 Component

In the life of an e-mail, one more component comes into play—the Post Office Protocol (POP). POP is a protocol by which users can retrieve their e-mail. It is typically referred to with its version number, such as POP3. A server that provides the POP3 service (a POP3 server) waits for connections from clients. When a client connects, it identifies itself with a user name and a password, which are validated by the server. When the user is validated, the POP3 server sends the user's e-mail messages from the SMTP message storage to the user's inbox. Typically the SMTP server has a directory for each mail user, which is analogous to a user's mailbox. This directory structure allows POP3 to efficiently retrieve all messages for the specified user.

Let's recap the process. E-mail is delivered to the appropriate SMTP server, where it is stored in a specific user's mailbox. The target client connects to this server via the POP3 protocol, and the message is finally delivered to the local mail client application such as Outlook Express. Two server processes, then, are involved in the sending and retrieval of e-mail: SMTP—which sends mail and uses port 25—and POP3—which retrieves mail and uses port 110. Figure 11.1 illustrates the relationship of SMTP to mail delivery.

It is possible to write an application that reads mail messages directly from SMTP message storage without using the POP3 protocol. After all, e-mail messages are just ASCII files on the SMTP machine. Retrieving mail from SMTP local e-mail storage to the client's inbox is a convenient option.

NOTE

Some systems (mostly UNIX platforms) provide a direct interface to SMTP message storage. Users can connect to their SMTP server and read e-mail directly from the SMTP mailbox. However, having e-mail delivered to the inbox folder of the e-mail client application, such as Outlook Express via POP3, is a much more convenient option. (For example, you can then use the various Inbox Assistant rules.)

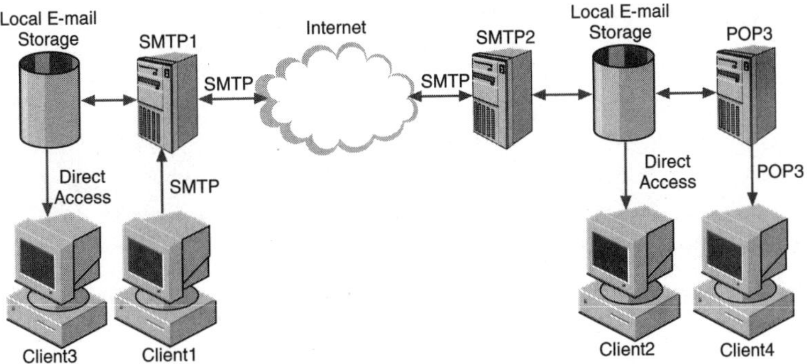

FIGURE 11.1

The role of SMTP in the e-mail delivery process.

As you can see in Figure 11.1, regardless of the final e-mail destination, Client1 always sends all outgoing mail to its SMTP server, SMTP1. Client1 and SMTP1 communicate via SMTP. If mail is sent to the domain directly serviced by SMTP1, the server simply deposits the mail message in the designated client's mailbox. From the mailbox, the client can retrieve the e-mail messages in one of two ways:

1. By directly accessing the mail message (as Client3 does in Figure 11.1). To do this the client must have direct access to the server's file system where the mail files reside.
2. By connecting to a POP3 server that has access to the file system containing the mail files. If the client does not have direct access to the server's file system, it can retrieve mail messages in this way. (See the Client4 machine in Figure 11.1.)

If mail sent by Client1 is addressed for a domain serviced by another SMTP server, the local SMTP server (SMTP1) establishes a network connection to the appropriate server (SMTP2 in this case) and transfers the mail via SMTP. Note that after the SMTP server deposits mail to the mailbox on the file system, it doesn't care what happens to the message. Its mission is accomplished. In fact, there is no formal connection between SMTP, which is used to send mail, and the POP3 protocol, which is used to deliver mail to local computers from the SMTP server.

IIS Mail Solution: CDO for NTS

Now that you have some background in Internet mail systems, you can better understand what IIS provides: IIS has an SMTP service but no POP3 service. The IIS SMTP service is a scaled-down version of the SMTP service provided by the Microsoft Site Server or Microsoft Commercial Internet System (MCIS), which supports mailboxes and the transfer of messages from users' mailboxes to their client applications (such as Outlook Express or QUALCOMM's Eudora).

The IIS SMTP service provides only mail delivery functionality; it is not intended to aid in the receipt of mail. With only one directory for all incoming messages, IIS SMTP does not sort messages for users into individual mailboxes. It either forwards messages to other SMTP servers (if the message is addressed to a remote domain) or stores messages in a global directory (\Mailroot\Drop by default).

You might wonder how SMTP can weed through potentially hundreds of files in the Drop directory (each file representing a single e-mail message) and find files destined for a particular e-mail recipient. Microsoft includes a special component with IIS, the Collaboration Data Objects for Microsoft Windows NT Server, also known as the CDO for NTS Library. The CDO for NTS Library exposes messaging objects that can be used in an Active Server Pages (ASP) script, a Microsoft Visual Basic application, or a C/C++ application to access and manipulate e-mail for a particular user. We can use a very simple ASP script to check for the local messages of a particular individual.

Let's review how CDO for NTS and SMTP work together. Clients send e-mail messages to the IIS SMTP service. If the mail is destined for a remote domain, the SMTP service looks up the address of the server for that domain and forwards the messages to that address. If the remote SMTP server is MCIS (or some similar system), mail is stored in the users' mailboxes until the clients retrieve their messages through the POP3 server. If the mail is targeted for the local domain, it will be stored in the Drop directory. CDO for NTS can then look through all the messages and find mail for a specific user.

Reading E-Mail with an ASP Script

Following is a simple ASP script (READMAIL.ASP) that uses the CDO for NTS Library.

```
<!--
    This sample script uses the CDO for NTS Library to
    read e-mail for a specific user.
    Leon Braginski & Matt Powell (c)
-->
```

```
<%@ LANGUAGE = "VBScript" %>
<%
If (Request.ServerVariables ("REQUEST_METHOD") = "POST") then
    Name = Request.Form("name")
    Email = Request.Form("ename")
else
    ' Assume it is GET
    Name = Request.QueryString("name")
    Email = Request.QueryString("email")
end if

If (Email = "") OR (Name = "") then
    Response.Write "You have to supply name and email <BR>"
    Response.End
End If

Set objSession = Server.CreateObject ("CDONTS.Session")
objSession.LogonSMTP Name, Email
Set objInbox = objSession.GetDefaultFolder(1)

If objInbox Is Nothing Then
    Set collMessages = Nothing
    Response.Write "Can't get folder. <br>"
    objSession.Logoff
    Response.End
End If

Set collMessages = objInbox.Messages

If (collMessages.Count = 0) Then
    Response.Write  "<center> User <b>"  & Name & "</b>" & _
        " (email:  <b>" & Email & "</b>) does not have messages"
    Response.End
    objSession.Logoff
end if

Response.Write  "<center> User <b>"  & Name & "</b>" & _
    " (email:  <b>" & Email & "</b>) has <b>"& _
    collMessages.Count & "</b> message(s) </center> <p>"

Response.Write "<TABLE BORDER WIDTH=100% >"
Response.Write "<TR> <TD WIDTH=10% > <i>ID</i></TD>" & _
    "<TD WIDTH=15% > <i>From</i></TD>" & _
    "<TD WIDTH=15% > <i>Subject</i> </TD> " & _
    "<TD WIDTH=60% > <i>Message Text</i></TD> </TR>"
```

(continued)

```
For Mes = 1 To collMessages.Count
    Set objMessage = collMessages.Item(Mes)
    Response.Write "<TR> <TD WIDTH=10% >" & Mes & "</TD>" & _
        "<TD WIDTH=15% >" & objMessage.Sender.Name & "</TD>" & _
        "<TD WIDTH=15% >" & objMessage.Subject & "</TD>" & _
        "<TD WIDTH=60% >" & objMessage.Text & "</TD> </TR>"
Next

Response.Write "</TABLE>"
%>
```

Without going into too much detail, let's look at the highlights of the script. We create a session object by using *Server.CreateObject ("CDONTS.Session")*. Once the session object is created, we log on to the server by using the *LogonSMTP* method of the session object. We set the Inbox as our default folder by using *GetDefaultFolder (1)* method so that we have access to the collection of messages stored there. Note that the SMTP server does not actually use an Inbox directory; it uses the \Mailroot\Drop server directory for the entire domain instead. Even though it uses the Drop directory to deposit messages for all users, CDO for NTS returns only the items destined for the specified user. At this point in the script, we iterate through each message in the collection and get the message's properties, such as its sender, subject, and text.

Our script accepts two parameters: name and email. You can specify values directly in the URL, like this: *http://server/scripts/readmail.asp?name=Leon&email=leonbr@leonbr-hm.* Or you can create an HTML form that would post data to the script.

NOTE

Even though a POP3 service is not included with IIS, you can easily write one or modify an existing service. For example, you could modify the POP3 service sample provided with the Microsoft Win32 Platform Software Development Kit (SDK) so that it uses the CDO for NTS Library to read mail based on the supplied user name.

Sending E-Mail from a Web Page

With IIS SMTP and CDO for NTS, you can send e-mail to anybody on the Internet directly from an ASP script. Why do you need an entire SMTP service to send e-mail from an ASP script, and why didn't Microsoft create a simple control that looks up the MX record and sends the mail? There are two reasons. First, sending messages can be a lengthy process. It involves looking up an MX record, and your potential communication could be with a server halfway around the world. And, of course, the lookup is only part of the e-mailing process. You have to connect to the server, make sure the server will accept new mail, and then transfer the message. Users would not want an application that required them to wait a long time for a response to their request to send a message.

Second, one of the main features of an e-mail message system, as opposed to other forms of immediate data transfer, is that once mail is posted to a server, its receipt is guaranteed or the sender receives notification of a problem. Unlike a simple lookup control, a permanently running process such as SMTP is capable of performing retries, handling errors, and queuing up mail if the mail can't be sent immediately. With all that said, the logical choice is to stick with the SMTP server and the CDO for NTS Library for sending e-mail.

The following simple script (SENDMAIL.ASP) allows you to send e-mail directly from a Web page. You can invoke the script directly from the URL or create an HTML form to execute it. Just make sure you provide all the required parameters in the script: from, to, subject, and body.

```
<!--
    This sample script uses the CDO for NTS Library to
    send email to a specific user.
    Leon Braginski & Matt Powell (c)
    Note: "To" is a reserved word, so we added an underscore to it.
-->

<%@ LANGUAGE = "VBScript" %>

<%
If (Request.ServerVariables ("REQUEST_METHOD") = "POST") then
    From = Request.Form("from")
    To_ = Request.Form("to")
    Subject = Request.Form("subject")
    Body = Request.Form("body")
else
    ' Assume it is GET
    From = Request.QueryString("from")
    To_ = Request.QueryString("to")
    Subject = Request.QueryString("subject")
    Body = Request.QueryString("body")
end if

Set objNewMail = Server.CreateObject ("CDONTS.NewMail")
objNewMail.Send From, To_, Subject, Body
Set objNewMail = Nothing
Response.Write "Message was sent"
%>
```

With the *NewMail* object, sending an e-mail message is simple. All you have to do is create the object, call its *Send* method, and set the object to *Nothing* (because the object can't be reused). Real code would always include error checking for user input, but just to make the code simpler, it was left out in this example.

With CDO for NTS, users can invoke a variety of e-mail features directly from a Web page—for example, they can add attachments or set message importance. Explore the objects in the CDO for NTS Library and see how easy it is to use them. Just remember—the SMTP Service must be installed for the *NewMail* object to work.

Installing SMTP

Before we look at the specifics of installing and configuring the SMTP service, we would like to make a couple of quick comments regarding our network configuration. Our setup has very few machines configured on a LAN. We do not use domains in our addressing; instead, we use the Fully Qualified Domain Name (FQDN), which by default is the computer name. So if our computer name is *leonbr-hm*, the FQDN is simply *leonbr-hm*. To send e-mail, we use the following format: *Joe@leonbr-hm*. If we had used a domain structure, the e-mail format would be different. For example, if our computer named *leonbr-hm* was located in the *cmpny.com* domain, then our FQDN would be *leonbr-hm.cmpny.com*. E-mail would have the following familiar format: *Joe@cmpny.com* or *Joe@leonbr-hm.cmpny.com.*

The SMTP service can be installed by selecting either the typical or custom installation option of the Microsoft Windows NT 4.0 Option Pack. For a custom setup, the first dialog box displayed allows you to select the components to install. In this dialog box, select Internet Information Server and click the Show Subcomponents button to open the Internet Information Server dialog box, which displays IIS subcomponents including the SMTP service, as shown in Figure 11.2.

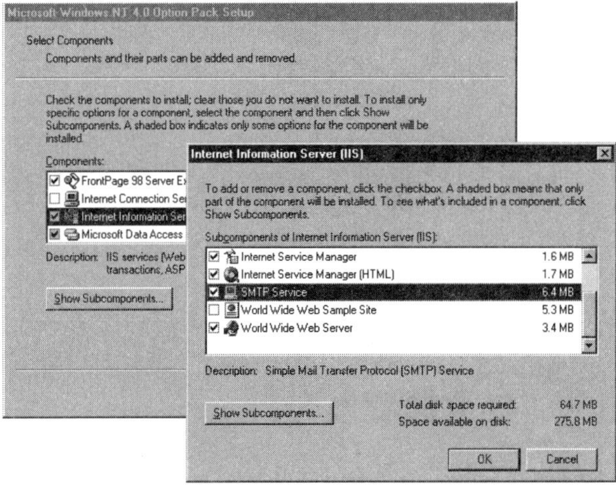

FIGURE 11.2

SMTP Service listed as one of several IIS subcomponents.

Once you make your component selections and continue with installation, a dialog box prompting for a mail root location is displayed; C:\Inetpub\Mailroot is a default location. When the installation of the SMTP service and the option pack is complete, the following directory structure will be created in the \Inetpub\Mailroot directory:

- **Badmail** This directory stores undeliverable messages.
- **Drop** This very important directory is where all mail for a specific SMTP domain is deposited. Each file in this directory represents one e-mail message. There is no way to determine the name and address of the recipient from the filename alone. CDO for NTS looks in this directory to find all messages for a specific user. (Don't confuse the Drop directory with the Pickup directory.)
- **Pickup** As soon as a mail message is placed in this directory, the SMTP service picks it up and either delivers it to the Drop directory or sends it to the SMTP server for the destination domain. You can use Notepad to create a properly formatted message and then copy the message to the Pickup directory. As soon as the message is copied to Pickup, the server will try to deliver it. Adding this handy feature to your application makes sending mail as easy as creating a text file and copying it to \Mailroot\Pickup.

NOTE

It is more efficient to create a message in a directory other than Mailroot\Pickup first and then copy or move the file to Mailroot\Pickup. (Remember that each message is just a text file.) If a new file is created in the Pickup directory, the SMTP service will automatically try to process it. But if the file is still open (because it is being typed in Microsoft Word, for example), the file may be locked and SMTP won't be able to access it. The SMTP process will waste CPU cycles by trying repeatedly to read the locked message.

- **Queue** If IIS can't deliver a message immediately because of a network problem or other issues, the message is queued up in this directory. The SMTP service will hold the message for a configurable length of time and then try to retransmit it.

- **Route, SortTemp and Mailbox** IIS uses these directories to sort and rearrange outgoing messages to make their delivery more efficient. If several messages need to be sent to the same remote host, IIS will try to send them all by using a single connection instead of transmitting each one individually by reconnecting multiple times.

◆ Creating a Mail File

We will learn about the mail file format in Chapter 26, but if you want to create a file now for the \Mailroot\Pickup directory, follow this format. Don't forget to insert an empty line between the header and the message text:

```
x-sender: mattpo@domain1.com
x-receiver: leonbr@domain2.com
From: mattpo@domain1.com
To: leonbr@domain2.com
Subject: Hello

This is the body of the message.
```

Checking the Status of the SMTP Service

After the SMTP service is installed, you can use several different methods to see whether it is running. One method is to go to the Control Panel and open the Services applet. The Microsoft SMTP Service status will be listed in the Services dialog box, as shown in Figure 11.3.

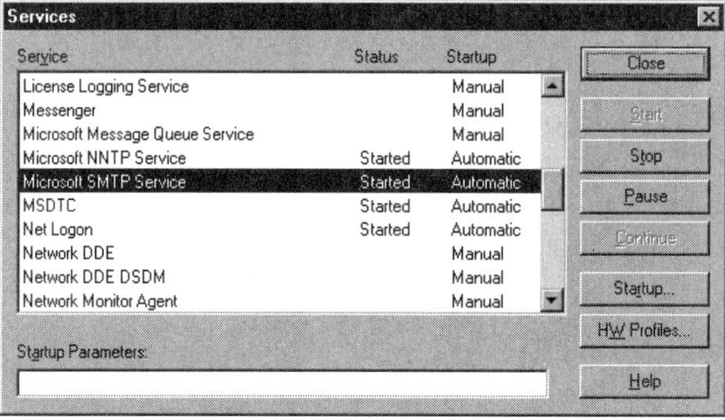

FIGURE 11.3

The Microsoft SMTP Service status.

You can also get a list of running services by invoking the Net Start command at a command prompt. Or you can check the status of the Start, Stop, and Pause buttons in the Microsoft Management Console when the SMTP site is selected in the left pane.

A more direct approach to checking the STMP service status is to establish a telnet connection with the SMTP port of the server. You can do this by entering the following command at a command prompt:

```
telnet localhost smtp
```

This command launches telnet, and you should see the server's welcome message in the telnet window:

```
220-leonbr-hm Microsoft SMTP MAIL ready at Sat, 31 Jan 1998 15:44:33
-0800 Version: 5.5.1774.114.11
220 ESMTP spoken here
```

To avoid leaving the connection in an idle state, type *quit* and press Enter. (We'll use telnet extensively when we learn about the SMTP protocol in Chapter 26.)

NOTE

Depending on how your telnet client is configured, you might or might not see what you've typed. To see your input, go to Terminal/Preferences and make sure that the Local Echo option is checked.

Starting the SMTP Service Manager

After the service is installed, changes to the SMTP configuration can be made either in the Management Console or from the HTML-based administration pages. The HTML-based administration pages used to modify SMTP options can be opened by selecting SMTP Service Manager (HTML) from the Microsoft SMTP Service group, or by connecting to *http://localhost/mail/smtp/admin/*. Even though the Management Console shown in Figure 11.4 looks a little different from the browser window shown in Figure 11.5, both have similar capabilities for configuring SMTP options.

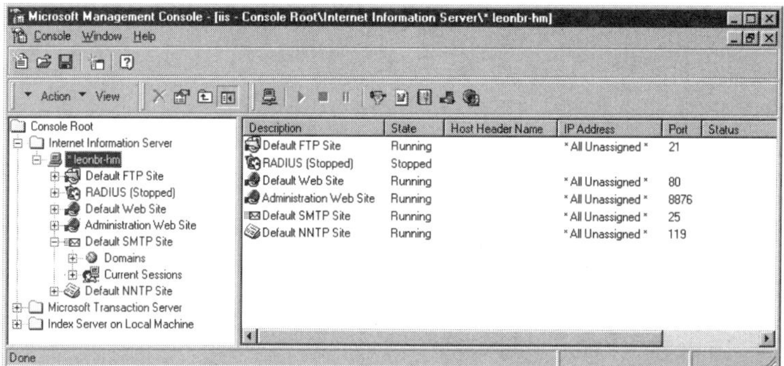

FIGURE 11.4

View of the Management Console with SMTP service, which can be used to modify SMTP options.

FIGURE 11.5

View of the HTML-based administration pages, which can be used to modify SMTP options.

We are going to use the Management Console to configure SMTP options, but you can perform almost all the same tasks through the HTML-based administration pages.

Setting Default Domain Properties

Let's start by taking a look at the default domain properties. The domain is the lowest unit of the server organization. The domains that SMTP operates with are identical to DNS domains discussed in Chapter 3. As mentioned earlier in this chapter, if a computer does not participate in a domain name system, the domain name for e-mailing purposes is just the computer name. IIS uses the default computer name from the TCP/IP protocol properties in the Network Control Panel applet as the default domain name. Figure 11.6 shows *leonbr-hm* as the default name.

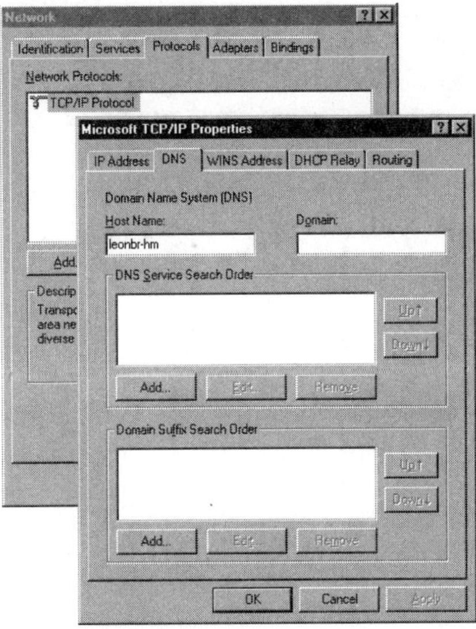

FIGURE 11.6

The default computer name, retrieved from the Network Control Panel applet, used as the default domain name.

To list the properties for a specific domain, click on the Domains entry in the left pane of the Management Console (shown in Figure 11.4). The right pane will show all the configured SMTP domains. Then right-click on the desired domain and choose Properties from the menu to invoke the Properties dialog box. Figure 11.7 shows the properties for the domain *leonbr-hm.*

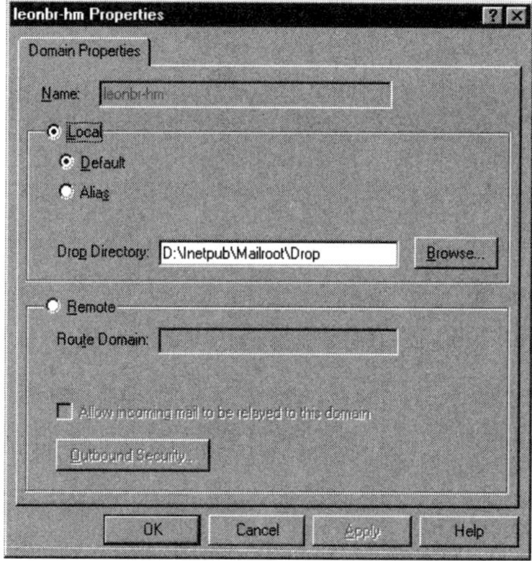

FIGURE 11.7

Domain properties for **leonbr-hm.**

Every machine must have at least one default local domain, so you cannot use the Alias or Remote radio buttons. (We will cover how to create a domain in the section "Creating a Domain" later in the chapter.) You can, however, change the default Drop directory for the domain. In Figure 11.7, the Drop directory is configured as D:\Inetpub\Mailroot\Drop.

◆ Remote and Local Domains

There are two kinds of domains: remote and local. Mail that is addressed to a *remote domain* isn't processed by a local server; it is passed along to the SMTP server responsible for that domain. The local server can locate the SMTP server that can process the mail via an MX record lookup. Mail that is addressed to the *local domain* is processed by the local host, just as the name suggests.

Using SMTP Server to Process Mail

The SMTP service is already set up to serve the *leonbr-hm* domain without any special configuration, so users specifying our server as the SMTP server in their favorite Internet e-mail program can send mail to the *leonbr-hm* domain. In our example, a few people have done exactly that. We use the READMAIL.ASP script we wrote earlier in this chapter to check e-mail for leonbr@leonbr-hm. Figure 11.8 shows all Leon's messages on the server.

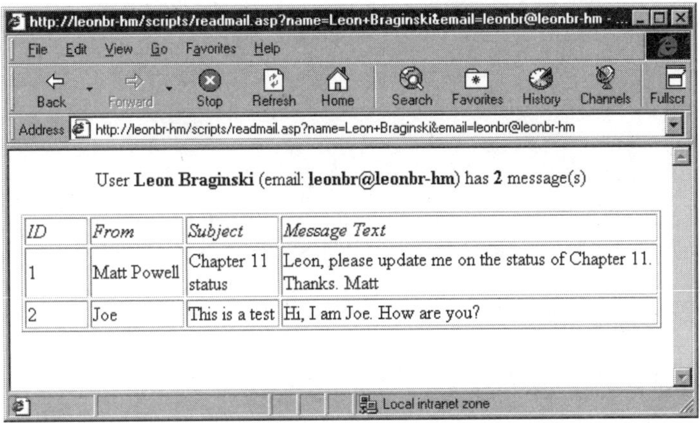

FIGURE 11.8

Using CDO for NTS in an ASP script to read all e-mail sent to **leonbr@leonbr-hm.**

As mentioned earlier in the chapter, the messages themselves are simply text files in the \Mailroot\Drop directory. Figure 11.9 shows such a text file opened in Notepad.

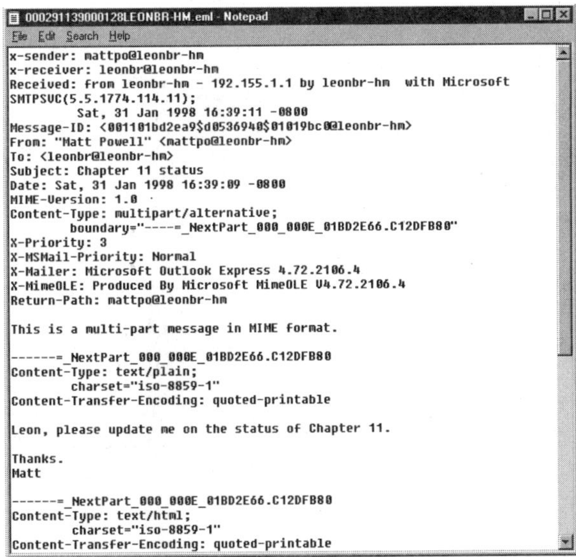

```
x-sender: mattpo@leonbr-hm
x-receiver: leonbr@leonbr-hm
Received: from leonbr-hm - 192.155.1.1 by leonbr-hm  with Microsoft
SMTPSVC(5.5.1774.114.11);
         Sat, 31 Jan 1998 16:39:11 -0800
Message-ID: <001101bd2ea9$d0536940$01019bc0@leonbr-hm>
From: "Matt Powell" <mattpo@leonbr-hm>
To: <leonbr@leonbr-hm>
Subject: Chapter 11 status
Date: Sat, 31 Jan 1998 16:39:09 -0800
MIME-Version: 1.0
Content-Type: multipart/alternative;
        boundary="----=_NextPart_000_000E_01BD2E66.C12DFB80"
X-Priority: 3
X-MSMail-Priority: Normal
X-Mailer: Microsoft Outlook Express 4.72.2106.4
X-MimeOLE: Produced By Microsoft MimeOLE V4.72.2106.4
Return-Path: mattpo@leonbr-hm

This is a multi-part message in MIME format.

------=_NextPart_000_000E_01BD2E66.C12DFB80
Content-Type: text/plain;
        charset="iso-8859-1"
Content-Transfer-Encoding: quoted-printable

Leon, please update me on the status of Chapter 11.

Thanks.
Matt

------=_NextPart_000_000E_01BD2E66.C12DFB80
Content-Type: text/html;
        charset="iso-8859-1"
Content-Transfer-Encoding: quoted-printable
```

FIGURE 11.9

Stored messages in the text file with long filenames and EML extensions.

As you can see in the Notepad title bar, the message has a rather user-*un*friendly name. It is impossible to reconstruct who the message is for by looking at the name alone; you have to look at the e-mail headers in the text file to determine who the sender and receiver are. CDO for NTS is used in the ASP script to locate all e-mail sent to a particular user—in our example, *leonbr@leonbr-hm*. It looks through all the text files in the directory and finds only those messages for a specific user.

We know that the SMTP service works fine for the *leonbr-hm* domain because messages sent to users in this domain are delivered without errors. But what happens when we send messages to someone like *Joe@cmpny.com*? Strangely enough, our mail client reported the error shown in Figure 11.10.

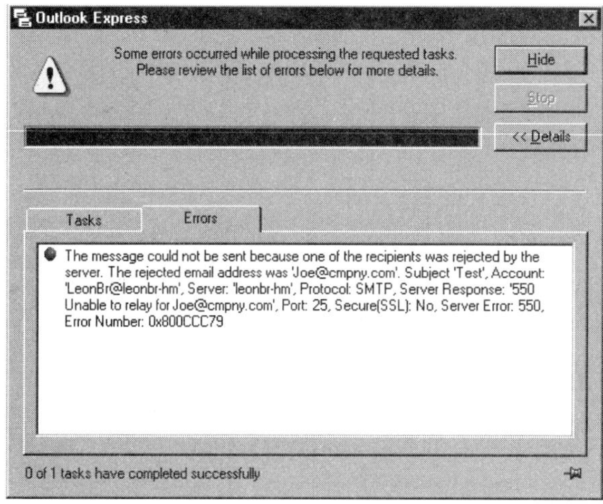

FIGURE 11.10

Outlook Express e-mail client error message.

The error message is a little difficult to understand, but the gist of it is that the server couldn't relay the e-mail to *Joer@cmpny.com*. Why? Because our server has no knowledge of the *cmpny.com* domain (at least not at this point). Our server would have to look up the MX record for *cmpny.com* by using a DNS server and then relay the e-mail message to the SMTP server responsible for receiving e-mail for the *cmpny.com* domain. By default, the Microsoft SMTP server does not relay e-mail to domains that are not configured in the SMTP site. This default prevents unrestricted transmittal of unauthorized messages. Without this restriction, almost anyone in the world could use your SMTP server and cause serious problems. For example, marketing companies could send thousands of spam messages about how to make $1,000 in a single day. All these messages would originate from your server, which is certainly less than desirable. The way around this restriction is either to create a remote domain (we'll do this a little later in the chapter) or to change the settings in the Relay Restrictions dialog box, which is invoked from the Directory Security property page for the SMTP site.

Let's suppose that we lift the relay restriction, by choosing the Allowed To Relay in the Relay Restrictions dialog box, and send e-mail to *Joe@cmpny.com* again. The message successfully leaves our favorite e-mail client (Outlook Express, of course) outbox. We check the status of our message to make sure that it has left the SMTP server by viewing the \Mailroot\Queue directory, but we find that the message is stuck in the queue along with a second file with an RTR extension:

```
D:\Inetpub\Mailroot\Queue>dir
 Volume in drive D has no label.
 Volume Serial Number is 6C83-F753

 Directory of D:\Inetpub\Mailroot\Queue

01/31/98  04:39p        <DIR>          .
01/31/98  04:39p        <DIR>          ..
01/31/98  04:39p                 1,652 000291139000128LEONBR-HM.eml
01/31/98  04:39p                   150 000291139000128LEONBR-HM.rtr
               4 File(s)          1,802 bytes
                            547,547,136 bytes free
```

It looks like we have a problem. To see what the problem is, we need to open the text file with the RTR extension. Here is what it says:

```
Connection to cmpny.com failed. No Ip address found from
   leonbr-hm-192.155.1.1
Joe@cmpny.com
Server received Winsock error Host not found.
```

This message tells us that in our sample configuration, we do not have a valid DNS server. This omission means that when the SMTP service running on our server tries to look up the MX record for *cmpny.com*, an error occurs. In our example, none of our computers have direct access to the Internet, so they can't resolve the addresses and look up MX records. The machines on our intranet don't know the IP address and MX record for *cmpny.com*, hence mail can't be sent successfully from within our intranet to the user on the Internet. In a more typical scenario, when IIS is connected directly to the Internet and the MX records can be obtained, the SMTP service would have the IP address of the SMTP server for *cmpny.com* and thus would be able to establish a connection and deliver the message.

Using a Smart Host

We can solve the lookup problem in the intranet example by using a great feature of IIS SMTP server called a smart host. A *smart host* is a machine that processes all outgoing messages bound for remote domains rather than sending the messages directly to the domain. A smart host can act as a mail gateway for the company because it is connected to both the Internet and intranet simultaneously. It can resolve domains like *cmpny.com* and freely connect to them.

The smart host also runs the SMTP service and has simultaneous connections to an internal LAN and to the Internet. All we have to do is configure the local SMTP service (running on *leonbr-hm*) so that it passes messages for all remote domains to the smart host, essentially using the smart host as mail gateway. It's almost like the TCP/IP default route for e-mail rather than for network packets. (Take a look at Chapter 3 to see the close resemblance.)When the smart host is configured, all outgoing messages to unknown domains are sent to the smart host for processing.

You might have a situation in which it makes sense to route most domains through a smart host, but you have other domains whose servers you can access via more efficient routes. In such a case, you have to create new entries for the domains that you know about and indicate a routing domain for each newly created domain. E-mail for those domains will be routed through the routing domain instead of through the smart host. (We'll discuss routing domains more towards the end of the chapter.) Now let's move—from e-mail delivery to configuring our mail server.

Configuring the SMTP Site

In the Management Console (shown in Figure 11.4 on page 270), right-click on the Default SMTP Site entry to bring up the Default SMTP Site Properties window. Here you can configure properties for the default SMTP site.

Setting site properties

The first sheet of the Default SMTP Site Properties window is shown in Figure 11.11. By default, the SMTP server listens on port 25 for all addresses assigned to the machine. You can change this default by clicking the Advanced button and bringing up the Advanced Multiple SMTP Site Configuration dialog box, where you configure the site to listen on different ports and on different IP addresses. The machine we are using has more than one IP address, so we could configure the server to listen on different ports for each address. This configuration wouldn't be very prudent, however, because port 25 is the default port known by all other servers and clients throughout the Internet. If any other port is used, all clients must be made aware of it.

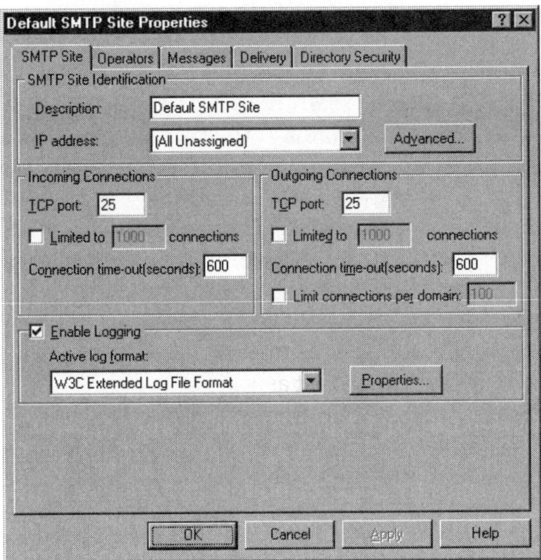

FIGURE 11.11

SMTP Site property page.

If you want the server to work efficiently and within its capabilities, you will need to properly specify the connection properties. For example, you probably wouldn't want to bring an old 486 machine to its knees by allowing thousands of simultaneous connections. On the SMTP Site property page, you can set a limit for incoming and outgoing connections and even set a timeout for disconnecting idle sessions.

The SMTP Site property page also allows you to set the standard logging options that are integral to each service installed with IIS. As with WWW, FTP, or NNTP, the mail server can generate logs in different formats with different log rotation frequencies.

Setting up security accounts

By default, anybody from the Administrators group can administer the SMTP server. On the Operators property page, shown in Figure 11.12, you can grant permissions for users or groups who can administer the server.

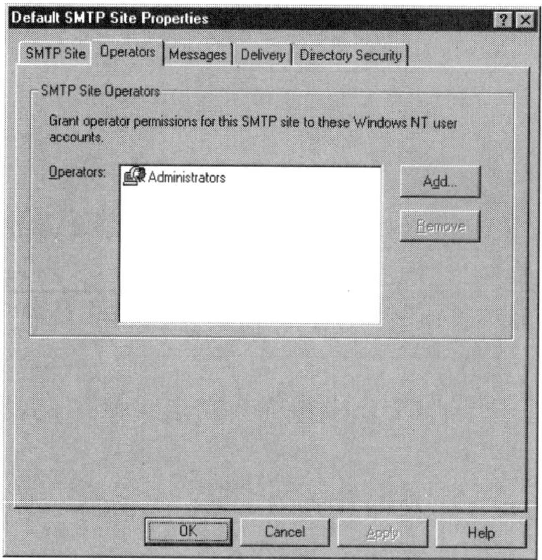

FIGURE 11.12

Operators property page.

Setting message properties

The Messages property page, shown in Figure 11.13, provides options for configuring message properties.

To prevent the server from accepting huge amounts of data from clients, you can limit the size of messages being sent to the server by indicating limits in the Maximum Message Size and Maximum Session Size text boxes. The Maximum Message Size parameter sets a limit on the size of a message that the SMTP service will accept. If a message is larger than this limit, it will not be accepted. Some mail applications may attempt to avoid this kind of problem by breaking large messages into multiple smaller messages. If all the messages being forwarded in a single session exceed the Maximum Session Size, the SMTP service will disconnect the client's connection. The Maximum Session Size must be larger than the Maximum Message Size.

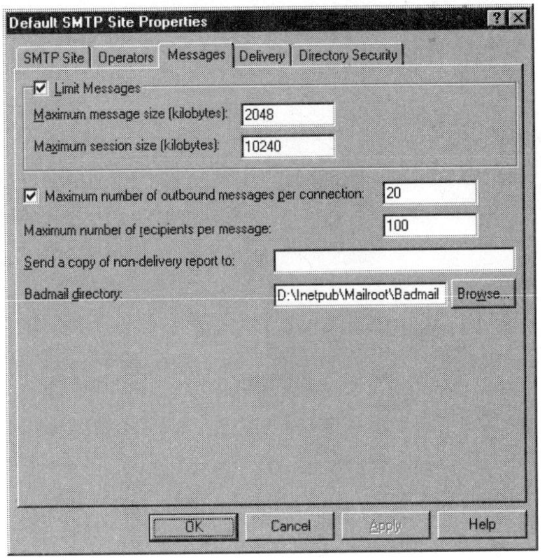

FIGURE 11.13

Messages property page.

These limits apply not only to clients directly connecting to this server, but also to other servers relaying messages to this one. These SMTP servers might be transmitting several messages over a single connection, so the amount of transferred data can easily exceed the Maximum Session Size. Choose this size carefully. Remote servers will try to resend messages after an unsuccessful attempt. When the connection is closed because the session size is exceeded, remote machines will automatically try to reconnect and resend the messages. This process is repeated until the messages are sent successfully or until a limit, such as the maximum number of retries, is exceeded. Constant retries from other servers might be more harmful to performance than a one-time attempt at posting a large block of messages.

Limiting the number of messages per connection is another performance-related parameter you can assign on the Messages property page. If there are many messages to send, it could be beneficial to make your server establish several connections—multiple messages could be sent simultaneously instead of individually, one at a time, over a single connection. To gain some context for determining a proper number of messages per connection, use the Microsoft Performance Monitor, which is part of Windows NT. Look at the Messages Sent/sec counter of the SMTP Server object. The limit set should be less than the maximum values viewed in Performance Monitor. This message limitation applies only to outgoing connections.

We can also limit the maximum number of recipients on this property page. RFC 821 limits the maximum number of recipients per message to 100. When this limit is reached, some clients generate an error called a non-delivery report (NDR). However, the Microsoft SMTP service won't; it will open a new connection so that it can deliver the message to those recipients beyond the 100-recipient limit. For example, if the message is sent to 110 people, 100 messages would be processed in one connection and then a new connection would be opened to process the 10 remaining messages.

When messages can't be delivered (for example, the message is targeted for a remote domain but the server can't establish a connection to the domain's server), an NDR is generated and sent to the e-mail originator. (You might be familiar with NDRs like this if you've ever misspelled a recipient's e-mail address.) You can designate a specific address to receive a copy of any NDRs that the SMTP server receives. Typically, the e-mail administrator would be the most appropriate person to receive NDRs. If for some reason the NDR can't be delivered to the originator, a copy of the message is placed in the Badmail directory. If you don't care about seeing NDR reports, leave the e-mail addresses blank.

Setting mail delivery properties

The Delivery property page lets you specify delivery-specific properties, as shown in Figure 11.14.

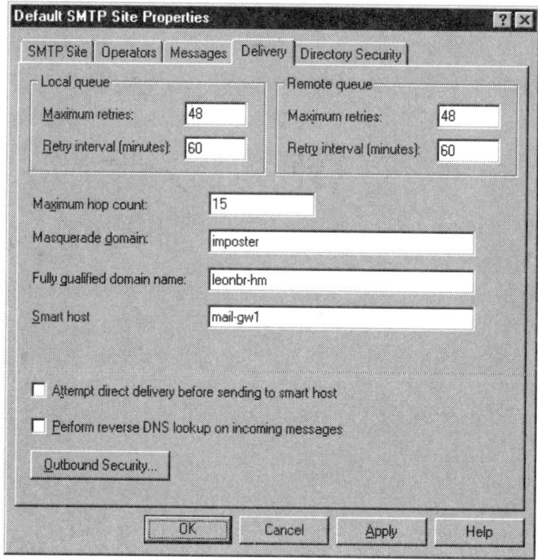

FIGURE 11.14

Delivery property page.

When a message can't be delivered after the first try, it goes back to the Queue directory. The server will resend the message the specified number of tries and wait the specified time between retries. When the maximum number of attempts is reached, an NDR is sent to the originator and any designated NDR recipient.

NOTE

The NDR is handled as ordinary mail and the same retry rules apply. However, when the number of retries are exceeded for an NDR message, the message is placed in the Badmail directory.

Before a message is delivered to its destination, it might be routed through many different domains and handled by many different servers. Each server the message encounters equals one hop. The number of hops can be determined by looking in the Received fields in the message header. Each server handling the message adds its own Received header to the e-mail message. (In our sample e-mail to *leonbr@leonbr-hm*, the number of hops is one—there is only one Receive header, as shown in Figure 11.9 on page 273.) As soon as the number of hops exceeds the preset limit, an NDR is generated.

Creating a masquerade domain The server automatically adds its default domain name to e-mail message headers, but you can change this domain stamp by entering a name in the Masquerade Domain text box. Changing the domain name makes the message look as though it was sent from someplace other than its originator. Suppose a message was sent from machine *leonbr-hm* by user leonbr to user Joe, and no masquerade domain had been entered. The x-sender field (which contains message sender identification) would show *leonbr@leonbr-hm*. But if we entered *imposter* as a masquerade domain, the e-mail message headers would display different information, as shown in Figure 11.15. Pay special attention to the x-sender and Return-Path headers.

In the x-sender field, notice that *leonbr@imposter* appears. (If the Masquerade Domain option was left blank, the x-sender field would display *leonbr@leonbr-hm*.) One header is not changed, however:

```
From: "Leon Braginski" <leonbr@leonbr-hm>
```

This From header is still correct—it came directly from our e-mail client, Outlook Express. If you want to change the identification of the client, you need to do so in the client software.

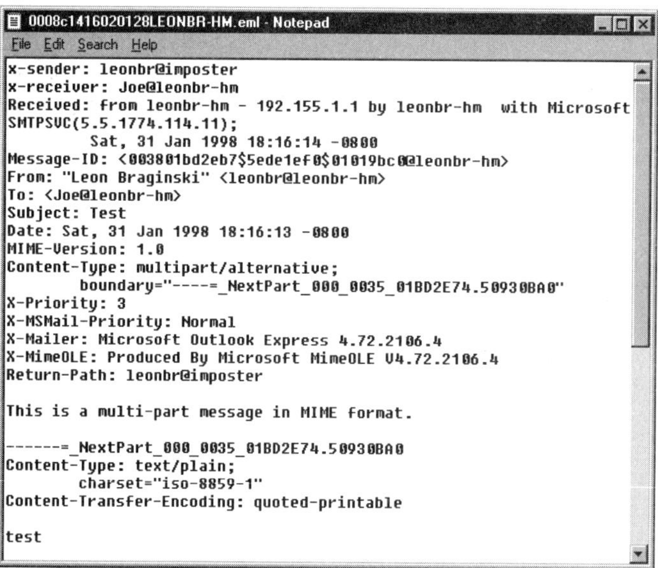

```
x-sender: leonbr@imposter
x-receiver: Joe@leonbr-hm
Received: from leonbr-hm - 192.155.1.1 by leonbr-hm  with Microsoft
SMTPSVC(5.5.1774.114.11);
         Sat, 31 Jan 1998 18:16:14 -0800
Message-ID: <003801bd2eb7$5ede1ef0$01019bc0@leonbr-hm>
From: "Leon Braginski" <leonbr@leonbr-hm>
To: <Joe@leonbr-hm>
Subject: Test
Date: Sat, 31 Jan 1998 18:16:13 -0800
MIME-Version: 1.0
Content-Type: multipart/alternative;
        boundary="----=_NextPart_000_0035_01BD2E74.50930BA0"
X-Priority: 3
X-MSMail-Priority: Normal
X-Mailer: Microsoft Outlook Express 4.72.2106.4
X-MimeOLE: Produced By Microsoft MimeOLE V4.72.2106.4
Return-Path: leonbr@imposter

This is a multi-part message in MIME format.

------=_NextPart_000_0035_01BD2E74.50930BA0
Content-Type: text/plain;
        charset="iso-8859-1"
Content-Transfer-Encoding: quoted-printable

test
```

FIGURE 11.15

Message sent from the imposter domain by using the Masquerade Domain option.

NOTE

It's very easy to fake a return address in e-mail. Faking an e-mail address is a somewhat common practice by unscrupulous advertisers and solicitors. Later in the chapter, we'll see how to make IIS check domains before accepting e-mail.

Setting the fully qualified domain name The Delivery property page also allows you to set your machine's fully qualified domain name. Because our sample machine (*leonbr-hm*) does not have a real Internet domain (like *leonbr-hm.cmpny.com)*, the FQDN displays as *leonbr-hm*, as shown in Figure 11.14. This name is automatically taken from information in the DNS configuration tab or from TCP/IP properties in the Network Control Panel applet.

Specifying the smart host The smart host option is also located on the Delivery properties page. In our sample scenario, all messages for domains that are not preconfigured on the server (i.e., domains other than local and remote domains) will go directly to *mail-gw1*, which is entered as the smart host on the Delivery property page. When a message is sent to *Joe@cmpny.com*, then *leonbr-hm* will not perform a DNS lookup for the MX record of *cmpny.com*. Instead it will send the message to *mail-gw1* for processing. As mentioned earlier, because *leonbr-hm* is a part of a self-contained LAN, it cannot connect to the remote server anyway, and it has no choice but to send the message to a mail gateway.

A more efficient way to specify a smart host is by its IP address. This approach relieves the server of having to resolve the name and then locate the appropriate IP address. You can specify the IP address in the Smart Host text box by enclosing it in square brackets. Brackets indicate that the entry is an IP address and therefore needs no resolution. By unchecking the Attempt Direct Delivery Before Sending To Smart Host option, you can avoid any local processing of the messages and force them to be sent to the smart host immediately.

Specifying a reverse lookup We mentioned before that it is possible to prevent mail spoofing (mail that appears to be sent from someone other than the originator). When the Perform Reverse DNS Lookup On Incoming Messages option is selected, the server will check (by doing a reverse lookup) that the IP address for the domain inserted in the From header matches the original IP address in the header. When the lookup is successful, the domain name is inserted in the Received field. When the lookup is unsuccessful, only the IP address is shown. This security feature, however, does not come cheap—performing a reverse lookup slows down the message handling process of a busy server.

Setting outbound message security Last but not least, the SMTP server can use various security schemes for its outbound connections. This capability increases the level of security when sending e-mail. Security features can be set for the entire site or for each domain configured on the system. In the Outbound Security dialog box (accessed by clicking the Outbound Security button), you can set familiar schemes: Clear text authentication (similar to Basic authentication for the WWW server) and Windows NT Challenge/Response authentication.

There is one more option: Transport Layer Security (TLS) encryption. This option is equivalent to Secure Sockets Layer (SSL) encryption for outbound connections. For this option, both machines (the SMTP server and its counterpart) must have a secure key pair installed. You'll learn much more about SSL security in Chapter 13.

Setting security options for inbound connections

On the Directory Security page, shown in Figure 11.16, you can configure server security for all inbound connections.

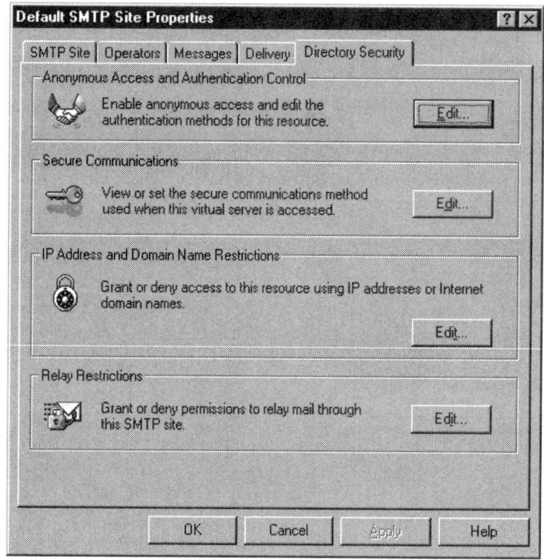

FIGURE 11.16

Directory Security property page.

The options configured on this page are very similar to the options of other services such as WWW and FTP. In addition to authentication schemes used for inbound connections and the ability to set data encryption via TLS (which is based on SSL) and IP address restrictions, the mail server has one more restriction— a relay restriction. Click the Edit button in the Relay Restrictions section to bring up the Relay Restrictions dialog box shown in Figure 11.17. This is where you can set the relay restrictions.

By default the server does not permit mail relays for any connections, unless an incoming connection was successfully authenticated. Recall that in an earlier example, the inability to relay messages was the problem we had while trying to send e-mail to *Joe@cmpny.com*.

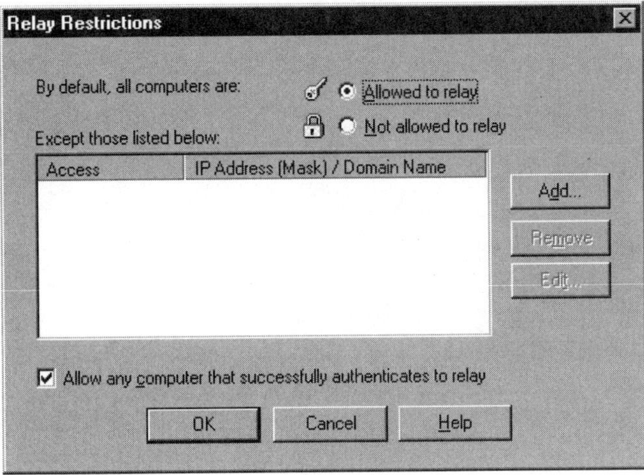

FIGURE 11.17

Relay restrictions dialog box.

Creating a Domain

At this point in our running example, the SMTP server *leonbr-hm* is configured. Now let's create a remote domain *cmpny.com* for the Cmpny Corporation. As soon as we configure it, users will be able to send mail to addresses such as *Joe@cmpny.com* without using a smart host.

The Management Console allows you to create a new domain for the default SMTP site through the New Domain Wizard. To display this wizard, right-click on the Default SMTP Site in the Management Console, choose New, and then select Domain. The wizard asks for two pieces of information: the domain type (local or remote) and the domain name. Figure 11.18 shows how the Management Console looks with the *cmpny.com* and *imposter* domains created.

You can also establish remote domains as routing domains via the Remote Domain Properties option. The option can be accessed by right-clicking on the domain in the Management Console and selecting Properties. A *routing domain* allows you to specify a route to an intermediate domain that may be more efficient than going to the smart host. (Recall that earlier in the chapter we did not want to use smart host for all domains configured on the server.)

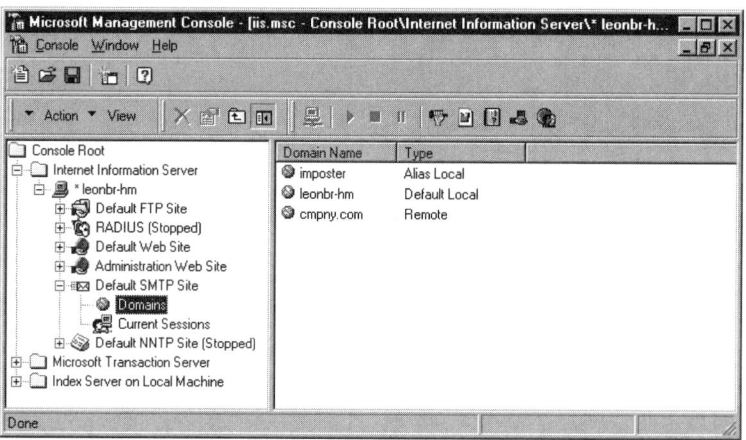

FIGURE 11.18

The domains cmpny.com and imposter as shown in the Management Console.

Since there can be only one default local domain, any other local domain that is created becomes an alias for the default local domain. For example, the *imposter* local domain shown in Figure 11.18 became a local alias for the default domain *leonbr-hm*.

Local aliases work well when you use a masquerade domain. When a masquerade domain is used, mail replies are sent to *Joe@mymasquerade.com* (who might not really exist), instead of to the correct address *Joe@myrealdomain.com*. Creating a local alias like *mymasquerade.com* avoids this problem. Now mail sent to *Joe@mymasquerade.com* will be correctly delivered to the server, and the sender won't get an NDR.

Individual domains can override global settings, and this can affect smart-host routing and SSL usage; for example, a domain might not use a specified smart host, or it might have different outbound security configurations. The idea is to make the SMTP server as flexible as possible.

One more interesting feature provided by the Management Console is the ability to see all current sessions connected to the SMTP server. Click on the Current Sessions icon to get a list of all users, IP addresses, and the connection times for each session. Figure 11.19 shows a list of all active connections.

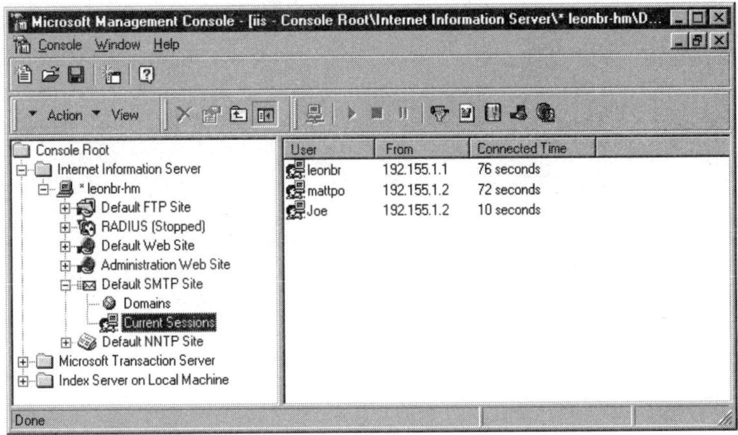

FIGURE 11.19

Current sessions shown in the Management Console.

In this chapter, we've covered the major capabilities of the SMTP service. If you've paid close attention to the components of IIS, you've noticed that many services appear to be similar—even the configuration options. Our next task is to look under the hood of these services and see whether they actually operate in a similar fashion. We will start learning about the under-the-hood components by looking into IIS security in more detail.

CHAPTER 12

Windows NT Security and IIS

Security is an integral part of any intranet or Internet application running on the Microsoft Windows NT platform. In this chapter, you'll learn about IIS security and how to limit user access to certain resources such as HTML files, Active Server Pages (ASP) scripts, Common Gateway Interface (CGI) applications, and ISAPI DLLs. We'll cover what happens behind the scenes when the browser requests names and passwords from users.

We'll also cover security for Windows NT services, which are special executables that run in the background and do not have a typical window or console. Because IIS is, in fact, a Windows NT service, it experiences all the benefits and burdens of native Windows NT security.

ISAPI is the interface provided by IIS to write Internet server applications through the use of DLLs that export specific entry points. The code in the DLLs can process requests and dynamically generate HTML for the responses.

CGI is another interface used to write Internet server applications. CGI applications are executable files that can communicate with information servers, such as IIS, via the standard input and output streams. Just like ISAPI extensions, CGI applications can process requests and dynamically generate HTML pages. However, unlike an ISAPI extension, a CGI application is created in a new process for each request, causing CGI applications to scale poorly. Chapter 20 will cover both ISAPI and CGI in more detail.

Security Descriptors and Access Tokens

One requirement of a secure system is the discretionary control of securable objects, such as files, registry keys, and pipes. Windows NT accomplishes this control with security descriptors and access tokens.

> **Glossary**
>
> **securable objects** *Objects that can be secured. Before an application can access a secured object, the operating system checks whether the application has access rights. Files and named pipes are examples of securable objects. Files and directories are not always securable objects. They can be secured only when they reside on the New Technology File System (NTFS), first introduced with Windows NT.*

Security Descriptors

Windows NT maintains security attributes for each securable object in the object's *security descriptor*. Think of the security descriptor as a single record in the Windows NT security database. The security descriptor is an internal structure that is not directly accessible by programmers, but it can be manipulated indirectly by using security APIs. The following information about an object is stored in a security descriptor:

- **Owner Security Identifier (SID)** The owner SID represents the object owner.
- **Group Security Identifier (SID)** The group SID represents the primary group of the object owner.
- **Discretionary Access Control List (DACL)** The DACL represents who can access an object and with what rights.
- **System Access Control List (SACL)** The SACL is used for auditing by the operation system. As a C2-level compliant system, Windows NT must be able to log any access activity for securable objects. When a particular object is configured for auditing, audit records will be available to the system administrator via the Windows NT Event Viewer under the Security Log.

Both DACLs and SACLs can be referred to as *Access Control Lists (ACLs)*. An ACL consists of one or more *Access Control Entries (ACEs)*. An ACE contains the following information:

- An account name such as a user account, a group, or logon account for a service
- A set of specific rights—for example, read, write, and execute
- A set of flags for controlling each right—for example, allow, deny, and audit

Suppose the GUESTS group has read access but not write access to the file DEFAULT.HTM. The ACL for DEFAULT.HTM would include the following ACE (along with others). Of course the following representation is only a generalization of the information included in an ACE. An actual ACE is just a bunch of 0s and 1s.

```
Account: group GUESTS:
         Right: Read - Allowed
         Right: Write - Denied
```

Not only would this information be in binary form, but the account itself would be represented by its SID.

SIDs

A *security identifier (SID)* is the lowest logical unit in the Windows NT security database. It is a unique binary value of variable length that cannot be accessed directly. An SID is used to identify a user, a group, or a logon session. (A logon session SID is the only nonunique SID). When a user logs on to the system, that user is issued a unique SID by the *security authority,* which is the facility that processes the logon.

Applications can access SIDs only via the security APIs (for example, APIs such as *LookupAccountName* and *LookupAccountSid*). Any process started by a user knows the user's SID and can access it. A user's SID becomes available to any processes that he starts via an access token.

Access Tokens

When a user logs on to to the system, his password is validated by Windows NT. In an interactive session, Windows NT validates the user when he enters his name and password in the Windows NT Logon dialog box. In a noninteractive session, validation occurs without any sort of interaction with the user interface. (We'll look at this form of logon a little later.)

If the user is successfully authenticated, the system generates an access token that is attached to every process started by the user. An *access token* is a binary value used to store all vital security information for the process. A partial list of the entries includes the user's SID, a list of group SIDs, a list of privileges, and impersonation information. (Don't confuse the access token with other tokens such as the Token Ring token-passing network discussed in Chapter 2.) Because the access token represents the process's security context, it governs the process's interaction with all securable objects. For example, when a process tries to access a file, the system checks each ACE in the file's ACL against the SID in the access token to determine whether the process can access a file.

Impersonation

When a process creates a thread, by default the thread has the same security context as the process that created it. A thread can, however, *impersonate*—that is, it can change its security context, pretending that it was started by a user other than the user who invoked the process. We could define *impersonation,* then, as the thread's ability to run in a security context other than the process that created the thread.

Consider the following example. A developer wants to write a program that allows a user named Joe to perform an administrative task, such as adding a user to the system. Joe, however, is not an administrator or a member of a group that has administrative rights. So if Joe were to run the program, the operating system would report an error about Joe not having proper permissions. The developer can work around this problem by using impersonation. All the developer has to do is add code that impersonates an administrator. When an administrator is impersonated, the thread runs in the administrator's security context. Now, when the thread accesses securable objects, it does so using the administrator's rights. Most other tasks performed by the thread will be performed in the new security context. When the developer has enhanced the program with impersonation, Joe can run the program and perform the administrative task of adding new users. When this administrative task is complete, the program can terminate the impersonation.

There is one important issue, however: if the thread, now running as an administrator, creates a new process by using the *CreateProcess* API, the new process will be created based on the security context of the original process. In other words, the new process will run in the security context of Joe. You can get around this situation by using the *CreateProcessAsUser* API, which takes an access token as one of its parameters and then starts a new process in the security context of that token.

The example just described is an appropriate situation for using impersonation. However, impersonation is most commonly used on the server side to impersonate the connected client's security context. The server can be a Web server with a Microsoft Internet Explorer client making a connection to it, or it can be any other network client/server application employing communication mechanisms that support security (for example, named pipes).

Glossary

named pipe *An end point used in one form of peer-to-peer network communications. Named pipes provide convenient two-way client/server communication. Microsoft Windows provides a set of functions to access and operate named pipes. In Windows, named pipes are implemented as securable objects.*

Typically, a server process runs as a Windows NT service. Services usually run in the security context of a special account named the Local System (or just System) account. (We examine the Local System account later in this chapter.) When a client connection occurs, the server impersonates the client's security context and performs the task on the client's behalf. Impersonating the client works in a similar manner as the impersonation in the Joe example we looked at earlier. The server process must first obtain the access token of the connecting user before it can use this token to impersonate the user. When the application is finished handling the client's request, it will terminate the impersonation and return to running as the Local System account.

When these actions are performed for a client/server application, the operating system does not necessarily have access to the password of the user for whom it created an access token. This is certainly the case when the server uses Windows NT Challenge/Response authentication (also referred to as NT LAN Manager, or NTLM, authentication). Although the server impersonates the client, it might not be able to do everything that the client can do. For example, it might not be able to establish a network connection in the client's context because the password is not passed directly to the server when NTLM authentication is used.

To prevent passwords from being transmitted over the network, the client and server use a handshake mechanism that involves encoding a random challenge. The server sends a random piece of data to the client, and the client encrypts that data with the password. The client then sends the encrypted data to the server for decryption by the server. After the server decrypts the data, it verifies that the end result—the unencrypted challenge—is what it expects. The server does not actually obtain the password from the client connection but instead confirms it with the NT security database. In the client/server interaction, the client's access token is obtained indirectly from the information passed across the client connection. (Actually, it's not really an access token that is obtained but rather an *impersonation token*, but we will ignore the difference for this discussion.)

The problem with accessing network resources is that password knowledge is required to establish a network connection; without that password, the connection fails. The same limitation applies to a process created with *CreateProcessAsUser.* This API takes a token representing a user's security context. When this token is obtained from an NTLM authenticated connection, the process gets created without direct access to the user's password. A more direct way to create an access token for a particular user is to use an API that requires a user name and password. For example, by using the *LogonUser* API, a process running under the Joe security context can programmatically log in as an administrator and obtain a corresponding access token. (That is, it obtains the logon session access token for the user "administrator" in the same way the system would create an access token when an administrator logs on interactively.) The following code fragment illustrates this impersonation sequence:

```
// The security context here is Joe. We need to logon as the
// administrator and get his access token (hUserToken.)
LogonUser("Administrator", "ComputerName", "Password",
    LOGON32_LOGON_INTERACTIVE, LOGON32_PROVIDER_DEFAULT,
    &hUserToken);
ImpersonateLoggedOnUser(hUserToken);
// We are now impersonating the administrator account. Note that
// if we called CreateProcess at this time, the new process would
// run in the context of Joe.
// Do all work here as the administrator and finish impersonation.
RevertToSelf();
```

◆ Threading Models and Security

Instantiating Component Object Model (COM) objects in threads when impersonation is involved has serious security implications. The security context in which an object runs depends on which apartment type it is.

Each thread in an application that uses COM objects must first initialize the COM library. One of the functions that initializes the COM library gives you the option of specifying whether the thread is part of a single-threaded apartment or part of a multithreaded apartment.

The term *apartment* refers to how many threads can call into a single instance of an object. Single-threaded apartments allow only one thread to call into a single instance of an object, so when you have multiple threads calling into your object, each thread gets its own instance of the object. Multithreaded apartments can have more than one thread call into a single instance of an object.

When a developer writes a COM object, she specifies whether it can be run in a single-threaded apartment or a multithreaded apartment. An object flagged as being able to run only in a single-threaded apartment is called an *apartment model* object. An object flagged as being able to run in a multithreaded apartment is called a *free threaded* object. If the thread's apartment type and the COM object's apartment type match (that is, a single-threaded apartment is paired with an apartment-model object or a multithreaded apartment is paired with a free-threaded object), the object's code will be called directly from the current thread. If the thread's apartment type and the COM object's apartment type do not match (that is, a single-threaded apartment is paired with a free-threaded object or multithreaded apartment is paired with an apartment-model object), the object's code will have to be launched in an apartment different from the current thread's. This means that in order for the method to execute, calls into the object must block the current thread and then be marshaled to a different thread. When the method is finished executing, the results must be marshaled back to the calling thread.

If a server's thread is currently impersonating a client, the impersonation is restricted to that individual thread. So if you call an object that must be executed in a thread that is different from the thread currently impersonating the client, the object code executes in the security context of the new thread. This usually means the code is running in the context of the process's owner. If, however, the apartment type for the object and the apartment type for the thread match, the call is made within the current thread and the object's code runs in the security context of the client that is being impersonated.

Privileges

Logging on a user programmatically and obtaining his access token with the *LogonUser* API is a security threat, so Windows NT implements a safeguard—*privileges*. A user whose process calls the *LogonUser* API must have a specified privilege: SE_TCB_NAME. (Users holding this privilege are identified as members of the Trusted Computer Base, or TCB.)

Earlier we learned that an access token contains information about a user's account, groups, and privileges. Now it's time to define what a privilege is. Privileges are mechanisms for discrete control of rarely performed or potentially dangerous tasks, such as shutting down the system or impersonating a user. They provide stricter control of tasks than DACLs do because you can enable a privilege directly before you perform a task and then disable it after the task is performed. This reduces the risk of unintentionally performing a crippling task.

A privilege is represented by a unique 64-bit value, which is referred to as a *locally unique identifier (LUID)*. All LUIDs for all Windows NT privileges are defined in the WINNT.H header file that comes with the Microsoft Windows Platform Software Development Kit.

A Windows NT administrator can add or revoke privileges for individual users via the User Manager application. This application can be found by default in the Administration Tools group. To establish privileges for a user, from the User Manager menu, choose Policies/User Rights to open the dialog box shown in Figure 12.1. Click the Show Advanced User Rights check box to activate it, and then in the Right drop-down list, choose the appropriate privilege. Click the Add button to add the selected privilege to the users or groups. In Figure 12.1, you can see that we have granted the IUSR_ LEONBR-HM account the privilege of acting as part of the operating system (although it might not be a good idea to grant such a powerful privilege).

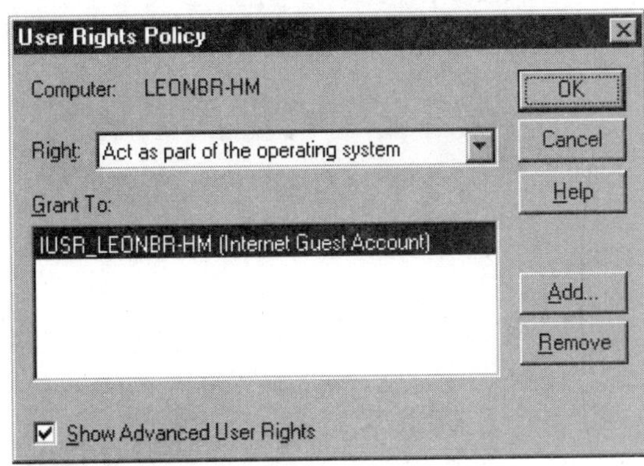

FIGURE 12.1

The User Rights Policy dialog box in User Manager.

◆ Friendly Privilege Names in User Manager

Why was the user account in our example granted the Act As Part Of The Operating System privilege instead of the SE_TCB_NAME privilege? Well, it actually was granted the SE_TCB_NAME privilege—the Act As Part Of The Operating System option in User Manager sets the SE_TCB_NAME privilege. The friendly privilege names shown in User Manager do not translate easily into the cryptic privilege constants defined in WINNT.H. Take a look at the Microsoft Knowledge Base article Q101366, "Definition and List of Windows NT Advanced User Rights," which maps other privileges to their friendly names.

The Big Picture

We've learned a lot about Windows NT security, but now we need to look at the information in the context of the full Windows NT security model, which is illustrated in Figure 12.2. On one side is a process, identified by an access token, and on the other is a Windows NT securable object being accessed by the process.

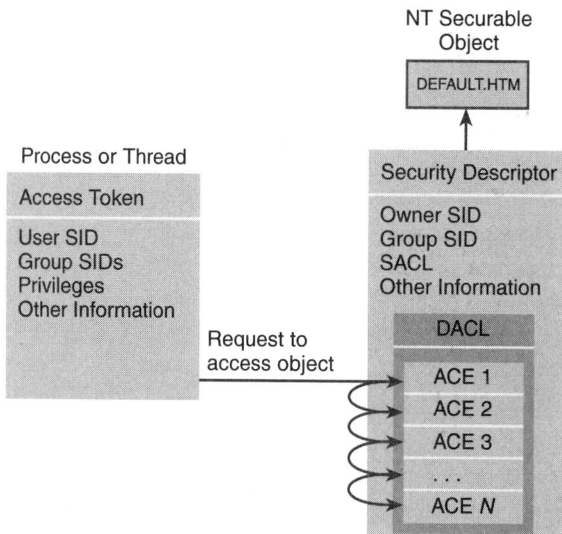

FIGURE 12.2

The Windows NT security model, showing the securable object (DEFAULT.HTM) being accessed by the process (or thread) with the corresponding access token.

Note in Figure 12.2 that the securable object has a security descriptor structure associated with it. This security descriptor structure has a DACL containing more then one ACE. When the process tries to access the securable object, the operating system extracts the user's SID from the process's access token. The user's SID is checked against each ACE in the security descriptor. An object can have more than one ACE for the same user, and when it does, the permissions specified in each ACE accumulate. Thus if one entry allows the group GUEST to read a file and the other entry allows the group to write to the file, any member of the GUEST group can both read the file and write to it. If one of the ACEs in the list denies access to the object, the system won't check any other entries and the requesting process won't be able to access the file. An ACE denying access takes precedence over an ACE allowing access.

When a new object is created, ACEs can be associated with it via the SECURITY_ ATTRIBUTES structure documented in the Platform SDK. Most securable objects have at least one ACE associated with them. However, an object might not have any, which renders the object inaccessible.

Even when an object has no ACE (and hence is inaccessible), the owner of the object can still change its permissions either programmatically or by using the following applications, which make it accessible again: Registry Editor (REGEDT32.EXE), Window NT Explorer (EXPLORER.EXE), or File Manager (WINFILE.EXE). Thankfully we don't have to write code to change ACEs programmatically because of the ACE editing capabilities incorporated into the applications mentioned above.

You can control access to registry keys by running the Registry Editor and choosing the Security menu. You can also control access to directories and files from Windows NT Explorer or File Manager for an NTFS partition. In Windows NT Explorer, right-click on a directory or file, choose Properties, and then click the Security tab. In File Manager, select a directory or file and choose the Security menu. Figure 12.3 shows the File Permissions dialog box, which was opened from Windows NT Explorer. This dialog box shows permissions (or ACEs) for the DEFAULT.ASP file. The administrator or a member of the Administrators group can not only control access to files and registry keys, but she can also take ownership of them and set auditing permissions for them. (SACLs, which were defined earlier in the chapter, are used by the operating system for auditing. We will look into auditing later in this chapter.)

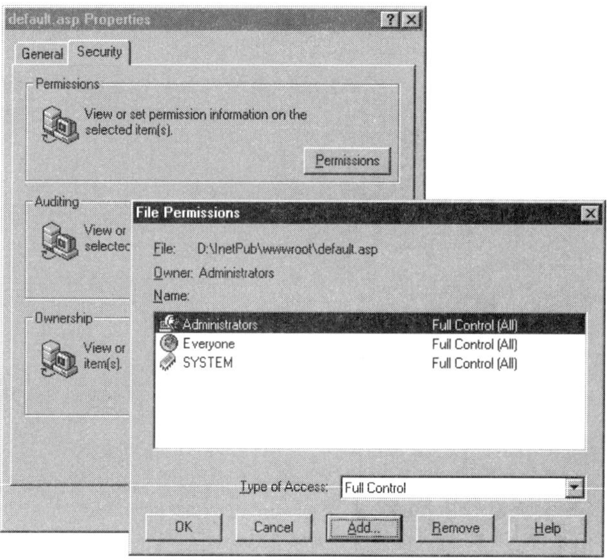

FIGURE 12.3

Security permissions on the NTFS file DEFAULT.ASP.

Securing the Desktop

If Windows NT is to be fully secure, even the windows on your desktop have to be protected. The following scenario illustrates why this is important. Suppose you have a Microsoft Word 97 window open under Windows NT and you are writing a book. If other users had access to your window, they could get its contents—that is, they could copy the text of your book—and potentially publish the book under their own names. This scenario is far-fetched, but it does illustrate a valid point. Without security, someone other than the interactive user could potentially access the contents of a window. How does the system ensure that users who connect to your machine over the network don't access your window? Windows themselves are not protected. If you tried to pass a window handle to a security API such as *SetUserObjectSecurity*, you would get an error.

Although a window itself is not a securable object, a window's parent object (named *desktop*) and the parent of the *desktop* object (named *window station*) are securable objects. The *window station* object contains items such as the clipboard. The fact that this object contains the clipboard is one more reason you would want to secure it—you wouldn't want the contents of your cut-and-paste operations to be visible to other users. The *window station* object also secures access to the graphical display device, the keyboard, and the mouse. Because the *desktop* object is a child object of *window station*, it inherits the security of *window station*. The *desktop* object secures access to the logical display surface that you see on your computer screen, including windows, hooks, and other Graphical Device Interface (GDI) elements.

At this point, we know enough about security to move on to the next topic, Windows NT services. Services are directly affected by NT security, and IIS runs as a service.

Windows NT Services

Services are special executables that run in the background and do not have a typical window or console. Services can be configured to start automatically when the system boots whether or not a user logs on.

The Windows NT *Service Control Manager (SCM)* controls services. It can start, pause, and stop them. You can use the Net commands to communicate with the SCM:

```
NET START enumerates all running services.
NET START servicename starts a service.
NET STOP servicename stops a service.
```

Windows NT also provides a graphical utility to control services. You can run this utility by opening the Services applet in the Control Panel. The dialog box that appears, shown in Figure 12.4, lists each installed service and its current status.

When a programmer creates a service, he writes code for the service as well as code that registers the service with the SCM. Each service can either run in its own process or share a process with other services. (A single executable can have more than one service—for example, INETINFO.EXE, the executable for the IIS, shares a process with the FTP, WWW, Admin Service, NNTP, and SMTP services.)

NOTE

When a service is registered with SCM, a registry entry for the service is created under HKEY_LOCAL_MACHINE\SYSTEM\CurrentControlSet\Services. *One of the keys under a specific service is ImagePath, which is the actual executable where the service code resides. For all services mentioned above, the ImagePath points to the same file—INETINFO.EXE.*

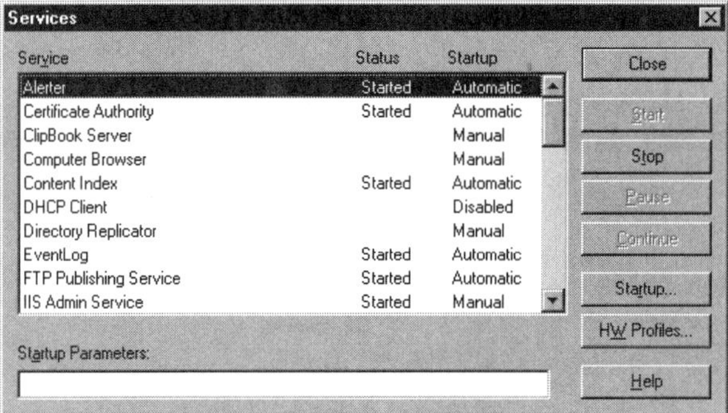

FIGURE 12.4

The Services dialog box, showing the status of all installed services.

The Service User Account

Every process running under a Windows NT system has to have an access token representing the security context of the user under whose account the process executes. Windows NT service processes are no exceptions. When a service is registered with the SCM by using the *CreateService* API, a user name (or account) and a password (if necessary) are specified as API parameters. When that service starts, the SCM logs on the specified account, gets an access token, and attaches the token to the service's process. From then on, all interaction among a service and securable objects takes place in the security context of the specified account. When the service tries to read a file on the NTFS partition, the service's access token is compared to the file's security descriptor.

Note that the SCM does not maintain information about the current password. If the password has expired, the service will fail to start and error messages will be logged in the NT Event Log. Logon accounts for services that are running as separate processes can be changed by the Service Control Manager. As with other options, modifications can be done programmatically or via the Services applet in the Control Panel. Figure 12.5 shows where you can set the user name and the password for the Schedule service. To access the Service dialog box, double-click on the service's entry in the Services applet list box. If a service is configured to run in the same process as other services, then its account can't be changed and must be the Local System account. Let's take a look at the implications of this situation.

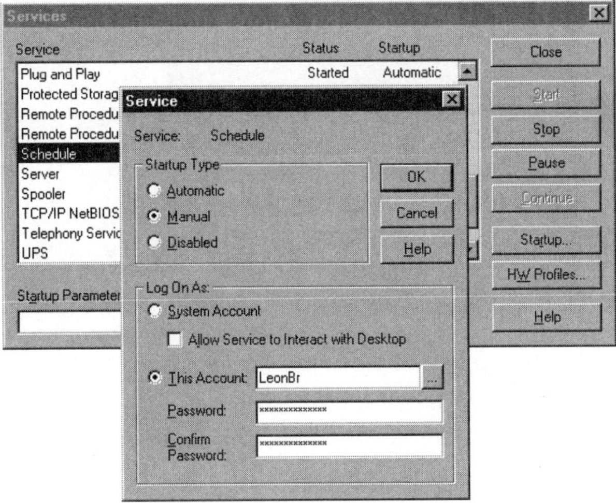

FIGURE 12.5

Configuring startup and logon properties for a service in the Service dialog box.

The Local System Account and the Network

The Local System account is a built-in system account. You won't see it in User Manager even though the system account is part of the Windows NT operating system. All system processes, including the SCM, run in the Local System security context. The Local System account is the default account used for starting services, and it has virtually unlimited authority on the local computer. Any process running in the context of the Local System account does not have typical security credentials (a user name, a password, and a domain) that could be used for validation by other computers on the network. Thus it has no access to network resources such as shared directories. Don't get confused by the fact that each Windows NT machine has an account with the name Local System. Accounts with the same name on different machines are different accounts. For example, *machine_1\Joe* and *machine_2\Joe* have distinct credentials.

The absence of credentials and the unlimited authority on the local machine for the process running under the Local System account suggest serious security issues. If a typical user gets contact with a process that runs in the Local System context, she could instantly have access to as many rights on the local machine as the operating system has. How could this happen? If a service running under the Local System account starts a batch file, and the interactive user interrupts the service by pressing Ctrl-C (more about service and desktop interaction a little later), the command window with the Local System security context remains.

To intentionally create and use a command window running under the Local System account, follow this procedure. First make sure that the Schedule service is running under the Local System account and that the Allow Service To Interact With Desktop option is checked. (You can see this option in Figure 12.5.) For this change to take effect, you'll need to restart the service. (Whenever you change the account or activate an option, the service must be restarted.) Now enter the following command at a command prompt to instruct the schedule service to start a console, where HH:MM is the military time for just a couple of minutes ahead of the current system time:

```
at HH:MM d:\winnt\system32\cmd.exe
```

At the specified time, a console window, like the one shown in Figure 12.6, will pop up on the screen. We displayed the environment variables to show the user name and user domain in this console.

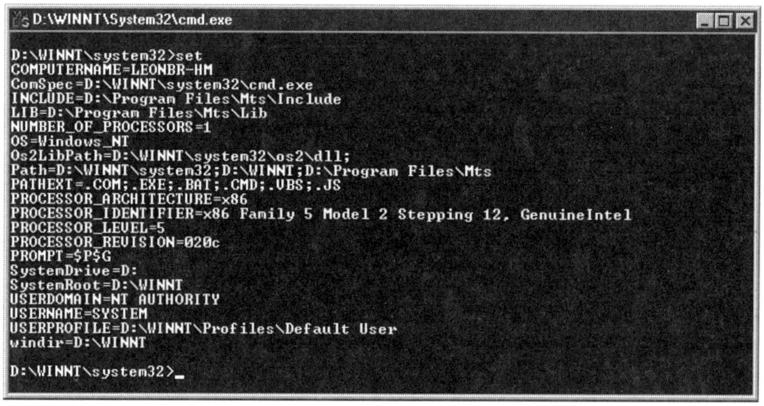

```
D:\WINNT\System32\cmd.exe

D:\WINNT\system32>set
COMPUTERNAME=LEONBR-HM
ComSpec=D:\WINNT\system32\cmd.exe
INCLUDE=D:\Program Files\Mts\Include
LIB=D:\Program Files\Mts\Lib
NUMBER_OF_PROCESSORS=1
OS=Windows_NT
Os2LibPath=D:\WINNT\system32\os2\dll;
Path=D:\WINNT\system32;D:\WINNT;D:\Program Files\Mts
PATHEXT=.COM;.EXE;.BAT;.CMD;.VBS;.JS
PROCESSOR_ARCHITECTURE=x86
PROCESSOR_IDENTIFIER=x86 Family 5 Model 2 Stepping 12, GenuineIntel
PROCESSOR_LEVEL=5
PROCESSOR_REVISION=020c
PROMPT=$P$G
SystemDrive=D:
SystemRoot=D:\WINNT
USERDOMAIN=NT AUTHORITY
USERNAME=SYSTEM
USERPROFILE=D:\WINNT\Profiles\Default User
windir=D:\WINNT

D:\WINNT\system32>_
```

FIGURE 12.6

The console started by the Schedule service inheriting the Local System security context.

Everything you do in this window is in the context of the Local System, so if you tried to establish a network connection to another machine, the connection would fail. Likewise, starting Task Manager (TASKMGR.EXE) from this console window allows you to end any system process because system processes run in the same security context of the Local System account. (We don't recommend doing this.) You can see that the console window running in the system's security context can be a very destructive tool in the wrong hands.

When Task Manager is started in the usual way—by right-clicking on the task bar—it runs in the security context of the user who is interactively logged on. Trying to end any system process at this point would certainly fail. This failure occurs because, by default, only the current owner of a process has permission to terminate it. If you wanted to change the permissions so that you could end the process, you would need to give your account PROCESS_TERMINATE access. To give your account this access, you would need to write a program that opened a handle to the process, took over ownership (you would need to be an administrator for this to work), and then adjusted the permissions. Once you had PROCESS_TERMINATE access, you could kill the process using the *TerminateProcess* API.

Services or processes running under the Local System account do not have the proper credentials to establish authenticated network connections. You can, however, configure certain shares and named pipes so that services can connect to them by using a *null session*.

Glossary

null session *A network session (connection), established by the process, that does not have a valid user name and password. By default, sessions established by a service are null sessions.*

By default, Windows NT shares and pipes prohibit null session connections, but you can overwrite this restriction by modifying the registry on the target Windows NT machine. This is the registry location:

```
HKEY_LOCAL_MACHINE
 \SYSTEM
  \CurrentControlSet
   \Services
    \LanmanServer
     \Parameters
```

This key contains the *NullSessionPipes* and *NullSessionShares* values, which list all the pipes and shares that will accept null session connections (that is, connections established by a service). Take a look at Figure 12.7. If you want to enable null session access to all pipes and shares, add the REG_DWORD value *RestrictNullSessAccess* and set it to *0*.

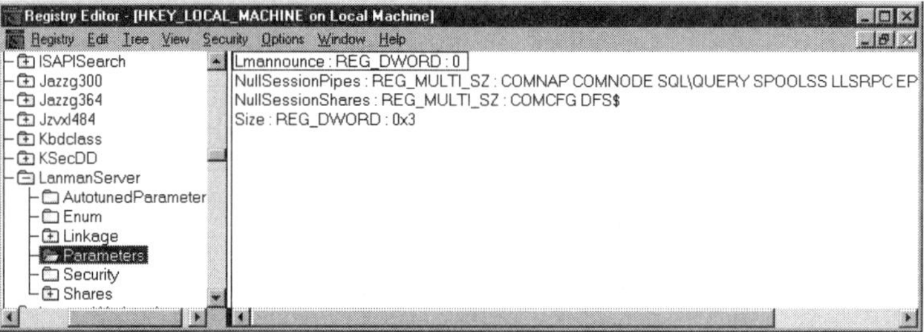

FIGURE 12.7

The **NullSessionPipes** *and* **NullSessionShares** *registry keys.*

Establishing a network connection is not the only tricky situation for services. Objects created by the services (pipes, memory-mapped files, processes, and so on) are not accessible to connections other than those of the Local System account. If you want to give everyone access to your service's objects, you can simply apply a NULL DACL to your object's security descriptor. A NULL DACL is a DACL that grants all users and groups full access to the object. Doing so effectively prevents the system from performing any access checks on the object. Don't confuse a NULL DACL, which grants everyone access to the object, with an empty DACL without ACEs, which denies everyone access to the object. The Win32 Security documentation explains how to programmatically set DACLs so that you can grant or deny access to objects.

Another situation that can cause problems with services occurs when a service can't open the *HKEY_CURRENT_USER* and *HKEY_LOCAL_MACHINE\SECURITY* registry locations. Services typically have access only to the default user profile. (See the *USERPROFILE* environment variable in Figure 12.6.) This makes simple tasks such as sending mail from a service complex because the default MAPI profile, which is stored in the *HKEY_CURRENT_USER* registry key, is not accessible.

Glossary

Messaging Application Programming Interface (MAPI) *A messaging architecture based on COM that enables applications to interact with multiple messaging systems.*

As if you haven't already seen enough problems with services, you're about to see that accessing the desktop from a service isn't a snap either. You learned earlier that the desktop is a securable object. Each service has its own secured desktop and by default uses its own instead of the interactive user's desktop. (Remember that we don't want services stealing content off the users' clipboards.) Recall that we had to run our schedule service as an interactive service, which enabled us to see the console created by CMD.EXE. Now try this: don't make the schedule service interactive and follow the same instructions as before to start CMD.EXE from the schedule service. You won't see the console window at the predefined time, but you will see the CMD.EXE process in Task Manager. The console window shows up but does so on the service's own hidden desktop, which you can't see and which does not accept your input.

If you want to enable a service to display windows on the interactive desktop, open the Service startup dialog box from the Control Panel Services applet and choose the Allow Service To Interact With Desktop option. (See Figure 12.5.) Note that this option is available only if your service is running as the Local System account because typically any other account would not have permissions to the interactive desktop. If you don't want to use the interactive desktop in your service, you can still perform the simple task of displaying a message box on the interactive desktop directly from the service, even if a user is not logged in. You do so by using a special flag named *MB_SERVICE_NOTIFICATION*, with the *MessageBox* API.

Debugging a Service

At this point in our discussion, services might seem like pretty scary things. Because services have so many strange characteristics, you might think that running a debugger on your service would be a huge challenge, but that's not necessarily true. There are a few different ways to debug a service.

The first option is to attach a debugger to a running service. The second option is to run your service as an interactive process. Some services are written in such a way that they can be run interactively as an application in addition to being run as a service. The third option is to use the Win32 *DebugBreak* API. When *DebugBreak* is executed, the system opens a dialog box that notifies the user that INT 3 (debug break interrupt) has been reached. If the system has the Just In Time (JIT) debugging option configured, clicking the dialog box's Debug button will start the debugger for the current process.

NOTE

JIT debugging allows the operating system to start a debugger when a process terminates abnormally or encounters an unhandled exception. Without JIT, Windows NT would report an error but not start the debugger. See Microsoft Visual C++ or your favorite Windows NT debugger documentation for more information.

When using *DebugBreak,* be aware of problems when the service and the desktop interact. For example, Visual C++ fails to initialize from a service (which is how Visual C++ starts when *DebugBreak* is called in a service and Visual C++ is configured to be your JIT debugger) that does not run in the Local System account. Visual C++ won't be able to interact with the desktop because it can't access the desktop object. Microsoft Knowledge Base article Q98890, "HOWTO: Debugging a service," talks more about this issue. We will revisit debugging when we talk about debugging ISAPI applications in Chapter 20.

Why have we spent half of this chapter reviewing security and Windows NT services? As it turns out, IIS is a Windows NT service that runs under the Local System account.

Security and IIS

Let's apply what we've learned about services and security thus far to the IIS. INETINFO.EXE is the executable that contains the WWW, FTP, and other services. The various IIS services share a single process, which means they are required to run in the context of the Local System account. But running ASP scripts, invoking ISAPI extensions, and even just accessing files on an NTFS partition in the context of the Local System account might not be a good idea. IIS uses impersonation to avoid servicing requests in the context of the Local System account.

When IIS is installed, two local accounts—or domain accounts, if Windows NT is the Primary Domain Controller (PDC)—are created: the IUSR_*computername* and the IWAM_*computername* accounts. (In both instances, *computername* would be replaced with the name of your computer. For example, the name of my machine is *leonbr-hm,* so the IUSR_LEONBR-HM account would be created on my computer.)

By default the IUSR_*computername* account is the account used by the IIS for anonymous requests. Now let's look at how IIS uses it.

◆ Local and Domain Accounts

Each Windows NT machine maintains a database of local users. These users are known to a particular machine and their logons are authenticated locally. An enterprise could have thousands of users and thousands of Windows NT machines. To allow every user the ability to log on to any of the Windows NT machines, each machine would have to maintain a database of all users in the company. Such a task has a serious drawback, in addition to being unrealistic. As we learned earlier in this chapter, a *machine_1\Joe* account is not the same as a *machine_2\Joe* account. Therefore, having accounts on all the machines does not enable Joe to easily access machines over the network.

There is a better solution: Windows NT account domains. To solve the problem, a group of Windows NT machines can be organized into logical units called *domains*. Each domain has one and only one Primary Domain Controller (PDC). The PDC maintains the user database for the entire domain, and its user accounts are said to be domain accounts. All Windows NT machines in the domain can have local accounts except domain controllers, whose local accounts database holds a copy of the domain accounts. When a user with an account in the domain tries to log on to a computer in the domain, the computer he logs on to won't be able to validate his credentials because it does not have his account information stored locally. To validate the user's credentials, the Windows NT machine sends the credentials to a domain controller. Each domain might have one or more Backup Domain Controllers (BDCs). These machines maintain a copy of the user database, which is regularly updated with any changes to the user accounts. The BDCs share with the PDC the load of authenticating all logon requests.

An enterprise might also have more than one domain. Each domain maintains its own user database, potentially creating the same type of problem mentioned earlier, in which each user might need an account on each domain. To avoid this problem, domains can maintain trust relationships. Consider the following: CMPNY corporation has three domains: *CORP*, *ENGNRNG*, and *ACCOUNTING*. The *CORP* domain is going to be what we call a top-level domain. The other two domains, *ENGNRNG* and *ACCOUNTING*, *trust* the *CORP* domain. This means that if a user tries to access machines on *ENGNRNG* or *ACCOUNTING* by using a valid *CORP* domain account, the machines will allow the *CORP* domain account to access their resources. This access is allowed only after the credentials of the user have been verified with a *CORP* domain controller.

The benefits of a domain structure are clear. A user needs to have only one account on the entire enterprise network. Due to trust relationships among domains, the user can potentially access resources in other domains using his *CORP* domain account. And finally, in terms of IIS, if the server is installed on a domain controller, the account of the form IUSR_*computername* actually gets the form IUSR_*domainname*. The benefit of this is that the account is known across the network and permissions can be set up accordingly. This is not the case if the IUSR_*computername* account exists only for a single machine's local accounts database.

Security and Web Applications

Every time a Web service receives an anonymous request from the Web client, the server impersonates the IUSR_*computername* account. An anonymous request from the client means that no user identification or password was supplied with the request. Before trying to access the requested resource via the all-powerful Local System account, however, IIS impersonates the IUSR_*computername* account. By default, the IUSR_*computername* account has only guest privileges.

Web applications run in the same memory space as the IIS process by default. (Recall our discussion about applications in Chapter 4.) So if an ISAPI extension behaves really badly, it could crash the W3SVC service. To avoid such a potentially catastrophic problem, a Web application can be loaded in a separate memory space.

◆ Running In-Process and Out-of-Process Applications

When a client request launches an ISAPI extension (including script-mapped applications such as ASP), the extension is wrapped in the WAM object and loaded by Microsoft Transaction Server (MTS). (See Chapters 16 and 20 for a discussion of MTS.) The WAM object is an in-process object, which means that it is implemented as a DLL instead of as an EXE. So for IIS applications flagged as running in process, IIS simply loads the in-process WAM object, which calls the ISAPI extension. For IIS applications flagged as running out of process, MTS creates a host process by using MTX.EXE, which in turn loads the in-process WAM object. Because the IIS application is running in the MTX.EXE process separately from the IIS service, the application cannot cause the IIS service to crash.

There is a slight performance hit when you run applications out of process, so you should run applications out of process only when you do not trust them. MTS further restricts the damage these "untrusted" applications can do by launching the MTX.EXE process in the context of the IWAM_*computername* account. This means that the code running in an out-of-process application will never run as the Local System account, which has virtually unlimited privileges on the local machine. So in certain situations, such as when a freethreaded component is called from an ASP page, applications running in process execute the component code in the context of the IIS process's owner—the Local System account. For applications marked as out of process, the free-threaded component executes in the context of the MTX.EXE process's owner—the IWAM_*computername* account. By default the IWAM_*computername* account has very limited privileges.

When applications run in a separate memory space, the user IWAM_*computername* comes into play. (Notice that this account starts with IWAM instead of IUSR.) WAM, which stands for Web Application Manager, is a special COM object that loads Internet server applications and communicates with the W3SVC service. The WAM process that is started, which runs in the context of the IWAM_*computername* account, still impersonates the IUSR_*computername* account for anonymous requests. In the worst case scenario, a misbehaving application will crash an instance of the WAM process, but IIS will continue running as if nothing ever happened.

We're going to examine a short ASP script that uses two ActiveX components: Permission Checker (PERMCHK.DLL), which checks file access permissions; and GetUserName (GETUSERNAME.DLL), which gets the user name under whose security context the ASP script runs.

NOTE

PERMCHK.DLL is available with the Exploration Air sample site that installs with the IIS\World Wide Web Sample Site subcomponent of the Windows NT 4.0 Option Pack. Once installed, PERMCHK.DLL is located in the Inetpub\iissamples\ExAir\Bin directory.

GETUSERNAME.DLL is available as part of the samples with the SDK that installs with the IIS\Documentation\SDK subcomponent of the Window NT 4.0 Option Pack. Once installed, GETUSERNAME.DLL is located in the \Inetpub\iissamples\sdk\isapi\extensions\com directory.

Both of these components must be properly registered before the PERMISSION-CHECK.ASP sample will work.

Here is the ASP script (PERMISSIONCHECK.ASP):

```
<%@ Language=VBScript %>
<center><h2> Access Check </h2></center>
<%
    Set Check = Server.CreateObject("MSWC.PermissionChecker")
    Set GetUserName = _
        Server.CreateObject("GetUserNameObj.GetUserNameObj.1")

    If (Request.ServerVariables ("REQUEST_METHOD") = "POST") then
        File = Request.Form("file")
    else
        ' Assume it is GET
        File = Request.QueryString("file")
    end if
    if (File = "") then
        File = Request.ServerVariables ("SCRIPT_NAME")
    end if
```

(continued)

```
        Response.Write "<b>Current user:</b> " & GetUserName.GetMyName & _
            "<br><b> File:</b> " & File & "<br><b> Access:</b> " _
            & Check.HasAccess (File) & "<br>"
%>
```

Invoke this ASP script to see who the default user is and to check whether that user has permission to access the file DEFAULT.ASP in d:\inetpub\wwwroot. After invoking the script through the URL *http://localhost/scripts/PermissionCheck.asp?file=d:\inetpub\wwwroot\default.asp*, the browser displays the text shown in Figure 12.8:

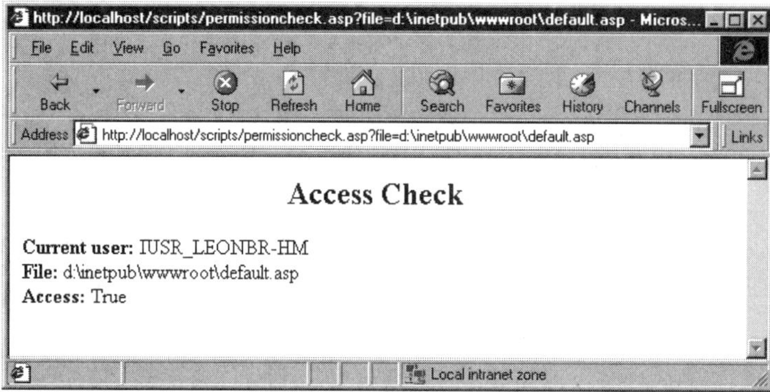

FIGURE 12.8

An ASP script that displays the user name for the context in which the script is running and displays whether this user has access to the specified DEFAULT.ASP file.

This is the expected result for an anonymous connection. When the Web browser makes an anonymous request, the user is not prompted for any identification information. Sometimes, however, you might want the user to be prompted. You can force the user to enter a user name and password. We'll look at how to do that next.

User Authentication and Impersonation

User authentication is a way of limiting the access of certain users to the server. If the requested resource (an HTML file, a directory, or an ASP script) is not accessible to the IUSR_*computername* account, or if anonymous access is disallowed, IIS won't be able to process the browser request. Instead of sending the requested document (or invoking a script), IIS sends the HTTP status code "401 Access Denied." The server response also includes information about which authentication schemes the server supports so that the client knows what method to use for transmitting them to the server. When the browser receives the 401 status code, it acquires user credentials (the user name and password) and resends the request with the credential information. We will discuss the details of server/browser interaction at the protocol level in Chapter 22 when we look more closely at the HTTP protocol.

Because the user's credentials are now available, the resubmitted request is not treated as anonymous anymore. After the credentials have been verified against either the local machine's database of accounts or a domain's database of accounts, the server accesses the resource or runs the script. Because the request has specified a user name, the request should be handled in the security context of the user, so the IUSR_*computername* account will not be used. As it turns out, the method for verifying the user's credentials returns an access token for that particular user. IIS impersonates the user with this token and then handles the request in the security context of the client. What happens when the server needs to run an ASP script or a CGI application? The same thing—to handle anonymous requests, IIS always impersonates the IUSR_*computername* anonymous user. (Remember, the service itself runs as Local System account.) When authentication is performed, the client's user account is impersonated instead of the IUSR_*computername* account.

NOTE

IIS via MTS maintains a thread pool to handle ISAPI extension requests. If the pool is exhausted, a new thread is created. (We talk more about this in Chapter 20 in the context of ISAPI extensions.) IIS changes the thread security context from the Local System account to the account of whatever user it needs to impersonate. Because ASP itself is implemented as an ISAPI extension, the same thing happens when scripts are processed.

To process CGI applications, the server needs to create a new process. It uses the CreateProcessAsUser *API to run the CGI executable in the desired security context.*

Forcing Authentication

There are two methods of forcing IIS to authenticate a user:

- Disallow anonymous access to the file, the virtual directory, or the entire application. To accomplish this, access the Authentication Methods dialog box for the directory or file in the Microsoft Management Console and clear the Allow Anonymous Access check box. The Authentication Methods dialog box can be accessed by right-clicking on the directory or file in the Management Console, choosing Properties, clicking on either the Directory Security or File Security tab, and then clicking the Edit button in the Anonymous Access And Authentication Control section.
- Change NTFS file permissions for the script or HTML file that needs to be secured so that you deny IUSR_*computername* access to it.

Figure 12.9 shows the file permissions for the file SECURE.ASP. Notice that the file is inaccessible to the anonymous user. Because the ACE denying user access has precedence over an ACE allowing access, the IUSR_LEONBR-HM account cannot access the file even though Everyone has full control. Both Windows NT Explorer and File Manager allow the owner of the file (or an administrator) to change file security.

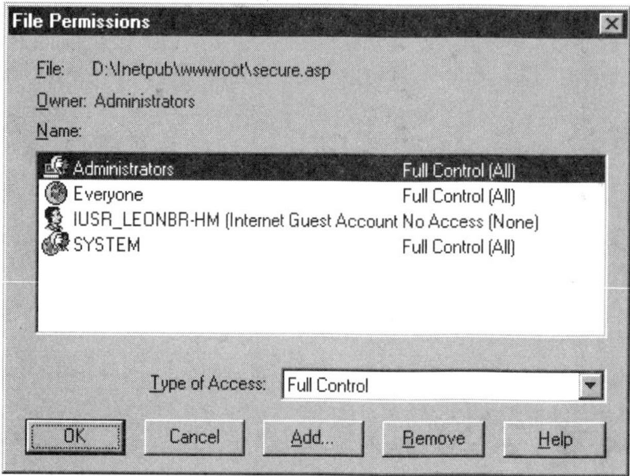

FIGURE 12.9

NTFS file permissions explicitly deny IUSR_LEONBR-HM access.

Verifying that SECURE.ASP is not accessible to the anonymous user could be done easily by running PERMISSIONCHECK.ASP. Figure 12.10 shows the script output for the URL *http://localhost/scripts/PermissionCheck.asp?file=d:\inetpub\wwwroot\secure.asp.*

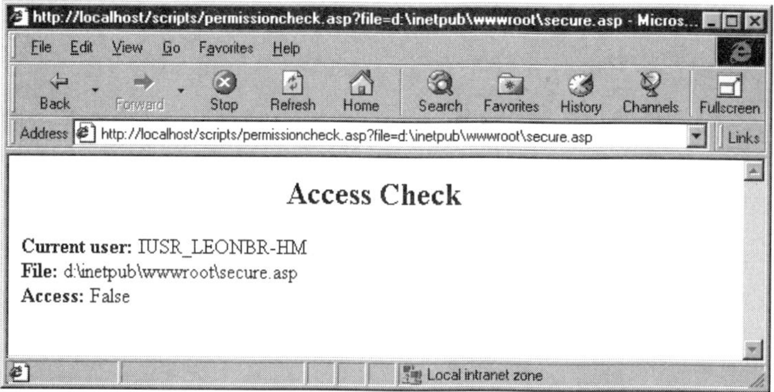

FIGURE 12.10

PERMISSIONCHECK.ASP verifying that SECURE.ASP is not accessible to the anonymous user.

If the browser had sent the request to SECURE.ASP directly, it would have invoked a dialog box that asks the user to enter her name and password. In our verification test, the ASP script PERMISSIONCHECK.ASP, running under the IUSR_LEONBR-HM account, tries to access SECURE.ASP. We can modify the script for PERMISSIONCHECK.ASP so that it can't be run by the anonymous user (in effect, requiring user authentication to be conducted programmatically within the ASP script rather than relying on IIS configuration settings):

```
<%@ Language=VBScript %>
<% if (Len(Request.ServerVariables("LOGON_USER")) = 0 ) then %>
    <% Response.Status = "401 Access Denied" %>
    <HTML><BODY><B>Error: Access is denied.</B><P></BODY></HTML>
<% else %>
<center><h2> Access Check 2 </h2></center>
' ...
' Rest of the old permissioncheck.asp
' ...
<%end if%>
```

When an anonymous user tries to run this script, the *LOGON_USER* variable is absent. Sending the "401 Access Denied" or "401 Unauthorized" status from the script forces the browser to get the user name and password and then resubmit the request. After entering the user name and password, the script runs in the context of a valid Windows NT account instead of the anonymous account. In Figure 12.11, we used the *leonbr* account:

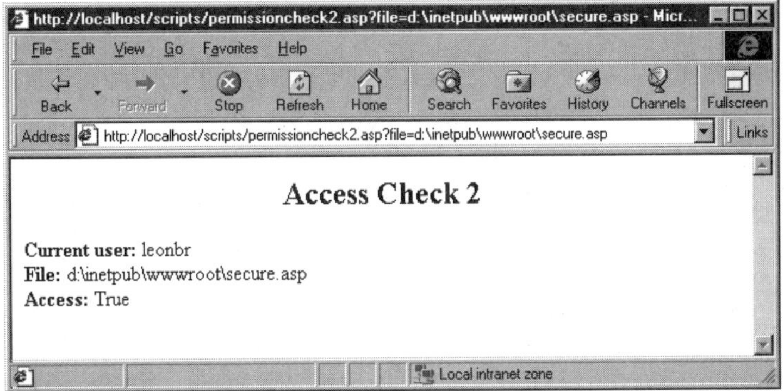

FIGURE 12.11

Modified PERMISSIONCHECK.ASP verifying that SECURE.ASP is now accessible to the **leonbr** *user.*

The ASP programmer could decide to compare the *LOGON_USER* variable with some predefined list of authorized users (*mattpo* and *leonbr*, for example), which would ensure that only *mattpo* and *leonbr* could access the file. To heighten security even more, the variable *REMOTE_ADDR* could be used. The *REMOTE_ADDR* server variable stores the IP address of the client's machine. Checking this variable implements IP-based access control. You don't need to add any code to the script, however, to disallow access to the anonymous user. Modifying NTFS file permissions for PERMISSIONCHECK.ASP has the same effect, forcing IIS to send a 401 status code to the browser.

Authentication Schemes

Having the default IIS directory (\Inetpub) located on an NTFS partition is a crucial part of authentication. Denying anonymous access to the resource is only one part of the authentication game—it merely forces IIS to send a "401 Access Denied" status to the browser. There is more to authentication than just sending a 401 status code to the browser. The server needs to have an authentication scheme selected. An authentication scheme is an agreement between the server and the client about how to transmit user name and password information from the browser to IIS. IIS supports the following authentication schemes:

- Basic
- Windows NT Challenge/Response (also called NTLM)
- SSL Client Certificate-based authentication

The administrator can choose any combination of the supported schemes from the Directory Security or File Security pages in the Properties window. The SSL Client Certificate authentication scheme is covered in Chapter 13, which addresses secure communications. We will examine the other authentication schemes here.

Basic authentication

Basic authentication is the simplest form of authentication. The browser displays the dialog box shown in Figure 12.12 to acquire the user name and password.

After getting the user name and password, the browser creates the following string: *UserName:UserPassword*. The resulting string is Base64 encoded and transmitted with the resubmitted request to the server. Anybody who wants to spy on a client/server transaction and knows how to view network packets by using a tool like Microsoft Network Monitor can easily steal a user name and password if Basic authentication is used. In other words, the Basic authentication scheme is not very secure. It does, however, offer the benefit of being supported by just about any browser running on any platform. In addition, firewalls and proxies do not create problems for Basic authentication.

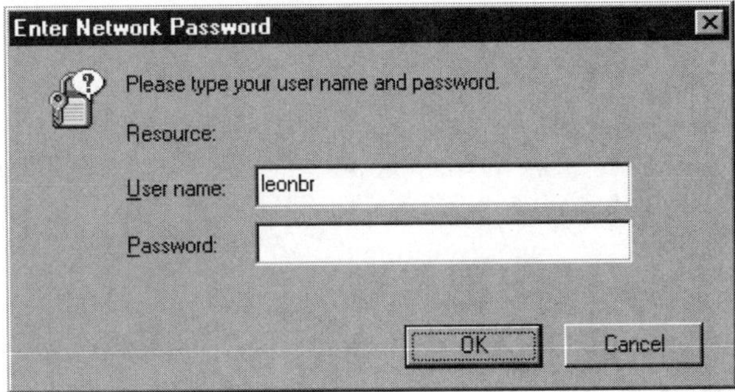

FIGURE 12.12

The browser displaying a dialog box in which the user enters a user name and password.

NTLM authentication

The NTLM authentication scheme is a much more secure method for authenticating users, and it is the same method used by Windows NT machines when they communicate with each other in the network environment. The password is never transmitted over the network, leaving network spies helpless when trying to determine a user's password. The browser automatically uses the credentials of the user who is currently logged on to the client machine; it displays a dialog box requesting the user name and password only when the credentials of the user who is currently logged on don't allow the user to access the requested object. In most cases, especially on an intranet where the network uses a Windows NT Domain structure, NTLM authentication is transparent to the user.

There are several problems, however. One is that NTLM is currently supported only by Microsoft browsers (although NTLM authentication services are available to all Windows applications). Another is that NTLM authentication must be performed on an HTTP Keep-Alive connection. If you are using a proxy and you specify the Keep-Alive connection option, the option applies only to your connection to the proxy. The connection from the proxy to the end server does not share the Keep-Alive connections status. Therefore, NTLM authentication will not work through a proxy.

Using Basic and NTLM authentication schemes simultaneously

Configuring a server to use both Basic and NTLM authentication schemes at the same time can be an excellent solution. NTLM takes precedence over Basic authentication, so NTLM will be used by the browser if the browser supports it. If the browser does not support NTLM, Basic authentication is used automatically.

NOTE

Keep in mind the Windows NT security model and impersonation process that we covered earlier in this chapter. When handling a request by impersonating a user, Basic and NTLM authentication function differently. NTLM authentication does not pass the user's password to the server, so although the server impersonates the user, the thread handling the request will not be able to access network resources.

Although an administrator can use any combination of authentication schemes on the server, disabling Basic and NTLM schemes at the same time is not a good idea (even when anonymous access is allowed). When a URL is inaccessible or an ASP script sends a "401 Access Denied" status, the server does not include any information about which authentication schemes it can handle. The browser prompts the user for a name and password, but because it does not know what method to use to submit them to the server, it does not submit them. Each time the browser retries, the server replies with a 401 status code. After a few unsuccessful attempts, the browser reports an error.

Other Mechanisms for Controlling Access

Supporting user authentication schemes is only one mechanism employed by IIS to control access. We'll go over the other mechanisms in this section to flesh out our understanding of IIS security.

Refusing connections from specific IP addresses or domains is the other level of the server's defenses against unwanted connections. Because the server knows the IP address and domain of each connecting client, it can easily implement access control based on the IP address and domain. You can access the IP Address And Domain Name Restrictions dialog box from the Directory Security property page or File Security property page in the Management Console.

Controlling read, write, and execute access to the directory is another level of IIS security, but the IIS administrator has to be very careful about adding unnecessary permissions for a directory. Directory permissions are set on the Home Directory property page or the Virtual Directory property page of the Management Console. For example, suppose a directory has write and execute permission at the same time. A user could upload a malicious script file with the Microsoft Posting Acceptor or just built-in HTTP functionality with the PUT method. (You will learn about PUT in Chapter 23.) Since the directory has execute permission, the user could run the malicious script, which could be a real danger.

An Overview of Security Logic

Now that we know all about authentication schemes and other access control mechanisms, let's look at how all these security features work together. Figure 12.13 shows a simplified diagram of the logic employed by the server when verifying incoming requests.

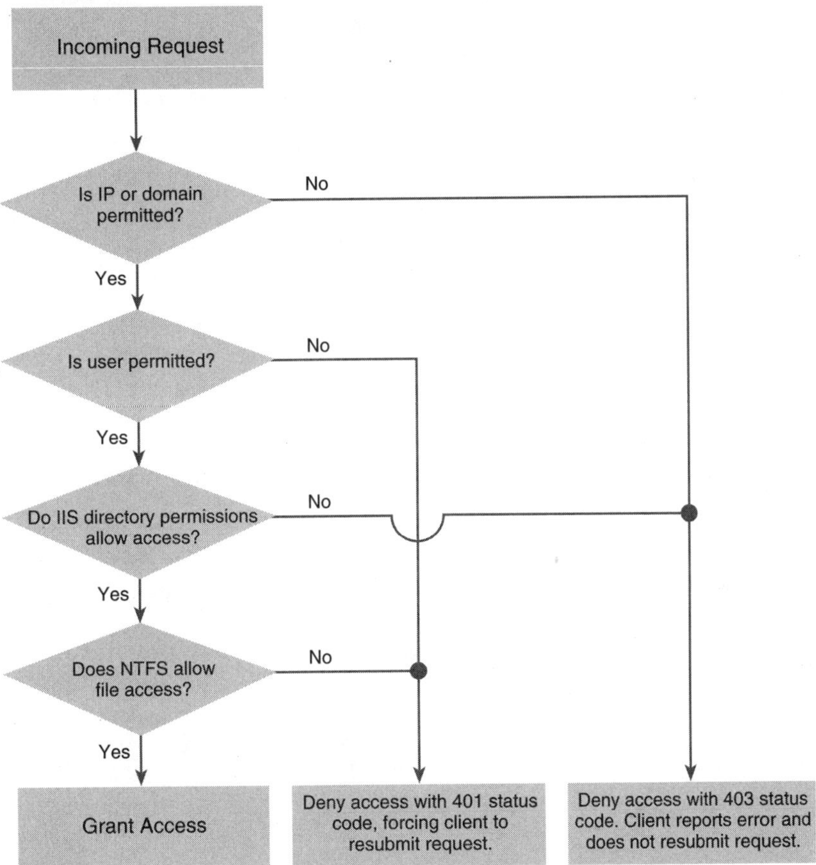

FIGURE 12.13

The logic used by IIS to check incoming requests and either grant or deny access.

As you can see from Figure 12.13, IIS first checks whether the client IP address or domain is allowed access. If not, the status code "403 Forbidden" is sent to the browser. The browser reports an error and does not resubmit the request for access. If the first check succeeds, then IIS checks whether the impersonated user has access to the object. If the request is anonymous, IIS tries to impersonate the

IUSR_*computername* account. If the request has credentials, IIS tries to authenticate the user's credentials. If the user can't be authenticated by the Windows NT server (because the user does not have a valid Windows NT account), the "401 Unauthorized" status code is sent to the client. The client prompts the user for credentials and resubmits the request. After all that has transpired, IIS checks the server's directory permissions and NTFS file permissions.

As you can see, IIS provides a full range of weaponry to secure itself and to control access from unauthorized users. The next security-related feature is *auditing*. Auditing is not a tool for controlling access or authenticating users, but it does enable the system to create a detailed log of events that have taken place.

Auditing

In Chapter 6, we used IIS logs to monitor the past activity of the server. The auditing features of Windows NT are somewhat similar, but they cover a much broader scope of activity. When auditing is enabled and certain objects such as a file located on an NTFS partition are accessed, an event is created in the Windows NT Event Log. If you want to perform file auditing, an NTFS partition is required. By now you probably realize that if security is important, you should use NTFS partitions.

NOTE

If you have a FAT partition on a drive, you can use the CONVERT.EXE utility installed with Windows NT to convert the partition to NTFS without losing the partition's data. Make sure you read all appropriate Windows NT documentation before using this utility!

Every process on the system carries security information that identifies the process owner. This user identity information can be used for auditing purposes, such as keeping track of who is doing what on the system. For example, you could audit every time a process is invoked. One reason to do this is to monitor which users start CGI applications.

The first step in setting up auditing on the system is to change the system policy. This can be done only by the administrator or by a member of the Administrators group. Start User Manager, and from the Policies menu choose Audit. This brings up the dialog box shown in Figure 12.14, where you choose which events you want audited.

Windows NT will log success or failure events when a new process is created. It will not, however, log access to the files on an NTFS drive without an additional step. To audit file access, the file's SACL must be changed either in File Manager or in Windows NT Explorer. Recall from the beginning of the chapter that the System Access Control List contains file auditing information.

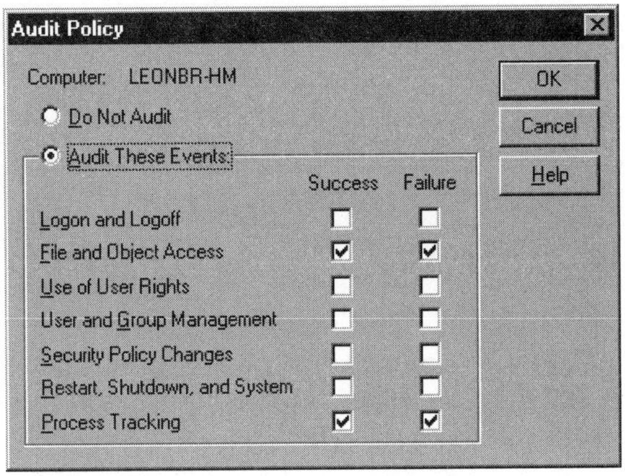

FIGURE 12.14

The Audit Policy dialog box.

In Windows NT Explorer, right-click on the file to bring up the Properties dialog box. On the Security tab, click the Auditing button to bring up the File Auditing dialog box, shown in Figure 12.15. Here you can add auditing information to the file (which adds an ACE to the SACL) in the form of a user name and the corresponding auditable events for that user.

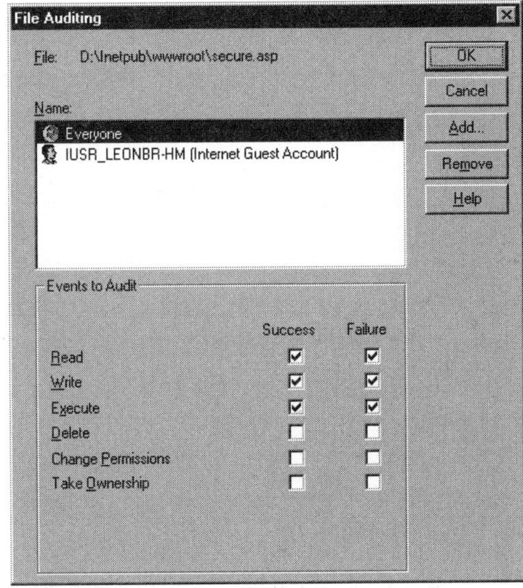

FIGURE 12.15

The File Auditing dialog box.

After you set up the auditing options, you can see the fruits of your labor. Start Windows NT Event Viewer, found in the Administrative Tools group, and choose Log/Security. Figure 12.16 shows quite a number of different audit events in our security log.

Event Viewer - Security Log on \\LEONBR-HM

Log View Options Help

Date	Time	Source	Category	Event	User	Computer
1/8/98	9:01:20 PM	Security	Detailed Tracking	593	leonbr	LEONBR-HM
1/8/98	9:01:20 PM	Security	Detailed Tracking	592	SYSTEM	LEONBR-HM
1/8/98	9:01:20 PM	Security	Object Access	562	leonbr	LEONBR-HM
1/8/98	9:01:20 PM	Security	Object Access	560	leonbr	LEONBR-HM
1/8/98	9:01:14 PM	Security	Object Access	560	IUSR_LEONB	LEONBR-HM
1/8/98	9:01:02 PM	Security	Detailed Tracking	593	leonbr	LEONBR-HM

FIGURE 12.16

List of audit events in the NT security log for **leonbr-hm.**

Filtering events by user or by category allows the system administrator to determine who tried to invoke which scripts and whether the startup was successful. Figure 12.17 shows details of an unsuccessful invocation of the SECURE.ASP file by *leonbr*. In this example, file permissions were set to deny *leonbr* access to SECURE.ASP. (After finding an event like this, an administrator might want to confront this user about why he tried to access the file.)

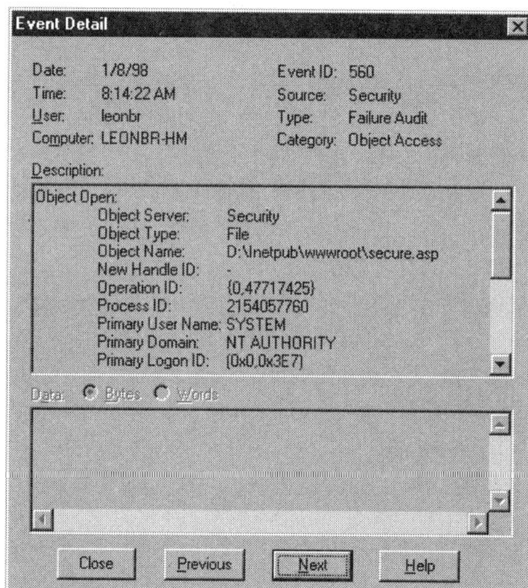

FIGURE 12.17

The Event Detail dialog indicating that the user **leonbr** *failed to access the SECURE.ASP file.*

Auditing is simple to set up, but don't let that fool you—it's a very powerful tool in the hands of a knowledgeable operator. If you are someone who deals with operating system security, you can appreciate the thought that went into the creation of a system with such rich security features. Now let's examine another service that takes advantage of NT security—the FTP service.

The FTP Service

FTP service security is much simpler than Web server security. Just like the Web service, the FTP service runs as the Local System account and impersonates the anonymous user IUSR_*computername* for anonymous connections. All other users must supply the name and password of a valid Windows NT user before they can log in.

With the FTP protocol, logon names and passwords are transferred over the network in clear text. So the most secure option is to allow *only* anonymous connections because it avoids the transfer of sensitive user information over the network. In terms of access control, the FTP service implements security in much the same way that the Web service does. When an FTP client tries to access a file or a directory, the directory permissions (read and write) that are set via the FTP Site Properties window are verified by IIS to determine whether access is allowed. This action occurs before the NTFS file permissions are verified on the requested local file or directory. If the anonymous user logs in and the default directory has a write permission but the NTFS permissions denies the IUSR_*computername* write permission, the file upload operation will fail. Here is how the "Access is denied" error is reported on the FTP client:

```
ftp> open leonbr-hm
Connected to leonbr-hm.
220 leonbr-hm Microsoft FTP Service (Version 4.0).
User (leonbr-hm:(none)): anonymous
331 Anonymous access allowed, send identity (e-mail name) as password.
Password:
230 Anonymous user logged in.
ftp> put cgi.cpp
200 PORT command successful.
550 cgi.cpp: Access is denied.
ftp>
```

Now you have learned about Windows NT operating system security, IIS Web server security, and FTP service security. Is there anything else left to learn about security? Certainly! In the next chapter, we'll learn about security and encryption.

CHAPTER 13

Secure Communications with SSL

In Chapter 12, you learned about a number of security measures used to authenticate and restrict access to various objects on the server. Another key feature of a secure system is private communication. No longer is the World Wide Web mainly used to download HTML pages. Through Microsoft Internet Information Server users have access to sensitive data on corporate intranets and the Internet via a user's authenticated identity. Even electronic financial transactions are taking place on the Web, and credit card numbers are being shuffled back and forth millions of times a day.

Data transmitted using the HTTP protocol, which is the client/server protocol used to access information on the Web, is very easy to read. If you have a network analyzer, like Microsoft's Network Monitor, you can see and interpret every HTTP request and response that a user makes. For most Web browsing, the capability to see what someone else is transmitting over the Web isn't a big deal because most Internet servers contain public information. However, sensitive, private data can be at risk because the data can be monitored and is not secure.

You can perform sensitive operations without worrying about a lack of privacy by establishing a secure underlying connection in which all the data passing between any two machines is encrypted. The Secure Socket Layer (SSL) and the Private Communication Technology (PCT) protocols allow for a very secure link between machines. This link not only keeps the data privileged but also allows the two machines involved to be authenticated. In this chapter, we'll review the technology for securing communications and then examine SSL configuration options.

Encryption

There are a wide variety of methods for encrypting data, from using cereal box encoder rings to using complex mathematical algorithms. It's important to understand some of the basic principles of modern encryption before looking at the mechanisms that enable us to apply those principles. Let's start out by considering a simple encryption scenario.

Take a simple phrase like "The sun is hot." The ASCII equivalent for this sentence is the following hexadecimal sequence:

```
T  h  e     s  u  n     i  s     h  o  t  .
54 68 65 20 73 75 6E 20 69 73 20 68 6F 74 2E
```

By converting our original sentence into ASCII, we have encrypted the data. Unfortunately this sort of encryption is rather easy to break because we are using the same principles as those underlying a cereal box decoder ring. But we have managed to convert our message into a numeric format, and now it can be manipulated using some mathematical principles.

For this type of encryption to work, two functions are necessary:

$f(x)$ and $g(x)$ such that if $f(x)=y$, then $g(y)=x$

This equation must be true for all values of x that we are encrypting. We refer to the function $g(x)$ as the inverse of $f(x)$. One example of a suitable set of functions that could be used to encrypt half a byte at a time is this:

```
f(x) = (3*x) mod 16
g(x) = (11*x) mod 16
```

The asterisks in this case indicate multiplication. The "mod," short for *modulus*, is an arithmetic operation whose result is the remainder when you divide the item to the left of mod by the item to the right of mod. In our ASCII phrase, we are going to interpret half a byte at a time. The result looks like this:

```
           T  h  e     s  u  n     i  s     h  o  t  .
x          54 68 65 20 73 75 6E 20 69 73 20 68 6F 74 2E
f(x) = y = FC 28 2F 60 59 5F 2A 60 2B 59 60 28 2D 5C 6A
g(y) =     54 68 65 20 73 75 6E 20 69 73 20 68 6F 74 2E
           T  h  e     s  u  n     i  s     h  o  t  .
```

The problem with this encryption scheme is that it wouldn't take a person too long to crack it with a little guessing and some simple analysis. The frequent use of the encoded value *60*, for example, would probably lead the decoder to conclude that *60* represents a space. Now that she's determined where the spaces are, she knows that the digit *6* represents *2* and that the digit *0* represents *0*. Since the message has only a handful of two-letter words, she would have to guess just a little more to come up with the third word, *is*. Once she infers that *2B* represents *i* and *59* represents *s* (or in more detail, that *5* represents *7*, *9* represents *3*, and *B* represents *9*), then we quickly find ourselves near the end of a Wheel of Fortune game with no "Lose a Turn" markers on the wheel.

In this example, we used some cryptoanalysis principles, such as looking at the reoccurring bytes in the contents of the encoded message to determine the original phrase. If the decoder were to take the next step in the encryption process, she would determine the percentages of the recurrence of certain numbers and match these percentages against the frequency percentage of letters in everyday conversation. The encoded letter that occurs most would be the letter *e* (which is the letter that appears the most frequently in standard English).

We can make this sort of encryption significantly more difficult by creating a rotating effect. In our encryption scheme, the function

```
f(x) = (3*x) mod 16
```

could be considered one of many functions that follow the same format. For example, we could replace the multiplier *3* with a value of *7* or with any number of values. In our case, it's important that the number is relatively prime to 16 (that is, it shares no common factors with *16*); if it weren't, we wouldn't be able to create a proper inverse function that produces our original values. If we replace the modulus of *16* with a prime number, then all values less than our modulus will be relatively prime to it. So if we set our modulus to the prime value *17* instead of *16*, all the following functions would create a valid encryption function for us:

```
f(x) = (1*x) mod 17
f(x) = (2*x) mod 17
f(x) = (3*x) mod 17
f(x) = (4*x) mod 17
f(x) = (5*x) mod 17
f(x) = (6*x) mod 17
f(x) = (7*x) mod 17
f(x) = (8*x) mod 17
f(x) = (9*x) mod 17
f(x) = (10*x) mod 17
f(x) = (11*x) mod 17
f(x) = (12*x) mod 17
f(x) = (13*x) mod 17
f(x) = (14*x) mod 17
f(x) = (15*x) mod 17
f(x) = (16*x) mod 17
```

In fact, we can refer to our function as the following, where *K* can be any one of the 16 values in our list:

$$f_K(x) = (K*x) \bmod 17$$

We refer to *K* as the *key* to our function. When we replace *K* with *3* in our new encryption function, we say that this encryption has a key value of *3* because in essence we have this:

```
f_3(x) = (3*x) mod 17
```

We already know that it would be simple to decrypt a message with any of these sorts of encryption schemes, but what we can do is change our key value while we are encrypting our message. For example, we might increase our original key by 1 for every 4 bits: if we encrypt a sequence of values *1,2,3,4,5,* and we start with a key value of *3,* our encryption would turn the values into the following:

```
f_3(1) = (3*1) mod 17 = 3
f_4(2) = (4*2) mod 17 = 8
f_5(3) = (5*3) mod 17 = 15
f_6(4) = (6*4) mod 17 = 7
f_7(5) = (7*5) mod 17 = 1
```

These changes make cryptoanalytic attempts at deciphering harder, but not impossible. One of the things we can do to make the scheme even more challenging is modify the way we change the keys, such as create a permutation function to mix the bits that represent the numbers we're going to use. We can even manipulate the inputs into our function by doing a bitwise "exclusive or" between our current element and the previous encrypted element.

Statistically, all these methods provide a more randomly encoded result, but the important fact is that any combination of these algorithms is completely reversible as long as the function, initial key, and method used to manipulate the key are known. If a person is going to decrypt the contents, she will need to have an inverse function (or sequence of functions) that ultimately provide the original text.

Symmetric Encryption Schemes

We have been looking at a "symmetric" encryption method because it uses the same key to both encrypt and decrypt a message. Even if the algorithm being used is known, as long as the key stays private, the message can be considered secure. In popular symmetric encryption schemes, the key is often referred to as the *session key* since it is usually used only for the length of the particular encryption session set up between the two communicators. Figure 13.1 illustrates a symmetric encryption scheme.

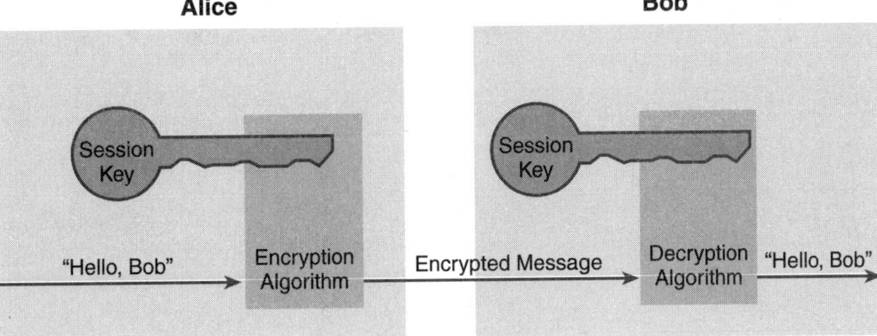

FIGURE 13.1

A typical symmetric encryption scheme.

One of the advantages of symmetric encryption over other forms of encryption is that it is relatively fast to encrypt and decrypt messages. For our purposes, a number of symmetric encryption schemes can be used as the basis for developing secure Web communication mechanisms.

Data Encryption Standard

Data Encryption Standard (DES) is a symmetric encryption scheme that was made a United States government standard in 1977. DES is considered a *block* cipher because data is typically encrypted in 64-bit blocks. The key for DES is 56 bits long, which is actually considered relatively short for most encryption algorithms. However, the use of DES is rarely approved for export to foreign countries.

RC2

RC2 is another block cipher that can take variable length keys. RSA Data Security developed it, and its algorithm is confidential. RC2 was given a special status by the United States government so that export to foreign countries could be approved quickly as long as the key length was limited to 40 bits. RC2 with 128-bit key support is commonly used within the United States.

RC4

RC4 is a *stream* cipher also developed by RSA Data Security. Unlike block ciphers, stream ciphers encrypt a message bit by bit rather than as an entire block. RC4 is similar to RC2 in that the algorithm can be implemented with keys of various lengths. Export of RC4 has been given special approval by the United States government as long as the key length is limited to 40 bits or less.

Public Key Encryption

We know that a message encrypted using symmetric encryption is only as secure as the mechanism used to transmit the key between the sender and the receiver. To transmit data across the Internet in an encrypted fashion, then, you would be wise to come up with some other mechanism for getting the key to the source. You could telephone the other party with the desired key, mail the key via a secure mail service, or transmit the key via a previously established secure channel, but these methods are not always convenient. One way of getting around these methods is through the use of public key encryption.

The public/private key pair

Public key encryption is an asymmetric encryption mechanism that uses two different keys: a public key and a private key. Instead of using a single key known by both parties (as is the case with symmetric encryption), public key encryption uses one key to encrypt data and another key to decrypt the data. One of these keys is called a public key because it is freely available to the public. The other key (the private key) is kept secret by the owner of the key pair.

The reason public key encryption mechanisms work is because they are based on a "one-way" function. A one-way function is simple to perform in one direction but difficult to perform in the opposite direction. For example, it's relatively easy to come up with two large prime numbers, but if you are given only the product of the two primes, then it is very difficult to factor the product back into the original two primes. Most public key encryption schemes currently in use are based on factoring large numbers into the product of two large primes.

The public and private keys for public key encryption can be used bidirectionally. For example, I can encrypt a message with my private key and it can only be decrypted with the corresponding public key. Similarly, someone who has my public key can encrypt a message but the message can be decrypted only with my private key. Figure 13.2 shows encryption being performed in both directions by using the public and private keys.

In public key encryption, the public key is well known and anyone with the public key can decrypt the message. In the top scenario in Figure 13.2, Alice should be well aware that the world knows she just said hello to Bob.

Privacy is guaranteed when encryption is performed with the public key and decryption requires the private key; in the bottom scenario of Figure 13.2, Bob is assured that his message is secure because Alice is the only person with knowledge of the private key. Anyone can grab Alice's public key, encrypt a message with it, and feel confident that Alice is the only person who can read the message.

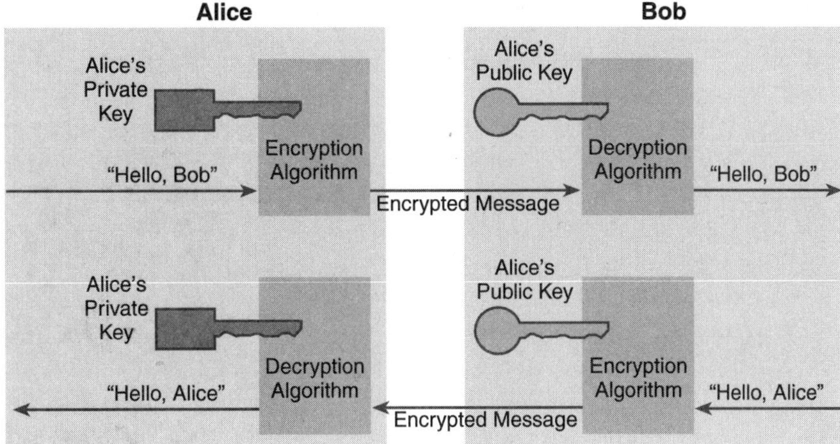

FIGURE 13.2

Using either the private key or the public key for encryption.

A simple way to ensure private communication in both directions is for Bob and Alice to have their own private and public keys. When Alice sends a message to Bob, she uses Bob's public key to encrypt the data. When Bob sends a message to Alice, he uses Alice's public key. Alice knows that Bob is the only person who can read the message she has sent, and Bob can feel confident that Alice is the only person who can read the messages that he is sending.

Public key encryption schemes have some unique characteristics that make them extremely useful in other circumstances, but for encrypting and decrypting simple messages like those of Bob and Alice, public key encryption is significantly slower than symmetric encryption schemes.

Using a public/private key pair for transferring a session key

Although public encryption schemes are slower than symmetric encryption schemes, public key encryption schemes can play an important role in security even when you are mainly using symmetric encryption schemes. You learned that one of the problems with symmetric encryption schemes is that you need a secure mechanism for transmitting the session key into the hands of the actual person to whom you want to send the information. Public key encryption provides this mechanism. If Bob wants to set up symmetric encryption with Alice, Bob simply generates a session key, then encrypts the session key with Alice's public key. Since Alice is the only one with knowledge of her private key, Bob knows that she is the only one who will receive the session key for performing the symmetric encryption.

Using a public/private key pair for authentication Another capability of public key encryption that symmetric encryption doesn't offer is a mechanism for performing authentication. If Alice sends Bob data encrypted with her private key and he can decrypt it with her public key, then he knows for a fact that the message came from Alice because she is the only one with access to her private key. If all Bob wants to do is authenticate Alice, he can send her a challenge (a random piece of data) that she in turn encrypts with her private key and then sends back to him. Bob decrypts the data using Alice's public key, and if it matches his original data, he knows it must be Alice who is responding.

Public key algorithm

A number of different public key algorithms are available, but almost all public key encryption performed today uses RSA, which was invented in 1977 by Ron Rivest, Adi Shamir, and Leonard Adleman. Other public key encryption schemes have either not held up to scrutiny or have been significantly more expensive computationally to perform.

The RSA algorithm involves the use of two large primes, p and q. The product of p and q is going to be used as the modulus for our computation and will be referred to as n. We pick a number e such that e is relatively prime to $(p\text{-}1)*(q\text{-}1)$. We then need to find a number d such that $(e*d)\text{-}1$ is divisible by $(p\text{-}1)*(q\text{-}1)$. It can be proved, by using algebraic theorems of Fermat and Euler, that for any number m less than n,

$$m^{e*d} \bmod n = m \bmod n = m$$

What this means in terms of our algorithm is that we can encrypt a value m to get the result c by using the following formula:

$$m^{e} \bmod n = c$$

And we can decrypt c by using d and the following formula:

$$c^{d} \bmod n = m^{e*d} \bmod n = m \bmod n = m$$

Thus we have a mechanism for encoding and decoding in which the public key is the combination of e and n, and the private key is the combination of d and n.

The size of the modulus determines the strength of the encryption. Most session key exchange mechanisms on the Internet use RSA with a modulus of 512 bits. Experts estimate that it would cost nearly $1 million for specialized encryption-cracking hardware and take that hardware eight months to successfully attack a message encrypted using RSA with a modulus of 512 bits.

Digital signatures

You learned that public key encryption can be used to authenticate a user, and in our example Alice received a piece of challenge data that she had to encrypt with her private key to prove her identity. One offshoot of that authentication mechanism is the digital signature. In essence, public key encryption can be used to sign a document in a way that guarantees the authenticity of the signature.

Hashes You can't simply add a static digital signature to the end of a document and expect it to be secure, because anyone could attach that same static signature to the end of any document. For a signature to be valid, it must indicate in some fashion that it corresponds to the particular document in question. To do this, *hash functions* are used to create a *document digest*. So before you can sign a document digitally, you need to understand what a hash is.

> **Glossary**
>
> **document digest** *A unique, fixed-length sequence of bits created by performing a hash function on a document's data. A document digest can be thought of as a digital fingerprint of the larger document.*

A hash function is a function that takes an arbitrarily long data string as input and then produces a fixed-length output. The output of a hash function must also have two properties:

- It must be impossible to determine the original message from the digest created by the hash function.
- The hash function can never create the same digest for two different messages.

If we have a document of arbitrary length, we can use a hash function to generate a digest that represents our document. To sign the document, we simply encrypt the digest with our private key. To verify the signature, the receiver of the signed document runs the document through the same hash function. He then decrypts the digital signature with the sender's public key to see whether the result matches the document's digest. If it does, the signature is valid. If it does not, either the signature was forged or the document was corrupted in transit. In either case, the document is considered invalid.

A number of different hash algorithms are used today, including several that have been accepted as Internet standards via the Request for Comments process:

- **MD2** This is the first of three message digest algorithms developed by Ron Rivest. It is defined in RFC 1319 and is optimized for use on 8-bit machines.
- **MD4** Defined in RFC 1320, MD4 is another message digest algorithm developed by Ron Rivest. It was optimized for 32-bit machines. Although it is a very fast algorithm, it has not held up to public scrutiny because it does not consistently create unique digests. MD4 should not be used as a secure mechanism.
- **MD5** Also developed by Ron Rivest, MD5 is like MD4 in that it is optimized for use on 32-bit machines. MD5 fixes many of the problems of MD4, although it does so at the cost of slower performance. MD5 digests are 128 bits long. MD5 is defined in RFC 1321.
- **SHA** This is the Secure Hash Algorithm defined by the United States government. It uses similar mechanisms as MD4 but is considerably more secure because it generates digests of 160 bits.
- **DES-DM** This is a hash function built around the DES block cipher. The blocks from DES are combined to create a fixed-length digest.

Certificates Using public key encryption to create digital signatures is a very powerful use of an encryption scheme, but one problem still needs to be addressed if public key encryption is to be useful for securing the transmission of a session key. How can we ensure that the public key used to perform a particular task belongs to the person we think it belongs to? The answer is to use *certificates* and *certificate authorities* to distribute public keys.

Glossary

certificate *A standardized document that includes a user's public key and is digitally signed by a certificate authority to prove its validity.*

certificate authority *A central authority that verifies the identity of the owner of a public key and then digitally signs the certificate used to distribute the key.*

The following example illustrates why certificates and certificate authorities are essential. Suppose we want to authenticate Alice by using her public key. We generate a random challenge, send it to the person claiming to be Alice, and then attempt to decrypt her response with her public key. How can we be assured we received Alice's public key? Suppose Charlie is trying to pretend he is Alice. If we simply ask the sender of the message for the public key, Charlie might give us *his* public key instead of Alice's. When we encrypt our data, only Charlie will be able read it.

There must be a way of publishing public keys so that it's clear whose public key belongs to whom. One idea would be to maintain a central repository of information that would verify an individual by using standard verification mechanisms like checking a picture ID or scanning fingerprints. After verification, the central repository would add the individual's public key to its store of public keys. When a person needed the public key, he could go to the central repository to get it instead of asking the unconfirmed individual for it.

The problem with a central repository of public keys, however, is that it is an inefficient mechanism for data storage on large networks—conceivably, you would want a public key for every individual on the Internet. Public key queries would occur thousands, if not millions, of times per hour, and commerce could come to a standstill.

How is the public key storage problem solved? Rather than keeping public key information in a central location, the central authority digitally signs a document containing a user's public key. Alice, then, can hold a copy of this signed document and pass it to anyone who wants to authenticate her identity.

Suppose Bob wants to verify that Alice is who she says she is. Bob doesn't have her public key at this point, so he asks her to provide it. Alice provides Bob with a document that both contains her public key and is digitally signed by the trusted certificate authority. Bob does have the public key of the certificate authority, which he uses to verify the digital signature of the document Alice gave him. Once Bob verifies the digital signature, he can trust that the document was signed by the certificate authority. The document, or certificate, would not only have Alice's public key, but it would also have several fields of unique information that lets Bob know the public key belongs to the particular Alice he's dealing with. Now he can send Alice the authentication challenge with the confidence of knowing exactly to whom the public key belongs.

To better understand what a certificate is, let's take a look at exactly what is included in a certificate document. The following table describes the fields of information contained in a certificate.

Field	Description
Certificate Version	The version of the certificate specification that the certificate follows.
Serial Number	A unique number for every certificate signed by the certificate authority.
Signature	Specifies the hash algorithm and public key encryption scheme used to sign the certificate. The digital signature is appended to the end of the certificate.
Issuer Name	The X.500 Distinguished Name of the certificate authority that is signing the certificate.
Validity Period	The start and stop dates specifying when a certificate is considered valid.
Subject Name	The X.500 Distinguished Name of the individual whose public key is contained in the certificate. Distinguished Names are universally unique.
Subject Public Key	The actual public key of the individual specified in the Subject Name field. In practice, this field usually contains two public keys: one used for performing session key exchanges, and one used for digitally signing documents.

Glossary

X.500 *A family of standards published by the International Standards Organization (ISO) designed to uniquely identify a directory. X.500 was created to promote the development of a white page directory much like the Internet's DNS.*

Certificate Authorities The certificate authority is responsible for verifying all the information contained in a certificate before actually signing it. The user requesting the certificate provides the public key or keys with her certificate request to the certificate authority. All the certificate authority has to do is verify the user and sign the certificate. Once the certificate is signed by the certificate authority, the certificate can be passed freely around the world.

To verify a certificate, you need to do the following:

- Verify that the validity period of the certificate is appropriate.
- Verify the digital signature of the certificate by using the certificate authority's public key.

- Verify that the certificate serial number is not on a list of revoked certificates published by the certificate authority.
- Verify that the subject name is the name for the desired individual.

You're probably wondering about the public key for the certificate authority. How do you get it? How do you know it belongs to the certificate authority you think it belongs to? The circular answer is, "We use certificates." Certificate authorities are supposed to be rare entities, so the act of verifying a certificate authority should be an infrequent task.

There are actually two kinds of certificate authorities—*root authorities* and *child authorities*. The difference between the two is that a root authority signs its own certificate.

The certificates with public keys for child authorities are signed by a separate certificate authority, called the parent authority. Because the parent authority itself might be a child authority for another certificate authority, verification can involve working through a complex hierarchy of certificate authorities. We can verify our certificate authorities by verifying each parent certificate authority until we reach the top of the hierarchy. At this point, we run into what is called a root authority.

Before a user adds a new root authority to his list of valid authorities, he needs to be very sure it came from a source that he can trust. In the best of all possible worlds, all child authorities are valid because their certificates were validated by a "higher authority." But what happens to the validity of certificates when a root authority is dishonest or its private key store has been compromised? When a root authority's private key is compromised, all certificates it signs are suspect.

One way certificate authorities avoid fraud is to maintain a Certificate Revocation List (CRL). A CRL is a list of certificate serial numbers that are no longer considered valid for reasons other than an expired validity period. For example, a certificate authority might provide a company with a CRL that includes serial numbers of certificates issued to employees who have left the company before their certificates expired.

Secure Socket Layer

We've examined symmetric encryption schemes, public key encryption schemes, authentication, digital signing, and certificates. Putting all these concepts together to create a standard mechanism for establishing a secure channel of communication is what the Secure Socket Layer (SSL) is all about. SSL provides an authenticated and encrypted link through which any sort of TCP socket communication can take place. We can use SSL to provide a secure conduit for HTTP requests and responses so that sensitive information like credit card numbers and finances can be transmitted securely across the World Wide Web.

There are two basic stages in SSL communication: the handshake stage and the data transfer stage. In the handshake stage, the secure connection is set up. As soon as algorithms are agreed upon, keys are exchanged, and the endpoints are authenticated, the data transfer stage starts. In the data transfer stage, information is passed to SSL, encrypted and decrypted, and then handed to a higher level entity. The routing of information is seamless to the higher-level application that is using SSL, as though encryption weren't being conducted at all. Figure 13.3 illustrates a typical SSL connection sequence.

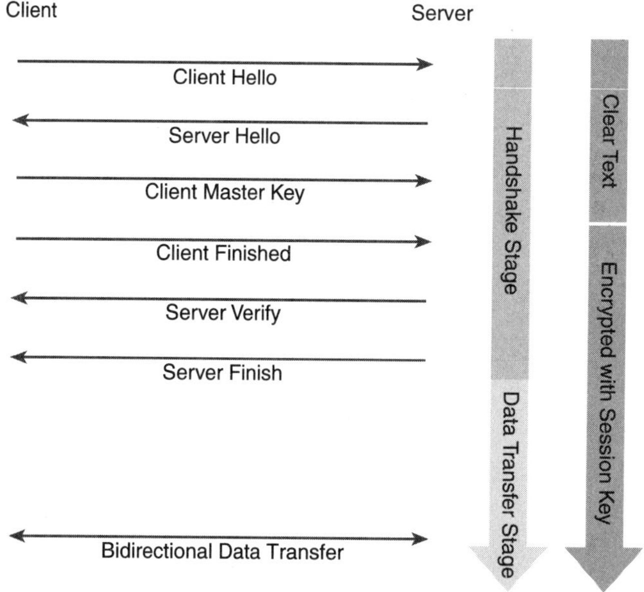

FIGURE 13.3

A typical SSL 2.0 session.

SSL requires that a communication channel be established between the client and the server. In the model we're looking at, the underlying connection is a TCP socket. Unlike typical HTTP, which uses TCP port 80, SSL uses TCP port 433. Once the TCP connection is established, the SSL handshake, shown in Figure 13.3, can begin.

In Figure 13.3, the first message to be sent across the underlying connection is the Client Hello message. The Client Hello message provides important information for setting up the secure channel: which version of SSL is being used, which symmetric encryption algorithms are supported by the client, which session key sizes are supported by the client, which key exchange mechanisms can be used, and which hashing algorithms are supported. The client also sends a randomly generated challenge as part of the Client Hello message.

The server responds to the Client Hello message with the Server Hello message. The Server Hello message responds to the client's list of supported encryption algorithms and hashes by sending a subset of algorithms that are also supported by the server. At this point, the list contains algorithms supported by both sides. The Server Hello message also contains a connection ID, which serves as a challenge of the client later in the handshake process, as well as the server machine's certificate.

When the client receives the Server Hello message, it verifies the server's certificate and then generates a Client Master Key message. The Client Master Key message includes the final encryption algorithms along with an appropriately generated session key, which will be used to perform symmetric encryption. The session key is actually encrypted by using the server's public key from the certificate in the Server Hello message. After the Client Master Key message is sent, all subsequent messages are encrypted using the specified symmetric encryption algorithm and the session key indicated in the Client Master Key message.

After the client has sent the Client Master Key message, it sends a Client Finished message to indicate to the server that it is ready to activate the channel. The Client Finished message includes the Connection ID sent by the server in the Server Hello message, but now the message is encrypted using the session key. This provides a degree of authentication of the client by the server.

The Server Verify message verifies that the server providing the certificate in the Server Hello message is the server currently communicating. The Server Verify message contains the challenge sent in the Client Hello message, encrypted with the session key from the Client Master Key message. This message is used to authenticate the server because only a machine with the server certificate's corresponding private key can decrypt the session key and use it. The client verifies that the challenge is encrypted correctly.

The Server Finish message is the server's way of indicating to the client that the server is ready to enter the data transfer stage. The encrypted Server Finish message contains a session identifier that can be used by the client later to expedite the SSL handshake process. Once the Server Finish message is sent, normal data transmission can occur. This means that the client can send its HTTP request across the secure connection and wait for the response.

In this long but simplified illustration, the server was the only portion of the connection with a certificate, meaning that the server was being authenticated but the client was not explicitly authenticated. SSL provides an optional means for authenticating clients by allowing the server to send a Request Certificate message before it sends its Server Finish message. The client must respond with its Client Certificate message, which includes the client's public key certificate along with the server's Request Certificate message digitally signed by the client. The server verifies the certificate along with the message's digital signature before sending the Server Finished message.

Once the connection enters the data transfer stage, data sent to the secure connection is broken up into messages that are both encrypted using the session key and digitally signed. The receiving end receives the encrypted messages and verifies the digital signatures before attempting to decrypt the data. Having data messages signed further secures the validity of the data source and the integrity of the data.

SSL 3.0

To illustrate the basic concepts, the example in Figure 13.3 shows a typical SSL 2.0 session. There have been a number of advances in secure communication since SSL 2.0 was first developed. SSL 3.0 provides greater flexibility in specifying supported encryption algorithms and parameters, so the SSL specification should remain fairly stable even if new encryption algorithms are developed. SSL 3.0 also provides a means for changing the current encryption key and algorithm on an existing secure channel.

Private Communication Technology

The Private Communication Technology (PCT) protocol, which is very similar to SSL, was developed by Microsoft to address a number of issues with SSL 2.0 and SSL 3.0. Among the advantages of PCT are the following:

- It reduces the number of packet transfers during the handshake stage.
- It provides an even more flexible means for algorithm negotiation.
- It allows for higher levels of message-signing security during the data transfer stage.
- It patches up a rather obscure security degradation that potentially could occur when a client certificate authentication uses less secure keys.

When communicating via a secure link between Microsoft Internet Explorer and Internet Information Server, the PCT protocol is used.

Setting Up IIS for Secure Web Communication

Now that you understand what secure Web communication is all about, let's look at the details of setting up Internet Information Server so that you can take advantage of its security options. First you must install one or more certificates on your server so that secure communications can be enabled, and then you select configuration options.

Key Manager

Before an SSL or a PCT link can be established to a server, the server must have a certificate installed so that authentication and session key exchange can occur properly. Certificates are purchased from a certificate authority or can be generated using Microsoft Certificate Server. You must run Key Manager to properly install a certificate on IIS. You can start Key Manager in several ways:

- By selecting Internet Information Server in the Scope Pane in the Management Console and then clicking its toolbar button (which shows a hand holding a key)
- By clicking the Key Manager button on the IIS Plugin's Directory Security property page
- By running the KEYRING.EXE program located in the C:\WINNT\SYSTEM32\INETSRV directory

Figure 13.4 shows the Key Manager application.

On the left side of the Key Manager window is a hierarchical view of our example machine and all the services for which you can install certificates. (We will focus on installing certificates for the World Wide Web service, but secure communications can be used for a number of different services.) Notice in Figure 13.4 that in the left-hand pane, two keys are listed under the WWW icon: the Admin Site Key and the Powell1 Site Key. You can highlight either key to display the details of its certificate in the right-hand pane. Details include the key's current functional status, the validity period details for the certificate, the key length, and the various components that make up the X.500 Distinguished Name for the server.

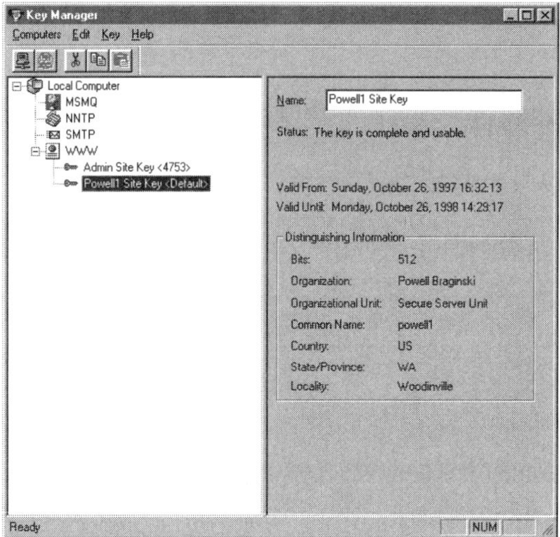

FIGURE 13.4

Installing a certificate on IIS from Key Manager.

You can double-click on a key's icon to invoke the Server Bindings dialog box. Figure 13.5 shows the Server Bindings for the Admin Site Key. The Server Bindings determine which keys will be used for the various Web sites. If on a single machine you have multiple virtual sites requiring secure communication, you will most likely need multiple keys installed. Be aware that you are binding SSL to specific IP addresses and ports. If you have multiple Web sites that use the same IP address and port, these sites must also use the same key.

NOTE

Binding multiple host names to the same IP address and port can be problematic because the Common Name in the key certificate must match the host name specified by the client's browser. If you have two host names using the same IP address and TCP port, only the host name that matches the Common Name in the certificate will actually work.

Figure 13.5 shows that the Admin Site Key is bound to the nonstandard port 4753. You can add, edit, or delete the IP address and ports this key is bound to by clicking the appropriate button. You can specify that the key be bound to specific IP addresses and ports or specify that it be used for any unassigned IP address or port. If you specify Any Unassigned for both the IP address and the port, the key becomes the default key for any secure connection not falling under any of the other explicitly defined bindings.

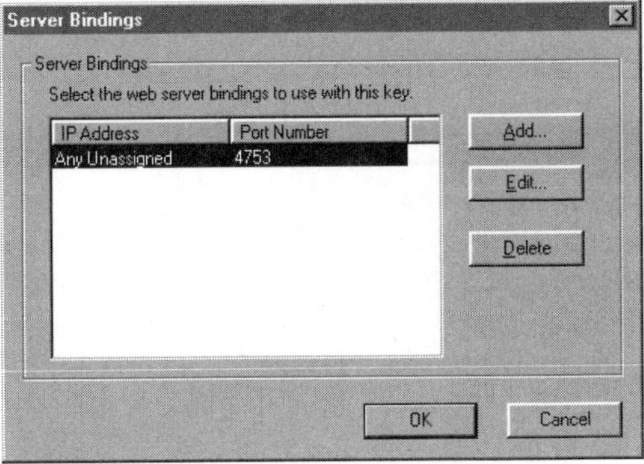

FIGURE 13.5

Binding a key to specific site information.

To begin creating a new key, choose the Create New Key wizard command from the Key menu. The wizard will guide you through the process of creating a new key. The first step is to create a request for a new key. You have to send the new key request to a certificate authority in one of two ways. The first option is to have the wizard create a certificate request file that stores the information in a text file. You are responsible for getting that request file to a certificate authority and then receiving and installing the corresponding certificate.

The second option, which is quite convenient, is to have the wizard automatically send the request to an online authority. If Certificate Server is installed on your machine, this option will be enabled for you. Otherwise you will have to create the request file, as we just mentioned.

The New Key wizard prompts you for a key name, a password to be used for verification purposes when you receive your certificate, the key length, and the X.500 Distinguished Name fields that identify your server. Be aware that if you want your secure connections to work, the Common Name must match the host name that your clients will be entering on their browsers. Once you have entered all this information, you will either need to submit the request file to a certificate authority (following whatever procedures the authority enforces), or your request will automatically be processed online if you selected the online option in the wizard.

If you chose to submit the request file manually, you will receive your certificate from a certificate authority in the form of a file for your Web server. After receiving this file, use Key Manager to install the certificate. In the left-hand pane of Key

Manager, select the disabled key that corresponds to the request you made and choose Install Key Certificate from the Key menu. You will be prompted for the filename and the password you specified for the request. At this point, your key should be installed, and you can specify any bindings that you want.

Key Manager also allows you to back up and restore server keys by using the Export and Import commands from the Key menu. Backing up your keys is a good idea because server key certificates can be relatively expensive—if you mistakenly delete a key within Key Manager and you don't have a backup, you have to request another key certificate from your certificate authority.

SSL Configuration Options in the Management Console

IIS is flexible when it comes to configuring SSL options. At the highest level, the Web Site property page, which can be accessed by selecting the IIS entry in the Scope Pane and then selecting the Properties button from the toolbar, allows you to determine what port will be used for SSL communication for a particular site. At the home directory, virtual directory, directory, and file levels, you can configure a fine granularity of detail. For example, you can specify whether a particular resource will use SSL and exactly how you want SSL to be configured for it.

Let's take a closer look at some of the options. Figure 13.6 shows the Secure Communications dialog box, which you access by clicking the Edit Secure Communications button on the Directory Security property page. For each resource on a particular machine, the Secure Communications dialog box offers the gamut of options for requiring, allowing, or denying the use of SSL and client certificates. At the top of the dialog box is one button that takes you back into Key Manager and an adjacent button that allows you to manipulate encryption settings.

NOTE

The Encryption Settings option lets you specify that the key length for the symmetric encryption portion of SSL must be 128 bits, allowing you to restrict secure connections to only the highest level of encryption. But this option is functional only on Microsoft Windows machines with built-in 128-bit security capabilities. Export restrictions dictate that this level of encryption is made available in only the United States and Canada.

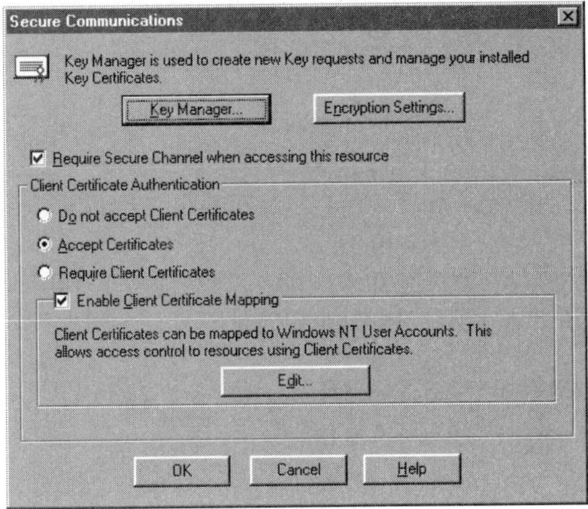

FIGURE 13.6

Configuring secure communications.

Certificate mapping

Another option available in the Secure Communications dialog box is the Enable Client Certificate Mapping option. You can choose this option as long as you are either accepting or requiring the use of client certificates for your secure connections. If client certificates are used for connecting to a secure resource, a high level of authentication has already been performed using public key encryption. Since you have already gone through this much effort to authenticate the client, it makes sense to take advantage of the public key encryption authentication scheme rather than rely on any of the higher level HTTP authentication schemes such as basic or NTLM authentication. In order to allow this to work, we use an IIS feature called client certificate mappings.

When you choose the Edit button to edit client certificate mappings, the Account Mappings window is displayed. From this window, you can map client certificates to actual Microsoft Windows NT accounts, so when a request comes in with a specific client's certificate, the server checks its certificate mapping list to see whether it has a valid certificate map for this particular certificate. If the server has a valid map, IIS impersonates the Windows NT account specified by the mapping when IIS executes the request. This process is similar to the way in which Windows NT impersonates a specified user when basic or NTLM authentication schemes are used, except that certificate mapping determines the account information used. Figure 13.7 shows the Account Mappings window.

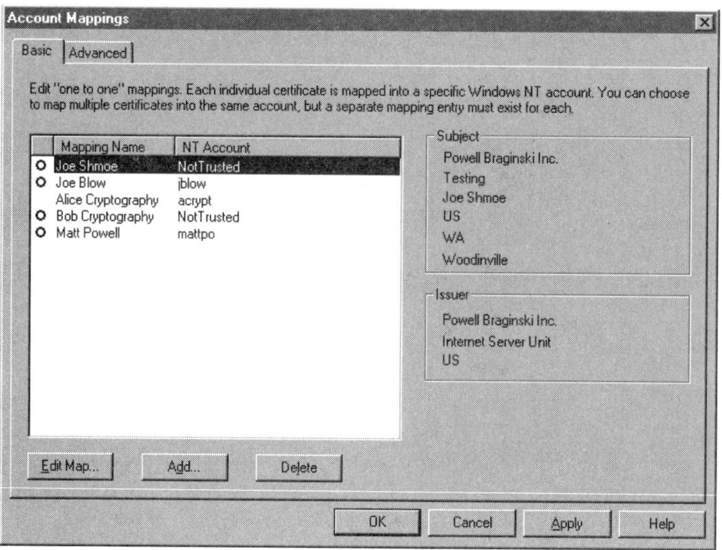

FIGURE 13.7

Setting up basic client certificate mappings to Windows NT accounts.

As you can see in Figure 13.7, the server already has a handful of certificate mappings set up for certain users. Each mapping is given a friendly name that should match the certificate's Common Name. Next to that name is the Windows NT account that Internet Information Server will impersonate when a session is established with the corresponding certificate. The small circles to the left of the mapping names indicate whether the particular mapping is enabled or disabled; a circle means that the mapping is enabled. Notice that the right side of the window contains a section that shows detailed information about a certificate when a mapping name is highlighted.

You can configure IIS so that it maps each certificate to a unique Windows NT account, or you can configure the server to map several certificates to a single account. For example, in Figure 13.7, we mapped both Joe Shmoe and Bob Cryptography to the same Windows NT account, an account we named "NotTrusted." Having a separate account for each individual uses up resources, and mapping more than one certificate to a single account avoids managing a separate NT account for each certificate.

To add a new certificate mapping to the list, click the Add button. If you add a mapping in this fashion, you will need to have a Public-Key Cryptography Standard (PKCS) #7 certificate file which is base 64 encoded with headers available as input. The PKCS #7 file might contain many certificates that specify the certification chain of authority that issued the certificate. Unfortunately, there really is no easy way to generate a PKCS #7 certificate file for a client certificate by using Internet Information Server.

However, we have found it relatively easy to add certificate mappings by creating a quick ASP script that uses the *IIsCertMapper* interface. One of the things ASP conveniently provides is easy access to the client's certificate. You can then pass the certificate, along with information identifying the Windows NT account and password that the certificate will map to, from ASP to the *IIsCertMapper* object. This creates a new entry in the list of certificate mappings. You'll learn more about ASP scripting in Chapter 17.

The following script receives the Windows NT account information from an HTML form that the user fills out. The data is posted to the ASP page, which must be in a virtual directory that requires SSL and client certificates. (This requirement ensures that the client certificate is passed to Internet Information Server so that you know it will be available to ASP.) We actually disable the mapping in this script to allow an administrator to decide at some later time whether she wants to enable the certificate mapping.

```
<%@ LANGUAGE="VBSCRIPT" %>

<HTML>
<HEAD>
<TITLE>Create Client Certificate Map</TITLE>
</HEAD>
<BODY>

<%
Dim CertMapper
Set CertMapper = GetObject("IIS://Powell1/W3svc/1/IIsCertMapper")

Dim ClientCert, NTAccount, NTPassword, Name
ClientCert = Request.ClientCertificate("Certificate")
NTAccount = Request.Form("NTAccount")
NTPassword = Request.Form("NTPassword")
Name = Request.Form("Name")

CertMapper.CreateMapping ClientCert, NTAccount, NTPassword, Name, False

Response.Write "Mapping has been completed!"
%>

</BODY>
</HTML>
```

After our script has added a certificate mapping, we can select the Edit Map button on the Basic page of the Account Mappings window (shown in Figure 13.7) to edit the account, password, and friendly name, and to specify whether the mapping is enabled.

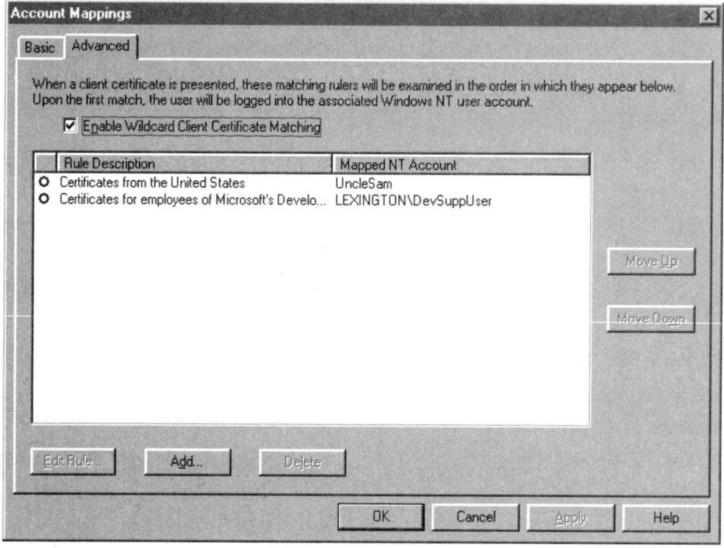

FIGURE 13.8

Advanced client certificate mapping features.

On the Advanced page of the Account Mappings window, you can activate an option for performing certificate mappings that isn't limited to mapping a single certificate to a particular account—you can specify wildcards so that exact mappings are not required. For example, Figure 13.8 shows an advanced mapping in which every certificate whose distinguished name has a US country code will be mapped to an account called "UncleSam." You can base the advanced mappings on any field value in the distinguished name, on the certificate authority that issued the certificate, on the client certificate's serial number, or on a number of other certificate properties.

Mapping rules can be combined to create a more specific mapping. Figure 13.9 shows the rules created to map certificates of individuals in Microsoft's Developer Support group to a particular account; the values of the Organization name and the Organizational Unit name were used to create the mapping. Wildcards were also used to avoid differentiation between certificates that say "Microsoft" and certificates that say "Microsoft Corp."

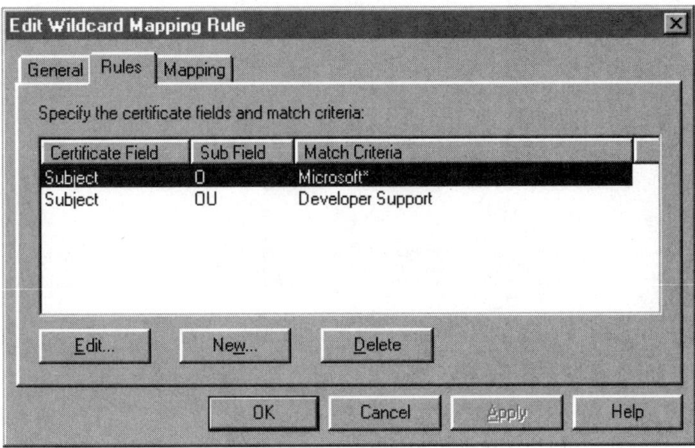

FIGURE 13.9

Using wildcards and distinguished name properties to create client certificate mappings.

In this chapter, you've learned a lot about secure communication and setting up Internet Information Server to take advantage of SSL capabilities—especially that certificates are a good way to ensure privacy. The cost of purchasing certificates and the lack of control in managing certificates, however, often limit their widespread use. Internet Information Server solves these cost and control problems by including Microsoft Certificate Server. With Certificate Server, you can be your own certificate authority and provide your own client (and server) certificates. You'll look at the details of Certificate Server in the next chapter.

CHAPTER 14

Certificate Server

Now that you understand a bit about the Secure Sockets Layer (SSL) and the role of certificates, you need to know how to go about getting a certificate. To get a driver's license, you must bring your birth certificate or other valid identification to the licensing office. The licensing people verify this information before they issue your license. Private companies also have positioned themselves as central authorities, issuing identity certificates to individuals around the world. Consider a common workplace situation. Almost everyone at your company has a driver's license, so, theoretically, the company could use drivers' licenses as a means of identifying its employees. The problem is that the company needs a way to differentiate between its employees and everyone else in the country who knows how to drive. It also needs to prevent individuals who are no longer with the company from identifying themselves as company employees. Therefore, it is common for companies to issue their own identification cards.

If you are using certificates to identify individuals in your company, you will probably want to issue the certificates yourself. For this reason, you might want to create your own certificate authority, but there are plenty of other reasons to do so. For instance, if you are an ISP, you might want to issue certificates to your customers to uniquely identify each one. If you are running a bank or other financial institution, you will want to issue certificates to control who is authorized to access various account information. Microsoft Certificate Server provides a safe and easy means for you to become your own certificate authority and issue your own certificates.

Is being able to create certificates all that is needed to become a certificate authority? Actually, there's quite a bit more to it. Although you can automatically issue a certificate to anyone who requests one, usually you will want to perform some sort of validation on the user. A certificate authority is also responsible for publishing a *Certificate Revocation List (CRL)*, which lists all the certificates that are no longer valid for reasons other than their normal expiration. Finally, it is critical for a certificate authority to guard the private key that it uses to create the digital signatures on the certificates it creates. If the private key has been compromised somehow, any certificate authentication performed from that point on cannot be trusted. Certificate Server helps you to perform all of these functions easily.

Probably the best way to get a feel for how Certificate Server works is to walk through what happens when a certificate request is submitted. Figure 14.1 illustrates this sequence of events.

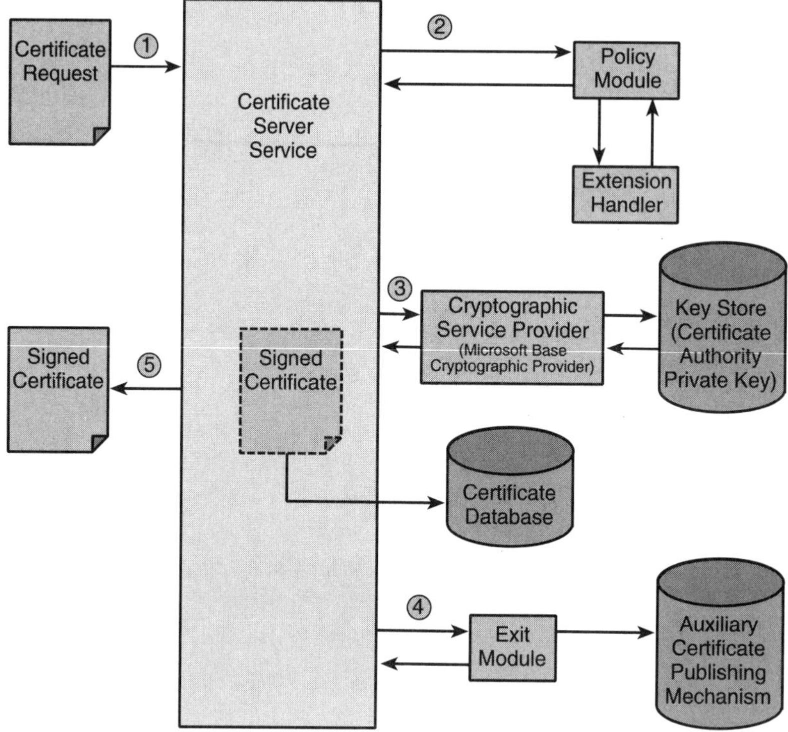

FIGURE 14.1

Handling a certificate request using Certificate Server.

The processing of a certificate request consists of five main steps, labeled 1 through 5 in Figure 14.1. In step 1, the certificate request is submitted to Certificate Server via the *ICertRequest* COM interface. *ICertRequest* can be called from a number of places. For the most part, we will be looking at how this interface is called from an Active Server Page (ASP), but you can also call it from a custom program or from a different scripting host. The request itself can be formatted in the public key cryptography standard (PKCS) #10 request format, or it can be in the format generated by the Key Manager utility (KEYRING.EXE).

Glossary

Key Manager *Graphical utility included in the Microsoft Windows NT 4.0 Option Pack that generates public and private key pairs and installs server certificates for IIS.*

In step 2, the Certificate Server runs the request using any installed policy modules. A *policy module* is a customizable object that implements the *ICertPolicy* COM interface. This object is responsible for implementing the policies your certificate authority requires before it will issue a certificate. For instance, you might want to enforce that the designated organization for a specified X.500 Distinguished Name be your company name, or you might accept certificate requests only from people in a certain area code. You can even set the state of the request to Pending until further verification has been performed—for example, if you needed to run a background check on the individual requesting the certificate or if you just wanted to have the request approved by a human instead of automatically generating the certificate.

The policy module can examine any "extra" information that came with the request. Certificate requests are capable of holding any proprietary information you want them to hold. For instance, you might want to know an individual's phone number, address, social security number, and mother's maiden name. This information isn't part of the standardized certificate request, but you can customize Certificate Server to support the addition of extra information by creating an *extension handler* to interpret the added proprietary information. Your policy module can query the extension handler to get at the extended information in the request. Now the decision to grant a request doesn't have to be based strictly on the rather limited standard information in the request; it can also be based on any included extended information.

If the policy module approves the request, the actual building of the certificate takes place in step 3. Certificate Server uses Microsoft CryptoAPI, a cryptography application programming interface, to digitally sign the certificate. CryptoAPI interfaces with cryptographic service providers that you have installed on your system. Theoretically, you might have several providers, each supplying a unique encryption service, but most likely the only provider you have installed is the Microsoft Base Cryptographic Provider. Not only is a service provider responsible for performing the hashing and signing of the specified data, it is also responsible for the secure storage of public/private key pairs. Key pairs are stored in the provider's *key store*, which for the Microsoft Base Cryptographic Provider is an encrypted database. In the case of a certificate authority, the cryptographic service provider uses the certificate authority's private signing key to create the digital signature. The cryptographic service provider signs the certificate request's data without Certificate Server even knowing what the certificate authority's private key is.

The result of step 3 is a completed, signed certificate. Before the certificate is sent back to the requester, however, some tracking is necessary. Certificate Server logs all the information about the certificate it has just created as well as information about the request itself in the certificate database. Without this information, you wouldn't be able to create a CRL if you needed to invalidate an individual's certificate. (We will talk more about CRLs in the "Administration" section later in this chapter.)

In step 4 of handling the certificate request, Certificate Server provides a means for exporting the certificate. Yes, the certificate is returned via the *ICertRequest* interface that the request came in on, but you might need to make your certificates readily accessible to other applications and components. Suppose you have an application that uses SSL and that will accept connections only from users with certificates on a predefined list, or perhaps you will use a collection of PKCS #7 certificate files to map client certificates to Microsoft Windows NT user accounts. In either case, you need to be able to customize the way certificate information is published. You can do this by writing a custom Certificate Server *exit module*. An exit module is implemented as a COM server that exports the *ICertExit* interface and is registered with the server. After the potential exit modules have been called, it's time for step 5—the final step—in which the certificate is returned to the entity that requested it.

Now that you have a general understanding of the certificate request process, let's take a look at some of the details involved in installing Certificate Server, using it to create certificates, and administering our certificate authority.

Installing Certificate Server

When you install the Microsoft Windows NT 4.0 Option Pack, Certificate Server is listed as an option in the Components list of the Setup window. Selecting the Certificate Server option and clicking Show Subcomponents displays the Certificate Server dialog box, shown in Figure 14.2.

You can install Certificate Server in its entirety, or you can disable some of the subcomponents. We suggest that you install all the subcomponents since they don't take up much room. The Certificate Server Certificate Authority provides the main functionality of Certificate Server. If disk space is tight, you could skip the Certificate Server Documentation option, but you might be left a bit helpless later.

The Certificate Server Web Client option provides the capability to request certificates via Web browsers and is installed automatically when you choose the Certificate Server Certificate Authority. This capability is probably one of the main reasons you would choose to install Certificate Server, although certificates can be used for a number of other purposes (such as e-mail encryption and signing).

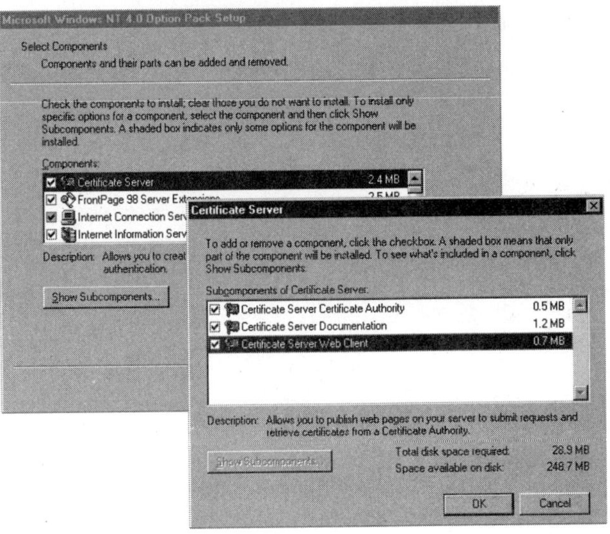

FIGURE 14.2

Certificate Server installation options.

Most components in the Windows NT 4.0 Option Pack use predefined configuration settings with a minimum of input from the user during installation. Certificate Server is an exception to this rule. After you select the subcomponents of Certificate Server you want to install and continue with the installation, the Microsoft Certificate Server Setup dialog box will appear, as shown in Figure 14.3. The Configuration Data Storage Location settings define the location of various exposable components of Certificate Server, including the certificate authority's root certificate, which needs to be made publicly available to anyone using or verifying certificates generated by your server. The Database Location and Log Location options specify the location of the files that hold the actual certificate information and the logs of the certificate requests. The format of the file is Microsoft Access, but you don't really need Microsoft Access itself. The Database Location specifies the location of the certificate database shown in Figure 14.1.

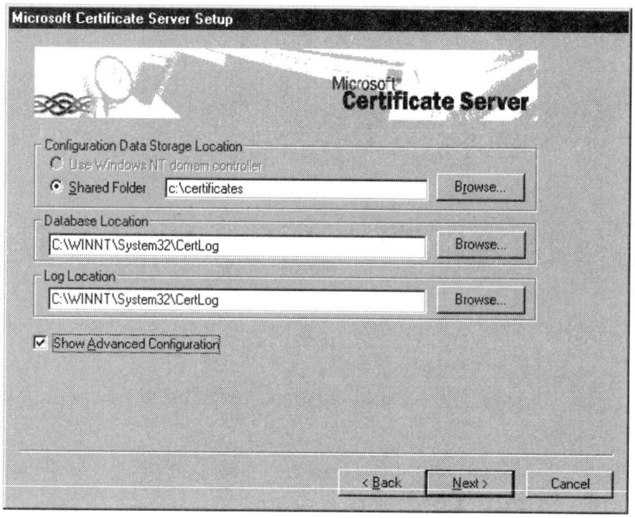

FIGURE 14.3

The first Microsoft Certificate Server Setup dialog box.

If you check the Show Advanced Configuration check box and click the Next button, an advanced Certificate Server configuration dialog box appears, as shown in Figure 14.4. From this dialog box, you can configure a number of more specific options concerning your installation of Certificate Server.

Although this dialog box seems to contain a lot of options, in reality there aren't that many. If you had multiple cryptographic service providers installed on your machine, you would be able to specify which one to use; however, as mentioned, in most instances the Microsoft Base Cryptographic Provider will be the only one installed. The Hash list lets you specify which hashing algorithm supported by the cryptographic service provider you want to use for the digital signatures your certificate authority will employ to validate certificates. As mentioned, cryptographic service providers are also responsible for storing the public/private key pairs that have been used for other applications. To use one of these previously created key pairs, check the Use Existing Keys check box. The Erase All Previous Configuration Information check box lets you remove the configuration files for any previous versions of Certificate Server you might have installed on your machine.

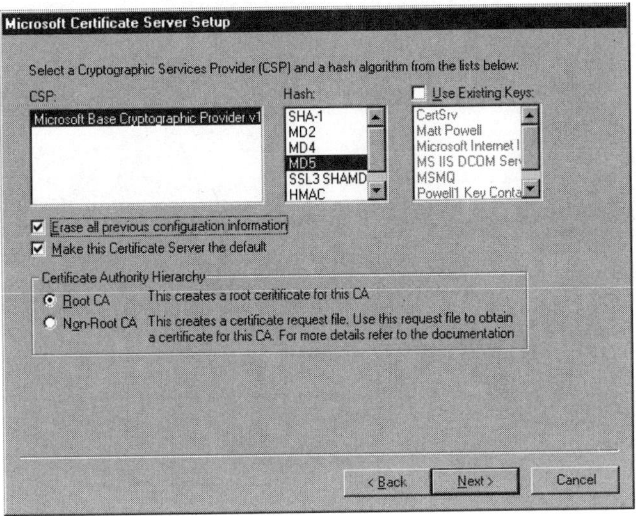

FIGURE 14.4

The Microsoft Certificate Server Setup dialog box used for advanced configuration.

The Certificate Authority Hierarchy area contains two options: Root CA and Non-Root CA. Because the underlying operating system support for certificate hierarchies is not available in the current version of Windows NT, Certificate Server can be installed with the Root CA option only. This means that your certificate authority's own certificate will be signed by itself (rather than being signed by one of the publicly available certificate authorities such as VeriSign Corporation).

The last step in the Certificate Server installation is to provide the information that will identify your certificate authority to the rest of the world. The options shown in the next Certificate Server setup dialog box in Figure 14.5—CA Name, Organization, Organizational Unit, Locality, State, and Country—are all part of building the X.500 Distinguished Name that will uniquely identify your certificate authority. At the bottom of this dialog box, the CA Description field provides a friendly description of the certificate authority that lets people know who you are and what your certificate authority is being used for.

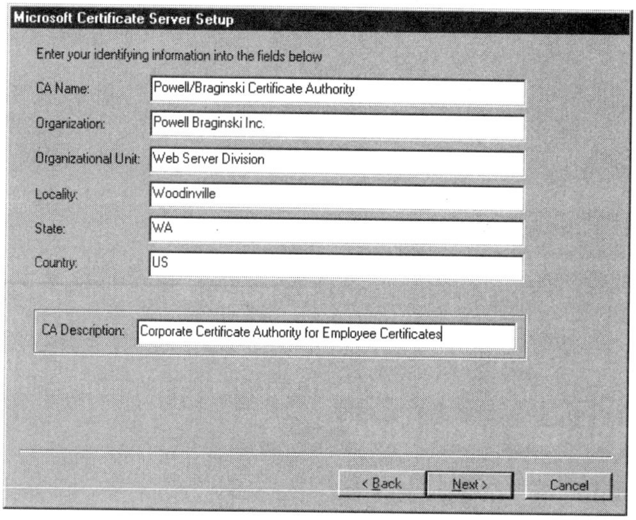

FIGURE 14.5

Identifying your certificate authority using the last Microsoft Certificate Server Setup dialog box.

We'll see the results of these configuration options in the next section, when we go through the steps of requesting a client certificate for our Web browser.

Managing Certificate Server

Now that Certificate Server is up and running, it's time to take advantage of your certificate authority. Let's start by going to the Certificate Server home page, shown in Figure 14.6. You'll find this page at *http://localhost/certsrv*, or you can use the specific local host name; in our example we accessed *http://powell1/certsrv*.

This home page provides links to the Certificate Administration Log Utility, the Certificate Administration Queue Utility, and the Certificate Enrollment Tools pages. It also provides a link to Certificate Server Documentation. We'll look at the administration pages later in this section; for now, let's discuss how to obtain a certificate. The Certificate Enrollment Tools page, shown in Figure 14.7, lists three options: Install Certificate Authority Certificates, Process A Certificate Request, and Request A Client Authentication Certificate.

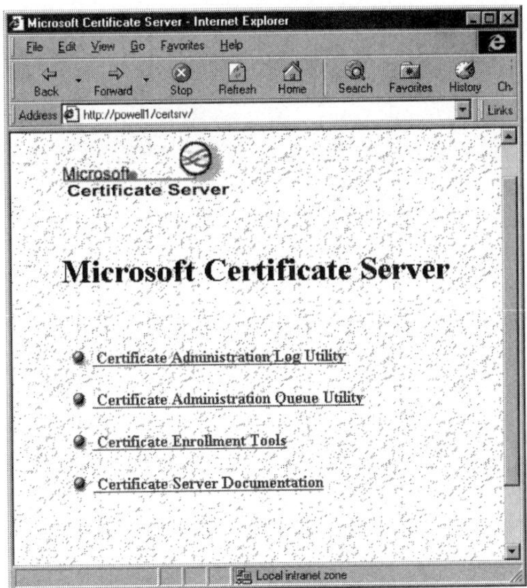

FIGURE 14.6

Your Certificate Server home page.

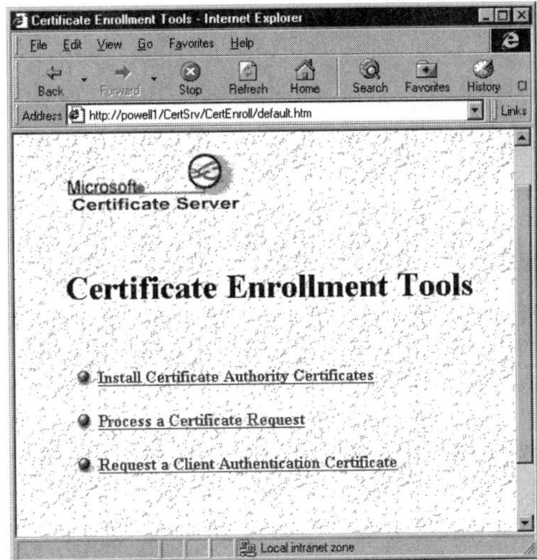

FIGURE 14.7

The Certificate Enrollment Tools page.

Requesting a Client Authentication Certificate

We'll look first at the process of requesting certificates for client browsers. One of the main fields of a certificate is the Subject field, which identifies the individual to whom the certificate is assigned. This Subject field contains an X.500 Distinguished Name in the form *C=US, O=Powell Braginski Inc., OU=Marketing, CN=Joe Employee*. For our browser to build a certificate request, it needs to let Certificate Server know the Subject for the certificate. Figure 14.8 shows the Certificate Enrollment Form page for Web browsers, where we provide the Subject information. To display this page, select the Request A Client Authentication Certificate option from the Certificate Enrollment Tools page.

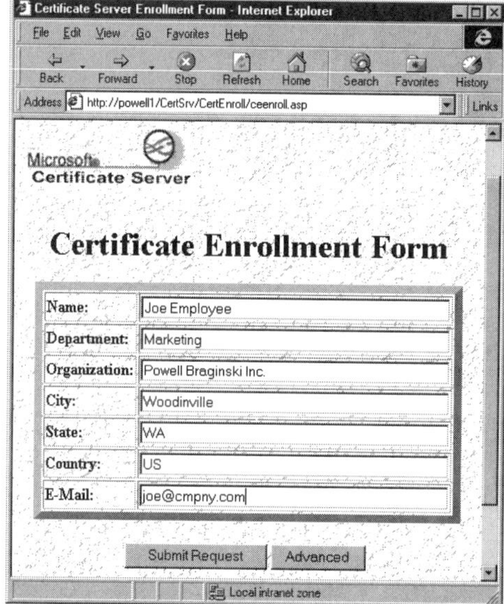

FIGURE 14.8

The Certificate Enrollment Form page.

The Advanced button at the bottom of the Certificate Enrollment Form page displays the Advanced Settings page (not shown here), which lets you specify such things as the type of certificate you want. Here we'll accept the default settings and simply get our client authentication certificate. To do this, click the Submit Request button. Clients running Internet Explorer will see another page that tells them to click a button to download the certificate. Netscape browsers have their own confirmation process for installing a client certificate.

Installing the Certificate Authority Certificate

After you have installed your client authentication certificate, you will be prompted to install the certificate authority certificate. This certificate is required for your client to exchange the session key for the secure connection. Downloading the certificate authority certificate is quite simple. You simply select the Install Certificate Authority Certificates option from the Certificate Enrollment Tools page to display the Certificate Authority Certificate List page, shown in Figure 14.9.

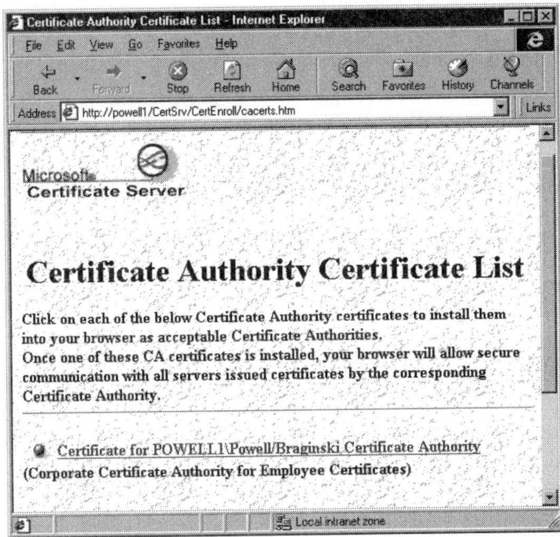

FIGURE 14.9

The Certificate Authority Certificate List page.

When you first install Certificate Server, you should see only a single option in this list. In our case, we see a certificate whose Subject consists of the CA Name and CA Description we specified in the Microsoft Certificate Server Setup dialog box shown in Figure 14-5. To install the certificate authority certificate, simply click on the link. Select Open This File From Its Current Location and click OK to display the New Site Certificate dialog box. Click the View Certificate button to open the Properties dialog box, which displays a list of fields on the left and their values on the right.

Notice that the details for the Subject field are the same as the details for the Issuer field, which means that this certificate authority signed its own certificate. This type of certificate authority is known as a *root certificate authority*. When you click OK in the New Site Certificate dialog box, the Root Certificate Store dialog box appears. This dialog box asks, "Do you want to ADD the following certificate to the Root Store?" and displays the Subject, Issuer, Time Validity, Serial Number, and Thumbprint values. Here too you can see confirmation that this is a "self-issued" certificate. Trusting root certificate authorities is a major security commitment. The root certificate authority has ultimate control over any certificates it issues. Before you specify yourself as a root certificate authority, you should be fully aware of the serious commitment you are making to confirm the identity of anyone you issue a certificate to.

Requesting a Server-Side Certificate

The other half of being able to establish secure connections is having a certificate for the server itself. We'll look at how Certificate Server provides this kind of functionality while discussing how to install a server-side certificate using IIS. We've seen in Chapter 13 how a server-side certificate can be created automatically in Key Manager if Certificate Server is already installed on your machine. But what if you are running IIS on a different machine? In that case, you must use the request file created by Key Manager to submit your request to Certificate Server.

When you create a request file in Key Manager, the file will look something like this:

```
Webmaster: mattpo@microsoft.com
Phone: (425)555-1212
Server: Microsoft Key Manager for IIS Version 4.0

Common-name: powell1
Organization Unit: Marketing
Organization: Powell Braginski Inc.
Locality: Woodinville
State: WA
Country: US

-----BEGIN NEW CERTIFICATE REQUEST-----
MIIBMDCB2wIBADB2MQswCQYDVQQGEwJVUzELMAkGA1UECBMCV0ExFDASBgNVBAcT
C1dvb2RpbnZpbGxlMR4wHAYDVQQKExVQb3dlbGwgQnJhZ21uc2tpIEluYy4xEjAQ
BgNVBAsTCU1hcmtldGluZzEQMA4GA1UEAxMHcG93ZWxsMTBcMA0GCSqGSIb3DQEB
AQUAA0sAMEgCQQDjTPS2HA9EVZBmFkyRTbr0pyKJvxSfitRFws7GQCLQi6SqmWq5
UeTuNbo5tMgsMl/9hub/RvsKpUu+vXcrirDLAgMBAAGgADANBgkqhkiG9w0BAQQF
AANBAHDPHryNEaYnrmPCeu4IzH95AtSzTrilHqGdT9qg5ethSu2JF+Ei732Pxagd
IWIEW5v1FW+LT5zUZBjtnt0LoRI=
-----END NEW CERTIFICATE REQUEST-----
```

We'll use the New Certificate Request portion of this file to submit this request to Certificate Server. To begin, we select the Process A Certificate Request option on the Certificate Enrollment Tools page shown in Figure 14.7 to display the Web Server Enrollment page, shown in Figure 14.10. This page consists of a simple form with a single text box. To process our server request, we simply cut and paste the portion of our request file between and including the Begin and End New Certificate Request lines.

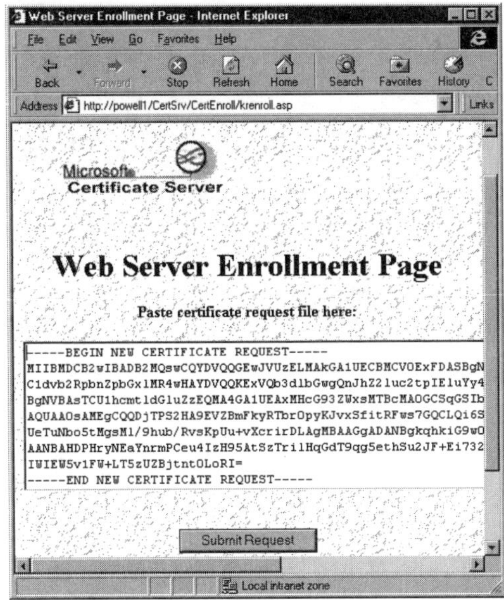

FIGURE 14.10

The Web Server Enrollment Page, showing the properly pasted request.

When we click the Submit Request button, we should see an acknowledgment page informing us that the request has been completed successfully. (If for some reason the request was not successfully processed, an error will be reported.) When the acknowledgment page appears, click the Download button to save the certificate in a file. The resulting encoded certificate is shown here:


```
-----BEGIN CERTIFICATE-----
MIICkjCCAjygAwIBAgIICNUjXgAAABEwDQYJKoZIhvcNAQEEBQAwaDELMAkGA1UE
BhMCVVMxJjAkBgNVBAoTHVBvd2VsbCBCcmFnaW5za2kgUHVibGljYXRpb25zMRsw
GQYDVQQLExJTZWN1cmUgU2VydmVyIFVuaXQxFDASBgNVBAMTC01hdHQgUG93ZWxs
MB4XDTk4MDEwNzAzMTM0MloXDTk4MTAyNjIyMjkxNlowgYkxCzAJBgNVBAYTAlVT
MQswCQYDVQQIEwJXQTEUMBIGA1UEBxMLV29vZGludmlsbGUxJDAiBgNVBAoTG1Bv
d2VsbCBCcmFnaW5za2kgUHVibGlzaGluZzEfMB0GA1UECxMWU2VjdXJlIFNlcnZl
ciBEaXZpc2lvbjEQMA4GA1UEAxMHcG93ZWxsMTBcMA0GCSqGSIb3DQEBAQUAA0sA
MEgCQQCLbBVXvh0G2UjicYZdB9eMlOy2c9wlSS8AxNOWcvw+1M9qpKhXQT3kPQLO
DflAl5XC4jzGNtIs1HcIXj3XJlzDAgMBAAGjgacwgaQwgaEGA1UdIwSBmTCBloAU
Z3pQdmEk2av73UR1nJcjdBQQYCuhbKRqMGgxCzAJBgNVBAYTAlVTMSYwJAYDVQQK
Ex1Qb3dlbGwgQnJhZ2luc2tpIFB1YmxpY2F0aW9uczEbMBkGA1UECxMSU2VjdXJl
IFNlcnZlciBVbml0MRQwEgYDVQQDEwtNYXR0IFBvd2VsbIIQAp0tBUAAQ78R0U5R
1KbnwjANBgkqhkiG9w0BAQQFAANBACTEv3OC5MJ2optN2XU66rlCjAClXsH3a2uR
rJfxiyn0BIm1tQx+iUj/GTQpYjPTyIBiD55Ryg1FsrYZcBsr2NI=
-----END CERTIFICATE-----
```

To install the key certificate, access the Key Manager from the toolbar in the Management Console window. When the Key Manager window appears, highlight your key request, and choose the Install Key Certificate option from the Key menu. When the Open dialog box appears, select the file we just downloaded, and the certificate will be installed.

But wait—there's one more step! If we accept or require client certificates for any pages on our site, our server will have to verify these client certificates by checking the digital signature. The digital signature was made using the certificate authority's private key, so IIS will need the certificate authority's public key. IIS also needs the certificate authority's certificate, and this information is obtained in a rather strange way. Since at this point IIS has no way to communicate with a certificate authority to get its certificate, IIS requires that you first copy the certificate to the machine by installing it using Internet Explorer. To do this, run Internet Explorer on the machine that IIS is running on and install the certificate authority certificate as described in the section "Installing the Certificate Authority Certificate" earlier in this chapter. The certificate authority's certificate will be added to the Internet Explorer certificate store on the server machine. Now we need to transfer the certificate to IIS's trusted certificate store by using a command-line utility named IISCA.EXE. This utility simply copies any certificate authority certificates from the Internet Explorer certificate store to the IIS certificate store. If your clients are receiving certificates from well-known certificate authorities such as VeriSign, that certificate authority's certificate will already be included in IIS's certificate store. However, if you are issuing client authentication certificates using Certificate Server, you will need to add your certificate authority certificate to the store manually using IISCA.EXE. The results of running IISCA should look like this:

```
C:\WINNT\system32\inetsrv>iisca
List of valid Certifiying Authorities ( CA ) successfuly
transferred to IIS
```

Now the clients to whom you issued certificates will be able to use them successfully to access secure resources on your machine.

Administration

When we talked about the Certificate Server architecture at the beginning of this chapter, we mentioned that all certificate requests and granted certificates were logged in the certificate database. Actually, a Web interface into the certificate database lets you see and administer the certificates. Figure 14.11 shows the Certificate Log Administration page, which lists all the certificates granted so far. To get to this page, select the Certificate Administration Log Utility from the Certificate Server home page (shown in Figure 14.6).

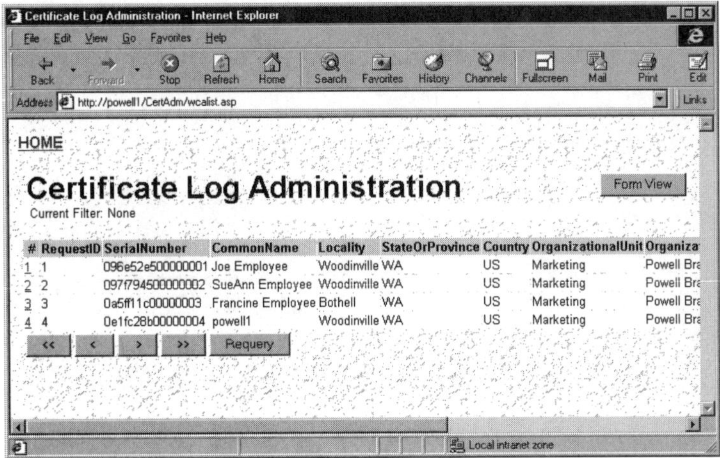

FIGURE 14.11

The Certificate Log Administration page.

You can also look at each certificate individually. To do so, either click the Form View button or click on a particular certificate's serial number. In form view, each field of the certificate is shown. More importantly, form view also provides a Revoke button that let's you revoke a certificate. Remember that certificates should be revoked when they are no longer valid. For instance, if an employee who had been issued a company certificate left the company, you would add that certificate to the CRL. The first step in doing this is to select the employee's certificate record in the database and click Revoke. The second step is to re-create the CRL by using the command-line utility CERTUTIL.EXE. To create a CRL, execute the following command:

```
C:>CERTUTIL -CRL -
```

The dash at the end of the command tells CERTUTIL to put this list in the default location, which is the enrollment virtual root. (The CERTUTIL file created for our certificate authority is named Powell/Braginski Certificate Authority.crl.) This file is the PCKS #7 standardized CRL file available on your Web site. The CRL must be publicly available so that servers and clients can determine whether their certificates have been revoked.

The Requery button at the bottom of the Certificate Log Administration page will refresh the contents of the list. This capability might be important if you need to determine whether additional certificates have been created since you first generated the list or whether other administrators have revoked any certificates.

The other administrative option available on the Certificate Server home page is Certificate Administration Queue Utility. Selecting this option displays the Certificate Server Queue Administration page shown in Figure 14.12. This page is similar to the Certificate Log Administration page; the difference is that the queue page shows us all the certificate requests along with their current status.

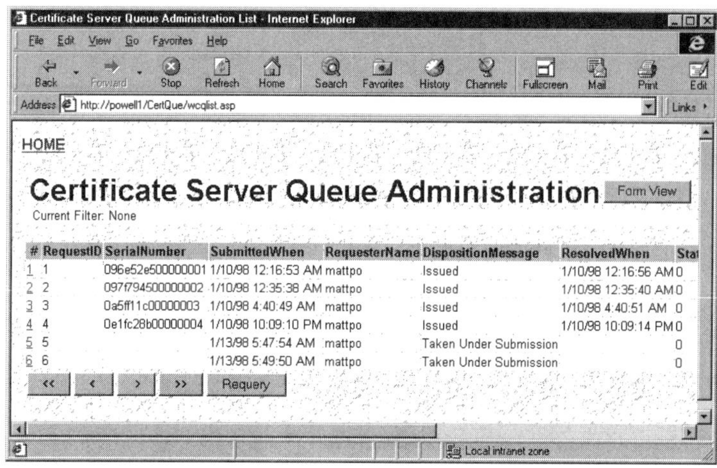

FIGURE 14.12

The Certificate Server Queue Administration page.

Notice that the last two records are somewhat different from the previous records. In particular, the DispositionMessage field shows Taken Under Submission, which tells us that the last two certificate requests have been submitted but have not yet been approved. Our policy module has specified that these requests have a status of "pending." The status of the requests will have to be rechecked to determine whether their status has changed. When this setting changes to Issued, the certificates can be downloaded by the client. The Certificate Server administrator can use this utility to see what requests have been submitted and determine the status of each request.

Command-Line Utilities

Certificate Server comes with two command-line utilities that expose much of its functionality. Some of this functionality is available through the Web interface, but some of it is not. For instance, we used CERTUTIL.EXE to publish a CRL, which you can't do through the Web interface. CERTUTIL has a number of other uses as well, including the ability to deny or resubmit pending requests, the ability to set certificate extension and attribute values, and the ability to revoke certificates. The command-line utility CERTREQ.EXE enables you to submit certificate requests without going through the Web interface. CERTREQ will also let you resubmit requests that were labeled as "pending" when you initially submitted them. These utilities can be quite useful, but you can actually add similar capabilities to your Web site simply by using the appropriate objects from your ASP code.

Programming and Scripting Interfaces

Before we look at a full-featured scenario in which we have implemented some of our own code to enhance the current Web interface, let's see what types of programming interfaces are available. Two basic kinds of programming interfaces are available with Certificate Server: front-end interfaces and back-end interfaces.

Front-End Interfaces

Front-end interfaces let you take advantage of the services provided by Certificate Server. The three front-end interfaces are *ICertConfig*, *ICertRequest*, and *ICertAdmin*.

The ICertConfig interface

The first front-end interface we'll look at is a relatively minor one: *ICertConfig*. Although the current version of Certificate Server cannot support multiple certificate authorities at the same time, the architecture has been designed to allow multiple certificate authorities to be supported in the future. Thus when you submit requests in your script to Certificate Server, you will need to identify the particular certificate authority you are interested in. The *ICertConfig* interface provides a means for enumerating and retrieving certificate authority configuration information. You will use *ICertConfig* simply to get the default configuration string; this is achieved with the following two lines:

```
Set ICertConfig = Server.CreateObject("CertificateAuthority.Config.1")
CAConfiguration = ICertConfig.GetConfig(0)
```

You'll need to pass the default configuration string obtained from this code to a number of other functions.

The ICertRequest interface

Next is the *ICertRequest* interface. The main purpose of this interface is to submit certificate requests to Certificate Server. *ICertRequest* is used by the ASP pages that make up the Web page certificate request mechanism. The two main methods you will need to use to request a certificate are the *Submit* method and the *GetCertificate* method. The *Submit* method sends a preformatted request to Certificate Server, and the *GetCertificate* method retrieves the certificate generated for the request. The following VBScript will request a certificate for the client:

```
bstrPKCS10 = Request.Form("CertReq")

Set ICertConfig = Server.CreateObject( _
    "CertificateAuthority.Config.1")
CAConfiguration = ICertConfig.GetConfig(0)

Set ICertRequest = Server.CreateObject( _
    "CertificateAuthority.Request.1")
Disposition = ICertRequest.Submit (257, bstrPKCS10, "", _
    CAConfiguration)

if Disposition = 3 then
    Certificate = ICertRequest.GetCertificate(257)
    ScriptFormatCertificate FormatedCert
end if
```

Our page receives a PKCS #10–formatted request from a client form, which builds the request from the various user inputs. (For more information, see the sidebar "Installing Certificates on IE 4 Using Xenroll Control.") We store the request in the *bstrPKCS10* variable. We then get the certificate configuration information using the *ICertConfig* interface. Last we create an instance of the *ICertRequest* object and call the *Submit* method. The first parameter of the *Submit* method is a flag with the value *257*. This value represents the combination of flags indicating that this is a PKCS #10–formatted request and that this request happens to be base 64–encoded, which is the type of request that was passed to us by the Xenroll control. The allowable flag values are defined in CERTCLI.H, which is included in the Microsoft Platform SDK. The second parameter is the certificate request itself. We pass a blank string as the third parameter, which indicates that we don't need any special attributes set on this request. The fourth parameter is the certificate authority configuration information that we just located using the *ICertConfig* interface.

Assuming that we built our request correctly, three basic types of results are possible. The first type indicates that the certificate authority denied our request—in this case, the *Submit* method returns a value of *2*. The second type indicates that the certificate authority has received our request but that the request is currently pending approval. In this case, the *Submit* method returns a value of *5*; we would have to check back later to see whether our request had been approved. The last type indicates that the certificate authority approved our request and created a certificate. In this case, the *Submit* method returns a value of *3*. If the certificate was issued, we can obtain it using the *GetCertificate* method. The *257* value passed to *GetCertificate* indicates that we want the certificate in base 64–encoded format and that we also want the "chain" of certificate authorities that have signed this certificate. In our case, the certificate authority is a root authority, so we will have only its added certificate in the result. The entire result is stored in a variable that we appropriately name *Certificate*. We then send the certificate to the client.

◆ Installing Certificates on IE4 Using Xenroll Control

Certificate Server is only half the certificate picture. After you issue certificates to Web clients, the clients have to install the certificates locally in their own certificate stores. This installation can be done in different ways, but Internet Explorer 4.0 provides a convenient control that makes this job much easier: the Xenroll control. The Xenroll control can be downloaded from the CertSrv virtual directory. It has two main purposes: to build certificate requests and to install the corresponding certificates in the local certificate store. The following script, executed on the client's browser, will create a PKCS #10 certificate request for the specified Distinguished Name:

```
<OBJECT
    classid="clsid:43F8F289-7A20-11D0-8F06-00C04FC295E1"
    CODEBASE="/CertControl/xenroll.cab#Version=5,102,1680,101"
    id=IControl
>
</OBJECT>

<SCRIPT LANGUAGE="JAVASCRIPT">
function SubmitRequest()
{
    Name = "C=US;"
    Name = Name + "S=WA;"
    Name = Name + "L=Woodinville;"
    Name = Name + "O=Powell Braginski Inc.;"
    Name = Name + "OU=Marketing;"
    Name = Name + "CN=FrancineBeth Employee;"
    IControl.KeySpec = 1;
    szPKCS10 = IControl.CreatePKCS10(Name, "1.3.6.1.5.5.7.3.2");
    document.ReqData.CertReq.value = szPKCS10;
}
</SCRIPT>
```

Once the request has been sent to the server and the certificate has been created, you can install the certificate using the Xenroll control again. The result is installed using the *acceptPKCS7* method, which takes a base 64–encoded certificate as its only parameter. Once *acceptPKCS7* has been called successfully, the new certificate will be added to the list of client certificates you can choose from when you are connecting to an SSL site that requests a client certificate.

The ICertAdmin interface

The remaining front-end interface is *ICertAdmin*. This interface can be used to perform a number of administrative tasks. As it turns out, the *ICertAdmin* interface does most of the same things as CERTUTIL.EXE. The following table lists the methods of the *ICertAdmin* interface and what they are used for.

ICertAdmin Method	Purpose
DenyRequest	Denies a certificate request.
GetCRL	Gets a pointer to the current CRL for the certificate authority.
GetRevocationReason	Returns a string indicating why a certificate was revoked; set by whoever calls *RevokeCertificate*.
IsValidCertificate	Checks whether a given certificate serial number matches a certificate in the certificate database and verifies that the specified certificate is not listed in the CRL.
PublishCRL	Causes Certificate Server to create a new CRL.
ResubmitRequest	Resubmits a certificate request that had received a Pending response to its original submission. Like the *ICertRequest::Submit* method, can return an Issued, Denied, or Still Pending response.
RevokeCertificate	Changes the status of a certificate to Revoked by a specified date. This certificate will be included the next time a CRL is created.
SetCertificateExtension	Sets an "extra" value for a certificate extension. Extensions are added pieces of information that will be included in the certificate to help identify the owner of the certificate.
SetRequestAttributes	Adds custom attribute information to a certificate request. Unlike a certificate extension, this information is not necessarily included within the certificate itself.

If you change the certificate policy so that it doesn't automatically issue certificates, you will need to use the administrative interfaces (or CERTUTIL.EXE) to manipulate the status of certificate requests. The following ASP script uses the *ICertAdmin* interface to set a certificate extension for a pending request and resubmits the request:

```
Approve = 1
ReqID = Session("rswcqJoin_AbsolutePage")
Set ICertAdmin = Server.CreateObject("CertificateAuthority.Admin.1")
Set ICertConfig = Server.CreateObject( _
    "CertificateAuthority.Config.1")
```

```
ConfigStr = ICertConfig.GetConfig(0)
ExtName = "1.2.3.4.5.6"
ICertAdmin.SetCertificateExtension ConfigStr, ReqID, ExtName, 1, _
    0, Approve
ICertAdmin.ResubmitRequest ConfigStr, ReqID
```

Again, you need to pass your certificate authority's configuration string to the *ICertAdmin* methods just as you had to do with the *ICertRequest* methods. Every server extension requires an Object ID—in our case, we are using the bogus ID *"1.2.3.4.5.6"*, but a number of predefined IDs are available that let you do things such as set the certificate type, include a URL to the CRL, and add an alternative name. Extensions can also hold different types of data, so we must specify a flag indicating that we want to store an integer (rather than a string or other type of data) in our extension. Next we include the data itself, which in this case is simply the number *1*. After we finally set our extension, we call the *ResubmitRequest* method to send the request back to the policy module to determine whether the certificate will now be issued.

Back-End Interfaces

The back-end interfaces of Certificate Server enable you to control how Certificate Server works. The main part of this capability involves manipulating the policy module, which enables you to determine under what conditions we will issue a certificate. In this section, you'll learn how to write your own policy module.

The ICertPolicy interface

A policy module is a COM server that supports the *ICertPolicy* interface. You can write a policy module in C++, Microsoft Visual Basic, or even Java. Our sample policy module is written in C++, uses the Active Template Library (ATL) from Microsoft Visual C++, and is based on the sample policy module (named Policy) provided in the Microsoft Platform SDK. Policy modules determine what criteria a certificate request must meet for a certificate to be issued. Our sample policy module will return a status of "pending" for all new certificate requests; it will issue the certificate only after the request has been manually approved. Clients must check back later to determine the current status of their requests and to download their certificates if they have been approved.

The *ICertPolicy* interface has four methods that the policy module will need to support. The *Initialize* and *Shutdown* methods simply provide the policy module with a convenient time in which to perform any necessary initialization and cleanup of internal modules. Because our simple policy module does not have anything to initialize or clean up, we simply return from these calls. The *GetDescription* method enables the policy module to provide an easy-to-read description of itself. The most important of *ICertPolicy*'s methods is the *VerifyRequest* method. *VerifyRequest* is called for each certificate request received by Certificate Server. It is the duty of *VerifyRequest* to analyze the certificate request and determine whether the request should be granted, denied, or assigned a "pending" status. The default policy module that comes with Certificate Server performs a simple request verification and then issues a certificate. The only reason it would deny a request is if the request were improperly formatted. Our sample policy module returns a "pending" status for each new request and requires the administrator to manually approve the request before a certificate is issued.

Certificate *request attributes* are used to hold customizable information about a request. When a client makes a certificate request, it can specify a series of attributes that will be submitted with the request. This custom information would not become part of the certificate as certificate extensions do. For instance, you might want to include your mother's maiden name with the request, although it wouldn't be included in the certificate itself. The policy module considers this extra information when it is handling the request. Administrators can also add attributes to a request using the *SetRequestAttributes* method of the *ICertAdmin* interface. Our policy module checks to see whether the *Approved* attribute is set before it will issue a certificate. The following code shows our policy module's *VerifyRequest* method and how we use the *Approved* attribute:

```
STDMETHODIMP CCertPolicy::VerifyRequest(
    /* [in] */ BSTR const strConfig,
    /* [in] */ LONG Context,
    /* [in] */ LONG bNewRequest,
    /* [in] */ LONG Flags,
    /* [out, retval] */ LONG __RPC_FAR *pDisposition)
{
    HRESULT hr;
    ICertServerPolicy *pServer = NULL;
    BSTR attrApproved = SysAllocString(L"Approved");
    BSTR ApprovedValue;

    hr = CoCreateInstance(
                    CLSID_CCertServerPolicy,
                    NULL,               // pUnkOuter
                    CLSCTX_INPROC_SERVER,
                    IID_ICertServerPolicy,
                    (VOID **) &pServer);
    if (S_OK != hr)
    {
        goto exit;
    }
```

```
    hr = pServer->SetContext(Context);
    if (S_OK != hr)
    {
        goto exit;
    }

    hr = pServer->GetRequestAttribute(attrApproved, &ApprovedValue);
    if ((hr == S_OK) && (lstrcmpW(ApprovedValue, L"1") == 0))
    {
        if (bNewRequest)
        {
            // Someone is trying to spoof our Approved attribute.
            // Deny this request.
            *pDisposition = VR_INSTANT_BAD;
            return S_OK;
        }
        // This request was approved.
        *pDisposition = VR_INSTANT_OK;
        return S_OK;
    }
    hr = S_OK;

exit:
    *pDisposition = VR_PENDING;
    return hr;
}
```

When Certificate Server calls our *VerifyRequest* method, it passes four arguments. One of these arguments, *strConfig*, is the certificate authority configuration string we've needed in some of the preceding interface methods. Another argument, *bNewRequest*, tells us whether this is a new request or a pending request that is being resubmitted. The *Flags* argument is currently unused and should be *0*. The remaining argument, *Context*, is used to take advantage of another interface, *ICertServerPolicy*.

The ICertServerPolicy interface

The *ICertServerPolicy* interface is supported by Certificate Server itself. It provides a convenient way for getting at the information in a certificate request. The first thing our policy module does is instantiate an instance of *ICertServerPolicy* using the *CoCreateInstance* function. We then synchronize the *ICertServerPolicy* interface with our current request by using the value of the context parameter passed to our *VerifyRequest* method to call *ICertServerPolicy::SetContext*.

We can now use the rest of the methods of *ICertServerPolicy* to pull out the certificate's attributes, any extension information, and the specific certificate properties. In our case, all we really care about is whether the *Approved* attribute is set, so we use only the *GetRequestAttribute* method. After we make the call to *GetRequestAttribute*, we check two things: whether the call completed successfully and whether the *Approved* attribute had a value of *1*. If both these conditions are true, we have a potentially approved certificate. Next we check whether this is a new request. Remember, we do this because the client that submitted the request could potentially have set attributes as well. If this is a new request and already has an *Approved* attribute set, we know that our administrator did not approve the request. Instead, a naughty client set the *Approved* attribute, presumably in an attempt to circumvent our administrator approval process. In this case, we explicitly deny the request by setting the disposition to *VR_INSTANT_BAD*. If this is a resubmit request and the *Approved* attribute is set, we can assume that our administrator has manually approved the request. (Clients submitting requests can set attributes only when they submit the initial request.) In this case, we issue the certificate by setting the disposition to *VR_INSTANT_OK*. If either the call to *GetRequestAttribute* failed (which usually means that the specified attribute is not there) or the value of the *Approved* attribute is not *1*, we can safely assume that this request has not yet been approved. In this case, we set the request's disposition to *VR_PENDING*. To indicate that our policy module handled the request successfully, we return *S_OK*; if we do not return *S_OK*, the request is automatically denied.

Certificate extensions

Our policy module is relatively simple. When you write your own policy modules, you might want to verify a few other things about any requests being submitted. You will probably want to verify that the Organization field of the Distinguished Name matches the name of your company. You might also want to include some optional properties in the request—for example, you might want to issue certificates only if the Distinguished Name includes an e-mail address. Certificate extensions also enable your certificates to include some extra information that might come in handy when a certificate is used to authenticate a user later. Hundreds of predefined extension values are available, or you can create your own extensions. You can require that users who submit a request add certain extensions, or you can add extensions yourself by using the *SetCertificateExtension* method of the *ICertServerPolicy* interface.

◆ Creating Customized Enrollment Pages

If you want to ensure that the certificates you issue have certain attributes or extensions, you can manipulate the Certificate Server Enrollment Form page (or create your own request page from scratch) to include these characteristics in the requests. You should, however, still verify the characteristics in your policy module because it is possible for people to create their own requests without using your request page. For instance, if you want to ensure that the Organization field in the certificates you issue contains the value *Powell Braginski Inc.*, you must create a request page that automatically sets this value in the request. You will need to verify that the Organization field still shows *Powell Braginski Inc.* in your policy module because users could easily create their own request pages and set the Organization field differently.

Certificate extensions can contain all types of data. You can create an extension that holds a string value, a numeric value, or even a customized structure. If your policy module is going to consider extension information, it will need a means of interpreting or setting the extension data. For this reason, Certificate Server includes the capability to create an extension handler. For instance, you might want to create an extension that holds an array of numbers. Certificate Server provides built-in support for extensions that hold numbers, strings, dates, and binary data, but it does not provide direct numeric array support. However, Certificate Server does provide the ability to create a certificate extension that supports numeric arrays. The extension would expose the *ICertEncodeLongArray* interface, which enables you to manipulate the data in your numeric array extension. Extension handler interfaces are also provided for date arrays, string arrays, bit strings, and CRL info. There are even a couple of sample handlers that show how to handle custom structures.

Extension handlers can also be used by exit modules to view the extra extension information after the policy module has approved a request. You can write your own exit module by creating a COM server that supports the *ICertExit* interface. Exit modules are notified of various Certificate Server events—for example, when certificates are issued, when certificates are rejected, when certificates are revoked, and even when CRLs are published. Exit modules are similar to policy modules in that they include an *ICertServerExit* interface that they can use once they set the *Context* argument, in the same way we included the *ICertServerPolicy* interface in our custom policy module. The exit module can then use the *ICertServerExit* interface to obtain information about the particular certificate.

Coordinating Front-End and Back-End Interfaces

When taking advantage of any of the back-end interfaces, you should be aware of the ramifications to the front end. If your policy module is going to approve only requests that have specific characteristics—for example, the elements of the Distinguished Name have set values or the request includes certain extensions or attributes—you should build your request pages to set those characteristics appropriately. But a policy module can also cause problems when it uses the "pending" request disposition. Our sample policy module returned a pending disposition for every new request. The effect on Certificate Server's standard certificate request enrollment pages was dramatic. The default enrollment pages made it appear that all certificate requests were denied even though they were pending manual approval, and there was no easy way to manually set our *Approved* attribute to actually complete the pending requests.

To overcome these problems, we had to manipulate the front-end interfaces to work with our new policy module. First we had to modify the CEACCEPT.ASP file, which submitted the actual request using the *ICertRequest's Submit* method. The default CEACCEPT.ASP file checks only for a disposition value of *3*, which indicates that the certificate has been issued. If the disposition has any other value, the request is considered denied. We added the following ASP script to handle a disposition of *5*, which indicates that the request is pending approval:

```
<% if DispositionCode = 5 then %>
    <H1>Certificate Request Accepted</H1>
    <B>
    <FONT SIZE=5>
    <BR>Your request has been successfully received and is
    currently waiting for approval.
    To check the status of your request, go to
    <a href=status2.asp> the Request Status Page. </a>
    You will need your Request ID, which is
    <H1><%=ICertRequest.GetRequestId()%>.</H1>
    </FONT>
    <BR><BR><BR><BR><BR>
<% End If%>
```

Our CEACCEPT.ASP page now provides a link to another page, on which we can check the status of our request. It also provides the Request ID, which will be needed for checking the status of the request at a later time. The Request ID is found by calling the *ICertRequest* interface's *GetRequestId* method. Our new page is shown in Figure 14.13.

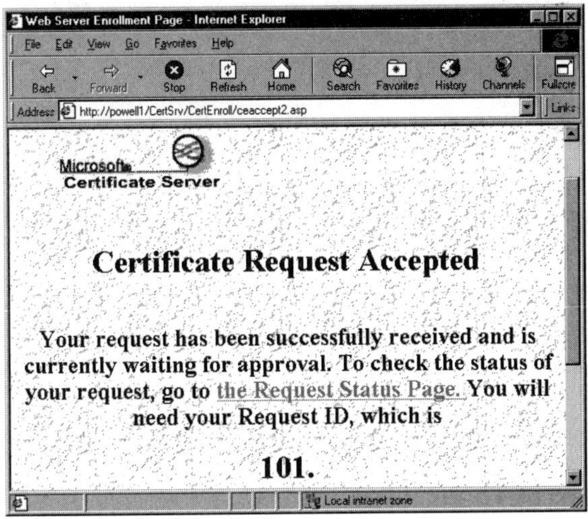

FIGURE 14.13

Our modified Web Server Enrollment page.

The Request Status page is a simple form that takes as input a single variable: the Request ID provided with our earlier request. The Request ID is submitted to another ASP page that does the actual check of the request. The ASP script is shown here:

```
<%@ LANGUAGE="VBSCRIPT" %>

<HTML>
<HEAD>
<TITLE>Certificate Request Status Page</TITLE>
</HEAD>
<BODY>

<%
    RequestID = Request.QueryString("RequestID")
    Set RequestObj = Server.CreateObject( _
        "CertificateAuthority.Request.1")
    Set ConfigObj = Server.CreateObject( _
        "CertificateAuthority.Config.1")
    ConfigString = ConfigObj.GetConfig(0)
    DispositionCode = RequestObj.RetrievePending(RequestID, _
        ConfigString)
```

(continued)

```
    if DispositionCode = 3 then %>
        <H1>Certificate Download</H1>
        <B>
        <FONT SIZE=5>
        <BR>Your request has been approved!
        </FONT>
        <FONT SIZE=4>
        <BR><BR><BR><BR><BR>
    <% else
        if DispositionCode = 5 then %>
            <H1>Your request is still pending</H1>
            <B>
            <BR><BR><BR><BR><BR>
        <% else %>
            <H1>Your request has been denied </H1>
            <B>
            <BR><BR><BR><BR><BR>
        <%End If%>
    <%End If%>
</BODY>
</HTML>
```

We use *ICertRequest*'s *RetrievePending* method to get the status of our earlier request. We check for the three possibilities: that our certificate has been issued (a value of 3), that it is still pending (a value of 5), or that it has been denied (any other value). Presumably, in the case in which a certificate has been issued, you would use *ICertRequest*'s *GetCertificate* method to actually download the request, as we did earlier, but in this case we omitted that step for the sake of simplicity.

Other front-end changes need to be made as well. We can view the certificate request queue by using the Certificate Server Administration Queue utility, but we need to somehow provide a mechanism for approving or denying the requests—that is, we need to somehow be able to set the *Approved:1* attribute that our policy module requires to accept a request. Again we accomplish this task by making some small modifications to the existing pages.

Figure 14.14 shows the form view of the certificate request queue available through the Certificate Server administration pages, specifically the Certificate Server Queue Administration Form. We've modified the WCQFORM.ASP page to include two extra hyperlinks that let us easily administer pending requests: the first link goes to an ASP page that will approve the pending request, and the second link goes to an ASP page that will deny the pending request.

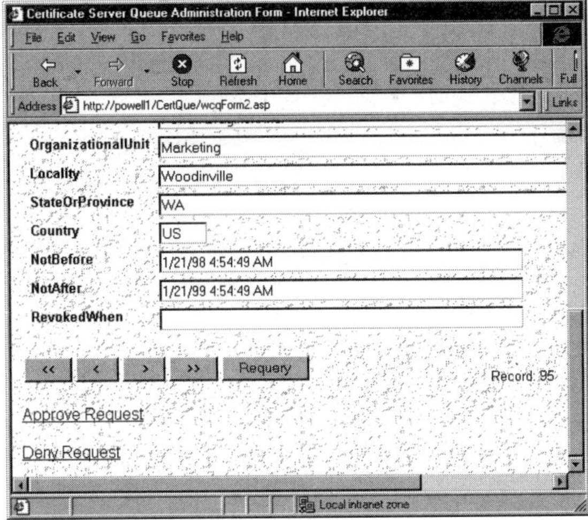

FIGURE 14.14

The certificate request queue in our modified form view.

The script for the ASP page that will approve the request is shown in the following code. The link we created on the previous page passed the Request ID in the query string of the URL.

```
<HTML>
<HEAD>
<TITLE>Certificate Approval Page</TITLE>
</HEAD>
<BODY>

<%
    RequestID = Request.QueryString
    Set AdminObj = Server.CreateObject( _
        "CertificateAuthority.Admin.1")
    Set ConfigObj = Server.CreateObject( _
        "CertificateAuthority.Config.1")
    Dim ConfigString
    ConfigString = ConfigObj.GetConfig(0)
    ApproveAttrib = "Approved:1"
    AdminObj.SetRequestAttributes ConfigString, RequestID, _
        ApproveAttrib
%>
<H1>Certificate Approval Page</H1>
<H3>Request <%=RequestID%> was approved.</H3>
```

(continued)

```
<%
    AdminObj.ResubmitRequest ConfigString, RequestID
%>
<H3>Certificate Created.</H3>
</BODY>
</HTML>
```

This code uses the *ICertAdmin* interface to add our *Approved* attribute to the specified request. We also resubmit the request using the *ResubmitRequest* method so that the policy module can appropriately approve the request and issue the certificate. Once this has been done, the client can go to the status page to find the current disposition of its request: *Issued*.

The deny request link on WCQFORM2.ASP also passes the Request ID to an ASP page via the query string in the hyperlink's URL. This link uses *ICertAdmin's DenyRequest* method, which sets the disposition of the request to *Admin Denied Request*. The code for the Certificate Denial page is shown here:

```
<HTML>
<HEAD>
<TITLE>Certificate Denial Page</TITLE>
</HEAD>
<BODY>
<%
    RequestID=Request.QueryString
    Set AdminObj = Server.CreateObject( _
        "CertificateAuthority.Admin.1")
    Set ConfigObj = Server.CreateObject( _
        "CertificateAuthority.Config.1")
    ConfigString = ConfigObj.GetConfig(0)
    AdminObj.DenyRequest ConfigString, RequestID
%>
<H1>Certificate Denial Page</H1>
<H3>Request <%=RequestID%> was denied.</H3>
</BODY>
</HTML>
```

Once this page has been executed, the client can see that its request has been denied the next time it checks the request's status page. Obviously, no certificates are created for denied requests.

We have now built a complete solution to match the policy module we created for our certificate authority. You can do much more with the various interfaces to further enhance the administration and end-user experience of Certificate Server. You can even provide requesting and administration capabilities within your own ASP pages. In Chapter 15, we will look at some of the other services you can take advantage of in IIS.

CHAPTER 15

Advanced Services

So far, we've looked at a number of services that sit on top of Internet Information Server, from Index Server to Certificate Server. Now we are going to look at two services, Microsoft Transaction Server (MTS) and Microsoft Message Queue Server (MSMQ), that are tightly associated with IIS but do not require IIS to be useful. These services can be used within IIS, however; in fact, IIS cannot run without MTS installed. We'll look at how IIS uses MTS and how you can easily create applications that take advantage of MTS and MSMQ in Part II. In this chapter, we will focus on installing MTS and MSMQ, configuring these services, and managing these services after they are up and running. Let's begin with MTS.

Microsoft Transaction Server

If you're not familiar with MTS or even with the concept of a database transaction, you might be a bit puzzled about what a transaction server is. When we hear the word "transaction," most of us think of purchasing merchandise at a cash register, and, in fact, that is precisely what transactions are all about. When you purchase a gallon of milk from your local grocery store, a transaction takes place. But this process involves more than simply handing your money to the cashier. In reality, a transaction is the coordination of two or more events. When you buy your milk, two actions occur: you give your money to the store (the clerk), and in return the store gives you the milk. If for some reason one of the actions is incomplete, all the actions need to be *rolled back* (returned to the state before the transaction). For example, if the milk costs 89 cents and you hand the clerk 75 cents, the money part of the transaction will fail. The clerk not only needs to discontinue the transaction (he doesn't give you the milk), but he also needs to roll back the initial transaction event (he returns your 75 cents).

MTS may not have much impact when it comes to buying milk, but it can definitely play a big role in dealing with other types of transactions. For instance, suppose you were a mail-order company processing a phone order. You might need to update a customer information database, an orders database, and an inventory database. If you weren't able to update the customer information database, you wouldn't want to update the orders database, and you would want to roll back any changes you had already made. Transactions provide a simple means for performing these kinds of tasks. MTS takes a collection of transactional objects and synchronizes their calls and completions. Each transactional object has a certain task it is responsible for completing. But the tasks themselves complete in two parts: the first part sets everything up so that there is no question that the task can complete successfully, and the second part is the actual commitment, which takes what has been set up and completes the request. If the object is unable to perform either the first or second part properly, it notifies MTS, which then informs all the objects within the transaction that they need to roll back their changes. When both parts of all tasks for all objects within the transaction have been completed successfully, the transaction is complete.

This model illustrates how a single transaction works, but real transactions are actually quite a bit more involved. For example, you might have two people launching simultaneous transactions using the same objects. Or you might be concerned about security issues within your transaction. MTS takes care of all these complexities for you. MTS allows you to build a simple component that doesn't worry about security, being called by multiple users at the same time, or even access to certain resources such as database connections. MTS manages all of these issues so that you can create a high-powered application with very simple component code.

Glossary

transactional object *An object that actively participates in Microsoft Transaction Server transactions. They may use the MTS object context to commit or abort transactional operations.*

MTS manages transactional components through elements called *packages*. By specifying a group of components and putting them into an MTS package, you are informing MTS that these components will be used in the same transaction. MTS gives each component an *object context,* which holds the transactional information about the component. The object context provides the link between the different components in the package so that they can cooperate to complete the transaction. MTS also provides security information to the package that the components can access through their object context. The components can even store transaction-specific data in the object context that can then be shared among the components in the package. IIS actually uses the object context to expose interfaces into its intrinsic ASP objects; we will learn more about this in Chapter 18.

The other defining characteristic of an MTS package, in addition to the components within the package, is the *role* of the various people who use the package. For instance, suppose you have defined a package that provides a mechanism for accessing employee salary information. You would probably want to limit access to any administrative aspects of this package to managers within your company. MTS allows you to define a group of users who are considered to fulfill the management role, which makes it easy for your application to query its object context for the role of the current user and allow appropriate access accordingly. If the user accessing the package happens to be in the group defined as having the manager role, that user will be allowed to view salary information. If the user is not in the manager group and in fact has only the employee role, that user will not be provided access to the information. Defining these roles and providing their information to the components within a package is another powerful feature provided by MTS.

Glossary

package *A collection of transactional objects that, when executed by a user, will share a single transaction context. If any object aborts a transaction, MTS will have the rest of the objects within the package roll back their changes as well.*

role *A collection of users or groups. When you authenticate users for your MTS transaction, you can base your object's logic on whether the calling user is part of a certain role.*

We will be getting into the details of transaction architecture and you will be writing your own transactional applications in the next few chapters, but for now we'll concentrate on installing and administering MTS.

Installing MTS

When you run the Microsoft Windows NT 4.0 Option Pack Setup program, MTS is automatically selected for installation. IIS itself uses MTS to manage things like its worker thread pools, so you cannot install IIS without also installing MTS.

MTS provides only a few installation options. If you select to install MTS from the Setup window and you click Show Subcomponents, you will see a list of three subcomponents, as shown in Figure 15.1. The Transaction Server Core Components option is the MTS service and components that make MTS work. If you plan on using MTS, you must select this option. The Transaction Server Core Documentation option lets you specify whether you want to install the online documentation. Last is the Transaction Server Development option, which consists of the various libraries, header files, documentation, and sample code—all of which provide the files you need to write your own MTS applications.

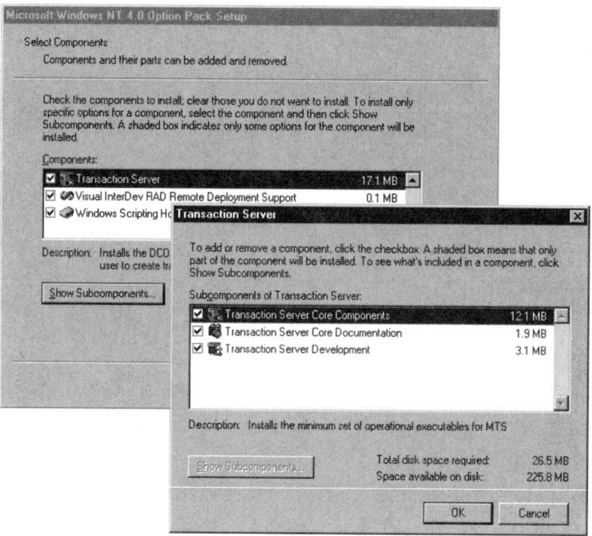

FIGURE 15.1

The MTS Setup window options.

After you choose your installation options, you will be prompted for the MTS installation directory. By default, MTS installs in the C:\Program Files\Mts directory, but you can change this setting to any directory you want. You can also specify whether you want to be able to administer MTS from a different machine. In the dialog box, shown in Figure 15.2, you can choose the Local or Remote administration option. If you do want to use remote administration, you will need to specify an account that will be used to communicate across the network. In this example, we have specified the *mattpo* account in the *Lexington* domain as the Administrator Account.

Managing MTS

After you have installed MTS, you still have to get everything configured and working properly. As with the other services we've looked at, MTS is managed using a snap-in to the Microsoft Management Console. The Management Console provides a seamless integration with the rest of the Windows NT Option Pack. Figure 15.3 shows the MTS management options available in the Management Console.

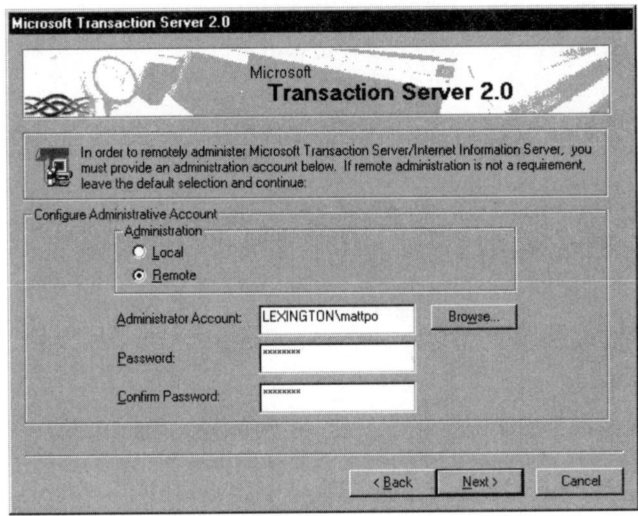

FIGURE 15.2

Configuring remote administration for MTS.

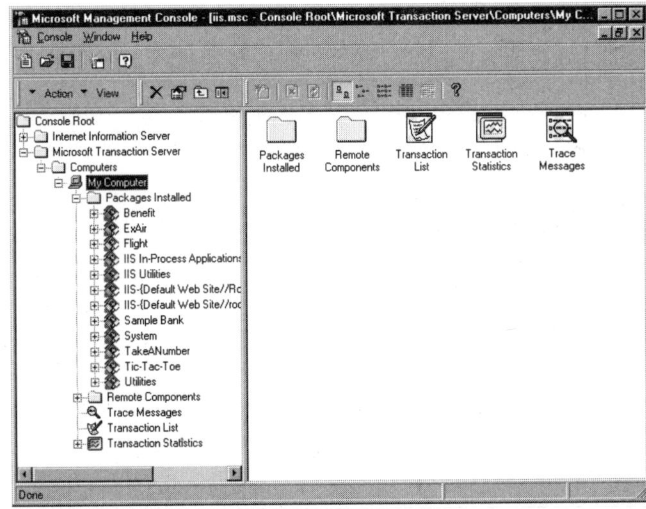

FIGURE 15.3

The MTS management options available in the Management Console.

Notice the folder below Microsoft Transaction Server named Computers. As with the other services, the Management Console can be used not only to administer the local machine, but also to remotely administer other MTS servers. If we were going to administer multiple machines, you would see other computers listed within the Computers folder in addition to My Computer.

When you select a computer under the Computers folder, five icons appear in the right-hand pane that provide access to a variety of configurable options and monitoring capabilities. We'll look at all of these options later in this chapter, but first we'll look at the folder that contains the heart of the MTS configuration, Packages Installed.

MTS packages

When you open the Packages Installed folder, you'll see a list of all the packages already set up in MTS. Each package consists of two main items: the components in the package and the roles defined for that package. Therefore, when you open each package in the list, you will see a Components folder and a Roles folder. Figure 15.4 shows the Management Console's MTS hierarchy for a single package named Benefit. (The Benefit package is installed with the World Wide Web Sample Site, a subcomponent of IIS.)

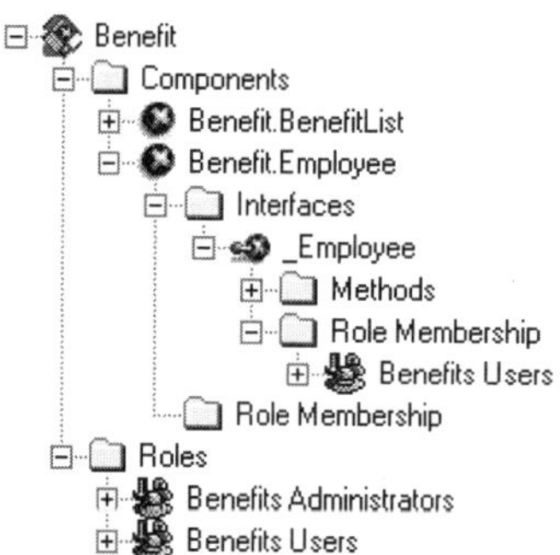

FIGURE 15.4

The example Benefit package expanded in the Management Console.

The sample Benefit package includes two components—*Benefit.BenefitList* and *Benefit.Employee*—and two roles—*Benefits Administrators* and *Benefits Users*. (You won't see these roles in your sample site. They were added for this discussion.) The roles will enable us to restrict access to certain components or their interfaces. You can define roles and manage the Windows NT accounts in each role under the package's Roles folder. Once a role is defined, you can then add that role as a requirement for access to a component or interface within the transaction. For example, the

Benefit package shows that the *_Employee* interface of the *Benefit.Employee* object has a *Role Membership* requirement, which means that MTS will allow only accounts in the *Benefits Users* role to access this interface. You can also define role restrictions at the component level, which means that only accounts included in the *Role Membership* folder for the component will be allowed to create an instance of the component. Thus, you have the flexibility of restricting access to the entire component or restricting access only to specific interfaces that the component supports.

NOTE

If there are no entries in the Role Membership *folder for a component or an interface, no role restrictions exist for that item. Such is the case for the* Benefit.Employee *component in this example.*

Creating packages To create a new package, highlight the Packages Installed folder in the left pane of the Management Console, choose New from the Action menu, and then choose Package. The Package Wizard will appear, as shown in Figure 15.5, to walk you through the process of creating a package. The Package Wizard has two initial options: Install Pre-Built Packages or Create An Empty Package. Let's examine what happens when we choose the Create An Empty Package option.

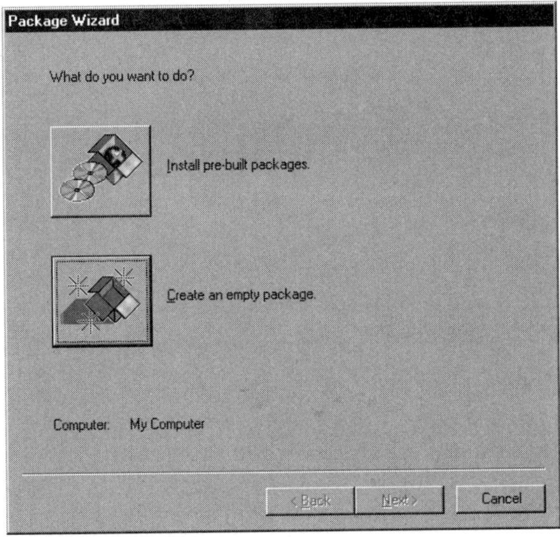

FIGURE 15.5

The Package Wizard.

The Package Wizard needs only two pieces of information to create an empty package: the package name and the identity information. The identity information is the account information used to launch the package components if the package is configured as a Server Package, which means it will run in its own process. Once you have supplied this information, your new package will appear in the list of packages under the Packages Installed folder.

Now that you have built a package, you need to also add some components to it. To do this, simply highlight the Components folder under the new package, choose the New option from the Action menu, and then choose Component. The Component Wizard will appear and walk you through the process of adding a component to your package. Two options for adding components are available: Install New Component(s) and Import Component(s) That Are Already Registered. Choosing the latter option displays the Choose Components To Import dialog box, as shown in Figure 15.6, which enumerates the Component Object Model (COM) objects registered on your local machine and lets you select the objects from the list.

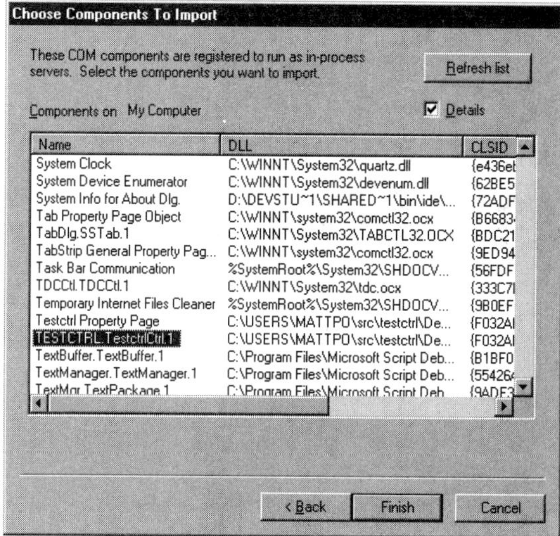

FIGURE 15.6

The Choose Components To Import dialog box.

This is a multiple-select list box, so you can highlight several components and import them at the same time. This option does not allow you to select objects that have not been registered.

NOTE

A component can be part of only one package at a time. If you attempt to add a component to your package that is already part of a different package, you will get an error message from the Management Console. If you select a component to import from the list of registered objects, keep in mind that objects in other packages will not appear in the list. If you can't find the component you're looking for in the list, you might want to see what components are being used by other packages on your system.

Choosing the Install New Component(s) option in the Component Wizard displays the Install Components dialog box, shown in Figure 15.7, which enables you to select the DLL or type library (TLB) files themselves, regardless of whether these files are registered. This technique makes it easy to install components on your system because MTS will register the components for you. Clicking the Add Files button lets you browse for the DLL or TLB file you want to install. Select the appropriate file, and it will appear in the Files To Install list; the components supported by the file will be displayed in the Components Found list.

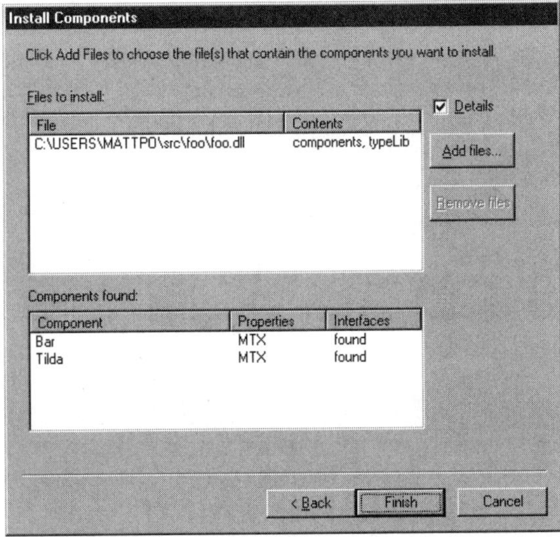

FIGURE 15.7

The Install Components dialog box, which lets you install unregistered COM components in your package.

After you have installed all your components, you can go about the process of configuring the various package options that are available.

Configuring packages A number of configurable options are available for each package within the Management Console. To see the details, right-click on the desired package and choose the Properties option from the pop-up menu. Figure 15.8 shows the Properties window for your Benefit package. Let's take a look at the different options available under the five different property pages.

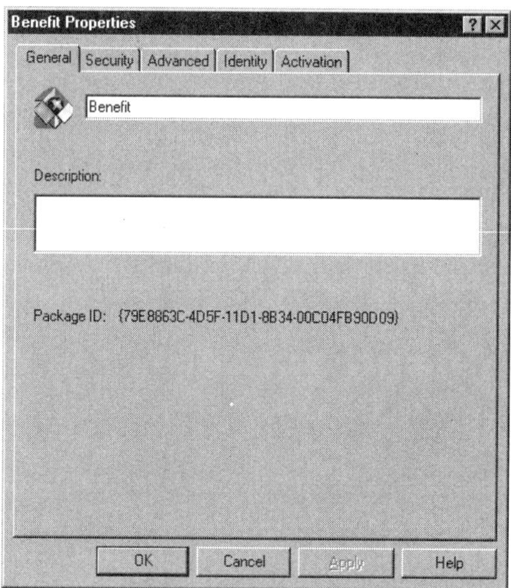

FIGURE 15.8

The Benefit Properties window, showing the General page.

The General page displays the name and an optional description of the package, both of which can be changed here. The name is the text that will appear within the Management Console next to your package. The Description can contain any notes you want to accompany the package. This information might include the purpose of the package or a brief overview of your transaction's architecture. You can add descriptions for your package's components, interfaces, and methods as well, so you don't need to describe them in detail at the package level. The Security page enables you to configure options for authentication and secure communications. The Enable Authorization Checking check box must be checked for MTS to use the role settings we discussed earlier. MTS needs some mechanism for determining who the client is so that it can find out what, if any, roles the client is in. If authorization checking is enabled, the Authentication Level For Calls list box lets you specify the level of authentication and secure communications that will be used to communicate with the components in the package. These security levels are listed in the following table.

Authentication Level	Description
None	No authentication takes place even if Enable Authorization Checking is checked.
Connect	Authentication takes place when a client makes the initial call to the object; these original credentials are then used for any calls that are made using the same connection.
Call	The user's authentication is verified for each method call of the object. This could be an important level of security if the client application is impersonating different users before calling the same instance of the object—IIS is a prime example of an application that impersonates other users before making object calls.
Packet	Packet authentication indicates that not only is the user authenticated but also that all the data received is guaranteed to be from the expected user.
Packet Integrity	Packet Integrity means that not only is the data verified as coming from the correct user but also the data is verified as free from any sort of corruption or tampering.
Packet Privacy	Packet Privacy provides all the previous levels of security as well as encryption of the data being transferred to and from the package, ensuring that no one can eavesdrop on the data being transmitted.

The options on the Security page are enabled only if you have flagged a package as a *server package* rather than a *library package*. Library packages run in the process of the client, and calls to components can go directly to the components instead of first going to MTS, where the different authentication levels can be implemented. Server packages, which run in their own process, require MTS interaction, and thus the different authentication levels can be controlled by MTS. The Advanced page provides options that let you shut down a package during idle periods and protect the current package configuration options. The Server Process Shutdown options let you specify whether you want your package to unload after a preset idle period. If you choose to enable an idle-time shutdown, you must also specify the number of minutes you want your package to wait before it shuts down and unloads the corresponding components. Shutdown options, like the Security page options, are available only for server packages. The Permission options let you prevent other people from changing the current package's characteristics. Two options are available. Disable Deletion doesn't allow your package to be deleted, and Disable Changes prevents any of the package settings from being modified. If you set the Permission options, your ability to configure a package's options will be limited. The Identity page lets you specify the account that the MTS process will use for server packages. (This is the same option we saw when we created our package.) By default, MTS server processes are launched using the Currently Logged On User setting. However, you can specify a different account (along with its password) that MTS will use to create the server process. The Identity page also is available only for server packages since library packages run in the same process as the application that launched them. The Activation page is where you flag your package as a library package or a server package. By configuring your package as a library package, you are indicating to MTS that the components within your package should be launched in the process of the application that is calling them. Doing so will provide a high level of performance, but it also means that any component can corrupt the memory space of the calling process. By running your package as a server package, you isolate the package components from the calling process, which avoids any unintended memory corruption for the client process. Server packages also provide many more security options that simply cannot be available when packages are run in the client's process.

Copying packages Once you have your package set up just the way you want it, you might want to provide a means for copying the package to other machines. This process is straightforward. Simply highlight your package in the Management Console, and choose Export from the Action menu. You will be prompted for the directory and filename that you want to export the information to and given the option of whether you want to include user information defined in the roles for the package. If you are planning to use your package on machines in your current domain, you might want to include the user information in the package. If you are planning to export your package for use on machines that are not in your personal domain structure, you should probably avoid including user information.

After you specify your options and click the Export button, the Management Console will copy all your package's components into the specified directory and will create a *package file* with a .PAK extension. The package file holds all the configuration information for the package. If you share this directory on the network, other machines can import this package as long as they can access your package file. All the properties for your package will be maintained, including the Disable Deletion and Disable Changes properties, which means that you can export your packages and feel confident that their configuration will not be tampered with. By the same token, you will not be able to modify the settings of any protected packages that you import. If the Disable Deletion option is selected, your imported package is there for good. To import an exported package, choose the Install Pre-Built Packages option from the Package Wizard. You will then be prompted to browse for the .PAK file that contains the configuration information for the appropriate package.

Component configuration options

We have talked a lot about packages and the various options for installing and configuring them. Some options can be configured on a per-component basis. For instance, you can provide a description that is specific to your component instead of describing your entire package. To configure component options, highlight the desired component in the left pane of the Management Console and select Properties from the Action menu. Figure 15.9 shows the Properties window for an imaginary *Foo.Bar* component added to your package.

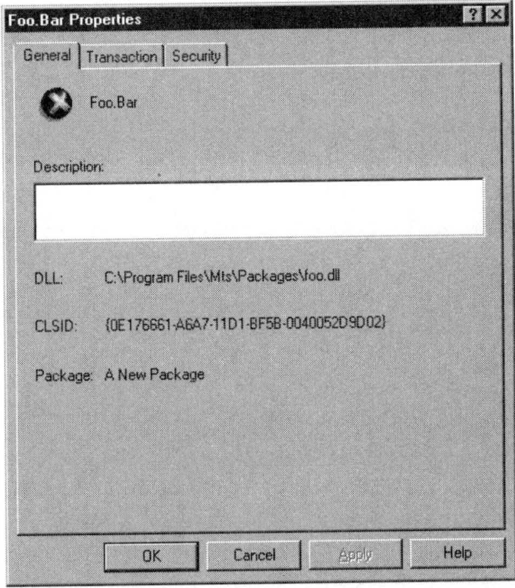

FIGURE 15.9

The Properties window for a component added to a package, showing the General page.

The General page lets you add a description for the component; the Security page enables authentication at the component level so you can rely on roles at the component level. The Transaction page lets you configure how the component interacts with MTS and the object contexts; several options are available.

- **Requires A Transaction** Indicates that the component's object context must have a transaction. If the program that calls this object is already executing within a transaction, the component will inherit that transaction's context. If the program that calls this object does not have a transaction, MTS will create a new transaction for the component.
- **Requires A New Transaction** Indicates that MTS will create a new transaction for the component regardless of whether the program that calls this object has a transaction. This transactional information will not be shared between this component and the application that calls it. Use this option for components that handle a transaction whose completion has no bearing on the transaction of the calling program.
- **Supports Transactions** Indicates that if the calling program has a transaction, this component will inherit that transaction. If the calling program does not have a transaction, MTS will not create a transaction for this component. This option should be used only by components that have the ability to run with or without a transaction.
- **Does Not Support Transactions** Indicates that the object context for this component cannot run within a transaction, regardless of whether the calling program has a transaction. This option should be used by components that were not designed to work with MTS.

You might be wondering why you would add a component to a package if that component either did not support transactions or required a new transaction. Such a component might still be used by the calling program or the other components in the package despite the fact that it does not share a transaction context with them. As long as the component is used by either the calling program or the other components within a package, it is convenient to include the component in the MTS package so that the package can be easily exported and then imported on different computers. This technique also makes it easier for administrators to determine all the components that are required for successful execution of an MTS application that uses this package.

Computer configuration options

Now that we have looked at configuration options at the package level and at the component level, we need to examine configuration options for the entire computer as well. To view these options, highlight the desired computer (for your local machine, choose My Computer) in the left pane of the Management Console, and choose the Properties option from the Action menu. Figure 15.10 shows the Advanced page of the Properties window for our local computer.

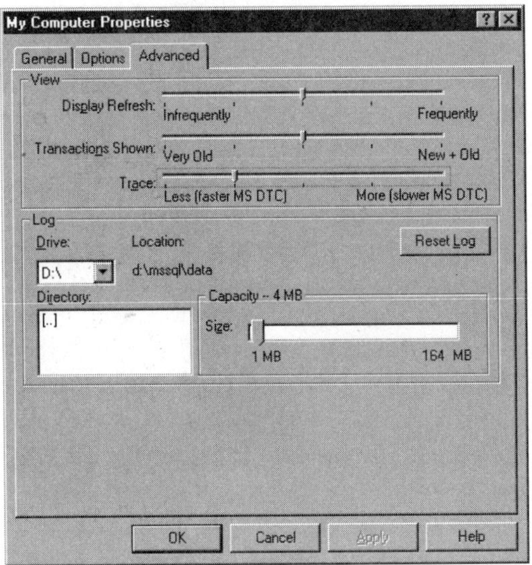

FIGURE 15.10

The My Computer Properties window, showing the Advanced page.

The General page again provides a place to add a description—in this case of the local computer. The Options page enables you to set a machinewide transaction timeout to control the length of time that a transaction can be active. If this timeout expires, MTS automatically sets an abort on the transaction and all changes are rolled back. The Options page also allows MTS to work with the Microsoft Cluster Server to replicate components between a cluster of computers. You can specify the server and share name of a common location from which MTS packages and components will be copied. This technique allows for the same packages to exist on a number of different machines.

Glossary

Microsoft Cluster Server *Microsoft's server clustering software that allows a group of servers to work together to provide high levels of availability and scalability.*

Perhaps the most significant page in the My Computer Properties window is the Advanced page, shown in Figure 15.10. The Advanced page basically provides a means for configuring various monitoring options for MTS. The View area lets you specify how often updates will appear for some of the monitoring options. (We will be looking at these options in the Monitoring MTS section.) The Display Refresh slider bar lets you specify how often the live monitoring options will update their displays. The refresh time ranges from once every 20 seconds for the Infrequently option to once every second for the Frequently option. The Transactions Shown option lets you specify how old a transaction must be before it appears in the utility that shows current transactions. If you want to see only transactions that have been active for a long period of time, select Very Old. Selecting the New + Old setting means that transactions older than 1 second will be displayed. The Trace option indicates what kinds of events are logged by the Microsoft Distributed Transaction Coordinator (MS DTC), which is the service component of MTS that provides most of the MTS functionality. This option lets you specify how many of the MS DTC events will be written to the MS DTC trace log. The five settings on the Trace slider bar correspond to the following actions:

- Don't log any MS DTC trace events.
- Trace only MS DTC error events.
- Trace MS DTC error and warning events.
- Trace MS DTC error, warning, and informational events (the default setting).
- Trace all MS DTC events.

The Log settings on the lower portion of the Advanced page indicate the maximum size and location of the MS DTC trace log. Clicking the Reset Log button allows you to clear the MS DTC trace log.

Action menu options In addition to configuring computer-wide MTS properties, you can perform some computer-wide actions by selecting the computer icon in the Management Console. If you click on the Action menu, you'll notice three computer-wide options that are not available at other levels in the Management Console: Stop MS DTC, Shut Down Server Processes, and Refresh All Components. The Stop MS DTC option simply stops the MS DTC service. If you select this option, you will notice that the screen of the computer icon in the Management Console will change from bright green to dark green (indicating that MTS is functionally powered off). The menu option will change to Start MS DTC. If you choose this option, you'll see the monitor return to bright green indicating that MTS is up and running again.

The Shut Down Server Processes option will find any server packages that are currently running and will unload the spawned MTS process that they are running in. You can shut down packages individually by highlighting the specific server packages and choosing the Shut Down Action menu option. The Shut Down Server Processes option, however, is most useful as a quick way to kill all the server packages running on the machine—for example, if you need to update a large number of components that span multiple packages.

The Refresh All Components option tells MTS to walk through the components in all of the MTS packages and re-read the component class and interface identifiers from the registry. This capability can be important if you are developing your own component and have rebuilt it using new class and interface IDs. Microsoft Visual Basic 5.0 changes these IDs every time a component is rebuilt.

Remote components

The Remote Components folder under the computer icon in the Management Console lets you configure components that can be used by the local copy of MTS but will execute on a remote MTS machine. MTS uses Distributed COM (DCOM) to launch these applications across the network and return the results to the local package. To add a remote component, you must be able to remotely administer another MTS machine within the Management Console. Once this is set up, one machine can export a package and then another machine can add a component from that package to its Remote Components folder. The Export Package option discussed earlier not only creates a .PAK package file, it also builds an *MTS Executable* for the package. An MTS Executable is a program that can be run on a machine that wants to add the components in the package to its Remote Components folder. The MTS Executable will make the appropriate registry entries on the machine to allow the remote execution of the components to succeed. On the MTS machine that wants to execute the components remotely, select the Remote Components folder in the left pane of the Management Console, choose New and then Remote Component from the Action menu. You will now be able to choose the exported components you want to add to your list of remote components from the computers you are currently administering. Once a component has successfully been added to the Remote Components folder, it can be used by an MTS application just as if it were on the local machine. However, the component will execute on the machine that exported the package.

Monitoring MTS

Now that we understand how we can manage MTS using the Management Console, let's look at the options for monitoring transaction activity. The three monitoring options provided by the Management Console and indicated by the three icons below the computer icon are: Trace Messages, Transaction List, and Transaction Statistics.

The Trace Messages window simply displays the MS DTC service log events that you can also view in the Microsoft Windows NT Event Viewer administrative tool. We saw how to configure the level of tracing using the Advanced page of our computer

Properties page. This window is usually used to trace any error conditions experienced by MS DTC, but you can also trace informational messages (such as when the MS DTC service is stopped), by setting the appropriate tracing option in the computer's Advanced property page.

The Transaction List option displays all transactions currently active on the machine. This option can be used simply to monitor how many transactions are in use, or it can be used to terminate "stuck" transactions. Figure 15.11 shows the Transaction List display for our computer.

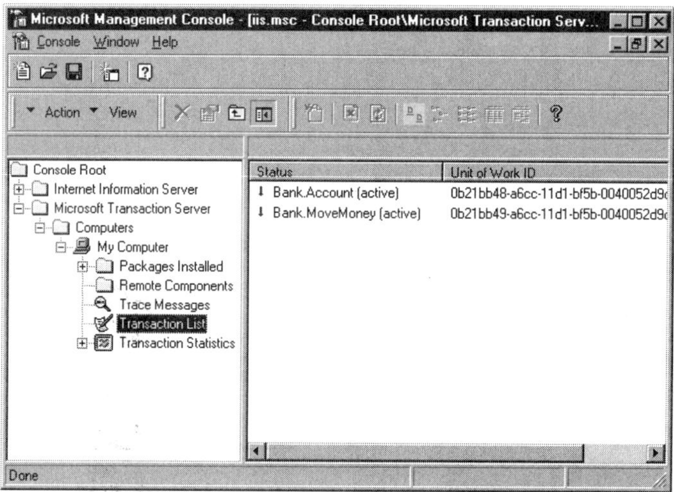

FIGURE 15.11

The Transaction List display.

Two active transactions are listed here: one involving the *Bank.Account* object and the other involving the *Bank.MoveMoney* object. Both transactions indicate their active status in the Status property field of the detail window. If you right-click on either of these transactions, a Resolve pop-up menu appears. From the Resolve menu, you can choose to Commit, Abort, or Forget the transaction. You should only resolve transactions with this menu if the transaction cannot be resolved through normal means. Most transactions tend to complete rather quickly and disappear in an instant from the Transaction List detail screen.

The Transaction Statistics option provides a simple snapshot of how active MTS has been. Selecting this utility displays a bar graph showing information about the current transactions, the maximum number of transactions, the number of times a transaction committed or aborted, the transaction response times, and information on the last time that the MS DTC service was started. Figure 15-12 shows the Transaction Statistics display for our local machine.

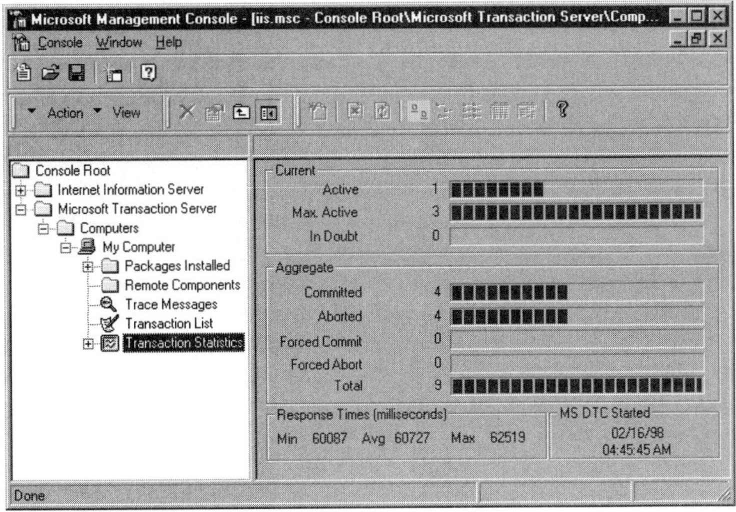

FIGURE 15.12

The Transaction Statistics display.

Now that we've seen how to administer MTS, from configuration options to monitoring capabilities, let's turn to another service that ships as part of the Windows NT Option Pack and can easily be used by applications written for IIS: the Microsoft Message Queue Server.

Microsoft Message Queue Server

Using transactions to guarantee the completion of certain tasks is a fine way to ensure integrity and consistency, but sometimes waiting for a task to complete is an unreasonable restriction to place on a collection of events. For instance, you might have an event that simply takes an extended period of time to complete or that requires communication over an unreliable network link. In either of these scenarios, you might not want to cause a whole package of components to hang around in a pending state while minutes, or even hours, go by until these potentially prolonged tasks complete. In these situations, it would be advantageous if we had a mechanism that could store all the information associated with a task and could ensure that the task would in fact complete at some point in the future. As it turns out, this is exactly what Microsoft Message Queue Server (MSMQ) can do.

Message Queue Concepts

When you think of messages on computers, you probably start imagining e-mail systems that deliver e-mail messages to various users. The concept of MSMQ is not significantly different. When you send e-mail to an individual in a different physical and logical location, your machine is rarely involved in the final delivery of the message. Your machine communicates solely with your local mail server, which is then responsible for getting the message to the appropriate person. As far as you're concerned, the message was successfully sent when it was passed to your local mail server. In reality, the message's journey might have just begun with the simple transmission from your local machine to your server. Once your server has received your message, it basically guarantees that the message will reach its destination. If links between your mail server and the destination fail, the message is simply kept in storage and the delivery is retried until the transmission succeeds. If such a drastic problem occurs that the message could not be delivered despite the retry mechanisms, an exception case is generated and a message is sent back to the sender's mailbox informing the user of the problem. This process is almost identical to how MSMQ provides message queue services.

Suppose you have a catalog company that sells tennis shoes. You need to be able to simultaneously update a customer information database, an orders database, and an inventory database. Everything would work smoothly if you could box up, label, apply postage, and ship a pair of tennis shoes within the standard period of time that a customer is willing to wait on the phone for her order to complete. Unfortunately, this is probably not a realistic requirement. It would make much more sense if we could simply store all the information required for shipping the tennis shoes via a mechanism that would guarantee that the task would ultimately complete. Once we have successfully stored all the information in our guaranteed storage mechanism, we could basically flag the transaction as complete and let the customer off the phone. We know that the shipping of the tennis shoes will eventually occur, but we don't have to worry about completing that portion of the task immediately. In this scenario, we say that we have "queued" the request to ship the tennis shoes since it has been added to the end of a list of other shoe shipments. The mechanism that performs the actual shipment of tennis shoes pulls shipment requests from the front of the queue and processes them at its own pace. Each shipment request is considered a single message.

MSMQ provides a number of features that aid in the creation of these message queues. First, MSMQ is designed to be able to span an enterprise of interconnected servers. A queue can exist on one server, but in order for a message to be placed in that queue it might have to be sent to many intermediate servers until it arrives at the destination. In this sense, MSMQ truly works like a mail server. And it is exactly this mail server quality of routing messages across a network that also provides its redundancy and fault tolerance. A message can be easily replicated between MSMQ servers, and if any machines or network connections fail, a new route can be found to the destination server through a different series of intermediate servers.

MSMQ also provides a means for prioritizing each message so that urgent messages can be sent to their destination faster than standard messages. And MSMQ can take advantage of the security features of Windows NT so that messages can be digitally signed to guarantee the identity of the sender, or encrypted to protect the message data. MSMQ can even integrate its messaging schemes with other messaging software so that you can take advantage of e-mail delivering schemes to forward messages between MSMQ servers.

MSMQ Server Roles

Let's first take a look at how MSMQ servers can be spread across a network and act in different roles. Figure 15.13 illustrates one potential enterprise configuration of MSMQ servers.

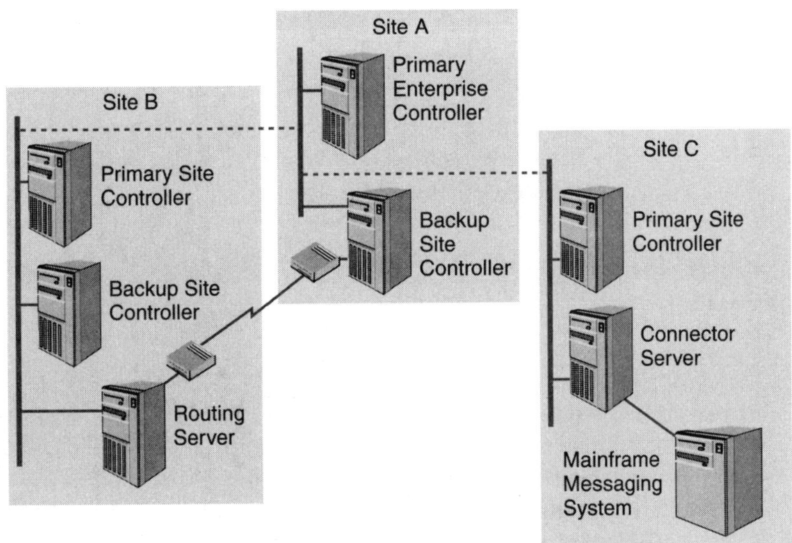

FIGURE 15.13

MSMQ servers fulfilling different roles throughout an enterprise.

Our sample enterprise has seven different MSMQ servers scattered across three sites. A site is usually defined as having relatively reliable, high-speed communication such as you might have with a LAN. Sites can then be linked via lower-speed lines that are often less reliable, such as dial-up connections, dedicated lines, or even Internet connections. The solid lines in this diagram indicate high-speed, reliable, network backbones. The dotted lines indicate some sort of lower-speed and geographically distant connection. Notice that we have created a second redundant link between sites A and B using a modem connection between two of the servers; this will provide a backup mode for transferring messages if our primary connection between the sites fails.

The several different roles played by the MSMQ servers in our diagram are described here:

- **Primary Enterprise Controller (PEC)** The main MSMQ server for the entire organization. There should be only one PEC, and it must be installed before any other site controllers can be created.
- **Primary Site Controller (PSC)** The main MSMQ server for each site. (The PEC also serves as the PSC for the site it happens to be in.) Each site controller is in charge of storing the hard data for any queues that exist at its site as well as handling client receipt and delivery of messages.
- **Backup Site Controller (BSC)** Holds a read-only copy of the PSC's database and so serves as a backup in case the PSC goes down. The BSC will also help to balance the load demand on the PSC by being able to service many kinds of client requests.
- **Routing server** Any MSMQ server that is not a PEC, PSC, or BSC. Routing servers provide intermediate message forwarding capabilities but do not keep a copy of the PSC's database. All MSMQ servers act as routing servers, even if they have other roles as well.
- **Connector server** An MSMQ server that communicates with another messaging scheme using additional software. In our example, we have a connector server communicating with a mainframe messaging package, but you could have connector servers communicating with other PC messaging servers as well. Microsoft provides the MSMQ Exchange Connector for linking MSMQ servers with Microsoft Exchange e-mail servers.

When a client connects to one of our MSMQ servers to send a message to a queue, it doesn't need to worry about what happens once the message has reached its MSMQ server. For example, if the routing server in site B receives a message destined for a queue in site C, the fact that the message may be forwarded to the PEC before it makes it to the PSC for site C is of no consequence to the client.

Our sample environment is relatively straightforward since all servers on our network are part of a single connected network (CN), which means every machine can communicate directly with every other machine on the network. You could have a situation in which two or more networks are not connected, meaning that it is simply not possible for a packet on one network to reach a machine on the other network. In a situation like this, you could have an MSMQ server with two network cards, each of which is connected to a disjoint network. The MSMQ server would have access to two connected networks and could then route messages between the two. Another situation in which a server would be connected to multiple CNs is if there are multiple protocols being used on a network. For instance, you could have a division of machines in your company that ran only Internetwork Packet Exchange (IPX) as their lower-level protocol while the rest of the company ran TCP/IP. You could have MSMQ servers routing messages between the two logical networks by having both protocols installed on at least one routing server.

The current version of MSMQ requires Microsoft SQL Server to be installed to provide a consistent means for the MSMQ servers to communicate with one another. The data that MSMQ saves in the SQL database is called the *MSMQ Information Store*; it contains information about the enterprise topology, the sites and locations of various MSMQ servers, and configuration information for queues stored on the network. When a new MSMQ server is installed or a change takes place on a server (such as the creation of a new queue), this information is replicated between all the MSMQ servers in the enterprise via messages passed to the servers telling them to update their SQL databases. The queues themselves—actually, the messages in the queues—are stored in memory-mapped files that are accessed directly by MSMQ.

Message Queues

The two main types of message queues that applications can take advantage of are public queues and private queues. *Public queue* information is replicated throughout the enterprise via the MSMQ Information Store and can be searched for and queried by applications. *Private queues*, on the other hand, do not have their information replicated by the Information Store. So if an application is going to use a private queue, it must have some outside knowledge of the complete name of the queue. Private queues by default are not shown in the MSMQ Explorer unless you explicitly enable their display for each server.

In addition to the standard private and public queues that applications send messages to, MSMQ provides a number of other types of queues that serve secondary roles but have features that enhance the direct use of private and public queues: journal queues, dead letter queues, transaction queues, administration queues, report queues, and system queues.

Journal queues are used by MSMQ to keep backup copies of messages that are being sent or received. MSMQ supports two types of journaling: *source journaling* and *target journaling*. Source journaling creates a copy of the message when it is first sent; it's up to the application sending the message to specify whether it will use source journaling. Each machine has a queue named journal that is not associated with a specific public queue. This journal queue contains the source journal copies of all messages that had source journaling turned on and copies of all source-journaled messages that were originally sent through that server machine. Target-journaled messages, on the other hand, are copies made of messages when they are received. Target-journaled messages are also kept in journal queues, but these queues are located under each normal queue on each machine. When a message is received from a standard queue, a copy is placed in its corresponding journal queue. Unlike source journaling, target journaling is enabled for an entire queue instead of for a single message. The extra copies created by journaling help to ensure the robustness of the queued messages in the case of loss or failure.

Dead letter queues are used to store messages that failed to be delivered. A message can end up in a dead letter queue for a number of reasons—for example, if the specified destination queue does not exist or if a time limit placed on the message has expired. Each server has its own dead letter queue.

Transaction queues are queues whose message receipt can be part of a transaction. MSMQ can act as a resource manager for transactions, which means that it will automatically work in a two-phase commitment scenario within an MTS transaction. For MSMQ, a transactional task is complete when a client's local MSMQ server successfully receives a sent message, but this does not mean that the transaction has actually reached its destination queue. However, because MSMQ guarantees delivery of a message once it is received, successful receipt of the message by the local MSMQ server is sufficient to complete a transaction. To mark a message as part of a transaction, you simply add a flag to a standard message. Transaction queues can hold only transaction messages, and nontransaction queues cannot receive transaction messages. Nontransaction messages sent to a transaction queue will fail and will be placed in the dead letter queue. Transaction messages that are sent to a nontransaction queue will fail as well, but these will be placed in the transaction dead letter queue. The transaction dead letter queue for an MSMQ server is named Xact Dead Letter and contains any failed messages that were flagged as transaction messages.

An application can specify an *administration queue* when it sends a message. The specified administration queue will receive an acknowledgment message indicating whether a message was successfully retrieved. If the message was not retrieved, a reason for the failure will be included in the message. When an application sets up an administration queue, it can specify what kinds of acknowledgments it wants sent to that queue. For example, an application might not be interested in having positive acknowledgments sent because it assumes that the message was sent successfully. Instead, the application might want to have only negative acknowledgments sent.

A *report queue* receives report messages that indicate the path a message made as it was propagated to its destination queue. Report queues can be useful tools for MSMQ managers who want to monitor the flow of messages across their enterprise.

And finally, each MSMQ server has a set of *system queues*. System queues are private queues that MSMQ uses to help communicate information across the enterprise. For example, MSMQ will send a message to one of the system queues of a server when MSMQ Information Store information needs to be replicated between the servers.

Now that we have a feel for the types of message queues and how MSMQ works, let's examine the process of setting up MSMQ and review the various configuration options.

Installing MSMQ

MSMQ is available with the Microsoft Windows NT 4.0 Option Pack. MSMQ is installed only under the Custom installation option. Figure 15.14 shows the Custom configuration option with the subcomponents for MSMQ displayed. The main components of MSMQ are installed by selecting the Microsoft Message Queue Core subcomponent. Once you have chosen to install the core service, you can choose whether to install the software development kit or the MSMQ Explorer. The documentation can be installed regardless of whether you install the core services.

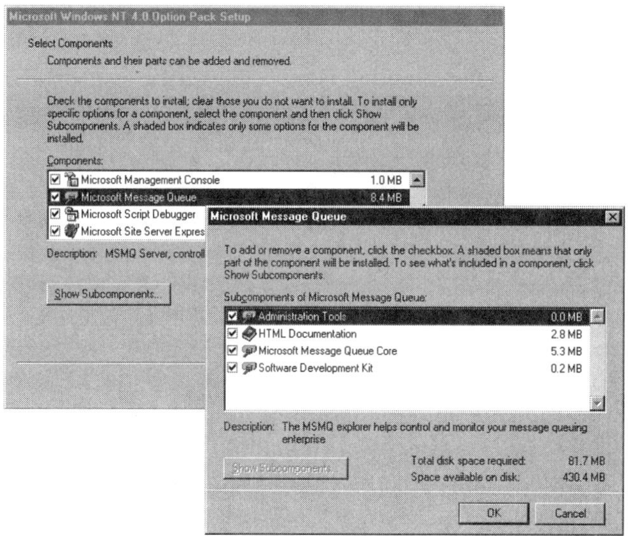

FIGURE 15.14

The subcomponents available with MSMQ.

Once you have chosen to install MSMQ, the dialog box shown in Figure 15.15 appears, in which you specify the role of your MSMQ server.

If you don't have any other MSMQ servers in your organization, you will need to make this server the PEC. All the other options will require you to specify the name of an already running MSMQ server. (Remember that Microsoft SQL Server must be installed on the local machine before you can install a PEC, PSC, or BSC.) If you choose to install a PEC, you will be prompted for the name of your enterprise as well as the name of your site since the PEC also serves as the PSC for its local site. The other installation options will require the name of a preexisting MSMQ server. To install a PSC, you will need the name of the PEC. To install a BSC, you will need the name of the PSC. To install a routing server, an independent client, or the MSMQ RAS connectivity service, you will need the name of a PSC or BSC. To install a dependent client, you will need the name of a routing server, PSC, or BSC. Any role besides the PEC gives your machine the option of communicating over a secure link with its parent machine, but for this to work the preexisting server must already have secure communications enabled.

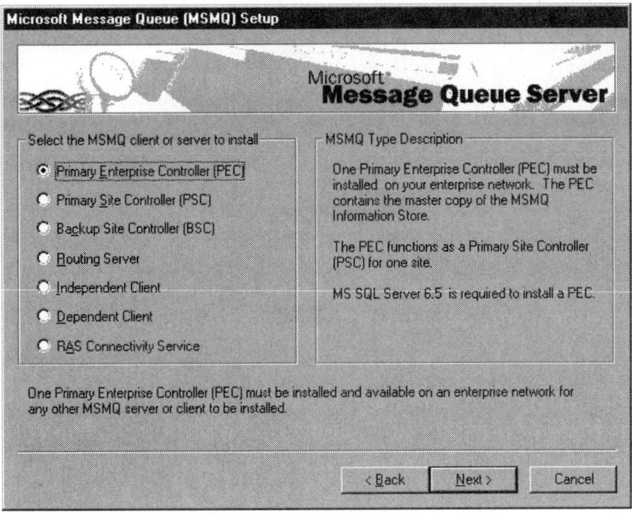

FIGURE 15.15

Choosing the role of your message queue server.

After you have specified your machine's MSMQ role and specified its parent server for non-PEC servers, the Setup program will prompt you for the directory in which you want to install MSMQ. By default, this directory is C:\Program Files\MSMQ, but you can choose any directory you want. For PEC, PSC, or BSC servers, you will need to choose the SQL Server database directory and size for your MSMQ server. Remember that the database only holds MQIS information, so it needs to be large only if you have a very involved MSMQ enterprise installation with many servers. If you have multiple network cards (including dial-up networking) or protocols installed, you will be asked to specify your connected networks in the MSMQ Connected Networks dialog box, shown in Figure 15.16. In most situations in which all your MSMQ clients and servers can connect to one another directly, you will have a single connected network—this is certainly the case with most corporate intranet scenarios. If you have MSMQ servers or clients that are not able to communicate directly with one another but must route messages across disjointed networks, at least one MSMQ server on the network will need to have both connected networks configured so that it can route messages between the two. In this example, we have a single connected network using the TCP/IP protocol for communications.

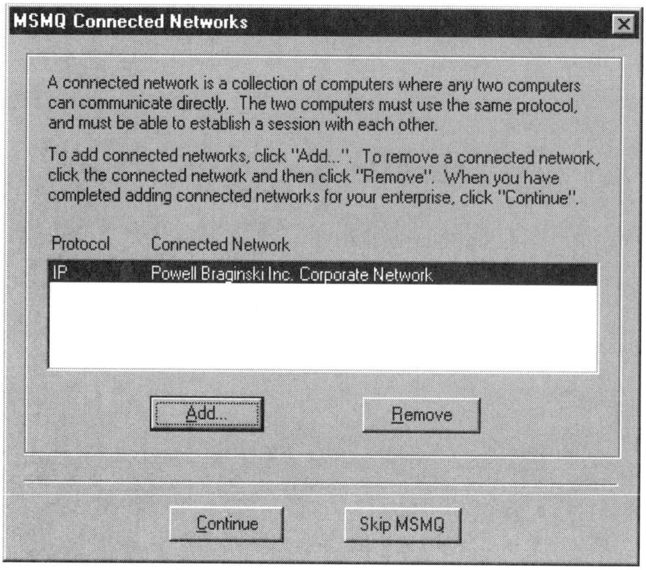

FIGURE 15.16

The MSMQ Connected Networks dialog box.

If you are installing a new PSC, you are effectively adding a new site to your MSMQ configuration. One of the pieces of information that you will need to provide when adding additional sites is the cost of your new site's links to the other existing sites. Link costs are simply numerical values you assign to each site that represent how hard it is to reach the specified site from your new site. For instance, if you have a very slow, nondedicated link to Site A, you might decide to set the cost rather high, perhaps to a value of 10. However, if you have a high-speed, direct connection to Site A, you might set the value to 1. A value of zero indicates that you cannot reach the specified site from your current location.

Your MSMQ servers use your link cost values to determine the most efficient way to route messages between sites. Routes with a smaller accumulative link cost will be used before routes with a larger accumulative link cost. If for some reason the more efficient route fails, then the routes with a higher value can still be used as backups. If all your sites have high-speed connections between them, you may want to specify a value of 1 for the link costs between all sites.

Figure 15.17 shows the link cost we are setting up for our site. We have a local ethernet connection between our two sites, so we have configured the link cost from our new site to headquarters to be 1. You will need to configure the link cost for each site on your network.

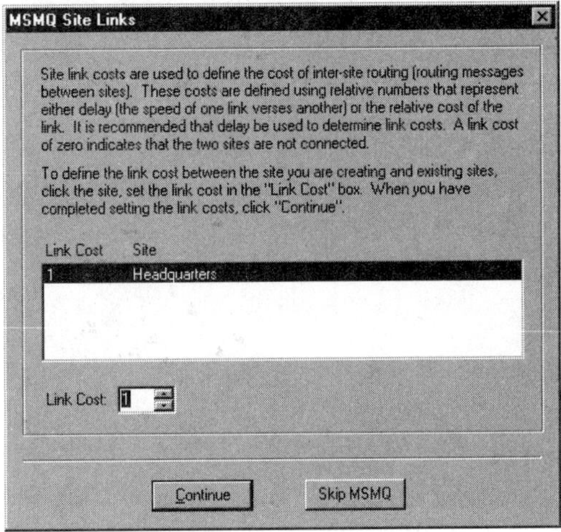

FIGURE 15.17

Configuring the link cost between sites.

Your MSMQ server or client is now set up and can be used to send and receive messages.

Managing MSMQ

Just like the other services we have administered up to this point, MSMQ is managed via a snap-in to the Microsoft Management Console, called the MSMQ Explorer. The MSMQ Explorer is shown in Figure 15.18.

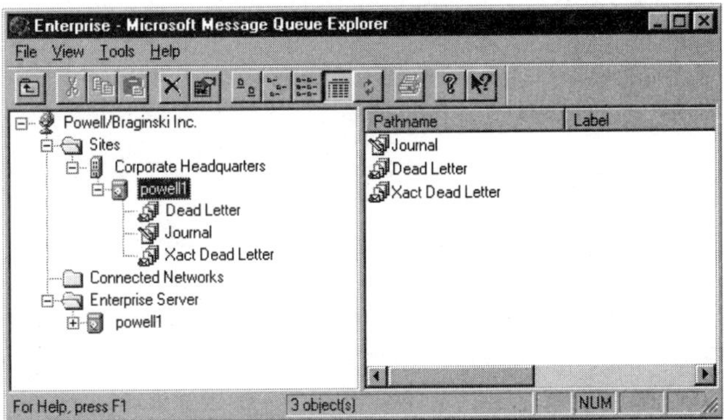

FIGURE 15.18

The MSMQ Explorer.

The MSMQ Explorer shows the MSMQ hierarchy in the left pane. At the top of the tree is the name of the enterprise, Powell/Braginski Inc. Just under the enterprise name are the Sites, Connected Networks, and the PEC (referred to as the Enterprise Server) folders. Because the enterprise we have created has only a single machine, *powell1*, it must serve as the PEC. It is also the only server in our only defined site, Corporate Headquarters. Although this might seem like a trivial message queue configuration, it can still provide a lot of functionality. We might lose the message forwarding benefits of a large corporate site with many servers, but we still get the benefits of a message store that allows for the asynchronous activation of our tasks. But with a single server solution, we obviously lose the level of redundancy provided by having multiple servers.

The Enterprise Properties window

Let's begin our examination of how the MSMQ Explorer works by looking at the properties of the enterprise itself. Right-click on the name of the enterprise and select the Properties option to display the Enterprise Properties window, shown in Figure 15.19.

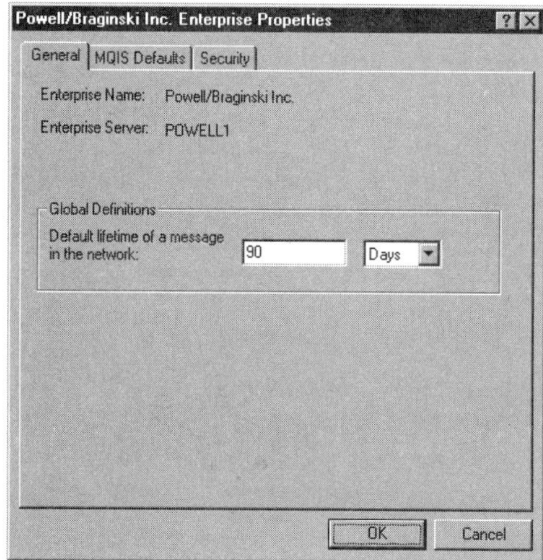

FIGURE 15.19

The Enterprise Properties window showing the General page.

The options that you set here are global options for the entire enterprise. For instance, on the General page you can change the default lifetime of a message in the enterprise. The lifetime is the amount of time that a message will continue to be stored in the message queues without being read until it is considered too old and is moved to the dead letter queue. You can set this option on a per-message basis as well, but if a value is not set for a message, the default takes precedence.

The MQIS Defaults page lets you set timers that control how often Information Store updates can be sent from any site controllers in the enterprise. You can set these values for specific sites as well, but by setting them at the enterprise level you are setting the defaults for any new sites created. You can set two timer intervals here, one for communications within the site (to back up site controllers) and one for Information Store communications to other sites (in particular, with the PEC). By default, internal-intrasite communication is set to 2 seconds and external-intersite communication is set to 10 seconds.

The last page in the Enterprise Properties window is the Security tab, shown in Figure 15.20. The various objects within MSMQ are securable objects. Recall from Chapter 12 that securable objects on Windows NT maintain certain security attributes. Basically, this means that each securable object has a security descriptor and access to that object is checked against the security descriptor before it is allowed. The security descriptor itself includes information about the owner of the object, the Discretionary Access Control List (DACL), and the System Access Control List (SACL). The DACL contains information about who is or is not allowed to access the object, and the SACL contains information about what actions should be audited. The Security page lets you configure the security descriptor for a particular object—in this case, the enterprise object.

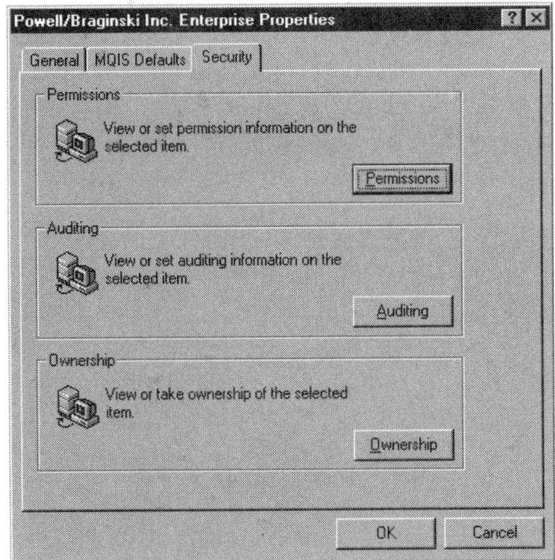

FIGURE 15.20

The Security page.

The Security page probably looks familiar. A similar page is used to set security descriptor information on a number of objects, including file security on an NTFS partition. Here the Security page is used to set security on the MSMQ enterprise object. And it probably comes as no surprise that you'll see a similar Security page for setting security on MSMQ site objects, server objects, and queue objects. The only difference between these and other securable objects is the access permissions you can specify for a particular object. The following table lists the access permissions and the MSMQ objects that apply for each access type.

Access Type	Enterprise Object	Site Object	Server Object	Connected Network Object	Queue Object
Create Site	✔				
Create CN	✔				
Create User	✔				
Create Routing Server		✔			
Create BSC		✔			
Create Computer		✔			
Receive Dead Letter			✔		
Peek Dead Letter			✔		
Receive Journal			✔		✔
Peek Journal			✔		
Create Queue			✔		
Open Connector				✔	
Receive Message					✔
Peek Message					✔
Send Message					✔
Get Properties					✔
Set Properties	✔	✔	✔	✔	✔
Delete	✔	✔	✔	✔	✔
Get Permissions	✔	✔	✔	✔	✔
Set Permissions	✔	✔	✔	✔	✔
Take Ownership	✔	✔	✔		✔

The Site Properties window

Let's see what other properties we can set from the MSMQ Explorer. Figure 15.21 shows the MSMQ Site Properties window. The site property options are fairly limited. On the General page, you can view the internal ID used to identify this site by MSMQ. The MQIS page enables you to override the default Information Store replication timeouts that we set at the enterprise level. On the Security page, you can set the security descriptor for the site. The only other information to be set here is the connection information on the Connections page.

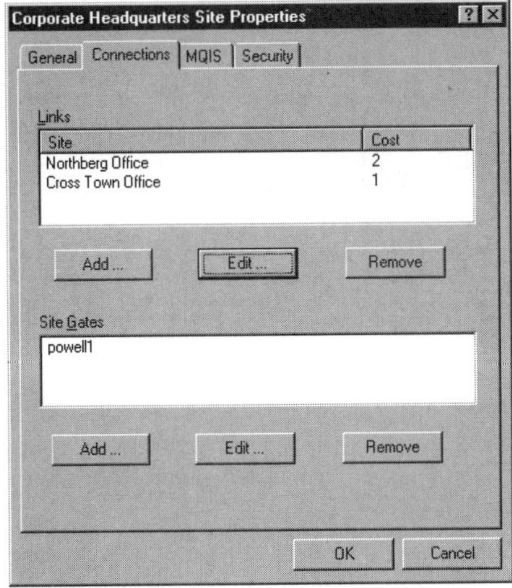

FIGURE 15.21

The Site Properties window showing the Connections page.

The connections shown here represent links to other sites on the network. When you have messages that need to be forwarded to other sites, this information determines how the messages will be sent. Each link to a site has an associated cost that provides a mechanism for determining which routes provide the best means for forwarding a message to its destination. You get to set the cost when you configure the link so that you can take into account connections over slow lines. The Site Gates list displays the servers through which all messages going in and out of this site should go. The Site Gates list cannot include MSMQ servers installed using the Windows NT Option Pack. If you want to make a server a site gate, you need to install Windows NT Server, Enterprise Edition. Site gates can be important because by funneling all traffic between sites through a single site gate, you use the connection between the sites more efficiently. This ability could be very important if your sites are connected via modem connections or low-bandwidth dedicated lines.

The Computer Properties window

If we look at the properties for a specific server, we might be a bit overwhelmed by the options available to us. Figure 15.22 shows the Computer Properties window for the *powell1* machine. Luckily, most of these property pages are monitoring tools for determining the current status of the server. Configuration options are limited to the General, Network, Tracking, and Security pages.

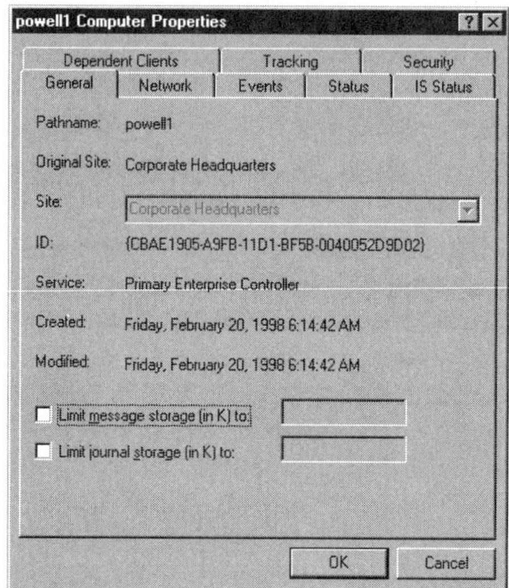

FIGURE 15.22

The Computer Properties dialog box showing the General page.

Figure 15.22 shows the General page for our server. For the most part, this information identifies our server and can't be changed. One option we can set is a limit (if any) on the amount of disk space we want MSMQ to use. By default, there is no limit for either message or journal storage, but you can set limits for one or the other here.

The Network page simply allows you to associate any physical or logical networks that your machine is connected to with any of the CNs that have been created for your MSMQ enterprise. Servers need to be connected to at least one CN, but they don't have to have a CN defined for each physical network that they are connected to.

The Tracking page enables us to turn on and configure the tracking of routing information. This concept of tracking how messages were routed through the enterprise was discussed earlier in the Message Queues section in relation to report queues. On the Tracking page, you can turn this option on or off and specify the corresponding report queue for the routing messages to be sent to. You also have the option of tracking all messages or only test messages.

The monitoring capabilities provided by the Computer Properties window are also very useful tools. The Events page lists all the MSMQ server events that have been written to the Windows NT Event Log. You can view the same events using the Event Viewer administrative tool except that all the non-MSMQ messages have been filtered out. The Status and IS Status pages list a collection of statistics for the server and for the Information Store, indicating such information as the number of active messages stored on the machine, the total number of bytes in all queues, the number of Information Store replication requests sent and received, and the number of errors that have occurred on the system. The Dependent Clients page lists all the active dependent clients with open connections to the server.

The Queue Properties window

To create a new queue on your server, simply right-click on the server in the MSMQ Explorer, choose the New option from the pop-up menu, and then choose Queue. Initially, you only need to give your queue a name and specify whether you want it to be transactional. Once you have done this, the queue is created. If you want to set further properties for your queue, you will need to use the Queue Properties window for the queue.

Figure 15.23 shows the Queue Properties window for a newly created queue, named Order Processing Queue, with the Advanced page displayed. The Queue Properties window should look familiar. The General page contains mostly identifying information, the Status page shows some statistics concerning your queue, and the Security page enables you to modify the security descriptor for the queue. You should be aware of one important property that you can set on the General tab: Type ID. The Type ID is simply a string that indicates to an application what the queue is for. In particular, you can use the Type ID field to help query for queues from the Information Store, which allows your application to quickly access a list of the queues that hold messages for it.

The Advanced page, shown in Figure 15.23, lets you configure a number of important characteristics for your queue. Here you can specify whether you want to limit the amount of storage used for your queue or whether you want to require that the message sender be authenticated before sending a message to your queue. Although you can specify whether a queue is transactional only when you first create it, the results of your decision are shown here as well. You can also specify whether you want this queue to be journaled. (Remember that journaling means a copy of messages read from the queue are kept in the queue's journal queue.) You can also limit the size of the journal queue, which can get large quickly if you store every message that goes through a queue. The Privacy Level option indicates whether the queue will accept encrypted messages. The None setting indicates that the queue will not accept encrypted messages, Optional indicates that the queue can accept both encrypted and nonencrypted messages, and Body indicates that all messages must be encrypted. Last you can specify the priority of the queue. Messages are forwarded across the enterprise based on their priority. Higher-priority messages are sent before lower-priority messages. The priority of the queue that you set here is the first factor taken into account, then the priority of the message itself is considered.

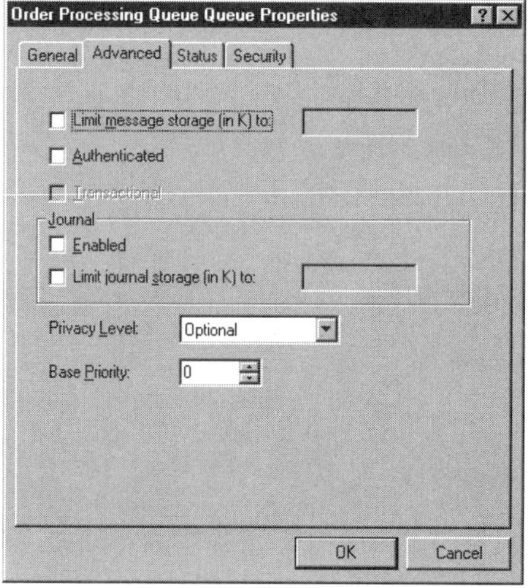

FIGURE 15.23

The Queue Properties window.

The Message Properties window

Finally, at the lowest level of the MSMQ Explorer you can look at the properties of the individual messages in the Message Properties window, as shown in Figure 15.24. To display this window, right-click on a message and choose properties. You cannot change any of the properties of a message, but you can view the different message characteristics, including the message identification information, the destination queue information, the body of the message itself, as well as information about the sender. This information can prove useful when you are trying to determine problems in your message queue routing structure.

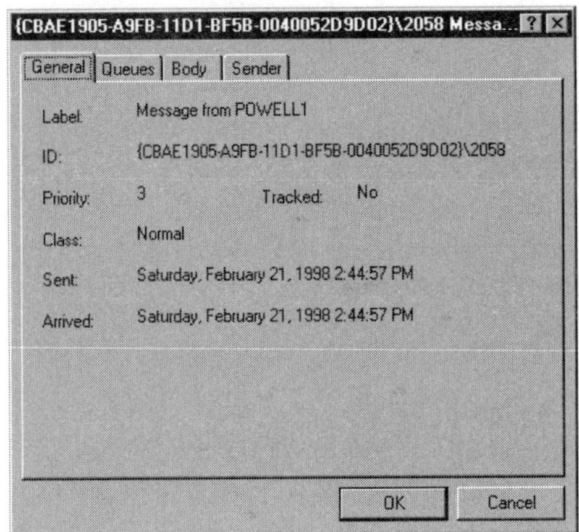

FIGURE 15.24

Message Properties window.

By now you understand something about MTS and MSMQ and know how to install and administer each. In the coming chapters, we will get into the specifics of writing applications for IIS, including writing applications that use MTS and MSMQ. But first we'll look at the architecture of IIS itself and the environment that IIS applications will be working in.

Part Two

The Microsoft Internet Application Server

CHAPTER 16

IIS and Application Architecture

In Part I of this book, we focused mainly on setting up, configuring, and administering IIS and its various services and add-ons. Now we'll shift our focus to running applications on IIS.

This chapter has something for everyone, whether or not you know Microsoft Visual C++. IIS is unique because it blurs the line between user and developer. Even if all you do is write a few lines of HTML code, you can consider yourself a developer.

Of course, writing HTML files is the most basic way to develop code for IIS. You can also write scripts that contain Server Side Includes (SSI) or use the Internet Database Connector (IDC), which is a bit more complex than writing HTML code. Active Server Pages (ASP) takes you one step farther than SSI and the IDC by providing a broad base of support that enables you to write a variety of code, from very simple scripts to large, involved script-based applications that are interwoven with custom COM components. If you are a C programmer and are familiar with the more traditional development process, you'll find that writing ISAPI extensions for IIS is straightforward, and you'll appreciate the development flexibility and power you have. And, of course, don't forget the old-fashioned Common Gateway Interface (CGI) applications. IIS provides full support for them as well.

In this chapter, we'll be looking at the different ways you can create applications that run on IIS. First let's look at running your applications on IIS and why doing so is a good idea.

Three-Tiered Client/Server Architecture

Traditional, or two-tiered, client/server computing typically involves a single server connected by a myriad of clients. This design isn't a bad one—it allows a single machine to control access to a resource like a SQL database—but each network connection adds a certain amount of overhead. A server can get bogged down quickly while managing that overhead, especially when many client connections are involved. An overloaded server has fewer resources available for performing tasks such as managing access to a database. Figure 16.1 illustrates this point. Notice that the overhead of managing network connections consumes a considerable portion of the total CPU power; in fact, less than half of the CPU processing power is available for handling access to the SQL database.

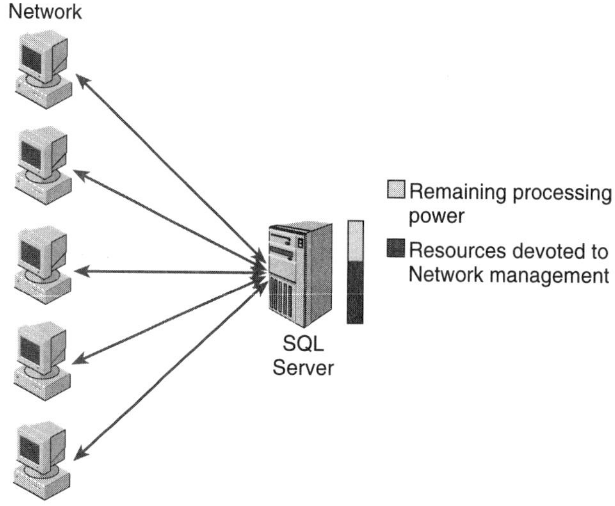

FIGURE 16.1

Two-tiered client/server computing, in which network management consumes a considerable portion of CPU resources.

To offload some of the overhead of network traffic, a middle layer—an intermediate server—can sit between the client and server (or servers). This architecture, called three-tiered client/server computing, is illustrated in Figure 16.2. Notice that the intermediate server handles the overhead of the network requests and then multiplexes the client requests over a single network connection to the SQL server. Because the SQL server has to manage only one network connection, the number of CPU resources used for network access is reduced, freeing up CPU resources for the SQL server and enabling it to service requests faster.

Multiplexing network connections is only one advantage of a three-tiered architecture. A typical client/server business solution does considerably more than send a single query to a SQL database. For example, it might handle multiple database calls while reading and writing to a file.

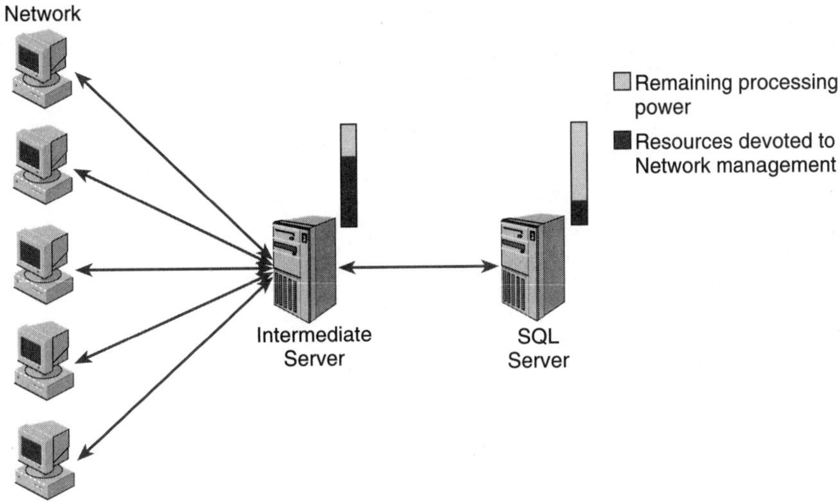

FIGURE 16.2

Simple three-tiered architecture, in which an intermediate server handles some of the network load.

Consider a situation in which an application has to update three different databases on a SQL server. In a standard two-tiered architecture, the client makes three separate requests to the server to update the databases. If the third update fails, the client has to make two additional requests to roll back the updates made to the first two databases. Unfortunately, these network requests take time and contribute to CPU usage. Obviously, it's more efficient to send a single request to the server requesting the server to perform the three updates simultaneously. Wouldn't it be nice if the server were smart enough to roll back the first two updates when the third update fails? A three-tiered approach is exactly what we need in a scenario like this.

Figure 16.3 shows a slightly more complex three-tiered architecture than Figure 16.2. In Figure 16.3, database updates are being made to two SQL servers and information is being read and written to a file storage mechanism. (The darker arrows in Figure 16.3 represent the request from a client, in the form of a transaction that is handled by the middle tier, or intermediate server.) The intermediate server offloads the lion's share of network traffic from the SQL servers and handles all the updates simultaneously when it receives a single transaction request from the client. In addition, the intermediate server is smart enough to commit the individual updates and roll back changes if errors occur along the way.

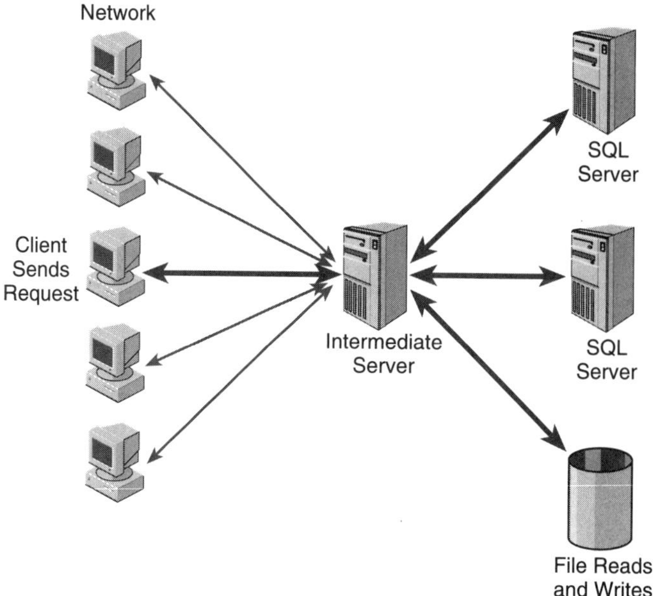

FIGURE 16.3

A more complex three-tiered transaction.

IIS enables you to use this three-tiered architecture easily and flexibly, providing the function of multiplexing client requests. You can write simple components, each handling one of the three basic server tasks (returning a static file, launching a CGI application, or launching an ISAPI extension), which will be explained shortly, and then assemble these components using a flexible ASP script. You can take that script and wrap it in an MTS transaction, which gives you rollback capabilities in case of an error situation. Updating files, then, becomes a simple extension of the transaction and can be easily rolled back in the case of an error. All this could be performed from a single client request.

NOTE

You can also add the asynchronous messaging capabilities of Microsoft Message Queue (MSMQ) server, which enables you to submit tasks and immediately continue processing.

What this means is that a smart and flexible middle tier can make high-powered business applications easy to create and inexpensive to implement. Let's examine how the IIS environment is put together and how applications can take advantage of the powerful features that it provides.

IIS Architecture

Before we discuss the details of developing powerful, three-tiered solutions, you need to understand the basics of IIS architecture and the ways in which IIS handles HTTP requests. Knowing the architecture will give you some insight into the way IIS handles your code—you'll be able to make informed decisions when choosing the preferred architecture for your own application and you'll be able to track down problems more easily.

The first aspect of IIS you need to understand is that IIS can perform only the following three types of tasks when handling a client request:

- Return a static file
- Launch a CGI application
- Launch an ISAPI extension

This assertion might seem hard to believe, but all the flexibility and power of IIS is generated from these three tasks. All functionality is based on these options, so let's take a look at each one.

Static Files

Static files are collections of data that are located on a hard drive and are accessible to IIS. When you send a request for *http://www.microsoft.com/index.htm*, you are simply asking that the file INDEX.HTM on your server be returned to your browser. IIS reads INDEX.HTM from the hard drive, creates an appropriate HTTP header, and sends the contents of the file to the client. The process is the same for an image file such as a JPEG or a GIF file, or for any other file type that IIS doesn't recognize. For efficiency, IIS might cache the contents of these files in memory, but it does not change the actual contents before sending the files to the client.

CGI Applications

CGI applications are executable files that IIS will launch in response to a request for a file that ends with the .EXE extension. So, for example, when a request for *http://www.xyz.com/scripts/input.exe* is received, IIS simply finds the INPUT.EXE file and runs it. A CGI file generates the response (usually in HTML) and hands that response to IIS. IIS then sends the response along to the client. Because the CGI application will need to know certain information about the request, IIS creates a number of environment variables for the process that was launched; these environment variables include information about the request. If the client request contains input data in the body of the request, the request is sent to the CGI application through the standard input (stdin) data stream. For standard console applications, this data stream is the same one that normally receives the input you enter by using the keyboard. The response that the CGI application creates is sent to IIS via the standard output (stdout) data stream, which for console applications is the output that you see on the console screen. IIS cannot determine whether an application is a legitimate CGI application, so if a URL requests NOTEPAD.EXE, for example, IIS will go ahead and start the application. Unfortunately, because Notepad does not communicate through stdin and stdout, it will begin but will do nothing. Luckily, by default IIS will timeout the CGI request and kill the process if it doesn't receive a response within 15 minutes.

ISAPI Extensions

Unsurpassed when it comes to performance, ISAPI extensions are dynamic link libraries (DLLs) that export certain functions. One of the exported functions, *HttpExtensionProc,* is analogous to the *main* function in an application. When a client requests a URL that specifies a .DLL extension, that DLL is loaded, and IIS calls the *GetExtensionVersion* function to get the version and text description of the DLL and then calls the *HttpExtensionProc* function. If IIS receives a request for *http://www.microsoft.com/scripts/input.dll* and the appropriate DLL is already loaded, IIS calls its *HttpExtensionProc;* otherwise, IIS finds INPUT.DLL, loads it into memory, and calls its *GetExtensionVersion* and *HttpExtensionProc* functions.

As we've seen, CGI applications are executables, so they run in their own process on Microsoft Windows NT and cannot access the process memory in which IIS is running. A poorly behaved CGI application that crashes or corrupts memory will have little impact on IIS. ISAPI extensions, on the other hand, are loaded and run in the process that calls them, which by default is the IIS process. So a poorly behaved ISAPI extension could potentially crash or corrupt memory in the IIS process. IIS avoids these kinds of problems in a number of ways, which we will look at in more detail later in this chapter.

Despite the potential for a poorly behaved ISAPI DLL to corrupt IIS's memory, ISAPI extensions actually have many advantages over CGI applications. For example, loading a DLL into memory requires fewer resources than starting a new process, as is necessary for CGI requests. Once an ISAPI DLL is loaded into memory, it doesn't have to be unloaded or reloaded, and it remains available for future requests.

Script Files

Now that you have a feel for the three tasks IIS can perform to service a request from a client, you might be wondering how ASP, IDC, and SSI are handled, since they aren't static files, CGI applications, or ISAPI extensions. Well, actually, they are scripts executed by ISAPI extensions through the use of a *script map.*

Script Maps

A script map is a list of file extensions, or types, associated with certain ISAPI extensions and CGI applications. When a request comes in for a URL with a file type listed in the script map, IIS executes the corresponding ISAPI extension or CGI application instead of simply returning the file. The application is then responsible for reading the physical file, interpreting the contents of the file, and building a response.

Figure 16.4 illustrates how IIS processes requests. Notice that below the box labeled "Map URL File Type," three possible options are listed: ISAPI extensions (DLLs), CGI applications (EXEs), and unknown files, which are simply downloaded, or returned, to the client. Before IIS can determine which of the three options it will perform, it must consult the script map. For example, when a client submits a request for *http://www.microsoft.com/sales/default.asp*, IIS finds the .ASP file type in the script map, sees that it is associated with the ASP DLL, and calls the *HttpExtensionProc* function inside the ASP DLL. One of the data items that an ISAPI extension can get from IIS is the physical file location for the requested URL, so the ASP DLL reads the requested file and interprets and executes the scripts that it contains.

Let's take a look at a few script map examples and determine how they work. We'll start with an SSI example SSIDEMO.STM:

```
<HTML>
<HEAD>
<TITLE>Sample SSI Page</TITLE>
</HEAD>
<BODY>
<H1>Sample SSI Page</H1>
<HR>
<I> This page was last modified at
    <!-- #flastmod file="ssidemo.stm" -->.
<HR>
Hello, <!-- #echo var="REMOTE_USER" --><BR>
Here is a list of the current TCP/IP connections that this
computer has open:<P>
<HR>
<PLAINTEXT><!-- #exec CMD="netstat -n" -->
```

As you can see, this code is similar to HTML. It is executed simply by the client requesting the file SSIDEMO.STM. In the default script map, .STM files are handled by the SSINC.DLL ISAPI extension. So SSINC.DLL will need to open our file (SSIDEMO.STM), read its contents, and perform any conversions necessary. In particular, SSINC.DLL looks for the HTML comment tag *<!* -- and then looks for

directives that it knows how to handle. For instance, the *#echo* command replaces the comment tag with the specified environment variable. In this case, the script is using *#echo* to display the logon name in a friendly greeting. The *#flastmod* command is used to display the last modification time for the SSIDEMO.STM file. At the end of the page, the *#exec* command will actually execute the NETSTAT –N command and insert the results from the command-line utility.

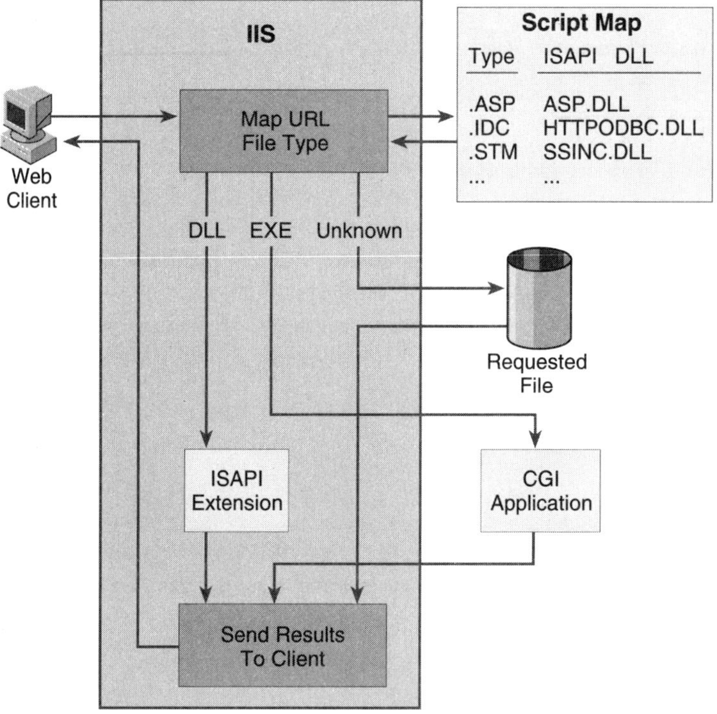

FIGURE 16.4

Request processing by IIS using script maps and URL file types to determine which of the three tasks it will perform.

NOTE

The SSI facility of IIS includes many other useful commands, which are explained in the IIS documentation under the following path: Microsoft Internet Information Server \Scripter's Reference\Server-Side Include Reference.

IDC Scripts

Another more involved type of script is the IDC. Files with the .IDC file type are handled by the HTTPODBC.DLL ISAPI extension. The IDC will let you query any database that supports ODBC. An IDC file also includes a reference to a template file that has an .HTX file type. Basically, .HTX files are HTML files with special tags that are placeholders for the various fields in the result set returned from the database query. The files also provide some rudimentary scripting capabilities that allow you to display a variable number of records by looping through a recordset. A sample IDC file, IDCSAMPLE.IDC is shown here:

```
Datasource: idcsample
Template: idcsample.htx
SQLStatement:
+ SELECT city, sales, costs, profits from cityrpt
```

This is a fairly simple IDC file—it retrieves information from an ODBC data source named idcsample. Note that the template file used to build the response is IDCSAMPLE.HTX. For an IDC file, the ISAPI extension HTTPODBC.DLL will need to read the IDC file, open up the appropriate data source, and pass the specified SQL statement to the database. When it receives the response to the SQL statement, it must open up the template file IDCSAMPLE.HTX. Let's take a look at the corresponding template file, shown here:

```
<HTML>
  <BODY>
    <H1>Sales by City</H1>
    <TABLE Border=2>
      <TD><B>City
      <TD><B>Sales
      <TD><B>Costs
      <TD><B>Profits<TR>

      <%begindetail%>
        <TD> <%city%>
        <TD> <%sales%>
        <TD> <%costs%>
        <TD> <%profits%><TR>
      <%enddetail%>
    </TABLE>
  </BODY>
</HTML>
```

The template file, for the most part, is straight HTML. The tags *<%begindetail%>* and *<%enddetail%>*, however, are a bit unusual. HTTPODBC.DLL looks for these tags to determine where it should put the information for the different records returned from its SQL call. For each record in the SQL response, HTTPODBC.DLL will fill in the requested information between these two tags. The tags in this section enclosed in <% and %> symbols indicate the names of the different fields requested from the database. HTTPODBC.DLL simply replaces those tags with the values of the fields for the record it is currently processing. The result is shown in Figure 16.5.

NOTE

The IDC supports a variety of commands in IDC files. HTX files can also be made much more complex by using an if-else-endif construct. For more information, see the IIS documentation under the following path: Microsoft Internet Information Server \Scripter's Reference\ Internet Database Connector Reference.

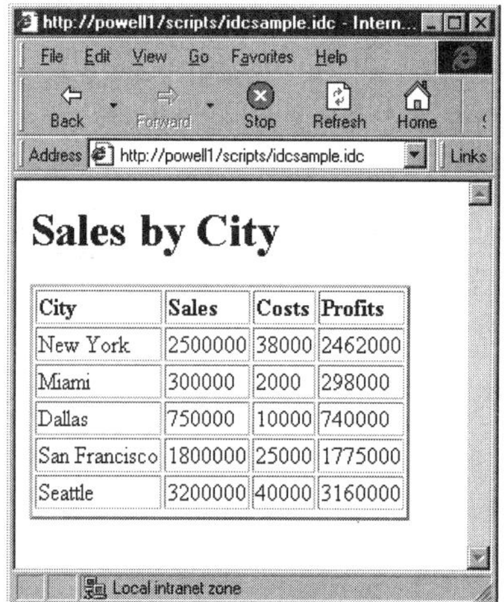

FIGURE 16.5

The results of a call to IDCSAMPLE.IDC.

We've looked at a few of the available script mappings implemented by IIS; there are others, of course, including ASP, the details of which we will be discussing later in this chapter and in chapters to come. Let's move now to some of the implementation details of launching ISAPI extensions.

ISAPI Thread Management

Because ISAPI extensions are the most efficient method for executing server-side code on IIS, Microsoft has put a lot of effort into designing the engine that executes ISAPI extensions. The result is a solution that addresses issues concerning concurrency, performance, and protection.

Worker threads

IIS uses the concept of a *worker thread* to perform many of its base functions. IIS creates a worker thread to handle any job that needs to be performed. It usually performs actions asynchronously, which means that it submits a request to perform an action and then gets control back even though the action has not yet completed. The thread is signaled when the asynchronous action it requested has completed. A large number of asynchronous actions might have to be performed, so the primary function of a worker thread is to loop continuously and wait for signals indicating that the actions have completed. Actually, if there are no actions to be performed the thread enters a sleep mode, relinquishing its processing time to other threads, and waits to be signaled. Once a signal is received, the worker thread must be smart enough to know which action was completed and then handle the event accordingly.

An example will clarify how this process works. Consider the task of receiving an HTTP request for the execution of an ISAPI extension. First a worker thread submits a request to receive the next HTTP request. Because there is no telling how long this might take, the worker thread submits this request asynchronously so that it can handle other events if necessary. Once the HTTP request is received, the event is added to the queue of events that the worker thread has to process.

When the worker thread gets to this event (the HTTP request is received), it performs the tasks necessary to get to the next step, which is calling the ISAPI extension's *HttpExtensionProc* function. These tasks include parsing the HTTP headers, authenticating the client, and building the internal structures that indicate the state of this request. Once the worker thread has completed its initial processing, it calls the *HttpExtensionProc* function of the DLL. The ISAPI extension then sends the HTTP response and returns from the *HttpExtensionProc* function. The worker thread then cleans up the resources associated with this request and submits a request to receive the next HTTP request.

The I/O thread pool

Although we talked about only a single worker thread, a pool of worker threads is actually operating on the same event queue. Because the state of any given request is stored in the internal structures associated with the request, any worker thread can handle the completion of an action even if that particular thread didn't submit the request. We will refer to this pool of worker threads as the *I/O thread pool*. To make the processing of the I/O thread pool as efficient as possible, and to handle potentially hundreds of pending asynchronous requests simultaneously, IIS uses something called *completion ports* to handle many of its operations. Completion ports allow IIS to minimize the number of times thread switches occur so that the CPU doesn't get bogged down with processing thread-switching logic. Completion ports also make IIS scale well on multiprocessor machines, which means that if CPU use is a bottleneck in your server processing, running your IIS server on a machine with multiple processors will significantly improve your performance.

Web Application Manager Objects and Microsoft Transaction Server

We will look at ISAPI extensions in detail in Chapter 20, but one thing you should know now about *HttpExtensionProc* functions is that they don't normally execute asynchronously—that is, when you call an *HttpExtensionProc* function, the function doesn't usually return control right away and then signal an event when it is finished. You might be wondering how a worker thread could asynchronously call the *HttpExtensionProc* function. The answer is that it doesn't call the *HttpExtensionProc* function directly. IIS has created a layer of abstraction, and the worker threads call this layer to indicate their desire to execute the *HttpExtensionProc* function of an ISAPI extension. The layer immediately returns, indicating that it will call the function. When it finally does call the function and the function returns, the layer signals the worker thread that the action has completed.

To create this abstraction layer, IIS took advantage of COM and created the Web Application Manager (WAM) object. The WAM object makes the actual calls to an ISAPI extension's *HttpExtensionProc* function. One of the pluses of making the WAM object a COM object is that we can take advantage of Microsoft Transaction Server (MTS)'s ability to manage COM objects. Not only does MTS handle the commitments and rollbacks of transactions, but it also handles the allocation of resources required to execute COM code. For example, MTS will allocate its own pool of threads, which will be used to call the various *HttpExtensionProc* functions of the ISAPI extensions. This capability is important because multiple HTTP requests might be executing at the same time. By having a pool of threads available to execute the *HttpExtensionProc* functions for each of the pending requests, MTS prevents the overhead of having to create threads from scratch. In addition to this, MTS will automatically increase the thread pool for the WAM object if more simultaneous requests are received than there are threads available to handle them.

As mentioned, using ISAPI extensions poses certain risks because they run within the same process space as IIS. What this means is that a poorly behaved ISAPI extension potentially can bring down IIS. IIS invokes a number of safeguards to avoid these risks, such as wrapping the calls to *HttpExtensionProc* functions in an exception handler. If the *HttpExtensionProc* function causes an access violation, IIS is notified that an error has occurred and is given the opportunity to handle the error appropriately instead of the process being shut down.

But this is only a small part of what IIS does to protect itself. The safest thing IIS can do is take advantage of MTS's ability run objects in a separate process. As you'll recall from our discussion of MTS in Chapter 15, MTS manages objects within *packages*. If you flag an MTS package as being a server package, MTS will create a separate process in which the package can run. So when you install IIS, MTS creates a package that includes various instances of the WAM object (one for each application configured on your system). By default, this package is a library package, which means that it runs in the same process as the application that called it. If you activate the Run In A Separate Memory Space option in the Microsoft Management Console of your IIS application, IIS creates a new package—a server package—and launches the WAM object in a new process of its own. So if an ISAPI extension in an application causes the process to die, only that specific application stops, not your IIS process. Figure 16.6 illustrates in-process execution and out-of-process execution of ISAPI extensions.

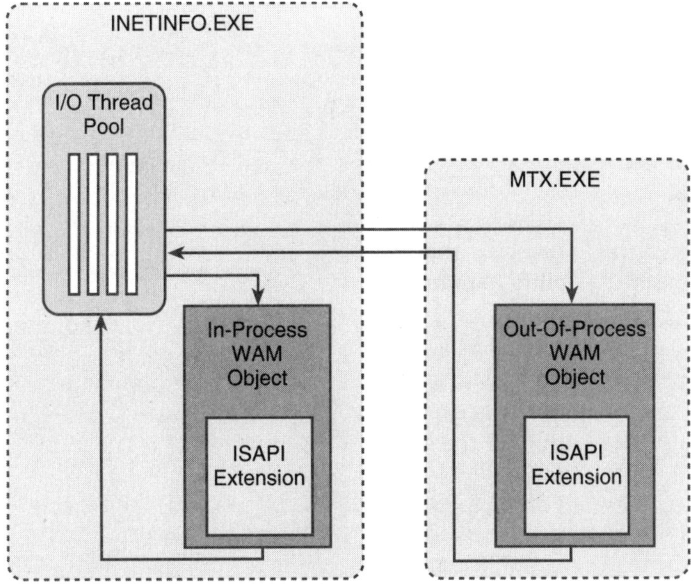

FIGURE 16.6

In-process and out-of-process execution of ISAPI extensions.

In this figure, the boxes bordered with a dotted line indicate the two processes involved: INETINFO.EXE is the process that the general IIS engine runs in and is where the I/O thread pool lives, and MTX.EXE is the executable MTS uses to launch a new process. After MTX.EXE loads, it hosts the components in the MTS package for which it was started. In our example, the component is a single instance of the WAM object. In both the in-process case and the out-of-process case, the WAM object wraps the ISAPI extensions to provide asynchronous function call support and to take advantage of MTS's ability to manage thread pools for its packages.

It's important to note that a WAM object is allocated for each IIS application. If multiple ISAPI extensions are being used from within the same application, they will share a single instance of the WAM object. For out-of-process applications, sharing a single instance of a WAM object means that one poorly behaved ISAPI extension has the potential to kill the process for all other ISAPI extensions running in the same process. This problem is minimized to a certain extent by MTS, which launches a new instance of the package when a previous instance crashes.

ASP Scripts

You already learned that ASP is just one more ISAPI extension set up as an entry in the script map. When a request comes in for an ASP file, ISAPI simply maps the .ASP extension to ASP.DLL, which reads the file and responds with the interpreted script.

But ASP is actually a little more complex than most script interpreters, for several reasons. First, ASP has a number of intrinsic objects that it makes available through its script. An instance of each of these objects must be created before the script can be interpreted. Second, ASP itself doesn't interpret the script; it uses script interpreters to parse and execute the code. Any installed script interpreter that supports the *IActiveScript* COM interface can be used by ASP to interpret script. IIS comes with two script interpreters, VBScript and JScript. The scripts in an ASP file are passed to the script interpreters, which in turn compile an image of the file that can be executed by the machine. This executable image of the script file is cached in memory so that the script won't have to be reinterpreted with each request for that page. If the file is changed, ASP reloads and recompiles the file so that the next request reflects the changes.

Because ASP is just another ISAPI extension, we already know how MTS wraps ASP.DLL in a WAM object for each application configured on a machine. ASP takes further advantage of MTS by using heavily the *object context* that MTS creates for each object that it launches. MTS creates an object context for each object that it launches in order to provide a means for storing and sharing information about the MTS package that the component is running within. For example, a component can determine whether it is part of an MTS transaction and what the state of the current transaction is.

Although each instance of an object within an MTS package has its own object context, the information for a specific request is shared among the different components through the object context. ASP uses the object context to store interface pointers to its intrinsic objects, which allows components launched by ASP to take advantage of the features provided by these intrinsic objects. So you can perform tasks such as retrieving information about a specific HTTP request by using ASP's intrinsic *Request* object from your component. Similarly, you can use the intrinsic *Response* object to build the HTTP response from your component.

Authentication and Impersonation

As we explained in Chapter 12, every process on Windows NT must run within the security context of a user account. By default, services are started in the context of a special account, named the Local System account, which exists on every Windows NT machine. IIS uses this default setting, which gives it the additional privileges necessary to impersonate users and log system events. Because the Local System account has nearly unlimited privileges on the server, IIS must restrict the capability of the code that is executed when a request is received—you certainly wouldn't want a user to launch an ISAPI extension that reformats your hard drive. IIS restricts access for code executed in response to a client request by impersonating the client before executing the request. For example, if SueEllen makes a request to IIS to access PAYROLL.HTM, IIS will impersonate SueEllen before trying to read and return the file. After the request has been handled, IIS reverts to the Local System account.

HTTP does not automatically implement authentication for each request that is sent to a server. Typically, requests are initially sent without any sort of authentication information included within the HTTP headers. These kinds of requests are called *anonymous requests*. When IIS receives an anonymous request, it wants to restrict access since it has no idea who is actually making the request, and it does so by impersonating the IUSR_*computername* account (where *computername* is replaced with the name of your computer). By default the IUSR_*computername* account has only guest privileges on the machine, so access to resources are relatively limited unless the administrator adds the account to the Administrators group or you enable certain privileges for the account in some other fashion. When you expand IUSR_*computername* privileges, you open the door to anyone who might want to perform undesirable tasks on your machine. Leaving the machine vulnerable might not be such a big deal when it comes to reading HTML files that you want to make available to the world. But it would become a very big deal if the client could somehow load and execute an ISAPI extension or an ASP page on the server. The client could then easily perform any task it wanted on your server.

The task of impersonating a client is fairly straightforward, but it is important to understand how impersonation works and what its limits are, particularly if you are writing your own ISAPI extension or ASP application. Since potentially IIS is handling multiple requests simultaneously, it is critical that IIS's impersonation of a client be restricted to the particular worker thread that is handling the request for that client. You might have several threads running at the same time, each impersonating a different user. Let's take a look at the effect of impersonation on each of the three tasks that IIS can perform: returning a static file, launching a CGI application, and launching an ISAPI extension.

Returning a Static File

Returning a static file is a fairly straightforward task and is basically handled within the worker thread from the I/O thread pool. After IIS has read the HTTP request and built the internal storage structures required to properly handle the request, the client's account or the IUSR_*computername* account is impersonated. This occurs before access to the file is attempted. After the account is impersonated, an attempt is made to read the file, and if the attempt is successful, the file is sent back to the client via the HTTP response. If the attempt fails, an "Access Denied" error is returned. After the file has been read, the task is complete and IIS can revert to the Local System account to complete the processing of the request and get ready for the next request.

NOTE

After a file is requested, it is cached in memory. Luckily, IIS is smart enough to detect whether a file or its permissions are modified so that security restrictions can be implemented immediately, even if the file was cached before the permissions were changed.

Launching a CGI Application

Impersonation for CGI applications is a little trickier than for returning simple static files, because IIS actually has to launch a process. To do this, IIS impersonates the client before making the call to launch the process. But all this type of impersonation does is check to make sure that the impersonated user has permissions to execute the program. By default, processes launched by another process are launched in the security context of the parent process, not in the security context of the thread that launched the process. Since IIS runs as the Local System account by default, processes would start in the security context of the Local System account—not a very secure system.

Luckily, Windows NT provides the capability to launch applications in the context of an impersonated user. Typically, you would call the function *CreateProcess* to launch an application, but if you wanted the new process to run in the context of a user different from yourself, you would use *CreateProcessAsUser*. By default, IIS uses *CreateProcessAsUser* to launch CGI applications. If SueEllen makes a request to *http://yourmachine/trashharddrive.exe*, the process will be created using her account privileges and the application will succeed only if you gave SueEllen permission to trash your hard drive.

◆ Configuring IIS to Use CreateProcess

IIS is flexible enough to allow you to configure it to use *CreateProcess* instead of *CreateProcessAsUser*. You can do this by editing the Metabase property *CreateProcess-AsUser* for the virtual directory. The following command uses ADSUTIL.VBS to change this setting for a virtual directory named myvdir:

```
ADSUTIL.VBS SET w3svc/1/root/myvdir/CreateProcessAsUser "FALSE"
```

By default, this setting is *TRUE*, meaning that CGI applications will be launched using *CreateProcessAsUser*. If the property is set to *FALSE*, CGI applications, located in the virtual directory, will be launched using *CreateProcess* and will run in the context of the Local System account. Obviously, using *CreateProcess* is a potential security hole, but occasionally it can be useful for specific CGI applications in specific user scenarios in which unlimited local permissions are required.

Launching an ISAPI Extension

ISAPI extensions are also relatively straightforward with regard to impersonation. The client is impersonated just before the DLL is loaded into memory, preventing access to the ISAPI extension if the impersonated user does not have access to the ISAPI DLL file. After the ISAPI extension is loaded, IIS reverts to the Local System account temporarily to perform a certain amount of initialization, including calling the *GetExtensionVersion* function in the ISAPI DLL. When IIS is ready to continue, the client is impersonated again, and the call is made to the *HttpExtensionProc* function in the ISAPI DLL. The function returns, and IIS reverts to the Local System account so that it can finish processing the current request and prepare to handle the next request. In the case of script maps such as ASP, the target file needs to be read and interpreted, both of which occur within the context of the impersonated user. So if the client cannot access the ASP file, the request fails.

Security issues

The handling of ISAPI extensions poses some security problems that you should be aware of and know how to address. Let's take a look at some of these issues.

Even though the *HttpExtensionProc* function of an ISAPI extension is called in the context of the impersonated client, an ISAPI extension can use several strategies to execute code in the context of the Local System account. We already looked at one of those strategies—calling *CreateProcess*.

Another strategy an ISAPI extension can employ is to call the function *RevertToSelf*, which ends an impersonation session. If you put in a call to *RevertToSelf* in the *HttpExtensionProc* function in an ISAPI extension, you would be in the security context of the Local System account. Any threads created by an ISAPI extension are created in the context of the owner of the process, which is the Local System account, and as mentioned earlier, the *GetExtensionVersion* function call is handled within the Local System account. An ISAPI extension can even launch a COM object which, if it is not an apartment model object, will run in the context of the Local System account. So if you don't trust an ISAPI extension, you should be very careful how you run it on your system. But how can you be careful?

In the context of preventing a poorly behaved ISAPI extension from bringing down your system, we discussed MTS and the WAM object and how you can force ISAPI extensions to run in a process different from the IIS process. Untrustworthy ISAPI extensions should be run out of process.

Let's extend our definition of untrustworthy extensions to cover the case in which a malicious ISAPI extension wants to hurt or spy on the system. If an ISAPI extension is running in the IIS process, it can call *RevertToSelf* and then it would gain full access to the local machine. However, if an ISAPI extension is running out of process by using the MTS option for the WAM object, calling *RevertToSelf* causes the security context to change to the owner of the current process—and this is where ultimate security is provided with IIS, even for ISAPI extensions.

When a new process is launched by MTS with the goal of running an ISAPI extension out of process, the new process is not started in the context of the Local System account. Instead, the new process is started in the context of a user called IWAM_*computername*. By default the IWAM_*computername* account has limited privileges on the machine, so an ISAPI extension's ability to perform mischief is greatly curtailed.

You do incur a performance hit for running ISAPI extensions out of process. (Running ISAPI extensions out of process is not nearly as slow as running a CGI application, but the time is a hit nonetheless.) So if you have an ISAPI extension from a trustworthy source, you are better off running it in process. If you have an ISAPI extension that might be buggy or otherwise suspect, run it out of process.

ISAPI Filters

Another kind of ISAPI DLL that IIS supports is an ISAPI filter DLL. Unlike ISAPI extensions, you cannot call an ISAPI filter directly from your browser. ISAPI filters are loaded into the IIS process space and receive notifications of particular events for every request received by IIS. For example, you can register to get notifications when a URL is mapped to a physical path. A filter not only receives the notification, but depending on the event, it can manipulate the handling of the request as well. So in the case of mapping the URL to a physical path, from a filter you can have a different file returned to the browser than the one that was requested.

ISAPI filters are very powerful and should be installed with caution. Filter notifications always occur within the security context of the Local System account, so they are basically unrestrained in the actions they can perform on the server machine. ISAPI filters always run in the same process as IIS, so a bug in a filter can bring down IIS.

Unknown filters can also be dangerous because they can literally monitor every byte sent to and from your server. Even encrypted SSL requests can be seen in their unencrypted form via an ISAPI filter, so you should be very confident of a filter's trustworthiness before installing it. You can take a fair amount of comfort in the fact that only IIS administrators on your server can install filters.

Global Filters and Site Filters

There are actually two kinds of filters, *global filters* and *site filters*. Site filters receive notifications only for the specific Web site for which they were installed. So if an Internet Service Provider (ISP) is hosting Web sites for multiple companies on the same machine, those companies can take advantage of filters without exposing their notifications to one another.

A global filter is a Web-service-wide filter, which means that the filter receives notifications for every request handled by the server regardless of the Web site. It's important to note that one kind of notification is available only to global filters: the read raw data notification. The read raw data notification is called when incoming data is received on a socket. When a request is first received, the HTTP headers have not yet been interpreted, so at the time of a read raw data notification, it is impossible to know which site the data is destined for. Therefore, only global filters receive read raw data notifications, and any site filter that attempts to receive them will not be loaded by IIS. A filter that IIS is unable to load successfully will generate an event in the Windows NT Event Log that includes a description of why the failure occurred.

SSPIFILT.DLL

When you install IIS, you will see that at least one global filter is already installed. The filter, named SSPIFILT.DLL, provides all the SSL support on the server. It does this by receiving read raw data notifications and sending read raw data notifications, which it uses to decrypt and encrypt data, respectively.

MSPROXY.DLL

Another Microsoft filter that demonstrates the power of ISAPI filters is the MSPROXY.DLL filter. This filter is installed when you install Microsoft Proxy Server and helps to turn your IIS machine into a secure HTTP proxy. It does this by analyzing the requested URL that is included in the HTTP request. Proxy requests include a full URL, such as *http://www.microsoft.com/msdn,* instead of a partial URL, such as */scripts/request.asp,* so that the proxy can relay the request to the proper server. The MSPROXY.DLL filter simply receives notifications of the event when the HTTP headers have been parsed. MSPROXY.DLL can then see what the format of the requested URL looks like, and if it is a proxy request the filter will relay the request to the proper machine. We will talk more about how HTTP proxy requests work in Chapter 23.

At this point, you should have a good feel for how IIS works and the environment it provides for building applications and solutions. The IIS platform is very flexible and powerful, providing a multitude of possibilities. In the remaining chapters in Part II, we will look at how you can create your own IIS applications. We'll start out by reviewing the basics of developing ASP, which provides an easy way to add server-side execution to an IIS installation.

CHAPTER 17

ASP Basics

Now that you have a good feel for transactions and applications and for IIS's exceptional ability to host applications, it's time to get down to the details of actually writing an application. Luckily, IIS provides an easy mechanism that enables even beginners to create effective applications.

Introduction to ASP

Let's start by looking at a simple HTML page as it might appear on your server:

```
<HTML>
    <HEAD>
        <TITLE>My HTML Page Title</TITLE>
    </HEAD>
    <BODY>
        Hello, World!
    </BODY>
</HTML>
```

We'll look at HTML in detail in Chapter 22, but for now you'll need to know some of the basics of HTML. First, HTML uses a number of *tags* to differentiate between different parts of the page. These tags are enclosed in angle brackets and usually occur in pairs—for instance, in the preceding code the <TITLE> tag is paired with the </TITLE> tag, which tells us that the contents between the two tags constitutes the title of our page. The page itself is identified by the <HTML> and </HTML> tags. Notice the two main sections within our HTML section: the body and the head. The head contains information and attributes—for example, the title—that apply to the entire page; the body contains the specific contents that will appear in the window of our browser. We will do some interesting things with the head later in this chapter, but for now we'll focus on the body.

Our simple HTML page doesn't do very much; in fact, it does only two things: it displays *My HTML Page Title* in the title bar of the browser, and it displays *Hello, World!* in the window of the browser. And to convert this page to an ASP page, we need to do only one thing: save this file on our server as HELLO.ASP instead of

HELLO.HTM. The output displayed by the renamed file is no different, but instead of the file being read and downloaded like a simple HTML file, it will now be interpreted by the ASP script map, ASP.DLL. (See Chapter 21 for more information about script maps.) The job of the ASP.DLL is to locate the physical file, read it into memory, and then locate the portions of the file that are to be interpreted as script. In reality, there is no requirement that an ASP page contain script; any nonscript portions of a file are considered straight HTML and are sent to the client as such. If we save our HTML file as HELLO.ASP, it will be sent to the client as an HTML file would be.

Well, it might be mildly interesting that you can rename HTML files using the ASP extension so that they will be interpreted by the ASP script map, but doing so is not particularly useful. Real usefulness comes from the way ASP.DLL will scan an HTML page for specific elements that it will then dynamically interpret. Here's a look at a slightly modified version of our original "Hello, World!" HTML page:

```
<HTML>
    <HEAD>
        <TITLE>My HTML Page Title</TITLE>
    </HEAD>
    <BODY>
        Hello, World! <br>
        I hope you are having a nice
        <%
            Dim today
            Dim NumericDay

            today = Date()
            NumericDay = Weekday(today)
            Response.Write(WeekDayName(NumericDay))
        %>
    </BODY>
</HTML>
```

Our page still provides the same friendly greeting, but we've added a line to customize our message. Scripting gives us the ability to create dynamic content for our client. Let's take a look at some of the details.

The difference between this page and the previous HTML page is that this page includes a new taglike element in the middle. Instead of the standard tag delimiters enclosed in angle brackets, here we have a new delimiter indicated by the <%

and %> symbols. These symbols tell ASP that the data contained within them is server-side script that it needs to execute—in other words, this is server-side script in the default language for this page. Since this page contains no other indication of what the default language is, ASP assumes that it is VBScript.

Now that we've determined that the script in our example is in VBScript and is to be run on the server, let's look at the script itself. If you're familiar with Microsoft Visual Basic, you'll recognize the first two statements in our script as variable declarations. We have declared two variables, *today* and *NumericDay*. In this case, we haven't bothered to declare them as any specific type of variable because VBScript has only one data type, Variant. A Variant is a special kind of data type that can hold different kinds of information. If a VBScript variable is used as a string, it will hold string information; if it is used as a number, it will hold numeric information.

The process of defining variables is straightforward, but a single variable can't include more than one data type. For instance, if you use a variable to hold a string, you cannot use the same variable to hold numeric data. The variable *today* is used in our example to hold date information. (Date data types are a variation of the numeric data type.) We set *today* to be equal to the value returned by the function *Date*. The *Date* function is one of a full-featured set of functions built into the VBScript engine. As you might expect, this particular function returns the current date, but all kinds of functions are available that enable you to do everything from calculating sines and cosines to reversing the sequence of characters in a string. The *Date* function does not require any parameters to obtain the current system date, so the parentheses following the *Date* call are empty. As you can see on the next line, however, the call to the function *Weekday* does have a parameter. The *Weekday* function takes a Date data type as its only parameter, and it returns a number corresponding to a day of the week (*1* = Sunday, 2 = Monday, and so on). Here we pass the current date, which was returned by the *Date* function, to the *Weekday* function.

The last line in our simple script gets a little complicated—we are actually making two function calls on a single line. The first function that is executed is the *WeekDayName* function, which takes the value returned by the *Weekday* function and returns the day of the week as an easily readable string. Technically, the second function is not a function at all—it is actually a method of the *Response* object. We'll take a look at objects, object properties, and object methods later in this chapter, but for now let's assume that *Response.Write* is just another function like *WeekDayName* that takes a string as its parameter. *Response.Write* writes this string to the Web client just as if it were inserted into the HTML that surrounds our script. In this case, our script will insert the current day of the week into our HTML page. Figure 17.1 shows the results of our scripting effort, an HTML page sent to the browser.

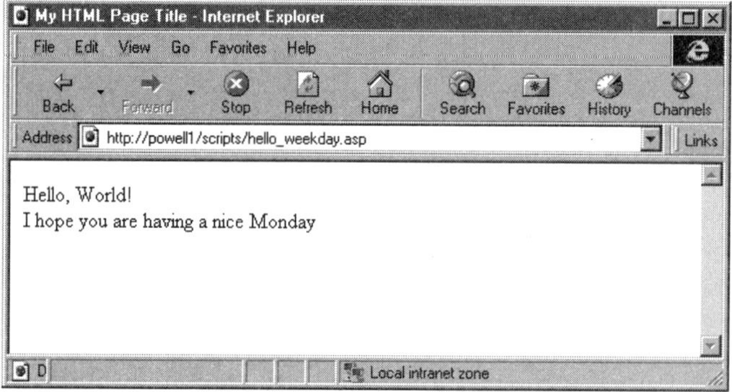

FIGURE 17.1

A simple ASP sample viewed in a browser.

Manipulating ASP Pages

We've written quite a lot of script just to display the day of the week. We can actually shorten our ASP script considerably, as shown here:

```
<HTML>
    <HEAD>
        <TITLE>My HTML Page Title</TITLE>
    </HEAD>
    <BODY>
        Hello, World! <br>
        I hope you are having a nice
        <%=WeekDayName(Weekday(Date))%>
    </BODY>
</HTML>
```

As you can see, seven lines of code have been reduced to a single line. Let's take a look at the aspects of ASP that allow us to do this.

As in the last line of our previous script, here we are calling several functions from a single line. We can do this because each of the functions returns a data type that will then be used as a parameter to the function it is wrapped within. We also took advantage of a little notation flexibility within VBScript. Our call to the *Date* function is made without the trailing parentheses since the VBScript engine is smart enough to realize what we mean when we just say "Date." This simplification tends to make our code a little easier to read as well.

ASP Directives

ASP provides three types of directives that enable you to manipulate how your ASP pages are processed: output directives, processing directives, and input directives. Let's look at each of these directive types in detail.

Output Directives

The simplification to the preceding example involved the use of an *output directive*. An output directive has the following format: <%= *expression* %>. A script delimiter immediately followed by an equals sign (<%=) tells ASP to evaluate and display the expression that follows the equals sign. An output directive is just performing a *Response.Write* of the expression. In this case, the expression is *WeekDayName(Weekday(Date))* and our script sends the following HTML to the client's browser:

```
<HTML>
    <HEAD>
        <TITLE>My HTML Page Title</TITLE>
    </HEAD>
    <BODY>
        Hello, World! <br>
        I hope you are having a nice
        Monday
    </BODY>
</HTML>
```

This output is exactly the same as that of our previous script. Note that the client never sees the script that was executed, even if the source of the HTML page is viewed in the client's browser.

Processing Directives

Our previous example used an output directive, but ASP also provides *processing directives*. A processing directive is indicated by an @ symbol immediately following the script delimiter; it has the following format: <%@ *directive=value* %>. Processing directives must appear before any other script in the ASP file because they provide ASP with the information needed to process the rest of the file. For instance, the processing directive <%@ *LANGUAGE=JScript* %> tells ASP that the default scripting language for this page is JScript. The following table lists the options that can be used as processing directives.

Processing Directive	Usage
@LANGUAGE	Specifies the default scripting language for the page. IIS supports VBScript and JScript, but third-party scripting engines can also be installed.
@CODEPAGE	Sets the character code page that tells ASP to use the specified character set instead of the system's default character set.
@LCID	Sets the locale ID, which handles the display of currency figures, as well as time and date formats if you want to use locale information different from the system's default locale setting.
@TRANSACTION	Specifies that an ASP page is transactional, which means that Microsoft Transaction Server (MTS) will manage transaction state information, including commits and roll backs. (Options for the transaction directive are discussed in Chapter 18.)
@ENABLESESSIONSTATE	Determines whether ASP session information will be stored for this page. ASP uses HTTP cookies to maintain state across multiple HTTP requests. Without the session state enabled, there will be no easy way to associate the execution of this page with the same user's execution of another page. Can be set to *TRUE* or *FALSE*.

Include Directives

Another capability that ASP provides for manipulating how ASP pages are processed is *include directives*. An include directive, indicated with a *<!--#include* delimiter, enables you to insert another file within an ASP page. This concept is not new; Server-Side Include (SSI) files have provided this kind of functionality long before ASP was around. Unlike SSI files, ASP does not provide a full-featured set of keyword mappings, but include directives are nevertheless a powerful tool.

Ordinary HTML editors use include files to insert a common header and footer in a series of pages. This technique lets you avoid having to copy the same HTML commands into each HTML file. Within a series of ASP pages, include files become extremely useful. For instance, you might have a series of pages that need to perform some of the same types of tasks. If your personal functions would be useful on two or more pages, you can simply put them in a single include file and then use an include directive to insert the file into each page.

The syntax of the include directive can take one of two forms, as shown here:

```
<!--#include virtual = "/scripts/globalfunctions.inc"-->
<!--#include file = "../morefunctions.inc"-->
```

Notice that the include directive is located within the standard HTML comment delimiters. This notation allows this file to be used on a Web server that doesn't support include directives; the server would ignore the text because it is inside of an HTML comment.

The *virtual* keyword tells ASP to locate this file based on the virtual path exposed by IIS virtual directories. In this example, the file GLOBALFUNCTIONS.INC needs to be located in the scripts virtual directory to work properly.

The *file* keyword tells ASP to locate the file based on the physical drive hierarchy. In this example, the MOREFUNCTIONS.INC file needs to be located in the parent directory of the current ASP file. This directory does not have to be directly accessible to Web clients.

One thing to watch out for is include files that are themselves allowed to include other files. You will run into problems if an include file tries to include itself or if two include files include each other. You could wind up with circular schemes that would cause ASP to include files ad infinitum. ASP is smart enough to detect this problem and will display an error message informing you of your mistake.

Writing Your Own Procedures

In our earlier example, we saw several techniques for using VBScript functions to perform a number of common tasks. Despite the power of VBScript and other scripting engines, undoubtedly there will be functions you would like to use that are specific to your Web application's needs. For instance, you might want a function that makes a certain kind of database query or a function that simply displays the user's name in HTML. Any code that is executed multiple times within your page is a prime candidate for moving into a function so that you can write the code once and reuse it many times. If you put your functions in include files, a single copy of a function could be used across your entire site. Here's a simple ASP page that implements its own function:

```
<HTML>
    <HEAD>
        <TITLE>My HTML Page Title</TITLE>
        <SCRIPT LANGUAGE=VBSCRIPT RUNAT=SERVER>
            Function Today()
                Today = WeekDayName(Weekday(Date))
            End Function
        </SCRIPT>
    </HEAD>
```

(continued)

```
    <BODY>
        Hello, World! <br>
        I hope you are having a nice <%=Today%>.<br>
        I really love <%=Today%>s.
        <br>
    </BODY>
</HTML>
```

This page is similar to our first scripting page, but here we have added some code to the page's head. As you can see, we have used the <SCRIPT> tag to indicate to ASP that we have script to run. But because client-side scripting uses the <SCRIPT> tag as well, we've included the *RUNAT* attribute to indicate that this script is actually supposed to be executed on the server.

◆ Server-Side Scripting vs. Client-Side Scripting

Both server-side scripting and client-side scripting allow the Web author to dynamically create HTML pages—the difference of course is where the script gets interpreted. So when do you choose one over the other? The decision might be obvious based on the resources the script is accessing. If, for example, your script is querying a database that is accessible only from the server, it makes sense to use server-side scripting. If the script needs to interact with the client's desktop via a Java applet or an ActiveX control, it obviously needs to be executed on the client. Be aware that client-side script is viewable by the client, whereas only the results of server-side script are viewable to the client. If you want to perform a single task that can be completed on either the client or the server, and the question of whether the code is viewable to the client is not important, you should probably choose client-side scripting. Although the task of executing most scripts is minimal, if a server is executing thousands or millions of requests, every little bit of CPU savings will be appreciated. A tied-up server CPU might mean that thousands of clients are waiting for the script to execute. If a client is tied up in a lengthy client-side script, the delay is affecting only that one client. And finally, be aware that if you do have a lot of server-side processing to perform, you should consider moving your code from a script into a COM component that can be called from your ASP page. With a custom COM component, you will have more control over how concurrent requests are handled and can take advantage of some of the performance enhancements provided by Windows NT that are not available from script.

You might be asking yourself why we are using the <SCRIPT> tag for our function when earlier we used the <% and %> delimiters. The <% and %> delimiters should be used within the body of your HTML page when you want to insert script-generated HTML among the standard HTML in your file. When ASP is parsing through the file and sending the HTML within the page to the client, the <% and %> delimiters indicate that the enclosed script should be executed and the results sent to the client before ASP continues downloading the HTML following the delimiters. Functions, on the other hand, are entities whose specific positions within the page are relatively meaningless. Their code is only executed when they are called. Therefore, functions apply to the entire page and as such belong in the head of an HTML document. In reality, since their position within the document is meaningless, we quite often see function declarations occurring even before the beginning <HTML> tag or after the closing </HTML> tag. But in order to indicate to ASP that this is script that should be interpreted only if the enclosed functions are called somewhere else within the page, we use <SCRIPT> tags instead of the <% and %> delimiters.

Our function is named *Today* and, as indicated by the *LANGUAGE* attribute of the <SCRIPT> tag, is written in VBScript. We use standard Visual Basic notation for our function definition after this. The *Today* function happens to use the same code that we used earlier to display the day of the week. By specifying Today = within our function, we are indicating that our function will be returning the results of our well-known script.

◆ Subroutines and Functions

If you're familiar with Visual Basic, you probably realize that two kinds of procedures are available to programmers: *subroutines* and *functions*. The difference between the two is that functions typically return a value, as we do with our *Today* function, whereas subroutines do not return a value. If you use a subroutine that accepts only one or no arguments, you are allowed to omit the parentheses when you call the subroutine. If a subroutine accepts multiple arguments, you must omit the parentheses. When calling functions, you use the syntax *value =functionName(arg1, arg2,...)*. When calling subroutines, you use the syntax *subroutineName arg1, arg2,...*. Enforcing parenthesis usage has always struck us as a small price to pay for being able to return data from your call.

In the body of our document, you'll notice that we have added another line of output to our page. The beauty of subroutines and functions is that we can use the code within them multiple times without having to insert the same code over and over again. Subroutines and functions also allow us to make our code easier to read, since we can replace a lengthy set of steps with a single name that clearly describes what the steps do. In our case, we use our *Today* function, not only to wish our users a nice day, but also to inform them that we personally love that particular day of the week.

Objects, Methods, Properties, and Collections

In our initial scripting sample, we mentioned the use of an odd-looking "function" named *Response.Write*. Actually, *Response.Write* is an example of an object being used within ASP. Although the term "object" is greatly overused in the world of computing, when we are talking about ASP, object refers specifically to a COM object that supports Automation (previously known as an OLE Automation object). The object used in our example is called the *Response* object. The *Response* object has to do with the request that activated the ASP page. In particular, the *Response* object has methods and properties related to the response that the ASP page is building to service the received HTTP request.

Glossary

COM object *An object that supports the Windows COM specification.*

Automation *An extension to the COM specification that allows an object's interfaces to be called by name without requiring the caller to know specifically how the interfaces were designed. Only COM objects that support Automation can be used from a script interpreter, such as ASP.*

The *Write* portion of *Response.Write* is known as a *method* of the *Response* object. Methods are functions made available by an object. In our case, *Response.Write* allows us to write HTML back to the client. The *Response* object has several other methods that we will describe later in this chapter, but it also provides a number of *properties*. Think of a property as a variable that you might set to a certain value. Sometimes it doesn't make sense to set certain properties, so you can only read them. The syntax for identifying a property is similar to the syntax for identifying a method—for instance, *Response.Status* identifies the *Status* property of the *Response* object. *Response.Status* indicates the HTTP status code for the given response. It certainly makes sense to set this property, but it also makes sense that you might want to read it as well. For example, the *Status* property might have been set earlier to some sort of failure condition, which requires further action.

Glossary

methods *Functions or subroutines made available through Automation that can be looked up by name and are frequently used by script interpreters such as ASP and Visual Basic.*

properties *Usually, the public variables of a COM object that supports Automation. The values of properties can be read or set as if they were variables from a script interpreter.*

Sometimes objects support *collections*. Similar to arrays, collections enable you to group related elements, such as strings, numbers, objects, or other values. You can then access the different elements in the collection by using an index or by specifying an element's name. For instance, the *Response* object has a collection named *Cookies*. You can identify each cookie by using a numeric index—for example, *Response.Cookies(2)* identifies the second element in the *Cookies* collection. Sometimes you don't want to have to walk through all the elements of a collection to find a specific element. Quite often you can use an element's name instead of an index to refer to a specific element. For instance, if you had a cookie named *UserID*, you could refer to its value as *Response.Cookies("UserID")*.

Glossary

collections *Can be interpreted almost as object properties in the form of an array for COM objects that support Automation. Unlike traditional arrays, the elements of collections often can be indexed by name instead of by simple numeric indexes.*

The *Response* object in ASP is one of a handful of special objects called *intrinsic objects* or *built-in objects* because you can automatically access them without having to do anything within your ASP page. Usually, if you want to access an object from an ASP page, you have to create an instance of the object yourself before you can use its methods or properties. This is done much like it is in Visual Basic, by using the *CreateObject* method. As it turns out, the *CreateObject* method in ASP is a method of another intrinsic object named the *Server* object. But you can use *CreateObject* to access any COM object that supports Automation on your machine, barring any security restrictions. This technique provides your ASP pages with a way to access the full set of resources on your server. You can make calls into a database, access a set of files on your server, maybe communicate with a special hardware device, or even access resources on another machine. The full high-powered Win32 programming interface is available within COM objects, so you potentially have the ability to do anything that you can do from any Windows-based application.

The following script excerpt shows how we can access any file on the server by using FileSystemObject object:

```
Set FileSys = Server.CreateObject("Scripting.FileSystemObject")
Set File = FileSys.OpenTextFile("c:\Phrases\PhraseOfTheDay.Txt", 1)
Response.Write(File.ReadLine)
```

We use the *CreateObject* method of the *Server* object to create an instance of *FileSystemObject*. Once we have an instance of the object, we can use its methods and properties. We use the *OpenTextFile* method to open the file in question.

OpenTextFile returns an instance of another object, the *TextStream* object. We can use the *TextStream* object's *ReadLine* method to read the first line of the file, which we then write back to our client using the *Response* object's *Write* method.

Application, Session, and Page Scopes

As with any application—in particular, client/server applications—there will be situations in which you want variables or objects to exist for the duration of the application. These variables or objects are referred to as having *application scope*. "Application scope" refers to those variables or objects that will live the entire time an application is running. For instance, you might want to keep a count of the total number of requests your application has serviced since it started, or you might have a resource such as a file that will be shared for all requests. "Page scope," on the other hand, refers to those resources that live only for the length of a single request. For instance, any VBScript variable declared in our ASP file has page scope because each request for the page gets a new copy of these variables, and each of these variables are destroyed when the specific request has completed. Obviously, in some instances it might be nice to have resources available with application scope instead of the short-lived page scope that we have seen so far.

Before we go into the details of how to implement application scope, we need to discuss a third type of scope: *session scope*. Since our HTTP server is working within a client/server paradigm, we might have any number of different clients requesting our resources over a specific period of time. In many situations, you would want to access and allocate resources per user. Perhaps your application is providing access to the clients' financial records, or maybe you just need to keep track of where each client has been and what should happen next. In and of itself, HTTP does not provide a means for maintaining any sort of state between requests, but with the use of HTTP cookies, Web applications are able to determine that a request came from a user who sent in a request for another ASP page a little earlier. ASP takes advantage of HTTP cookies to provide session scope. Session scope allows ASP to allocate resources and objects per user, but unlike request scope resources, these resources are not destroyed when a single request completes. Instead, objects with session scope stay around for any number of requests made by the same user. Session scope objects are destroyed only after a user session has been idle for a lengthy period of time (the default is 20 minutes) or after an ASP page has specifically asked to end the session. Figure 17.2 illustrates the correlation between application scope, session scope, and page scope.

Both application scope and session scope capabilities are made available to ASP applications through the use of two other intrinsic objects, appropriately named the *Application* object and the *Session* object. An *Application* object is instantiated the first time an ASP page in an application is requested. The *Application* object is then destroyed either when IIS is shut down or if the application is specifically unloaded, as can be done through the Microsoft Management Console by clicking the Unload button in the application's Properties window. *Session* objects are optional and will not work for browsers that either don't support or have disabled the use of HTTP cookies. A *Session* object is created only if ASP has detected that the application is actually making use of *Session* object functionality. A *Session* object can be created by storing variables using the *Session* object, by including scripts that hook *Session* object events, or by creating an object with the *SCOPE* attribute set to *Session*.

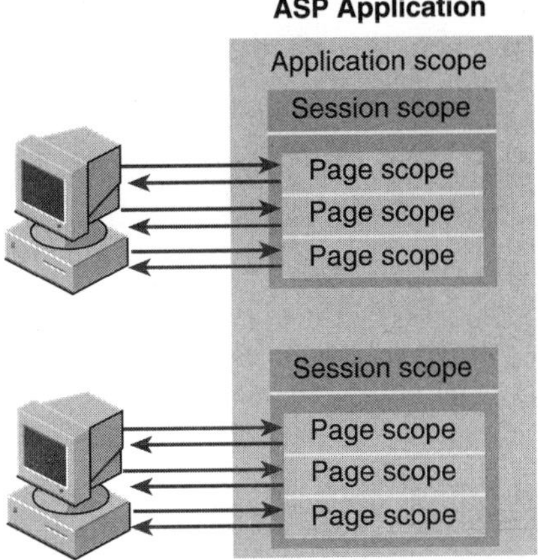

FIGURE 17.2

The relationship between application scope, session scope, and page scope.

GLOBAL.ASA

You might be wondering how application and session processing is performed because so far we have seen only code within specific ASP files. It's not hard to figure out that ASP pages in general have page scope since they are executed at each page request. Certainly the state of an ASP page has no direct way of existing between requests; for this reason, a special file named GLOBAL.ASA was created. GLOBAL.ASA is a script file that exists in an application's root directory. It contains script just like an ASP page, but unlike an ASP page, its contents aren't executed for every request. In particular, GLOBAL.ASA code is executed during an *Application* or *Session* object's startup or shutdown. ASP provides these two objects to manage application and session scope, and it is through the events of the *Application* and *Session* objects that an application is provided a means for doing some processing during application and session startup and shutdown.

In addition to handling events, GLOBAL.ASA gives you the ability to instantiate an object with application or session scope. For example, instead of creating a new instance of your object for each request, you might want your object to exist for the entire lifetime of an application or a session. In this way, you avoid the penalty of reinstantiating an object on subsequent calls. Any objects with application or session scope are immediately available within any ASP pages in the application just as if they were intrinsic objects. Their methods and properties can be accessed within an ASP page as if *CreateObject* was already called on them.

Unlike the object creation syntax in a standard ASP page, the syntax for creating objects in the GLOBAL.ASA file is almost the same as the syntax used when creating client-side objects in a page. Here's an example of a GLOBAL.ASA file:

```
<OBJECT
    RUNAT=Server
    SCOPE=Application
    ID=Counter
    PROGID="MSWC.Counters">
</OBJECT>

<SCRIPT LANGUAGE=VBSCRIPT RUNAT=SERVER>
Sub Application_OnStart
    Application("StartTime") = Time
    Application("TotalPagesSinceStart") = 0
    Application("TotalSessionsSinceStart") = 0
    Application("CurrentSessions") = 0
    Counter.Increment("MyAppStarts")
End Sub

Sub Session_OnStart
    Counter.Increment("TotalSessions")
        Application.Lock
        Application("TotalSessionsSinceStart") = _
        Application("TotalSessionsSinceStart") + 1
        Application("CurrentSessions") = _
        Application("CurrentSessions") + 1
        Application.Unlock
        Session("SessionPages") = 0
End Sub

Sub Session_OnEnd
        Application.Lock
        Application("CurrentSessions") = _
        Application("CurrentSessions") - 1
        Application.Unlock
End Sub
</SCRIPT>
```

This GLOBAL.ASA has two main sections: an object section and a script section. The object section is defined using the <OBJECT> tag and includes four attributes. The *RUNAT* attribute is used here much like we used it earlier with the <SCRIPT> tag. It might seem obvious that if an object is mentioned in the GLOBAL.ASA, it must run on the server, but if *RUNAT=Server* is not specified, the object will not load properly. The next attribute, *SCOPE*, lets ASP know whether we want this object to have application scope or session scope. Because we specified *Application*, our object will exist as long as we don't unload our application or restart our server. The *ID* attribute is the name that we will use later to refer to this object in our script. As it happens, we are creating an instance of the *Counters* object , which is available with the Counters component (COUNTERS.DLL) in the IIS Resource Kit. The *Counters* object is not one of the intrinsic objects, which means that we have to explicitly create an instance of it before it can be used. The *PROGID* attribute is the identifier that ASP uses to track down the proper object to load. We could have instead specified the *Counters* object's class identifier using a similar *CLASSID* attribute, but the *PROGID, MSWC.Counters*, is a lot easier to remember than the *CLASSID, 89B9D28B-AAEB-11D0-9796-00A0C908612D*.

In the script section of our GLOBAL.ASA, delimited by <SCRIPT> tags, we actually use the *Counters* object that we instantiated in the object section. We can use the *ID* we specified, *Counter*, as if it were just another object available to us. We are going to create counters that count the number of pages, sessions, and times our application has started, using the scope of our various counters. The *Counters* object, although instantiated in application scope, provides a conduit to permanent storage. In fact, the counters created by the *Counters* object are stored in a text file named COUNTERS.TXT, which basically allows the *Counters* object to provide us one more level of scope that we'll call *global scope*. The counters provided will continue to exist even after an application is stopped and restarted—they don't just disappear when our *Application* object goes away—so the call to *Counter.Increment("MyAppStarts")* inside our *Application_OnStart* routine keeps a tally of just how many times our *Application* object is restarted.

In our sample, we have taken advantage of some other objects as well. Our *Application_OnStart* routine uses four variables provided with the *Application* object to keep track of application scope information. In this case, we are keeping track of the time that our application started, the number of pages accessed since our application started, the number of different user sessions that have been created since our application started, and the number of sessions that are currently active. We will keep all of this information in application scope. In our *Session_OnStart* routine, we use some global, application, and session scope counters. We increment the global number of sessions by using our Counters component, we increment the number of sessions since our application started by using an application scope variable, we increment the number of current sessions by using an application scope variable, and finally we initialize a session scope variable to keep a count of the number of pages accessed on this particular session. The *Application.Lock* and *Application.Unlock* calls are used to avoid problems when two scripts attempt to access application scope variables at the same time.

Note that you are somewhat restricted as to what you can and cannot do in a GLOBAL.ASA file. Some of the standard intrinsic objects—for example, *Request* and *Response* objects—are not always available to code being executed in GLOBAL.ASA. Also be aware that the threading model of the objects you use in the GLOBAL.ASA file should be set to *Both* so that they can be used without marshaling from multi-threaded apartments (MTA) and single-threaded apartments (STA). (We will look at component threading models in the section "Writing Your Own Components" later in this chapter.)

The scopes of our objects finally come to life when we actually access a page within our application. Here is the script for one of the pages in our application:

```
<%@ LANGUAGE="VBSCRIPT" %>
<HTML>
<HEAD>
<TITLE>My ASP Application</TITLE>
</HEAD>
<BODY>
<H1>My ASP Application</H1>
This particular session has accessed
<%
    Session("SessionPages") = Session("SessionPages") + 1
    Response.Write(Session("SessionPages"))
%>
pages.<p>
There have been
<%
    Application("TotalPagesSinceStart") = _
        Application("TotalPagesSinceStart") + 1
    Response.Write(Application("TotalPagesSinceStart"))
%>
pages accessed since the last time this application was started.<p>
The total number of pages accessed since this application was
created is <%=Counter.Increment("TotalPages")%>.<p>
</BODY>
</HTML>
```

This page tells us how many pages have been accessed in the user's current session (session scope), how many pages have been accessed since the last time the application started (application scope), and how many total pages have been accessed since the application was started for the first time (global scope). The results are shown in Figure 17.3.

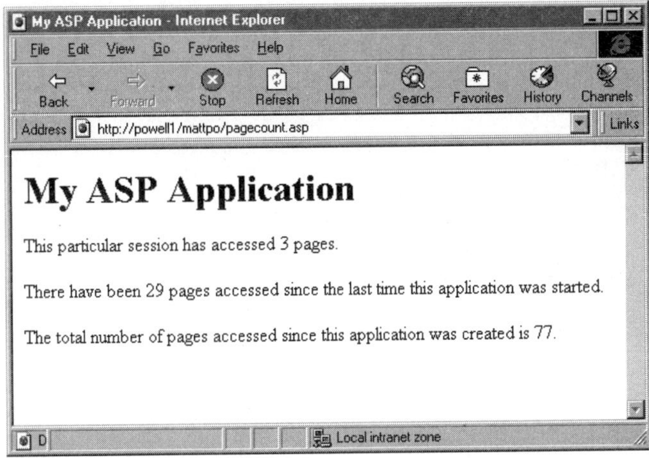

FIGURE 17.3

An ASP application that uses GLOBAL.ASA and the Counters component to demonstrate session, application, and global scope.

As you would expect, the number of pages accessed in the session is less than the number of pages accessed in the application, and that in turn is less than the number of pages accessed since the application has existed. Now let's take a look at the details of some of the objects provided for use within ASP, beginning with the intrinsic objects.

ASP Built-In Objects

We've seen a number of objects in the context of our scripting samples. For instance, we saw how the *Response* object could be used to write HTML back to the client and how the *Application* and *Session* objects provide a level of scope to our ASP application. As mentioned, these intrinsic objects are special because we do not have to instantiate them ourselves; ASP has instantiated them for us so that they are immediately ready for use. The six objects that provide some of the core functionality within ASP are shown here:

- **The *Request* object** Provides information about the HTTP request that was sent from the client's browser to the server.

- **The *Response* object** Provides the means by which we build the response to the client's request. *Response* enables us to manipulate all the characteristics of the HTTP response, from the status code, to the various response headers, to the contents of the response body.
- **The *Server* object** Provides access to global resources and utilities, such as our object creation method and URL and HTML encoding methods. It also enables us to lengthen the global script *Timeout* property.
- **The *Session* object** Provides session scope within our ASP application. The settings made with the *Session* object can be considered user-specific settings.
- **The *Application* object** Provides application-wide scope. For the most part, the *Application* object is used simply to store global application data. It also provides a means for locking the application data so that simultaneous requests do not cause reentrancy problems.
- **The *ObjectContext* object** The means used by ASP to provide transaction support. The ObjectContext object provides a means for setting transaction aborts and completes as well as for receiving notifications of abort and commit events.

The specifics of these intrinsic objects are discussed in the following sections.

The *Request* Object

When you enter a URL in your Web browser, the browser builds an HTTP request and transmits it to the host machine where the requested page lives. IIS picks up this request and hands it to ASP. ASP then provides the page with as much information as possible about the request using the *Request* object.

Request properties

The *TotalBytes* property is the total number of bytes sent in the body of the HTTP request. For most requests, this value will be *0* since HTTP requests usually do not include a body. However, if you have a form that uses the *POST* method instead of the *GET* method, the contents of the form fields will be included in the body and the *TotalBytes* property will be greater than 0.

Request collections

The *ServerVariables* collection provides a plethora of information about the client's request. This information is roughly equivalent to the information available in environment variables for Common Gateway Interface (CGI) applications or more directly through the ISAPI *GetServerVariable* callback function (discussed in Chapter 20). This collection includes information about the URL requested, the physical path of the file, the corresponding Metabase paths to the page, the client certificate, authentication credentials, and the HTTP headers as well as information about the underlying connection, such as the IP address of the client and the port being used. In fact, the *ServerVariables* collection contains in one location all the information available in all the other *Request* object properties and collections except the *Form* collection. Although you can get all this information from the *ServerVariables* collection, it is sometimes packaged more nicely in the other collections.

The *QueryString* collection takes the raw string you obtain from *Request.ServerVariables("QUERY_STRING")* and parses the different elements into variable names and values. This breakdown is especially helpful if you have used a form to transmit a number of variables to your page that uses the *GET* method. For instance, if you used a text input in your form named *Greeting* and a check box input named *Day*, you might have the query string *Greeting=Hello%2C+World%21&Day=Sunday*. You can use the *QueryString* collection to retrieve the specific values you're after. For example, *Request.QueryString("Greeting")* will return the string *Hello, World!* Notice that the collection not only pulls out the appropriate value from the list, but it also decodes the URL-encoded value from the query string. In this case, the *%2C*, *+*, and *%21* characters are appropriately converted to a comma, a space, and an exclamation point. Be aware that some forms will return multiple variables with the same name. For instance, you might have several check box inputs, all named Day, that could legitimately be checked by the user. In this case, you'll get the query string *Day=Sunday&Day=Saturday*. *Request.QueryString("Day").Count* will tell you the total number of *Day* variables.(In our example, it will return 2.) You can then use an index to retrieve the different values—here*Request.QueryString("Day")(1)* is *Sunday* and *Request.QueryString("Day")(2)* is *Saturday*.

The *Form* collection is similar to the *QueryString* collection; the only difference is in how the data is passed from the client to the server. If a form in an HTML page uses the *GET* method, variables will be passed in the URL simply by placing a *?* at the end of the URL and then URL encoding the parameters after the question mark. In that case, you will need to use the *QueryString* collection to retrieve the data. If the HTML form uses a *POST* method, the variables will be passed in the body of the HTTP request, which can be a benefit for two reasons. First, if you have a lot of data to pass, you might run into limits on the size of the URL that your form is building if you use the *GET* method. Second, post data is not usually cached on the client. Therefore, if you specify the URL used earlier for a *POST* method request, it will send the request to the server for processing instead of just pulling the page out of the client's local cache. The *GET* method requests that put the parameters in the URL will attempt to simply display a locally cached copy instead of sending a request to the server to execute. So if your form uses the *POST* method, you will need to use the *Form* collection to retrieve your variable values.

The *Cookies* collection is very similar in its implementation to the *QueryString* and *Form* collections. We discuss HTTP cookies in detail in Chapter 23, but suffice it to say that cookies are a way to maintain state between HTTP requests. As it happens, a server can set name and value pairs that will be returned in subsequent requests in the HTTP cookie header. Thus, we can retrieve the value of a cookie named *Greetings* using the *Cookies* collection like this: *Request.Cookies("Greetings")*. A single cookie value can have several subvalues, or *keys*. For instance, the value *Global=Hello%2C+World%21&Individual=Hi.* indicates that our *Greetings* cookie has a key *Global* whose value is *Hello, World!* and a second key, named *Individual*, whose value is *Hi*. To retrieve the values of the keys within our cookie, we add the key name to the end of our earlier syntax, so *Request.Cookies("Greetings")("Global")* returns *Hello, World!* Notice again that the *Request* object decodes the URL-encoded string. Because many cookies will not include keys, you can use the *HasKeys* attribute to check whether a cookie has any keys. Note that ASP requires the use of HTTP cookies to maintain session scope. These cookies are dynamically generated and encoded so that they do not make much sense to anyone but ASP. Luckily, ASP session cookies are stripped out of the *Cookies* collection before the collection is provided to your ASP page.

The *ClientCertificate* collection is provided only for sessions that are created over secure links using SSL or Private Communication Technology (PCT) and that have been configured to require client certificates. (See Chapter 13 for details on configuration options for secure sessions.) The *ClientCertificate* collection consists of the *Subject*, *Issuer*, *ValidFrom*, *ValidUntil*, *SerialNumber*, *Certificate*, and *Flags* properties. (The different fields in a certificate are discussed in Chapter 13.) As mentioned, you can also retrieve this information, as well as some other information, from the *ServerVariables* collection, but it is not presented quite as nicely there. For instance, you can get the *Issuer* string by using *Request.ClientCertificate("Issuer")*; this string might look something like *C=US, O=Certificates-R-Us, OU=Cert Issuer Unit, L=Akron, S=OH*. You might recognize this format as following standard X.500 directory naming conventions. If you want to get just the organization name, add an *O* subfield to the name like this: *Request.ClientCertificate("IssuerO")*. This method will return the string *Certificates-R-Us*.

Request methods

The only method provided by the *Request* object is the *BinaryRead* method. This method is used to directly access the data in the body of the HTTP request. Since an HTTP request that uses the *POST* method can contain any sort of data (not just form data), it is important that we have a way of getting at the data being sent. Keep in mind that the *BinaryRead* method immediately invalidates access to the *Form* collection, and accessing the *Form* collection immediately invalidates the use of *BinaryRead*. The following code uses the *BinaryRead* method, which attempts to read 100 bytes of raw data:

```
ReadBytes = 100
BinArray = Request.BinaryRead(ReadBytes)
```

When the *BinaryRead* call returns, the variable *ReadBytes* will contain the actual amount of data in bytes read, which will be *100* or less. *BinArray* will contain the actual data. If you want to read all of the data at once, set *ReadBytes* to *Request.TotalBytes* (and be ready to receive a lot of data).

The *Response* Object

The *Response* object provides access to the HTTP response that our ASP page is building to send back to the client. This response includes the HTML that we send back as well the HTTP headers that will precede the HTML. The *Response* object also provides optional buffering functionality.

Response properties

The *Buffer* property indicates whether the output we are generating is immediately sent to the client or whether we should hold on to the data until ASP has finished processing our entire page. By default, buffering is turned off, so we send data to the client as soon as any portion of our script being executed generates output. If we turn buffering on, we can do things like set our HTTP headers even after we have composed some of the body of our request. (If buffering had been turned off, the headers would have already been sent and this would create an error in our script.) Since this property determines how the script is handled for the entire page, if you are going to turn buffering on, you should set the *Buffer* property in the first line of your script, like this: *Response.Buffer=TRUE.*

The *IsClientConnected* property is a read-only property that indicates whether the underlying TCP connection is still available. During a lengthy script, the client might have stopped the downloading of your response, which would break the connection. It would be nice to check whether the client is still connected before we start some lengthy processing so that if necessary we could quit our script quickly and avoid using our server's processor for no reason.

The *Status* property is where we can set the HTTP status code that is returned to the browser. By default, the "200 OK" status is sent, but we could send any other status property we want. (See Chapter 23 for a list of HTTP status codes.) For instance, if we want to redirect the client to a different URL, we could use *Response.Status = "302 Object Moved".*

The remaining properties of the *Response* object allow us to set specific HTTP headers in a straightforward fashion. The *CacheControl* property can be used to set the HTTP Cache-Control header to *Private* or *Public*. By default, this header is set to *Private*, but you can have your page set it to *Public* so that proxies can share the cached page with other users.

The *ContentType* property sets the HTTP Content-Type header to the appropriate Multipurpose Internet Mail Extensions (MIME) type. The default setting is *text/html,* but you can return any type of data using the *Response.BinaryWrite* method (which we will discuss shortly). You should thus set the content type to the corresponding MIME type for the data you are returning so that the browser knows how to handle the data. The *Charset* property adds the *charset* parameter to the HTTP Content-Type header; the default *charset* is *ISO-8859-1*. The following code sends the HTTP header *Content-Type:text/text; charset=ISO-8859-4*:

```
Response.ContentType = "text/text"
Response.Charset = "ISO-8859-4"
```

The *Expires* and *ExpiresAbsolute* properties set the HTTP Expires header. The Expires header takes a date and time in HTTP time format, specified in GMT time. The *Expires* property can be used to specify the number of minutes from the current time after which the data will expire. The *Response* object will then perform the conversion to the proper time format for you. Note that *Response.Expires =0* is a valid use of the *Expires* property and will basically prevent the client from caching the response. The *ExpiresAbsolute* property simply allows you to specify a specific date and time for the expiration. Again, the *Response* object will convert this value to the proper HTTP time format.

The *PICS* property sets the HTTP PICS-Label header. (PICS stands for the Platform for Internet Content Selection.) The PICS-Label header is usually used to rate the content of the returned information to prevent children from being exposed to explicit material. The Recreational Software Advisory Council (RSAC) has created a rating system for the Internet called RSACi. The format of an RSACi rating PICS label looks like this:

```
(PICS-1.0 "http://www.rsac.org/ratingsv01.html" l by <email> on
<date/time> exp <date/time> r (v <violence rating> s <sex rating>
n <nudity rating> l <language rating>))
```

The *<email>* placeholder is the name of the individual who rated this site. The various rating values range from 0 through 4 and are defined at the specified URL at the RSAC site. If we wanted to rate the content of our ASP page so that it would not be blocked out to children, we could use the following code:

```
PicsLabel = "(PICS-1.0 " & chr(34)
PicsLabel = PicsLabel & "http://www.rsac.org/ratingv01.html"
PicsLabel = PicsLabel & chr(34)&" l by "& chr(34)
PicsLabel = PicsLabel & "mattpo@microsoft.com"
PicsLabel = PicsLabel & chr(34)&" on " & chr(34)
PicsLabel = PicsLabel & "1997.10.24T08:15-0500"
```

```
PicsLabel = PicsLabel & chr(34)&" exp " & chr(34)
PicsLabel = PicsLabel & "1999.12.31T23:59-0000"
PicsLabel = PicsLabel & chr(34) & " r (v 0 s 0 n 0 l 0))"
Response.PICS(PicsLabel)
```

NOTE

Because the PICS time format requires quotation marks, we must insert chr(34) *codes into our labels.*

Response collections

The *Reponse* object contains only one collection: *Cookies*. This *Cookies* collection is similar to the *Cookies* collection in the *Request* object except that here we are setting cookies instead of receiving them. The information will be sent in the HTTP Set-Cookie header and will be returned to us in future requests. As with the *Cookies* collection in the *Request* object, we have access to cookie values and keys with the *Response* object. But now we have a number of additional attributes available. The *Expires* attribute sets the date after which a cookie should no longer be sent. If this attribute is not set, the default value of *0* is assumed, indicating that the cookie is not written to the client's hard disk. This means that as soon as the current browser process ends, the cookie will stop being sent. The *Domain* attribute allows the cookie to be sent to other servers on the same domain. The *Path* attribute specifies the virtual path to which a cookie should be sent, and the *Secure* attribute indicates that the cookie should be sent only over a secure connection. You can set these attributes simply by appending them to the specific cookie reference. For instance, *Response.Cookies("Greeting").Expires = "1/1/2000"* indicates that the cookie will no longer be sent after January 1, 2000.

Response methods

The *AddHeader* method provides a means for adding specific HTTP headers not available using the properties we've discussed up to now. For instance, you could add your own proprietary header *Foo: Bar* by using the following syntax:

```
Response.AddHeader "Foo", "Bar"
```

The *Redirect* method provides an easy means for returning an HTTP redirect response. It automatically sets the HTTP status to "302 Object Moved" and fills in the HTTP Location header with the specified URL. For example, to redirect to a page named NewLocation.htm, you would use the following code:

```
Response.Redirect "NewLocation.htm"
```

The *Write* and *BinaryWrite* methods provide the means for writing data to the body of the HTTP response. The *Write* method writes a string (usually in HTML format) back to the client. The *BinaryWrite* method writes nontext data back to the client.

The *End* method causes the script to stop executing immediately. If the *Buffer* property has been set to *TRUE*, any buffered data already generated will be sent to the client. If the data is not buffered, the termination of the script processing simply means that no more data will be sent to the client. If you don't want to send buffered data when you call the *End* method, you should use the *Clear* method (discussed next) immediately before calling the *End* method.

The *Clear* and *Flush* methods provide a means for manipulating the buffered response data assuming that buffering has been turned on using the *Buffer* property. The *Clear* method clears all data generated to that point, and the *Flush* method simply sends any buffered data immediately to the client. Once *Flush* has been called, you usually will not be able to manipulate any of the HTTP headers in subsequent script.

The *AppendToLog* method allows an ASP page to add an extra text string to the end of the IIS log record for the particular request, which means that an application can add its own proprietary information to the IIS log files. For instance, to monitor the value of the *UserID* cookie, you could add the following code to your ASP page:

```
Response.AppendToLog Request.Cookies("UserID")
```

The *Server* Object

The *Server* object provides a set of frequently needed utilities and access to global functionalities. Unlike the other intrinsic objects, it does not really encompass any particular aspect of IIS applications or HTTP transactions.

Server properties

The only property provided by the *Server* object is *ScriptTimeout,* which basically provides a page with the means for extending the default script timeout. For instance, for a lengthy script you might want to allow your page more time than the default 90 seconds to execute. Of course, you should use this property with caution because it might result in your clients twiddling their thumbs, not knowing whether a script is ever going to finish executing.

Server methods

The *MapPath* method is used to convert virtual paths on your Web server to the corresponding physical path. Although you can access this information for a specific ASP page by using the *Request.ServerVariables("PATH_TRANSLATED")* call, you can use the *MapPath* method to retrieve the physical location for any path you specify. *MapPath* will also convert relative paths, although it does not support the . or .. syntax. Any paths that do not start with a leading slash are considered relative paths.

The *HTMLEncode* and *URLEncode* methods provide a means for converting strings to appropriately encoded formats. URL encoding is often required when you are building a list of parameters to be passed as the query string for a URL. HTML encoding can be used to quickly run through some text and replace the less than and greater than symbols with their HTML-encoded equivalents so that they will be displayed in a page (instead of being interpreted as HTML tag delimiters).

The *CreateObject* method is the usual means by which nonintrinsic objects are instantiated. *CreateObject* takes the ProgID of the object as its parameter. These nonintrinsic objects must support Automation to get any use from them within our script. We will look at quite a few objects later in this chapter that we can take advantage of using the *CreateObject* method.

The *Session* Object

The *Session* object embodies the session scope capabilities discussed earlier. Its main capability is probably to provide a means for storing session scope variables—that is, variables that are available per user session.

Session properties

The *LCID* and *CodePage* properties enable us to set and retrieve the locale identifier and system codepage for a particular user, which lets us generate internationalized content using the proper character sets, abbreviations, and time and money formats.

The *SessionID* property is the dynamically assigned session identifier that ASP uses to track a session. It can potentially be used by your ASP application as an index value for a list of records, but be aware that *SessionID* values can be reused if the server is stopped and restarted. If you are using any persistent data, you should probably come up with your own indexing scheme.

The *Timeout* property allows an ASP application to set the length of time an ASP session will be allowed to stay idle before being terminated. *Timeout* enables a page to extend or reduce the default session timeout of 20 minutes.

Session collections

The *Contents* collection is the means by which we provide session scope variables. When we create a session variable by setting *Session("MyVariable")=320*, we are adding an item to the *Contents* collection, even though we haven't specifically indicated it. The *Contents* collection can contain any sort of variable, including objects, and so provides another means for creating session scope objects in addition to using the GLOBAL.ASA file.

The *StaticObjects* collection is similar to the *Contents* collection except that it contains only those objects that were instantiated using the <OBJECTS RUNAT= Server…> tags. These kinds of objects are considered *static* because they are automatically instantiated for the session. Objects instantiated using the *Server.CreateObject* method are instantiated only when the actual call is made, and they can be killed by resetting their *Contents* entry. Static objects are around for the length of the session.

Session methods

Abandon is the only method supported by the *Session* object. The *Abandon* method basically destroys the *Session* object, which means that all the variables with session scope will be destroyed. If the client accesses other pages in the same application after *Abandon* was called, a new session will be invoked. Usually, *Abandon* is used to free up server resources when you know the user will not be returning. Note that even if *Abandon* is called, the session will not be deleted until the current page has finished executing.

Session events

Earlier in this chapter, in the section "GLOBAL.ASA," we discussed the *Session_OnStart* and *Session_OnEnd* startup and shutdown routines that can be used in the GLOBAL.ASA file. These callbacks are actually events triggered by the *Session* object itself; they enable an application to do some initialization and cleanup tasks for session scope entities.

The *Application* Object

The *Application* object provides a means for creating global application variables that can be shared among all users of our ASP application. These variables are said to have application scope, and they exist for as long as our application is loaded. Applications can be unloaded manually through the Management Console, but they are also unloaded when IIS is shut down so that they are not persisted forever.

Application collections

As with the *Session* object, the main benefit of the *Application* object is to provide a *Contents* collection for holding application scope variables. Similarly, the *StaticObjects* collection is also available for the objects created using the <OBJECT> tag with application scope, enabling you to create COM objects in your ASP pages that can then be reused for other requests for as long as your application is running.

Application methods

The *Lock* and *Unlock* methods are required to synchronize potentially simultaneous access to the variables in the *Application* object's *Contents* collection. Since multiple users could certainly access these global variables at the same time, it is important that manipulation of the variables by other users can be locked out while our page is using their values. Therefore, you will often see *Lock*/*Unlock* calls surrounding access to application scope variables, as shown in the following code:

```
Application.Lock
Application("GlobalIndex") = Application("GlobalIndex") + 1
Application.Unlock
```

Keep in mind that the locks are for the entire collection of application scope variables, so a lock on any particular variable freezes access for all other variables. This technique might not be the best means for synchronizing access for heavily stressed servers.

Application events

The *Application_OnStart* and *Application_OnEnd* routines that an ASP application writer can implement in the GLOBAL.ASA are obviously called when an application loads and when it unloads. As with the corresponding *Session* object routines, the *Application* object startup and shutdown routines can be used to perform any initialization and cleanup except these routines are performed at application scope.

The *ObjectContext* Object

The *ObjectContext* object is used by ASP to provide transactional capabilities for database commits, aborts, and rollbacks. *ObjectContext* provides methods for aborting and completing transactions, as well as events for getting notifications when other components have completed their transactional tasks or have triggered an abort. We will discuss the *ObjectContext* object in detail in Chapter 18.

Installable Components for ASP

ASP lets you utilize any COM object that supports Automation. The code modules that serve up these objects are typically called *components*. When you install IIS, many components intended to be used with ASP are automatically installed. A number of these components provide Web server–specific functionality; others provide more generic functionality. We'll look at a number of these components in the following sections, beginning with the Ad Rotator component.

The Ad Rotator Component

The Ad Rotator component enables you to display new advertisements on an ASP page each time the page is accessed. This component provides a convenient way for Web authors to earn money for their pages by charging others to display their ads. The Ad Rotator component provides the standard capabilities you would want for an advertising space, such as the ability to rotate the ad images displayed on a page, the ability to track the number of times a particular advertisement was displayed, and the ability to track the number of times clients clicked on an ad.

The Ad Rotator component works by reading a file, called the Ad Rotator schedule file, that includes information about the location of the image files to be displayed as well as the various attributes of each image. Here's a look at an Ad Rotator schedule file:

```
REDIRECT /mattpo/hitcount.asp
WIDTH 440
HEIGHT 60
BORDER 0
*
/adimages/trivets.jpg
http://www.TrivetsRUs.com
Click here to check out Trivets-R-Us!
2
/adimages/GrassClippings.jpg
http://www.GrassClippingsRUs.com
For the best in Grass Clippings, click here!
3
/adimages/slugad32.jpg
http://www.SlugsRUs.com
Slime with the best! Slugs-R-Us!
5
```

The first four lines of this code contain the global settings for the ad. The *REDIRECT* line indicates the URL that the ad will be a hotlink to—this is not the URL for the specific ad itself but will instead be an intermediate page that will be called so that you can track the number of times the ad was clicked. This *REDIRECT* URL will be called with a query string that contains two parameters: the URL of the particular ad's home page, and the URL of the image file. We will look at how this works later, when we talk about the redirection file. The remaining three lines above the asterisk simply describe how the ads are displayed. The width is set to 440 pixels, and the height is set to 60 pixels. In this example, we have a border with a width of *0*.

The lines following the asterisk describe the specifics for each ad in four-line increments. Here we have twelve lines following the asterisk, describing three ads. Each ad description contains the URL for the image file, the home page URL for the ad, the alternative text for the image, and a weight value that indicates how often this page will be displayed compared to the others. Ultimately, the component will simply insert HTML code that will embed an image in the document with the corresponding properties. The preceding schedule file will build the following HTML for the second of our sample ads:

```
<A HREF="/mattpo/hitcount.asp?
    url=/GrassClippingsRUs.asp&
    image=/adimages/GrassClippings.jpg" >
    <IMG SRC="/adimages/GrassClippings.jpg"
        ALT="For the best in Grass Clippings, click here!"
        WIDTH=440
        HEIGHT=60
        BORDER=0>
</A>
```

The image is a hotlink to our redirect page, which, has two values set in the query string, *url=/GrassClippingsRUs.asp* and *image=/adimages/GrassClippings.jpg*. The image itself is given the global attributes *WIDTH*, *HEIGHT*, and *BORDER*, and the *ALT* attribute for the image is set to the third line of the description for this advertisement in the schedule file. To determine how often an ad will be displayed, sum the weight values for all the ads in the schedule file. In our case, the total is *10*. The Grass Clippings ad has a weight of *3*, which means that it will be displayed three times for every ten times the Ad Rotator component is called.

The redirection file is a simple ASP page that does two things: it increments a counter for the URL reference associated with the ad, and it redirects the user to that same reference. By incrementing the counter, we can keep track of how many times users clicked on the ad and then bill the advertiser accordingly. Incrementing the counter and redirecting the user is performed using the following two lines of ASP script:

```
Counter.Increment(Request.QueryString("url"))
Response.Redirect(Request.QueryString("url"))
```

So now let's look at how the Ad Rotator component is used in a page. First we have to instantiate the *AdRotator* object using the *Server.CreateObject* method. The *PROGID* attribute for the Ad Rotator component is *MSWC.AdRotator*. Once we have an instance of the *AdRotator* object, we call the *GetAdvertisement* method to actually insert the HTML that we looked at earlier. The complete code looks like this:

```
<% Set MyAd = Server.CreateObject("MSWC.AdRotator")%>
<%= MyAd.GetAdvertisement("ScheduleFile.Txt") %>
```

Ad Rotator properties

The Ad Rotator component enables you to control some of the ad characteristics directly through the object properties to override the settings in the schedule file. For instance, the *Border* property lets you set the width of the border to a value different from the schedule file's border setting. The *Clickable* property lets you turn off the hotlink associated with the advertisement so that only the image is displayed. The *TargetFrame* property lets specify the name of the frame in which you want the ad to be displayed.

Ad Rotator methods

The only method supported by the Ad Rotator component is the *GetAdvertisement* method, which takes a single parameter: the name of the Ad Rotator schedule file. The path to the file is a relative path from the current virtual directory. Physical paths are not allowed.

The Browser Capabilities Component

The Browser Capabilities component enables you to identify the capabilities of certain browsers. It is able to do this because of the HTTP User-Agent header that each version of a browser is supposed to send when making a request. The Browser Capabilities component maps the User-Agent to a browser that is described in the file named BROWSCAP.INI. The browser capabilities can then be identified through the properties of the *BrowserType* object. For instance, the following code uses the *ActiveXControls* property to write text back to users telling them whether their browsers support ActiveX Controls:

```
Set BrowseCap = Server.CreateObject("MSWC.BrowserType")
if BrowseCap.ActiveXControls = TRUE then
    Response.Write("Your browser supports ActiveX Controls.")
else
    Response.Write("Your browser does not support ActiveX Controls.")
end if
```

A BROWSCAP.INI file is provided for you by default in the system32\inetsrv directory. This file already contains information for versions of Microsoft Internet Explorer, Netscape Navigator, a version of Oracle's browser, and a default browser. You can modify this file yourself by adding your own properties or updating the file based on a newly released version of a browser.

Some of the properties that the Browser Capabilities component can identify are: *ActiveXControls, backgroundsounds, beta, browser, cdf, cookies, frames, Javaapplets, javascript, platform, tables, vbscript, version.* Check out the documentation for the Browser Capabilities component and the BROWSCAP.INI for more information.

Be aware that the identified capabilities are simply static for the available versions of the browsers. If, for example, you have turned off cookies and ActiveX Controls as part of your Internet Explorer 4.0 configuration, the Browser Capabilities component will simply report that Internet Explorer 4.0 supports cookies and ActiveX Controls.

ActiveX Data Objects

One of the most common tasks performed from a server application is accessing a server-side database. ActiveX Data Objects (ADO) are available for use from ASP and can be used to access any ODBC-compliant database, including Microsoft SQL Server, Microsoft Access, Oracle, and others. Although designed specifically for use from ASP, ADO can also be used in other areas, such as from a Visual Basic application or even from an application written in C++. We will discuss data access in Chapter 18, along with the transactional capabilities IIS provides.

The Content Linking Component

The Content Linking component provides the means for creating a table of contents for a series of pages. The Content Linking component also makes it easy for pages to include previous and next links. Of course, you can do all this in straight HTML, but with the Content Linking component you can take a series of pages that do not have any navigation capability in them and insert all the navigation code by adding only a single include file. Let's take a look at how this is done.

To use the Content Linking component, we need to create a Content Linking List file. The Content Linking List file contains information for all the pages we want to link. This file is simply a text file in which each line represents a page. Each line can have as many as three parts (the last part being optional); tabs separate the different parts. The format is shown here:

```
<PageURL>    <Page Description>    <Comment>
```

PageURL is the URL of each page, *Page Description* is a short description of that page, and *Comment* is additional text used for commenting purposes, but is not processed. The order of the lines in the list file determines the order of the different pages in our table of contents. A sample list file is shown below; it doesn't happen to contain any comments:

```
ChooseHammer.asp      Choosing a Hammer
PickingNails.asp      Picking the Right Nail
Positioning.asp       Positioning the Picture
DrivingNail.asp       Driving the Nail
HangingPicture.asp    Hanging the Picture
```

We saved this file as PICTURE.TXT, which we can now use in our ASP page. The following ASP page builds a table of contents for our list of pages:

```
<%@ LANGUAGE="VBSCRIPT" %>
<HTML>
<HEAD>
<TITLE>Table of Contents</TITLE>
</HEAD>
<BODY>
<H1> Table of Contents </H1>
<% Set CL = Server.CreateObject("MSWC.NextLink") %>
Total Parts: <%=CL.GetListCount("picture.txt")%> <p>
<% For i = 1 to CL.GetListCount("picture.txt") %>
    Part <%=i%>: <a href=<%=CL.GetNthURL("picture.txt", i)%> >
    <%=CL.GetNthDescription("picture.txt", i) %> </a><br>
<% Next %>
<!--#include file="foot.txt"-->
</BODY>
</HTML>
```

We open our *ContentLinking* object using *Server.CreateObject* and specifying the *PROGID* attribute as *MSWC.NextLink*. Next we display the number of different parts using the *GetListCount* method. Then we loop through each entry, display its description, and then make the description a hotlink to the actual URL. To do this, we use the *GetNthDescription* and *GetNthURL* methods.

In this table of contents, we didn't actually have any knowledge of the pages themselves. The Content Linking component provides a generic means for making a table of contents as long as a list file and the actual content pages are provided, which could be very useful, particularly for a site in which the contents change regularly.

Notice at the end of our table of contents that we have included a file named FOOT.TXT. The one requirement we have for the content files within our list is that they include this same line at their end. FOOT.TXT uses the Content Linking component to create previous and next links as well as a link back to the table of contents. Notice that you can create the previous and next links using the same code for all the pages in our list. The code for FOOT.TXT looks like this:

```
<% Set CL = Server.CreateObject("MSWC.NextLink")%>
<hr>
<center>
<a href=<%=CL.GetPreviousURL("picture.txt")%>> &lt;&lt;Prev </a> -
<a href=<%=CL.GetNextURL("picture.txt")%>> Next&gt;&gt;</a><p>
<a href=contents.asp>Table of Contents</a>
```

We create the previous and next links using the *GetPreviousURL* and *GetNextURL* methods of the *NextLink* object. Again, note that this code has no knowledge of the actual files in our list. As long as we are provided with the list file, PICTURES.TXT, this same code will work for any list of files. The result of our FOOT.TXT is that our content pages have a functioning footer, as shown in Figure 17.4. Note that calling *GetPreviousURL* on the first page in the list will return a URL to the last page. Similarly, calling *GetNextURL* on the last page will return a URL to the first page. Depending on your application, you might not want this kind of circular link. If not, you should add additional code that uses the *GetListIndex* method to determine whether the current page is the first or last page in the list and handle the links accordingly.

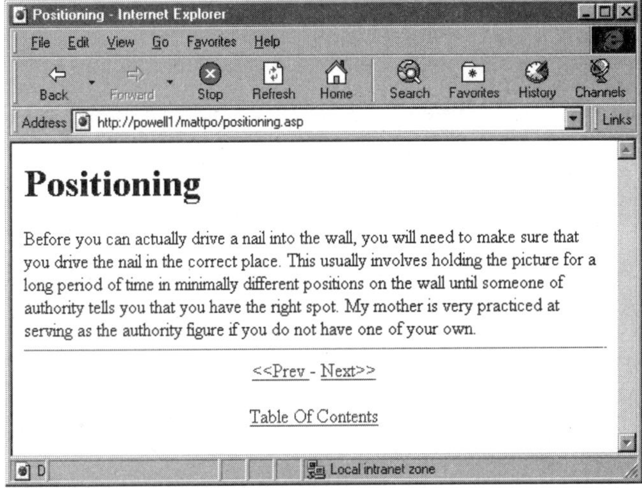

FIGURE 17.4

A sample page showing the footer created using the Content Linking component.

Content Linking methods

The Content Linking component provides a number of methods, most of which are used to access the various entries in the list file by different means. Since there are only two function elements for each entry, the methods come in pairs, with one retrieving the URL for the entry and the second retrieving the description.

The *GetNthURL* and *GetNthDescription* methods get the corresponding entry's elements. These methods require not only the list filename, but they also take an index as one of their parameters. Using these methods, we can walk through the entire list just as we did when we created our table of contents.

The *GetNextURL*, *GetNextDescription*, *GetPreviousURL*, and *GetPreviousDescription* methods get the entry information relative to the current page. The Content Linking component finds the entry for the current page and then determines what the next and previous entries are for that particular page. We use this information to create our previous and next links in our footer. The only parameter any of these methods use is the name of the list file.

The *GetListCount* method simply returns the number of entries in the specified list file, and the *GetListIndex* method can be used to determine the index of the current page in the list file.

The Collaboration Data Objects for NTS

The Collaboration Data Objects for Microsoft Windows NT Server, also known as the CDO for NTS , exposes messaging objects that enable your ASP page to send Internet mail. It will also allow your ASP page to read mail delivered to your server. The CDO for NTS requires the use of the SMTP service and is explained in depth in Chapter 11.

The Tools Component

The Tools component, which is available with the IIS Resource Kit, provides some standard functionality that isn't easily available through standard scripting. In particular, its *FileExists* method provides an easy way to determine whether files exist on the Web server. *FileExists* looks at the Web virtual directories instead of the physical file locations. The other function available on IIS is the *Random* method, which simply provides a random number between –32,768 and +32,767. The Tools component is also how some of the specific features for Personal Web Server and Personal Web Server for Macintosh are implemented.

The Counters Component

The Counters component, available with the IIS Resource Kit, was designed to provide a means for maintaining global counters. We looked at the Counters component in the section "GLOBAL.ASA" earlier in this chapter. The Counters component works exceptionally well for keeping track of page hit counts, but you can also use it to keep any global count information you want. The Counters component stores its data in a file, COUNTERS.TXT, which you will find by default in the system32\inetsrv directory.

Counters methods

Four methods are available with the Counters component: *Get*, *Set*, *Increment*, and *Remove*. All these methods are fairly self-explanatory. If you're wondering where the *Create* method is, it doesn't exist. To create a counter for the first time, you simply call the *Set* method using a counter name that has not yet been used.

Other Components Available from ASP

You can call any COM object that supports Automation from an ASP page, but a few additional objects are provided with some of the other services installed with the Microsoft Windows NT 4.0 Option Pack. These objects are discussed in the following sections.

Index Server Query and Utility Objects

Microsoft Index Server 2.0 now provides Automation objects for performing queries instead of the HTM/IDQ/HTX technique used in the past. These objects enable you to build query forms and responses with all the power that ASP provides for versatility and customization. Obviously, you can use the default pages that Index Server provides for creating queries, but you can also add querying capabilities from your own pages. Details on the use of these objects are provided in Chapter 7.

Certificate Server Request, Config, and Admin Objects

Certificate Server, which provides certificates for SSL communication, has a set of objects that enable you to take advantage of all of Certificate Server services. These objects can be used from ASP pages, and in fact that is how all the Web administration pages for Certificate Server are provided. You can provide access to Certificate Server through your own pages, or you can enhance the capabilities of the current Certificate Server pages. The Certificate Server components are described in Chapter 14.

IIS Admin Objects

Internet Information Server 4.0 provides objects for controlling the configuration options of IIS. The IIS Admin Objects provide an easy means for setting all the various configuration options that are stored in the Metabase. You can use the Admin Objects to do everything, including setting up access permissions, creating a new virtual directory, setting up an application, restarting a server, and setting any of the myriad of different configuration options possible from the Internet Service Manager. In fact, the HTML version of the Internet Service Manager is just a series of ASP pages that use the Admin Objects to control the server configuration. Be aware that appropriate permissions are required to do much of this kind of configuration, so your ASP pages would need to be set up with an appropriate authentication scheme. Details on using the Admin Objects can be found in Chapter 5.

Posting Acceptor

The Posting Acceptor is a part of Microsoft Site Server Express, which is included in the Windows NT 4.0 Option Pack. The Posting Acceptor actually has two parts: one that sits on the client to provide a means for specifying a local file on the client for uploading to the server, and one that sits on the server to accept the file uploaded to it and place the file in the appropriate location on the server. The Posting Acceptor can be used to allow clients to upload their own HTML or ASP files or to provide business sites with a means for uploading various reports and spreadsheets. Site Server provides the server component through an ISAPI extension that receives the input file sent to the server using the RFC 1867 specification for uploading data. On the client side, you can use Netscape's built-in file upload capability; for clients such as Internet Explorer that support ActiveX Controls, you can use the File Upload Control provided with Site Server. The advantage of the File Upload Control is that you can simply drag and drop files onto it or you can double-click on it to display the standard Open dialog box for finding the appropriate file to upload.

The File Upload Control is a client-side component and so isn't actually used like an ASP component. We use ASP to build the file upload pages on our server because of ASP's ability to detect the type of client and act accordingly if we need to provide client-side script for activating the File Upload Control. ASP can also build the appropriate form for Netscape's HTML upload. Plus the ASP page can adjust the various parameters for upload by setting locations based on the connected user, so you won't get people trying to upload files to places they have no rights to upload to. The following sample page provided with Site Server shows how ASP code is used to build the appropriate options for the File Upload Control. Notice that this page even provides a path on your server where the client can install the File Upload Control. This file, named UPLOADX.ASP, is copied to your scripts virtual directory by default.

```
<% Response.Buffer = TRUE %>
<% if (Len(Request.ServerVariables("LOGON_USER")) = 0 ) then %>
    <% Response.Status = "401 Unauthorized" %>
    <B>Error: Access is denied.</B><P>
<% end if %>
<HTML>
<HEAD>
<TITLE>File Upload Control</TITLE>
</HEAD>

<BODY LEFTMARGIN=20 TOPMARGIN=20 BGCOLOR=#FFFFFF
    TEXT=#000000 LINK=#FF0066 VLINK=#330099
    ALINK=#000000 language="VBS" onload="InitializeControl">

<FONT FACE="ARIAL" SIZE=2>
```

```
<CENTER>
<P><FONT SIZE=5><B>Welcome</B></FONT>
</CENTER>

<H3>File Upload</H3>
<P>
You can upload your HTML content using this control.
<OBJECT
    classid="clsid:886E7BF0-C867-11CF-B1AE-00AA00A3F2C3"
    id=IFlUpl1
    width=100
    height=100
    align=textmiddle
    color=blue
    codebase=
        http://<%= Request.ServerVariables("SERVER_NAME") %>
        /FlUpl.cab#Version=6,1,10,0
>
</OBJECT>
You may drag and drop files onto this. Or double-click on
it to get an FileOpen dialog box.

<SCRIPT LANGUAGE="VBS">

Sub InitializeControl
    IFlUpl1.CreateTempBinding
        "http://<%= Request.ServerVariables("SERVER_NAME") %>
        /users/<%= Request.ServerVariables("LOGON_USER") %>",
        "{8B14B770-748C-11D0-A309-00C04FD7CFC5}"
End Sub

</SCRIPT>

</FONT>

</BODY>
</HTML>
```

Writing Your Own Components

As mentioned, the term "object" is greatly overused. And it doesn't help matters when, even within Microsoft's COM framework, we start referring to entities as objects and, in the same breath, as controls or components. Add to this a variety of object descriptors such as ActiveX, OLE, COM, COM+, Doc, Activation, and Automation, and it's probably safe to say that everyone is confused.

From our ASP perspective, we will focus here on one specific kind of object: COM objects that support Automation, currently referred to as an ActiveX control. Our scripting paradigm, although very flexible in many ways, is limited in the sorts of OLE functionality it can support. Therefore, it supports only the use of ActiveX controls. Without going too far into a description of COM, let's take a look at what specifically makes up an ActiveX control.

As with any COM object, an ActiveX control is required to support the IUnknown interface. In the case of server scripting, it doesn't make sense for our component to have any sort of user interface through a window or form, so none of the interfaces required for user interface concepts such as in-place activation are required. Instead, we need a nice generic interface named IDispatch. What's nice about IDispatch is that it allows an application to access the object's functions in a way that doesn't require the caller to know anything about the format of the functions beforehand. For instance, if you had an application that needed to use an object through the IFoo interface, your application would basically have to be linked with the definitions of the IFoo interface when it was built. For a single interface, this requirement isn't a big deal, but what if we need to access a myriad of different objects with different interfaces, and perhaps some with interfaces that haven't been developed yet? This situation is typical for scripting engines that will want to be able to invoke any object but certainly won't know the specific interfaces when the scripting engine is built.

IDispatch is a clever interface in that it allows an application to access the exposed functions via the names of the functions instead of requiring the application to know the interface ID. For scripting applications, this means we can use an easy-to-remember text string to reference a function instead of having to link a bunch of globally unique identifiers (GUIDs). This capability is critical to a scripting engine because it doesn't have any prior knowledge of the object. The IDispatch interface of the object exports a function named GetIDsOfNames that allows a scripting engine to get identifiers for the named properties or methods, and then the IDispatch::Invoke function provides a generic means for calling the methods or getting/setting the properties. Last is the concept of an object providing a *sink*. The idea behind a sink is that the user of an object can provide an interface for the object to call when certain events take place, which is how Visual Basic and scripting languages can provide event notifications.

Glossary

sink *A mechanism whereby a COM object can communicate with its client. This communication is sometimes called "firing an event" and is how various event notifications, such as the* Application_OnStart *event, are implemented. The interface that the COM object uses to communicate with the client is defined by the COM object itself, but implemented by the client with an object called a* Sink *object.*

Although creating a COM object that supports Automation from scratch can be fairly involved, a number of tools are available that can make developing COM objects easy. For C++ programmers, the Active Template Library (ATL) and Microsoft Foundation Class(MFC) Library provided with Visual C++ can make COM development much easier. Another option is to use Visual Basic, which makes the task of writing an Automation object that we can use from our ASP pages quite easy.

Let's take a look at the code for a sample object that we have created in Visual Basic. Here's a set of functions that will help us further enhance our page's greeting:

```
Function Hello(Name)
    Hello = "Hello, " + Name + "!"
End Function

Function NameLength(Name)
    NameLength = Len(Name)
End Function

Function NumberOfMs(Name)
    Count = 0
    Start = 1
    Start = InStr(Start, Name, "m", 1)
    While Start > 0
        Count = Count + 1
        Start = InStr(Start + 1, Name, "m", 1)
    Wend
    NumberOfMs = Count
End Function
```

These three functions take a name and manipulate it in various ways. Although quite simplistic, you can see that they seem to share a common aspect: each of these functions takes a name as its parameter. Because we want to create a warm HTML greeting page, we are going to use these functions to do various things with the client's name. In the course of creating a dynamic greeting, we will pass the same name to each of these functions to help build some text that might pique the client's interest. We could easily make the three function calls, passing each one the same name, or we can take our page to the next level by introducing it to server-side controls.

Next we need to provide a means of grouping our simple set of functions and enabling them to share information with each other. For instance, we can set up a system whereby we supply the name to these functions only once, and from then on when we call our *NameLength* and *NumberOfMs* functions the name doesn't have to be specified in the function's parameters. To do this, we will group our data (the name) and our functions into an object named *Welcome*.

In one sense, an object is just a means for grouping data. What makes objects useful is that any special kind of data usually has some actions that are specific to it as well. For instance, suppose we have a bank transaction object. The data would be the actual value of the bank transaction and some other peripheral information such as the date the transaction occurred, who was paid, the account number, and maybe a code that tells us this was a written check as opposed to a cash machine withdrawal. But bank transactions have a lot of actions that need to be performed on them in order to debit the correct account and validate a few pieces of information. For example, if we had a whole bunch of bank transaction objects and wanted to go through them and deduct money from appropriate accounts for various types of debits, we might want a function for doing this. We could call the *DebitAccount* method, which would perform the complete act of removing the money from the account specified for the given transaction. The code that calls *DebitAccount* would not need to know the amount of money involved, the name of the account, or even the mechanics of how *DebitAccount* works. All it would need to know is that as soon as all the data about the transaction had been entered, it would simply have to call *DebitAccount* and the whole transaction would be complete. The account is simply debited, and we can go on to processing the next transaction object.

But let's get back to our *Welcome* object. Our new "object-ized" code might look something like this:

```
Public m_Name As String
Function Hello()
    Hello = "Hello, " + m_Name + "!"
End Function
Function NameLength()
    NameLength = Len(m_Name)
End Function
Function NumberOfMs()
    MCount = 0
    Start = 1
    Start = InStr(Start, m_Name, "m", 1)
    While Start > 0
        MCount = MCount + 1
        Start = InStr(Start + 1, m_Name, "m", 1)
    Wend
    NumberOfMs = MCount
End Function
```

Our object has three member functions and one property. In this case, the property is the name that we want to use in our different functions. Notice that we no longer pass the *Name* parameter to our functions because our object will know the name as soon as we set the *Name* property. Here's the ASP code that will now be using our object:

```
<%@ LANGUAGE="VBSCRIPT" %>
<HTML>
<HEAD>
<TITLE>Welcome to Our Site!</TITLE>
</HEAD>
<BODY>
<% if Request.QueryString("Name") = "" then %>
    <FORM ACTION=myobj.asp METHOD=GET>
        Please enter your name:
        <INPUT NAME="Name" TYPE=TEXT> <br>
        <INPUT TYPE=SUBMIT>
    </FORM>
<% else %>
    <% Set a = Server.CreateObject("Welcome.Welcome2")
    a.m_Name = Request.QueryString("Name")%>
    <%=a.Hello()%><br>
    Did you know your name has <%=a.NameLength()%>
    characters in it?<br>
    And it also has <%=a.NumberOfMs()%> Ms in it!!
<% End If %>
</BODY>
</HTML>
```

This page checks to see whether the query string contains a *Name* value. If it does not, the page prompts the user for a name using a trivial form. Assuming that the form has a name entered on it, the ASP page will display a pleasant greeting that includes some interesting facts about the user's name. The result is a page that looks something like the one shown in Figure 17.5.

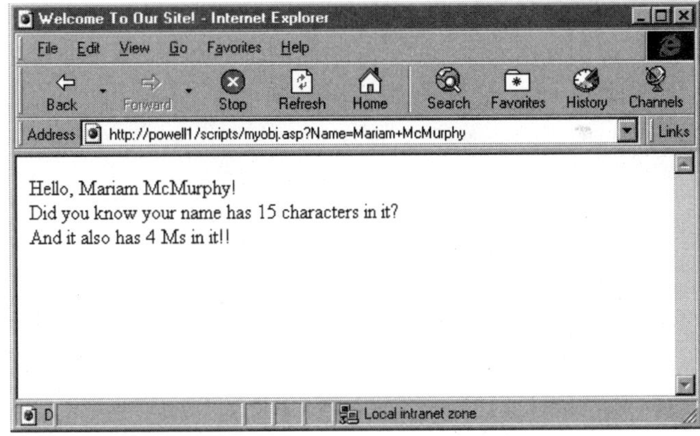

FIGURE 17.5

A sample ASP page using our Welcome object.

If you look at the URL displayed in the address of Figure 17.5, you'll notice that the *Name* parameter appears in the query string of the request URL. This indicates that this page was apparently created from the form version of the same page.

Threading Models

We created our *Welcome* object using Visual Basic, but you can create an object using a number of different languages. You will probably want to write high-powered, high-performance objects in C++ to take advantage of the direct link to the powerful Win32 function set provided by Microsoft Windows. Some other advantages of writing your Automation objects in C++ have to do with *threading models*. Because you might have hundreds or thousands of clients that access your site, there is a distinct possibility that two clients will make a request at the same time. Even on a site with only a few hits a day, there is always a possibility that two requests will occur at the same time. This potential collision raises some interesting issues with server-side objects because multiple threads handling simultaneous requests could end up accessing our object at the same time. How access to our object is controlled depends on the threading model of the object.

The two basic kinds of threading models for COM objects are *apartment model* and *free-threaded*. To understand the difference between these two models, we must first come to grips with the term "apartment." An apartment is basically an object and the set of threads that might be calling into the object. A single-threaded apartment (STA) consists of an object (or objects) that can be called by only one thread at a time. A multithreaded apartment (MTA) consists of an object or objects that can be called by multiple threads at the same time. We make this distinction because sometimes a call to an object has to change apartments, and the underlying layers of COM need to marshal access to the object.

Glossary

marshaling *A mechanism used to pass data across a boundary. For example, when calling a function, parameters and return values might need to be passed across apartment, process, or system boundaries. Marshaling can involve changing the format of the passed data. For instance, if you were passing an integer in a 16-bit application to a 32-bit COM object, the internals of COM would marshal the 16 bit integer into a 32 bit integer.*

Single-threaded objects

We'll start by looking at a simple kind of object—an object that was not designed to be called from multiple threads but, in fact, was designed to be used by a process with a single thread. This object falls under the trivial STA model. What becomes interesting about single-threaded objects is how they are handled by a multithreaded application such as IIS.

ASP declares its threads to be STAs. But to access a single-threaded object that was not designed to be run in multiple threads, it simply launches the object in the main *WinProc* thread. ActiveX then marshals access to this thread by forcing all calls to it to go through the single *WinProc* thread. Thus, if two requests come in at the same time we might see the scenario illustrated in Figure 17.6.

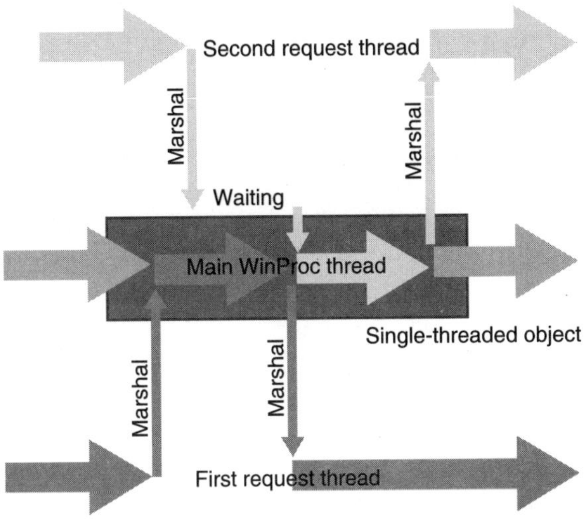

FIGURE 17.6

Two simultaneous requests for a single-threaded object being marshaled to the main* WinProc *thread. Only one request is processed at a time, so the second request must wait for the first request to complete.

In this example, the first request comes in on the thread on the bottom. Because it is a single-threaded object, it is launched in the main *WinProc* thread. The first thread blocks, while access to the object is marshaled between the two apartments. The object is actually instantiated, as indicated by the rectangle, by the main *WinProc* thread. The second request comes in and is handled by the thread on the top. It tries to access the object by marshaling, but since our main thread is already handling the first request, the second request is now blocked while it waits for the first request to complete. When the first request completes and frees up the main *WinProc* thread, the second request can be serviced. Eventually, the main *WinProc* thread completes the second request and the results are marshaled back to second request's thread. Obviously, the major flaw in this model is that the second request had to sit around doing nothing while it waited for the first request to complete. So let's look at an alternative arrangement.

Apartment model objects

Apartment model objects are objects that can run only in an STA. Unlike single-threaded objects, however, apartment model objects can exist simultaneously in multiple threads. Therefore, in a multi-threaded application such as IIS, apartment model objects must treat each thread like a separate apartment. This technique actually works quite well since each thread will get its own copy of the apartment model object, thus eliminating any waiting around for one request to complete before another request can run. And because each thread is its own apartment, there is no need for crossing apartment boundaries when accessing the object, so no marshaling is involved. Figure 17.7 illustrates multiple requests to an apartment model object; here each thread gets its own instance of the object, as indicated by the rectangles. Notice that no marshaling is involved.

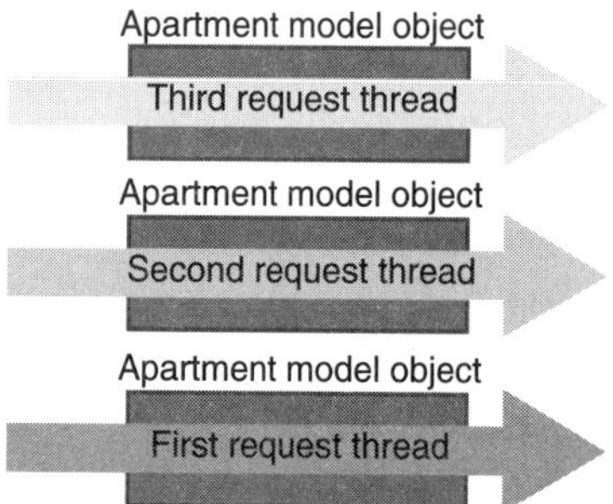

FIGURE 17.7

Apartment model objects executing in the same thread that called them since they are being called from STAs.

The problem with apartment model objects is that because each thread has its own copy of the object, there can be no shared resources among the different instances of the object. For example, suppose these objects were making calls to a database. If we had 50 clients making requests at the same time, we would be using 50 different database connections. It might be more efficient to somehow share a single connection among the different instances of the object.

Free-threaded objects

Free-threaded objects provide a mechanism for sharing global resources similar to the database connection we just mentioned; however, this capability might come at a price. Free-threaded objects run in an MTA, which on the surface can be a good deal. You'd think that because a free-threaded object can handle requests from multiple threads at the same time, it avoids the limitations of the single-threaded object while still being able to share global resources. But this is not always the case.

The problem with straight free-threaded objects is that the threads of IIS initialized ActiveX by presenting themselves as STA threads. When a free-threaded object is called, COM must create an MTA to run it in. This doesn't necessarily mean that it will be creating multiple threads, but it needs to create at least one thread that is flagged as an MTA thread. Therefore, because our access to this object must cross apartment boundaries, it must be marshaled. And so we get into many of the same problems that we had with a single-threaded objects, and we end up with an arrangement that looks just like the one illustrated in Figure 17.6.

Apartment model and free-threaded objects

The way to have nonmarshaled calls and still be able to share global resources is to create an object that is both apartment model and free-threaded. When IIS sees that the object is marked as *Both*, it realizes that the object can be handled as if it were an apartment model object, and therefore no marshaling occurs when we call our object. If we now instantiate our object in our GLOBAL.ASA with application scope, only a single instance of our object is created. Thus, we avoid the performance hit of marshaling our object's interfaces and we get the benefit of sharing global resources. Figure 17.8 illustrates how an object marked as *Both* is handled.

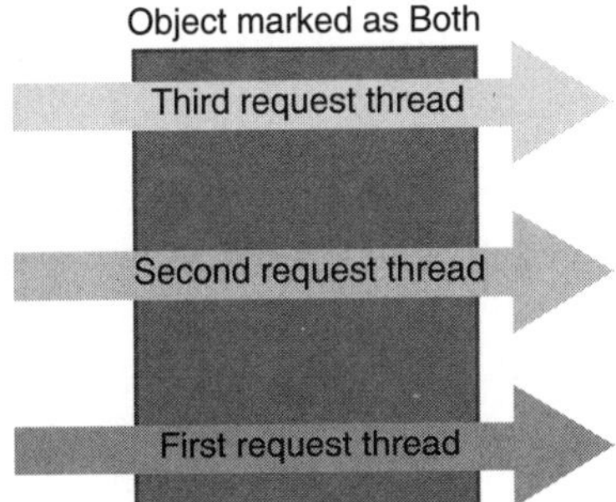

FIGURE 17.8

Object marked as* Both *executing in the threads that called it, but now the object can share resources between the calling threads.

Be aware that performance for objects marked as *Both* can be great, but if there are global resources being shared, access to these resources needs to be synchronized in some fashion. For instance, if you were writing information to a file, you wouldn't want two threads moving the end-of-file pointer at the same time. Therefore, you will need to use one of the many Windows synchronization mechanisms to avoid having multiple threads corrupt global data and resources.

If you create your objects in Visual Basic, as in our example, you will have the option of choosing between two threading models. You can configure your COM object to be a Single or Apartment model in the Project Properties dialog box. If you want to create a free-threaded object or an object marked as *Both*, you will need to write your object in C++, which makes a lot of sense since the synchronization objects needed to avoid corruption to global resources are easily available from C++.

Transactional Objects

IIS uses Microsoft Transaction Server (MTS) to manage its thread pooling and object access. Any object called from an ASP page can use the *GetObjectContext* function to get the transaction context for the request. The object context actually contains interface pointers to the built-in objects of ASP. Therefore, your components can get all the information from the ASP *Request* object, write data to the client using the methods of the *Response* object, and basically do anything else that you can do from an ASP script.

We will talk about object context and MTS in further detail in our Chapter 18.

Script Debugging

The Windows NT Option Pack comes with a generic scripting interface debugger called the Microsoft Script Debugger. This debugger, which has been used for some time to step through script on the client side, now works seamlessly on the server side as well. With the Script Debugger, you can set breakpoints, step through code, and look at the values of variables just like a normal debugger. At this time, however, you cannot edit your code from within the debugger.

You do have to run the Script Debugger on the server itself. And you have to enable your page's application for debugging, which can be done in the Management Console from the App Debugging page of the Application Configuration dialog box. To open your ASP file, your page will need to be loaded into memory, which means that you will have to request it from a browser at least once before trying to debug it. Once it has been accessed, you can find your file in the debugger by opening the Running Documents window, accessed through the View menu item. You will probably see a Microsoft Internet Explorer entry in this window since this debugger can debug client-side scripts as well. For now, select the Microsoft Active Server Pages entry so that you can expand the tree view in the window. Below the Microsoft Active Server Pages entry, you will see a hierarchy similar to the Internet Service Manager, with the different sites and virtual directories listed on your machine for pages that have been accessed and have had debugging turned on. Select the page you want to debug to open it. You can now set breakpoints within your page. When you refresh the page in your browser and a breakpoint within your page is encountered, you can view the values of variables by typing *? variablename* in the Command window. Figure 17.9 shows the Script Debugger in the process of debugging one of our sample ASP pages.

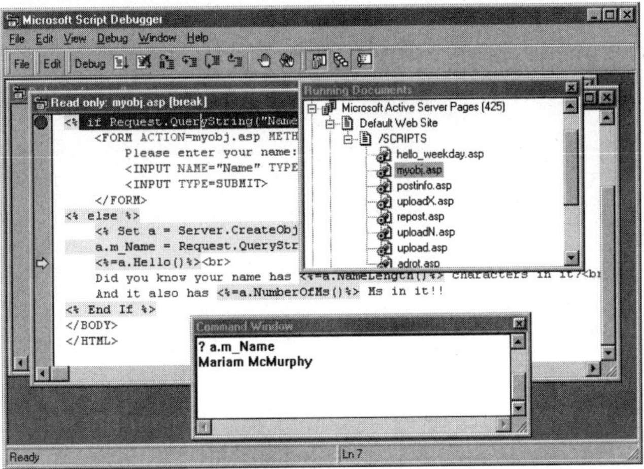

FIGURE 17.9

The Microsoft Script Debugger at work.

You now have a good understanding of the basics of ASP, the various objects provided for your use within ASP, and how to write your own ActiveX controls that can be used within your ASP pages. In the next chapter, we'll show you how to take advantage of IIS's transaction capabilities, including accessing a database.

CHAPTER 18

Transactional ASP

Microsoft Internet Information Server 4.0 has redefined the role of the Web server. IIS has moved beyond the traditional HTTP server and now encompasses numerous other application processes, including transactions, certificates, messaging, indexing, and more. It truly is an enterprise Web server.

In this chapter, we'll look at how to create transactional applications using Active Server Pages (ASP), which means we'll be looking at both IIS and Microsoft Transaction Server (MTS) and how the two can be leveraged to create transactional, browser-based applications. It's worth noting that transactional ASP is just one way that you can use MTS. You can also write transactional applications using Visual Basic, Visual C++, or Visual J++ for your client-side presentation layer.

MTS is based on the Component Object Model (COM), which allows you to use various development tools to access the objects and components installed in MTS. For example, you can use the same components in MTS by calling them from applications developed in Visual Basic, Visual C++ or ASP. You might do this if you wanted to make MTS components available to both Web-based users (perhaps mobile workers) and LAN-based users.

To fully understand transactions, you'll need to be familiar with some of the basic concepts of MTS—specifically, MTS packages and components, transactions, transaction attributes, and the *ObjectContext* object. We covered MTS packages and components in Chapter 15. In this chapter, we'll focus solely on transactions and how to incorporate them into your code.

Transactions

Those of you familiar with client/server applications should be accustomed to dealing with transactions. A transaction can be defined as a logical unit of work; it is performed as an atomic operation, meaning that it either succeeds or fails as a whole. A typical example of a transaction is the transfer of money from a savings account to a checking account. This transaction includes both the withdrawal of money from savings and the deposit of the same amount of money into checking. If you are unable to withdraw the money from savings, the transaction fails. The transaction also fails if you get the money from savings, but you are unable to deposit it into checking. In this case, the step of getting the money from savings is rolled back—the money is returned to savings—and the situation returns to the same status as before the transaction was attempted. The use of MTS simplifies the task of developing application components because it provides monitoring and transaction handling that no longer has to be included in each component. MTS also protects applications from anomalies caused by concurrent updates or system failures.

Transactions have the following properties, known as the ACID properties:

- **Atomicity** This property ensures that regardless of various actions, a transaction is treated as an atomic entity. All actions within a transaction must succeed—the failure of any single action causes a failure of the entire transaction. In the preceding example, the withdrawal from the savings account and the deposit to the checking account are parts of the atomic transaction.
- **Consistency** This property ensures that a transaction is a correct transformation of the system state, preserving the state invariants. By using transactions, you can ensure that all related items are updated and reflect the same state. In our bank example, the *Consistency* property ensures that when the money transfer is complete, both accounts are left in a consistent state that indicates the debit from one account and the credit to the other.
- **Isolation** This property protects concurrent transactions from viewing each other's partial and uncommitted results, which might create inconsistencies in the application state. Various synchronization protocols are employed by MTS (and other transaction-aware applications) to take care of the isolation of uncommitted transactions. In our bank example, the *Isolation* property ensures that if we were to somehow check the balance of our accounts during the transaction—even if we had already taken money from savings but hadn't yet deposited it in checking—we would get the correct balance.
- **Durability** This property ensures that committed updates to managed resources (such as a database record) survive failures, including communication failures, process failures, and server system failures. Transactional logging even allows you to recover the durable state of the system after certain failures (such as disk media failures). In our banking example, if money is withdrawn from savings to be deposited into checking and the checking account is temporarily unavailable, the transaction is kept in an uncommitted state until access to the checking account becomes available. (In the case of an unrecoverable failure, the transaction is aborted.)

The intermediate states of a transaction are not visible outside the transaction since all other transactions and applications view these states as part of the whole transaction. You get all or nothing: either the entire transaction works or everything fails. This limitation greatly simplifies the development of components for each transaction because programmers can safely ignore concurrency issues and assume that transactions execute sequentially.

The *ObjectContext* Object

An MTS object is an instance of an MTS component. Remember from Chapter 15 that an MTS component is a COM component that is installed in MTS; on disk this component is an ActiveX DLL. The MTS component can contain any number of methods and usually provides a certain category of service. For example, a finance component might contain many different types of financial methods and is therefore a collection of a particular category of business logic.

MTS maintains a *context* for each object. This context, which is implicitly associated with the object, contains information about the object's execution environment, such as the identity of the object's creator and, optionally, the transaction encompassing the work of the object. The object's context is similar in concept to a process's context, which an operating system maintains for an executing program. MTS stores the context information and makes it available to the developer in an object named *ObjectContext*.

Figure 18.1 shows an MTS object and its associated context object.

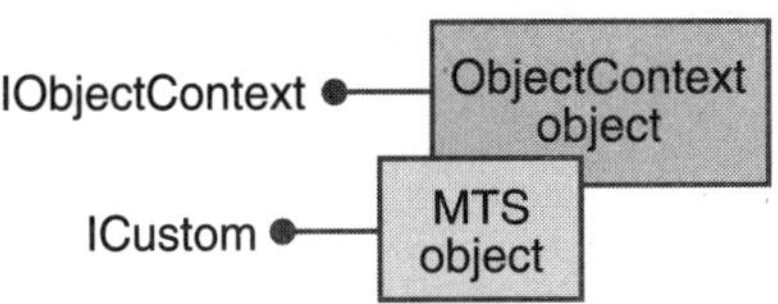

FIGURE 18.1

An MTS object and its associated context object.

An MTS object and its associated context object have corresponding lifetimes. MTS creates the context object before it creates the MTS object, and it destroys the context object after it destroys the MTS object.

ObjectContext and ASP

In IIS 3.0, the ASP framework provided five built-in objects: *Application, Session, Request, Response,* and *Server*. In Chapter 17, we discussed how these objects are special because they are built into ASP pages and do not need to be created before you can use them in scripts. For example, to send output to the browser you would use the *Write* method of the *Response* object. You simply call *Response.Write* and pass it a string. You don't have to create an instance of the object before you can use its methods.

IIS 4.0 provides a sixth built-in object: *ObjectContext*. You can use the *ObjectContext* object to either commit or abort a transaction that has been initiated by a script contained in an ASP page.

When an ASP page contains the *@TRANSACTION* directive, the page runs in a transaction and does not finish processing until the transaction either succeeds completely or fails. We'll come back to the *@TRANSACTION* directive in the section "ASP Transaction Basics" later in this chapter.

ObjectContext Methods

The *ObjectContext* object has 11 methods that can be called from your applications. These methods allow you to carry out a number of tasks, including those listed in the following table.

Method	Description
Count	Returns the number of context object properties.
CreateInstance	Instantiates another MTS object.
DisableCommit	Declares that the object hasn't finished its work and that its transactional updates are in an inconsistent state. The object retains its state across method calls, and any attempts to commit the transaction before the object calls *EnableCommit* or *SetComplete* will result in the transaction being aborted.
EnableCommit	Declares that the object's work isn't necessarily finished but that its transactional updates are in a consistent state. This method allows the transaction to be committed, but the object retains its state across method calls until it calls *SetComplete* or *SetAbort* or until the transaction is completed.
IsCallerInRole	Indicates whether the object's direct caller is in a specified role (either directly or as part of a group). An MTS role is a symbolic name that defines a logical group of users for a package of components.
IsInTransaction	Indicates whether the object is executing within a transaction.
IsSecurityEnabled	Indicates whether security is enabled. MTS security is enabled unless the object is running in the client's process.
Item	Returns a context object property.
Security	Returns a reference to an object's *SecurityProperty* object.

Method	Description
SetAbort	Declares that the object has completed its work and can be deactivated on returning from the currently executing method but that its transactional updates are in an inconsistent state or that an unrecoverable error occurred, which means that the transaction in which the object was executing must be aborted. If any object executing within a transaction returns to its client after calling *SetAbort*, the entire transaction will abort.
SetComplete	Declares that the object has completed its work and can be deactivated on returning from the currently executing method. For objects that are executing within the scope of a transaction, this method also indicates that the object's transactional updates can be committed. When an object that is the root of a transaction calls *SetComplete*, MTS attempts to commit the transaction on return from the current method.

This table lists the methods that are available to Visual Basic applications. Visual C++ and Visual J++ do not have direct access to the *Count* and *Item* methods because they gain access to the current object's context through the *IObjectContext* interface, as we shall see later in this chapter. ASP has access to only two of these methods: *SetComplete* and *SetAbort*.

NOTE

More details on how Visual C++, Visual J++, and Visual Basic handle the ObjectContext *object can be found in the Windows NT Option Pack documentation under Microsoft Transaction Server\Microsoft Transaction Server Programmer's Guide\MTS Reference. Details on accessing* ObjectContext*'s properties and methods from ASP can be found in the "Built-In ASP Objects Reference" section of the Windows NT Option Pack documentation.*

ObjectContext Events

Two events are possible after an *ObjectContext* method has executed: *OnTransactionAbort* and *OnTransactionCommit*. The *OnTransactionAbort* event occurs if the transaction is aborted. When the *OnTransactionAbort* event occurs, IIS will process the script's *OnTransactionAbort* subroutine, if it exists. As you might expect, the *OnTransactionCommit* event occurs after a script's transaction commits. Then when the *OnTransactionCommit* event occurs, IIS will process the script's *OnTransactionCommit* subroutine, if it exists.

In the next section, we'll see some examples of how to use these events within your ASP script.

ASP Transaction Basics

As mentioned, to have ASP take advantage of the reliability provided by MTS, you need only include the *@TRANSACTION* directive in your script. This directive tells MTS that any changes occurring on that page, such as database manipulation or Microsoft Message Queue (MSMQ) message transmission, should be considered transactions. A change that is being managed by transaction services can be either committed, making the change durable (permanent), or aborted, which would result in the database, or queue, being rolled back to the state before the changes were made.

To familiarize ourselves with transactional ASP scripts, let's dissect one of the samples included with the IIS SDK, shown in the following code. The IIS SDK is not installed by default. To install the SDK, select IIS in the Windows NT Option Pack setup Components list and click the Show Subcomponents button, which causes the IIS subcomponent window to be displayed. Then select Documentation from the subcomponent list and again click the Show Subcomponents button. Finally, from the Documentation window, you can select SDK from the subcomponents list. Once SDK is installed the sample can be found in \Inetpub\iissamples\sdk\asp \transactional\ SimpleTransaction_VBScript.asp.

NOTE

You can also see an overview, run the example, and even see the Visual Basic script source from the Windows NT Option Pack Online documentation. Open the interactive documentation by selecting the Product Documentation menu item from the Windows NT 4.0 Option Pack program group. Then, using the contents page, expand Microsoft Internet Information Server, Developer Samples, ASP Transaction Services, and then select Basic Transaction to see the sample.

As you can see, the code starts with the *@TRANSACTION* directive. If the *@TRANSACTION* directive is used, it must appear on the first line within the ASP file or an error will be generated.

```
<%@ TRANSACTION=Required LANGUAGE="VBScript" %>

<HTML>
    <HEAD>
        <TITLE>Simple Transactional Web Page</TITLE>
    </HEAD>

    <BODY BGCOLOR="White" topmargin="10" leftmargin="10">
```

```
        <!-- Display Header -->

        <font size="4" face="Arial, Helvetica">
        <b>Simple Transactional Web Page</b></font><br>

        <hr size="1" color="#000000">


        <!-- Brief Description blurb.  -->

        This is a simple example demonstrating the basic
        structure of a Transacted Web Page.

    </BODY>
</HTML>


<%
    ' The Transacted Script Commit Handler.  This sub-routine
    ' will be called if the transacted script commits.
    ' Note that in the example above, there is no way for the
    ' script not to commit.

    Sub OnTransactionCommit()
        Response.Write "<p><b>The Transaction just comitted</b>."
        Response.Write "This message came from the "
        Response.Write "OnTransactionCommit() event handler."
    end sub


    ' The Transacted Script Abort Handler.  This sub-routine
    ' will be called if the script transacted aborts
    ' Note that in the example above, there is no way for the
    ' script not to commit.

    Sub OnTransactionAbort()
        Response.Write "<p><b>The Transaction just aborted</b>."
        Response.Write "This message came from the "
        Response.Write "OnTransactionAbort() event handler."
    end sub
%>
```

Figure 18.2 shows the resulting output after the code has been run inside the online product documentation.

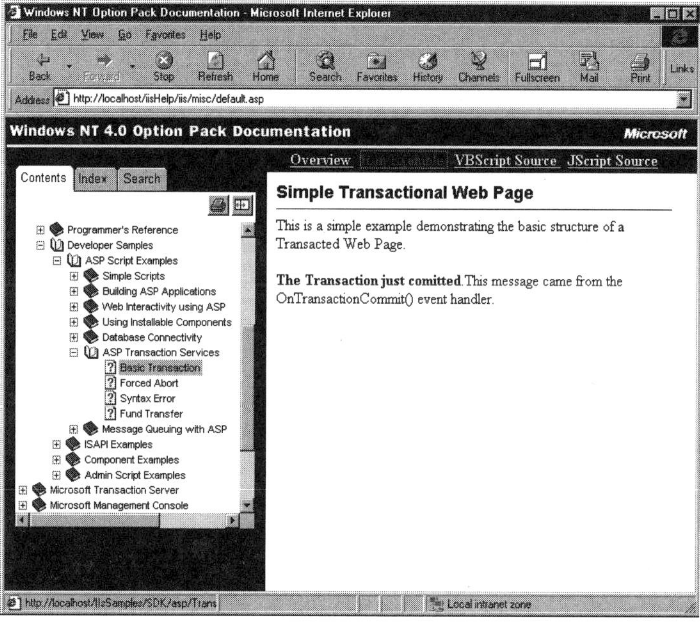

FIGURE 18.2

The browser output that results after running the preceding code.

Transaction Directive Attributes

First let's look at the available transaction attributes that can be used in the *@TRANSACTION* directive. Note that the same transaction attributes apply to all objects that use MTS transactions, not just ASP scripts. The valid attributes are shown in the following table.

Attribute	Description
Requires_New	Denotes that a new transaction should be initialized for the page. Regardless of whether this component is part of another transactional application, MTS will initiate a new transaction.
Required	The page must execute within the scope of a transaction. A new transaction is created unless the page is called within a transaction (that is, as a part of the transactional ASP application).
Supported	A transaction is not created for this page although it can execute within a transaction. If the object is called within a transactional application, it inherits the transaction from the context of the application.
Not_Supported	Denotes that the page should not be executed within the scope of a transaction. Even if an object is called within a transactional application, its ObjectContext object is created without a transaction.

Why would you choose one attribute over another? To fully explain these attributes, let's discuss a transactional application (such as a COM object) rather than an ASP script. *Not_Supported* is the simplest attribute. Suppose you have an object that implements a complex transaction, such as reserving an airline flight, processing the payment for the purchased tickets, and then submitting the order to the company that will mail the tickets to the traveler. All these steps constitute a single atomic transaction. In the middle of this transaction, the prospective buyer might want to invoke another object that implements some value-added service, such as providing tourist information about points of interests at the final destination. To denote this object as not being a part of the whole transaction, the *Not_Supported* attribute can be used.

The *Required* and *Requires_New* attributes look similar, and their usage might be confusing. With the *Required* attribute, the object is handled in the context of the existing transaction, meaning that if the transaction fails, whatever the object just did is rolled back. With the *Requires_New* attribute, the object is handled in a new transaction. Returning to our airline tickets example, if for some reason the transaction was aborted (due to a lack of available seats on a flight, for example), the application would want to log the reason for the failure. If this logging is handled in the context of the original transaction, in the event of a problem the logging action is rolled back as well. To prevent this automatic rollback of logging information, you would have to require a new transaction for the logging action. If the ticket purchase fails, this failure won't affect the completely separate transaction of logging an error.

The difference between the *Required* and *Requires_New* attributes is not all that apparent in an ASP application. Because transactions can't spawn multiple pages or be declared in the GLOBAL.ASA file, each transactional ASP page has a completely different transaction. There is no way to force one transactional ASP script to be executed in the object context of a different transaction.

The preceding code specifies that a transaction is required to start a new transaction. You'll also notice two subroutines within the page. These are the event handlers for the *OnTransactionCommit* and *OnTransactionAbort* events for the *ObjectContext* object. These handlers give you a way to trap the event and take the appropriate action. In this example, the event handlers simply print a message to the browser declaring the success or failure of the transaction. Of course, in this example, there is no way for the script not to commit.

Just to prove to yourself that our example ASP page is truly included as a transaction, select the Transaction Server Explorer from the Microsoft Transaction Server program group. This opens the Microsoft Transaction Server snap-in in the Microsoft Management Console. In the Management Console, select Transaction Statistics from the left-hand pane, as shown in Figure 18.3. Each time you run the ASP example, you'll see the Committed and Total counters in the Aggregate section increase by one.

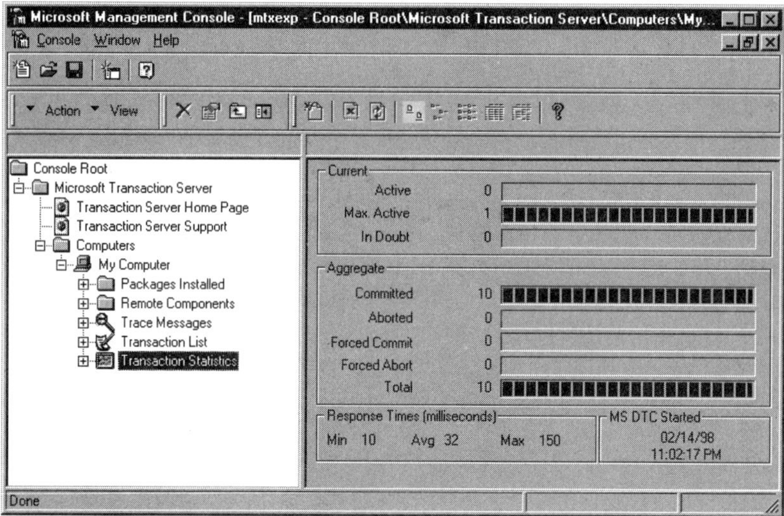

FIGURE 18.3

The Microsoft Transaction Server snap-in in the Management Console, showing the total number of committed and aborted transactions.

Notice in Figure 18.3 that the Management Console also displays the minimum, average, and maximum response times for the transactions. This window is a good way to monitor how quickly your transactions are executing.

As an example of how you might use these event handlers, suppose your transaction aborted for some reason. MTS is capable of rolling back only changes made to the database. It does not roll back changes to files on your hard disk, ASP session and application variables, and so on. The *OnTransactionAbort* event handler would be an ideal place to roll back these kinds of changes.

You can explicitly commit or roll back transactions using the *SetComplete* or *SetAbort* methods of the *ObjectContext* object. A transaction is committed when either the script has successfully completed or the *ObjectContext.SetComplete* method has been called. Likewise, the transaction is aborted when the script encounters some kind of processing error, the script times out, or the *ObjectContext.SetAbort* method has been called.

NOTE

Keep in mind that a transaction cannot span multiple ASP pages. If a transaction requires objects from several transactional components, you should group operations that use those objects into a single ASP page. Also, a transaction can't be declared in the GLOBAL.ASA file.

Transactions Using ADO from ASP

In this section, we'll look at how an ASP page can participate in a true database transaction. To keep things simple, we'll start off by using just ActiveX Data Objects (ADO) to access the data; we won't use MTS components.

The code for this example is shown below. This listing is taken from the ASP Script Examples included in the IIS SDK (at \Inetpub\iissamples\sdk\asp\transactional\ under the name FUNDTRANSFER_VBSCRIPT.ASP). The sample ASP page obtains information from the SQL 6.5 Pubs database regarding a book sale. It then increments the quantity of books sold by a value of *1* and changes the zip code of the store in which the book was sold. Because there are two phases to this operation and because they are both contained within this transactional ASP page, both must succeed or the transaction will be rolled back.

```
<%@ TRANSACTION=Required LANGUAGE="VBScript" %>

<!--#include file="adovbs.inc"-->

<HTML>
    <HEAD>
        <TITLE>Transactional Database Update</TITLE>
    </HEAD>

    <BODY BGCOLOR="White" topmargin="10" leftmargin="10">


        <!-- Display Header -->

        <font size="4" face="Arial, Helvetica">
        <b>Transactional Database Update</b></font><br>

        <hr size="1" color="#000000">


        <!-- Brief Description blurb.  -->

        This is a simple example demonstrating how to
        transactionally update a SQL 6.5 database using ADO and
        Transacted ASP. The example will obtain information
        regarding a book sale from the SQL 6.5 "Pubs" database.
        It will then increment the quantity of books sold by one,
        as well as change the zip-code of the store in which the
        book was sold.
```

(continued)

```
    <p> Because the two database operations are wrapped within
    a shared ASP Transaction, both will be automatically rolled
    back to their previous state in the event of a failure.


<%
  Dim oConn   ' object for ADODB.Connection obj
  Dim oRs     ' object for recordset object
  Dim oRs2    ' object for recordset object


  ' Create Connection and Recordset components

  Set oConn = Server.CreateObject("ADODB.Connection")
  Set oRs   = Server.CreateObject("ADODB.Recordset")
  Set oRs2  = Server.CreateObject("ADODB.Recordset")


  ' Open ADO Connection using account "sa"
  ' and blank password

  oConn.Open "DSN=LocalServer;UID=sa;PWD=;DATABASE=pubs"
  Set oRs.ActiveConnection = oConn
  Set oRs2.ActiveConnection = oConn



  ' Find a random book sale

  oRs.Source = "SELECT * FROM sales"
  ' use a cursor other than Forward Only
  oRs.CursorType = adOpenStatic
  ' use a locktype permitting insertions
  oRs.LockType = adLockOptimistic
  oRs.Open


  ' Change quantity sold

  If (Not oRs.EOF) Then
     oRs("qty").Value = oRs("qty").Value + 1
     oRs.Update
  End If



  ' Find the store in which the book was sold
```

```
    oRs2.Source = "SELECT * FROM stores where stor_id='" _
        & oRs("stor_id") & "'"
    ' use a cursor other than Forward Only
    oRs2.CursorType = adOpenStatic
    ' use a locktype permitting insertions
    oRs2.LockType = adLockOptimistic
    oRs2.Open


    ' Change zip code

    If (Not oRs2.EOF) Then
        oRs2("Zip").Value = oRs2("Zip").Value + 1
        oRs2.Update
    End If
  %>


    </BODY>
</HTML>


<%
    ' The Transacted Script Commit Handler.  This sub-routine
    ' will be called if the transacted script commits.

    Sub OnTransactionCommit()
        Response.Write "<p><b>The update was successful</b>."
    End sub


    ' The Transacted Script Abort Handler.  This sub-routine
    ' will be called if the script transacted aborts

    Sub OnTransactionAbort()
        Response.Write "<p><b>The update was not successful</b>."
    end sub
%>
```

Once again, this ASP script begins with the *@TRANSACTION* directive. The script proceeds to create one connection object and two recordset objects. It then uses a *SELECT* statement to obtain information about a random book sale from the sales table. Using the first recordset object, it changes the quantity sold and performs an update. Then, using the second recordset, it uses a *SELECT* statement to obtain information about the current store from the stores table. The current store ID for this query comes from the first recordset. Finally, the zip code for the current store is changed to show multiple database edits within the transaction.

At the end of the ASP script, the event handlers are used to write a message to the browser to indicate whether the update was successful. If either the first or the second update (or both) failed, the entire transaction is automatically aborted by MTS. Of course, the entire transaction might fail for some other reason, such as a failure of the SELECT statement because of ADO connection errors. This technique relieves the developer from having to write code to handle these scenarios. By placing all the database operations in a single ASP page, they are made part of a single transaction. If both updates are successful, the transaction commits automatically when the script finishes execution.

Transacting Components Called from ASP

In the previous section, we saw how to work with transactions within ASP pages. In this section, we'll look at working with transactions within MTS components that have been called from ASP. This type of application architecture, using ASP to access components installed in MTS, is often used to create scalable Web applications. The architecture uses a browser-based client for the presentation layer, MTS components in the middle tier for the business rules layer, and a Relational Database Management System (RDBMS) for the data layer. Rather than having ASP communicate directly with the database via ADO, the ASP script calls methods within COM components in MTS that then communicate with the database. These COM components can also use ADO for their database access. ADO has a simpler object model than Data Access Objects (DAO) or Remote Data Objects (RDO).

This application architecture is also a nice way to create a more object-oriented code. Instead of having your business logic embedded within ASP pages (and often intermingled with the presentation logic), the logic resides in components that can be managed, easily maintained, and administered within MTS. Unlike an ASP page, a component can also be reused by other applications written in languages such as C/C++ or Visual Basic.

In this section, we'll create a server-side component using Visual Basic 5.0 and then place it under MTS control. We'll then create an ASP page to call the component and we'll see how the ASP page and the component can work together in a single transaction.

Creating a Transactional Component

For our transactional component, we need to create an ActiveX DLL project in Visual Basic 5.0 and define a class with one method, as shown in the following code. This project, named MTS_EXAMPLE.VBP, can be found on the companion CD in the \Chap18\MTS_Example folder:

```
Public Function CommitOrAbort(ByVal TransType As Integer)

    Dim strResult As String
```

```
    On Error GoTo ErrorHandler

    Dim ctxObject As ObjectContext
    Set ctxObject = GetObjectContext()

    ' Take the appropriate action based on the TransType code
    If TransType = 1 Then
        ' Commit
        ctxObject.SetComplete
        CommitOrAbort = "Committed"
    Else
        ' Abort
        ctxObject.SetAbort
        CommitOrAbort = "Aborted"
    End If

    Exit Function

ErrorHandler:

    ctxObject.SetAbort

    CommitOrAbort = "Aborted" ' Indicate that an error occurred

    Err.Raise Err.Number, "MtsExample.Transaction.CommitOrAbort", _
        Err.Description

End Function
```

The *CommitOrAbort* method shown in this code listing takes an integer as input and then explicitly commits or aborts the transaction based on the TransType input variable. If the value of the *TransType* variable is *1,* the method will commit the transaction; otherwise, it will abort. The method also returns a text string to the calling program describing the action that took place.

Notice that the method gets its context by calling the *GetObjectContext* method. The context is stored in a *ContextObject* object variable named *ctxObject.* To commit the transaction, the method calls *ctxObject.SetComplete,* and to abort the transaction it calls *ctxObject.SetAbort.*

After compiling the project to create an ActiveX DLL (MTS_EXAMPLE.DLL), you'll need to install it within MTS using the Management Console. To do this, first create a package and then use the Component Wizard to import the already registered component.

To create a new package, you can use the Package Wizard. To do so, select Packages Installed in the left pane of the Management Console. The Packages Installed item is located under the My Computer item in the Computers folder. Next click the Create A New Object button on the toolbar to start the Package Wizard. To create a new package, click the Create An Empty Package button. The Create Empty Package step of the Package Wizard will prompt you for a name for the new package—for this example, enter *MTS Example*. The next step, Set Package Identity, will prompt you for the user account that this package should be run under. Select the default, Interactive User The Current Logged On User. Click the Finish button in the Package Wizard to create your new empty package.

Now that your package is created, you can access the Component Wizard to install the component by selecting the Components folder inside your new package folder and clicking the Create A New Object button on the toolbar. If you have built and registered the example using Visual Basic, you can click the Import Components That Are Already Registered button and select the *mtsexample.transaction* component in the Choose Components To Import wizard step. Figure 18.4 shows the *mtsexample.transaction* component in the Management Console.

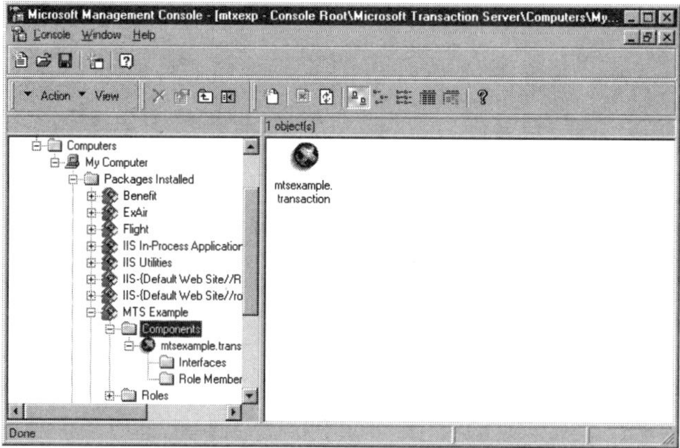

FIGURE 18.4

The **mtsexample.transaction** *component in the Management Console.*

For an MTS component to be transactional, its transaction attribute must be defined in the Management Console. You can do this by right-clicking on the component and choosing Properties. In the Properties dialog box, select the Transaction tab and then choose the Requires A Transaction option in the Transaction Support area. Choose OK, and you're done—your transactional component has been installed in MTS.

Calling the Transactional Component from ASP

To call a transactional component from an ASP page, you simply instantiate the object using the *Server.CreateObject* syntax and then reference the object's methods, as shown in the following code:

```
<%
Dim myObject
Set myObject = Server.CreateObject("mtsexample.transaction")
rtnString = myObject.CommitOrAbort(TransVal)
Response.Write "Return status is '" + rtnString + "'.<p>"
%>
```

Continuing our transactional component example, let's look at an HTML page and an ASP page. The HTML page lets you specify the action the component should take—that is, whether the component should commit or abort the transaction. The ASP page captures this input (sent via an HTML form) and sends the appropriate code to the *CommitOrAbort* method of the *mtsexample.transaction* component. The ASP page displays the resulting status returned from the component and also the final status of the entire transaction. The following code shows the CMP_TRANS.HTM page.

```
<HTML>
<HEAD>
    <META NAME="GENERATOR" Content="Microsoft Developer Studio">
    <META HTTP-EQUIV="Content-Type" content="text/html;
    charset=iso-8859-1">
    <TITLE>Simple Transactional Web Page Using ASP and
    Components</TITLE>
</HEAD>

<BODY BGCOLOR="White" topmargin="10" leftmargin="10">


    <!-- Display Header -->

    <font size="4" face="Arial, Helvetica">
    <b>Simple Transactional Web Page Using ASP and
    Components</b></font><br>

    <hr size="1" color="#000000">


    <!--  Brief Description Blurb -->

    This simple example demonstrates the basic
    structure of a transacted Web page using ASP and components.
```

(continued)

```
        <p>
        The ASP page calls the CommitOrAbort method in the
        mtsexample.transaction component. You can make this
        component either commit or abort by specifying the action
        to take on the CMP_TRANS.HTM page.
        <p>



        <!-- HTML form lets you make the component either
        commit or abort. -->
        Specify whether you want the mtsexample.transaction
        component to commit or abort, and then click the Submit button.
        <FORM METHOD=POST ACTION="cmp_trans.asp">
        <TABLE>
            <TR>
            <TD><input type="radio" checked name="TransFlg"
                value="Commit">Commit</TD>
            </TR>
            <TR>
            <TD><input type="radio" name="TransFlg"
                value="Abort">Abort</TD>
            <TR>
            </TR>
            <TR>
            <TD><INPUT type="submit" name="Submit" value"Submit"></TD>
            </TR>
        </TABLE>
        </FORM>

        <P>

    </BODY>
    </HTML>
```

The CMP_TRANS.HTM page simply sends the value of the currently selected radio button (Commit or Abort) to the CMP_TRANS.ASP page via an HTML *Post* method. The CMP_TRANS.ASP page is shown here:

```
<%@ TRANSACTION=Required LANGUAGE="VBScript" %>

<HTML>
<HEAD>
    <TITLE>Simple Transactional Web Page Using ASP and
    Components</TITLE>
</HEAD>
```

```
<BODY BGCOLOR="White" topmargin="10" leftmargin="10">

    <!-- Display Header -->

    <font size="4" face="Arial, Helvetica">
    <b>Simple Transactional Web Page Using ASP and
    Components</b></font><br>

    <hr size="1" color="#000000">


    <!--  Brief Description Blurb -->

    This simple example demonstrates the basic
    structure of a transacted Web page using ASP and components.
    <p>
    The ASP page calls the CommitOrAbort method in the
    mtsexample.transaction component. You can make this
    component either commit or abort by specifying the action
    to take on the CMP_TRANS.HTM page.
    <p>

    <!-- Find out whether the user wants to commit or abort. -->
    <%
    If Request.Form("TransFlg") = "Commit" Then
      TransVal = 1
    Else
      TransVal = 0
    End If
    %>

    <!-- Instantiate the Transaction component, and then
        call the CommitOrAbort method. -->
    <%
    Dim myObject
    Set myObject = Server.CreateObject("mtsexample.transaction")
    rtnString = myObject.CommitOrAbort(TransVal)
    Response.Write "The component transaction status is '" + _
        rtnString + "'.<p>"
    %>


</BODY>
</HTML>
```

(continued)

```
<%
' The Transacted Script Commit Handler. This subroutine
' will be called if the transacted script commits.
' Note that in the example above, there is no way for the
' script not to commit.

Sub OnTransactionCommit()
    Response.Write "<p><b>The transaction just committed</b>."
    Response.Write "This message came from the "
    Response.Write "OnTransactionCommit event handler."
End Sub


' The Transacted Script Abort Handler. This subroutine
' will be called if the transacted script aborts
' Note that in the example above, there is no way for the
' script not to commit.

Sub OnTransactionAbort()
    Response.Write "<p><b>The transaction just aborted</b>."
    Response.Write "This message came from the "
    Response.Write "OnTransactionAbort event handler."
End Sub
%>
```

In the preceding code, the value from the HTML form is obtained using the *Form* method of the *Request* object, as shown here:

```
Request.Form("TransFlg")
```

The *mtsexample.transaction* component is instantiated using the *Server.CreateObject* syntax, and the *CommitOrAbort* method is called with the *TransFlg* variable passed as a parameter. Finally, the ASP page prints out the return status from the *CommitOr-Abort* method. Figure 18.5 shows the results of clicking the Commit button on the CMP_TRANS.HTM page.

Notice that the transaction as a whole completed successfully. Because the component's transaction was successful (it fired the *SetComplete* method), the ASP page was able to capture the event in its *OnTransactionCommit* event handler. If you look at the Transaction Statistics in Management Console, you'll see just one transaction for this entire process.

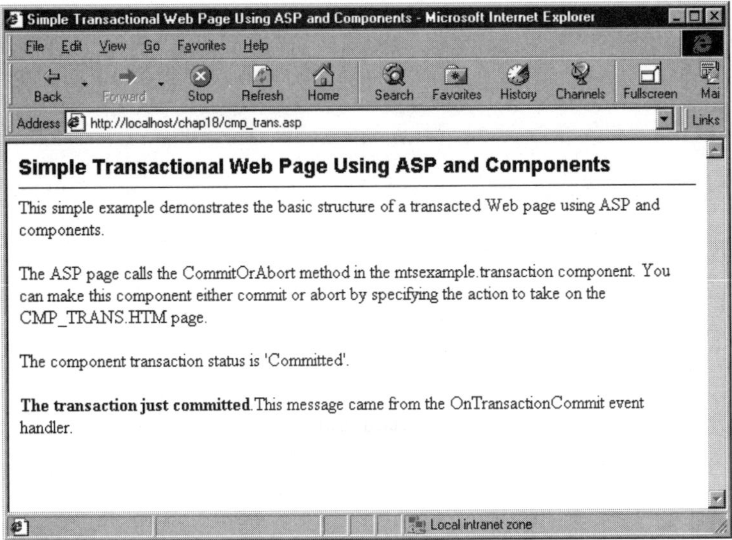

FIGURE 18.5

Output from the CMP_TRANS.HTM page after the user chooses the Commit option and clicks the Submit Query button.

If you select the Abort option and then click the Submit Query button on the CMP_TRANS.HTM page, you'll see that the entire transaction aborts. The CMP_TRANS.ASP page captures the event using the *OnTransactionAbort* event.

Using Built-In ASP Objects from *ObjectContext*

As mentioned, within your Visual Basic server-side components you can also use the *ObjectContext* object to access the built-in ASP objects of IIS: *Request*, *Response*, *Server*, *Session*, and *Application*. You can do this by calling the *Item* method of the *ObjectContext* object. The following sample code retrieves the value of the server name from the *ServerVariables* collection of the *Request* object. In this example, *oc* is the object variable for the *ObjectContext* object.

```
Dim oc As ObjectContext
Set oc = GetObjectContext()
oc("Request").ServerVariables("SERVER_NAME")
```

The ability to access the built-in ASP objects from within a server-side Visual Basic component yields some very interesting possibilities. For example, you can actually write output to the browser from your component—you don't have to return the output to your ASP code for processing. The following code defines a class with one method. This project, called MTS_EXAMPLE.VBP, can be found in the \Chap18\MTS_Example folder:

```
Public Function BuiltInAsp() As String

    Dim strResult As String

    On Error GoTo ErrorHandler

    ' Get the context object
    Dim oc As ObjectContext
    Set oc = GetObjectContext()

    ' Print some text to the browser using the Response object
    oc("Response").Write "<p>Here's some text from the Visual " + _
        "Basic component!</p>"

    ' Print the server name using the Request object
    oc("Response").Write "<p>Server Name: " & _
        oc("Request").ServerVariables("SERVER_NAME") & "</p>"

    ' Print the user's first name using the Request object
    oc("Response").Write "<p>First Name: " & _
        oc("Request").Form("FirstName") & "</p>"

    oc.SetComplete

    BuiltInAsp = "Committed"

Exit Function

ErrorHandler:

    oc.SetAbort

    BuiltInAsp = "Aborted" ' Indicate that an error occurred

    Err.Raise Err.Number, "MTSExample.ASP.BuiltInAsp", Err.Description

End Function
```

We looked at this project file earlier in the chapter, but this code is stored in a class named *ASP* instead of in a class named *Transaction*.

As you can see from this code, you can do a lot of things by accessing the ASP built-in objects. The code uses the *Write* method of the *Response* object to send output to the browser. It prints a simple line of text, the server name from the *Request* object, and finally the value of the *FirstName* variable from an HTML form.

To run this example, open the CMP_BUILT-IN.HTM file from the \Chap18 folder. This file captures the user's first name and then calls CMP_BUILT-IN.ASP. The ASP file calls the *BuiltInAsp* method shown in the preceding code. You'll also want to install the *mtsexample.asp* component in MTS using the Management Console if you have not already done so.

NOTE

There's nothing significant about the names of these files and methods. These examples are intended simply to demonstrate how to access the ASP built-in objects from within a server-side component.

Figure 18.6 shows the output from this example as it appears in Internet Explorer. Note that the ASP page and the component are once again part of a transaction.

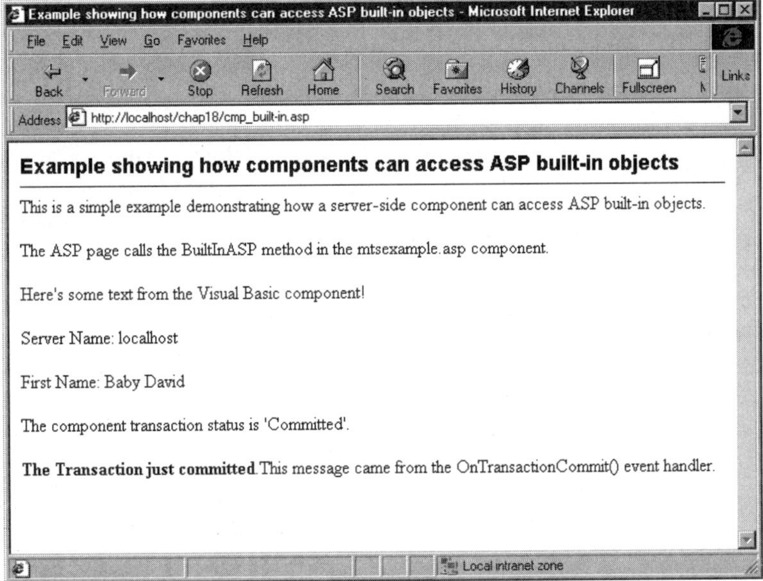

FIGURE 18.6

Output from the CMP_BUILT-IN.HTM page after entering **Baby David** *for the user's first name and clicking the Submit Query button.*

Transactional C/C++ Components

Working with transactions and the context object from C/C++ components is similar to using Visual Basic, but as you would expect, the syntax is slightly different. Let's examine how to access an object's context using C/C++.

The *IObjectContext* interface provides access to the current object's context. You can obtain a reference to the *IObjectContext* interface by calling the *GetObjectContext* function. As with any COM object, you must release the *ObjectContext* object when you have finished using it.

The *IObjectContext* interface exposes the following methods:

- *CreateInstance*
- *DisableCommit*
- *EnableCommit*
- *IsCallerInRole*
- *IsInTransaction*
- *IsSecurityEnabled*
- *SetAbort*
- *SetComplete*

These *methods* provide the same functionality as their Visual Basic counterparts. Notice that the *Item* method is not included here, although it was for Visual Basic. The *Item* method enabled us to access the ASP built-in objects. To do this within C/C++ components, you can use the *IGetContextProperties* interface, which has a method named *GetProperty*.

The *IGetContextProperties* interface also has a method named *Count* that returns the number of context object properties and a method named *EnumNames* that returns a reference to an enumerator that you can use to iterate through all the context object properties. You use the *EnumNames* method to obtain a reference to an enumerator object. The returned *IEnumNames* interface exposes several methods you can use to iterate through a list of BSTRs (Automation string data type) representing context object properties. Once you have retrieved a property name, you can use the *GetProperty* method to obtain a reference to the context object property it represents. In the case in which your object is launched from a transactional ASP page, you can use *GetProperty* to get interface pointers to the intrinsic *Request*, *Response*, *Server*, *Session*, and *Application* objects.

Glossary

BSTR *A string data type defined by Automation (formerly called OLE Automation) that consists of a header, which includes information about the length of the string, and the string itself.*

In this chapter, we've examined how to work with transactions, specifically within ASP pages and within components inside MTS. We've seen what a transaction is, what a context object is, how to declare an ASP page as transactional, how to declare a component as transactional, and how these elements can communicate via the *ObjectContext* object to signal their completion status. We've also seen how the *ObjectContext* object can be used within a component to access the ASP built-in objects.

MTS unleashes the power of transactional applications, but this is not the only service available through the Windows NT Option Pack that can add extra value to your ASP applications. Microsoft Message Queue (MSMQ) server is another powerful addition to the Internet server family. We will be looking at the details of using MSMQ server from ASP in Chapter 19.

CHAPTER 19

Using Microsoft Message Queue Server

In Chapter 18, you learned how to take advantage of the transaction capabilities of Microsoft Transaction Server (MTS) from your Active Server Pages (ASP) applications and that MTS transactions are an integrated part of ASP. In this chapter, we'll examine another middle-tier functionality available to ASP applications: asynchronous requests. An *asynchronous request* is a submitted request that will be processed at a later time—we do not wait for the request to complete before we return from our processing. There are several good reasons for using asynchronous requests from within an ASP application.

If you haven't dealt with any sort of message queueing service before, you might be wondering why being able to submit a request that you don't wait to complete is a benefit. In fact, you perform these types of transactions regularly in your day-to-day activities. For instance, if you order take-out pizza, you are free to do whatever you want until the pizza is ready. In a more computer-centric setting, you might need a colleague to perform a task for you. You could send an e-mail message outlining your request and then can continue working on something else until you receive the results. E-mail and message queueing are very similar conventions, and in fact they can be used together in some situations.

But how do we bring asynchronous communications into our IIS environment? We've seen how to perform multiple tasks in the context of a transaction, but what would happen if one of those tasks took a long time to complete? For example, suppose you have a complex computation to process, or you need to perform a lengthy database sort. You might need to access remote resources over slow, unreliable network lines or over the Internet. Or you might simply have a task that needs to be processed at a later time—perhaps because the task requires a resource that is not constantly accessible. Having the clients who access your server staring at their browsers for even a couple minutes while a task is being completed isn't a very practical scenario. And when we talk about tasks that could take many minutes or even hours or days to complete, we can see the value of being able to return some sort of immediate status to the client and having a reliable way to schedule the pending task. Microsoft Message Queue Server (MSMQ) provides exactly this kind of service.

NOTE

MSMQ is a powerful product with many capabilities, almost all of which can be taken advantage of from within your ASP application. Because MSMQ provides so many capabilities, it would be impossible to cover all the material in a single chapter. In this chapter, we introduce you to how MSMQ can be used from ASP to perform some common tasks such as sending messages, receiving messages, and taking advantage of ASP transactions. To learn about all the capabilities of MSMQ, you might want to look at the documentation in the MSMQ Software Development Kit (SDK) included with the Microsoft Windows NT 4.0 Option Pack. You can then use the samples in this chapter as templates for integrating your MSMQ environment with your ASP applications.

In Chapter 15, we described what's involved in setting up a message queue and how message queue servers can be linked in order to transport messages across a network. Although you could also create and configure your message queues from within your ASP pages, in this chapter we'll focus on accessing these message queues in the context of sending messages to and receiving messages from them.

Messages

We've looked at a couple of scenarios in which submitting asynchronous requests might be valuable, but to be useful these requests must be capable of storing information. For instance, if you are processing orders for widgets, you need to be able to include in the order information such as the number of widgets ordered, the kind of widgets ordered, who to ship the widgets to, and what sort of mailing options to use. Or suppose that you need to perform some processing at a different location—say, at a place that has access to some SQL databases not available from your current location. In this case, you might want to send more than just some simple information about the request at hand.

You can conceptually send a COM object in an MSMQ message. Suppose you have created an ActiveX control to perform database requests. Usually, this is done in two stages: first you must set the various properties from which the control builds the corresponding database query, and then the control submits the actual database query. With MSMQ, you can set the properties appropriately for the first stage of the object's implementation. Your object could then have an export function that would effectively pass all its current state information to a variant that you could then place in the body of an MSMQ message. The message could then be sent to a remote location. At the remote location, a new instance of the object could be created and its properties set based on the state information sent in the MSMQ message. The object would have the same state as the original object before the message was sent. Next, the method to perform the database query could be called. In this way, the request submitted to MSMQ has the ability to store the information needed to perform the task at hand.

Message Properties Set by the Sender

In the previous example, we talked about storing an object's data in the body of a message. The body of the message is probably the most important aspect of an MSMQ message, but other properties of a message can be set that enable you to describe your message and control the way in which it is delivered. For instance, you can use the *Label* property to include a brief description of your message, much like you would include a Subject line in an e-mail message or a memo. The *AppSpecific* property provides a flexible means of including an extra pointer or index with your message that could hold data in addition to what is included in the body of the message. Other properties let you specify how a message is sent, how long an unread message is retained, and how acknowledgments and responses should be sent. Let's take a look at each of these properties in more detail.

The primary property that controls how a message is sent is the *Delivery* property. The *Delivery* property lets you specify express or recoverable delivery. Express delivery is faster than recoverable delivery, but can be less reliable. Express delivery is indicated by setting the *Delivery* property to *MQMSG_DELIVERY_EXPRESS* or *0*. Recoverable delivery stores redundant copies of a message in case of computer failure on any of the remaining links to the destination queue. Recoverable delivery is indicated by setting the *Delivery* property to *MQMSG_DELIVERY_RECOVERABLE* or *1*.

NOTE

The MSMQ SDK, which is a subcomponent of the Microsoft Message Queue component in the Windows NT 4.0 Option Pack, includes the definitions for the constants referred to in the online documentation for the various properties. If you install this SDK, you can find the definitions in the default C:\Program Files\MSMQ\sdk\include directory in the C include file MQ.H. Because there is no easy way to import these constants so that they are available to your ASP script, you must define them yourself.

You can set message priority using the *Priority* property. This numeric value indicates the order in which messages are routed and the order in which messages are placed in the queue. The *Priority* property values range from 0 through 7; 7 is the highest priority, and the default value is 3.

The *PrivLevel* (short for "privacy level") property specifies whether the message body is encrypted. Encrypted messages can be sent only to queues that are configured to accept them. The *EncryptAlgorithm* property specifies which encryption algorithm should be used to encrypt the data. The two available options are RC2 and RC4, which (as you'll remember from our discussion of encryption in Chapter 13) are public key encryption ciphers based on RSA encryption. RC2 is a block cipher, and RC4 is a stream cipher, but which cipher you choose makes little difference to your application.

The *Trace* property tells MSMQ to trace the route that the message will take through the various message queue servers until it reaches the destination queue. MSMQ will send a message to the report queue indicating the final route for the message. To turn tracing on, set this property to *MQMSG_SEND_ROUTE_TO_REPORT_QUEUE* or *1*; to turn it off, set the property to *MQMSG_TRACE_NONE* or *0*. Similarly, you can use the *Journal* property to indicate whether you want your message to be journaled. As you'll remember from Chapter 15, journaling creates a copy of the message for redundancy purposes. The *Journal* property has three possible settings. To turn journaling on, set the *Journal* property to *MQMSG_JOURNAL* or *2*; to turn journaling off, set *Journal* to *MQMSG_JOURNAL_NONE* or *0*. If you set *Journal* to *MQMSG_DEADLETTER* or *1* and the timeout period for reaching the destination queue expires or the timeout period for the message being received expires, the message becomes a dead letter and a copy of the message will be kept in the dead letter queue of the machine on which the message expired.

The *MaxTimeToReachQueue* and *MaxTimeToReceive* properties specify the message time limits. *MaxTimeToReachQueue* specifies the maximum time, in seconds, that a message has to reach its destination queue, and *MaxTimeToReceive* specifies the maximum time, in seconds, that a message will wait after it has reached the destination queue until it is retrieved. If the maximum time specified by either the *MaxTimeToReachQueue* property or the *MaxTimeToReceive* property has elapsed and if the *Journal* property is set to *MQMSG_DEADLETTER*, a copy of the message will be placed in the dead letter queue of the machine on which the message expired.

The remaining properties you can set when sending a message have to do with acknowledgments and responses. Acknowledgments are messages generated by MSMQ that are sent to indicate whether a message has reached its destination queue and whether it has been read from its queue. The *Ack* property lets you specify exactly what kind of acknowledgments you want to receive. The acknowledgments can be positive, which indicates success, or negative, which indicates failure. Positive and negative acknowledgements include the act of reaching the destination queue and the act of being retrieved. You can even indicate that you want to receive no acknowledgments (the default). Acknowledgment messages are sent by MSMQ to the queue specified by your message's *AdminQueueInfo* property. The *CorrelationId* property of the acknowledgement message will be set to the *Id* property of your original message.

Response messages are responses generated by an application that are sent to the sender's response queue. For example, if you are creating a message that contains a widget order, you might want to receive a response when that order has been shipped. You can specify a response queue by using the *ResponseQueueInfo* property of the message. When you are sending responses, you should set the *CorrelationId* property equal to the *Id* property of the message you are responding to; this allows the receiver to make the correlation between the two messages.

Other Message Properties

A number of other message properties are set by MSMQ itself when your message is sent. These properties let you track your messages and help to identify messages for the receiving application and any other application or administrative tool that is monitoring the messages in the queue. The *SentTime* and *ArrivedTime* properties indicate the time the message was sent and the time it arrived in the destination queue. *Id, SenderId, SenderIdType,* and *SourceMachineGuid* are all properties that MSMQ assigns based on where the message came from. As mentioned, the *Id* property is a unique number generated by MSMQ for each message sent; the *SenderId* and the *SourceMachineGuid* properties indicate who generated the message and what machine it was generated from. The *DestinationQueueInfo* property simply indicates the destination queue.

Sending a Message

The act of sending a message is probably the most common use of MSMQ from an ASP application. To send a message, open the queue the message will be sent to and build a message. Once this is done, you simply call the *Send* method of the message object. When you are sending messages, you will most often use the *MSMQMessage* and *MSMQQueue* objects. *MSMQMessage* is the object that contains the actual message, and *MSMQQueue* is simply the destination queue for the message.

The following code sample sends a trivial message to a test queue:

```
<%@ LANGUAGE="VBSCRIPT" %>
<HTML>
<TITLE>Test Message Queue Page</TITLE>
<BODY>
<%
    Set Query = Server.CreateObject("MSMQ.MSMQQuery.1")
    Set QInfos = Query.LookupQueue(,,"TestQueue")
    QInfos.Reset
    Set QInfo = QInfos.Next
    Set Queue = QInfo.Open(2, 0)
    Set Message = Server.CreateObject("MSMQ.MSMQMessage.1")
    Message.Label = "Test Message Label"
    Message.Body = "Hello, World!"
    Message.Send Queue
%>
</BODY>
</HTML>
```

The first thing the code must do is open an instance of the destination message queue. This step isn't as easy as you might expect. To obtain an instance of the queue in question, we must first query MSMQ to see whether such a queue exists. To do this, we must create an instance of the *MSMQQuery* object whose *Lookup-Queue* method allows us to query MSMQ for any queues that match our search criterion. In this case, we are looking for a queue whose *Label* property is *TestQueue. LookupQueue* returns an *MSMQQueueInfos* object, which is simply a list of *MSMQQueueInfo* objects. Before we can find the needed *MSMQQueueInfo* object in this list, we must first scroll to the beginning of the list using the *Reset* method. If multiple queues match our search criterion, we can walk through this list of queues supplied by the returned *MSMQQueueInfos* object using its *Next* method. In our case, we know that only one queue matches our search criterion, so we simply take the first queue returned with a single call to the *Next* method. Once we have the correct *MSMQQueueInfo* structure, we can finally open an instance of the queue by using the *Open* method of the *MSMQQueueInfo* object to provide the interface pointer we need to send our message. When you are opening message queues, it is important to pass the appropriate access flag to the *Open* method. In this case, we pass the *MQ_SEND_ACCESS* flag, which has a value of 2 and indicates that we need the ability to send messages to the queue.

The *Server.CreateObject* method is used to create a new instance of the *MSMQ-Message* object. We set the *Label* and *Body* properties of our message and call the *Send* method, passing it the instance of the *MSMQQueue* object we opened earlier. We could also have set any number of the advanced properties for sending our message, including the options for acknowledgments and privacy. For simplicity, this sample does not check for errors either in finding the queue or when sending the message, although a properly robust application would perform this error checking.

Receiving Messages

When you map the traditional concept of client/server computing to message queueing, usually the client sends a message and the server receives it. Since ASP sits as a middle tier between the client and the server, in most circumstances you will want your ASP pages to send messages, acting as a proxy for the client. Although receiving messages from an ASP page is a bit unusual, we will look at a scenario in which we can see what messages are available to be read from MSMQ. The following code shows a script that reads the first message in our test queue:

```
<HTML>
<HEAD>
<TITLE>MSMQ Receiving Test Page</TITLE>
</HEAD>
```

```
<BODY>
<H1>ASP MSMQ Receiving Test Page</H1>
Message Info:<p>
<%
    Set Query = Server.CreateObject("MSMQ.MSMQQuery.1")
    Set QInfos = Query.LookupQueue(,,"TestQueue")
    QInfos.Reset
    Set QInfo = QInfos.Next

    Set Queue = QInfo.Open(1, 0) ' 1=Read Access
    Set Message = Queue.Receive
%>
    Message.Label: <%=Message.Label%> <br>
    Message.Body:  <%=Message.Body%>  <br>
</BODY>
</HTML>
```

As you can see, this script is quite similar to the previous example. The primary differences are that in this case we use a different flag in the call to open the queue, and we call a *Receive* method on the message instead of a *Send* method.

NOTE

*When you are setting permissions on your queue, as discussed in Chapter 15, be aware that if you want to read your messages from your ASP scripts, you'll probably have to change the default permissions. By default, everyone has send access to message queues, but only the owner of the queue has receive access. Because your ASP page might be executing in the context of the IUSR_*computername *account or impersonating a client, a number of security contexts might become involved. You can grant permissions to the queues through the MSMQ Explorer. First right click on the queue in question, choose Properties, and select the Security tab. Next click the Permissions button, and then modify the permissions settings accordingly. The accounts that you want to receive messages must have Receive access permission.*

After the queue has been opened, we need to call the *Receive* method of the *MSMQQueue* object. The result is an *MSMQMessage* object that contains all the properties we set previously. We are receiving these messages from a queue, which by definition implies that the messages will be received in the order in which they arrived in the queue. Figure 19.1 shows the results of our message query.

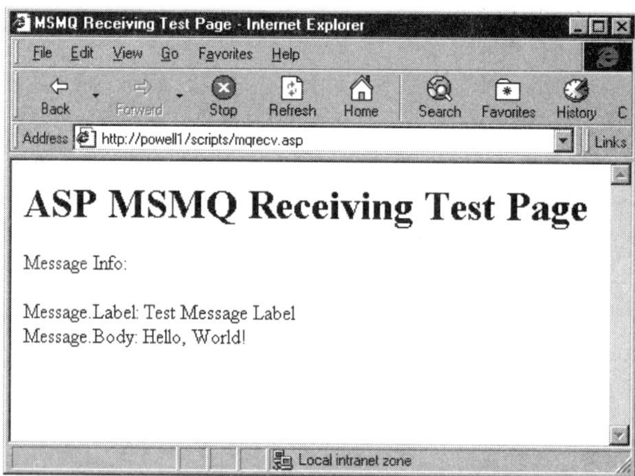

FIGURE 19.1

Receiving an MSMQ message from an ASP page.

Keep in mind that when you make your request to receive a message, there might not be any messages in the queue. If this is the case, by default your request will wait indefinitely until your browser times out. You can modify this default behavior by adding a timeout to your *Receive* method call. For example, if you wanted to set a 10-second timeout, you would replace the *Receive* method call and the label and body property statements in the previous script with the following code:

```
<%
    ...
    Set Message = Queue.Receive (,,,10000)
    if Message Is Nothing then%>
        Receive timed out; no messages in queue. <br>
<%  Else%>
        Message.Label: <%=Message.Label%> <br>
        Message.Body:  <%=Message.Body%>  <br>
<%  End If%>
```

The *10000* parameter in the *Receive* call itself indicates a 10,000 millisecond timeout. If we do timeout, we will catch the error by checking for the error condition *MQ_ERROR_IO_TIMEOUT*, which has the value *C00E001Bh*, as indicated here.

Transactional Messaging

You now know how to send and receive MSMQ messages from your standard ASP pages. One of the exciting features of MSMQ is that it is a *transactional resource manager*. This might sound a bit confusing, but basically it means that MSMQ messages can be treated as part of an ASP transaction just as calls to ActiveX Data

Objects (ADO) are. The underlying infrastructure will handle the two-phase commits and the potential rollbacks on error conditions. Unlike immediate database transactions, however, we do not wait until the task is complete before we return from our message queue transaction. In the case of MSMQ, we are simply committing to the fact that a message has been placed into the system. This commitment should be adequate, considering that once a message has been submitted to an MSMQ server, its delivery to the destination queue is guaranteed unless you receive notification otherwise.

Let's return to a familiar scenario in which this sort of transactional model makes perfect sense. If we are handling widget orders, we do want some sort of guarantee that the order is in the pipeline without having to wait until the order is boxed up and shipped out. Remember that while we are committing our asynchronous request, we might be processing a charge to the customer's credit card or updating our customer profile database. If for some reason we failed at sending the MSMQ message that included the actual order, we would definitely want to roll back the entire transaction to avoid upsetting our customers.

Let's take a look at some of the details of making a message queue call from within an ASP transaction. The first thing you need to do to send your message as part of a transaction is to enable your destination queue for transactions. Queues can be configured to be transactional only at the time they are created. If you want to make an existing queue transactional, you're out of luck. If you have already created a queue, simply delete it and create a new queue with the *Transactional* flag set. Figure 19.2 shows the Queue Name dialog box, which is displayed when you are creating a new queue, with the Transactional option checked.

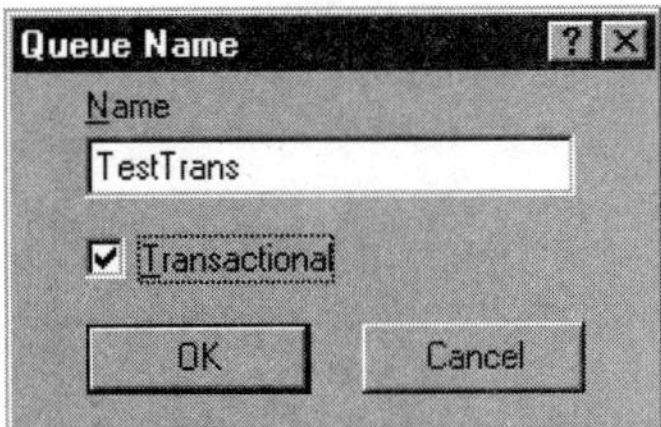

FIGURE 19.2

Creating a transactional message queue.

The next step in sending a transactional message is to change the ASP code to enable transactions and to indicate that MSMQ should use the transaction that MTS is providing for the ASP page. The following code shows these changes.

```
<%@ TRANSACTION=Required LANGUAGE="VBSCRIPT" %>
<HTML>
<TITLE>Test Transaction Message Queue Page</TITLE>
<BODY>
<%
    Set Query = Server.CreateObject("MSMQ.MSMQQuery.1")
    Set QInfos = Query.LookupQueue(,,"TestTrans")
    QInfos.Reset
    Set QInfo = QInfos.Next
    Set Queue = QInfo.Open(2, 0)
    Set Message = Server.CreateObject("MSMQ.MSMQMessage.1")
    Message.Label = "Test Message Label"
    Message.Body = "Hello, World!"
    Message.Send Queue, 1
    Queue.Close
%>

<% Sub OnTransactionCommit %>
    Transactional message sent and committed.
    </BODY></HTML>
<% End Sub %>
<% Sub OnTransactionAbort %>
    A problem occurred, and your message was not sent.
    </BODY></HTML>
<% End Sub %>
```

For the most part, this script is the same as the script we used earlier to send a message, but here we have made a few changes. As you can see, we have added another value to our @ directive on the first line. The *TRANSACTION=Required* value indicates to ASP that we need this page to be executed in the context of an MTS transaction. MSMQ relies on having some sort of transaction available, so it is important to provide one. By using the built-in ASP transaction support (instead of having to initialize the transaction support that MSMQ is capable of providing itself), we can roll together multiple transactional requests within our ASP page such as writing to a database or sending other transactional messages.

Once we have configured the queue and our ASP page to be transactional, the rest is easy. The only other change we made was in the actual call to send our message. In this case, we have included a previously omitted second parameter to the *MSMQMessage* object's *Send* method. This second parameter is designed to take an instance of a transaction object, but it can also accept a few constants. Here we have passed the value *MQ_MTS_TRANSACTION* or *1*, which tells MSMQ to use the built-in MTS transaction for this request. As it turns out, this value is the default for transactional message sending; we have explicitly set this parameter here for illustrative purposes.

NOTE

Because the default setting for the transaction parameter of the MSMQMessage *object's* Send *method is to use the built-in MTS transaction, be aware that using this default will cause problems if you are trying to send messages to nontransactional message queues. If the directive* TRANSACTION=Required *is included, messages sent to nontransactional message queues with no second parameter in the* Send *method will fail. To avoid this problem, use the* MQ_NO_TRANSACTION *flag or* 0 *as the second parameter of the* Send *method if you want to send a message to a nontransactional queue.*

The last difference between this script and our previous message sending script is the addition of the *OnTransactionCommit* and *OnTransactionAbort* subroutines. These subroutines are the built-in *ObjectContext* object's event handlers for transactions that we discussed in Chapter 18. We use these routines to determine whether we have successfully completed sending our message.

You now know how to take advantage of MSMQ from within your ASP applications. You can use MSMQ to submit asynchronous requests and retrieve messages, and you can even send messages within the context of an ASP transaction. In Chapter 20, we will examine the Internet Server Applications Programming Interface (ISAPI) and the power it can bring to your applications.

CHAPTER 20

Web Server Applications

As we've seen, passing static HTML pages to a Web browser is entertaining for only a short time. Every experienced Web surfer knows that an interactive experience makes the Internet more fun to use. In the realm of business and intranets, the ability to write server-side applications is a must. Web pages that display stock quotes, make custom database queries, collect user input, and render custom pages (much like *www.msn.com*) are all examples of *Web server applications* in action. In this context, we are using the term "Web server application" to describe any application that runs on the Web server and that dynamically creates HTML output that is in turn sent to the browser. Web server applications are behind almost every HTML form that has a Submit button.

In Chapter 17, you learned about Active Server Pages (ASP)—the powerful addition to IIS that allows Webmasters to create dynamic and interactive pages. Once you saw the power and ease of ASP scripts, you probably lost interest in learning about any other type of Web server application. The objective of this chapter is to respark your interest and show you the power and possibilities available with Web server applications. Two principal techniques are available for creating a Web application that will run on the server: one method is to force the Web server to start a process that will do the work of generating HTML pages (and any other programming task you might imagine); the second method is to force the server to load a Dynamic Link Library (DLL) that encapsulates the needed functionality. Programmers use both methods, although launching a new process has some performance problems, which will be discussed shortly. Let's begin by taking a look at the specification that allows the Web server to launch a new process for each client request.

NOTE

We will be referring extensively to some of the details of the HTTP protocol in this chapter, including HTTP methods, headers, status codes, and URLs. If you are unfamiliar with these concepts, you might want to skip ahead to Chapter 23 before continuing with this chapter.

Common Gateway Interface

The Common Gateway Interface (CGI) is simply a specification that defines how a Web server can launch executable modules (applications) and communicate with them. CGI applications have been around as long as the first Web servers (such as

HTTPd). In Microsoft Windows NT, CGI applications are console-based programs that can read from and write to the standard input and output data streams.

Usually, a client sends a request to the Web server that invokes a CGI application to handle either an HTTP *POST* or an HTTP *GET* request. Of course, nothing stands in the way of a programmer who wants to write a CGI application that handles any HTTP request, method, or verb, as described in Chapter 23.

CGI Invocation

Both the *POST* and the *GET* requests are able not only to invoke a CGI application but also to provide it with data—for example, interactive user input from an HTML form can be provided to a CGI application for processing. The difference between a *POST* and a *GET* request is the way in which the data is provided. The data provided by the *POST* request is read by the CGI application from the standard input data stream. The *POST* request also uses an environment variable named *CONTENT_LENGTH* to inform the CGI application of the amount of the data to be read from standard input. The *GET* request, however, sets the environment variable *QUERY_STRING* equal to the data provided. In the *GET* request, the data is provided, by the client, as parameters on the URL line separated by a question mark from the URL itself. For example, an HTML page might have the hyperlink *http://server/scripts/cgi.exe?param1=value1*; this URL line can also be entered directly in the Address line of the browser. This URL line invokes the CGI application CGI.EXE and sets the environment variable *QUERY_STRING* equal to *param1=value1*. The CGI application, CGI.EXE, can then retrieve the string *param1=value1* from the environment variable and process it appropriately.

Data sent using the *GET* method should not exceed command-line or environment variable size limitations set by the Web server. (A common maximum for *GET* is 256 bytes, even though a larger query string might still work.) The *POST* request data, on the other hand, has no size limit, so the data provided can be as long or as short as you want. A *POST* request is often used to post large amounts of data, such as when you upload a file. When reading *POST* data, the CGI application should not rely on the presence of an end of file (EOF) marker as a data terminator. Instead, the CGI application should read as many bytes from the standard input stream as indicated by the *CONTENT_LENGTH* variable, which is mandatory for all *POST* requests.

NOTE

URLs are encoded in the format—known as URL-encoded—described in RFC 1738 titled "Uniform Resource Locaters (URL)." In this format, all spaces are replaced by plus signs, and special characters are given in the hexadecimal form %xx. *For example,* "Hello, World!" *would be encoded as* "Hello+World%21".

That's all we'll cover here about the communication mechanisms that link a CGI application and a Web server. You can find more information about the CGI specification at *http://hoohoo.ncsa.uiuc.edu.* Let's look at how IIS handles CGI applications.

◆ CGI and Thread Pool Configuration

By default, IIS uses a thread pool to handle communications with Web clients. The *MaxPoolThreads* registry key located in *HKEY_LOCAL_MACHINE\SYSTEM\CurrentControlSet\Services\InetInfo\Parameters* controls the maximum number of threads per CPU in this pool—by default, this value is set to *4*. In this case, because each CGI process takes one thread from the pool (to handle the actual client/server communications) and there are only four threads, a maximum of four CGI applications can run concurrently.

If your server will be handling many CGI requests, you might want to set *MaxPoolTreads* to a higher number. Note, however, that this value cannot be greater than the *PoolTreadLimit* value, in the same registry path. The limit on the number of threads that IIS can create is, by defalut, twice the number of megabytes (MB) of physical memory on your machine—on a machine with 32 MB of RAM, the limit is 64 threads.

Alternatively, you can configure IIS not to use a thread pool for CGI applications by setting the *UsePoolThreadForCGI* value (located in *HKEY_LOCAL_MACHINE\SYSTEM\CurrentControlSet\Services\W3SVC\Parameters*) to *0* (which means *FALSE*). Setting this value to FALSE can significantly decrease performance if many CGI applications are being launched on your server, however. Use this value only if you have CGI applications that take a long time to respond to a single request.

In general, having a huge number of threads running on your machine is not a good idea. Having a huge number of different processes running on your machine is an even worse idea. In both cases, the operating system spends too much time switching between the various processes and the threads running in them. Since a single CPU can run only one thread at a time, the highest possible performance is obtained from an application that uses the same number of threads as CPUs on the system. On a system with two CPUs, for example, only two threads can truly run in parallel (without spending any time performing context switching). However, most applications do not require all of the processor time, leaving a large number of processor cycles available for other applications and threads. Adjusting the settings for *MaxPoolThreads* and *PoolThreadLimit* to obtain the best performance is a balancing act and is best performed by analyzing your CPU usage. Leaving the settings at their relatively low default values is probably safe, but if your CPU is sitting idle at peak usage, you should consider increasing *MaxPoolThreads* and perhaps *PoolThreadLimit.*

Glossary

thread pool *An efficient method of reusing threads and limiting the number of concurrent threads. Rather than creating a new thread to perform a task, an existing thread, which might have been used previously and has finished its task, can be reused for the current task. This practice reduces the overhead of creating a new thread for each task and also can be used to limit the number of threads created by forcing the task to wait until a thread in the pool is available.*

CGI Internals

CGI applications are essentially stand-alone executables started by IIS. For each request, a new process is created. Poorly written CGI applications are not a major threat to the server because any memory leaks, opened resources, or access violations are contained within the CGI process. As soon as a CGI application is unloaded, all memory is freed and all handles are closed; any access violations would have affected only the CGI process itself. One major scalability and performance problem exists with CGI: the overhead of creating a new process is very high. It takes much more time and memory resources to create a process using CGI than using other forms of Web server applications.

As we saw in Chapter 12, in Windows NT each process runs in the security context of a valid Windows NT account. A CGI application started by an anonymous HTTP request runs in the context of the configured anonymous user: IUSR_*computername*. If the anonymous user can't access the CGI executable file (or the directory in which it is located), IIS will impersonate the user whose credentials were supplied by the client.

A Sample CGI Application

To verify all this information—that is, the different processes and security contexts—we wrote a simple CGI application, shown here:

```
#include <iostream.h>
#include <stdlib.h>
#include <windows.h>

char *szHtmlUserName = "<html><h1>Sample CGI Application</h1><hr>"
  "User Name from getenv (blank means anonymous was used): "
  "<i>%s</i><br>"
  "User Name from Win32 API GetUserName (actual user context "
  "of the thread): <i>%s</i> </html>";
```

```
char *szHtmlPID = "<html><h1>Sample CGI Application</h1><hr>"
  "CGI is running in Process ID: %lu <br></html>";

char *szDefaultHtmlOut = "<html><h1>Sample CGI Application</h1><hr>"
  "<font=+3>Select from the following:</font><br>"
  "\n<a href=%s?getproc> Get process ID </a><br>\n"
  "<a href=%s?getuser> Get user ID </a><html>\n";

int main ()
{
  char szHtmlOut[1000];
  char *lpszQueryString, *lpszScriptName;

  cout << "Content-type: text/html\r\n\r\n";
  if (! (lpszQueryString = getenv("QUERY_STRING")))
  {
    // QUERY_STRING is missing, assuming that CGI is called
    // without parameters.
    if(! (lpszScriptName = getenv("SCRIPT_NAME")))
      wsprintf(szHtmlOut, "Can't get SCRIPT_NAME. ERROR!: %lu",
               GetLastError());
    else
      wsprintf(szHtmlOut, szDefaultHtmlOut, lpszScriptName,
               lpszScriptName);
    cout << szHtmlOut;
    return 1;
  }
  if(!_stricmp(lpszQueryString, "getuser"))
  {
    char *lpszGSVUserName, szWin32UserName[256];
    // Get remote user name using environment variable.
    lpszGSVUserName =  getenv("REMOTE_USER");

    // Get user name of the current thread using Win32 API.
    DWORD dwSize = 30;
    if(! GetUserName(szWin32UserName, &dwSize))
    {
      cout << "GetUserName error: " << GetLastError();
      return 0;
    }
    // Send the data to the client.
    if(! lpszGSVUserName) // No remote user name
      wsprintf(szHtmlOut, szHtmlUserName, "", szWin32UserName);
```

(continued)

```
        else
          wsprintf(szHtmlOut, szHtmlUserName, lpszGSVUserName,
                   szWin32UserName);
        cout << szHtmlOut;
        return 1;
      }
      // If process information requested,...
      if(!_stricmp(lpszQueryString, "getproc"))
      {
        // ...get the process ID and send it to the client.
        wsprintf(szHtmlOut, szHtmlPID, GetCurrentProcessId());
        cout << szHtmlOut;
        return 1;
      }
      cout << "Unknown command was entered.\n";
      return 1;
    }
```

Here's how this sample works. This CGI application makes use of the *QUERY_STRING* environment variable, which should be used only with the *GET* method (because to handle the *POST* method we would need to read the number of bytes specified by the *CONTENT_LENGTH* environment variable from the standard input data stream). When the client invokes the CGI.EXE application but does not provide any data—for example, as in *http://leonbr-hm/scripts/cgi.exe*—the executable returns the HTML shown in Figure 20.1 to the Web server via the standard output data stream.

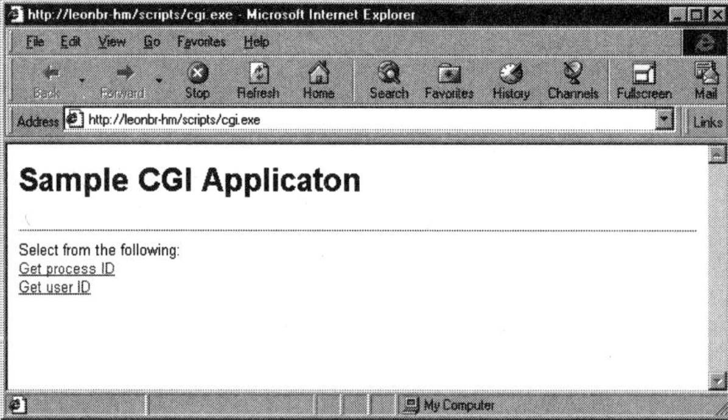

FIGURE 20.1

Default output when CGI.EXE is invoked without parameters.

The rendered page allows the user to invoke the CGI application again, but this time with two different parameters: *getproc* and *getuser*. The *getproc* parameter tells the application to return the process ID (PID) for the CGI application, and the *getuser* parameter tells the application to return the user ID in whose security context the CGI application is running. The user name can be obtained by calling the Win32 API *GetUserName*—which gets the user name for the current thread—or by getting the *REMOTE_USER* environment variable. *REMOTE_USER* is set by the Web server, based on the Authorization header from the browser trying to access the URL, and is set only if the request is not anonymous.

If you click on the Get Process ID hyperlink, shown in Figure 20.1, and then keep refreshing the page, you'll notice that a new PID is reported for each request. This result shows that a new process is created each time the browser accesses the CGI application. Clicking the Get User ID hyperlink produces equally interesting results. If we placed the CGI.EXE executable in our d:\inetpub\scripts directory, which is accessible to the IUSR_*computername* account, the browser does not need to send any credentials, and therefore the *REMOTE_USER* environment variable is blank. Of course, the CGI process (just like any other process in Windows NT) runs in the security context of a valid Windows NT user: the IUSR_LEONBR-HM account on our machine. Figure 20.2 shows the browser after we have accessed *http://leonbr-hm/scripts/cgi.exe?getuser.*

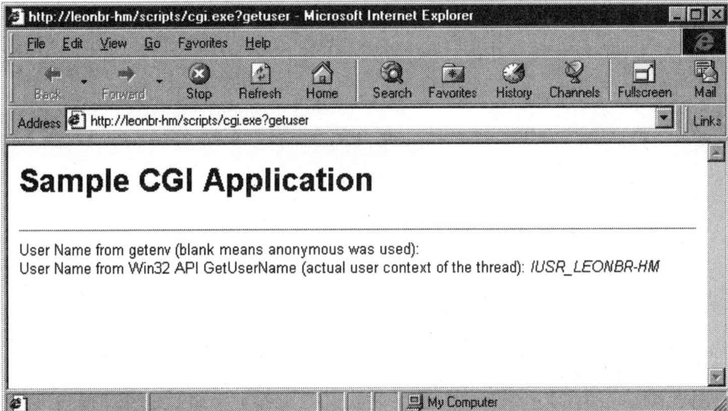

FIGURE 20.2

Sample browser output when CGI.EXE is invoked with the* getuser *parameter.

Moving the CGI executable to a directory that is inaccessible to IUSR_LEONBR-HM forces the browser to send credentials and starts the CGI process in the security context of the provided user. Figure 20.3 shows the browser output after we supply credentials for a local user account named JoeB.

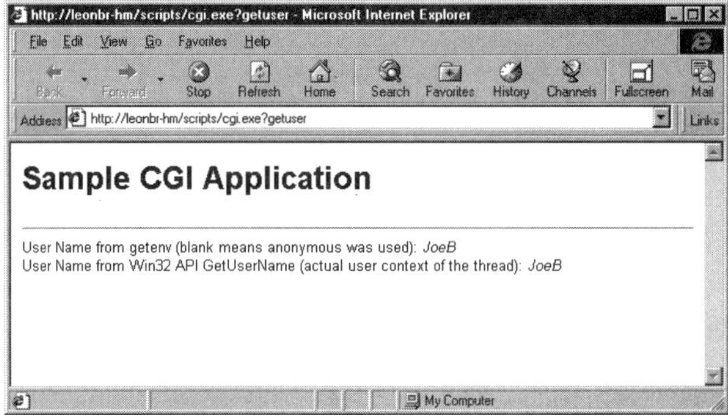

FIGURE 20.3

Sample browser output when CGI.EXE is invoked with* getuser *parameter with a user context of JoeB.

In addition to obtaining the user name and PID, this CGI application also performs the necessary tasks of receiving and sending data. Receiving data is as easy as getting the environment variable *QUERY_STRING*. Sending data back to the browser is accomplished simply by writing to the standard output data stream. (*Cout* is a standard output stream used in C/C++.) Along with the data visible in the browser, our CGI application must send HTTP headers as well. (In fact, all the same rules about sending headers apply to Internet Server Application Programming Interface (ISAPI) applications, which are covered in the second half of this chapter.) Headers are also sent to *cout,* and each header is terminated with a *\r\n*—a carriage return–linefeed (CR-LF) pair. The last header must be terminated with a *\r\n\r\n*. For simplicity, we send only one header that indicates the type of data that the CGI application sends to the server, as shown here:

```
cout << "Content-type: text/html\r\n\r\n"
```

CGI Application Creation

When IIS starts a CGI application, it uses the *CreateProcessAsUser* API, thus creating a new process in the security context either of the IUSR_*computername* user (for anonymous requests) or of the user name supplied by the browser for authenticated connections. You can force IIS to use the *CreateProcess* API to start a CGI application, which means that a CGI process will run in the same context as the main IIS process itself—the Local System account. The *CreateProcessAsUser* Metabase property (which can be set to *TRUE* or *FALSE; TRUE* is the default) indicates whether the Local System account is used for the new CGI process. When

CreateProcessAsUser is set to *FALSE*, a CGI process runs under the Local System account regardless of the credentials supplied by the client. Even if a CGI application does not allow anonymous access and the Web browser is forced to provide a valid Windows NT user name and password, the CGI process will still be started under the Local System account context. *CreateProcessAsUser* is available for the following IIS Admin Objects: *IIsWebService, IIsWebServer, IIsWebVirtualDir, IIsWebDirectory*, and *IIsWebFile*. Keep in mind that a process running under the Local System account has a much broader range of security permission than a process running under the IUSR_*computername* account (which by default is a member of the Guest group and has only Guest privileges).

To illustrate this concept, we have copied CGI.EXE from the default \scripts directory to the newly created virtual root named \test, which has only execute permissions. The next step is to use the ADSUTIL.VBS script, located by default in the %SystemRoot%\system32\inetsrv\adminsamples directory, which allows direct manipulation of IIS Metabase values, as shown in the following command. (Notice that the command line appears on two lines here because of page width limitations but must be entered on a single line at the command prompt.)

```
D:\WINNT\system32\inetsrv\adminsamples>adsutil set /w3svc/1/root/test/
CreateProcessAsUser FALSE
CreateProcessAsUser           : (BOOLEAN) False
```

NOTE

ADSUTIL.VBS, one of the sample scripts included with IIS, is located in the %SystemRoot%\system32\inetsrv\adminsamples directory. To learn more about what can be done with ADSUTIL.VBS, run the command adsutil help. *You'll need to have the Windows Scripting Host installed to run any of the admin samples.*

After the command completes, the script prints a confirmation that *CreateProcessAsUser* is set to *FALSE*. The CGI.EXE executable residing in the \test virtual root can be accessed by the anonymous user; therefore, if we enter the *http://leonbr-hm/test/cgi.exe?getuser* URL in the browser, we are not prompted for credentials. Since this is an anonymous request, we get a blank user name from the *REMOTE_USER* environment variable and the real user name from *GetUserName*, as shown in Figure 20.4.

Notice that *GetUserName* does not report IUSR_LEONBR-HM. Instead, it reports *SYSTEM*, which is the user name for the Local System account. We next deny the anonymous Internet user access to the CGI executable in the \test directory. Essentially, we will need to enter valid credentials in the browser that will be passed to the server. When we make this change, the output shown in Figure 20.5 is produced from the CGI.EXE application.

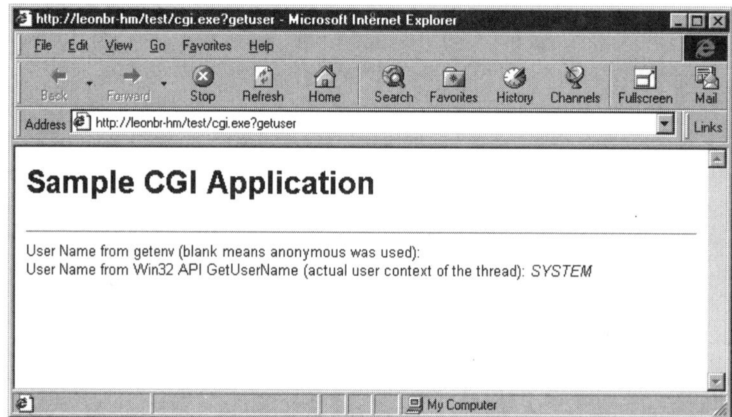

FIGURE 20.4

Default output when CGI.EXE is invoked by an anonymous request.

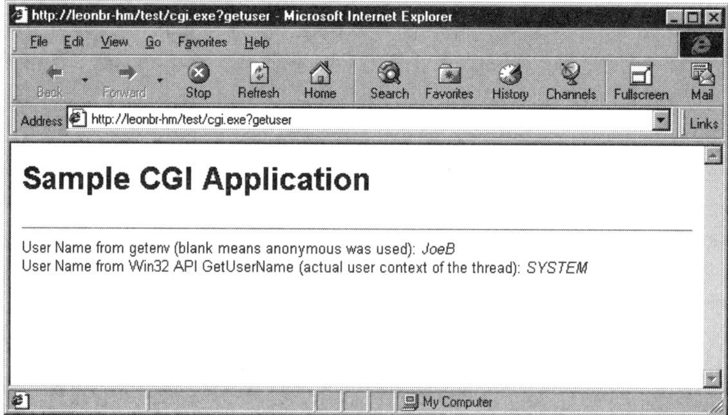

FIGURE 20.5

Default output when CGI.EXE is invoked with a user context of JoeB.

Even though the server has successfully received credentials for the user JoeB from the client (shown by obtaining the *REMOTE_USER* environment variable), the CGI process still runs under the *SYSTEM* security context. This illustrates that once *CreateProcessAsUser* is set to *FALSE* in the IIS Metabase, a CGI process will always run in the Local System account's security context. Running under the Local System account is a potential security threat but can simplify the debugging of a CGI application. If simplifying CGI testing outweighs any potential security risk in your particular environment, you might want to set *CreateProcessAsUser* to *FALSE*.

The Local System account has unlimited access to the default desktop, so if *CreateProcessAsUser* is set to *FALSE*, CGI would have easy access to the default desktop. Another reason to run a CGI application in the context of the Local System account is to access remote shares on the network machines from the CGI application without fancy user impersonations or adding network rights to the IUSR_*computername* user. (Recall Chapter 12, in which we talked about accessing network shares from services.) This process will be a snap if a remote share is added to the list of Null session shares (also discussed in Chapter 12). To set the *Metabase* property to its original value, execute the following command:

```
adsutil set /w3svc/1/root/test/CreateProcessAsUser TRUE
```

Debugging CGI Applications

What should you do if the CGI application you wrote doesn't work? As with any other application, the debugger comes to the rescue. However, unlike many other applications, CGI applications are started by a service. As you'll remember from Chapter 12, it's the little details that complicate debugging: the security context, secure desktop problems, and other things that come with any service process or any process created by a service.

You can always try to run a CGI application as a stand-alone process in Windows NT since it is, after all, a console-based application. Before the application can be started from the command line (or from the debugger), certain environment variables (such as *QUERY_STRING*) must be set in the correct format. If your CGI application handles the *POST* method, you will need some helper application or a utility that can pipe data to the standard input stream for the CGI process, such as the following:

```
d:> echo Hello,+World%21 | cgi.exe
```

Unfortunately, invoking the CGI executable from the command line might not reflect the conditions that exist when it's started by IIS. When you feel you need to debug your CGI application in the "natural habitat" of the service, you can try attaching the debugger to the CGI process. To do this, you need to get the PID for the CGI application (using either *GetCurrentProcessId* or the Windows NT Task Manager). The real challenge is pausing the CGI application's execution so that you have a chance to start the debugger and attach it to the process. Otherwise, the CGI process terminates before you have a chance to attach. There is more than one way to pause a CGI application so that the process will still be running when your debugger is started. The simplest technique is to call the *Sleep* API, which causes the process to just sit there and wait. A more complex technique is to open a global synchronization object (such as a named mutex), and wait until it becomes signaled. One problem with this solution is that it requires you to write a helper application that would set this object to the signaled state.

NOTE

One more way to debug your CGI application is by using the DebugBreak *API, which causes an application to stop and display a dialog box containing a button that starts the default system debugger for the process. This solution might present some difficulties because the CGI process runs in a different desktop from the debugger's desktop. If you are using the Microsoft Visual C++ debugger, for example, it might not be able to initialize its user interface properly. Microsoft Knowledge Base article Q98890, titled "How To: Debugging a Service," explains the potential problems of using this method to debug services and possible solutions.*

The major shortcoming of a CGI application is that it requires you to create a new process for each request. It would be much more efficient to cache the code that is used over and over throughout multiple client requests. Although such caching is not possible when a new process is created for each request, caching code that is used over and over is the cornerstone of ISAPI applications.

Internet Server Application Programming Interface

The limitations of CGI have inspired an entirely different architecture for Internet applications. The main design consideration and goal for the new application model was to minimize any needless request-processing overhead—the logical solution would be to load the code that processes the request only once and then reuse it for future requests. Because a DLL is the perfect component for accomplishing this goal, Microsoft and a company named Process Software have jointly developed a specification that governs how a DLL can be written to process Web client requests: Internet Server Application Programming Interface (ISAPI).

ISAPI Extension Architecture

An ISAPI extension is a DLL that is loaded by IIS—specifically, by the World Wide Web Publishing Service—in its own process space. (IIS 4.0 can also load ISAPI in a separate process; more about this in a bit.) The DLL has an entry point, a function, which is called for each client request. The major improvement of ISAPI over CGI lies in the server's ability to cache ISAPI extension DLLs for an extended period of time. After a DLL is loaded for the first request, all subsequent requests for the same application are lightning fast because the code does not need to be reloaded. Any and all initialization code can be run just once, when the DLL loads for the first time. The loading of a DLL once and the caching of it by IIS have brought a considerable speed gain over executing CGI applications. Even the first request that forces the ISAPI extension DLL to load is faster than a CGI application because calling *LoadLibrary*, the API used to load DLLs, uses less overhead than creating a new process does.

NOTE

Caching DLLs is great for a production server, but it is a major headache for a programmer in the midst of the development cycle. Because any DLL being used by an application cannot be overwritten, the Web Publishing Service must be stopped each time the developer creates a newer version of the DLL. As you'll recall from Chapter 4, individual applications can be configured to prevent ISAPI extension DLLs from caching. (See Figure 4.14.)

The speed improvement offered by ISAPI extensions does not come for free, however. ISAPI extensions can pose some very real dangers to the IIS service. Malicious or buggy ISAPI extensions can crash the entire IIS service because it runs directly in the IIS process space. Even though IIS tries its best to handle possible problems by using exception handling around the calls to the ISAPI entry points, not all errors can be handled gracefully. In the past, this architecture forced developers to choose between slower and safer CGI applications and faster but potentially dangerous ISAPI applications. The issue of making ISAPI safer has been addressed with IIS 4.0. Changes in the way ISAPI extensions are loaded by the server without changing the specification itself have made a major difference in the ability of badly behaved ISAPI extensions to impact the IIS service. Let's explore how ISAPI works with IIS 4.0 before we dive into the details of an actual ISAPI implementation.

IIS 4.0 and ISAPI

It's worth mentioning that although the way in which ISAPI extensions are invoked in IIS 4.0 is very different from how they were invoked in earlier versions of IIS, these changes are completely transparent to the DLL itself. The server still calls the same entry point functions (which we will discuss shortly) with the same parameters.

IIS 4.0 is tightly integrated with the Microsoft Transaction Server (MTS). MTS plays a direct role in the ISAPI extension invocation. We covered the internal architecture of IIS in Chapter 16, so here we'll touch on just components relevant to ISAPI extensions. The major difference between IIS 4.0 and earlier versions is that an ISAPI extension can be loaded by IIS 4.0 indirectly. Simply stated, this means that the main IIS process never calls *LoadLibrary* on the ISAPI extension DLL itself; instead, this call is made using the Web Application Manager (WAM) object.

The WAM component is a COM object that performs the actual loading of the ISAPI extension DLL. Each IIS Web application configured in the Management Console is serviced by its own instance of the WAM object. The WAM object itself is contained in an MTS package and is implemented in %SystemRoot%\system32\inetsrv\wam.dll. Remember that each Web application is based on a virtual directory (recall how we created a Web application in Chapter 4), so a single application could be loading multiple ISAPI extensions or ASP pages and any COM objects those ASP pages might be launching. All the components of an application, loaded by the WAM object, reside in the same process memory space. Depending on how the application is configured, the WAM object can be loaded by IIS either in its own memory space, referred to as running *in-proc*, or in a separate memory space, referred to as running *out-of-proc*. When loaded in-proc, IIS 4.0 is susceptible to the same problems with ISAPI extensions that earlier versions experienced. Memory leaks, heap corruption, and access violations in an in-proc ISAPI extension can possibly crash IIS. Configuring applications to run out-of-proc is a whole different story.

When a Web application containing an ISAPI extension, is configured to run in a separate process, the WAM object is loaded by a process other than the IIS service. The application is loaded into the MTS's MTX process, which is implemented in %SystemRoot%\system32\mtx.exe. Now if an ISAPI extension DLL crashes, the failure will be contained in the MTX process; the IIS service is not affected. (Of course, a crash of the ISAPI DLL will also bring down all other components of the same Web application, such as running ASP scripts or COM objects.) Once it has crashed, MTX.EXE will be restarted for the next request to the ISAPI extension. Launching ISAPI extensions in their own process with MTX.EXE might sound a lot like how CGI applications are launched, but there is one significant difference: MTX.EXE is created only once for a particular application and remains in memory for all subsequent requests (if a buggy ISAPI extension does not crash it, of course). Some overhead is used when you create the new process, but this is a one-time cost. Using the WAM object to load an ISAPI DLL out-of-proc gives us the speed of ISAPI with the safety of CGI.

NOTE

When an out-of-proc ISAPI application crashes, IIS will start a new instance of the process the next time the Web server receives a request for that ISAPI application. This restarting won't continue forever, however. The number of times an application is restarted is controlled by the AppOopRecoverLimit *identifier, which is available with the* IIsWebServer, IIsWebVirtualDir, *and* IIsWebDirectory *Metabase objects. By default, this value is set to* 5, *which means that after the MTX process has crashed and been restarted five times, it will not be restarted again and clients will receive an error message if they request further resources from ISAPI invocations.*

Along with the out-of-proc benefits provided by MTX, MTS manages another crucial aspect of applications: the creation of threads to handle requests. Earlier versions of IIS maintained a thread pool that was used by extension DLLs. ASP components, on the other hand, maintain their own thread pool for ASP scripts. Needless to say, having two different thread pools is far from ideal. The integration of IIS and MTS has successfully resolved these threading issues. Now MTS takes care of creating thread pools for ISAPI extensions and ASP scripts.

Don't forget that each process in Windows NT has a process token that indicates the user account under whose security context the process is running. For the versions of MTX.EXE that IIS is launching, this account is the IWAM_*computername* user account (not to be confused with the IUSR_*computername* account, which is used for anonymous requests). The ISAPI extension itself does not run in the context of IWAM_*computername*, but it still impersonates either the IUSR_*computername* user for anonymous connections or the user whose credentials were submitted by the browser.

Loading an ISAPI Extension DLL

In order for IIS to be able to load an ISAPI extension DLL, it must export two mandatory functions: *GetExtensionVersion* and *HttpExtensionProc*. IIS calls the first function only once, when the ISAPI extension DLL is loaded for the first time. The second function, *HttpExtensionProc*, is where the actual request processing takes place. *HttpExtensionProc* is called every time an ISAPI extension receives a request. When *HttpExtensionProc* is called, it receives a pointer to a special structure that contains information about the request. We will talk about these two functions and the structure a little later.

Because an ISAPI extension is a DLL, it enjoys all the benefits of DLLs in the Win32 realm, including the ability to use *DllMain*. Any DLL is free to export a *DllMain* entry point. This function is called by the operating system when the DLL is loaded or unloaded by the process and when new threads in the process are created. You can use the *DLL_PROCESS_ATTACH* notification to perform initialization of your ISAPI extension and *DLL_PROCESS_DETACH* to perform any cleanup you might need to do. Another function, *TerminateExtension*, can be exported by your ISAPI extension DLL and will be called by IIS when it is unloading your DLL. The *TerminateExtension* function can be a nicer place to perform your cleanup since memory pointers owned by the main process of an application might no longer be available when *DllMain* is called using the *DLL_PROCESS_DETACH* notification.

NOTE

If you search the Win32 Platform SDK documentation, you won't find DllMain *right away. You will, however, find a Win32 function named* DllEntryPoint. DllMain *is the default name for a DLL entry/exit function if you use the Microsoft Linker. The linker embeds the address of the default entry/exit function in the DLL image. When the* /DLL *flag is used to tell the linker that the target is a DLL, the function entry point is* _DllMainCRTStartup. *This function is part of the Microsoft Visual C++ run-time library. After performing some initialization tasks, this function calls your* DllMain *function. Other 32-bit C/C++ development products may use a function name other than* DllMain.

The following sections look into the ISAPI extension entry points in detail.

GetExtensionVersion

GetExtensionVersion is a simple function. Here's how it is defined:

```
BOOL WINAPI GetExtensionVersion(HSE_VERSION_INFO* pVer);
```

NOTE

All function prototypes, various structures, and definitions are located in the HTTPEXT.H header file included with the Microsoft Platform SDK and the IIS SDK found in the Windows NT 4.0 Option Pack. Note that Microsoft Visual C++ versions 4.2 and later also include this header file; however, this file is an older version and does not have the additions available in IIS 4.0. The older header does not reflect the changes for IIS filter applications either. We will examine IIS filters in Chapter 21.

An ISAPI DLL uses this function to fill in the *HSE_VERSION_INFO* structure and pass this information back to the server. The structure has only two fields: *dwExtensionVersion* is used to hold the numeric version of the ISAPI specification being used, and *lpszExtensionDesc* is used to hold a string describing the extension. HTTPEXT.H defines this structure as follows:

```
typedef struct _HSE_VERSION_INFO
{
  DWORD  dwExtensionVersion;
  CHAR   lpszExtensionDesc[HSE_MAX_EXT_DLL_NAME_LEN];
} HSE_VERSION_INFO, *LPHSE_VERSION_INFO;
```

The *lpszExtensionDesc* variable should contain a text description of the ISAPI DLL and can be anything you want; *dwExtensionVersion* corresponds to a version of the ISAPI specification supported by IIS. Setting the *dwExtensionVersion* variable to a version of the ISAPI specification indicates to IIS which version of ISAPI your DLL conforms to. If the ISAPI specification were to change, your ISAPI DLL would still operate correctly because IIS would mimic the older version of ISAPI that your DLL conformed to. When you build your ISAPI DLL, you can simply use the version number defined in the HTTPEXT.H file you are using to build your DLL. Here's how you would properly set *dwExtensionVersion* using the *MAKELONG* macro:

```
MAKELONG(HSE_VERSION_MINOR, HSE_VERSION_MAJOR);
```

Again, *GetExtensionVersion* is called by IIS only once, when the DLL is loaded for the first time. The Boolean return value of the *GetExtensionVersion* function is used to indicate success or failure. The *GetExtensionVersion* function is a good place to initialize any global variables you might use in your DLL. But loading ISAPI and initializing data is only half the job—all the communications with IIS to handle HTTP requests happen in the *HttpExtensionProc* function.

HttpExtensionProc

Here's where all the magic happens. The *HttpExtensionProc* function is called once for each client request. The function receives all request information through a pointer to the Extension Control Block (ECB), which is the only parameter passed to *HttpExtensionProc*. Even though this pointer is the only parameter passed to the function, it contains ample information for handling the request. The prototype for *HttpExtensionProc* looks like this:

```
DWORD WINAPI HttpExtensionProc(LPEXTENSION_CONTROL_BLOCK lpECB);
```

Notice that instead of a simple *TRUE* or *FALSE* value, this function returns a *DWORD*. All the client request processing is conducted in this function, and therefore returning from the function usually indicates that the processing of the request is complete. When the request processing is complete, the server must know how the client connection should be handled. The return values from *HttpExtensionProc*, listed in the following table, indicate to IIS how it should handle the underlying client connection.

Value	Description
HSE_STATUS_SUCCESS	The extension has finished processing, and the server should disconnect and free up allocated resources. If the client and server communicate via the HTTP 1.1 (not the HTTP 1.0) protocol, the server will not disconnect the client session—that is, it will leave the TCP connection open for further requests. For HTTP 1.1, this return code is similar to *HSE_STATUS_SUCCESS_AND_KEEP_CONN*. Chapter 23 covers the details of the HTTP protocol, including the differences between HTTP 1.0 and HTTP 1.1.
HSE_STATUS_SUCCESS_AND_KEEP_CONN	The extension has finished processing, and the server should wait for the next HTTP request if the client supports persistent connections. The extension should return this value only if it was able to send the correct Content-Length header to the client. The server is not required to keep the session open. The client has two ways to determine whether all the data from the server has been received: ◆ The server closes the session by closing the socket. ◆ The server keeps the connection open but sends a special header (Content-Length) that indicates how much data the client should expect to read. As soon as the client reads all the data, it closes the connection.
HSE_STATUS_PENDING	Indicates that the request was queued for processing by the DLL and that the ISAPI extension is releasing this thread back to the pool. IIS still keeps the client connected. This value is a special case that we will describe later in this chapter.
HSE_STATUS_ERROR	The extension has encountered an error while processing the request, and the server can disconnect and free allocated resources.

TerminateExtension

One more optional entry point in the extension DLL is the *TerminateExtension* function. When an ISAPI extension DLL is going to be unloaded (either because the server is configured not to cache ISAPI extensions or because the server is being shut down), *TerminateExtension* is called. Here is the function prototype:

```
BOOL WINAPI TerminateExtension(DWORD dwFlags);
```

The *DWORD* parameter passed to the function indicates whether the ISAPI extension can refuse to unload and hence stay loaded. If *TerminateExtenstion* is called with a *dwFlags* value of *HSE_TERM_ADVISORY_UNLOAD*, the ISAPI extension can choose whether it will unload. Returning *FALSE* from *TerminateExtension* will indicate to the server that the ISAPI extension has refused to be unloaded, IIS 4.0 does not try to unload ISAPI extensions that have not been accessed for a long time, but future versions of IIS might. A *dwFlags* value of *HSE_TERM_MUST_UNLOAD* leaves the extension with no choice; it is merely a notification that the extension will be unloaded. When the IIS service is stopped, all DLLs are unloaded, like it or not. *TerminateExtension* is a good place to perform cleanup if needed. (As mentioned earlier, the other place to perform any cleanup is in your *DllMain* function.)

Extension Control Block

The variety of return codes from *HttpExtensionProc* and their importance is not the only interesting aspect of ISAPI extensions. The *lpECB* parameter, the pointer to the ECB, is equally intriguing. Before we look at the details of this parameter, let's take a look at how it is defined:

```
typedef struct _EXTENSION_CONTROL_BLOCK {

    DWORD   cbSize;             // Size of this struct
    DWORD   dwVersion;          // Version info of this spec
    HCONN   ConnID;             // Context number not to be modified!
    DWORD   dwHttpStatusCode;   // HTTP status code
    CHAR    lpszLogData[HSE_LOG_BUFFER_LEN];
            // Null-terminated log info for this extension DLL

    LPSTR   lpszMethod;         // REQUEST_METHOD
    LPSTR   lpszQueryString;    // QUERY_STRING
    LPSTR   lpszPathInfo;       // PATH_INFO
```

```
    LPSTR   lpszPathTranslated; // PATH_TRANSLATED

    DWORD   cbTotalBytes;       // Total bytes indicated from client
    DWORD   cbAvailable;        // Available number of bytes
    LPBYTE  lpbData;            // Pointer to cbAvailable bytes

    LPSTR   lpszContentType;    // Content type of client data

    BOOL (WINAPI * GetServerVariable) ( HCONN    hConn,
                                        LPSTR    lpszVariableName,
                                        LPVOID   lpvBuffer,
                                        LPDWORD  lpdwSize );

    BOOL (WINAPI * WriteClient)  ( HCONN    ConnID,
                                   LPVOID   Buffer,
                                   LPDWORD  lpdwBytes,
                                   DWORD    dwReserved );

    BOOL (WINAPI * ReadClient)  ( HCONN    ConnID,
                                  LPVOID   lpvBuffer,
                                  LPDWORD  lpdwSize );

    BOOL (WINAPI * ServerSupportFunction)( HCONN    hConn,
                                           DWORD    dwHSERequest,
                                           LPVOID   lpvBuffer,
                                           LPDWORD  lpdwSize,
                                           LPDWORD  lpdwDataType );

  } EXTENSION_CONTROL_BLOCK, *LPEXTENSION_CONTROL_BLOCK;
```

The ECB is the only mechanism provided that enables an ISAPI extension to communicate with IIS. Each ECB is uniquely identified by the *ConnID* (connection ID) parameter, which means that regardless of how many ISAPI extension DLLs are executing simultaneously, the connection ID is guaranteed to be unique. When an ISAPI extension completes a request, however, the *ConnID* is released back to IIS so that the server can reuse it. The ECB delivers all the information to the ISAPI extension in its different structure members. For instance, by examining *lpszMethod*, an ISAPI extension can determine what HTTP method (*POST* or *GET*, for example) was used by the client to invoke the request.

As with a CGI application, data submitted via a *GET* request is received via the HTTP query string. Unlike a CGI application, however, an ISAPI extension does not have to retrieve the value for this variable from the environment. The *GET* data, separated by a question mark in the URL sent by the client, is held in the *lpszQueryString* field of the ECB structure. When an ISAPI extension is invoked using the *POST* HTTP method, incoming data is handled very differently. First the *cbTotalBytes* member of the ECB is set to the total size of the posted data, which is equivalent to the *CONTENT_LENGTH* CGI environment variable. The *POST* method does not restrict the size of the data that the client sends to the server. Occasionally, not all the incoming *POST* data is immediately available for ISAPI extensions. In this case, the *cbAvailable* member of the ECB structure is the number of available bytes out of the total bytes (*cbTotalBytes*) that the client has submitted. The *lpbData* field points to the currently available data. To read large amounts of incoming data, the programmer should implement a loop that reads chunks of data until the entire *cbTotalBytes* amount of data is read using a callback function, as described in the next section. Most of the time, *cbTotalBytes* is equal to *cbAvailable,* indicating that the extension doesn't have to read data; instead, it can simply use the *lpbData* pointer directly.

◆ IIS Read-Ahead Buffer

When an ISAPI extension is invoked using the HTTP *POST* method, IIS itself will read a chunk of data from the client and store it in its read-ahead buffer before setting the ECB fields and invoking the ISAPI extension. After the invocation, the ISAPI extension is responsible for reading the rest of the data. The size of the read-ahead buffer is controlled by the UploadReadAhead value, which is located in the registry in *HKEY_LOCAL_MACHINE\SYSTEM\CurrentControlSet\Services\W3SVC\Parameters.* The read-ahead buffer is set to 48 KB by default.

The read-ahead buffer is also controlled via the Metabase, which allows you to set this buffer size for individual applications (unlike the registry, which controls the global default value). In IIS Admin Objects, this value is referred to as the *UploadReadAheadSize* property. This property can be set for the following objects: *IIsWebService, IIsWebServer, IIsWebVirtualDir, IIsWebDirectory,* and *IIsWebFile.* In IIS Admin Base Object (an alternative way of accessing the Metabase from C/C++ applications covered in Chapter 5), this property is referred to as the *MD_UPLOAD_READAHEAD_SIZE* property and can be accessed through the following keys:

```
/LM/W3SVC,
/LM/W3SVC/n,
/LM/W3SVC/n/,
/LM/W3SVC/n/ROOT/WebVirtualDir,
/LM/W3SVC/n/ROOT/WebVirtualDir/WebDirectory,
/LM/W3SVC/n/ROOT/WebVirtualDir/WebDirectory/WebFile
```

The ECB is not only used to receive data, but also a few of its fields are used to send data back to IIS from an ISAPI extension. The *lpszLogData* field contains the message that the server appends to the IIS log. An ISAPI extension DLL is free to place any string shorter than *HSE_LOG_BUFFER_LEN* (defined as 80 characters) in this buffer. Doing so essentially allows an extension DLL to alter the W3SVC log. Although usually ISAPI extensions don't need to set the *dwHttpStatusCode* field, it can be modified to indicate to the server the status of the request after it has been completed.

Extension Control Block Callback Functions

The *dwHttpStatusCode* normally isn't set by an ISAPI DLL because the ECB structure contains pointers to callback functions located inside IIS that can be used to report the HTTP status code. All the important function tasks of reading and writing data, setting headers, and retrieving server variables are accomplished using callback functions. ISAPI extensions do not themselves contain functions that can be used to communicate with the server. Reading, writing, and other important functionalities that an ISAPI extension must make use of reside in the IIS code itself. A DLL can use any function implemented in IIS if it receives a pointer to the function. One of the ECB's duties is to provide pointers to the callback functions implemented in IIS. Once an ISAPI extension gets hold of these callback functions, it can use them in the same way any other Win32 API would be used. We'll examine, in the following sections, each of the four callback functions contained in the ECB structure. As we examine these callback functions, you might want to refer to the ECB structure declaration in the section "Extension Control Block" earlier in this chapter to see the actual callback function prototypes.

Glossary

callback function *A function whose address is passed as a parameter to another routine so that the callback function can be accessed by the other routine. Callback functions are generally used for event notification. When you call a routine to do some lengthy processing, it's helpful to also pass a pointer to your callback function as a parameter. The routine can then access your callback function to perform such tasks as reporting processing status.*

GetServerVariable

The name of this function says it all. *GetServerVariable* is the ISAPI alternative to obtaining environment variables in a CGI process. The first parameter to the function is a pointer to *ConnID* from the ECB. The three remaining parameters indicate a variable name (such as *SCRIPT_NAME*), a buffer in which to copy the value of the retrieved variable, and the size of the buffer. It might not be possible to determine the size of the buffer beforehand; therefore, when the API is called with *lpdwSize* pointing to a value of *0*, *GetServerVariable* fails with an error *122* (*ERROR_INSUFFICIENT_BUFFER*) but returns the size of the buffer in *lpdwSize*. This gives you a chance to dynamically allocate the buffer of the needed size and call the API once again—this time to get the buffer itself.

WriteClient and ReadClient

These similar functions take as parameters the *ConnID* from the ECB, a pointer to a data buffer and a pointer to a variable that holds either the size of the buffer or the number of bytes written or read upon return. The buffer is either sent to the client using the *WriteClient* function or filled with the data using the *ReadClient* function. *WriteClient* takes one additional parameter: *dwReserved*. This parameter controls the asynchronous mode of the API. We'll talk about these functions in detail in the section "Asynchronous API Calls in ISAPI Extensions" later in this chapter. Internally, both of these functions send and receive data to and from the underlying socket. As a consequence, *WriteClient* and *ReadClient* exhibit behavior similar to the Windows Sockets APIs *send* and *recv*—namely, they block execution, or wait, while data is being received or being sent. For example, when *WriteClient* is called to send 1 MB of data, the entire ISAPI execution on the current thread is blocked and cannot continue until the *WriteClient* function call returns. Calls are not guaranteed to send or receive buffers in their entirety. The *lpdwSize* parameter returns the actual byte count, which can be less than the original value specified when the call was made.

ServerSupportFunction

ServerSupportFunction is the most universal function IIS has to offer. The *ServerSupportFunction* callback accomplishes different tasks depending on the *dwHSERequest* parameter passed. Tasks that can be accomplished using this function vary from simple ones, such as sending HTTP status codes and HTTP headers, to advanced ones, such as setting up an asynchronous callback function to monitor a request's progress. Like CGI applications, ISAPI extensions can simply write HTTP headers to IIS (to send them to the client) using *WriteClient*. However, the *ServerSupportFunction* is much better equipped for this task. Calling *ServerSupportFunction* with *HSE_REQ_SEND_RESPONSE_HEADER* as the *dwHSERequest* parameter sends the desired header to the client. Similar to CGI (according to the HTTP specification), each header is terminated with a *\r\n* and the final header terminates with *\r\n\r\n*.

Using *HSE_REQ_SEND_RESPONSE_HEADER_EX* as the *dwHSERequest* parameter enables the use of an improved header-sending facility. Instead of supplying headers as parameters to the *ServerSupportFunction* callback as was done with

HSE_REQ_SEND_RESPONSE_HEADER, an *HSE_SEND_HEADER_EX_INFO* structure is filled with header and status codes and passed as the *lpvBuffer* parameter. This structure is defined as follows:

```
typedef struct _HSE_SEND_HEADER_EX_INFO {
  //
  // HTTP status code and header
  //
  LPCSTR  pszStatus;  // HTTP status code, e.g., "200 OK"
  LPCSTR  pszHeader;  // HTTP header
  DWORD   cchStatus;  // Number of characters in status code
  DWORD   cchHeader;  // Number of characters in header
  BOOL    fKeepConn;  // Keep client connection alive?
} HSE_SEND_HEADER_EX_INFO, * LPHSE_SEND_HEADER_EX_INFO;
```

Using this structure instead of sending headers directly accomplishes two things: it sends headers and specifies that the connection is kept alive by setting *fKeepConn* to *TRUE*.

The next two values for *dwHSERequest* deal with mapping the URL to its physical location. Using *HSE_REQ_MAP_URL_TO_PATH* enables you to map a URL such as */scripts/myscript.asp* (or simply */scripts*) to its physical location in the form d:\inetpub\scripts\myscript.asp. This technique is fine for simple URL mappings, but it does not return any information about the virtual root should */scripts* happen to be a virtual root. *HSE_REQ_MAP_URL_TO_PATH_EX* is a more complex approach to mapping a URL to its physical path and provides even more information about the mapping. The following structure is used in conjunction with *HSE_REQ_MAP_URL_TO_PATH_EX*:

```
typedef struct _HSE_URL_MAPEX_INFO {
  CHAR  lpszPath[MAX_PATH]; // Physical path root mapped to
  DWORD dwFlags;            // Flags associated with this URL path
  DWORD cchMatchingPath;    // Number of matching characters in
                            // physical path
  DWORD cchMatchingURL;     // Number of matching characters in URL
  DWORD dwReserved1;
  DWORD dwReserved2;
} HSE_URL_MAPEX_INFO, * LPHSE_URL_MAPEX_INFO;
```

Upon the function's return, *dwFlags* has information about the virtual root properties in the form of the values listed in the following table OR'd together.

Flag	Description
HSE_URL_FLAGS_READ	Allows reading
HSE_URL_FLAGS_WRITE	Allows writing
HSE_URL_FLAGS_EXECUTE	Allows execution
HSE_URL_FLAGS_SSL	Requires an SSL connection
HSE_URL_FLAGS_DONT_CACHE	Does not cache (for virtual roots only)
HSE_URL_FLAGS_NEGO_CERT	Allows client SSL certificates
HSE_URL_FLAGS_REQUIRE_CERT	Requires client SSL certificates
HSE_URL_FLAGS_MAP_CERT	Maps SSL client certificates to Windows NT accounts
HSE_URL_FLAGS_SSL128	Requires an 128-bit SSL connection
HSE_URL_FLAGS_SCRIPT	Allows script execution

As you can see, using *HSE_REQ_MAP_URL_TO_PATH_EX* might spare you from writing complex code to get the same information via the IIS Admin Objects or the IIS Admin Base Objects.

By now, you are probably impressed with the possibilities offered by the *ServerSupportFunction* function. And we haven't even covered half of the API's capabilities. Taking advantage of this functionality is as simple (or as complex) as finding the correct value for *dwHSERequest* and calling the APIs with the correct parameters. The following table lists the values for *dwHSERequest* not already mentioned and a short description of what they are used for.

dwHSERequest Value	Description
HSE_APPEND_LOG_PARAMETER	When logging is enabled, this value appends a string contained in lpvBuffer to the log record.
HSE_REQ_ABORTIVE_CLOSE	Once an ISAPI extension has finished, this value requests that the ISAPI extension abortively close the underlying socket connection. Abortively closed sockets do not wait for outstanding data to be sent or received but close immediately. This value will actually improve performance upon termination.
HSE_REQ_GET_CERT_INFO_EX	Retrieves the security certificate information for the client's connection.
HSE_REQ_GET_IMPERSONATION_TOKEN	Retrieves the impersonation token that reflects the security context of the ISAPI application. The obtained token can be used in calls to the *ImpersonateLoggedOnUser* function and the *SetThreadToken* Win32 API.

dwHSERequest Value	Description
HSE_REQ_GET_SSPI_INFO	Returns a structure related to the Security Support Provider interface. This value works only for in-proc ISAPI extensions.
HSE_REQ_IS_KEEP_CONN	Obtains the current status of the underlying TCP connection. The lpvBuffer parameter of *ServerSupportFunction* is set to TRUE or FALSE according to the connection status.
HSE_REQ_REFRESH_ISAPI_ACL	Forces IIS to dynamically recheck the Access Control List (ACL) in the ISAPI extension DLL. If the DLL is loaded, changing its ACL (as we saw in Chapter 12) will not affect IIS's ability to use it unless the ACL was refreshed using this call.
HSE_REQ_SEND_URL_ REDIRECT_RESP; HSE_REQ_SEND_URL	Two ways to issue a client redirect: HSE_REQ_ SEND_URL_REDIRECT_RESP sends a "302 Redirect" HTTP status code to the browser, thereby forcing the browser to resubmit the request. The *HSE_REQ_SEND_URL* option does not force the browser to resend a request for the new URL; instead, it changes the URL as if the client had requested a new URL.*

* *The IIS documentation mistakenly refers to a* ServerSupportFunction dwHSERequest *parameter of* HSE_REQ_SEND_URL_EX. *If you look in the HTTPEXT.H file, you won't find this value there. This is a problem with the documentation, and you can ignore this parameter since it does not exist.*

We won't go through all the *ServerSupportFunction* capabilities in detail here, but if you want to learn more about the mysteries of this "monster" API, look in the IIS SDK documentation. We will refer back to the *ServerSupportFunction* a few more times, however, in our discussion of the asynchronous read/write facilities of ISAPI.

Threads and ISAPI Extension Behavior

Before we talk about asynchronous functionality, let's look at the ISAPI extension architecture once again—specifically, ISAPI extensions and thread management. As mentioned, thread pools are a cornerstone of IIS architecture and its ability to handle requests efficiently. In Chapter 16, you learned about the thread pool maintained by MTX for Web applications (including ISAPI extensions). For the remainder of this section, we will be talking about the MTX thread pool that governs threads used by ISAPI extension DLLs.

IIS is designed to handle thousands of simultaneous requests. If requests are aimed at an ISAPI extension, having to start a new thread for each ISAPI request will probably bring Windows NT to a complete halt. If any application spawns thousands of threads, the entire CPU's power is wasted on context switches between running threads as well as the cost of creating each thread. IIS does not create a new thread for each ISAPI invocation. For each ISAPI extension request, a thread is taken from the thread pool. After an ISAPI extension has finished, the thread is released and placed back in the thread pool.

There's a good chance that the same ISAPI extension DLL will be invoked by multiple clients at the same time, which means that more than one thread will be using the ISAPI extension DLL and executing *HttpExtensionProc* at exactly the same time. If an ISAPI extension DLL uses any global data that can be written and read, access to all such data must be strictly controlled using synchronization objects. (We'll see how to use synchronization objects in Chapter 21.)

Access to global data is a minor issue compared to our next topic: blocking. If an ISAPI extension DLL blocks (either intentionally, by waiting for an API that takes a long time, such as waiting for a database connection, or unintentionally, because of a bug), thread execution is stopped. This means that the thread is taken from the pool and is not placed back in a timely fashion. Suppose a thread pool has *n* threads and there are *n* requests for the ISAPI DLL that blocks. The picture is clear: the entire thread pool will be depleted. IIS is capable of creating a new thread for a new request if needed, but that's not the point. The point is that we now have quite a few threads on the system. Granted, blocked threads don't burn many CPU cycles, but each thread still needs some nonpaged memory and other system resources. Usually, when a scenario like this occurs, the performance of IIS suffers. But there is a solution for this problem.

Glossary

blocking *Halting the execution of a thread until a certain condition occurs or a blocking function completes. Processes or threads can block intentionally by waiting for certain objects or by waiting for blocking function calls such as writing data to or reading data from a file.*

Consider the following: an ISAPI extension submits a database query or performs some other time-consuming task. It would be nice if we could create our ISAPI extension's own queue or thread pool to manage all the lengthy tasks for all possible DLL invocations. Well, we can do this by creating additional threads to do our processing; these are known as *worker threads*. One or more worker threads, created only once (in *DllMain* or *GetExtensionVersion*) can queue up and then handle at their leisure potentially hundreds of time-consuming tasks. What happens to the original ISAPI thread that called *HttpExtensionProc*? We should simply release it back to IIS and indicate that a worker thread is still alive. There is a great performance benefit in using such an architecture. An ISAPI extension is invoked, submits its tasks to the worker thread, and then releases its original thread back to the pool.

The system is not cluttered with hundreds of threads; instead, a limited number of worker threads (or a single worker thread, for that matter) does the job.

ServerSupportFunction and *HttpExtensionProc* are both used to provide support for a worker thread architecture. Here's how it works:

1. *HttpExtensionProc* returns *HSE_STATUS_PENDING*, which indicates that the request was queued for processing by the DLL and that the ISAPI extension is releasing the thread back to the pool. IIS still keeps the client connected.
2. Once the thread has finished request processing for a particular request (uniquely identified by the ECB *ConnID* structure field), the thread notifies IIS by calling *ServerSupportFunction* with *dwHSERequest* set to *HSE_REQ_DONE_WITH_SESSION*. This value indicates to IIS that the request has been completed.

Using an ISAPI extension's private thread pool enables a programmer to create truly powerful applications that otherwise would not be possible if the DLL were intended to perform a long task. Without implementing a private thread pool, extensions performing lengthy tasks would not scale well when used intensively because of the constant CPU thread switching and depletion of system resources. The system would also become cluttered with hundreds of threads. Remember one very important point, however. All this will work only if IIS caches ISAPI applications (which is the default). Otherwise, unloading the ISAPI extension while there are executing threads would have disastrous consequences. You are certainly guaranteed to get an access violation if this were to occur. The way to prevent this problem is to first ensure that IIS caches the ISAPI extensions and second ensure that your ISAPI extensions gracefully handle ISAPI termination calls. Here is where you might find *TerminateExtension* handy. When the *TerminateExtension* function is called, in the case of an unload event, you could either shut down all running threads (by setting a global synchronization object, for example) or, if the event is an advisory unload, refuse to unload.

NOTE

*In the case of a mandatory unload, ISAPI extensions can't prevent IIS from unloading them. It is possible, however, to add ISAPI filter entry points (*GetFilterVersion *and* HttpFilterProc*) to your DLL so that it will also become an ISAPI filter. ISAPI filter DLLs load on site startup and are not unloaded unless the site shuts down. ISAPI filters will be covered in more detail in Chapter 21.*

◆ Where Do You Go from Here?

The Windows NT 4.0 Option Pack comes with the IIS SDK optional component, available through the Custom Installation option. The IIS SDK comes with two samples: \Inetpub\iissamples\sdk\isapi\extensions\WorkerThread and \Inetpub\iissamples\sdk\isapi\extensions\KeepAliveWithThreads

The first sample demonstrates how to create a worker thread in your *HttpExtensionProc* and how to perform processing in this thread. While this sample demonstrates how to perform time-consuming processing in a separate thread, it does not reduce the total number of threads on the system.

The second sample is much more functional (and much more complex). It demonstrates how to create and manage a thread pool in an ISAPI extension DLL. Regardless of how many times *HttpExtensionProc* is invoked (that is, regardless of the number or requests), only a fixed number of running threads can exist. Another important function of the thread pool is keeping clients connected while the pool thread handles a lengthy task—in other words, if the Web browser has submitted a form with a database query, the client must remain connected in order to receive the query results. Without maintaining a thread pool (keeping threads running), keeping clients connected would not be possible. Once the thread exits, the client will be disconnected.

Asynchronous API Calls in ISAPI Extensions

The advanced functionality of an ISAPI extension DLL is not limited to the ability of *HttpExtenstionProc* to return *HSE_STATUS_PENDING*, thus releasing the thread to the IIS thread pool. Other high-performance features of IIS include asynchronous input and output capabilities.

Asynchronous WriteClient

As mentioned, by default *WriteClient* blocks for the duration of time it takes the function to send its data. *WriteClient* can work asynchronously, however, by setting the last parameter to *HSE_IO_ASYNC*. This setting means that we can now submit a large buffer to *WriteClient* and not be blocked while IIS is sending the data to the browser. Since we are not keeping ISAPI threads blocked, we have a chance to exit (return *HSE_STATUS_PENDING* from *HttpExtensionProc*), to complete processing in the ISAPI extension's own thread, or to perform some other task (such as updating a database record). If you decide to use asynchronous capabilities, be prepared for some heavy-duty programming. The sequence of calling *WriteClient* asynchronously is as follows:

1. Your ISAPI extension calls *ServerSupportFunction* with *dwHSERequest* set to *HSE_REQ_IO_COMPLETION* and *lpvBuffer* pointing to a callback

function in your ISAPI DLL. This sets the callback function, which is defined as:

```
VOID WINAPI * PFN_HSE_IO_COMPLETION
(
  EXTENSION_CONTROL_BLOCK * pECB,
  PVOID  pContext,
  DWORD  cbIO,
  DWORD  dwError
);
```

2. Once the callback function is set, the application calls *WriteClient* with *HSE_IO_ASYNC* as the *dwReserved* parameter.

The callback function will be called by IIS if an error occurs or on completion of the asynchronous *WriteClient* request. This function will be called with the following parameters:

- **pContext** A unique value identifying the request that was passed to *ServerSupportFunction* when the callback was installed
- **cbIO** The number of bytes transmitted
- **dwError** A Win32 status code

If there is more data to send (say, the first call to *WriteClient* sent only 1 out of 10 MBs of data), any additional I/O requests would be resubmitted here. If there is nothing else to do (say, I/O has completed and all data has been sent or received), *ServerSupportFunction* is called with *HSE_REQ_DONE_WITH_SESSION* to indicate to IIS that the session is complete. In fact, this technique is similar to what we did earlier to create an additional thread to handle lengthy requests.

Asynchronous TransmitFile

As if *WriteClient* wasn't complicated enough, one more feature can make ISAPI send data to the client at the speed of light. This functionality tightly integrates with the Win32 *TransmitFile* API. Without going into too much detail, we will tell you that the *TransmitFile* API uses some Windows NT kernel "trickery" to be the most efficient API to transmit an entire file from one network peer to another. If an ISAPI extension needs to send an entire file to a client (say, a picture file), *TransmitFile* is the way to go. Incidentally, this call can be made only asynchronously, which makes sense because we are going to great lengths here to create a truly high performance application. The *TransmitFile* capability is accessible indirectly from the *ServerSupportFunction* callback by supplying *HSE_REQ_TRANSMIT_FILE* as the *dwHSERequest* parameter.

Although this idea is similar to using *WriteFile*, once the call is made the implementation is slightly different. The callback function could be installed either using *ServerSupportFunction* and *HSE_REQ_IO_COMPLETION* as the *dwHSERequest* parameter or by passing a pointer to an *HSE_TF_INFO* structure, as the *lpvBuffer* parameter, used in conjunction with *ServerSupportFunction* and *HSE_REQ_TRANSMIT_FILE* as the *dwHSERequest* parameter. This structure provides information about the file to be transmitted, HTTP status codes, and optional headers to be sent before the file, as well as information about the callback function in the absence of a previously called *ServerSupportFunction* with *HSE_REQ_IO_COMPLETION* as the *dwHSERequest* parameter. Here is the *HSE_TF_INFO* structure:

```
typedef struct _HSE_TF_INFO {
  //
  // Callback and context information
  // The callback function will be called when I/O is completed.
  // The context specified will be used during such a callback.
  //
  // These values (if non-NULL) will override the one set by
  // calling ServerSupportFunction with HSE_REQ_IO_COMPLETION.
  //
  PFN_HSE_IO_COMPLETION  pfnHseIO;
  PVOID  pContext;
  // File should have been opened with FILE_FLAG_SEQUENTIAL_SCAN
  HANDLE hFile;
  //
  // HTTP header and status code
  // These fields are used only if HSE_IO_SEND_HEADERS is present
  // in dwFlags.
  //
  LPCSTR pszStatusCode; // HTTP status code--e.g., "200 OK"
  DWORD  BytesToWrite;  // Special value 0 means write entire file.
  DWORD  Offset;        // Offset value within file to start from
  PVOID  pHead;         // Header buffer sent before file data
  DWORD  HeadLength;    // Header length
  PVOID  pTail;         // Tail buffer to be sent after file data
  DWORD  TailLength;    // Tail length
  DWORD  dwFlags;       // Includes HSE_IO_DISCONNECT_AFTER_SEND...
} HSE_TF_INFO, * LPHSE_TF_INFO;
```

The flexibility of this structure helps make the transmission of the file from the server to the client a one-shot deal; you don't even need to send separate headers and a status code. Everything is taken care of. With all this said, we've hopefully showed you some new ways to send data to the client more efficiently from an ISAPI extension.

◆ Where Do You Go from Here?

The IIS SDK includes two asynchronous samples: \Inetpub\iissamples\sdk\isapi\extensions\io\ASyncWrite and \Inetpub\iissamples\sdk\isapi\extensions\io\AsyncTrans. These samples demonstrate how to use the asynchronous *WriteFile* and *TransmitFile* functions. Unfortunately, both samples erroneously state (in the corresponding README.TXT files) that they can be used to send GIF files to the browser. This is not the case. Both samples send an HTTP Content-Type: text/html header to the browser, thereby forcing the browser to render incoming data as HTML text instead of displaying any image formats.

You can use the samples as they are (they do demonstrate the concepts) with HTML files. Or better yet, you can find the place where the Content-Type HTTP header is set and modify the sample so that correct headers would be sent for various file types.

Data reading

Unlike *WriteClient*, the *ReadClient* API does not provide direct support for asynchronous operation, which means that if you need to read data in a nonblocking fashion, you might as well forget about using *ReadClient*. As you've probably guessed by now, this functionality is exposed via *ServerSupportFunction*. To read data asynchronously, you must first call the *ServerSupportFunction* function using *HSE_REQ_IO_COMPLETION* (as described in the previous sections, "*Asynchronous* TransmitFile" and "*Asynchronous* WriteClient") to set a callback in your ISAPI DLL. After the callback is set, you can call the *ServerSupportFunction* using *HSE_REQ_ASYNC_READ_CLIENT* as the *dwHSERequest* parameter and *HSE_IO_ASYNC* as the *lpdwDataType* parameter. When reading has been completed, the callback function will be called with the number of bytes read. How do you know when to stop reading? If a read completes indicating 0 bytes read, the client has gracefully closed the connection. By the way, if you are using any kind of asynchronous API, you should become familiar with Win32 error *998* (*ERROR_IO_PENDING*). When an API is submitted asynchronously, it will fail with this error, which does not indicate a problem but rather that the Windows NT Operating System has accepted the request and is working on it.

◆ Where Do You Go from Here?

The IIS SDK includes an \Inetpub\iissamples\sdk\isapi\extensions\io\ASyncRead sample that demonstrates how to read data asynchronously. This sample uses *ServerSupportFunction* with the *HSE_REQ_ASYNC_READ_CLIENT* option to implement asynchronous reads in an ISAPI extension. The sample also uses the *ServerSupportFunction* to set a callback function that is called upon completion of the I/O operation.

A Sample ISAPI DLL

Whew! Enough hardcore programming for now. Let's do some fun stuff. In this section, we'll create a sample ISAPI DLL that demonstrates some of the principles we've been examining.

Recall our sample CGI application earlier in this chapter. This ISAPI extension application will work in exactly the same way. It is not going to use standard input and output, but it will accomplish the same task. Here's the code:

```
#include <windows.h>
#include <httpext.h>

// HTML Form Templates
char *szHtmlUserName = "<html><h1>Sample ISAPI Extension</h1><hr>"
  "User Name from GetServerVariable (blank means anonymous was "
  " used)<i>%s</i><br> User Name from Win32 API GetUserName "
  "(actual user context of the thread): <i>%s</i> </html>";

char *szHtmlPID = "<html><h1>Sample ISAPI Extension</h1><hr>"
  "ISAPI is running in Process ID: %lu <br></html>";

char *szDefaultHtmlOut ="<html><h1>Sample ISAPI Extension</h1><hr>"
  "<font=+3>Select from the following:</font><br>\n"
  "<a href=%s?getproc>"
  "Get process ID </a><br>\n<a href=%s?getuser> Get user ID </a>"
  "<html>\n";

BOOL WINAPI GetExtensionVersion(HSE_VERSION_INFO *pVer)
{
  pVer->dwExtensionVersion = MAKELONG(HSE_VERSION_MINOR,
                                      HSE_VERSION_MAJOR);
  lstrcpyn(pVer->lpszExtensionDesc, "ISAPI Sample",
           HSE_MAX_EXT_DLL_NAME_LEN);
  return TRUE;
}

DWORD WINAPI HttpExtensionProc(EXTENSION_CONTROL_BLOCK *lpEcb)
{
  char szHtmlOut[1000];
  DWORD dwSize;
  char szScriptName [256];
  // Send headers to the client;
  // terminate with double Carriage Return - Line Feed: \r\n\r\n.
  lpEcb->ServerSupportFunction(lpEcb->ConnID,
                         HSE_REQ_SEND_RESPONSE_HEADER, NULL, NULL,
                         (LPDWORD)"Content-type: text/html\r\n\r\n");
```

```
// Different functions are performed based on QueryString
// if user name requested.
if(!_stricmp(lpEcb->lpszQueryString, "getuser"))
{
  char szGSVUserName[30], szWin32UserName[30];
  // Get user name using GetServerVariable.
  dwSize = 30;
  if(!lpEcb->GetServerVariable(lpEcb->ConnID,
                               "REMOTE_USER",
                               szGSVUserName,
                               &dwSize))
    wsprintf(szGSVUserName, "ERROR!: %lu", GetLastError());

  // Get user name of the current thread using Win32 API.
  dwSize = 30;
  if(!GetUserName( szWin32UserName, &dwSize))
    wsprintf(szWin32UserName, "ERROR!: %lu", GetLastError());

  // Send the data to the client.
  wsprintf(szHtmlOut, szHtmlUserName,
           szGSVUserName, szWin32UserName);
  dwSize = lstrlen(szHtmlOut);
  lpEcb->WriteClient(lpEcb->ConnID, szHtmlOut, &dwSize, 0);
  return HSE_STATUS_SUCCESS;
}

// If process information requested,...
if(!_stricmp(lpEcb->lpszQueryString, "getproc"))
{
  // ...get the process ID and send it to the client.
  wsprintf(szHtmlOut, szHtmlPID, GetCurrentProcessId());
  dwSize = lstrlen(szHtmlOut);
  lpEcb->WriteClient(lpEcb->ConnID, szHtmlOut, &dwSize, 0);
  return HSE_STATUS_SUCCESS;
}
// If no function or unsupported function requested,
// send default page.
dwSize = sizeof(szScriptName);
if(!lpEcb->GetServerVariable(lpEcb->ConnID, "SCRIPT_NAME",
                             szScriptName, &dwSize))
  wsprintf(szHtmlOut, "ERROR!: %lu", GetLastError());
else
  wsprintf (szHtmlOut, szDefaultHtmlOut, szScriptName,
            szScriptName);
```

(continued)

```
    dwSize = lstrlen(szHtmlOut);
    lpEcb->WriteClient(lpEcb->ConnID, szHtmlOut, &dwSize, 0);
    return HSE_STATUS_SUCCESS;
}
```

As you can see, this simple extension handles only *GET* requests (because it looks only at the *lpszQueryString* field of the ECB). As we did in the CGI application, here we send the Content-Type header to the browser, but this time we are using *ServerSupportFunction*. *ServerSupportFunction* also takes care of sending "200 OK," which is the HTTP status code when the third parameter (*lpvBuffer*) is *NULL*.

Let's see what our ISAPI extension does. Invoking it without parameters, as in *http://leonbr-hm/scripts/isapi.dll*, renders the HTML page shown in Figure 20.6.

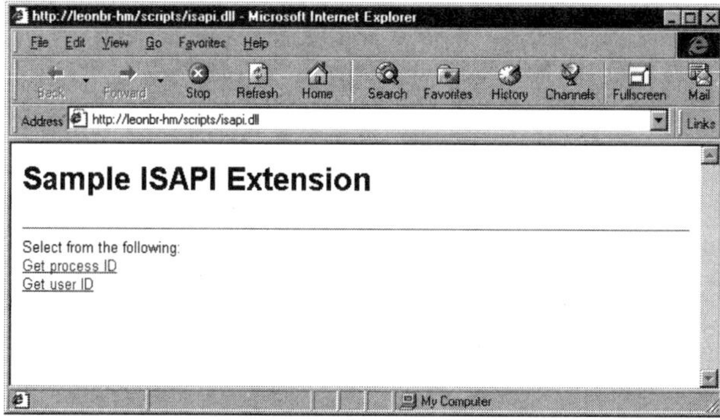

FIGURE 20.6

Default output when ISAPI.DLL is invoked without parameters.

As with the CGI sample application, we can get both the process ID and the user name by invoking our ISAPI extension with different parameters. Let's run our sample through the same tests that we ran our CGI application through. First let's get the user name when the anonymous user is allowed, as shown in Figure 20.7.

If we don't allow an anonymous connection, our Web browser will send credentials that will cause our ISAPI extension to create the output shown in Figure 20.8. (In this example, we've provided credentials for a user named JoeB.)

This is exactly what we expected to see. Anonymous ISAPI extensions impersonate the built-in user IUSR_LEONBR-HM, and when credentials are supplied, the entered user—in this case, JoeB—is impersonated.

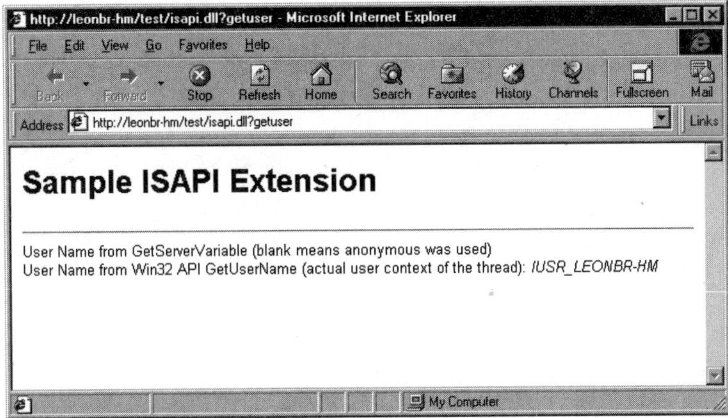

FIGURE 20.7

Default output when ISAPI.DLL is invoked with an anonymous user context.

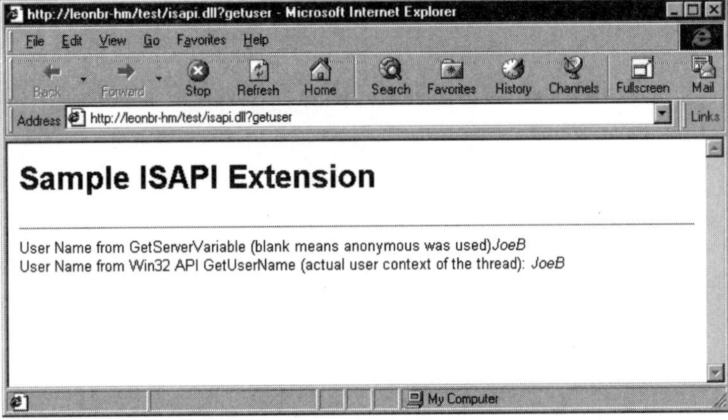

FIGURE 20.8

Default output when ISAPI.DLL is invoked with a user context of JoeB.

Let's now obtain the ISAPI DLL PID. First we'll get the PID when our application is configured to run in-proc, and then we'll get the PID of an ISAPI extension that is running out-of-proc. To accomplish this, we've copied ISAPI.DLL to two virtual directories. Both directories are configured as separate Web applications (we learned how to do this in Chapter 4) and run applications in either the same process (the *scripts* directory) or in a separate process (the \test directory). Following are the results of the extension invocation with the corresponding URLs.

- *http://leonbr-hm/scripts/isapi.dll?getproc,* in-proc ISAPI output:

```
ISAPI is running in Process ID: 244
```

- *http://leonbr-hm/test/isapi.dll?getproc,* out-of-proc ISAPI output:

```
ISAPI is running in Process ID: 162
```

These numbers don't match! Let's take a look at Task Manager, shown in Figure 20.9.

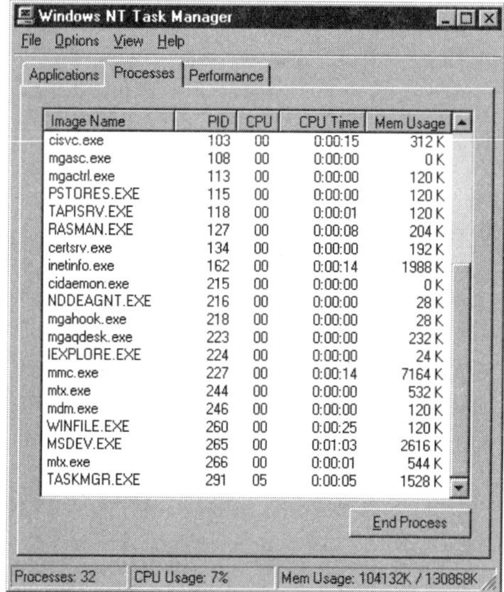

FIGURE 20.9

Windows NT Task Manager.

It's not difficult to discover that PID 244 corresponds to the INETINFO.EXE process and PID 162 corresponds to MTX.EXE. These are the expected results. INETINFO.EXE is the actual executable that contains the Web Publishing Service and loads in-proc applications. MTX.EXE is the MTS component that loads out-of-proc applications. Note that the system can run more than one instance of MTX.EXE at a time. Even though MTX.EXE runs under the IWAM_LEONBR-HM account (the WAM account) on our machine, the ISAPI extensions themselves are still invoked after IIS impersonates the IUSR-LEONBR-HM account for anonymous connections.

ISAPI Debugging

This sample ISAPI extension demonstrates some very important concepts. It was easy to write and did not require debugging. But how would we go about debugging our ISAPI extension code?

When you are debugging ISAPI extensions, remember that they are either loaded by the IIS service process or by a process that is started by the IIS service process. Thus, all the rules and difficulties of debugging services apply. There are at least two ways of debugging an ISAPI extension DLL. (You can undoubtedly find other techniques, such as using *DebugBreak*, but be aware that the complications we discussed earlier when talking about debugging CGI applications also apply here.)

Before we examine the particulars of debugging an ISAPI extension, take a look at the following location in the Windows NT 4.0 Option Pack documentation: Microsoft Internet Information Server\Advanced Web Application Development\Debugging Your Application\Establishing a Debugging Environment. This documentation describes the exact steps to follow to debug ISAPI extension DLLs. (By the way, the same steps apply when you are debugging ISAPI filter DLLs, which we will discuss in Chapter 21.) To avoid simply repeating the documentation, here we'll give only a quick overview of the debugging process.

One method of debugging ISAPI extensions consists of attaching the debugger to the running INETINFO.EXE process for in-proc applications. For out-of-proc applications, you will need to attach the debugger to MTX.EXE. Be careful here, because you might have more than one MTX.EXE process running on your system. It can be helpful to include code in your ISAPI extension DLL that reports the PID in which it is running. The other method for debugging consists of running INETINFO.EXE interactively as a process in the debugger, instead of running it as a service. This method changes the security context of INETINFO.EXE, however, to the security context of the interactively logged on user who starts the process.

Running INETINFO.EXE interactively was trivial with IIS 3.0. Supplying the *–e w3svc* parameter to the INETINFO.EXE process did the trick. This approach is no longer possible with IIS 4.0. To accomplish the same task, several registry entries must be modified. The documentation mentioned above lists the steps of this process in detail and explains the modifications that need to be made. Attaching the debugger to INETINFO.EXE (or to MTX.EXE) while it runs as a service tends to be a much easier method of debugging.

NOTE

Hunting down the correct registry location and modifying it just to debug an ISAPI extension might seem like a lot of work. And it really is! However, the IIS SDK includes two .REG files that will make the appropriate registry modifications for you. Hold on, though. Before you rush out to run these files, please review the explanation file in the same directory: \Inetpub\iissamples\sdk\components\IIS_as_process.txt.

◆ How Do I Debug a DLL That Fails to Load?

There are two common reasons why IIS fails to load an ISAPI extension DLL. (Of course, when the DLL doesn't load, you can't even get as far as running the debugger, which poses some obvious difficulties.) One reason an ISAPI extension DLL might not load is due to a dependency on other DLLs. Assume that ISAPI.DLL was written using the Microsoft Foundation Classes (MFC). Such a DLL imports a variety of functions from the MFC and C run-time environment. If the appropriate DLLs are missing from the current directory or are not in the search path, IIS won't be able to load the ISAPI extension DLL.

The other reason that IIS might fail to load an ISAPI extension is because of a failure to export the mandatory ISAPI entry points. If your ISAPI DLL does not export *GetExtensionVersion* and *HttpExtensionProc*, it won't be loaded.

Both these problems can be easily identified by using a special utility named DUMPBIN.EXE included with Microsoft Visual C++. Along with many other capabilities, this utility can display all the exports and imports for a DLL or an executable file. To see what DLLs are imported by ISAPI.DLL, enter the following at the command-line prompt:

```
Dumpbin isapi.dll /imports
```

Exports are shown by entering the following command:

```
Dumpbin isapi.dll /exports
```

DUMPBIN.EXE often produces lengthy output. If this is the case with your DLL, pipe it to the *more* utility so that you can view one screen at a time (for example: *Dumpbin isapi.dll /exports | more*).

We've covered a lot in this chapter. We've covered CGI applications, ISAPI extensions, and IIS's way of handling both, and we've looked at some debugging techniques. We've even covered some of the advanced techniques for writing high-performance asynchronous applications. Now that we've seen the reach and power of writing ISAPI extension DLLs, one question comes to mind: What can ISAPI extensions do?

The answer is: many things. You can create ISAPI applications for online transaction processing (such as credit card validation) that is capable of handling thousands of clients without creating thousands of threads. Web applications consisting of multiple ASP scripts might benefit greatly from working with ISAPI extensions to perform some of the more intensive tasks. The coolest thing that ISAPI extensions allow you to do, however, is to write custom *script interpreters*. Script interpreters provide a means for ISAPI extensions to preprocess files (or run scripts) before sending them to the client. ASP, the Internet Database Connector (IDC), and Server-Side Includes (SSI) are all implemented as ISAPI extension DLLs. Many other script interpreters are available out there, but the best of them are implemented as extension DLLs. Sounds intriguing, doesn't it? In the next chapter, you'll learn how to write a custom script interpreter and how to use ISAPI filters.

Chapter 21

ISAPI Filters, Extensions, and Custom Script Interpreters

In our discussion of the Internet Server Application Programming Interface (ISAPI) extensions in Chapter 20, we saw that ISAPI provides the programmer with a powerful tool. ISAPI extensions can accomplish a wide variety of tasks with greater efficiency than higher-level components such as ASP because they have access to the low level architecture of IIS. ISAPI extensions are a good choice for performing most advanced tasks, but several more options that provide even greater functionality are available, including ISAPI filters and server-side custom script interpreters.

Up to now, we've talked about all the various options and services available for configuring IIS to fit your needs, but in this chapter we'll take IIS customization to the next level. Here you'll learn how to write *ISAPI filters*—dynamic link libraries (DLLs) that affect various aspects of server request processing. You'll also learn how to create your own scripting capabilities by writing a server-side custom script interpreter (also known as a script processor). As it turns out, you already know how to use a number of script interpreters that are part of the IIS installation, including ASP, Server Side Includes (SSI), and the Internet Database Connector (IDC). By writing your own script interpreter, you'll get a better feel for how script maps work. (Script maps were discussed in Chapter 16.) Let's begin by looking at ISAPI filters.

ISAPI Filters

Even though the logic of a client's interaction with the server is not too complex (how hard can it be to receive a request and send back a reply?), to effectively process a client's request, IIS must do a lot of work. Here we'll look at a way to change the default behavior of IIS and modify how HTTP requests are handled. In effect, this technique will enable the programmer to write a custom building block that plugs into the IIS framework. This building block is, of course, an ISAPI filter, which can be used to greatly extend (or impair) IIS functionality.

ISAPI Filter Architecture

The processing of a client request can be separated into several steps, as shown here:

1. IIS reads the raw request data.
2. IIS processes the HTTP request headers.
3. IIS maps the URL, in the form *http://server/document.htm*, to a physical path on the machine such as d:\inetpub\wwwroot\document.htm.
4. If this is the first request over the connection, IIS authenticates the user.
5. If the client sends *POST* data with its request, the server begins to read the data in chunks.
6. IIS, and potentially a Web server application, sends HTTP headers to the client.
7. The server sends the response data to the client.
8. The server ends the processing of the request. Note that the session might remain open.
9. The server writes request information to the log. (See Chapter 6 for more information about event logging.)
10. The server session is closed.

IIS was designed to handle each of these steps. Writing an ISAPI filter enables the programmer to write code that will be executed by the server for each step. Therefore, if you don't like how IIS maps a requested URL to a physical drive location, you can write a filter that will change how the URL is mapped. You might want to redirect a client request to different documents depending on the type of browser being used by the client. A filter can easily handle this situation. The greatest feature of filters is that they are completely transparent to higher-level IIS applications. ASP applications, ISAPI extensions, and anything else invoked on the server side don't know whether filters were involved.

Filter Implementation

Filters are implemented as DLLs; they are registered with IIS and loaded in its process space on server or site start-up. (Chapter 4 describes how to register filters with IIS using the Management Console's ISAPI Filters page.) After the filter is loaded, it advises IIS of which steps in the server request processing it needs to be notified about. For example, if a programmer wants to modify the default action performed by the Web server when a URL is mapped to a file, the filter would need to register its interest in receiving URL mapping notifications. Because a filter can request a number of different notifications, IIS in turn notifies the filter DLL about what step is currently taking place in the processing of the request. It does so by calling one of the functions in the filter with a specific notification value. Each step described in the filter architecture has a specific value associated with it.

The fundamental difference between an ISAPI extension and an ISAPI filter is that an ISAPI extension is loaded and called only when requested. Although ISAPI extensions are cached, they are eventually unloaded. ISAPI filter DLLs are loaded by the server at start-up and stay in memory until the server or site is shut down. Filters are called for each request arriving at the server, whereas extensions are called only when they are specifically requested. For example, if our ISAPI filter requests to be notified of URL mappings and 1000 different clients each generate 10 URL map requests, our ISAPI filter will be called 10,000 times. On the other hand, if one of the URL mappings that each of the clients requested resulted in an ISAPI extension being executed, the extension would be called only 1000 times.

A poorly written filter can have disastrous consequences to IIS. It can either shut down IIS or slow it to an unusable speed. Since an ISAPI filter can be called to handle every request made, it is very important that the filter be written so that it is as efficient as possible. Also, remember that an ISAPI filter executes in the process space of IIS. So forgetting to close a handle or free an allocated resource could quickly reduce the performance of IIS, if not stop it all together.

The core of a filter DLL is simple. It must export two mandatory entry points: *GetFilterVersion* and *HttpFilterProc* functions. The *GetFilterVersion* function provides filter information to the server and supplies a list of events that the filter will be handling. It is called only once—when the server or site starts. Because more than one filter can be registered with IIS at one time, filters specify a *priority level.* Filters with a higher priority level have the first shot at handling notifications. If several filters have the same priority level, their load order is determined by the order in which they appear on the Management Console's ISAPI Filter page.

HttpFilterProc is the main function in an ISAPI filter. For each event that a filter has registered an interest in, *HttpFilterProc* is called with the notification type and the appropriate data structure. In the case of URL map notifications, this structure will include information about the URL and its physical path.

A filter can also provide an optional entry point named *TerminateFilter,* which will be called when the filter is being unloaded. This call will happen only when IIS is stopped or, for a site filter, when the site is stopped. As we saw in Chapter 4, IIS is able to host multiple sites. Individual filters can be loaded on a site specific basis, which means that a filter installed for one site will not affect the behavior of another site running on the same server machine. Remember one very important point, though: if the filter handles raw read (*SF_NOTIFY_READ_RAW*) notifications, it can be loaded only as a global filter. If it is configured as a site specific filter, the filter will fail to load and an error event with explanations will be logged to the Windows NT Event Log. To install a global filter via the Management Console, you must go to the WWW Service Master Properties window instead of the Site Properties window (again, as discussed in Chapter 4).

One other entry point might be useful for your filter because, after all, a filter is a DLL: *DllMain*. You can use *DllMain* to perform a certain amount of initialization and cleanup. The operating system calls this optional function in the DLL to notify it of attaching and detaching processes and threads. (We discussed *DllMain* in detail in Chapter 20.)

In the following sections, we'll examine some of the details of the different functions that an ISAPI filter exports.

NOTE

All the values and filter-related structures are defined in the HTTPFILT.H header file included with the Microsoft Platform SDK and the IIS SDK found in the Microsoft Windows NT 4.0 Option Pack. Note that Microsoft Visual C++ versions 4.2 and later also include this header file; however, this file is an older version and does not provide the additions available in IIS 4.0

GetFilterVersion

The objective of the *GetFilterVersion* function is to set the filter priority level and register for the event notifications of interest to the filter. In the following code from our sample filter, we specified a high filter priority by using *SF_NOTIFY_ORDER_HIGH*. This setting ensures that when multiple filters are loaded, this filter is handled before filters of a lower priority. The notification we're interested in handling is *SF_NOTIFY_URL_MAP*, which is triggered by IIS when it maps a URL to its physical location. In *GetFilterVersion*, the filter also registers a short description with the server and indicates whether it wants notifications for secure, encrypted connections over SSL links, non-encrypted connections, or both. Our sample filter's description string, *"Smart Redir Filter"*, will work for connections coming to secure ports (indicated by *SF_NOTIFY_SECURE_PORT*) and to nonsecure ports (indicated by *SF_NOTIFY_NONSECURE_PORT*).

```
BOOL WINAPI GetFilterVersion(PHTTP_FILTER_VERSION pFilterVersion)
{
  pFilterVersion->dwFilterVersion = HTTP_FILTER_REVISION;
  strcpy(pFilterVersion->lpszFilterDesc, "Smart Redir Filter");
  pFilterVersion->dwFlags = (SF_NOTIFY_ORDER_HIGH      |
                             SF_NOTIFY_SECURE_PORT     |
                             SF_NOTIFY_NONSECURE_PORT  |
                             SF_NOTIFY_URL_MAP);
  return TRUE;
}
```

This function is called only once—when the filter is loaded by IIS. If you need to perform initialization, *GetFilterVersion* would be a good place to do it.

HttpFilterProc

The next step is to add the code that does the real work of your filter. As mentioned, *HttpFilterProc* is the core function of an ISAPI filter DLL. It is similar to the *HttpExtensionProc* function for ISAPI extensions that you learned about in Chapter 20. *HttpFilterProc* is called by the server with a pointer to an *HTTP_FILTER_CONTEXT* structure as the first parameter. (The *HTTP_FILTER_CONTEXT* structure is similar to the *EXTENSION_CONTROL_BLOCK* structure, which the *HttpExtensionProc* of an ISAPI extension receives.) Here is the *HttpFilterProc* prototype:

```
DWORD WINAPI HttpFilterProc(PHTTP_FILTER_CONTEXT pfc,
                            DWORD notificationType,
                            LPVOID pvNotification);
```

The *HTTP_FILTER_CONTEXT* structure is unique for each request. It not only carries request identification information, but it also carries pointers to other functions that can be used in your filter. The *HTTP_FILTER_CONTEXT* structure is defined as follows:

```
typedef struct _HTTP_FILTER_CONTEXT
{
   DWORD  cbSize;
   DWORD  Revision;
   PVOID  ServerContext;
   DWORD  ulReserved;
   BOOL   fIsSecurePort;
   PVOID  pFilterContext;
   BOOL   (WINAPI * GetServerVariable);
   BOOL   (WINAPI * AddResponseHeaders);
   BOOL   (WINAPI * WriteClient);
   VOID * (WINAPI * AllocMem);
   BOOL   (WINAPI * ServerSupportFunction);
} HTTP_FILTER_CONTEXT, *PHTTP_FILTER_CONTEXT;
```

GetServerVariable, *AddResponseHeader*, *WriteClient*, *AllocMem*, and *ServerSupportFunction* are pointers to the corresponding functions implemented by IIS. This point is a bit tricky since the functions themselves are not implemented in the filter. For a programmer to call a function residing in the server code, he or she must have pointers to these functions. That is precisely what the *HTTP_FILTER_CONTEXT* structure is doing: the structure returns pointers to the functions that can be used in the filter code. These callback functions are used by the filter to communicate with IIS (just as was done with the ISAPI extension callback functions we discussed in Chapter 20).

The second and third parameters of the *HttpFilterProc* function are the notification type and a pointer to the data structure specific to the notification. Notification-specific structures can contain a combination of data (such as the requested URL for a URL map notification) and pointers to other functions that make sense only for a specific notification. For example, here is the structure that is received by the filter when IIS has finished preprocessing an HTTP request's headers:

```
typedef struct _HTTP_FILTER_PREPROC_HEADERS
{
  BOOL   (WINAPI * GetHeader);
  BOOL   (WINAPI * SetHeader);
  BOOL   (WINAPI * AddHeader);
  DWORD  HttpStatus;
  DWORD  dwReserved;
} HTTP_FILTER_PREPROC_HEADERS, *PHTTP_FILTER_PREPROC_HEADERS;
```

Notice that *GetHeader, SetHeader,* and *AddHeader* are pointers to functions specific to the HTTP header manipulation and make sense only for preprocessing HTTP request and response headers.

The following table summarizes the notification types and the corresponding data structures received by ISAPI filter DLLs for each notification

Notification Type and Structure	Description
SF_NOTIFY_AUTHENTICATION *HTTP_FILTER_AUTHENT*	The server is authenticating an incoming user; this happens once per session. (See Chapter 12 for more information about authentication.)
SF_NOTIFY_END_OF_REQUEST no structure used	The server has finished processing the re quest. Note that the session to the client might still be open because of the HTTP Keep-Alive connection option. (Keep-Alive connections are explained in Chapter 23.) This notification is mainly used to enable you to clean up any request-specific data used by your filter.
SF_NOTIFY_READ_RAW_DATA *HTTP_FILTER_RAW_DATA*	The server is reading raw data from the underlying socket. By handling this notification, a filter can access the raw data being sent by the client. This notification can be posted more than once for each request.
SF_NOTIFY_PREPROC_HEADERS *HTTP_FILTER_PREPROC_HEADERS*	The server is about to process the request's headers. Server variables will become available at the next notification for this request.

Notification Type and Structure	Description
SF_NOTIFY_URL_MAP *HTTP_FILTER_URL_MAP*	The server is mapping the URL address (such as *http://machine/hello.htm*) to its physical path (such as d:\inetpub\wwwroot\hello.htm). The filter can specify a different physical path for this request at this notification.
SF_NOTIFY_SEND_RAW_DATA *HTTP_FILTER_RAW_DATA*	The server is sending data back to the client on the underlying socket; this can occur more than once for each request. The filter can change outgoing data by handling this notification. Note that you can't just replace the physical path for HELLO.HTM with HELLO.ASP and expect the server to execute ASP script. This notification comes too late in the chain of events and instead of running the script, the server will return ASP content to the client. If you need to change a request for a static file to a request for a script, you must change the URL header in the preprocessing header notification.
SF_NOTIFY_LOG *HTTP_FILTER_LOG*	The server is writing an entry to the IIS log. The filter can alter this information by handling this notification.
SF_NOTIFY_END_OF_NET_SESSION no structure used	The session between the client and the server has been closed. This notification is used mainly to clean up any session-specific data.
SF_NOTIFY_ACCESS_DENIED *HTTP_FILTER_ACCESS_DENIED*	The server couldn't access the requested document because access was denied. A "401 Access Denied" response status code is about to be sent to the client.
SF_NOTIFY_SEND_RESPONSE *HTTP_FILTER_SEND_RESPONSE* (the same as *HTTP_FILTER_PREPROC_HEADERS*)	The server is about to send HTTP response headers to the client. The filter can alter these headers by handling this notification.

Once *HttpFilterProc* has been called with certain notifications and the filter has processed the information, we need to return from *HttpFilterProc*. It's important that we do this as quickly as possible because IIS cannot do anything for the request while the filter DLL is handling a notification. That's why filters should be as efficient as possible. The server expects *HttpFilterProc* to return a *DWORD* value. This return value tells the server what to do next with the client's connection and the client's request. The following table lists the possible return values.

Return Value	Description
SF_STATUS_REQ_FINISHED	The request is complete; the server needs to close the session with the client.
SF_STATUS_REQ_FINISHED_KEEP_CONN	This is similar to *SF_STATUS_REQ_FINISHED*, except that if the Keep-Alive option was negotiated, the session should remain open.
SF_STATUS_REQ_NEXT_NOTIFICATION	If more than one filter is installed, the next filter in the chain should be called. For example, if a filter handles raw read or write operations (for instance, to perform custom data encoding), after the raw data has been changed, the next filter should be called (for example, to check certain custom headers).
SF_STATUS_REQ_HANDLED_NOTIFICATION	The notification was handled by this filter. Other handlers should not be called to handle this request.
SF_STATUS_REQ_ERROR	An error occurred in the filter. The filter can obtain an error code using the *GetLastError* API or set it using the *SetLastError* API. The server aborts the HTTP session if *HttpFilterProc* returns this value. There is no way to return a friendly error message to the client browser with this return code.
SF_STATUS_REQ_READ_NEXT	The filter is an opaque stream filter, reading large amounts of data from the server. Such a filter can perform decryption or compression and, for now, it just reads certain connection configuration parameters in the read raw data notifications. This value indicates to the server that the filter did not read all of the data. The server should post another read notification to the filter so that the filter will continue reading data.

Although the sequence of events in *HttpFilterProc* might seem straightforward, it is not so for all requests. When a server uses the NT LAN Manager (NTLM) authentication scheme, as discussed in Chapter 12, a client and a server might typically exchange three requests / responses in order to authenticate the client. The filter will be called for each request. Even a simple *SF_NOTIFY_URL_MAP* notification might be posted more than once for the same request. This redundancy occurs when a client invokes an ISAPI extension that calls the *ServerSupportFunction* with the *HSE_REQ_MAP_URL_TO_PATH* parameter to map a URL location to its physical path. Because an ISAPI extension can't map a URL to its physical path, it resorts to using a filter to do the mappings, thereby causing one more *SF_NOTIFY_URL_MAP* event in the filter to be out of its normal sequence.

NOTE

While handling the SF_NOTIFY_URL_MAP *notification you can't replace the physical path for an HTML file with an ASP file and expect the server to execute the ASP script. This notification comes too late in the chain of events and instead of running the script, the server will return ASP content to the client. If you need to change a request for a static file to a request for a script, you must change the URL header in the preprocessing headers notification* (SF_NOTIFY_PREPROC_HEADERS).

TerminateFilter

TerminateFilter is an optional entry point that is called by the server when the filter is going to be unloaded from memory. Here is the prototype:

```
DWORD WINAPI TerminateFilter(DWORD dwFlags);
```

In IIS 4.0, neither the *dwFlags* parameter nor the return value is used. Thus you can ignore *dwFlags*, return *1* as the *DWORD* value from the function, and everything will work just fine.

A Sample Filter: *SmartRedir*

Now let's apply our theoretical knowledge and write a sample filter. First let's look at what we want our sample filter (named *SmartRedir*) to do. Suppose we have a Web server that has a directory named IEONLY and that all documents in this directory use features (such as Dynamic HTML) that can be handled only by Internet Explorer version 4.0 or 4.01. Because no other types of browsers can correctly display the pages in the IEONLY directory correctly, they should not be able to access the directory or the files in the directory. Our filter will monitor the URLs requested by clients, and if the *IEONLY* string is present anywhere in the URL, the filter will check the User-Agent header to obtain a description of the client's browser. If the browser is not Internet Explorer 4.0 or 4.01 and the request is for files in the IEONLY directory, the filter does not allow the browser to access the requested document. Instead, it will redirect the browser to the GETIE.HTM file, which explains that the user must install the latest version of Internet Explorer in order to access this resource. You can even improve the code so that the filter allows not only Internet Explorer 4.0 or 4.01 but also all future browsers to access the resource. To do so, you will need to include some smart code to compare User-Agent header strings.

As we will see, the process of writing a filter that controls access to the specific directory based on the browser type is quite simple.

NOTE

You might be wondering why we would even bother to write such a filter. If the IEONLY directory contains only ASP files, we could add VBScript or JScript code in each file to check the user agent and redirect browsers other than Internet Explorer 4.0. However, this solution would not work for HTML files that don't have any script that executes when they are processed. If an HTML file contains features understandable only by Internet Explorer 4.0 (such as Dynamic HTML), other browsers won't be able to correctly render the file. (They might not even be capable of running client scripts that check for the browser version.) Converting current HTML files to ASP files might not be practical. A redirection filter fits this task perfectly because it will work for any kind of files in the IEONLY directory.

HttpFilterProc

We've already looked at our sample's *GetFilterVersion* function, which registered for the notifications we are interested in receiving, set the priority level, and set our filter's description. Now let's look at the heart of our sample, the *HttpFilterProc* function:

```
DWORD WINAPI HttpFilterProc(PHTTP_FILTER_CONTEXT pFC,
                            DWORD dwNotificationType,
                            LPVOID pvNotification)
{
  HTTP_FILTER_URL_MAP *pUrlMap;
  CHAR  szTemp [256], *lpszUserAgent, *lpszServer;
  DWORD dwSize = 0;

  if(dwNotificationType == SF_NOTIFY_URL_MAP)
  {
    pUrlMap = (HTTP_FILTER_URL_MAP *)pvNotification;
    if(strstr(strlwr((CHAR *)pUrlMap->pszURL), "ieonly"))
    {
      // This call should fail with ERROR_INSUFFICIENT_BUFFER error.
      // Check for other errors.
      pFC->GetServerVariable(pFC,"HTTP_USER_AGENT",
                             lpszUserAgent,&dwSize);
      lpszUserAgent = (CHAR *)pFC->AllocMem(pFC,dwSize,0);

      // Request is to IEONLY directory; check user agent.
      if(! pFC->GetServerVariable(pFC,"HTTP_USER_AGENT",
                                   lpszUserAgent,&dwSize))
```

```
        {
          pFC->ServerSupportFunction(pFC, SF_REQ_SEND_RESPONSE_HEADER,
                                     (PVOID)"200 OK", 0, 0);
          wsprintf(szTemp, "GetServerVariable failed: %d",
                   GetLastError());
          dwSize = lstrlen(szTemp);
          pFC->WriteClient(pFC, szTemp, &dwSize, HSE_IO_SYNC);
          return SF_STATUS_REQ_FINISHED;
        }
        if(! strstr(strlwr(lpszUserAgent), "msie 4"))
        {
          // Not an IE 4.0 or 4.01 browser; redirect client.
          // Get the name of the server, but first determine the
          // size of the buffer.
          dwSize = 0;
          pFC->GetServerVariable(pFC,"SERVER_NAME",
                                 lpszServer,&dwSize);
          lpszServer = (CHAR *)pFC->AllocMem(pFC, dwSize, 0);
          if(! pFC->GetServerVariable(pFC,"SERVER_NAME",
                                      lpszServer,&dwSize))
            return SF_STATUS_REQ_FINISHED; // Perform error check here.

          wsprintf(szTemp, "Location: http://%s/%s\r\n\r\n",
                   lpszServer, FILENAME);
          pFC->ServerSupportFunction(pFC, SF_REQ_SEND_RESPONSE_HEADER,
                                     (PVOID)"302 Redirect",
                                     (DWORD)szTemp, 0);
          return SF_STATUS_REQ_FINISHED;
        }
      } // If URL contains "ieonly"
    } // If notification handler,...
    return SF_STATUS_REQ_NEXT_NOTIFICATION;
  } // ...end HttpFilterProc.
```

This function warrants an explanation. The first thing the code does is verify that we handle only *SF_NOTIFY_URL_MAP* notifications by checking the *dwNotificationType* variable. This code is actually redundant because the filter registered an interest in receiving only *SF_NOTIFY_URL_MAP* notification in the *GetFilterVersion* functions, but here we wanted to illustrate how to go about handling multiple notifications types in the same filter by checking notification type parameters. In our case, if we were to see a notification that we were not looking for, we would quickly return.

Checking for the requested URL

The next step is to determine what URL the client has requested. The filter receives the URL via the *pszURL* member of the *HTTP_FILTER_URL_MAP* structure. The correct procedure would be to carefully scan the entire URL to determine whether it includes an IEONLY subdirectory, as exemplified in the following URL: *http://server/ieonly/subdir/hello.htm*. (We use the term "carefully" because we wouldn't want to be confused by a URL such as *http://server/wrong_ieonly_url/hello.htm*, which shouldn't trigger our filter.) For illustration purposes, however, we chose to go the short route and simply scan the URL string for presence of an *ieonly* substring. Just to ensure that there won't be a problem with mixed uppercase and lowercase strings, we converted the URL to lowercase and searched for the lowercase substring *ieonly*. If the *ieonly* substring does not exist in the requested URL, the *SmartRedir* filter simply exits with *SF_STATUS_REQ_NEXT_NOTIFICATION*, thereby allowing other filters (if they are installed) to handle the request.

Checking the browser software

If the URL contains the *ieonly* string, the next step is to determine what software the client is using. We need to prevent browsers other than Internet Explorer 4.0 and 4.01 from accessing any resources in the /ieonly directory. The client's browser sends the User-Agent header, which identifies the browser. If the filter was using the *SF_NOTIFY_PREPROC_HEADERS* notification, we could simply use the *GetHeader* callback function, exposed via the *HTTP_FILTER_URL_MAP* structure, to obtain the User-Agent value. Our filter, however, handles the URL map notification, which comes after any preprocessing headers, so we must use something other than *GetHeader* to obtain the User-Agent value.

By this time, the server has had a chance to get each header and set the corresponding server variable, so we need to get the value of the *HTTP_USER_AGENT* variable. This variable is a string, and the *GetServerVariable* callback function, exposed via the *HTTP_FILTER_CONTEXT* structure, will do the job. As always, there is a catch: we don't know ahead of time how large this agent string will be. It can be as short as a few characters for some browsers or as long as the string *"Mozilla/4.0 (compatible; MSIE 4.01; Windows NT)"* sent by Internet Explorer 4.01. To dynamically allocate the buffer for the variable, the first time we call *GetServerVariable* we set the size of the buffer to *0* (*dwSize = 0*). This value causes the *GetServerVariable* call to fail with error *122* (*ERROR_INSUFFICIENT_BUFFER*), but it will return the size of the actual string in the *dwSize* parameter. In our filter, we don't check the first call for any errors for the sake of making the code simple to understand. In production code, you will probably want to verify that all functions return successfully. After all, a filter should gracefully handle any situation even if the client didn't send a User-Agent header.

Once we know the buffer size for the variable, we can allocate the memory we need, and therefore we call *GetServerVariable* again, now with a real buffer to get the value of the variable. This time, we do check the error code. If *GetServerVariable* fails, we create a *szTemp* string with the error code and send it to the browser. Because the client and the server use the HTTP protocol, we can't just send error messages as text to the client—instead, we must send the HTTP status code first and then and only then the HTML data. The call to *ServerSupportFunction* sends a "200 OK" response status message, and *WriteClient* sends *szTemp* to the browser. If an error occurred in the filter, the request should not be handled by any other filters and should be disconnected. In this scenario, our filter returns *SF_STATUS_REQ_FINISHED*.

Allocating memory in the filter

There are many ways to allocate memory in C or C++, and plenty of memory allocation APIs are available through the Microsoft Win32 SDK. Each memory allocating API has a corresponding API to release the memory—otherwise, the filter will have a memory leak. To spare the programmer from running into the memory allocation and deallocation mess, IIS exposes the *AllocMem* function via the *HTTP_FILTER_CONTEXT* structure. The great thing about this function is that all allocated memory will be automatically released when communication with the client is terminated. Again, in production code you might want to check the success of the *AllocMem* call. Although *AllocMem* is a useful and convenient method exposed by IIS, you should be aware that the dynamic allocation of memory is costly and can have a negative impact on performance. *AllocMem* automatically deallocates memory upon session termination. Note that if Keep-Alives are used, the client might be sent more than one request over the established session. If each request calls *AllocMem*, it is possible to observe memory increase as long as the client is connected and sends multiple requests over the same connection. All memory will be deallocated, however, once the client terminates the session—that is, once the underlying TCP/IP connection is closed.

Now that we have allocated our buffer and copied the name of our browser software into that buffer, what do we do next? We need to check the user agent for the presence of the *msie 4* substring, which would indicate that the browser is Internet Explorer 4.0 or 4.01. To prevent case-sensitivity problems, we have converted the user agent string to lowercase and searched for the lowercase *msie 4* substring. Even though we know that the user agent string for Internet Explorer uses uppercase, by insuring both strings are lowercase we avoid any case-sensitivity problems.

If *msie 4* is present in the user agent string, the browser is allowed to access the /ieonly directory. In this case, *HttpFilterProc* returns and allows the next filter in the chain (if any more exist) to process the request. If *msie 4* isn't found, the browser is not allowed to access the restricted location. In this case, we must perform the job of redirecting the browser to a URL that explains where to get the latest version of Internet Explorer.

Redirecting the browser

Well, our worst dreams may have come true: a browser other than Internet Explorer 4.0 or 4.01 has tried to access our secret URL /ieonly. What do we do? We need to crash the offending browser, of course! Just kidding—the filter can't really crash a browser, but it can redirect the browser to a different location. The filter's job is to send a "302 Redirect" status code to the browser and set the HTTP Location header to the new URL. The *\r\n* (carriage return/linefeed pair) at the end of our location string indicates the end of our HTTP header. The second *\r\n* indicates the end of all the headers we are sending.

SmartRedir has a hard-coded name for the HTML file used as a redirection target, as defined in the following line of code at the beginning of our C++ source file:

```
#define FILENAME "getie.htm"
```

Because the constant *FILENAME* doesn't include a path, the file GETIE.HTM must reside in the root directory of the site (wwwroot by default). Therefore, sending the HTTP Location header *http://server/getie.htm\r\n\r\n* forces the browser to display the GETIE.HTM file. Setting this header does require the filter to replace *server* in the URL with the correct server name, however. To ensure that the filter will work on any installation of IIS, the filter should determine the name of the computer it is running on and use this name in the header. Getting the server name is simple when you use the *SERVER_NAME* server variable. This server variable contains the host name of the server (or sometimes the IP address of the server). The following code actually creates the Location header and sends it to the server with the "302 Redirect" HTTP status code:

```
wsprintf(szTemp, "Location: http://%s/%s\r\n\r\n",
         lpszServer, FILENAME);
pFC->ServerSupportFunction(pFC, SF_REQ_SEND_RESPONSE_HEADER,
                           (PVOID)"302 Redirect",
                           (DWORD)szTemp, 0);
```

After redirecting the client to another URL, the filter notifies the server that this request is complete by returning *SF_STATUS_REQ_FINISHED* from *HttpFilterProc*.

Adding an ISAPI extension interface to SmartRedir

The *SmartRedir* sample filter is functional enough to be used in real life, but there is a drawback in our implementation: the user agent string (*msie 4*) and the protected directory (/ieonly) are hard-coded into the filter source code. To change these values, the filter needs to be recompiled—which is probably an unacceptable solution for any reasonable software. Is there a convenient way to change some values in the filter while it is loaded? Suppose we want to dynamically change the redirection target without unloading the filter or restarting IIS. We can accomplish this task quite easily by adding an ISAPI extension interface to our ISAPI filter.

Both ISAPI filters and ISAPI extensions are implemented as DLLs. Nothing prevents SMARTREDIR.DLL from exporting two more entry points that would make it an ISAPI extension and filter at the same time, so we can have our filter export the *GetExtensionVersion* and *HttpExtensionProc* functions. Adding ISAPI extension entry points to the filter enables the filter to be invoked in the same manner as any other ISAPI extension DLL—for instance, with a URL such as *http://server/scripts/smartredir.dll*. Now we can declare strings that identify the user agent (*msie* 4) and the redirection target (*http://server/getie.htm*) as global parameters, which would make them accessible from the *HttpFilterProc* and *HttpExtensionProc* functions. A programmer could then add code to the *HttpExtensionProc* function that would modify the global strings by invoking the ISAPI extension with parameters such as this: *http://server/scripts/smartredir.dll?agent=NewAgent&redir=http://server/getienow.htm*.

By adding an ISAPI extension interface, we allow our filter's behavior to be modified without having to unload the filter, restart IIS, and recompile. But before you rush out to modify the *SmartRedir* sample, here's a word of caution: there's a good chance that the ISAPI filter functions and the ISAPI extension functions will be invoked by multiple clients at the same time. If one client invokes the ISAPI extension and tries to modify the user agent string while the ISAPI filter tries to use the global variable, we could run into some problems. To avoid this problem, access to all global variables should be controlled via a *synchronization object*. Windows NT uses synchronization objects to control threads that access the same variable (or other shared data) at the same time. In our case, access to global variables can be guarded using a synchronization object called a *critical section*. Critical sections are objects used to delineate blocks of code. When a critical section is used to mark the beginning and ending of multiple blocks of code, the critical section guarantees that no more than one thread is executing any of the code in all of the blocks. Thus we use the critical sections to insure that no more than one thread reads or changes our global data at any one time.

You can use the following code skeleton to add an ISAPI extension interface to the *SmartRedir* filter sample. Although it is not complete, this code demonstrates all the necessary steps to give you a solid idea of what needs to be done.

```
// Declare critical section object and user agent substring
// as file scope data.
CRITICAL_SECTION g_CritSect;
CHAR g_szUserAgentId[256];
```

(continued)

```
BOOL WINAPI GetFilterVersion( ... )
{
  // Critical section should be initialized first,
  // either in GetFilterVersion or in DllMain
  // when it is called for PROCESS_ATTACH.
  InitializeCriticalSection(&g_CritSect);
  // Set the default user agent.
  strcpy(g_szUserAgentId, "msie 4");
  ...
}

DWORD WINAPI HttpFilterProc( ... )
{
  ...
  // Implement code that searches for the user agent substring.
  EnterCriticalSection(&g_CritSect);
  if(!strstr(strlwr(lpszUserAgent), g_szUserAgentId))
  {
    ...
  }
  LeaveCriticalSection(&g_CritSect);
  ...
}

DWORD WINAPI HttpExtensionProc( ... )
{
  ...
  // Implement code that changes g_szUserAgentId based on the
  // parameters passed to our ISAPI extension.
  EnterCriticalSection(&g_CritSect);
  Change_User_Agent(g_szUserAgentId);
  LeaveCriticalSection(&g_CritSect);
  ...
}

DWORD WINAPI TerminateFilter( ... )
{
  // Critical section must be deleted, either here
  // or in DllMain when it is called for PROCESS_DETACH.
  DeleteCriticalSection(&g_CritSect);
  ...
}
```

Advanced Filter Tasks

An ISAPI filter can do many things. For example, a filter can implement a custom authentication scheme by handling an *SF_NOTIFY_AUTHENTICATION* event. Both Basic and NTML authentication methods control access based on valid Windows NT accounts—that is, if a Windows NT account does not exist for the supplied credentials, the user won't gain access to the secure resource. You can write a filter that accesses the user name and password for a request (the user name and password are members of *HTTP_FILTER_AUTHENT* structure) and then performs authentication based on a proprietary user account's database instead of Windows NT's user accounts. If the check against the database is successful, the filter replaces the supplied user name and password with the name and password of a valid Windows NT account. In this manner, the user's credentials may still allow the client to access the protected resource, even when there is no corresponding NT account for these credentials. The IIS SDK included with the Windows NT 4.0 Option Pack provides a sample that demonstrates this concept. You can find the *AuthFilt* sample at \Inetpub\iissamples\sdk\isapi\filters\AuthFilt.

Another common task performed using ISAPI filters is writing your own logging software by creating a filter that gets the *SF_NOTIFY_LOG* notification. ISAPI filters can also be used to encode and decode the raw data being sent across the socket. In fact, this technique is how Secure Socket Layer (SSL) is implemented—a global filter named SSPIFILT.DLL registers for the *SF_NOTIFY_READ_RAW_DATA* and *SF_NOTIFY_SEND_RAW_DATA* notifications to encrypt and decrypt the data accordingly. ISAPI filters also enable you to add your own authentication scheme. We've talked about creating your own user database, but you could also create another authentication scheme similar to Basic or NTLM authentication or the new Digest Authentication scheme currently being considered as part of the HTTP specification. Digest Authentication is similar to NTLM in that the user password is never transmitted over the network. To create such an authentication scheme, you would register for the *SF_NOTIFY_ACCESS_DENIED* notification and build the appropriate HTTP headers to perform your custom authentication handshake. When the response is returned, you would need to also be notified for the *SF_NOTIFY_PREPROC_HEADERS* event to read the custom response headers that contained your authentication information and react appropriately. Finally, ISAPI filters allow you to monitor the various events so that you can track down problems on your server. For instance, if you are writing an ISAPI extension and you want to see the exact response data you are generating, you could write an ISAPI filter that registers for the *SF_NOTIFY_SEND_RAW_DATA* event and displays the data being sent. This can be a great tool for developers trying to debug their applications.

By now, your mind is probably filled with ideas about all the powerful things you can accomplish by writing your own ISAPI filters, but let's step back and look at another way to customize IIS: by writing your own script interpreter.

Custom Script Interpreters

In Chapter 16, you learned how to use the built-in SSI facility. This helpful addition to IIS lets you create dynamic pages based on HTML-like template files. In this section, we'll look at the insides of an SSI interpreter and write our own custom interpreter. Consider the following scenario: CMPNY Corporation needs to build a set of Web pages from predefined templates, similar to the SSI capabilities, for advertising garden supplies on the Web. The pages might consist of the item names and prices for each item. Since there could be hundreds of different items on a page, updating the price of each item one at a time would cause a huge headache for the Webmaster. If the prices changed daily, the overhead of editing such a document would be unacceptable. A smarter solution would be to use certain tags—such as SHOVEL_PRICE, SCOOPER_PRICE, and so on—in the initial documents to indicate where the appropriate information should be inserted. Then when a request for the page arrived, we could somehow dynamically replace the tags with the actual prices. We could then store the real values in either a database or a text file. You might already be thinking that we could solve the problem of updating item prices in several ways: we could use the Internet Database Connector (IDC), write our own ASP pages, or even write a raw data filter that would replace the data placeholders with the appropriate values. There is another solution, however: writing a custom script interpreter.

You might protest that with all the other tools already available, creating anything from scratch would be a waste of time, but this is not necessarily the case. If you already have a proprietary mechanism for creating templates for displaying information, you could write your own script interpreter to read your file format and create the appropriate HTML. You could add a script map entry to associate your proprietary file type to a particular script interpreter that will convert the files to HTML on the fly so that they can be displayed on a browser. In fact, as we saw in Chapter 16, that is how IDC works: a file with the proprietary file type (in this case, with the extension .HTX) is converted on the fly to valid HTML format by the script processor (in this case, HTTPODBC.DLL).

Script interpreters are ISAPI extension DLLs just like any other ISAPI extensions, with one exception: instead of referring to the extension DLL explicitly in the URL, a script map is used to associate certain file extensions with the ISAPI extension

DLL. IIS will run the ISAPI extension when a request is received for a file with the corresponding file extension. (We saw how to configure custom script interpreters to IIS using the Application Mapping Properties window in Chapter 4.) Adding a new entry for a particular file type will allow IIS to invoke our custom DLL for this file type. Of course, IIS already has a number of mappings for certain file types, such as ASP. That's right, ASP is implemented in this same way.

A Sample Script Interpreter: *SSIDemo*

To create this sample script interpreter, we wrote an ISAPI extension, SSIDEMO.DLL, and used the script map to associate .BPI files with it. As soon as a request to a file with the extension .BPI arrives, IIS will load SSIDEMO.DLL, just as it does any ISAPI extension request. For example, a request for *http://MyServer/MyTestFile.bpi* does not refer to SSIDEMO.DLL directly, it refers to the .BPI file, but IIS now knows to load SSIDEMO.DLL for this file extension. Once the DLL is loaded, we can access the full file path of MYTESTFILE.BPI via the *lpszPathTranslated* member of the Extension Control Block (ECB) structure. At this point, we can open this file, read it, and send its modified version to the client using the *WriteClient* callback function.

Let's look at the details of our SSIDemo sample. The purpose of this sample is to replace all tags in a template file. (In our case, the files have the .BPI extension.) Each of our template file's tags has a text string associated with it. These tag-string associations are stored in a special file that we can edit to create any associations we want. The filename and location are configured via the registry location *HKEY_LOCAL_MACHINE\SYSTEM\CurrentControlSet\Services\W3SVC\SSI*. The registry value is named *DictFile* and is of type REG_SZ. In our sample, we have complied with the SSI format, so our tags have the format <!-- #TAG -->. SSIDEMO.DLL will parse the .BPI file for all tags and will replace them with their string values from the dictionary file. The dictionary file consists of one string pair per line—for example, *TAG1 = This is a tag.* (Note that tags are case sensitive.)

We also decided to do something more than simple text substitution by adding extra capabilities. If a tag is preceded by a special character (we use the @ character by default), our DLL will handle the tag as a server-side variable and replace it with the value returned from the callback function *GetServerVariable*. (The special tag character can be changed by adding a *VariableCharacter* registry entry to the preceding registry location. Although *VariableCharacter* is type REG_SZ, only its first character is significant.) For example, if you put the entry <!-- #@HTTP_USER_AGENT --> in the .BPI file, it will be replaced with the actual value from the User-Agent header.

GetExtensionVersion

We'll use the *GetExtensionVersion* function to perform our one-time initialization. First we must read the parameters from the registry: the filename with the tag-string pairs (referred to as the dictionary file) and the character that is used to indicate server variable tags. We also need to open the dictionary file. In this sample, we assume that our file will fit into a buffer allocated using the *LocalAlloc* Win32 API. These initialization tasks need to be performed only once for the entire life of the DLL, so it works out well to do them in our *GetExtensionVersion* function, which will be called only once. Once the dictionary file is read, we can close the registry and the file.

We check for locking and sharing violations when the dictionary file is opened using the *CreateFile* function, and we read it using the *ReadFile* function. If the dictionary file is locked (for instance, if someone is editing it), the program waits 100 milliseconds and then retries the operation. It will retry three times. If for some reason we can't read the dictionary file, we continue execution of the program. Because a .BPI file can have only server variables and no other tags, the absence of a dictionary file is not a critical error.

Here is our *GetExtensionVersion* code:

```
BOOL WINAPI GetExtensionVersion(HSE_VERSION_INFO *pVer)
{
  // We will open the dictionary file here and read its
  // contents into our global memory buffer.
  //
  // If an error occurs we set the global pointer to NULL.

  HANDLE hFileDict;
  DWORD dwSizeDict, dwError, dwRead;
  int i = 0;
  BOOL bCriticalError = FALSE;
  HKEY hKey;
  CHAR szDictFile[256], temp[2];

  pVer->dwExtensionVersion = MAKELONG(HSE_VERSION_MINOR,
                                      HSE_VERSION_MAJOR);
  lstrcpyn(pVer->lpszExtensionDesc, "HTTP SSI Application",
           HSE_MAX_EXT_DLL_NAME_LEN);

  if(ERROR_SUCCESS == RegOpenKeyEx(HKEY_LOCAL_MACHINE, REGKEY, 0,
                                   KEY_READ, &hKey))
```

```
{
  // We don't care if we can't read the registry.
  dwRead = sizeof (temp);
  if(RegQueryValueEx(hKey, "VariableCharacter", NULL, NULL,
     (LPBYTE)temp, &dwRead) == ERROR_SUCCESS)
    g_cVarChar = temp[0];

  dwRead = sizeof(szDictFile);
  if(RegQueryValueEx(hKey, "DictFile", NULL, NULL,
     (LPBYTE) szDictFile, &dwRead) != ERROR_SUCCESS)
  {
    DebugOut("Can't get reg value DictFile, error: %d\n",
             GetLastError());
    RegCloseKey(hKey);
    return TRUE;
  }
}
else
{
  DebugOut("Unable to read the registry.\n"
           "No data read, g_cVarChar is @\n");
  return TRUE;
}
RegCloseKey(hKey);

// Open the dictionary file,and handle possible error conditions.
while(((hFileDict = CreateFile(szDictFile, GENERIC_READ,
      FILE_SHARE_READ | FILE_SHARE_WRITE, (LPSECURITY_ATTRIBUTES)
      NULL, OPEN_EXISTING, FILE_ATTRIBUTE_READONLY,
      (HANDLE)NULL)) == INVALID_HANDLE_VALUE))
{
  if((dwError = GetLastError()) == ERROR_SHARING_VIOLATION)
  {
    DebugOut("File: %s is locked (sharing). Still trying...\n",
             szDictFile);
    Sleep(100);
  }
  else
  {
    DebugOut ("Error opening: %s Error: %d\n", szDictFile);
    return TRUE;
  }
  if(i++ == 3)    // Try to open the file at least
    return TRUE;  // 3 times before giving up.
}
```

(continued)

```
    dwSizeDict = GetFileSize(hFileDict, NULL);
    g_lpDataDict = (CHAR *)LocalAlloc(LPTR, dwSizeDict + 1);

    i = 0;
    while(! bCriticalError && ! ReadFile(hFileDict, g_lpDataDict,
          dwSizeDict, &dwRead, NULL))
    {
      if((dwError = GetLastError()) == ERROR_LOCK_VIOLATION)
      {
        DebugOut ("File: %s is locked (lock). Still trying...\n",
                  szDictFile);
        Sleep(100);
        if(i++ == 3)              // Try to read the file at least
          bCriticalError = TRUE;  // 3 times before giving up.
      }
      else
      {
        DebugOut("Error opening: %s Error: %d\n",szDictFile,dwError);
        bCriticalError = TRUE;
      }
    }
    if(bCriticalError)
    {
      LocalFree(g_lpDataDict);
      g_lpDataDict = NULL;
    }
    else
      g_lpDataDict[dwRead] = '\0';
    CloseHandle(hFileDict);

    DebugOut("Dictionary file %s is read into memory\n", szDictFile);
    return TRUE;
  } // GetExtensionVersion()
```

You might have noticed an interesting function here: *DebugOut*. *DebugOut* is used to send our DLL's debugging output to the debugger window. The *DebugOut* code looks like this:

```
  #ifdef _DEBUG
    void DebugOut(CHAR *lpszFmt, ...)
    {
      CHAR szBuff[1024];
      va_list vargs;
      va_start(vargs,lpszFmt);
```

```
    vsprintf(szBuff, lpszFmt, vargs);
    va_end(vargs);
    OutputDebugString(szBuff);
    return;
  }
#else
  void DebugOut(CHAR *lpszFmt, ...)
  {
    return;
  }
#endif
```

The *OutputDebugString* API used in *DebugOut* sends *szBuff* to the debugger window, when our DLL runs in the debugger and only if it is built using debug compiler and linker flags. You don't have to run the DLL in the debugger, however. The DBMON.EXE utility from the Microsoft Platform SDK, also enables you to view the debugging output. DBMON.EXE creates a console window that displays all debugging output.

HttpExtensionProc

At this point, the dictionary file has been read and the stage is set for reading the .BPI file and parsing all the tags in it. Because the full path of the .BPI file is passed in the ECB structure, opening this file is straightforward, as shown here:

```
hFile = CreateFile(pECB->lpszPathTranslated, GENERIC_READ,
                   FILE_SHARE_READ | FILE_SHARE_WRITE,
                   (LPSECURITY_ATTRIBUTES)NULL, OPEN_EXISTING,
                   FILE_ATTRIBUTE_READONLY, (HANDLE)NULL);
```

We still want to verify that the file is not locked and that there are no sharing violations. We want to keep this file open for as short a time as possible so that it's not locked up if someone needs exclusive access in order to edit it. As soon as the file contents are read to the buffer, we close the file.

One way to handle the substitution of all the tags is to go over the entire buffer and replace the tags with their values. The problem with this approach is that we don't know beforehand what size buffer is required. The new buffer can be either smaller (if the string values from the dictionary file are shorter than the tags) or larger than the original one. We need to change the buffer length dynamically. Once the original buffer—that is, the buffer containing the .BPI file—is modified, we can issue a single call to *WriteClient* to send the buffer to the browser.

In this sample, we have chosen an easier and more sensible approach to the substitution process, with the drawback that we will be making potentially many calls to *WriteClient*. Here's what we're going to do:

1. Find the first occurrence of the characters <!--. These characters indicate the possible beginning of a tag (or the possible beginning of the HTML comment).
2. Send the contents of the buffer immediately preceding this possible tag to the browser using the *WriteClient* ISAPI callback function.
3. Search for an occurrence of the characters -->, which indicate the end of the tag (or the possible end of the HTML comment).
4. If the tag is an HTML comment (that is, it contains no # characters), we send it to the browser as is.
5. The presence of a # character between the HTML comment delimiters <!-- and --> indicates that this is a possible tag value. Replace the entire comment from <!-- to --> with the tag's value and send it to the browser using *WriteClient*.
6. Search for the next <!-- characters and go through the process all over again.

The following code represents this procedure. The *lpData* element is a pointer to the buffer containing the .BPI file:

```
DWORD WINAPI HttpExtensionProc(EXTENSION_CONTROL_BLOCK *pECB)
{
  HANDLE hFile;
  DWORD dwLen = 0, dwError, dwSize, dwRead;
  int i = 0;
  BOOL bCriticalError = FALSE;
  CHAR *lpData = NULL, *lpIncStart, *lpIncEnd,  *lpDataForDelete;
  CHAR szTagBuffer[256], szValueBuffer [256], szBuff [256];

  DebugOut("Opening File: %s for HTML\n",
          pECB->lpszPathTranslated);

  // Open the .BPI file and handle possible error conditions.
  while((hFile = CreateFile(pECB->lpszPathTranslated, GENERIC_READ,
        FILE_SHARE_READ | FILE_SHARE_WRITE,
        (LPSECURITY_ATTRIBUTES)NULL, OPEN_EXISTING,
```

```
      FILE_ATTRIBUTE_READONLY, (HANDLE)NULL))
      == INVALID_HANDLE_VALUE)
{
  if((dwError = GetLastError()) == ERROR_SHARING_VIOLATION)
  {
    DebugOut("File: %s is locked (sharing). Still trying...\n",
             pECB->lpszPathTranslated);
    Sleep(100);
    if(i++ == 3)                   // Try to open the file at least
      return HSE_STATUS_ERROR;     // three times before giving up.
  }
  else
  {
    DebugOut("Error opening: %s Error: %d\n",
             pECB->lpszPathTranslated, dwError);
    return HSE_STATUS_ERROR;
  }
}
// Determine .BPI file size; allocate buffer for the entire file.
dwSize = GetFileSize(hFile, NULL);
lpData = (CHAR *)LocalAlloc(LPTR, dwSize + 1);

i = 0;
// Read entire .BPI file into lpData buffer.
while(! bCriticalError && ! ReadFile(hFile, lpData, dwSize,
                                     &dwRead, NULL))
{
  if((dwError = GetLastError()) == ERROR_LOCK_VIOLATION)
  {
    DebugOut("File: %s is locked (lock). Still trying...\n",
             pECB->lpszPathTranslated);
    Sleep(100);
    if(i++ == 3)                  // Try to read the file at least
      bCriticalError = TRUE;      // three times before giving up.
  }
  else
  {
    DebugOut("Error opening: %s Error: %d\n",
             pECB->lpszPathTranslated, dwError);
    bCriticalError = TRUE;
  }
} // While no error and data left to read
CloseHandle(hFile);
```

(continued)

```
if(bCriticalError)
{
  LocalFree(lpData);        // If an error, free allocated memory
  return HSE_STATUS_ERROR;  // and return error status.
}
lpData[dwRead] = '\0';
// We will lose lpData as we parse the file;
// preserve its value for buffer deletion.
lpDataForDelete = lpData;

wsprintf(szBuff, "Content-Type: text/html\r\n\r\n");
dwLen = lstrlen(szBuff);
pECB->ServerSupportFunction(pECB->ConnID,
                            HSE_REQ_SEND_RESPONSE_HEADER,
                            "200 OK",
                            &dwLen,
                            (LPDWORD)szBuff);

// This is a <!-- #TAG --> sample.

while((lpIncStart = strstr(lpData, "<!--")) != NULL)
{
  // Send data before <!--tag directly to the client.
  dwSize = lpIncStart - lpData;
  pECB->WriteClient(pECB->ConnID, lpData, &dwSize, HSE_IO_SYNC);

  // Find end of the --> tag.
  if((lpIncEnd = strstr(lpData, "-->")) == NULL)
  {
    // We did not find end of tag; bail out.
    DebugOut("No --> found. Bailing out\n");
    dwSize = lstrlen(lpIncStart);
    pECB->WriteClient(pECB->ConnID, lpIncStart, &dwSize,
                      HSE_IO_SYNC);
    LocalFree(lpDataForDelete);
    return HSE_STATUS_SUCCESS;
  }

  // Move lpData to the beginning of the tag.
  lpData = lpIncStart + lstrlen("<!--");
  while(ISWHITE(*lpData))
    lpData++;
```

```
        // Start copying the tag buffer.
        i = 0;
        while((! ISWHITE(*lpData)) && (lpData != lpIncEnd))
           szTagBuffer[i++] = *lpData++;
        szTagBuffer[i] = '\0';
        DebugOut("Tag found: %s\n", szTagBuffer);

        lpData = lpIncEnd + lstrlen("-->");
        // Output proper value here.
        if(szTagBuffer[0] == '#')
        {
          // It was a tag; get rid of the #.
          CHAR *p = szTagBuffer + 1;
          DebugOut("Looking up: %s\n", p);

          dwSize = GetValueFromTag(szValueBuffer, p, pECB);
          pECB->WriteClient(pECB->ConnID, szValueBuffer, &dwSize,
                            HSE_IO_SYNC);
        }
        else
        {
          // It was a comment; just print it.
          DebugOut("Comment found (not a tag)\n");
          dwSize = lpData - lpIncStart;
          pECB->WriteClient(pECB->ConnID, lpIncStart, &dwSize,
                            HSE_IO_SYNC);
        }
      }

      dwSize = lstrlen(lpData);
      pECB->WriteClient(pECB->ConnID, lpData, &dwSize, HSE_IO_SYNC);

      LocalFree(lpDataForDelete);  // Free file buffer.

      return HSE_STATUS_SUCCESS;
    }
```

Notice that we used *GetValueFromTag* in our code. This procedure is where we get the text string value for the found tag. The text string value comes from the dictionary file, which is currently in a memory buffer pointed to by a global variable. Since we use the global variable only to read data, we don't need to perform any synchronization to access it. We also need to know how big the string associated with our tag is. The following function returns the lengths of the strings.

```
DWORD GetValueFromTag(CHAR *szValue, CHAR *szTag,
                      EXTENSION_CONTROL_BLOCK *pECB)
{
  // The tag dictionary file line format is Tag = This is tag1.
  // Tags proceeded with @ or g_cVarChar are the server variables.

  DWORD dwLen = 256, dwError, dwTag = lstrlen(szTag);
  CHAR * pch = g_lpDataDict;        // Pointer into dictionary file
  CHAR *p;                          // Pointer to the tag
  int i;

  if(*szTag == g_cVarChar)
  {
    p = szTag + sizeof(CHAR);
    // This is a server variable.
    if(! pECB->GetServerVariable(pECB->ConnID,   // Connection ID
                                 p,              // Variable
                                 szValue,        // Buffer
                                 &dwLen))        // Length
    {
      if((dwError = GetLastError()) == ERROR_INVALID_INDEX)
        wsprintf(szValue, "<br><i>Variable %s does not exist. "
                 "Please notify Webmaster about this.</i><br>", p);
      else
        wsprintf(szValue, "<br><i>Error %d occurred while getting"
                 " %s variable</i><br>", dwError, p);
    }
  }
  else
  { // This is a real tag. Do the job of looking for it.
    if(pch == NULL)
    {
      // Our buffer is empty.
      wsprintf(szValue, "<br><i>Can't find match for %s</i><br>",
               szTag);
      return lstrlen(szValue);
    }

    if(! (p = strstr(pch, szTag)))
      wsprintf(szValue, "<br><i>Tag %s not found. Please notify "
               "Webmaster about this.</i><br>", szTag);
    else
    {
      // Skip to the tag value.
      while((*p != '='))
        p++;
      p++;
```

```
      // Skip from = to the actual value.
      while(ISWHITE(*p))
        p++;

      i = 0;
      // Copy the tag value to szValue.
      while((*p != '\n') && (i < 256))
        szValue[i++] = *p++;
      szValue[i] = '\0';
    }
  }
  return lstrlen(szValue);
}
```

That's the core of our custom SSI extension. All that's left is to deallocate the global memory that holds the dictionary file buffer when our DLL is unloaded. Adding *DllMain* to our DLL will do the trick, as shown here:

```
BOOL WINAPI DllMain(HANDLE hInst,
                    ULONG  ul_reason_for_call,
                    LPVOID lpReserved)
{
  if(ul_reason_for_call == DLL_PROCESS_DETACH)
  {
    DebugOut("DLL_PROCESS_DETACH for instance: 0x%X\n", hInst);
    LocalFree(g_lpDataDict);
  }
  return TRUE;
}
```

Before we enjoy the results of our hard labor and look at SSIDEMO.DLL in action, you should be aware of one more point: it's not necessary to implement a script interpreter as an ISAPI extension. You can use a Common Gateway Interface (CGI, discussed in Chapter 20) application instead, although it will be much slower. In fact, some script processors, such as some Perl interpreters, are available in CGI (EXE) or ISAPI (DLL) versions. Should you decide to create a new mapping for a CGI script interpreter, be sure to add *%s %s* to the EXE filename in the IIS script map (accessible via the Application Configuration window in the Management Console). For instance, a script map entry might look like this: C:\Winnt\System32\SSIDemo.exe %s %s. The first *%s* will be mapped to the physical path of the .BPI file, similar to *lpszPathTranslated* member of the ECB structure. The second *%s* will be mapped to the query string—for example, in a request for */scripts/foo.bpi?Foo=Bar*, *%s* will be the value of the *Foo=Bar* string. Notice that we don't use query strings in our sample.

Taking SSIDemo *for a test*

Let's see how *SSIDemo* works. The first step is to create a registry entry for the dictionary file and to optionally set the special character indicating server variable tags (if we're not happy with the default @ character). Our dictionary file is located in d:\inetpub\wwwroot\dictfile.txt; we created the registry entry *DictFile* to reflect its location. Figure 21.1 shows the contents of our dictionary file.

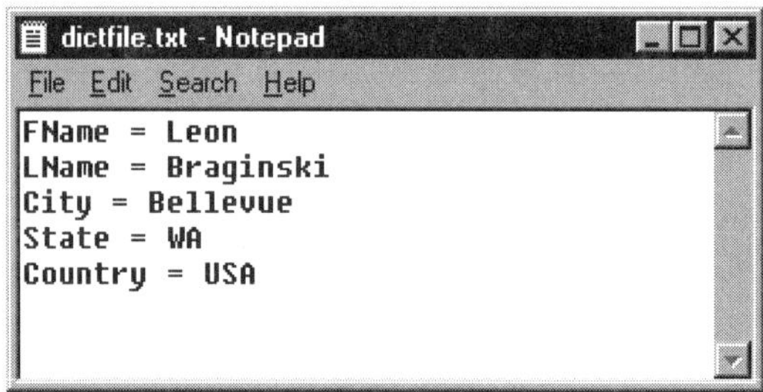

```
FName = Leon
LName = Braginski
City = Bellevue
State = WA
Country = USA
```

FIGURE 21.1

The contents of our DICTFILE.TXT file.

The dictionary file is just an ASCII file; it shows the following tags and their values: FName, LName, City, State, and Country.

The next step is to create a template .BPI file. The .BPI file uses all valid HTML tags and comments. Figure 21.2 shows the HELLO.BPI file, which includes comments, tags, and server variables that would be processed by SSIDEMO.DLL.

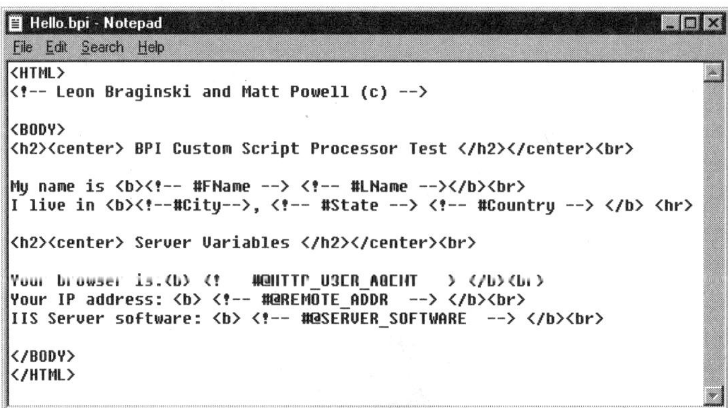

```
<HTML>
<!-- Leon Braginski and Matt Powell (c) -->

<BODY>
<h2><center> BPI Custom Script Processor Test </h2></center><br>

My name is <b><!-- #FName --> <!-- #LName --></b><br>
I live in <b><!--#City-->, <!-- #State --> <!-- #Country --> </b> <hr>

<h2><center> Server Variables </h2></center><br>

Your browser is:<b> <!-- #@HTTP_USER_AGENT --> </b><br>
Your IP address: <b> <!-- #@REMOTE_ADDR --> </b><br>
IIS Server software: <b> <!-- #@SERVER_SOFTWARE --> </b><br>

</BODY>
</HTML>
```

FIGURE 21.2

The HELLO.BPI template file.

All that's left to do at this point is to access *http://leonbr-hm/hello.bpi* and enjoy the ride. Figure 21.3 shows what users see in their browser. Notice that all the tags have been replaced by their text string values from the dictionary file DICTFILE.TXT.

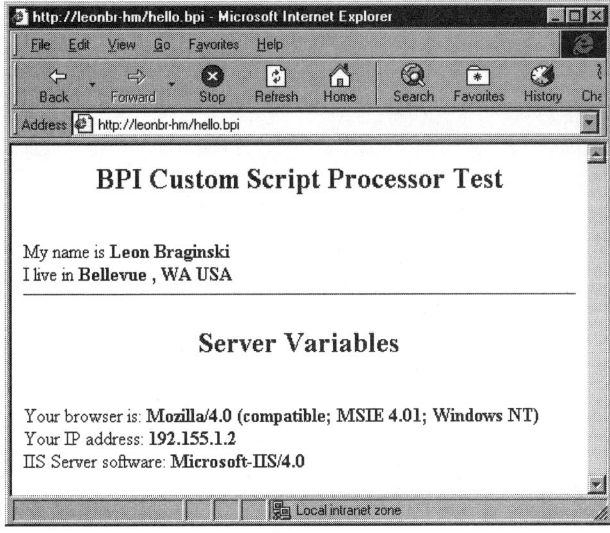

FIGURE 21.3

HELLO.BPI after processing by SSIDEMO.DLL.

By the way, because we used the debug version of the DLL, we can view the debugging output using the DBMON.EXE utility. The output for our request is shown in Figure 21.4. Because this is the first time *SSIDemo* is invoked, *GetHttpExtension* is called and DICTFILE.TXT is read into memory.

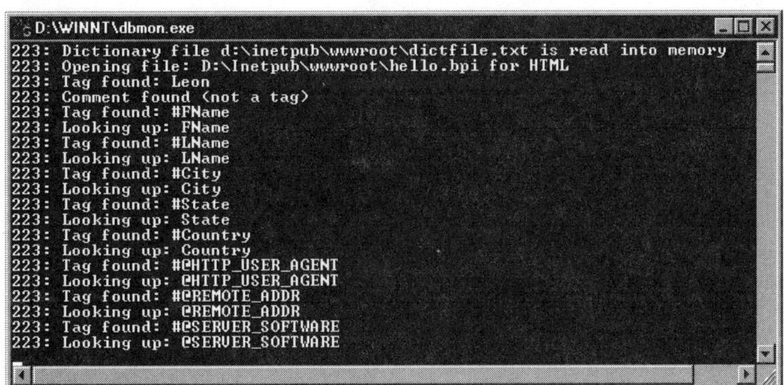

FIGURE 21.4

The debugging output from SSIDEMO.DLL as displayed by DBMON.EXE.

Now we have a working script interpreter that has customized the use of certain types of files. We have also seen how an ISAPI filter can be used to modify how HTTP requests are processed. These customization capabilities enable us to make IIS handle HTTP requests in almost any manner that we see fit.

This chapter concludes our discussion about writing code and components for IIS. You've learned about many things in this part of the book, including ASP scripts, transactional objects, CGI, ISAPI extensions, filters, and script interpreters. All of these elements are the building blocks of Internet applications running under IIS. In Part III, we will look inside IIS and unveil the mystery of the various networking protocols, but if you've come all this way and still feel unfamiliar with HTML, don't worry—HTML is the topic of the next chapter.

Part Three

Under the Covers of Internet Information Server

CHAPTER 22

The Hypertext Markup Language (HTML)

We dedicated the previous portion of this book to explaining how to take advantage of the powerful Web application environment that IIS provides. We focus in the remaining chapters on understanding the details of the different specifications that make IIS possible. If you already have a thorough grasp of the underlying specifications, you'll gain a broader understanding of the product and how to take advantage of it. We begin by explaining HTML.

The ability to send HTTP requests and receive responses is only part of the underlying infrastructure that makes the World Wide Web so powerful. Much of the current popularity of the Web can be attributed to two primary capabilities of HTML. The first of these capabilities is the ease of merging text and graphics to create professional-looking Web pages, which is possible for even graphic design novices. The second is the inherent characteristic that gives the Web its name. *Hyperlinks* allow content creators to associate remote pieces of information with each other to form virtual strands that link content together in patterns that resemble a spider's web.

Enabling relatively easy Web page layout and creating links may be the current reasons that HTML has gained popularity, but the next development, creating interactive content, is just beginning. With the addition of scripting capabilities, objects, ActiveX Controls, and Dynamic HTML, the client environment has moved from being a simple file-downloading environment to a real interactive application. We'll look at some of the basic concepts behind HTML and show how it can be used to make such applications later in this chapter. But first, the basic concepts.

Architecture: How Browsers Interpret HTML

To display an HTML file, you initiate an HTTP request for the HTML file; the HTTP response then returns the contents of the file in the body of the response. The Web browser must now interpret the HTML contents in order to display it properly. In the case of Internet Explorer, MSHTML.DLL parses the contents of the HTML file and formats the display that you see in the Internet Explorer window.

An HTML document is broken up into elements by what are commonly called *tags*. In its simplest form, a tag consists of a keyword surrounded by angle brackets. Tags are often used in pairs to delineate elements of the document. The element is preceded by the appropriate *start tag* and followed by the appropriate *end tag*. The end tag is altered slightly by an added slash (/) directly before the keyword. For instance, the following shows an example of some HTML:

```
<TITLE> This Is the Document Title </TITLE>
```

The keyword in this case is TITLE. The phrase between the <TITLE> start tag and the </TITLE> end tag defines the document title. The result is that a browser interpreting this HTML should show the title of this document as *This Is the Document Title*. Internet Explorer interprets a title as being the text displayed in the title bar of the Internet Explorer window.

Setting the title is a simple example of what can be done with HTML tags, but you can't legitimately do much else with the <TITLE> tag other than specifying the title string. On the other hand, the <TABLE> tag, which allows you to define the layout of a table within your HTML document, provides a lot more options. When you create a table, you might want to specify that the table has a border 5 pixels wide. You do this by adding an *attribute* to the <TABLE> tag. Attributes typically appear in this form:

attribute=value

When you're setting the border width of a table, the name of the attribute you want to use is *BORDER*, and the value specifies the number of pixels that you want the border to be, as shown here:

```
BORDER=5
```

A sample table might be defined as follows:

```
<TABLE BORDER=5 CELLPADDING=3>
<TR>
<TD> Hello, <TD> World!
</TABLE>
```

This table has two attributes, one that defines the border width and one that defines *CELLPADDING* as three pixels. (*CELLPADDING* is the distance between the cell borders in a table and the actual contents of a cell.) The <TR> tag indicates that a new row is starting. The <TD> tags indicate where a new cell is starting. The <TR> and <TD> tags indicate *child elements* of the TABLE element because they define elements within the larger TABLE element. Notice that you don't see a </TR> tag or any </TD> tags. These end tags are optional because browsers are smart enough to figure out that if a new cell is beginning, the previous cell must be ending. The end result is a table that looks like the one shown in Figure 22.1.

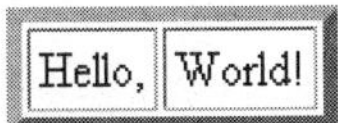

FIGURE 22.1

A simple HTML table.

Let's use what we know about tags and elements to look at the general layout of an HTML document, shown here:

```
<!DOCTYPE HTML PUBLIC "-//W3C//DTD HTML 4.0//EN"
    "http://www.w3.org/TR/REC-html40/strict.dtd">
<HTML>
<HEAD>
<TITLE>This Is the Document Title</TITLE>
...
</HEAD>
<BODY>
...
</BODY>
</HTML>
```

Most of this HTML template is straightforward. The first line is in need of some explanation, however. The first line is the *document type declaration* and is based on the Standard Generalized Markup Language (SGML) specification. The <!DOCTYPE> declaration is used to specify the document type and the version. In our example, we have indicated that this document type is compliant with the HTML 4.0 specification. In practice, the !DOCTYPE declaration isn't frequently used, but if your document doesn't contain it, it's not HTML 4.0–compliant. By specifying the version of HTML for which your document was written, you allow your document to be displayed accordingly, even if the HTML specification changes in the future.

Glossary

Standard Generalized Markup Language (SGML) *A standard for markup languages defined by the International Standard ISO 8879. SGML is very flexible but also much more convoluted than simple HTML. The SGML definition of HTML is included in the HTTP 4.0 specification. It is to this definition that the !DOCTYPE declaration in the example refers.*

Once we get past the !DOCTYPE declaration, we notice that an HTML document has two main parts: a head and a body. The head consists of information, such as the title, that corresponds to the general document entity and is not so much concerned with the specific layout of the actual contents. The body contains the main portion of information to be displayed in the browser window. Notice that the HEAD and BODY elements are child elements of the more global HTML element, which simply provides a nice wrapper to indicate where the document starts and where it ends.

The table on page 604 shows the complete list of HTML 4.0 elements.

Embedded Images

So far we've talked about the various attributes of an HTML document. When you view a Web page, you typically see objects on your screen in addition to text—for example, images placed directly within the page itself. You insert these images in the layout of your document by adding references to the image files. For instance, you might have a picture of yourself in JPEG format in a file named ME.JPG. To display your picture at the beginning of your home page, you would use the IMG tag. The image itself would have to be accessible to the users, so you would probably want to copy it to your server as well. The line that you would use to include this image file would look something like this:

```
<IMG SRC=/IMAGES/ME.JPG TITLE="My Picture">
```

The *SRC* attribute lets your browser know where it can get the image, and the *TITLE* attribute is used by most popular browsers as the text that will display while the user waits for the image to download. You also might want background images, either for the entire document or for things like specific cell backgrounds in a table. In these cases, the *BACKGROUND* attribute of the BODY or TD element must point to the location of the image

Hyperlinks

The ability to click on a reference and have it transport you to the intended document is the single most powerful feature of the Web. The result is that the resources of the entire Internet are made available to anyone developing content. Let's take a look at how you can add hyperlinks to your document. Consider the following element:

```
<A HREF=http://www.microsoft.com> Go to Microsoft's home page. </A>
```

The tag used in this case is the <A> tag, which stands for *anchor*. The A element is anchored to the reference specified by the *HREF* attribute. You can also name an anchor using the *NAME* attribute. In this case, the *HREF* attribute tells the browser that this element is a hyperlink to *http://www.microsoft.com*. The browser typically indicates this fact to the user by displaying the *Go to Microsoft's home page* text in a different color than standard text and underlining it. Now if you click on the specified text in your browser, you'll be whisked away to the Microsoft site.

But A elements don't have to be simple text. You can have any number of child elements within your A element. For instance, you often see IMG elements used within an A element so that clicking on the picture takes you to the specified reference. So now you can display a picture of the Microsoft logo instead of the simple text we had previously and use it as the link to Microsoft's site. You could also use images that look like push buttons or some other intuitive navigational control.

Linking to other HTML pages is certainly a worthwhile thing to do, but keep in mind that almost all the power of a URL is available to you from a hyperlink. This means that your reference could be pointing to an FTP resource such as *ftp://ftp.microsoft.com,* or it could launch your mail client using a URL such as *mailto:mattpo@microsoft.com*. You can even use an HTTP URL to point to something other than an HTML document. Based on the reader's browser and how it is configured, your hyperlink could display a Microsoft Excel spreadsheet, open up a Microsoft Schedule+ archive, or display your own proprietary document type. This capability is particularly useful in intranet scenarios because the hyperlink allows your information to be made available in its most current form.

HTML Tags That Affect the Server

We could write an entire book on the details of all the HTML tags, including the various properties that they support and what each means, but obviously that isn't what this book is about. However, a number of HTML tags not only influence what's happening on the client, but also have an effect on the server. A standard hyperlink is one simple example, but we'll look at some other HTML elements that affect the HTTP requests a document might make.

Image maps

The hyperlinks we've looked at so far have been defined by HTML elements. This solution is fine when we're associating a piece of text with a hyperlink because HTML's text-based architecture allows us to break down the text in a document to even a single letter. We can anchor this single letter to a URL by making the letter the only content of an A element. However, when we bring other types of objects, such as images, into our document we lose the granularity that we have with HTML text. For instance, we might have an image of a floor plan of our building. We'd like this image to have multiple references associated with it. When we click on a person's office, for example, we'd like it to link to that person's home page. When we click on someone else's office in the same floor-plan image, we'd like that to link to the second person's home page. We can't achieve this kind of functionality using simple A elements and a single floor-plan image.

HTML 4.0 Elements

- **HTML** document
  - **HEAD** general data
    - **TITLE** document title
    - **STYLE** style sheet
    - **SCRIPT** client-side script
    - **ISINDEX** simple input
    - **BASE** base URL
    - **META** document properties
    - **LINK** relationships to other documents
  - **BODY** displayed data
    - **H1...H6** headers levels 1 – 6
    - **ADDRESS** author or company address
    - Block Elements
      - **P** paragraph
      - **UL** unordered list
      - **OL** ordered list
      - **DIR** directory list
      - **DL** definition list
      - **MENU** menu list
      - **PRE** preformatted text
      - **DIV** document division
      - **SPAN** generic container
      - **CENTER** centered text
      - **BLOCKQUOTE** quoted passage
      - **FORM** user input
      - **FRAME** subwindow
      - **FRAMESET** group of subwindows
      - **IFRAME** inline frames
      - **NOFRAMES** content displayed when frames are unavailable
      - **NOSCRIPT** content displayed when scripting is not performed
      - **OBJECT** data to be rendered by an external application
      - **PARAM** parameter passed to an OBJECT
      - **ISINDEX** simple form
      - **HR** horizontal rule
      - **TABLE** table
    - Text-Level Elements
      - Font Style Elements
        - **TT** monospace
        - **I** italic
        - **B** bold
        - **U** underlined
        - **STRIKE** strikethrough
        - **S** strikethrough (same as STRIKE)
        - **BIG** large font
        - **SMALL** small font
        - **SUB** subscript
        - **SUP** superscript

Phrase Elements

- **ABBR** abbreviation
- **ACRONYM** acronym
- **BDO** language direction
- **DEL** deleted text
- **INS** inserted text
- **DD** definition description
- **DT** definition term
- **Q** quotation
- **EM** basic emphasis
- **STRONG** strong emphasis
- **DFN** definition
- **CODE** program code
- **SAMP** sample
- **KBD** text typed by a user
- **LI** list item
- **VAR** variables
- **CITE** citation

Form Fields

- **BUTTON** button
- **FIELDSET** set of form's controls and labels
- **INPUT** form control
- **LABEL** label for one of the other controls on the form
- **LEGEND** caption to a fieldset
- **OPTGROUP** groups of options within a SELECT list
- **OPTION** options within a SELECT list
- **SELECT** user input selected from a list
- **TEXTAREA** multiline text input

Table Elements

- **CAPTION** table description
- **COL** subset of columns in a table
- **COLGROUP** explicit group of columns
- **TBODY** table body
- **TD** table data cell
- **TFOOT** table footer
- **TH** table header cell
- **THEAD** table header
- **TR** table row

A anchor
AREA image map area
IMG image
APPLET Java applet
FONT character font
BASEFONT standard document font
BR line break
MAP image map

Luckily for us, *image maps* were created. With an image map, different areas of an image are associated with their own hyperlinks. For instance, Figure 22.2 contains an image created for the corporate sales department's home page.

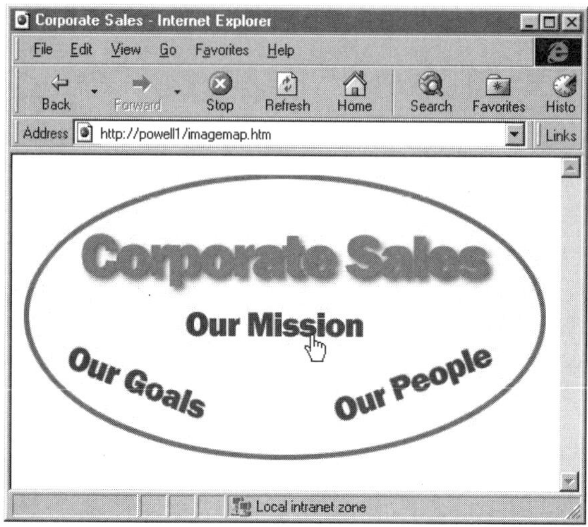

FIGURE 22.2

An image in which the areas Our Mission, Our Goals, and Our People link to three different pages by means of an image map.

The corporate sales department wants the *Our Goals, Our Mission,* and *Our People* areas to link to different pages on their Web server. Since these words are part of a single image file, we can't use a simple anchor to create the link. Instead, we use an image map to define areas within the picture and what links they belong to. In our example, the HTML might look like this:

```
<MAP NAME="CorpSalesMap">
    <AREA SHAPE="RECT"
        COORDS="132, 107, 283, 132"
        HREF="mission.htm">
    <AREA SHAPE="POLYGON"
        COORDS="40, 132, 158, 175, 145, 201, 31, 150"
        HREF="goals.htm">
    <AREA SHAPE="POLYGON"
        COORDS="251, 179, 378, 127, 390, 152, 255, 199"
        HREF="people.htm">
</MAP>
<IMG SRC="/images/corpsales.jpg"
    BORDER="0"
    WIDTH="430"
    HEIGHT="230"
    USEMAP="#CorpSalesMap">
```

The <MAP> tag defines our image map. It has child elements, defined by the <AREA> tags, that define the different regions within our image. The first <AREA> tag has an attribute named *SHAPE*, which is defined as the string *RECT*. This attribute tells the browser that the *COORDS* attribute contains the *xy*-coordinates for the upper left corner, followed by the *xy*coordinates for the lower right corner. Then the associated hyperlink reference for the given area is defined. In our example, the coordinates form a rectangle around the words *Our Mission* in the image. When we click on these words; we link to MISSION.HTM.

The second and third <AREA> tags have the *SHAPE* attribute set to the value *POLYGON*. Because the words *Our Goals* and *Our People* are tilted on the image, defining a polygon shape to surrounding these words would work better than defining a horizontal rectangle. The *POLYGON* value tells the browser that the *COORDS* attribute is in the format of a list of *xy*-coordinates for a series of points in the image. We happen to have a list of eight values, which means that our area has four points. If we plot these points, we'll see that they create something close to a rectangle around the words *Our Goals* and *Our People*.

How did we come up with the numbers in the *COORDS* attribute for these areas? The numbers that correspond to *x*-coordinates are the numbers of pixels from the left edge of our image. The numbers that correspond to the *y*-coordinates are the numbers of pixels from the top edge of the image. Unless you think that we used a magnifying glass to count pixels or played a lengthy game of trial and error, you probably realize that a tool allows us to do this—in this case, we used Microsoft FrontPage to build the coordinate values, although other tools are available.

The image map definition that we have demonstrated here is a client-side image map, meaning that the client browser is given the image map information and then must interpret the areas itself. Formerly, the use of image maps meant that the client included an *ISMAP* attribute for a displayed image, which anchored the URL for what was called a map file to the image. When the user clicked on the image, an HTTP request was made to the specified link using the *xy*-coordinates of the image on which the user clicked as parameters to the request. The server had to have support for the image map files so that it could interpret the request, read the areas defined in the map file, and then send the browser a redirect request to the specified location.

IIS does not natively support server-side image maps, although there are probably third-party CGI applications or ISAPI extensions that can do the trick. However, the use of client-side image maps solves many problems. For instance, the area processing occurs on the client instead of the server, which is probably busy handling many other requests and doesn't need to be interpreting image maps as well. Also, client-side image maps work whether you're making an HTTP request or accessing the HTML file directly (for instance, using a URL such as *file:c:\inetpub\wwwroot\corpsales.htm*). Server-side image maps work only if you're using HTTP. Client-side image maps also allow the browser to give the user feedback when she passes her mouse over a hot region within the image. Passing the mouse over the words *Our Mission* in our sample image causes Internet Explorer to display the link to MISSION.HTM in its status bar. The only feedback you get from a server-side image map is that the entire image is a link to the map file. You should always use client-side image maps in your HTML documents.

<META> tags

The <META> tag is a child element of the HEAD element and thus applies to the entire contents of a document. In its base form, it provides a way to associate properties, such as the name of the author or the software that generated the file, with the document. The *NAME* attribute defines the name of the property you're setting, and the *CONTENT* attribute contains the value of the property. You can specify whatever property names you want; the names have little meaning to most Web browsers and servers. However, the <META> tag can be a useful element for creating search indexes for your Web site. For example, by setting *Author="Matt Powell"* or *Security=high* using the <META> tag, you allow for a search engine to find all the documents authored by a certain individual or all the documents flagged as needing high security. Here's an example of how to use the <META> tag to set the author for our document:

```
<META NAME="Author" CONTENT="Matt Powell">
```

The <META> tag can also be used to specifically control the HTTP headers that are sent along with the requested document. Instead of supplying a *NAME* attribute, you supply an attribute named *HTTP-EQUIV*, which indicates the name of the HTTP header you're trying to set. The following code sets the HTTP Expires header to the date and time specified:

```
<META HTTP-EQUIV="Expires" CONTENT="Mon, 22 Mar 1999 14:11:52 GMT">
```

By adding this element to your HTML document, you're letting the browser that downloads it know that it shouldn't read the document out of its cache after the specified date and time. <META> tags with the *HTTP-EQUIV* attribute can also set up redirections, set refresh times, set rating information, and set numerous other HTTP actions on a per-file basis by manipulating only the HTML document itself. It's the responsibility of server software such as IIS to read the HTML file and look for META information that might need to be sent in the HTTP headers.

Forms

Probably no other HTML tag is used for business-related activity more than the <FORM> tag. As its name suggests, the <FORM> tag is used to create a form that lets the user supply requested information and submit that information to the server. The information entered by the client is made available to the server application for processing. A form could be used by a data entry division of a company to input transactions into a database, or a form could be used to submit feedback on an idea presented in a page. Figure 22.3 shows how a simple form might look in your browser.

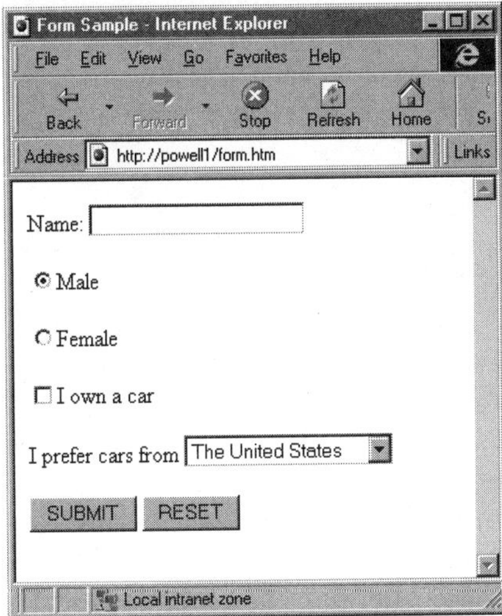

FIGURE 22.3

A sample HTML form.

In this example, we used five different kinds of input mechanisms: a text box, two radio buttons, a check box, a drop-down list box, and two buttons. Let's take a look at the HTML source code for this form:

```
<FORM ACTION="/SCRIPTS/SURVEY.DLL" METHOD="POST">
    <P>Name: <INPUT TYPE="TEXT" SIZE="20" NAME="NAME"></P>
    <P><INPUT TYPE="RADIO" CHECKED NAME="SEX" VALUE="M">Male</P>
    <P><INPUT TYPE="RADIO" NAME="SEX" VALUE="F">Female</P>
    <P><INPUT TYPE="CHECKBOX" NAME="OWN" VALUE="TRUE">I own a car</P>
    <P>I prefer cars from
    <SELECT NAME="COUNTRY" SIZE="1">
        <OPTION>the United States</OPTION>
        <OPTION>Japan</OPTION>
        <OPTION>the United Kingdom</OPTION>
        <OPTION>Germany</OPTION>
        <OPTION>Italy</OPTION>
        <OPTION>Russia</OPTION>
        <OPTION>Sweden</OPTION>
    </SELECT></P>
    <P><INPUT TYPE="SUBMIT">
    <INPUT TYPE="RESET"></P>
</FORM>
```

The FORM element lives inside the body of our document. FORM elements themselves can be very simple or quite large, depending on how many input controls are required. We created most of the input mechanisms in our form by using the <INPUT> tag. The <INPUT> tag's *TYPE* attribute determines what kind of control we need to display. The exception to this is the drop-down list, which we use the <SELECT> tag to create. Each of the input mechanisms has a *NAME* attribute, and a couple have a *VALUE* attribute. The idea is that a list of parameters will be passed to the specified server in the form of *attribute=value* when the Submit button is clicked. In the case of a drop-down list, the value submitted will be the text string selected in the list.

The attributes of our <FORM> tag are probably the most important of the entire form. The *ACTION* attribute specifies the URL to which the information will be sent. The *METHOD* attribute specifies the HTTP method to be used in the request. Usually, a form uses the *POST* or *GET* method to submit the request. The difference between a *POST* request and a *GET* request is that a *GET* request appends the parameter information to the end of the indicated URL. A *POST* request, on the other hand, puts the parameter information in the contents of the HTTP body. Figure 22.4 shows two versions of the same request from our form; one is made with the *POST* method and the other with the *GET* method.

Using a POST method

```
POST /SCRIPTS/SURVEY.DLL HTTP/1.0
Accept: image/gif, image/x-xbitmap, image/jpeg, image/pjpeg,
        application/vnd.ms-excel, application/msword,
        application/vnd.ms-powerpoint, */*
Referer: http://powell1/form.htm
Accept-Language: en
Content-Type: application/x-www-form-urlencoded
User-Agent: Mozilla/2.0 (compatible; MSIE 3.01; Windows NT)
Host: powell1
Content-Length: 57
Pragma: No-Cache

NAME=Matt+Powell&SEX=M&OWN=TRUE&COUNTRY=Japan
```

Using a GET method

```
GET /SCRIPTS/SURVEY.DLL?NAME=Matt+Powell&SEX=M&OWN=TRUE&COUNTRY=Japan
HTTP/1.0
Accept: image/gif, image/x-xbitmap, image/jpeg, image/pjpeg,
        application/vnd.ms-excel, application/msword,
        application/vnd.ms-powerpoint, */*
Referer: http://powell1/form.htm
Accept-Language: en
User-Agent: Mozilla/2.0 (compatible; MSIE 3.01; Windows NT)
Host: powell1
```

FIGURE 22.4

HTTP requests generated from an HTML form using the* POST *method and the* GET *method.

Usually, it doesn't matter which method you use, but you should be aware of a couple of issues. First of all, the response to a *POST* request is never cached, which might be good or might be bad, depending on the kind of application you happen to be writing. The advantage of caching is that your server won't have to process as many requests if you allow the use of cached information. The disadvantage is that the user might be seeing old information if they're looking at a cached version. You can be certain with a *POST* request that you are looking at recent information. A *GET* request, on the other hand, contains the parameters *in* the URL. Because HTTP responses are cached based on the URL, subsequent requests for the URL will most likely be retrieved from cache. One more thing to note: although there's no limit to the size of a URL according the URL specification, a number of client and server implementations impose a limit on the size of a URL. Therefore, if your parameter list is large, information could potentially be lost in a *GET* request. A *POST* request avoids these problems by placing the parameters in the body of the HTTP request, where there's no size limit.

Client Scripting

When we talked about image maps, we noted that one of the reasons that client-side image maps are so useful is that they make it possible for the server to do less processing per request. Keeping a server's load to a minimum is usually a good thing because of the multiuser nature of servers. Because clients are relatively underburdened, it's a nice trade-off if we can have the client do some of the computing for us.

Consider the task of validating form input. Figure 22.5 shows a form prompting the user to enter a year between now and 2025. We could very easily end up getting values that won't make much sense to our server application. For instance, a user might enter 98 instead of 1998. He might enter 1996 by mistake, or he might even try to write out a word instead of entering the numeric year. A static HTML document would simply pass these parameters to the server when the form was submitted, and the server form-handling application would then need to validate the year that was entered properly. If the year didn't validate properly, the server software would have to generate the form again and send it back to the client to replace improper information.

Client-side scripting allows code to be included in an HTML document to perform a certain level of computation when certain events are triggered. For instance, our HTML file could include code that was executed when the Submit button was clicked. This code could check to verify that the values in the form were in the proper format without having to send the entire request to the server. If the input was invalid, the code would alert the user to the error and have the user fix the problem. If the code determines that the input is valid, it submits the request to the server for processing. In this fashion, we can eliminate a large number of superfluous HTTP requests.

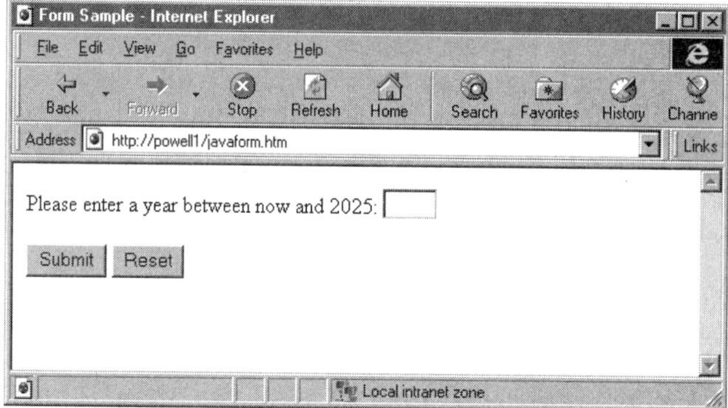

FIGURE 22.5

A simple form on which client scripting is used to validate the user's input before the request is sent to the server.

JavaScript

Now that we've determined the sort of thing that we would like client scripting to do, let's look at the specific code needed to perform this validation. We'll start by looking at an HTML file with JavaScript embedded in it, shown here:

```
<!DOCTYPE HTML PUBLIC "-//W3C//DTD HTML 4.0//EN">
<HTML>
<HEAD>
<TITLE>Form Sample</TITLE>
<SCRIPT LANGUAGE="JavaScript">
<!--
function isvalidyear(f)
{
    intvalue = parseInt(f.Year.value)
    if (isNaN(intvalue))
    {
        alert("You must enter a numeric value.")
    }
    else
    {
        if (intvalue > 1997)
        {
            if (intvalue < 2025)
```

```
                {
                    f.submit()
                }
                else
                {
                    alert("The year must be less than 2025.")
                }
            }
            else
            {
                alert("The year must be greater than 1997.")
            }
        }
}
// -->
</SCRIPT>
</HEAD>

<BODY BGCOLOR="#FFFFFF">
<FORM NAME="yearform" ACTION="/SCRIPTS/SURVEY.DLL" METHOD="GET">
    <P>Please enter a year between now and 2025:
    <INPUT TYPE="TEXT" SIZE="4" NAME="Year"></P>
    <P><INPUT TYPE="button" Value="Submit"
        onclick="isvalidyear(document.yearform)">
    <INPUT TYPE="RESET"></P>
</FORM>
</BODY>
</HTML>
```

The *isvalidyear* function checks the value entered in our text control to verify that it's numeric and within the range of acceptable values for our field. If the value isn't valid, an alert is displayed indicating to the user that he must fix the entry. If the value is acceptable, our function submits the request to the server application for processing. The SCRIPT element is used as a child element of our HEAD element because script functions are defined for the entire document. This sample happens to be in JavaScript as is indicated by the *LANGUAGE* attribute of the <SCRIPT> tag. Since many browsers don't support scripting, we include the contents of our SCRIPT element within a COMMENT element (indicated by the <!-- and --> delimiters). Browsers that support scripting understand that they must read through the comments section. JavaScript comments are indicated with two slashes (/ /). When the Submit button is clicked, an *onclick* event is generated. The Submit button's <INPUT> tag indicates that the *isvalidyear* function should handle the *onclick* event The form is passed as a parameter to the *isvalidyear* function, which then uses the value of the Year text box to determine whether the user entered a valid year.

VBScript

Internet Explorer also supports the VBScript language. The HTML for the same validation functionality in VBScript would look like this:

```
<!DOCTYPE HTML PUBLIC "-//W3C//DTD HTML 4.0//EN">
<HTML>
<HEAD>
<TITLE>Form Sample</TITLE>
<SCRIPT LANGUAGE="VBScript">
<!--
Function isvalidyear(f)
    If IsNumeric(f.Year.Value) Then
        If f.Year.Value > 1997 Then
            If f.Year.Value < 2025 Then
                f.submit
            Else
                MsgBox "The year must be less than 2025."
            End If
        Else
            MsgBox "The year must be greater than 1997."
        End If
    Else
        MsgBox "You must enter a numeric value."
    End If
End Function
// -->
</SCRIPT>
</HEAD>

<BODY BGCOLOR="#FFFFFF">
<FORM NAME="yearform" ACTION="/SCRIPTS/SURVEY.DLL" METHOD="GET">
    <P>Please enter a year between now and 2025:
    <INPUT TYPE="TEXT" SIZE="4" NAME="Year"></P>
    <P><INPUT TYPE="button" Value="Submit"
        onclick="isvalidyear(document.yearform)">
    <INPUT TYPE="RESET"></P>
</FORM>
</BODY>
</HTML>
```

If you compare the VBScript to the JavaScript version, you'll notice many similarities. For instance, we still declare the functions using the <SCRIPT> tag in the head of the document. The *isvalidyear* function is still being used to handle the Submit button's *onclick* event. The parameter being passed to the *isvalidyear* function is exactly the same in the two versions. The similarities are due to the underlying object model exposed by Internet Explorer, which is the same whether you are using JavaScript or VBScript. The small differences are simply the syntax of the scripting language. Let's take a closer look at the objects available for scripting.

Objects

If you aren't accustomed to using COM objects, you might have had a few questions about some of the references and calls that we were making in our scripting code. For instance, the *document.yearform* parameter that we passed to our *isvalidyear* function might not make sense to you. The rationale for this strange-looking syntax is the object-oriented nature of COM.

COM objects, like other kinds of objects, are a combination of code and data. Each object exposes its data and functionality through a unique combination of properties, methods, and events. A *property* is a piece of data that the object stores, such as the value in a text box. A *method* is something that the object can do, such as submit a request. An *event* is something that happens to the object, such as being clicked on. Sometimes related objects are grouped together, similar to an array of values, to create what is called a *collection*. Consider one of the objects in our scripting sample.

Internet Explorer provides a *document* object for use by the script embedded in an HTML document. The *forms* collection of the *document* object is an array of the forms included in the document. An array of forms wouldn't really make much sense if it weren't for the fact that Internet Explorer creates a *form* object for each FORM element in our HTML document. So in reality the array of forms is an array of *form* objects, each with its own methods and properties. When we call our *isvalidyear* function, the parameter we pass is *document.yearform*. This is shorthand notation for the *yearform* form in the array of *form* objects that are contained within our HTML file's *document* object. By passing the pointer to this *form* object to our function, we make its methods and properties available within our function. One of the form's collections is an array of the input objects within the form. Again, Internet Explorer has simplified the use of the INPUT elements in our form by creating an object for each one. The *value* property of our text input object contains the actual text entered by the user. We check this value to see whether it's numeric and in the given range. If the entry is valid, we call the *form* object's *SUBMIT* method to send the form's information to the server. If it's not valid, we use another object, the *window* object, to display a dialog box indicating that there's a problem. You might have noticed that in the case of JavaScript's *alert* function and VBScript's *MsgBox* function we don't seem to be using any dotted object notation. The reason for this is that the actual script interpretation takes place within the scope of the current *window* object. This means that there is an implied "*window.*" before the name of any function that's called. In this case, *alert* becomes *window.alert*. So what looks like an inherent function is actually just another method of our current object.

A number of different types of objects are exposed by Internet Explorer for JavaScript and VBScript. Netscape Navigator exposes similar objects for its implementation of JavaScript. A fundamental understanding of the nature of these objects and their hierarchical associations is critical to the effective writing of HTML scripts. Figure 22.6 shows the relationships between the various objects.

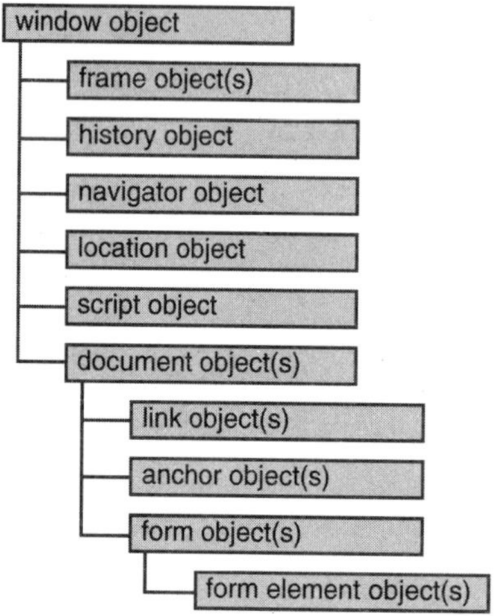

FIGURE 22.6

HTML scripting object hierarchy.

The objects exposed by the browser provide a sturdy foundation for usage within your HTML script, but you can raise your interactive HTML even one more level. The OBJECT tag allows you to include external objects, such as Java classes and ActiveX controls, within an HTML document. This capability gives your document the freedom to access and manipulate any resource to which your browser's operating system allows programmatic access. You can now kick off an interactive game, provide timer-event-driven processing, access hardware resources, and even access other network resources, all within the context of your HTML document. The power of your operating system is truly unleashed. What this means for anyone developing Web applications is that even the most highly interactive tasks can be performed today within the context of an HTML document. Obviously, certain security concerns will need to be addressed when you are using objects that have access to operating system resources. If you use objects designed by a third party, be sure that they are from a reputable source. Luckily, trustworthy objects will be digitally signed with the name of the company that developed them.

Dynamic HTML

With Internet Explorer versions 4.0 and later, a new object model has been created for HTML scripting. Instead of having only a small set of objects available for scripting, effectively every element within a Web page is an object. The different attributes for our elements can now be used as properties of our objects, and almost every element includes support for a number of different object events, such as when someone clicks on our element. The total group of objects exposed for scripting in Internet Explorer 4.0 is called the Dynamic HTML object model. Figure 22.7 shows the scripting object hierarchy used in Internet Explorer 4.0.

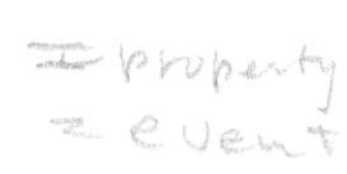

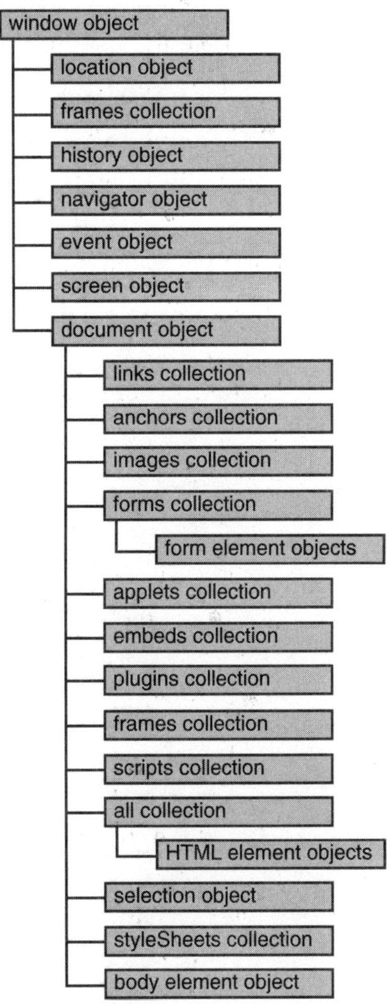

FIGURE 22.7

Scripting object hierarchy used in Internet Explorer 4.0.

Dynamic HTML is a general term that describes the combination of HTML, scripting, and cascading style sheets to create Web pages that are more interactive. The following sample uses Dynamic HTML to provide a truly interactive experience to the user:

```
<HTML>
<HEAD>
<META HTTP-EQUIV="Content-Type"
    content="text/html; charset=iso-8859-1">
<TITLE>DHTML Sample Page</TITLE>
</HEAD>
<BODY>
<H1> DHTML Sample Page </H1>
<OL>
    <LI>
        <SPAN ID="Item1">This is some text. </SPAN>
    <LI>
        <SPAN ID="Item2">This is another line of text. </SPAN>
    <LI>
        <SPAN ID="Item3">And yes, this is a third line. </SPAN>
</OL>

<SPAN ID="HelperText">
As you move your mouse over the options above, the text here will
change to display context-sensitive help for each of the options
above.</SPAN>

</BODY>
</HTML>

<SCRIPT LANGUAGE = "VBScript">
function Item1_onmouseover()
    Item1.style.fontWeight = "bold"
    Item1.style.cursor = "default"
    HelperText.innerText = _
        "This is the helper text for Item 1 in our list."
end function
function Item2_onmouseover()
    Item2.style.fontWeight = "bold"
    Item2.style.cursor = "default"
    HelperText.innerText = _
        "This is the context-sensitive help for Item 2 in our list."
end function
```

```
function Item3_onmouseover()
    Item3.style.fontWeight = "bold"
    Item3.style.cursor = "default"
    HelperText.innerText = _
        "This is, of course, the helper text that will " & _
        "appear when you hold the mouse over Item 3 in our list."
end function
function Item1_onmouseout()
    Item1.style.fontWeight = "normal"
end function
function Item2_onmouseout()
    Item2.style.fontWeight = "normal"
end function
function Item3_onmouseout()
    Item3.style.fontWeight = "normal"
end function
</SCRIPT>
```

In this example, we use a new element, SPAN. The SPAN element is simply a way to define regions within a document. We use it to manipulate the text in an ordered list that we've created. We've added script functions to handle six different Dynamic HTML events. Each of the three elements in our ordered list has two events associated with it: the *onmouseover* event and the *onmouseout* event. The event handlers themselves are named in VBScript using the *ID* attribute and the event separated by an underscore. For instance, we've named the first element in our list *Item1* using the *ID* attribute. The two event handlers for that item are *Item1_onmouseover* and *Item1_onmouseout*.

Our three *onmouseover* event handlers all do basically the same thing. Each event handler changes the underlying text to bold, changes the mouse cursor image to the default cursor (normally, the mouse cursor changes to a crossbar when passing over text), and finally changes the text of the *HelperText* object to some context-sensitive help for our list item. The *onmouseout* functions simply change the underlying text font back to normal after it was changed to bold when the mouse moved over the item. The result is a page that gives us immediate feedback about which item is being pointed to by changing the text to bold while also displaying context-sensitive help. Figure 22.8 shows what happens when our mouse moves over a list item.

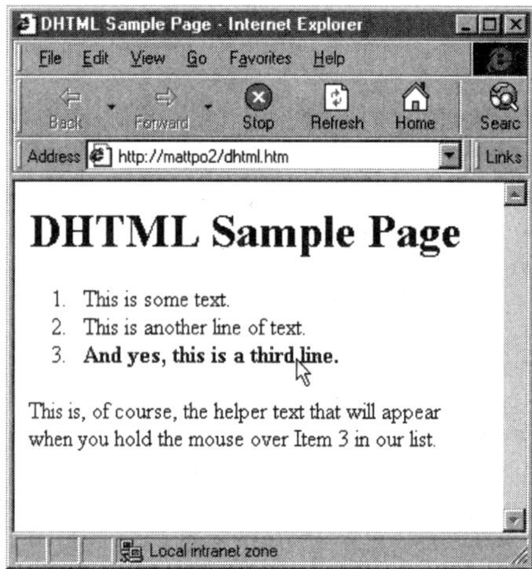

FIGURE 22.8

A Dynamic HTML page that changes a list item to bold and displays the helper text when the mouse is moved over the item.

You can do much more with Dynamic HTML, including creating interactive games. Your experience can be as interactively satisfying as many traditional applications are today, but will require only a minimum of programming knowledge. You can learn more about Dynamic HTML from the Microsoft Internet Client SDK or from the World Wide Web Consortium at *http://www.w3.org*.

Now that you have learned some of the basics of HTML and how your Web site's experience can take advantage of it, let's look at some of the protocol specifications that IIS supports. We'll be looking at FTP, NNTP, and SMTP in the coming chapters, but we'll start off with the protocol that's the base support of the Web: HTTP.

CHAPTER 23

The Hypertext Transfer Protocol (HTTP)

Let's begin our discussion of HTTP by answering two questions: "What is a protocol?" and "Why is it important to know a protocol?" Protocols are nothing more than a set of rules that client and server computers follow to communicate. These rules can be simple—for example, specifying that a server must respond to every request from a client—or more advanced—for example, rules that govern custom authentication schemes and security. So how does understanding all this low-level information help you create terrific interactive Web pages and applications? With a solid knowledge of HTTP, you will not only understand why IIS and server applications work the way they do, you will also have a feel for the power of HTTP and how you can take advantage of its capabilities for your site.

In this chapter, we will review the latest versions of HTTP and describe some of HTTP's key features. You can find more information about HTTP, as well as the RFC references in this chapter, at the World Wide Web Consortium site at *http://www.w3.org*.

In this chapter, we will also talk about *cookies*. Using cookies, we can build a shopping mall type of application or enable users to customize Web pages according to their individual tastes. In short, cookies are a "magic wand" that helps us build state-aware solutions using the stateless HTTP protocol. We will also learn about server status codes, which can be used to alert the browser that certain information or pages are secured and that the server expects the browser to supply a user name and password. By the end of this chapter, you will understand how a browser and a server negotiate and support access to password-protected resources.

An Overview of HTTP

HTTP is the backbone of the Web. Compared to other network protocols such as TCP/IP, HTTP is relatively new. In its first implementation, version 0.9, HTTP supported only simple *GET* requests and responses—enough to get a hypertext (HTML) document from a remote machine by providing a machine address. Today almost every server uses HTTP version 1.0 or 1.1. Each of these versions has significantly expanded the capabilities of HTTP.

HTTP/1.1 includes many provisions to make information transfer as efficient as possible. These performance improvement features include *persistent connections* (partially supported in HTTP/1.0) and *pipelining*. Persistent connections is a mechanism that enables the server to keep the underlying TCP connection open for reuse for subsequent HTTP requests and responses. Pipelining is a mechanism that enables a client to make multiple requests without waiting to receive the responses on a single underlying TCP connection.

The Internet RFC governing the HTTP version 1.1 specification (RFC 2068, "Hypertext Transfer Protocol -- HTTP/1.1") is almost three times larger than the similar document for HTTP/1.0 (RFC 1945, "Hypertext Transfer Protocol -- HTTP/1.0"). As of this writing, at least four revisions to RFC 2068 are in the works, but we will concentrate on the released documents and will not discuss proposed changes.

To talk about network protocols, we must return to the Open Systems Interconnection (OSI) network architecture model, which we discussed briefly in Chapter 2. HTTP provides the OSI model's application layer support. The application layer is the top layer in the OSI model, which means that the functionality provided relies on lower layers to perform tasks such as transmitting data reliably and establishing connections over routed networks. The higher-level HTTP protocol is not burdened with these routine tasks. Instead, it implements only those services needed to accomplish a specific task: submitting requests to get specific URLs, which usually results in the transfer of HTML files. Of course, these days not only HTML data travels from the server to the browser (and from the browser to the server). Modern browsers can download ActiveX controls, Java applets, and a bunch of other binary and text data directly from the server—all using HTTP as a vehicle.

HTTP and TCP/IP

The Internet is a TCP/IP-biased world, and HTTP is no exception. Nothing prevents HTTP from running over other network protocols that would provide low-level services, but in reality the world has standardized on HTTP running over TCP/IP. TCP provides HTTP with guaranteed delivery and guaranteed packet sequencing capabilities, so HTTP doesn't have to worry about whether the machine at the other end received the data sent and whether that data is in the order in which it was sent. Figure 23.1 illustrates what we mean when we say that HTTP is carried on top of the TCP/IP protocol.

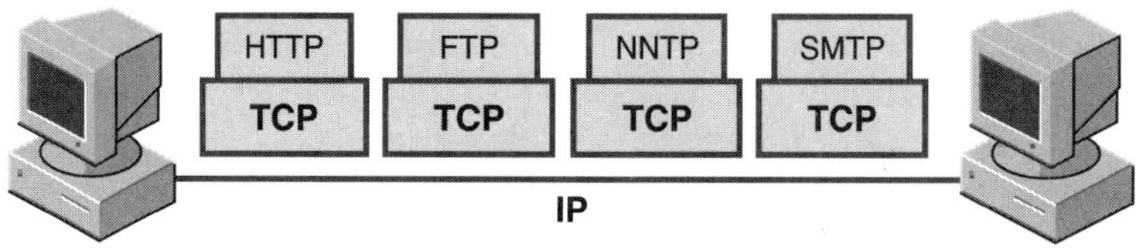

FIGURE 23.1

The relationship between application layer protocols and TCP/IP.

NOTE

This chapter is the first in a series of four chapters discussing the various network protocols. These other application layer protocols—File Transfer Protocol (FTP), Network News Transfer Protocol (NNTP), and Simple Mail Transfer Protocol (SMTP)—are also carried on top of TCP/IP, so keep this figure in mind for the coming chapters as well.

The fact that TCP / IP provides the low-level connection services for HTTP enables us to access TCP directly and manually create HTTP requests. If we do so, we won't be able to see the nicely rendered pictures and other HTML markup elements typically found on an HTML page; instead, we will get raw HTTP data. Sockets provide the interface to the TCP layer, so we could write a Microsoft Windows Sockets (Winsock) application that will dump the raw HTTP data in a simplified Web browser. Or we could use a telnet client application to access TCP. By default, the Web browser listens for client connections on TCP port 80 (or on port 443 for SSL connections). If we start telnet and connect to our WWW server's port 80, we can issue any HTTP command we want. Towards the end of this chapter, we will use the telnet client application to make HTTP requests and spy on HTTP responses.

The HTTP Request/Response Format

HTTP typically follows a general transaction paradigm. A client sends a request to the server, which then sends back a response, hopefully containing the requested information. This request / response model can end up being slightly more complicated if any proxies or gateways are acting as intermediaries in our transactions. For example, the client might send its request to a proxy and then wait for the proxy to send back a response. The proxy receives the request from the client and then forwards that request to the actual destination server. The destination server perceives the proxy as the client, and so it sends the response to the proxy. The response is received and then immediately forwarded to the client as if it came from the proxy originally. In this case, the proxy simply acts as a subserver to the client.

An HTTP request has the following format:

```
<method> <request_URI> <HTTP_Version>
<header1_fieldname>: <field1_value>
<header2_fieldname>: <field2_value>
  ...
<headerN_fieldname>: <fieldN_value>

<data>
```

The first line, the Request-Line, holds the general information about our request: the type of a request we are making (*<method>*), the file or entity we are requesting (*<request_URI>*), and the version of HTTP we understand (*<HTTP_Version>*).

Each of these fields is separated by a single space. A carriage return/linefeed pair separates this line from the other headers in our request.

NOTE

URI stands for Uniform Resource Identifier and is part of a specification used to identify resources. URL (short for Uniform Resource Locator) is a subspecification of URI and is also used to identify resources. For the purposes of our discussion of HTTP, URI is synonymous with URL.

Depending on the type of request, a number of headers might be required in order to provide more information to the server handling our request. This header list has a variable list of entries, each one separated from the others by a carriage return/linefeed pair. The end of the header list is indicated by two carriage return/linefeed pairs in immediate succession. Any specific data that should accompany this request would then follow this header list.

The second part of our HTTP transaction is the response sent from the server back to the client. The response format is shown here:

```
<HTTP_Version> <Status_Code> <Reason_Phrase>
<header1_fieldname>: <field1_value>
<header2_fieldname>: <field2_value>
  ...
<headerN_fieldname>: <fieldN_value>

<data>
```

The first line of our response, the Status-Line, contains the HTTP version of the response (*<HTTP_Version>*), the numeric status code (*<Status_Code>*), and a short phrase that describes what the numeric status code means (*<Reason_Phrase>*). The Status-Line is separated from the rest of the HTTP headers by a carriage return/linefeed pair. As with the HTTP request, the response has a variable list of headers containing information about the response, each separated by a carriage return/linefeed. Here too, two carriage return/linefeed pairs indicate the end of the headers list and the beginning of the accompanying data. Before we look at the details of requests and responses, let's talk about connection management.

HTTP Connection Management

HTTP uses lower-level TCP to establish and tear down connections. Establishing new connections is a costly task. TCP needs to send at least three network packets as part of a three-way handshake just to establish a connection. Having to spend extra time setting up connections takes its toll on the browser's speed and on the user's experience of surfing the Web.

As we've seen, HTTP was designed to use a request/response model. If the requested document contains other links, such as images, the browser needs to submit a separate request for each image. This process involves opening and closing a connection (that is, a TCP socket) with each request. Accessing a password-protected page also generates more than one request (you will learn the details of this authentication process in the "HTTP Credential Management" section later in this chapter) and results in connection termination and reestablishment. All of this handshaking and connection establishment obviously doesn't help overall performance. To remedy the situation, HTTP has a special provision to keep a connection open rather than closing the socket after each request/response pair.

The original version of the HTTP/1.0 protocol always closed a connection after the server sent a response. To prevent this, the client could negotiate a persistent connection by sending a Connection: Keep-Alive header. Once a server receives this header, it does not close its socket after sending a response. But if the server does not close the socket, how does the client know when all of the intended data has been received from the server so that it can stop indicating to the user that it is still working (as Microsoft Internet Explorer does with its little spinning globe)? The client relies on the presence of the Content-Length header, which indicates the number of bytes the client should read. If the Content-Length header is missing, the client assumes that it needs to read data for as long as the connection is kept open by the server. Therefore, if there is no Content-Length header, the Keep-Alive header must not be used.

HTTP/1.1 was designed with performance improvements in mind. All connections are persistent by default. If a client sends a request with HTTP/1.1 as the protocol version, it does not need to send any Connection headers. But HTTP/1.1 servers are usually backward compatible with earlier versions of the protocol and understand the Connection header if one is received. Sure enough, an HTTP/1.1 server can close a connection immediately after a response is sent. In this case, the server closes its socket and sends a Connection: close header. The server still sends a Content-Length header as is required by the HTTP/1.1 specification. When a client sends data to the server (for instance, by using the *POST* method), it must also send the Content-Length header so that the server knows how much data the client is sending with the request.

HTTP Credential Management

HTTP has special provisions to negotiate access to secure resources. Such negotiation relies heavily on both request and response headers. Here's how it works. The client first issues a request for a secured resource to which the server responds with a "401 Access Denied" status code. The server's response includes a WWW-Authenticate response header containing a challenge for the client. The client then resubmits the request with the added Authenticate request header. This header contains the response corresponding to the server's challenge, usually including the encrypted user name and password information.

One of the simplest authentication schemes is Basic authentication, in which the user name and password are encrypted via the Base64 encoding method. (Base64 encoding is defined in RFC 1521 "MIME [Multipurpose Internet Mail Extensions] Part One: Mechanisms for Specifying and Describing the Format of Internet Message Bodies.")

Here's how Basic authentication works:

1. The client sends a request, such as this:

   ```
   GET /default.htm
   ```

2. Assume that DEFAULT.HTM is a password-protected resource and that an anonymous user cannot access it. The server sends the following response:

   ```
   HTTP/1.1 401 Access Denied
   WWW-Authenticate: Basic realm="Foo"
     ...
   ```

   This response indicates that the server is requesting the client to use the Basic authentication scheme with a *realm* of *Foo*. The *realm* element is a special attribute (usually a string) that defines a unique protected space on the server (such as a directory). By using different *realms*, multiple user name/user password pairs can be supported on the same server.

3. If the client does not support the Basic authentication scheme (which is very unlikely), an error is reported. Otherwise, the client asks the user to enter credentials (name and password) and resends the original request to the server with the acquired credentials in the Authorization header, as shown here:

   ```
   GET /default.htm HTTP/1.1
   Authorization: Basic XXXXXXXXXX
   ```

   XXXXXXXXXX represents the Base64-encrypted user name and password separated by a colon before the encoding.

4. Upon receiving the resubmitted request, the server decodes the credentials and verifies whether they are valid. If they are not valid, the server starts over again from step 3. Usually, the server sends a "401 Access Denied" status code three times. If after three attempts the client can't supply a valid name and password, the server reports an error and does not resend any more responses.

Basic isn't the only authentication scheme available with HTTP. IIS also uses Microsoft Windows NT Challenge/Response authentication, which is sometimes referred to as Windows NT LAN Manager (NTLM) authentication. NTLM authentication is a more secure option than Basic because with NTLM the user's password is never physically transferred over the Internet. Instead, the password is used as a one-way encryption key for a random chunk of data sent between the client and the server as a challenge. The NTLM challenge/response handshake requires a much more intricate sequence than Basic authentication. The original anonymous request is sent to the server, which responds with a "401 Access Denied" status and a WWW-Authenticate header with NTLM specified as the authentication scheme. Included with the NTLM authentication is a randomly generated challenge. The challenge is used by the client to one-way encrypt the client's user name. The server then replies with another "401 Access Denied" response that includes a challenge to be used as a public key to encrypt the user's password. The password itself is unknown to IIS; however, the encrypted response can be validated. NTLM authentication requires that all requests from the server with the challenge for the same session arrive on the same socket, which can be accomplished only by using the Keep-Alive HTTP option. This limitation also prevents NTLM from being used through a proxy.

In addition to the server requirement for authenticated connections, an HTTP proxy can require clients to supply a user name and password just to pass through it. Although the authentication mechanism is identical, the proxy uses the Proxy-Authenticate header instead of the WWW-Authenticate header. And the client returns a Proxy-Authorization header rather than an Authorization header.

HTTP Requests

As mentioned, the HTTP/1.1 specification is a superset of the HTTP/1.0 specification and provides for backward compatibility with HTTP/1.0 requests. If an HTTP/1.1 server receives an HTTP/1.0 request, the server is obligated to respond with an HTTP/1.0 response.

For those of us relatively familiar with the Web, a reference such as *http://www.microsoft.com/intdev* seems fairly straightforward, but there's more to an HTTP URL (or URI) than you might expect. The general format for an HTTP URL is *http://<host>.<domain>:<port>/<path>*. The *http:* at the start of the URL specifies the protocol being used. The *<host>* field (often *www*) is the name of the server you are connecting to, the *<domain>* is the rest of the fully qualified name of the host. You can specify which TCP port you want HTTP to use; if you leave the *<port>* field blank, it defaults to port 80. The *<path>* is the specific hierarchical reference to the entity you desire.

When you see the request URI in a request packet, you are almost always looking at a relative URI. The fully qualified host name is already apparent because the TCP connection is already established by the time an HTTP packet is built. The URIs in this case are relative to the default base path of the server.

Request Methods

The request method is a cornerstone of HTTP. Methods denote an action that the client wants to perform with the associated URL. Seven common case-sensitive (uppercase) methods are defined in RFC 2068; IIS provides support for each of these methods. Realize that if a server supports a certain method, only Web clients supporting this method can take advantage of it. Any server can also implement its own extension methods.

Methods can be grouped in two categories: safe and unsafe. Safe methods merely read the contents of a certain URL; they can't change the contents of the server or the URL itself. For example, issuing a *GET* request for /default.htm can't change the content of DEFAULT.HTM. Of course, a client can invoke a server application (ISAPI, CGI, ASP, and so on) using a *GET* request that in turn formats the hard drive, but this is considered a side effect of the application and not of the method. Unsafe methods, on the other hand, do change the contents of the Web server. Certain methods can create or delete files on the server; the success of such actions depends on the server configuration. For example, if a virtual directory does not have write permission, the method that deletes or creates a new file referred to in the URL won't succeed. The following sections describe the individual request methods and their potential side effects.

OPTIONS

The *OPTIONS* method enables a client to request information about all of the supported methods for a particular server and for the URL in particular. It is much more efficient to check whether posting data to the specific directory is allowed than to try to post a huge amount of data (therefore wasting network bandwidth and time) and have it fail. Two properly formatted *OPTIONS* requests are shown here:

```
OPTIONS /myurlpath/myurl.htm HTTP/1.1
OPTIONS * HTTP/1.1
```

The first request obtains all supported methods for the */myurlpath/myurl.htm* relative URL. The second request inquires about the entire server, as indicated by the asterisk (*).

A successful response to the *OPTIONS* request contains strictly headers; it does not include a BODY element. Two headers are of particular interest. The Public header indicates all publicly implemented methods on the server. The Allow header represents methods that apply to the specific URL sent with the request. Depending on the URL, the allowed methods may change. For a directory that does not allow writing, for example, methods that create files wouldn't be allowed. When an *OPTIONS* request is sent to the server via a proxy, the proxy edits the server's response to delete any methods that the proxy does not support. The client can't take advantage of the methods supported by a server if it has to send the request through a proxy that does not support those methods.

TRACE

TRACE is a simple method designed mostly for debugging purposes. A *TRACE* request invokes a loopback test, which means that the entire data set sent to the server, including headers and body, is echoed back to the client. To indicate that the response is an echo of sent data, the server sets the Content-Type headers to *message/http*. This method is useful for testing configurations involving multiple proxies and gateways. In such cases, a message is forwarded from proxy server to proxy server. Each proxy server participating in the request chain adds its name using the Via header. Thus, an echo message contains a fingerprint of each proxy server, which allows the administrator to determine the path the message took. What happens if a series of proxies has been misconfigured and HTTP requests are being passed infinitely from machine to machine? *TRACE* can be used to help resolve such problems. The initial *TRACE* request might contain a Max-Forwards header that specifies how many times the request is allowed to pass from machine to machine.

GET

The *GET* method is undeniably today's most widely used form of HTTP request. When your Internet browser reads an HTML file, it uses a *GET* request to retrieve the data. *GET* can also be used to retrieve the contents of any image, sound, and video files embedded in your HTML page. *GET* can be optimized by adding a condition header such as If-Modified-Since. This header allows the server to transmit data only if it is a newer version than the data the client may have cached locally. Other condition headers include If-Unmodified-Since, If-Match, If-None-Match, and If-Range. The document is transmitted only if the condition is met. These modified *GET* requests are called *conditional GET* requests. A *partial GET* is an HTTP/1.1 enhancement that lets you achieve better performance by sending only a portion of the requested entity. Partial *GET*s use a special header to determine the byte range that needs to be sent. Both conditional *GET*s and partial *GET*s improve network performance and don't clutter bandwidth if the requested document can be read from the browser's cache.

HEAD

The *HEAD* method is similar to the *GET* method with one exception: the *HEAD* request asks the server to reply with the response headers only and not include any of the entity's data. This technique is useful for checking the validity of a hyperlink without transferring the entity itself; it can also be a convenient means of checking the validity of cached data by comparing the Content-Length headers or the optional Content-Version headers with the size and version of a locally stored copy.

POST

If the *GET* method represents the "read" request, the *POST* method represents the "write" request. A *POST* request contains entity data that is submitted to the specified URL. Because a *POST* request contains entity data, the server must know the size of the request. For this reason, either the Content-Length header is required or the request must use chunked encoding for all *POST* requests. The chunked encoding method means that the HTTP data consists of multiple data chunks. (We discuss chunked encoding later in the "Handling Posted Data" sidebar.) The URL in the *POST* request is a script or a server application of some sort that will perform the actual processing of the data. For instance, you might use a *POST* request to submit HTML data to a script or application that will store it as a local file. (That 's how the Microsoft Posting Acceptor works for HTTP uploads, as we saw in Chapter 8.) Or you might use a *POST* request to submit a database record to be inserted into a database.

A server can react in a variety of ways to a *POST* request, depending on the application involved. Although it's nice to think of a *POST* request as a "write" operation, a successful *POST* request does not require that any sort of persistent information be stored on the server. Nothing specifies that the Content-Length header of the *POST* request can't be *0*. (But be careful here—zero-length content does not mean the absence of the Content-Length header.)

PUT

The *PUT* method is similar to the *POST* method, except that the URI specified for a *PUT* method indicates the actual requested destination for the data instead of indicating the gateway application that should handle the posted data. Consider the first line of the *PUT* request, shown here:

```
PUT /myurlpath/myurl.htm HTTP/1.1
```

This request forces the server to get the body of the request (which would normally be supplied by the client), create the MYURL.HTM file (if it doesn't already exist) in the /myurlpath directory, and store the data in the file. As you can see, there's no need to write a specific script to handle the data—IIS creates a file and stores the data all by itself. *PUT* is a simple way of creating and storing data remotely, but it is not as flexible as *POST* because the server does not invoke any external process to handle the data. Of course, a directory must have write permission before the client can create any files in the directory.

WARNING

Allowing a directory to have both write and execute permissions is asking for a potential security disaster. Clients can upload any malicious script or application and then run it. IIS displays a warning alerting the user when it detects that a directory has write and execute permissions.

DELETE

If you can remotely create an entity identified by a URL using *PUT*, there must also be a way to delete an identified entity. Sure enough, the *DELETE* method does exactly this. The *DELETE* method is probably the simplest method of all—all it does is delete the resource specified in the URL. Of course, the same rules regarding write permissions apply to *DELETE* as apply to *PUT*.

Request Headers

When an application uses HTTP, often the information stored in the headers is the most useful. Some headers are mandatory for accurate processing, however, many other headers are optional. If a request leaves out the optional headers, the Web server will still accept and process the request. But let's take a look at some available request headers.

The From header enables a client to specify an Internet e-mail address to be sent with the request. This header can be particularly useful when automated requests are being submitted and a problem occurs. Without this header, you would have no way of determining who to contact about the errant request. The From header is optional.

The If-Modified-Since and If-Unmodified-Since headers are used to create a conditional *GET* request. As we'll see in the "HTTP Protocol Details" section later in this chapter, a conditional request can be used to get data only if the data has changed since it was cached. In some cases, changes in the document date do not necessarily mean that the contents of a document have been modified, so the If-Modified-Since header is not enough to determine whether a new copy of the document should be transferred.

The ETag (short for Entity Tag) header can help with this difficulty. The ETag header is a special cache validation header that uniquely identifies the HTML document. It can be anything: any unique string of letters or numbers, or a combination of the two. Don't get confused here—ETag is an HTTP response header. It identifies content transferred from the server to the client. Other headers used for conditional requests include If-Match and If-None-Match, which are used in conjunction with the ETag header. When a client wants to receive only a certain byte range instead of an entire document, the If-Range header is used.

The Connection header provides information that is specific to the connection itself. (We saw this header already, in the "HTTP Connection Management" section earlier in this chapter.) HTTP/1.0 clients use the Keep-Alive value to indicate that the server should not close the lower-level connection after it sends the response. This allows the client to submit further requests without tearing down and reestablishing the TCP connection each time. The client submits the request with the Connection: Keep-Alive header to request a persistent connection, and the server includes the same header in its response to indicate that it will keep the session open. For clients that support the more recent HTTP/1.1 specification, keeping the underlying connection open is the default action, so the Connection: Keep-Alive header is no longer needed. Instead, the Connection: Close header is used to indicate when the underlying connection should be terminated.

The Referer header (which is deliberately misspelled) specifies the URI that referenced the current request. This information can be interesting for a server to keep track of if it would like to see who has hyperlinks pointing to it. The Referer header will not be present unless the URI was accessed via a hyperlink.

The User-Agent header is a text string describing the client application. It can be used by the server to respond appropriately to different clients depending on the client application's capabilities. This header might be used to determine whether you are running Internet Explorer 4.0 or later, for instance, in which case your response might contain a custom ActiveX control. (We used this header in Chapter 21, when we wrote a custom ISAPI filter.)

The Accept header provides a list of content types that are supported by the client for the specified request. These types are normally in the form of MIME content pairs separated by semicolons; however, an Accept header can also specify a preferred content type. A typical Accept header might look like this:

```
Accept: text/html; application/msword; image/gif
```

The Accept-Charset, Accept-Encoding, and Accept-Language headers indicate the character sets, encoding schemes, and languages the client supports. The server is obligated to respond in a specified manner. Omitting any of these headers indicates to the server that any of the respective character sets, encoding schemes, or languages are acceptable.

As mentioned, the client is free to omit any of these headers. However, one header is mandatory with HTTP/1.1: the Host header. If a server receives an HTTP/1.1 request without this header, it will reply with an error code indicating an incomplete request. The Host header represents the name of the host, taken directly from the URL. Thus, if an HTTP/1.1 client makes a request to *http://leonbr-hm*, the Host header will have the value *leonbr-hm*. This header is useful for multiple servers running on a single machine; it allows more than one name to be associated with a single IP address. IIS uses the Host header to identify each unique site when it has more than one Web site. (Chapter 4 describes how to configure your IIS server to support multiple Web sites.)

HTTP Responses

Now that we've looked at a number of options for the client request, let's look at the options for a server response. Like the client request, the response header includes the *HTTP_Version* field, which is used to indicate the version of the response. To provide backward compatibility, the server should respond to HTTP/1.0 requests only with headers that the client will recognize while still indicating its support for HTTP/1.1.

Response Status Codes

After the version number, the server must indicate the general status of the request/response with both the *Status_Code* field and the *Reason_Phrase* field, a text field describing the code. The five categories of status codes and their corresponding levels are shown here:

100	Informational
200	Successful
300	Redirection
400	Client Error
500	Server Error

The 100-level Informational status codes are used to indicate server events that are more or less independent of a client's request. Informational status codes are not supported by HTTP/1.0 clients; however, HTTP/1.1 clients are required to support them. The 200-level Successful status codes indicate that the requested action has completed as expected. The 300-level Redirection status codes tell the client that the requested action could not be performed but that it might be able to be performed if the client redirects the request to a different entity. The 400-level Client Error status codes indicate that the client request itself is in error. This level includes not only malformed requests but also requests that do not meet security and entity restrictions. The 500-level Server Error status codes tell the client that its request was fine, but that some sort of server problem prevented the server from replying successfully. The following table lists the available status codes and provides a short explanation of each.

Status Code	Reason Phrase	Description
100 Informational		
100	Continue	A partial request has been received, and the remainder of the request should be submitted.
101	Switching Protocols	Agreement to switch the application protocol.
200 Successful		
200	OK	The request completed successfully.
201	Created	The request resulted in the creation of a new resource, which can be referenced by the returned URI.
202	Accepted	The request has been accepted for processing, but the processing is not finished.
203	Non-Authoritative Information	The data returned is not necessarily from the original source (could be from a proxy, for example).
204	No Content	There is no entity data to go along with the response, and the client should not change the current document view.
205	Reset Content	The client should reset the current document view.
206	Partial Content	The server is responding with the results to a partial *GET* request.
300 Redirection		
300	Multiple Choices	There are multiple locations that satisfy the client's request.
301	Moved Permanently	The client should reset the current URI to the specified permanent URI.
302	Found	The client should note that the current URI has changed temporarily to the specified URI.
303	See Other	The client should get the response from a different URI by performing another *GET* request.
304	Not Modified	The target URI has not changed since the client's cached version was retrieved.
305	Use Proxy	The requested entity must be accessed through a proxy.
307	Temporary Redirect	The request is temporarily relocated but the client should still send future requests to this location.

Status Code	Reason Phrase	Description
400 Client Error		
400	Bad Request	The request was not understood by the server.
401	Unauthorized	The request requires user authentication.
402	Payments Required	The request requires a payment by the client.
403	Forbidden	The authenticated user does not have permission to access this resource.
404	Not Found	The specified resource does not exist.
405	Method Not Allowed	The request method is not supported by this server.
406	Not Acceptable	The resource exists, but it might not be in the proper format required by the client as indicated in the Accept request header.
407	Proxy Authentication Required	The client must first authenticate itself with the proxy.
408	Request Timeout	The client did not complete the request in time.
409	Conflict	The request could not be completed due to a resource conflict.
410	Gone	The resource is no longer available.
411	Length Required	The server requires a Content-Length header in the client's request.
412	Precondition Failed	A precondition in the request failed and prevents the requested method from being applied.
413	Request Entity Too Large	The requested entity exceeds the server's limit, and the server might close the connection.
414	Request-URI Too Long	The request URI exceeds the server's limit.
415	Unsupported Media Type	The request is in a format unsupported by the requested resource.
416	Requested Range Not Satisfiable	The request is for a range within the entity that is no longer valid.
417	Expectation Failed	The expectation given in an Expect header could not be met.

(continued)

Status Code	Reason Phrase	Description
500 Server Error		
500	Internal Server Error	Some unexpected condition prevented the server from completing the request.
501	Not Implemented	The server does not support the request received.
502	Bad Gateway	The gateway could not access the upstream server.
503	Service Unavailable	The server is unable to handle the request at this time.
504	Gateway Timeout	The upstream server did not respond to the gateway in time.
505	HTTP Version Not Supported	The server does not support the HTTP version specified in the request.

Like client requests, server responses can contain a variety of headers. These headers are divided into two groups: response headers, which describe the response itself, and entity headers, which describe only the body of the request. We touched on some of the response headers earlier in this chapter; the following section describes some of the other most often used response headers.

Response Headers

At times, a requested document might not be available at the specified location. In this case, the server can redirect the browser to the new location. (We saw in Chapter 4 how to configure IIS to perform a redirection.) When the redirection does occur, the server sends a 300-level status code (usually "302 Found") and a Location header. This header contains the URL for the new location of the resource.

The Public and Allow headers specify the methods that the server generally supports. These headers are used in response to an *OPTIONS* request. The Public header indicates all the methods supported by the server, whereas the Allow header indicates what methods are applicable to the specific URL used in the *OPTIONS* request.

Just as the client identifies itself with the User-Agent request header, the server identifies itself with the Server header. The Server header contains the name of the server application and potentially software version information as well.

Under certain conditions, the server might encode an entire response—for example, to expedite its transmission. If encoding is used, the Transfer-Encoding header denotes what kind of encoding scheme or combination of schemes was applied. The scheme IIS uses most frequently is the chunked method, which is designed to optimize the sending of dynamically generated content, such as that sent by ASP. Using this scheme, the HTTP response data is sent in chunks, with each chunk preceded by a value indicating its size.

Entity Headers

This section describes a class of headers known as *entity headers* because they describe characteristics of the entity data sent with the response. In reality, many of these headers can be used with requests as well to describe entity data that might be included with the request. However, since most requests do not include any entity data, we tend to label these other headers "response headers."

The objective of the server is to always accurately describe the data it's sending to the client. Not only should it indicate the size of the data for persistent connections, but it should also describe the data type and other details. Without a description of the data, the browser will have a hard time figuring out what do to with it. Should it start a helper application, invoke Automation to launch Microsoft Word or another Microsoft Office application (if the requested entity is a .DOC or .XLS file, for example), or just try rendering the data itself? The entity headers dealing with the description of the data contained in the body of the response include Content-Length, Content-Encoding, and Content-Language. For the most part, these headers are fairly self-explanatory. One might be confusing, however: Content-Encoding. Like Transfer-Encoding, Content-Encoding indicates the encoding method used in the response. Unlike Transfer-Encoding, however, Content-Encoding applies only to the body of the request.

One more task of the server is to facilitate efficient caching mechanisms by HTTP clients. Of course, the server can't directly manipulate a client's cache, but it can help by supplying special headers that specify when content was received and when it expires. Several headers deal with controlling the client cache; the most prominent and often used of these are the Cache-Control and Expires headers. Cache-Control defines the caching that can be applied to the document. This header can be set to *no-cache*, indicating that the content should not be cached, or to *private*, indicating that the client should use its own mechanism to cache the data but that proxies should not cache this data. The Expires header specifies a date after which the document cached by the client shouldn't be used. Even when the document is in the client's cache, the browser should not use its cached version but should send a request to the server directly.

NOTE

HTTP/1.0 clients might not understand the Cache-Control: no-cache directive. They should use the Pragma: no-cache header instead. If a response travels through proxies or gateways, the no-cache directive should apply for them too. If, however, a proxy or gateway does not understand the directive, it should ignore it.

Extension Headers

Extension headers are request/response headers that are not part of the HTTP specifications. They can be used to provide additional functionality to client and server applications that understand the new headers. If a client or server receives an extension header that it does not understand, it simply ignores the header. Extension headers should be used in such a fashion that the client or server that specifies this header does not rely on its counterpart's ability to understand the header. Before we look at one of the more popular extension headers, the Set-Cookie header, we need to talk about cookies.

Cookies

HTTP was originally designed to be a stateless protocol. Web servers could log incoming client transactions, but they did not have the facility to track clients from one request to another. In certain instances, it would be nice if a Web server could assign a unique ID to a client and then monitor the activity of the client by using this ID. Now this concept is available to the public. Most Web servers and Web browsers now support *cookies*, persistent information kept by the client. The introduction of cookies to HTTP made a wide variety of new Web server applications possible, such as virtual shopping malls and customized Web pages. A cookie is a piece of information that the Web server passes to the browser. The browser caches this information and makes it available for a server upon its next request. RFC 2109, "HTTP State Management Mechanism," outlines the cookie concept in detail. Let's use a simple example to demonstrate cookies.

Suppose it's the middle of winter and you're wearing a heavy coat. You go to the theater, and the first thing you do is go to the coatroom. You give your coat to the attendant, who gives you a claim ticket with a unique number. This ticket can be considered your cookie. The coatroom attendant now knows who you are by the number on your ticket. (He might not know your name, but he will know how to locate your coat.) Once your coat has been checked, you are free to go anywhere else—you might even go to some other place and check your briefcase. Now you have two claim tickets. This is equivalent to visiting another Web server that supplies your browser with another cookie. Now assume that it's time to go home and you want to retrieve your coat and briefcase. Back at the coatroom counter, you suddenly realize that you have two tickets but you don't remember which is which. No problem. All you have to do is show both tickets to the coatroom clerk, and he'll pick the correct ticket for your coat.

A similar situation happens with the Web browser when it connects to a server and the server supplies it with a cookie. The browser caches all the cookies to a file so that an appropriate server can receive the cookies later. If the browser has cached cookies from more than one server, it searches for the correct one by matching the Internet domain for which the cookie has been set. Optionally, the URL path can also be used for cookie identifications. Cookies may or may not have an optional Expires field. If the Expires field is present, the browser will cache the cookie and send it to the server each time it makes a request before the date indicated in this field. In the absence of the Expires field, the cookie is still cached by the browser, but it's only stored for the duration of the browser session. Once the browser session ends, the cookie is gone forever. Expired cookies are considered deleted for all practical purposes. Browsers will never send them to the server and can delete them as they would any other stale cached contents.

NOTE

*In Internet Explorer 4.0, the cookies are part of the cache. To view the cookies, choose Internet Options from the View menu, select Settings from the Temporary Internet Files area, and click View Files. You'll probably see a few cookies among the different files; they are text files that typically have a name in the form Cookie:*username@domain.

Keep in mind that IIS (or any other server, for that matter) does not give any cookie preferential treatment; it treats cookies just as it would any other header. In this case, the header name is Set-Cookie. Web applications such as ASP scripts or ISAPI extensions can access this header just like any other request header. If the server application wants to delete a cookie that was sent to the client earlier, it can set the same cookie (using the Set-Cookie header) with the Expires field set to a time in the past. For example, by sending the following header the cookie named *CookieName* is deleted:

```
Set-Cookie: CookieName=CookieValue; path=/; Expires=Wed,
    17 Dec 1969 11:30:00 GMT
```

An excellent example of an application that utilizes cookie technology is a virtual shopping mall. By using a Web browser, you can go from page to page, selecting items and placing them in your virtual shopping cart. Every time you choose a new item, the server modifies the cookie and the browser caches it. You can leave the shopping mall at any time, but all the information about your selected items will be preserved until the next time you visit the same mall (that is, the same Web server).

Another application that uses cookies extensively is ASP, which uses them to create user sessions and to keep session-persistent information (such as session variables). The user can roam from one ASP script to another, and all session information is preserved. ASP does not add an Expires field to the cookie, and thus once the user closes the current browser session, the session information is deleted.

HTTP Protocol Details

As we all know, the best way to learn is through practice. So let's give the HTTP protocol a try. One way of looking into what's going on between a client and a server application is to use special network analyzing tools. Quite a few network analyzing tools are currently on the market. For example, Microsoft offers Network Monitor, a special network debugging tool that enables you to capture and view network traffic. This tool parses all packets according to the specific protocol. One of the drawbacks of using Network Monitor is that it requires that the client and server run on two different machines. If a Web browser runs on the same machine as IIS, for example, no frames will be captured by the tool, for one reason. The TCP/IP driver in Windows NT is smart enough not to put anything on the physical network wire unless absolutely necessary.

NOTE

Network Monitor is included with Microsoft Windows NT Server 4.0. You can install it from the Services tab in the Network control panel. After clicking the Add button, choose Network Monitor Tools And Agent. Note that this version might not have an HTTP protocol parser (that is, it shows only TCP frames and you will have to look at the payload to see the HTTP data), and it allows you to capture all traffic only to and from the local machine (that is, you can't trace network traffic between machines A and B if Network Monitor is running on machine C). The full version of Network Monitor is part of Microsoft System Management Server (SMS).

Peeking at the communication between a Web client and server can be interesting. For learning purposes, however, it's much better to have a tool that allows you to directly enter any protocol command and monitor server responses. A telnet session is perfect for doing this. We will use a telnet client throughout the remainder of this book to view the protocols we are discussing. To get a feel for the telnet interface, look at Figure 23.2, which shows a telnet session with a Web server. *OPTION* and *TRACE* are the commands sent to the server. This session was initiated by entering the following command at the command prompt:

```
D:\> telnet leonbr-hm 80
```

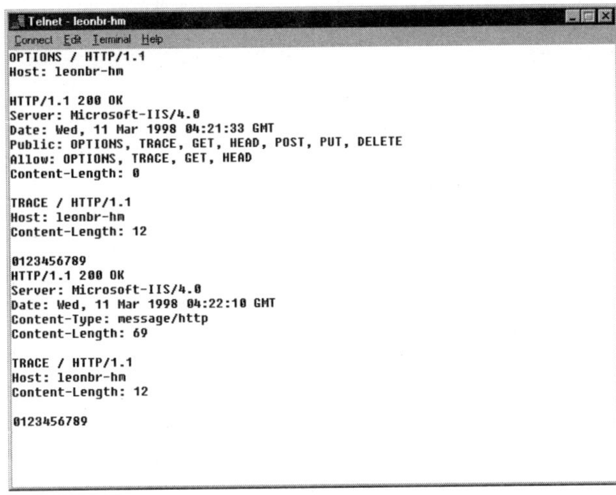

FIGURE 23.2

A telnet session with a Web server, where* OPTIONS *and* TRACE *requests have been sent to the server.

We'll go into the details of this request shortly. Meanwhile, we'll continue to enter HTTP requests in the same telnet session. We've logged this telnet session to a file instead of providing figures illustrating telnet windows. The contents of this file are shown below with our input in boldface. For brevity's sake, we've deleted the text of the extended error message reported by the server.

```
PUT /telnet/newfile.htm HTTP/1.1
Host: leonbr-hm
Content-Length: 12

HTTP/1.1 100 Continue
Server: Microsoft-IIS/4.0
Date: Wed, 11 Mar 1998 04:24:57 GMT
```

(continued)

```
0123456789
HTTP/1.1 201 Created
Server: Microsoft-IIS/4.0
Date: Wed, 11 Mar 1998 04:25:05 GMT
Location: http://leonbr-hm/telnet/newfile.htm
Content-Type: text/html
Content-Length: 67
Allow: OPTIONS, TRACE, GET, HEAD, PUT, DELETE

<body><h1>/telnet/newfile.htm was created successfully.</h1></body>
GET /telnet/newfile.htm HTTP/1.1
Host: leonbr-hm

HTTP/1.1 200 OK
Server: Microsoft-IIS/4.0
Date: Wed, 11 Mar 1998 04:26:05 GMT
Content-Type: text/html
Accept-Ranges: bytes
Last-Modified: Wed, 11 Mar 1998 04:25:05 GMT
ETag: "708bc9aaa54cbd1:2083"
Content-Length: 12

0123456789
GET /telnet/newfile.htm HTTP/1.1
Host: leonbr-hm
If-Modified-Since: Wed, 11 Mar 1998 04:27:00 GMT

HTTP/1.1 304 Not Modified
Server: Microsoft-IIS/4.0
Date: Wed, 11 Mar 1998 04:30:26 GMT
ETag: "708bc9aaa54cbd1:2083"

HEAD /telnet/newfile.htm HTTP/1.1
Host: leonbr-hm

HTTP/1.1 200 OK
Server: Microsoft-IIS/4.0
Date: Wed, 11 Mar 1998 04:31:01 GMT
Content-Type: text/html
Accept-Ranges: bytes
Last-Modified: Wed, 11 Mar 1998 04:25:05 GMT
ETag: "708bc9aaa54cbd1:2083"
Content-Length: 12

DELETE /telnet/newfile.htm HTTP/1.1
Host: leonbr-hm
```

```
HTTP/1.1 200 OK
Server: Microsoft-IIS/4.0
Date: Wed, 11 Mar 1998 04:31:43 GMT
Content-Type: text/html
Content-Length: 67

<body><h1>/telnet/newfile.htm was deleted successfully.</h1></body>
GET /telnet/newfile.htm HTTP/1.1
Host: leonbr-hm

HTTP/1.1 404 Object Not Found
Server: Microsoft-IIS/4.0
Date: Wed, 11 Mar 1998 04:32:13 GMT
Connection: close
Content-Length: 461
Content-Type: text/html

<html><head><title>Error 404</title>
  ...
Detailed error message from the server has been deleted.
  ...
</html>
POST /scripts/post.asp HTTP/1.1
Host: leonbr-hm
Content-Type: application/x-www-form-urlencoded
Content-Length: 25

HTTP/1.1 100 Continue
Server: Microsoft-IIS/4.0
Date: Wed, 11 Mar 1998 04:58:08 GMT

message=Hello,+World%21
HTTP/1.1 200 OK
Server: Microsoft-IIS/4.0
Date: Wed, 11 Mar 1998 04:58:26 GMT
Content-Length: 108
Content-Type: text/html
Set-Cookie: ASPSESSIONIDGGQGGGFG=GHHNMDLCJPIDJEPNEENLPNEL; path=/
Cache-control: private


<HTML>
25 bytes were posted to the
/scripts/post.asp <br>
Message field is "Hello, World!"
</HTML>
```

NOTE

If you type commands in the telnet window and don't see your typing, the Local Echo option is turned off. To turn it on, choose Preferences from the Terminal menu and check the Local Echo check box.

This example demonstrates several things. We start our experiment by sending an *OPTIONS* request to the server. This is a logical first step if we want to know what methods are supported by the server. Figure 23.2 shows the *OPTIONS* request for the / virtual root URL. Notice that we've added a Host header, which is required for HTTP/1.1 requests. The server responds with a successful "200 OK" status code and includes the HTTP/1.1 methods supported by IIS 4.0. Of course, not all of these methods apply to the / virtual root. The virtual root does not have write permission, so *PUT* and *DELETE* are not supported. The virtual root is not an application (like /myscript.exe), so a *POST* request would not work here either. But we can issue a *TRACE* command to conduct a loopback test.

The *TRACE* request appears as the third chunk of text in the telnet window, beginning with the *TRACE / HTTP/1.1* line. Because we are sending data with the request, we supply a Content-Length header. One interesting fact: we specified a Content-Length of 12 bytes, but after inserting one empty line to separate the data from the headers, we typed only 10 digits (0 through 9). After typing *9*, we press Enter, adding two invisible characters that indicate a new line will be sent to the server, making the total length 12 bytes. As soon as the server receives all 12 bytes of data, it echoes back the request in its entirety. Because the echo consists of the original headers and body, the Content-Length of the reply is much greater than 12. Summing all the originally sent headers and all the two-byte linefeeds gives a total of 69 bytes. Just as the HTTP specification describes, the Content-Type for the *TRACE* method is *message/http*.

Let's move on from the telnet window to the telnet session transcript shown in the preceding code. Here we use the *PUT* method to create a new file named NEWFILE.HTM in the virtual directory /telnet. The /telnet directory was created with write permissions prior to the telnet session. Once again, we've added two characters to the total Content-Length to account for the carriage return/linefeed pair after the body. Interestingly enough, the server does not give us a chance to enter content immediately after the headers. As soon as we press Enter twice, to separate the headers from the body with two carriage return/linefeed pairs, the server sends a "100 Continue" status code. This code indicates that IIS has accepted the information so far and now expects to receive the rest of the data—namely, the number of bytes specified by the Content-Length header. Here we enter the data (*0123456789*) and press Enter.

The status code "201 Created" means that the /telnet/newfile.htm file was created successfully. Being the untrusting souls we are, we don't take the success code on faith; instead, we endeavor to verify on our own that the file is indeed there. A simple *GET /telnet/newfile.htm* request will do the trick. Along with the contents of the file (*0123456879*), the server sends a Last-Modified header. This header helps us test the conditional *GET* request, which looks like a normal *GET*, but now it contains an If-Modified-Since header. We specify a time about two minutes later than when the file was last modified. In fact, we are simulating the work of a real browser when it has a cached version of a file. If a file has not been modified since it was cached, there is no need to download it again. Indeed, the server sends a "304 Not Modified" response to allow the browser to use the file from the cache.

The next method on the list is *HEAD*, which produces similar results to *GET*, except here only headers are sent to the client and the body is missing. Using the *DELETE* method, we can delete the file, NEWFILE.HTM, created on the server earlier with the *PUT* request. Once the file is deleted, we want to verify this fact by trying to get the file once again. Because the file was deleted, the status code "404 Object Not Found" is no surprise. Along with this status code, the server sends a long friendly message explaining what might have gone wrong. For the sake of brevity, the telnet session transcript does not show the entire text of that message.

One more test remains to be run. We wrote a script that accepts information via the *POST* method and prints the value for the field *message*. This script simulates form processing by an ASP script. The important detail for posting form data is supplying the correct Content-Type request header. The data should be URL encoded, meaning that spaces are converted to plus signs and special characters such as "!" are converted to their hexadecimal values. Not only have we encoded *"Hello, World!"* as *"Hello,+World%21"*, but we have also described the contents as *application/x-www-form-urlencoded* in the request header.

The response from IIS is generated from an ASP script, POST.ASP, that handles posted data. ASP uses cookies to preserve the session state, so the Set-Cookie header you see in the reply is the ASP-issued cookie.

◆ Handling Posted Data

The ASP script, POST.ASP, that we used to handle the posted data is shown here:

```
<% Response.Buffer = TRUE %>
<HTML>
<%= Request.TotalBytes %> bytes were posted to the
<%= Request.ServerVariables ("SCRIPT_NAME") %> <br>
Message field is "<%= Request.Form ("message") %>"
</HTML>
```

You might wonder why we inserted the *Buffer = TRUE* line at the beginning of this script. When buffering is not enabled (which is the default setting, unless it is set to *TRUE* using the application configuration options), ASP streams data to the client as it processes the script (instead of preparing the buffer and then sending it as one piece). When the data is not buffered, the chunked encoding method is used, which means that the HTTP data consists of multiple data chunks. Each chunk starts with a hexadecimal value indicating the number of bytes that follow. For example, we saved the following HTML text as SIMPLE.ASP (so that IIS will think it's a script and will process it):

```
<HTML>
Hello, this is a simple ASP script.
</HTML>
```

The following code is a telnet transcript showing the request for this script. The text shown in boldface is the contents of the SIMPLE.ASP file sent by the server:

```
GET /scripts/simple.asp HTTP/1.1
Host: leonbr-hm

HTTP/1.1 200 OK
Server: Microsoft-IIS/4.0
Date: Wed, 11 Mar 1998 05:02:27 GMT
Content-Type: text/html
Set-Cookie: ASPSESSIONIDGGQGGGFG=HHHNMDLCGAFLFJIBGNDPGPGE; path=/
Cache-control: private
Transfer-Encoding: chunked

34
<HTML>
Hello, this is simple a ASP script.
</HTML>
0
```

Notice that the hexadecimal value *34* (decimal 52) precedes the actual text in the first chunk, and yet the total number of characters doesn't appear to be 52. Here too we've added two carriage return/linefeed pairs, which makes 48 characters for the message plus 4 characters for the two new lines—for a total of 52 bytes. The second chunk contains 0 bytes, hence it starts with *0*.

This chapter marks the beginning of our voyage into the "underworld" of the Internet—the world of protocols used under the covers of user-friendly browsers, mail applications, and news readers. The FTP protocol is our next topic. In Chapter 24, we'll see what happens on the network when you start your favorite FTP application or just type *ftp://ftp.microsoft.com* in your browser.

CHAPTER 24

The File Transfer Protocol (FTP)

FTP is a specification for moving files; it is one of the most common communication protocols used on the Internet today. Even though the FTP doesn't deliver fancy text and graphics directly to the client application in the way that HTTP and Web browsers do, an FTP server is still a powerful tool and a welcome addition to an Internet or intranet site. More precisely, FTP is a specification governing the transfer of files from one machine to another. Various aspects of the specification are contained in more than one document, the primary document being RFC 959 titled "File Transfer Protocol (FTP)." The beauty of FTP lies in its ability to work not only across different computer types but also across different character sets. Text files might be stored in EBCDIC format on a mainframe machine but in ASCII format on a PC. FTP has no trouble getting a file from a mainframe computer and delivering it to a PC in the correct ASCII format.

NOTE

That files can be transferred from one host on the network to another doesn't mean that a client has direct access to files on the server. Other network protocols, in particular the Network File System (NFS), allow direct file access across the network. FTP doesn't work that way.

As is the case with any network client/server application, two FTP applications are required in order to communicate: the server on the back end (such as IIS with FTP services, described in Chapter 9) and the client. There are various types of client FTP applications. Their designs vary from those having an elaborate user interface, such as Microsoft Internet Explorer, which supports *ftp://* URL (and therefore allows the user to see and download files on the server specified on the URL line), to those bare-bones command-line FTP clients, such as the ones included with Microsoft Windows NT and various forms of UNIX. Regardless of the user interface implementation, all clients support the same basic tasks: logging on to the server, enumerating directories, uploading files, and downloading files. Client designers may choose not to implement certain functions, of course. For instance, you might have noticed that Internet Explorer can't upload files to an FTP server.

In this chapter, we'll look at FTP clients and the FTP service. We'll be using the FTP client included with Windows NT, which might be a boring command-line utility but is at least as functional as most Windows FTP clients.

FTP Implementation

As with many other high-level Internet protocols such as HTTP, FTP relies on the low-level TCP layer for some very important services. TCP takes care of establishing reliable connections, delivering data in the order in which it was sent, and exposes functions that ensure that data is successfully delivered between the FTP client and the server. Before we talk further about FTP, let's look into the connection mechanism used by TCP.

Socket Interface

TCP employs *sockets* to establish and transfer FTP data from one point to another. As we've seen, a socket is an endpoint for network communication. The client/server network computer paradigm warrants that a slightly different set of socket calls (or APIs) be used by clients and servers. But first both client and server need to open a socket. The server opens a socket and waits for clients to connect. (In network jargon, it listens for connections.) When a client's connection request arrives, the server accepts it and executes the client's requests that are sent across the socket connection. Either side can initiate closing the connection by closing the socket.

Before clients can send a connection request to the server, certain steps for opening a connection should take place, just as dialing a phone number is the first step in establishing a telephone conversation. The client initiates the connection; this step is referred to as an *active open*. The server isn't doing anything active yet; it just waits passively for the incoming connection request. Incidentally, the server's side of establishing a connection is called *passive open*.

Just as in telephone communication the caller must know the callee's phone number, network clients performing an active open must know the server's address. Two pieces of information uniquely identify the socket for a server process (such as the FTP service): the IP address of the server, and the *port*—an integer identifying the network process that listens for incoming connections.

If you're wondering why we are going into a detailed explanation of sockets at this point, it's because FTP opens a new network connection (in addition to the existing one) each time a file is transferred or a directory listing is requested by the client. A basic understanding of socket connection management is important for understanding certain aspects of FTP data transfers.

FTP Connection Management

Few people who use FTP realize how many TCP connections (sometimes referred to as *virtual circuits*) are open between the client and the server at any given time. You might assume that only one TCP connection could reliably carry FTP commands requested by the client to the server for execution. Although there is *some* truth to this assumption, it's not fully accurate.

FTP employs two connections at the same time and is the only protocol using two connections that we'll cover in this book. Commands (such as LIST, which requests a directory listing; USER and PASS, which ask for user credentials; and CWD, which changes the working directory) and server replies travel over the control channel, or control connection. The FTP server listens for new control connections on the well-known port 21.

> **Glossary**
>
> **well-known ports** *Ports numbered 1 through 1023. These ports are centrally managed by the Internet Assigned Numbers Authority (IANA). All computers supporting TCP/IP are aware of the default ports (which is why they are called well-known) used by various networking protocols such as FTP, HTTP, NNTP and SMTP.*

By performing an active open, the client connects to the server's port 21 to establish a working control connection. Both the client and the server FTP software applications include a special component responsible for command interpretation and execution over the control connection: this component is known as the Protocol Interpreter (PI).

Once the control channel is established, the channel is used in a half-duplex fashion, meaning that both the server and the client take turns communicating on the socket. The client sends FTP commands and then waits for the server to reply before doing anything else. The server sends replies for each command it receives. Note that the client does *not* send commands directly to the server's PI. On the client side, commands are acquired from the user interface by the client's PI. The commands are transmitted over the control channel to the server's PI for execution. The client maps the commands you enter into something the server PI can understand. So when you type *DIR* or *LS* at the FTP prompt, the client actually sends a LIST or an NLST (Name List, the filename only) command to the server. Some clients can bypass their PI and send commands directly to a server's PI. Sending pass-through commands from the FTP client included with Microsoft Windows NT or Microsoft Windows 95 is achieved by using the QUOTE or LITERAL commands. (Don't be confused: the QUOTE and LITERAL commands aren't FTP protocol commands—they're commands supported by the client program.)

A server reply consists of a three-digit numeric status code and a text message (very similar to HTTP). A reply might look something like this:

```
214 HELP command successful.
```

In fact, we'll see in the following chapters that Simple Mail Transfer Protocol (SMTP) and Network News Transfer Protocol (NNTP) use similar replies. If the FTP server's reply consists of more than one line of text (in other words, a multiline reply), each line except the last one separates numeric codes from the text message with a hyphen (-). The last line of the server reply has space between the numeric code and the description text. (Note that more than one space is possible.) Each digit of the status code carries important information about the status of the command. The client's PI evaluates the status code and, depending on the success or failure of the command, performs the necessary steps, which might be resubmitting user credentials, reporting an error to the user, or any number of actions.

Assuming that the reply code is in the form

xyz Text Message

the following table shows the meaning of the first digit of the status code.

First Digit of Status Code	Meaning
1yz	Positive preliminary reply. The server has begun request processing. The client should expect to receive another reply before the action can be completed. The client shouldn't send another command immediately after getting this response, but if it does the server should be able to queue the new command. Only one *1yz* reply per command should be sent.
2yz	Positive completion reply. The command completed OK. The client can send a new request.
3yz	Positive intermediate reply. The command has been accepted so far. The client should provide more information to complete the request. An example would be entering the USER command, which sends the user name to the server. Because the password must follow the user name (PASS command), the server replies with a *3yz* status code to the USER command.
4yz	Transient negative reply. The command has failed, but recovery is possible. If a client retries the same command with the same parameters, it might succeed.
5yz	Permanent negative reply. The command is either not implemented or not correct (misspelled, for example). Serious problems might have occurred.

Knowing that the command has failed when an error occurs is a good thing. It is, however, much better if the client knows exactly what went wrong, or at least in what area the error resides. The second digit of the numeric status code serves to clarify the category of the error. The possible values and their categories are shown in the following table.

Second Digit of Status Code	Category
x0z	Syntax error. The command is misspelled or doesn't exist.
x1z	Information reply. Applies to requests for status information, such as the SYST (returns the server system type) command or the STAT (return status of the connection) command.
x2z	Connection category. The reply relates to the connection established between the client and the server.
x3z	The reply relates to authentication and accounting systems. The USER and PASS commands are followed by this type of a status code.
x4z	Not used.
x5z	The reply is from the server's file system.

The RFC doesn't explicitly specify the meaning of the third digit. FTP servers are free to use the third digit to supply the client with more detail than has already been indicated by the first and second digits. Each FTP server therefore determines its own meaning for the third digit.

Up to this point, the client/server communication has been straightforward. The client and the server have established a control connection. The client sends commands to the server. The commands are executed, and replies are sent back. But this is only half of the picture. The objective of FTP isn't just to execute commands—we have plenty of other protocols for that. Remember, FTP is the *File Transfer Protocol,* which means that it's used when we want to transfer files among different computers on the network. To do this, a second socket connection, a data connection, is opened between the client and the server in order to upload or download files or to receive a directory listing from the server.

Data Connection

Opening an additional TCP connection every time a file transfer or a directory listing occurs presents certain challenges (not to mention adding overhead). The server closes this data connection as soon as the file transfer or the directory listing is complete. In fact, the closing of a data connection indicates to a client that the requested file was transferred in its entirety. Both the client and the server FTP software contain a component known as a Data Transfer Process (DTP), which is responsible for initiating and accepting data connections.

The main challenge of managing data connections is the need for the client or server DTP process (whichever performs the active open on the data connection) to know the address and the port of its counterpart, which passively accepts the connection. The control connection is used to transfer the port and the address for data connections between the client and the server. We'll look at all the details of the interactions between an FTP client and an FTP server later in this chapter, but first let's put together the concepts we've covered so far. Figure 24.1 shows the relationships between the PI, the DTP, and the two kinds of connections that are used when the FTP client and the FTP server are communicating.

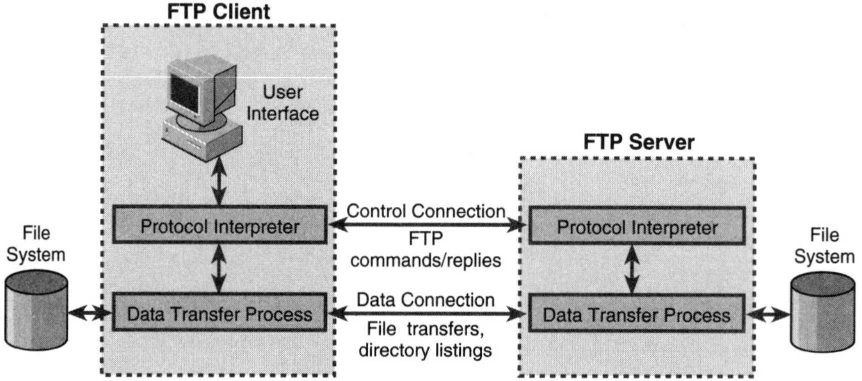

FIGURE 24.1

The FTP architecture.

Even though the architectural details might be clear now, the specific sequence of steps that occur when FTP is transferring a file might not be so clear. In fact, there's more than one way for a client and a server to establish and control the data connection. We'll begin to understand this process by looking at the active FTP semantics.

Active FTP Semantics

By default, the FTP client manages the creation of a data connection. The client gets direct input from the user, so it knows what commands require the opening of a data connection. The following list shows the default steps for establishing a control channel and a data channel between an FTP client and server:

1. The client connects to the FTP server's control connection port 21 (thereby performing an active open).

2. Once the control channel is open, the client is authenticated by means of the USER and PASS commands. Other commands might also be exchanged.
3. When a client needs to upload or download a file or get a directory listing, the client creates a new socket and starts listening for a connection on a port randomly assigned by the operating system. The port, which the client has performed a passive open on, is known as an ephemeral port.
4. The client sends the port number at its end of the data connection to the server via the control connection using the PORT command. The PORT command takes six parameters that reflect the IP address and port number of the listening process, as shown here:

   ```
   PORT h1, h2, h3, h4, p1, p2
   ```

   The parameters *h1* through *h4* are the corresponding octets of the IP address. (We described IP addresses in detail in Chapter 3.) The parameters *p1* and *p2* are the high and low 8 bits of the 16-bit port number. To get the entire port number, use this formula:

   ```
   Port = p1 X 256 + p2
   ```

   Sending the command PORT 192,155,1,1,7,165 to the server indicates to the server that it should connect to IP address 192.155.1.1 on port 1957 ($7 \times 256 + 165 = 1957$) to establish a data connection.
5. After the server receives the port number from the client, it initiates the data connection (performs an active open).
6. The data connection is closed when the data transfer is complete and a new data connection will be opened again if needed.
7. The control channel connection stays open during the entire FTP session. The connection is closed when either the client or the server closes the FTP session.

Glossary

ephemeral ports *Ports with a short life span. These ports exist only as long as the application that opened them is running. They are typically used in the client process of networking software because, unlike a server process that runs for a long time, clients run only long enough to execute a specific set of commands. Client software usually does not specify an ephemeral port directly; instead, it lets the operating system choose the next available port.*

Because the FTP server uses TCP, we can use virtually any application that can directly access the TCP layer and send typed commands as the client. The telnet client application included with Windows NT or Windows 95 can perform this kind of activity quite well. The telnet client can perform only active opens—that is, it must initiate connections. This technique is perfect for control connections, but it isn't sufficient for data connections. In the case of data connections, the client shouldn't initiate the connection; instead, it needs to wait for the server to connect. Even though telnet can't perform a passive open, we still use telnet for data connections by using the passive FTP semantics.

Passive FTP Semantics

When you use the passive FTP semantics, you change the roles of the client and the server in establishing the data connection. Instead of the server actively connecting to the client's end of the data connection, the client actively connects to the server. The client, however, can't connect to the server unless it knows the server's port, where the server is waiting to accept the connection. Keeping this change in mind, the following passive FTP semantics steps are similar to the active FTP semantics with the exception of steps 3, 4, and 5.

1. The client connects to the FTP server's control connection port 21 (thereby performing an active open).
2. Once the control channel is open, the client is authenticated by means of the USER and PASS commands. Other commands might also be exchanged.
3. When the client needs to upload or download files or get a directory listing, it sends a PASV command to the server. The PASV command doesn't require any parameters.
4. Once the server has received the PASV command, it creates a new socket for the data connection and starts waiting for connections—that is, it performs a passive open. The server's reply to the PASV command contains the port number that the server uses for its DTP, which waits for the connection. The syntax of the reply, shown below, is similar to the PORT command. Notice that the IP address and port number are relayed to the client.

   ```
   227 Entering Passive Mode (192,155,1,1,7,166)
   ```

5. After the client receives the reply to its PASV command (meaning that the server is now waiting for the client to connect), it connects to the server's data port (performs an active open).

6. The data connection is closed when the data transfer is complete and a new data connection will be opened again if needed.

7. The control channel connection stays open during the entire FTP session. It's closed when either the client or the server closes the FTP session.

The passive FTP semantics aren't used by default, but we use them here because our example uses telnet to illustrate the details of FTP.

Benefits of Using Multiple Connections

FTP connection management isn't as straightforward as you might like. The first questions that come to mind are these: "Why does FTP need two connections?" and "Can't the directory listings (or even the files) be transferred over the control connection?" But there are good reasons for establishing additional connections between a client and a server. Imagine what would happen if you started transferring a 20-MB file over the control connection and then you changed your mind and wanted to cancel the request. You have no way to send a cancel command over the control connection because it's already in use. Had that data been flowing over a separate data connection, however, canceling would be a breeze. The client could request the server to stop the data transfer at any point by sending an FTP ABOR (Abort) command over the control connection.

Another benefit of having a second connection is that it enables one machine to act as a "master" over the data transfer between two other machines without actually receiving and forwarding any data itself. Figure 24.2 shows how this can be done.

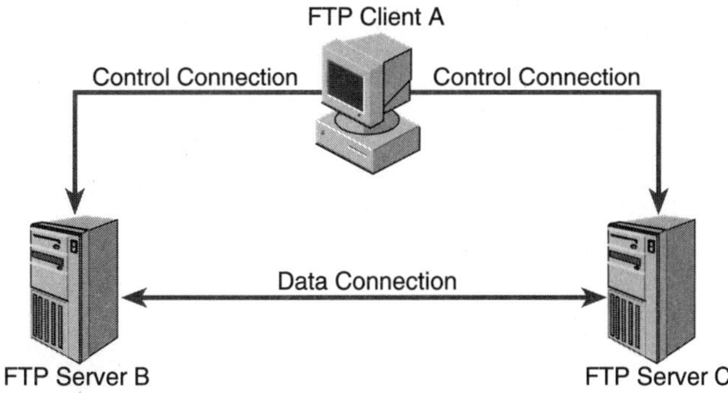

FIGURE 24.2

Transferring data between two hosts.

The following scenario could take place in orchestrating the transfer of data from machine B to machine C with user input from machine A. Machine A (a client machine) sends a PASV command to machine C. Machine C receives the command and executes a passive open for the data connection. It sends the port for its end of the data connection back to machine A. Machine A now sends a PORT command to machine B. The port command specifies the IP address of machine C and the port for the data connection on machine C. Sending the PORT command to machine B causes B to perform an active open for the data connection, effectively establishing a data connection between machines B and C. At this point, if you request a directory listing or a file transfer from machine B the data will be sent to machine C. This is an efficient way to transfer data between two remote machines without having to transfer the data first to machine A and then have machine A transfer the data again to machine C. This technique is particularly efficient if machine A is connected to the other two machines via a slow modem line.

FTP is certainly more complex than the other protocols covered in the following chapters. If you're a bit confused at this point, don't worry—we'll clear everything up by seeing FTP in action.

FTP in Action: Using the FTP Client

First let's take a high-level look at using the standard FTP client included with Windows, FTP.EXE. Our server allows anonymous logins, which means that any user can log in by supplying *anonymous* as the user name and her e-mail name as the password. (Actually, the validity of the e-mail account isn't checked, so anything works as a password for an anonymous login.) Here's the session transcript; our input is shown in boldface:

```
ftp> open leonbr-hm
Connected to leonbr-hm.
220 leonbr-hm Microsoft FTP Service (Version 4.0).
User (leonbr-hm:(none)): anonymous
331 Anonymous access allowed, send identity (e-mail name) as password.
Password:
230-Welcome to LEONBR-HM Default FTP Site!
230 Anonymous user logged in.
ftp> help
Commands may be abbreviated. Commands are:

!               delete          literal         prompt          send
?               debug           ls              put             status
append          dir             mdelete         pwd             trace
ascii           disconnect      mdir            quit            type
bell            get             mget            quote           user
```

```
binary          glob            mkdir           recv            verbose
bye             hash            mls             remotehelp
cd              help            mput            rename
close           lcd             open            rmdir
ftp> quote help
214-The following commands are recognized(* ==>'s unimplemented).
   ABOR
   ACCT
   ALLO
   APPE
   CDUP
   CWD
   DELE
   HELP
   LIST
   MKD
   MODE
   NLST
   NOOP
   PASS
   PASV
   PORT
   PWD
   QUIT
   REIN
   REST
   RETR
   RMD
   RNFR
   RNTO
   SITE
   SIZE
   SMNT
   STAT
   STOR
   STOU
   STRU
   SYST
   TYPE
   USER
   XCUP
   XCWD
   XMKD
   XPWD
   XRMD
```

(continued)

```
214  HELP command successful.
ftp> stat
Connected to leonbr-hm.
Type: ascii; Verbose: On; Bell: Off; Prompting: On; Globbing: On
Debugging: Off; Hash mark printing: Off
ftp> quote stat
211-leonbr-hm Microsoft Windows NT FTP Server status:
     Version 4.0
     Connected to leonbr-hm
     Logged in as leonbr@leonbr-hm
     TYPE: ASCII, FORM: Nonprint; STRUcture: File; transfer MODE: STREAM
     No data connection
211 End of status.
ftp> ls
200 PORT command successful.
150 Opening ASCII mode data connection for file list.
file1.txt
file2.txt
file3.txt
226 Transfer complete.
33 bytes received in 0.02 seconds (1.65 Kbytes/sec)
ftp> dir
200 PORT command successful.
150 Opening ASCII mode data connection for /bin/ls.
02-13-98  09:18AM                  226 file1.txt
02-13-98  09:17AM                  105 file2.txt
02-13-98  09:17AM                   71 file3.txt
226 Transfer complete.
150 bytes received in 0.00 seconds (150000.00 Kbytes/sec)
ftp> quit
221 Thank you for visiting
```

This looks like an ordinary FTP session. If you've used FTP before, I'm sure you have performed similar tasks. But now we're empowered with knowledge of the PI, the DTP, and other pieces of information about FTP. This knowledge gives us a different perspective.

Here are some interesting facts about our simple FTP session. We've opened the FTP session to the LEONBR-HM machine as an anonymous user. Each entered command is acknowledged by the server with a reply status code. Even though we have entered our password at the corresponding prompt, for security reasons the FTP client does not display the actual characters. Notice that multiline replies, such as the welcome message confirming the login, do not include hyphens between the status code numeric value and the text message on the last line. We start by typing *help* at the FTP prompt. In response to *help*, we get a list of all supported commands. Don't get confused here. This is the list of commands supported by our client (FTP.EXE, included with Microsoft Windows NT) or, to be exact, the commands supported by our client's PI. These aren't FTP commands. The client is free to implement any command it wants, but of course only commands supported by FTP should actually be sent to the server.

Ordinary users typically don't worry about FTP commands supported by the FTP server. We're not ordinary users, however, so we're interested in getting a list of commands supported directly by the server. As we've seen, we have a way of passing commands directly to the server's protocol interpreter: the QUOTE command. In this case, we pass the HELP command directly to the server's PI by entering the QUOTE HELP command. Compare the list of commands supported by the server with the list of client commands. They are quite different. We won't go into the details of each command here, but if you're interested in learning more about commands that we don't cover, you can read about them in RFC 959.

The next thing we want to do is to get the status of the FTP connection. Entering *STAT* at the client's prompt accomplishes this. The client doesn't really send anything to the server at this point; it merely prints its own current state parameters. Getting the status of the server is a different process. The QUOTE STAT command passes the STAT command directly to the server for execution. Indeed, the output is very different. Along with a number of parameters that aren't particularly interesting to us (but informative to the client software), the *Logged in as* line is rather interesting. We've logged in as the anonymous user. The anonymous user usually identifies itself via the e-mail name that is used as the login password. We typed *leonbr@leonbr-hm* as our password, so this is our identification for the current session and how the FTP server will log our actions.

Before closing our FTP session using the QUIT command, we want to list the contents of the default (or home) directory. We can choose one of two ways of doing this: using the LS client command or using the DIR client command. When LS is received by the client's PI, the client sends the NLST FTP command over the control channel to the server. The NLST command causes the server to send only names of the files in the directory; no other data (such as the file size, date of creation, and so on) is sent. The DIR command is treated differently. It causes the client to send a LIST command to the server. The LIST command generates a directory listing that includes a number of file details.

But enumerating files in the directory isn't as simple as it might look. As we've seen, directory listings aren't transferred over the control connection. The FTP client and server must establish a data channel in order to transfer the directory listing information. By default, the client performs a passive open and supplies the server with the port number with which to connect. This is what happened when we executed the LS and DIR commands in the previous session transcript. The client executed the FTP PORT command to send its data channel port number twice, once for the LS command and once for the DIR command. We can't see the entire port command, but we definitely see the status response that the PORT command completed successfully.

An FTP session usually involves sending commands to the server's PI; data channels are then established when needed. We can accomplish both these tasks by using the telnet client application. This way, we can see the details of FTP being transferred between the client and the server.

More Action: Using the Telnet Client

The telnet client included with Microsoft Windows NT or Microsoft Windows 95 uses TCP sockets and can connect to any TCP port. By connecting to the server's default FTP control connection port, port 21, you can send any command directly to the server's PI. Of course, you could use the FTP client QUOTE command to provide this same direct functionality, but then you wouldn't see the details of FTP commands being sent across the wire. If the passive FTP semantics are used, the FTP server waits for data connections instead of actively initiating them, which is its default behavior. We can use a second instance of telnet to connect to the server's data port. In a way, we're building a fully functional FTP client by using two telnet connections. Once you understand how to do this, you probably won't want to use this method to perform your day-to-day FTP tasks, but you can use it to impress your family and friends with your knowledge of FTP.

The first step is to establish the control connection to the FTP server. You can specify the server name and port as parameters to the telnet application at the command prompt. The following line launches the telnet client and connects to the LEONBR-HM host on the default FTP port: *telnet leonbr-hm ftp*. (Remember that our computer knows the well-known port for FTP, so we can use the protocol name instead of directly specifying port 21.) At this point, we can enter commands in the telnet window that are sent directly to the server. The transcript of our telnet session is shown below; our input appears in boldface. We have also added comments that should not be entered in the telnet window; these comments begin with >>> and serve as a cue indicating when and how to start the second instance of telnet. Set the Local Echo option in telnet so that you can see what you are typing.

NOTE

The Local Echo setting is available in the Terminal Preferences dialog box of the telnet application. To turn on Local Echo, open the Terminal Preferences dialog box by choosing the Preferences command from the Terminal menu. Once the dialog box is displayed, check the Local Echo checkbox to turn it on. Then click the OK button to close the dialog box, and you're ready to go.

```
220 leonbr-hm Microsoft FTP Service (Version 4.0).
user anonymous
331 Anonymous access allowed, send identity (e-mail name) as password.
pass leonbr@leonbr-hm
230-Welcome to LEONBR-HM Default FTP Site!
230 Anonymous user logged in.
stat
211-leonbr-hm Microsoft Windows NT FTP Server status:
     Version 4.0
     Connected to leonbr-hm
     Logged in as leonbr@leonbr-hm
     TYPE: ASCII, FORM: Nonprint; STRUcture: File; transfer MODE: STREAM
     No data connection
211 End of status.
pasv
227 Entering Passive Mode (192,155,1,1,7,236).
>>> At this point, we need to start the second instance of telnet as
>>> follows: "telnet 192.155.1.1 2028"
list
125 Data connection already open; Transfer starting.
226 Transfer complete.
site
214-The following SITE commands are recognized(* ==>'s unimplemented).
   CKM
   DIRSTYLE
   HELP
   STATS
214  HELP command successful.
site stats
200-ABOR : 1
    HELP : 14
    LIST : 16
    NLST : 10
    PASS : 20
    PASV : 12
    PORT : 14
    QUIT : 10
    RETR : 3
    SITE : 7
    STAT : 5
    SYST : 1
    USER : 22
200 End of stats.
quit
221 Thank you for visiting
```

We need to send the same commands that the client's PI normally sends. Therefore, we use the USER and PASS commands to send the user name and password. To get the status of the connection, we use the STAT command. Notice that the STAT command generates exactly the same output as the QUOTE STAT command, entered at the prompt of the full-fledged FTP client.

Now we want to obtain a directory listing of the default FTP directory. This requires that we open a data connection. Remember again that the telnet client can't accept incoming connections; it can only initiate them, so here we use the passive FTP semantics and enter the PASV command. Now we need to use the server's reply to the PASV command to open the data connection, as shown here:

```
227 Entering Passive Mode (192,155,1,1,7,236).
```

This reply indicates that our second instance of the telnet application should connect to 192.155.1.1 on port 2028 ($7 \times 256 + 236 = 2028$).

The second instance of telnet should be started like this (see the comments preceded by >>> in the telnet session transcript) :

```
telnet 192.155.1.1 2028
```

At this point, as soon as the LIST command is entered at the control connection, the server sends a file listing to the second telnet client over the newly established data connection. Here's the transcript from the telnet client connected to the data port:

```
02-13-98  09:18AM                  226 file1.txt
02-13-98  09:17AM                  105 file2.txt
02-13-98  09:17AM                   71 file3.txt
```

All done! We have a directory listing from the server. Because the data connection is closed immediately after the data is sent, getting new directory listings or performing file transfers requires establishing a new data connection each time. The same control connection is maintained throughout the session.

Before we close the FTP control connection using the QUIT command, we want to get some server statistics—that is, we want to determine how many times each type of command has been received by the server. You can get this information by using the SITE STATS command. The SITE command is designed to get or set server-specific parameters for the current FTP session. Because other servers might not implement analogous commands, site-specific commands aren't part of the FTP specification.

Getting a directory listing using two telnet instances is fun, but uploading and downloading files is even better. Two FTP commands accomplish this: STOR (Store) to store (that is, upload) files on the server and RETR (Retrieve) to get (that is, download) files from the server. It might surprise you that FTP doesn't use the standard PUT and GET commands that you pass to the FTP client's PI. The FTP client simply converts the commands that you pass to STOR and RETR commands, which it then passes to the server.

Performing file functions with two telnet clients is simple. The first step, of course, is to establish a data connection by using the PASV command. The port will be different for each new data connection, but the steps for making the connection are the same as we saw earlier in this chapter. Now sending the RETR FILE1.TXT command over the control connection sends the contents of FILE1.TXT over the data connection. You will see the contents of FILE1.TXT displayed in the window of the second instance of the telnet client. When the server closes the data connection, you know that the entire file was transferred. Uploading a file to the server is similar. Again, we must first establish a data connection. Once we have established the data connection, we can send STOR FOO.BAR over the control connection. At this point, the server creates the FOO.BAR file (if the logged-on user has write permissions) and saves all the data that comes over the data connection in this file. In the second instance of the telnet client (that is, the instance connected to the data port of the server), you can start typing anything you want. As soon as you close the telnet session, the new file FOO.BAR with your data appears in the server's directory.

As we've just seen, transferring files is easy with FTP. But in our example, we used the same type of machines (Intel x86) to move our files. What happens if a file transfer takes place between two different systems that use different standards to represent textual data, such as mainframe machines and PCs? In this case, the protocol is responsible for translating data from one system to the other. Let's look at how this is done in more detail.

Data Representation

The FTP specification was written in an age when mainframe computers ruled the cyberworld. FTP accounts for the different techniques used to encode files (ASCII vs. EBCDIC) as well as a file's physical structure. Many FTP commands used to set file transmission and representation parameters aren't needed (and aren't even implemented) on modern servers such as IIS's FTP server, but a number of them are needed. Our description of FTP would be incomplete if we didn't look into these commands.

Keep in mind that many FTP clients might not even implement some of these commands; the client therefore imposes its own limitations on FTP sessions. Because we're using telnet to directly communicate with the server's PI, we aren't running into FTP client software limitations. Three major FTP protocol commands control transmission and data representation modes: TYPE and STRU (Structure), which control how data is represented; and MODE, which controls how bits of data are sent between the client and server.

Transmission Types

When two different systems exchange textual data, they usually convert the data to ASCII representation for transmission, and then each site converts the data to its own specific format for storage. Some of you have probably downloaded a text file from a UNIX machine to Windows and haven't noticed any difference in the way the file looked. Your FTP software takes care of text file data conversion from UNIX to Windows because of the difference in the way the two systems represent the newline character. UNIX systems normally use a carriage return symbol only, whereas Windows machines use a carriage return/linefeed pair. Such conversions take place automatically when the transfer type is set to ASCII. The TYPE command helps us do this, as shown in the following code. The argument *a* for the TYPE command stands for ASCII.

```
type a
200 Type set to A.
```

Text conversions work fine for text files, but conversion is more tricky for binary data. For example, you might be sending data from 32-bit systems to systems that use a larger number of bits to store a single unit of data (36, for example). It's questionable where and how data received from a 32-bit system should be padded with zeros—at the beginning or at the end. To correct this problem, the binary (or image) transfer type is used. In this mode, the sender transmits a contiguous stream of bits (packed as 8-bit words) to the receiver. Because each bit of data is important, sites don't perform any conversion (as is done for ASCII transfers). If the receiver needs to pad the data with zeros, it can do this only at the end of the file. The binary type is used each time non-text files are exchanged. The binary, or image, transfer mode can be set using the TYPE command, as shown in the following code. The *i* argument for the TYPE command stands for image.

```
type i
200 Type set to I.
```

Again, don't forget that we're entering these commands directly to the server's control connection. Client implementation might be different, so to set image transfer mode we might need to enter a different command in the client. For instance, look at the following transcript from the standard Windows FTP client; our input is shown in boldface.

```
ftp> type i
i: unknown mode
ftp> type image
200 Type set to I.
ftp> type
Using image mode to transfer files.
```

File Structure

The transmission type (image or text) might not be enough to completely describe incoming or outgoing files. Files might not be structured internally. Files without structure don't have any internal logical elements and instead consist of contiguous arrays of bits. Structured files consist of logical records of a specified size. In addition to records of fixed size, FTP also supports *page-structured* files.

Page-structured files consist of multiple pages; each page is assigned a page header, without which the page can't be processed. The page header includes page information such as the type of the page (first, last, ordinary page), the page index (number), the page size, and so on. Unlike record files, in which all records are the same size, each page can have a different size.

To indicate the type of the file, you use the STRU command. It's worth mentioning that IIS supports only plain files—that is, files that don't have any internal structures (or at least internal structures known to IIS). Look at the following FTP session transcript, in which *f* stands for file, *r* for record, and *p* for page:

```
stru f
200 STRU F ok.
stru p
504 Unimplemented STRU type.
stru r
504 Unimplemented STRU type.
```

Transmission Mode

Setting file types and their internal structures still doesn't describe how data transmission should take place. You can choose from three different transmission modes: *stream*, *block*, and *compressed*. Transmission mode is set using the MODE command, and only unstructured file types are supported by IIS.

In stream mode, the file travels as a stream of data over the data connection. If this is a binary file and it's corrupted somewhere in the middle, the entire file must be considered invalid.

In block mode, the file is sent in logical blocks. This is a good way to transfer structured files. Each block has a header field that indicates the number of bytes in the block. Knowing the number of bytes in the current block makes it easy to determine where the next block begins. A header also includes a specific field (referred to as the *descriptor code*) that indicates the type of data block used. One of the possible uses of the descriptor code is to indicate that a block might be corrupted. It's not intended for error recovery; it's merely an indicator to the receiving machine. The receiver might not store the file with the corrupted block. The receiver could store all the uncorrupted blocks but simply flag the questionable block and report its number (or other information about the block) at a later time.

As we've seen, a lot of different parameters are involved in the transferring of files. Setting the correct parameters for file transmission mode, structure, and type are the variables in the big equation of successful file uploads and downloads. Although we didn't cover all the details of FTP in this chapter, you should certainly have a good feel for how FTP works. In fact, you know enough to read the output of the STAT command that was shown in our first telnet session transcript:

```
TYPE: ASCII, FORM: Nonprint; STRUcture: File; transfer MODE: STREAM
```

What does all this mean? It's pretty simple: the type is set to ASCII, the next file to transmit won't have any internal structures, and the file will be transferred in stream mode. One field we didn't mention, however, is *FORM: Nonprint*. This is a special character (or sequence of characters) used to separate pages in text files in the event that the receiver is to print the file instead of storing it. *Nonprint* is the default setting, indicating that page separation markings are omitted.

FTP is one of the more complex protocols covered in this book. In the next two chapters, we'll look at two other protocols, NNTP and SMTP, that are much easier to work with—at least they don't need second connections for transferring data.

CHAPTER 25

The Network News Transfer Protocol (NNTP)

In Chapter 10, you learned about the Microsoft news server—an integral part of IIS. By now, you know how to configure and operate a news server, but we still haven't talked about the language spoken by news servers and newsreaders. As with any computer network communication, if two or more computers want to exchange data over a network, they need to agree on a common set of rules—that is, a network protocol. We looked at a variety of protocols in Chapter 2. In this chapter, we'll examine the Network News Transfer Protocol (NNTP) in detail. But first let's go over some fundamentals.

Internet News Delivery Systems

One of the things that made the Internet popular is that it enabled potentially millions of users to exchange news and other public information. One way of exchanging this information is by using mailing lists; another is to use a news system. We'll explore each of these approaches in the sections that follow.

Internet Mailing Lists

A *mailing list* contains the e-mail addresses of all the list's subscribers. An e-mail message sent to the mailing list causes the message to be sent to each member, and the latest mailing list software can automatically maintain lists of subscribers. Usually, a subscriber can simply send e-mail to the mailing list using a special keyword such as *delete* or *subscribe* in the message text to remove or add his or her e-mail address to the list. But even if a mailing list system is fully automated, it can have serious drawbacks. A lot of overhead is required to update and maintain a list of correct e-mail addresses; the system administrator (computer or human) needs to stay on top of address changes, new list subscriptions, and so on. If a list has more than a hundred users, resending each e-mail message to all subscribers could generate a large amount of network traffic. A better solution is to use some method of centralized storage and distribution.

USENET News

Today's news servers take advantage of the USENET Internet news system, which offers the benefits of centralized news storage and easy distribution. The cornerstone of such a system is a single news server that contains the entire news repository. Clients connect to the news server and view a list of news article headers (similar to e-mail headers). If the client wants to read a particular article, the entire article can then be downloaded from the server.

The USENET news system has clear advantages. For example, clients with limited disk space can select only the messages they want to read from the list of articles stored on the server. The entire overhead of news processing now rests on a single news server computer. Centralized news storage necessitates the introduction of a specific protocol to describe commands used by a client to post new articles, enumerate a server's newsgroups, and perform other tasks not required with the Internet mailing list system. NNTP is the protocol used by news clients and servers. This protocol is just complex enough to accomplish news-related tasks, but it doesn't have to worry about establishing reliable client/server connections and other lower-level tasks. Like HTTP, discussed in Chapter 23, NNTP rides on top of TCP which takes care of the mundane tasks of establishing connections, verifying data delivery, and so on. The news server runs a specific background process that awaits client connections on the news port (by default, port 119) and services them when they arrive. IIS implements the news server using the NNTP service.

News Distribution

News clients (such as Microsoft Outlook Express) use NNTP to connect to a centralized host to read and post news articles. As you'll recall from Chapter 3, the Internet consists essentially of many interconnected LANs. For example, the LAN maintained by Microsoft Corporation is connected to the LAN maintained by California State University Northridge. According to the USENET architecture, each LAN can have only one centralized news host. (Actually, some backup, or "slave," computers can also be used.) Our example would thus consist of two centralized news servers: *news.microsoft.com* and *news.csun.edu*. Because of the global nature of the news system, a question posted by a CSUN student on *news.csun.edu* would eventually be accessible to a Microsoft engineer who gets her newsfeed from *news.microsoft.com*. (And if the Microsoft engineer has time, she might respond to the query.)

How does a news article posted on one centralized host get to another host, possibly located on the other side of the world? Again, the answer is NNTP. Individual news servers are interconnected, but because of the physical size of the Internet they can't all be connected to every other news server. Instead, each news server needs to be connected to just one or more peers. The individual servers communicate constantly via NNTP to propagate new articles from one server to the other. So even if *news.microsoft.com* never connects to *news.csun.edu* directly, news articles from one server will eventually get to the other via intermediate hosts (such as *news.uunet.net*).

The way news is fed from one machine to another is also important. Because a server can be connected to more than one peer, sending the entire news database from one server to another doesn't make sense. For example, if Server1 received news messages in the *rec.climbing* group from Server2, it would have to discard the same message group content when it was received from Server3, wasting the network bandwidth used to send the contents of *rec.climbing* a second time. NNTP implements an alternative to this simple flooding scheme: the receiving host obtains a list of new articles from the sending host and then decides which articles it needs to receive. Usually, the system administrator can configure the news server to receive certain groups from certain hosts.

Figure 25.1 illustrates how all this works. Clients connected to *news.csun.edu* post news articles. *news.csun.edu* provides a newsfeed to *news.uunet.net*, which in turn feeds news to *news.microsoft.com*. Even though no direct connection exists between *news.csun.edu* and *news.microsoft.com*, newsreaders at Microsoft still can view the articles.

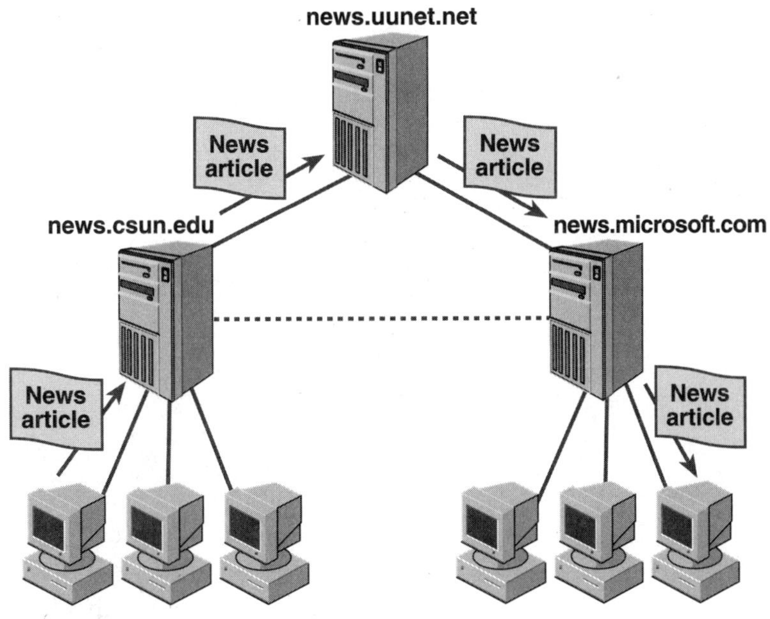

FIGURE 25.1

Internet news operations.

NOTE

The NNTP server included with IIS is capable of communicating with other news servers in only one direction. Other news servers can connect to IIS and receive news; however, they cannot send news articles to IIS. Therefore, the NNTP server can build its news database only from locally connected clients. To have a full-fledged news server, you should install the NNTP server included with the Microsoft Commercial Internet System (MCIS).

News Articles

Before we delve into the depths of the news transfer protocol, let's look at how news messages are organized. At the bottom of the news storage hierarchy is the news article. News articles are simply messages that contain information. They are similar to e-mail messages, but instead of being sent to your coworkers they are posted in a public forum. The formats of news articles and e-mail messages are described in the same specification, RFC 1036, "Standard for Interchange of USENET Messages."

News articles in turn are organized into groups. Theoretically, articles dealing with the same topic should be grouped together. For example, the newsgroup *rec.climbing* contains articles about mountaineering and rock climbing, whereas *comp.compilers* contains articles about various compilers.

An article on the news server still has a format similar to that of the older e-mail–based news system. To view the format of a news message, you can open an actual posted message file from your NNTP server message store. Figure 25.2 shows a message opened in Notepad; notice that it looks similar to the mail messages described in Chapter 11.

Let's go over the headers visible in this message. The From, Subject, Date, and Lines headers are fairly self-explanatory. The X-Newsreader and X-MimeOLE headers identify the software used to post the message. Message-ID is a mandatory header that uniquely identifies the particular news article anywhere on the Internet.

NOTE

RFC 1036 suggests how unique Message-ID headers can be generated. Because a Message-ID header is part of the message itself, the same message on any server would have the same ID.

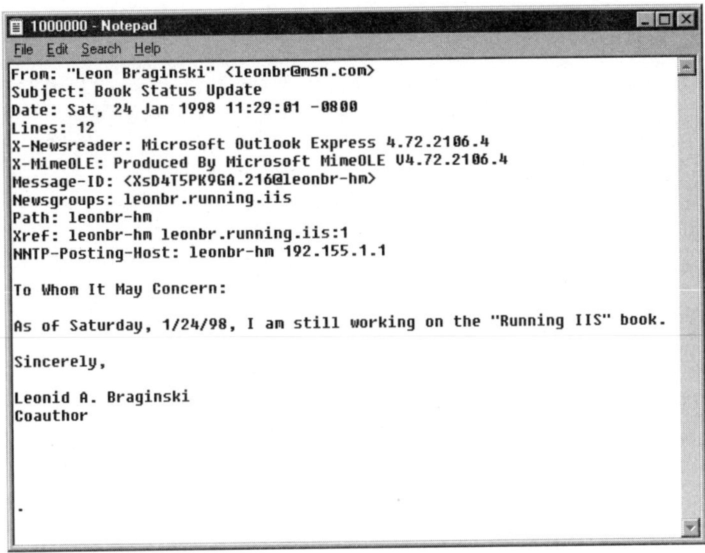

```
From: "Leon Braginski" <leonbr@msn.com>
Subject: Book Status Update
Date: Sat, 24 Jan 1998 11:29:01 -0800
Lines: 12
X-Newsreader: Microsoft Outlook Express 4.72.2106.4
X-MimeOLE: Produced By Microsoft MimeOLE V4.72.2106.4
Message-ID: <XsD4T5PK9GA.216@leonbr-hm>
Newsgroups: leonbr.running.iis
Path: leonbr-hm
Xref: leonbr-hm leonbr.running.iis:1
NNTP-Posting-Host: leonbr-hm 192.155.1.1

To Whom It May Concern:

As of Saturday, 1/24/98, I am still working on the "Running IIS" book.

Sincerely,

Leonid A. Braginski
Coauthor

.
```

FIGURE 25.2

The format of a news message stored in an ASCII file on the news server.

The Newsgroups header specifies which existing newsgroup or newsgroups the message belongs to. The Path header specifies the path used to reach the current news system. Because this example message was posted directly to the *leonbr-hm* machine, the path in this case is very short. Typically, messages travel from one server to another server, in which case the Path header might be something like *news.microsoft.com!gateway!localhost*. The Xref header indicates by message number the presence of this message in other groups on the local server. In this case, *leonbr-hm leonbr.running.iis:1* indicates that this message is present in only one group on the local server; the message is filed by the server as message number 1. The NNTP-Posting-Host header identifies the host that accepted the posted message directly from the client.

Glossary

Message number *An integer value used by a particular news server to uniquely identify a message in a newsgroup.*

Each message maintains a header trail (similar to a paper trail) long enough to identify the message's origin, the accepting news host, and the message's location. Nevertheless, an experienced user can always forge any and all of these headers by directly connecting to a news server using software such as telnet. We'll see how to do this shortly.

The Internet contains thousands and thousands of newsgroups. Discussion topics range from daytime TV soap operas to complex mathematical problems. Our server is not connected to the Internet and contains only a few newsgroups. Actually, even if our server were connected to the Internet, the number of newsgroups or articles would not be affected because the IIS NNTP service is unable to receive news from other servers.

On our server, we created a newsgroup named *leonbr.running.iis* that is dedicated to the ongoing process of writing this book. Presumably, anyone who connects to our server can share ideas and progress reports. Figure 25.3 shows a news message with the Subject header *Book Status Update* displayed using the newsreader client, Microsoft Outlook Express; we saw this same message in Figure 25.2 displayed in Notepad.

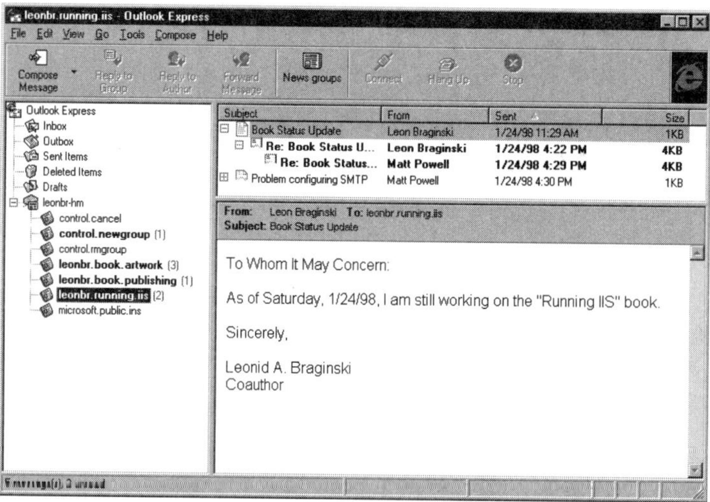

FIGURE 25.3

A new message in the* leonbr.running.iis *newsgroup.

This message was created and read using Outlook Express. This message traveled from the client, to the server (where it was stored in an ASCII file), and back to the client (where it was read).

NNTP Overview

NNTP is similar to HTTP, which was discussed in Chapter 23. In fact, all the presentation layer Internet protocols we discuss in Part III (HTTP, FTP, NNTP, and SMTP) use many of the same concepts. All rely on the lower-level, stream-oriented TCP for services such as connection establishment, reliable data delivery, and so on. This layered architecture enables NNTP to focus on its particular job: communicating with news servers for the purpose of accessing news databases. The news server itself is implemented as a Microsoft Windows NT service that listens for connections on the NNTP port (by default, port 119). As mentioned, NNTP is implemented on top of TCP, and therefore by using an application that has direct access to the TCP layer we can manually create NNTP protocol packets and submit them to the server. Just as we have done with other protocols, we will be using the telnet client included with Microsoft Windows to connect to port 119 and execute NNTP commands. This can be done by running the following command on your system:

```
telnet News_Server_Name 119
```

Don't forget to turn on the Local Echo option in the telnet client, as we did in the Chapter 24.

NNTP Commands

NNTP's similarity to other presentation layer protocols is not limited to its architecture. The structure of the protocols is similar as well. Clients (newsreaders) and servers exchange specific commands that describe tasks one peer wants the other to perform—for example, listing all the newsgroups on the server or sending a specific article. NNTP commands are simply case-insensitive ASCII strings that may have one or more optional parameters separated by spaces or tab characters. Just as with HTTP, NNTP commands end with a carriage return/linefeed pair (*\r\n* in C language syntax). Again similar to HTTP, the server can respond to an NNTP command in two ways: with a status response or with a text response. The legal NNTP commands are described in RFC 977, "Network News Transfer Protocol."

NNTP responses

The status response is a three-digit code that notifies the client of the status of the sent command and provides a short description string. The following table lists the possible meanings of the first digit of the status code.

First Digit of Status Code	Description
1*yz*	Informative message.
2*yz*	Command was OK.
3*yz*	Command is OK so far; send the rest of it.
4*yz*	Command was OK, but task could not be performed.
5*yz*	Command was not implemented, not correct, or a serious problem occurred.

The second digit of the status code indicates the category of the response, as listed in the following table. (Notice that the numbers 5, 6, and 7 are not used.)

Second Digit of Status Code	Category
*x*0*z*	Connection, connection setup, or miscellaneous message
*x*1*z*	Newsgroup selection
*x*2*z*	Article selection
*x*3*z*	Distribution function
*x*4*z*	Posting
*x*8*z*	Private implementation extension
*x*9*z*	Debugging output

Although the NNTP specification does not explicitly specify the third digit of the status code, this digit can be used to further describe the status of the command. For example, codes ranging from 190 through 199 would indicate various informative debugging output messages.

The text response can be sent by the server only when the status code indicates that text will follow. For example, when the client connects and asks the server to list all its newsgroups (potentially thousands of groups), the server sends a status code indicating that the operation has completed and that more text (the group list) will follow. When text is returned, multiple lines are separated by carriage return/linefeed pairs. A single period on a separate line indicates the end of the text response. If the text itself contains a single period on a line, a double period must be used. The idea behind the status and text responses is that news clients, such as simple text-based terminals, can view the status code first, without showing it to the user. The client software then decides whether more information, such as the group list, should be shown to the user.

Obtaining a list of commands

The Internet RFC governing NNTP describes quite a few commands, and some news servers might not implement all of them. Before we look at some specific commands, let's get a list of all the commands supported by the IIS news server. And what better place to obtain such list than from the server itself! As we explained earlier, we'll use the telnet client to send the HELP command to the news server and get its response. Because our server name is *leonbr-hm*, the command issued to start telnet is as follows:

```
telnet leonbr-hm 119
```

The telnet communication with the server is shown in the following code; our input is shown in boldface:

```
200 NNTP Service Microsoft® Internet Services 5.5 Version:
5.5.1774.13 Posting Allowed
help
100 Legal commands are :
article [MessageID|Number]
authinfo [user|pass|generic|transact] <data>
body [MessageID|Number]
check <message-id>
date
group newsgroup
head [MessageID|Number]
help
ihave <message-id>
last
list [active|newsgroups[wildmat]|srchfields|searchable|
    prettynames[wildmat]]
listgroup [newsgroup]
mode stream|reader
newgroups yymmdd hhmmss ["GMT"] [<distributions>]
newnews wildmat yymmdd hhmmss ["GMT"] [<distributions>]
next
post
search
slave
```

(continued)

```
stat [MessageID|number]
xhdr header [range|MessageID]
xover [range]
xpat header range|MessageID pat [morepat ...]
xreplic newsgroup/message-number[,newsgroup/message-number...]
takethis <message-id>
.
quit
205 closing connection - goodbye!
```

This quite interesting output warrants some explanation. As soon as the new connection has arrived at the server, the welcome message is sent to the client. The "200" numeric status code indicates that everything is OK so far. The server replies to our HELP command with the "100 Legal commands are :" status message. The numeric status code is followed by the list of legal commands supported by the server. Each line contains a single command, and the text response ends with a single period on a separate line. The QUIT command requests the server to close the connection.

Navigating through groups and articles

A server can have thousands of different newsgroups, each containing thousands of messages. The efficient navigation of these groups and messages is a task of utmost importance. To use network bandwidth efficiently, the server needs to avoid sending any unnecessary information to the client. NNTP supports an easy, and at the same time efficient, command set for navigating through the forest of groups and news articles.

A client can access an article in a number of ways. As mentioned, each article has a unique ID. (Remember the Message-ID header in Figure 25.2.) Each article also has a number (not the same as Message-ID) under which it is filed in the newsgroup by the server. Each article can therefore be identified either by its number or by its ID. The client can retrieve the entire article, only the article headers, or only the article body without its headers. The ARTICLE, HEAD, and BODY commands provide these capabilities; all three commands take either the Message-ID or the article number in the newsgroup. To distinguish between the Message-ID and the number, the Message-ID is surrounded by angle brackets.

Before getting the article or its parts, the client must know the article's Message-ID or its article number. Article numbers can be obtained indirectly by listing the newsgroups using the LIST command. The LIST command returns a list of all groups, the total number of articles in each group, and the numbers of the first and last article. Before you can get specific group information, you must first make that group active. An individual group can be made active using the GROUP command.

The GROUP command also returns the total number of articles in the group and the numbers of the first and last articles. All article numbers in a group can be listed using the LISTGROUP command. Called without parameters, the LISTGROUP command displays the numbers of all articles in the active group. LISTGROUP can also be called with a parameter that specifies a group in order to list the article numbers in that group.

NOTE

Using the LIST, LISTGROUP, and GROUP commands is similar to using the DIR and CD commands at the command prompt. The LIST and LISTGROUP commands enumerate newsgroups and article numbers, similar to how the DIR command enumerates directories and files. The GROUP command makes a specified newsgroup the active newsgroup, similar to how the CD command makes the specified directory the active directory.

The news server maintains an internal *current article pointer*. When a particular group is selected, the current article pointer is set to the first article in the group. The pointer can be moved forward using the NEXT command and can be moved back using the LAST command. When the article is accessed using the ARTICLE, BODY, or HEAD command by its number in the group, the current article pointer is set to the specified article. If the news client wants to move a pointer without receiving any part of the article, the STAT command with the article number can be used. The STAT command can also be used to obtain the Message-ID when only the article number is known. Note that the ARTICLE, BODY, HEAD, and STAT commands don't affect the current pointer when the article is referred to by its Message-ID rather than its number in the group. When the above commands are called without parameters, the server uses the current active article (that is, it uses the current article pointer).

And now let's put all this information together. Here are the steps for reading an article:

1. The client connects to the server and obtains a list of all the newsgroups from the server (unless the client already has the list) by using the LIST command.
2. The client specifies the group it wants to make active using the GROUP command.
3. The client lists the article numbers in the group using the LISTGROUP command.

4. The client accesses any part of an article by its number using the ARTICLE, BODY, or HEAD command.
5. The client calls the STAT command to obtain the Message-ID for a specific article number.
6. The client accesses any part of the article by its Message-ID (returned from the previous STAT command) by using the ARTICLE, BODY, or HEAD command.

Note that the client does not need to perform step 3 of this process. Because the first article in the selected group is made current, the ARTICLE, BODY, HEAD, and STAT commands can be called without parameters to read it. The current article pointer can then be moved to the next article using the NEXT command (or to the previous article using the LAST command).

As you can see, the steps for reading news messages are quite simple. In fact, if you know Windows Sockets programming you can write a news client that is functional enough to connect to the server and read news without too much effort. We won't be writing such a client any time soon, but we will use telnet to put our NNTP knowledge to the test. The following code shows the log of a telnet session with our news server; again, our input is shown in boldface. The numbers preceding the commands are for reference only; they weren't part of the actual telnet session.

```
200 NNTP Service Microsoft® Internet Services 5.5
    Version: 5.5.1774.13 Posting Allowed
1) list
215 list of newsgroups follow
control.cancel 0 1 y
control.newgroup 1 1 y
control.rmgroup 0 1 y
leonbr.book.artwork 3 1 y
leonbr.book.publishing 1 1 y
leonbr.running.iis 5 1 y
microsoft.public.ins 2 2 y
.
2) group leonbr.running.iis
211 5 1 5 leonbr.running.iis
3) head 1
221 1 <XsD4T5PK9GA.216@leonbr-hm>
From: "Leon Braginski" <leonbr@msn.com>
Subject: Book Status Update
Date: Sat, 24 Jan 1998 11:29:01 -0800
Lines: 12
```

```
X-Newsreader: Microsoft Outlook Express 4.72.2106.4
X-MimeOLE: Produced By Microsoft MimeOLE V4.72.2106.4
Message-ID: <XsD4T5PK9GA.216@leonbr-hm>
Newsgroups: leonbr.running.iis
Path: leonbr-hm
Xref: leonbr-hm leonbr.running.iis:1
NNTP-Posting-Host: leonbr-hm 192.155.1.1
.
4) body 1
222 1 <XsD4T5PK9GA.216@leonbr-hm>

To Whom It May Concern:

As of Saturday, 1/24/98, I am still working on the "Running IIS" book.

Sincerely,

Leonid A. Braginski
Coauthor




.
5) next
223 2 <Y#8EbdSK9GA.214@leonbr-hm>
6) next
223 3 <5e7pUhSK9GA.235@leonbr-hm>
7) stat 4
223 4 <KSinAiSK9GA.235@leonbr-hm>
8) article <KSinAiSK9GA.235@leonbr-hm>
220 0 article <KSinAiSK9GA.235@leonbr-hm>
From: "Matt Powell" <mattpo@msn.com>
Subject: Problem configuring SMTP
Date: Sat, 24 Jan 1998 16:30:56 -0800
Lines: 7
X-Newsreader: Microsoft Outlook Express 4.72.2106.4
X-MimeOLE: Produced By Microsoft MimeOLE V4.72.2106.4
Message-ID: <KSinAiSK9GA.235@leonbr-hm>
Newsgroups: leonbr.running.iis
Path: leonbr-hm
Xref: leonbr-hm leonbr.running.iis:4
NNTP-Posting-Host: leonbr-hm 192.155.1.1
```

(continued)

```
Hello,

My SMTP service does not work correctly. Please help me fix it.

Matt


.
9) quit
205 closing connection - goodbye!
```

It's clear from this log that we have connected to the server and read a couple of messages. Let's go over each command that was sent to the server.

1) list The first thing the client needs to do upon connecting is to get the list of all the newsgroups on the server. (In our example, the telnet client is a news client.) The LIST command does just that. In response to the LIST command, the server sends a numeric status code with a short description: "215 list of newsgroups follow." Because this status code implies that more information is to follow, the server sends a text response. This text consists of a list of newsgroups on the server. Each group is in the form *groupname last first P*. The *last* variable indicates the number of the last article in the group; *first* indicates the number of the first article in the group. The *P* variable is the letter "y" if posting to this newsgroup is allowed and "n" if posting is not allowed. Notice that the list ends with a single period on a separate line.

NOTE

You might be wondering why the number for the first message in the group would not always be 1. The news server keeps articles for a limited number of days—after a specified period of time, the article expires and is deleted by the server. (We saw how to create expiration policies in Chapter 10.) Because the first few articles in the group have probably expired, the first existing article is no longer 1.

2) group leonbr.running.iis The group *leonbr.running.iis* is now the default group. Along with making this group the default, the GROUP command returns important information in the form *xyz N F L group*. *xyz* is a status code—here, *211* indicates that the group selection succeeded. *N* is the estimated number of articles in the group, *F* is the number of the first article in the group, *L* is the number of last article in the group, and *group* is the currently selected group.

3) head 1 This command retrieves the header for only the first message in the group. The server's response to this command includes the status code 221 with the Message-ID (*<XsD4T5PK9GA.216@leonbr-hm>*) followed by the message's headers.

As usual, the text response sent by the server is terminated with a single period on a separate line.

4) body 1 Here, after examining the headers, the client wanted to get the body of the message. The status code 222 is followed by the message body.

5) next; 6) next These two steps are the same. By calling the NEXT command twice, we moved the current article pointer twice. The currently selected article is 3. At this point, we could have just typed *ARTICLE*, without a Message-ID or number to show the text of article number 3.

7) stat 4 We didn't want to see article number 3, and instead decided to get the Message-ID for article number 4. In reply to the STAT command, the server sends the Message-ID for article number 4: *<KSinAiSK9GA.235@leonbr-hm>*. Recall that the angle brackets indicate that this is the Message-ID, not the message number.

8) article *<KSinAiSK9GA.235@leonbr-hm>* Here we finally retrieve the entire article by its Message-ID, which was obtained from the previous STAT command.

9) quit The client wants to close the connection.

Looking at something that is rarely seen is always an interesting experience. If reading the news using a standard newsreader was always a bit of a mystery to you, now you know the rest of the story (specifically, the NNTP conversation between a newsreader and the server). A more experienced reader might have noticed one especially interesting detail: this particular news server did not ask the client for a user name and password. This laxity is not common practice. The majority of news servers on the Internet require some sort of client authentication. The following code shows what would happen if a news server did not allow anonymous connections:

```
200 NNTP Service Microsoft® Internet Services 5.5
    Version: 5.5.1774.13 Posting Allowed

list

480 Logon Required


authinfo user JoeB
381 Waiting for password
authinfo pass test
281 Authentication ok
list
215 list of newsgroups follow
control.cancel 0 1 y  ...
```

When the server requires client authentication, the client can't issue a command before the AUTHINFO command is used to submit a user name and password. The first time the LIST command is sent to the server, the server replies with a status code message of "480 Logon Required." As we saw in the tables of status codes earlier in this chapter, the first digit of this status code indicates that even though the command was correct, for some reason it could not be completed. The second digit specifies the implementation-specific status code category. To submit user credentials, AUTHINFO should be called twice because the user name and password are submitted in different transactions.

We've learned a lot about how NNTP is used to read news, but we have not yet looked at how a message is posted to a news server and at how servers communicate to send news to and receive news from each other.

Posting news

Posting news is a simple process. It requires only one command: POST. When the client sends this command to the server, the server reads the client input line by line. It stops reading when the client sends a single period on a separate line, indicating the end of the input. Simulating the POST command in the telnet client is not as simple as the previous commands we have tested because the server expects to receive a message that strictly conforms to the format described in RFC 1036. This means that the message should have all the mandatory headers, such as Subject and Date. Every message needs a valid and unique Message-ID header. We cheated by adapting a Message-ID header from a message posted using Outlook Express. The telnet session that posts a message to the *leonbr.book.publishing* newsgroup is shown here, with our input in boldface:

```
200 NNTP Service Microsoft® Internet Services 5.5
    Version: 5.5.1774.13 Posting Allowed
post
340 Continue posting - terminate with period
From: "Leon Braginski" <leonbr@msn.com>
Subject: My test post
Date: Sat, 24 Jan 1998 20:03:50 -0800
Lines: 3
X-Newsreader: Telnet Client
Message-ID: <In8Epjdk9GA.237@leonbr-hm>
Newsgroups: leonbr.book.publishing
Path: leonbr-hm
Xfer: leonbr-hm leonbr.book.publishing:1
```

```
Hello
This is a test post. Will it work?
Good-bye
.
240 Article Posted OK
quit
205 closing connection - goodbye!
```

Seeing is believing. The results of our labor are shown in Figure 25.4.

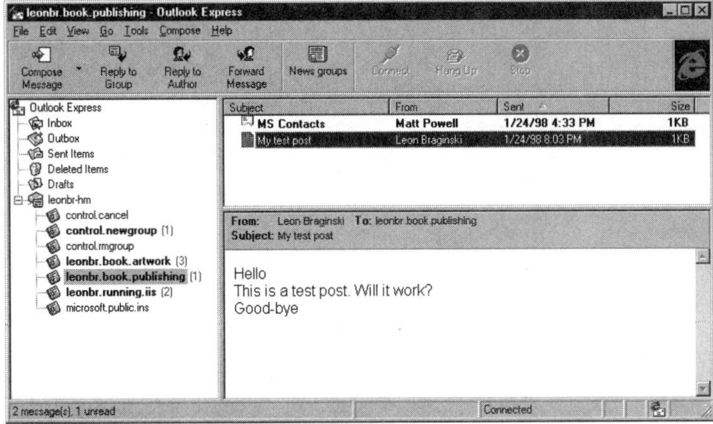

FIGURE 25.4

Our test message as displayed in Outlook Express.

News Distribution Between Servers

The beauty of Internet news is that it enables a newsreader to see a message posted from across the world. Earlier in this chapter, we explained how news servers communicate with one another to share news. In this section, we'll discuss the commands NNTP provides to support this server-to-server collaboration.

Receiving news using the IHAVE command

When one server offers news articles to another server, the offering server does not use the POST command; instead, the IHAVE command is used. The IHAVE command takes a Message-ID, so it can reject a duplicate article before network bandwidth is wasted to transfer the entire message. When a server is offered news using the IHAVE command, it might also perform other validations based on some internal rules. For example, if a server is configured to take a newsfeed for *rec.climbing* from *news.uunet.net*, new messages from other servers to this group will be rejected. We can't demonstrate how IHAVE works in a telnet session with IIS because the news server does not support news uploads from other servers. The IIS NNTP server replies to the IHAVE command with the status code message "502 Access Denied." Recalling our status code tables again, *5* as the first digit of the status code indicates that the command is not implemented.

Sending news to other servers

IIS is capable of providing a newsfeed to other servers. The NEWGROUPS and NEWNEWS commands are used by connecting servers to list new groups and new messages created after a specified date and time. To avoid confusion, in this section we will call the server that initiates the connection to the "client" (even though it is still a server running the NNTP service). The machine that accepts the connection will be referred to as the "server." In our telnet session, we will simulate a client. But remember that we are talking about a server-to-server news exchange. Therefore, the client is not a newsreader program; instead, it is another server that wants to receive a newsfeed from the machine it is connecting to.

Using the NEWGROUPS and NEWNEWS commands is a fairly straightforward process. The client connects and requests a list of new groups created after a specified date. Once the list is received, the client may create new groups in its own news storage location. If a new group is created on one news server, there is a potential for the same newsgroup to eventually propagate to different servers. Once newsgroups are created, the connecting server can request a list of new articles added since a specified date and time. If new articles exist and the client is configured to accept the newsfeed of these articles from the server, the client requests the articles using the ARTICLE command. The following telnet session shows this news retrieval process in action:

```
200 NNTP Service Microsoft® Internet Services 5.5
    Version: 5.5.1774.13 Posting Allowed
newgroups 980124 090000
231 New newsgroups follow.
leonbr.book.artwork 3 1 y
leonbr.book.publishing 2 1 y
leonbr.running.iis 5 1 y
.
newnews leonbr.book.* 980124 090000
230 list of new articles by message-id follows.
<rctvDlSK9GA.214@leonbr-hm>
<KtBLDjSK9GA.235@leonbr-hm>
<ZZjKaiSK9GA.235@leonbr-hm>
```

```
<In8Epjdk9GA.237@leonbr-hm>
<In3EpjSK9GA.235@leonbr-hm>
.
article <In3EpjSK9GA.235@leonbr-hm>
220 0 article <In3EpjSK9GA.235@leonbr-hm>
From: "Matt Powell" <mattpo@msn.com>
Subject: MS Contacts
Date: Sat, 24 Jan 1998 16:33:51 -0800
Lines: 8
X-Newsreader: Microsoft Outlook Express 4.72.2106.4
X-MimeOLE: Produced By Microsoft MimeOLE V4.72.2106.4
Message-ID: <In3EpjSK9GA.235@leonbr-hm>
Newsgroups: leonbr.book.publishing
Path: leonbr-hm
Xref: leonbr-hm leonbr.book.publishing:1
NNTP-Posting-Host: leonbr-hm 192.155.1.1

Hello

Please post names and contact numbers of MS Press technical editors.

Thanks.



.
quit
205 closing connection - goodbye!
```

Let's look at this session line by line. The client news server (represented by the telnet application) has connected to *leonbr-hm* and requested a list of new groups using the command *newgroups 980124 090000*. The two numeric values after the command stand for the date and time—in this case, the client has requested a list of all new groups created since January 24, 1998, at 9:00:00 AM. If *GMT* is not appended after the time, the time is assumed to be in the server's time zone. If *GMT* is appended, the time is assumed to be in Greenwich mean time. In both cases, the time uses a 24-hour system. The server responds with a list of new groups followed by their now familiar numbers. And don't forget, the list ends with a single period.

The NEWNEWS command has a similar format in terms of date and time, but there is one difference with the parameters: the command is followed by the name of the group that should be checked for new messages. This group name can contain wildcard characters. For example, "*" means "anything" and "!" means "except."

Thus, *leonbr.book.** would include *leonbr.book.artwork* and *leonbr.book.publishing*, and *!leonbr.book.*,** would list all groups except *leonbr.book.<anything>*, leaving off such groups as *leonbr.book.artwork* and *leonbr.book.publishing*. In reply to the NEWNEWS command, the server sends a Message-ID for each new article. (Remember that the connecting client needs to know the Message-ID instead of the message number so that it can check for duplicate messages before actually getting articles using the ARTICLE command. The whole idea is to make news transfer as efficient as possible.)

Control Messages

By now, you have a good sense of most of the NNTP commands and understand what is going on under the hood between newsreaders and news servers. You might have noticed that NNTP does not provide a command to create or delete groups or existing messages. Message management is not the responsibility of the protocol. NNTP is simply a vehicle used to carry news from one machine to another. Message and group management is still possible by posting specially formatted messages in specific newsgroups. These messages are called *control messages* and are posted in the control newsgroups (which we saw when we executed the LIST command earlier in this chapter). Control messages are usually generated by news clients or specific software (or even manually, using a telnet client) and contain direct commands to the news server. All of these commands are defined in RFC 1036, but not all of these commands are implemented by every server. Some of the more frequently used commands are CANCEL, NEWGROUP, and RMGROUP.

For a message to be considered a control message, it must be specifically formatted. Two aspects transform an ordinary message into a control message: the Control header or a specially formatted Subject header. The body of the Control header contains a command for the server software. A message with a Control header such as *Control: cancel <SpdkOJSK9GA.235@leonbr-hm>* requests the server to delete the article with the specified ID. The body of a cancel control message can be left blank. If the Control header is missing, the Subject header can be used to carry out a command. In this case, the Subject header must contain a string starting with *cmsg*. Here's how an article would be deleted using the Subject header: *Subject: cmsg cancel <SpdkOJSK9GA.235@leonbr-hm>*.

It's worth mentioning that control messages travel from server to server just like an ordinary news article. They are usually posted in special control groups: *control.cancel*, *control.newgroup*, and *control.rmgroup*. Theoretically, anyone who reads RFC 1036 and knows the format for a control message can create one and post it to the control group. To prevent someone else from using control messages to manipulate your news server, control groups can be moderated. Moderated groups accept posts only after they have been reviewed and approved by the administrator or other designated entity. (We explained how to create and manage moderated groups in Chapter 10.) NNTP is indeed similar to HTTP. In both cases, we have requests coming from clients. The server processes the request and returns a status code and data back to the client. In Chapter 26, we will talk about the Simple Mail Transport Protocol (SMTP), and you'll learn about what happens below the surface of your e-mail system when you send mail to a colleague or friend. We will also see some similarities between SMTP and NNTP.

CHAPTER 26

The Simple Mail Transfer Protocol (SMTP)

E-mail messaging is one of the oldest uses of the Internet. Long before "surfing the Web" became an everyday activity, scientists at universities worldwide were exchanging electronic messages. These early Internet users did not have fancy-looking e-mail applications such as Microsoft Outlook Express; instead, they used command-line–based mailing utilities. Many of these utilities are still in use in the UNIX world, but nowadays almost no one is required to learn how to use an application that does not have an intuitive user interface. Interestingly enough, the mechanics of e-mail delivery used by the various Internet mail systems are the same now as they were in the early 1980s. E-mail delivery is based largely on the Simple Mail Transfer Protocol (SMTP), which is outlined in RFC 821, "Simple Mail Transfer Protocol." To appreciate the complexity of SMTP, you need to look at this RFC—it takes a stack of 67 pages to describe how e-mail gets from point A to point B. We won't be looking into all the protocol details, but by the end of this chapter you'll have a good understanding of how an e-mail message is sent to an Internet user.

SMTP Overview

SMTP is used by mail delivery agents (such as IIS's SMTP service) to transfer mail messages to one another. It is also the language spoken by mail clients that use it to transfer mail to the SMTP server for delivery. SMTP is not used, however, for delivering mail messages from the SMTP server to an end user's mail client software (as you'll recall from our extensive discussion in Chapter 11). As with HTTP, File Transfer Protocol (FTP), and Network News Transfer Protocol (NNTP), SMTP rides on top of connection-oriented TCP. (Nothing prevents SMTP from being used over a different connection-oriented protocol, but in reality it is used almost exclusively over TCP.) Figure 26.1 shows a typical SMTP architecture. The sending machine transfers a message, either in the form of user input or from its local file system, over the network to the receiving SMTP server, where the message is stored somewhere in the local file system.

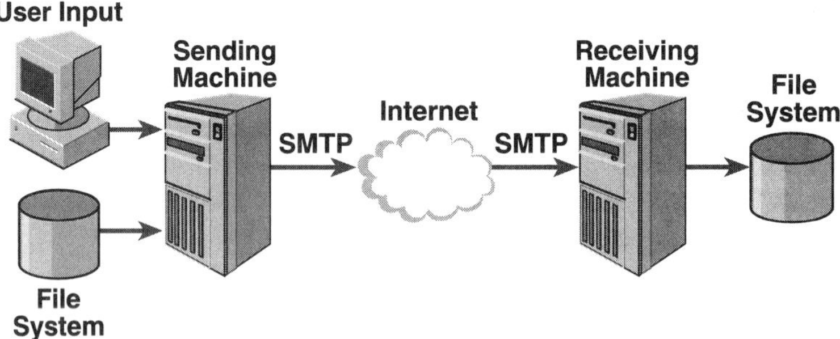

FIGURE 26.1

SMTP being used to send mail to a mail server.

Different SMTP servers might organize their file storage differently. As we saw in Chapter 11, the IIS mail server by default puts all mail messages in the \Mailroot\Drop directory. It's not important to the user or the sending machine how the messages are stored in the local file system.

Mail messages look a lot like the news articles we saw in Chapter 25: ASCII data with auxiliary headers (identifying the sender, the recipient, and so on) followed by the body of the text message. We'll begin our discussion of SMTP by examining the protocol itself, and then we'll discuss the message details.

SMTP Implementation

SMTP uses a simple command/reply mechanism. One application (which we'll call the "client" for the sake of simplicity, even though it could be either an SMTP server process or a client such as Outlook Express) establishes a connection to an SMTP server. Once the connection is established, the client sends a command to the server. Commands are not case sensitive and are terminated with a carriage return/ linefeed (CR-LF) pair. The end of the text input is denoted by a period preceded and followed by a CR-LF pair. If the client needs to send a line containing a period, a double period (..) is sent. The success or failure of each command is indicated by the status code in the server's reply.

Mail transactions usually consist of several commands that must be executed in a specific sequence. The identification of the mail sender and the recipient is followed by the message (data) itself. The simple task of sending a single message can be accomplished using five SMTP commands issued in sequence, as follows:

- **HELO** Used to identify the connecting server
- **MAIL FROM** Used to specify the address of the sender

- **RCPT TO** Used to specify the address of the recipient
- **DATA** Used to enter the message data
- **QUIT** Used to quit the transaction and disconnect

Several other useful SMTP commands exist to control and assist in mail transactions. The client can abort mail transactions at any time by using the RSET (Reset) command. The VRFY (Verify) command is used to obtain the full user name and the given user's e-mail address (in other words, the mailbox). The EXND (Expand) command returns a list of e-mail addresses for a given mailing list (or alias). Because IIS does not provide mailboxes for individual users, the VRFY command can be used successfully for any address—in other words, IIS doesn't even care whether a particular user exists. The mailing list EXND command is not supported by IIS. Mail transactions vary from sending a simple mail message to sending a message with user name verification to performing a complex mail relay. Regardless of the command or the nature of the mail transaction, each command is followed by a server reply.

Server Command Reply Status Codes

Like the protocols we've looked at up to now, the SMTP server replies to each command with a status code consisting of a three-digit number and a message string in the following form:

xyz Text message

The server's reply to a command can take more than one line. Each line except the last of a multiline server reply includes a hyphen between the status code and the text message. The client can thus determine the end of the reply because the last line does not contain a hyphen.

The three-digit status code serves an important purpose. The client receiving the status code can quickly examine the code and then decide on its course of action. In many cases, the client might skip all reply lines containing a hyphen between the status code and the text message. It might then search for a numeral followed by a space, indicating the final line of the reply. Depending on the status code, the client might need to submit the next command, resubmit the previous command, report an error, or do any number of things. The first digit of the reply status code indicates the general success or failure of each command. The following table lists the five possible values for the first digit of the status code and their meanings.

First Digit of Status Code	Description
1*yz*	Positive preliminary reply, meaning that the command was accepted but that the server is waiting for the client before executing the command. The sender should process this status code and submit the command specifying whether the action should continue. Although this is one of the possible status codes, no current SMTP commands allow this kind of reply—this value was provided for future enhancements to SMTP. Therefore, you should not see an SMTP reply starting with *1*.
2*yz*	Positive completion reply. The command completed successfully, so the sender can send its next command.
3*yz*	Positive intermediate reply. The command was accepted successfully, but further information is needed to complete the action. This status code is used when the server receives a DATA command, which must be followed by text input from the sender.
4*yz*	Temporary negative completion reply. The command was not accepted, and the server could not perform the requested action. The command sequence might still be recovered, however. For instance, the client can return to the beginning and retry the entire command sequence.
5*yz*	Indicates a permanent negative completion reply. The server did not accept the command for some reason. (Perhaps a syntax error occurred or the command was not implemented.) Mail transactions consist of a sequence of single commands. If one of these commands fails with a 5*yz* reply, the sender can retry sending it (after fixing the problem). Therefore, the permanent failure of one command might not mean the failure of the entire mail transaction.

When the sending client receives a reply status code that identifies either a warning or an error condition, the client can use the second digit of the status code to help determine the cause of the problem. The second digit of the reply status code provides the category or the server facility that generated the code. The table on the facing page shows the possible values for the second digit and their meanings.

The SMTP specification does not explicitly assign meanings to the last digit of the reply status code. This digit can be used to further narrow the category of the reply, but the value and its meaning might be server specific. To ensure that various SMTP servers (and clients) can successfully communicate with one another, it's important to follow the reply status code conventions outlined here. Servers should not create new status codes for specific replies; instead, they should try to conform their replies to the current categories.

Second Digit of Status Code	Category
*x*0*z*	The command syntax category. A second digit *0* might indicate a command syntax error, but replies to syntactically correct commands that don't fit any other category can also have *0* as the second digit.
*x*1*z*	The information category. Indicates a reply to a request for information—for instance, a reply to the HELP command.
*x*2*z*	The transmission channel category. These status codes refer to the underlying transmission channel.
*x*3*z* and *x*4*z*	Not currently used.
*x*5*z*	The mail system category. Indicates the status of the mail system—almost all replies that relate to the general mail system (responses to commands such as HELO, MAIL, and so on) have *5* as the second digit.

Sending or Mailing a Message

As we've seen, sending mail, the basic transaction around which the Internet e-mail delivery system revolves, requires at least five SMTP commands. The sender uses the different commands to supply the following information: the names of the connecting host, the mail sender, the mail recipient, and the data (the mail message) itself. In this chapter, we use the term "sending mail" frequently, but this usage isn't quite correct. SMTP supports two separate mail commands: SEND, which *sends* a mail message; and MAIL, which *mails* a message. As we'll see, there is a big difference between these two commands.

The SEND command originated in the early days of computers, when mail recipients usually logged on to the SMTP server using a serial connection from a dumb terminal. These users would receive e-mail messages directly to their terminal. As e-mail was delivered, instead of being deposited in an inbox, it would by typed directly on the user's terminal—sometimes on top of whatever text happened to be displayed on the screen. Another problem with the SEND command was that it failed if the recipient was not logged on at the time of mail delivery. This probably doesn't sound all that convenient, but the SEND command did have a good side: ready or not, the user was able to view all e-mail at the moment it arrived, without having to check a separate inbox.

The MAIL command was designed to compensate for the SEND command's deficiencies. The MAIL command doesn't mess with the user's screen; instead, it directs the server to deposit the mail in the user's inbox for later reading. As you probably guessed, the MAIL command is much more popular than the SEND command and is used almost exclusively today to send e-mail. One minor problem with the MAIL command, however, is that the user does not know immediately when new mail messages have been deposited in his or her inbox. The user needs to check the inbox periodically to determine whether new mail has arrived. But this inconvenience is a small price to pay for not interfering with the user's terminal.

One more command incorporates the convenience of immediate mail notifications available with the SEND command and the robustness of the MAIL command: SAML, short for "send and mail." The SAML command works just like the SEND command except that it won't fail if the user is not currently logged on. If the user is logged on to a terminal that accepts terminal messages, SAML will deliver the message directly to the terminal in addition to depositing it in the user's inbox. If the user is not logged on, no problem: the message is simply deposited in the user's inbox. And of course, if there's a way to "send and mail" a message, there must be a way to "send or mail" a message: the SOML command. The SOML command offers the best of both worlds. It will send a message to a user's terminal screen if he or she is logged on and accepting messages. However, if the send message is not successful because the user is not logged on or does not accept messages, the SOML command will mail the message.

NOTE

The mail server included with IIS does not support the SEND, SAML, and SOML commands; only the MAIL command is supported.

Supported Commands

Lucky for us, SMTP uses TCP to do its job. Both peers participating in the SMTP transaction rely on the TCP layer to establish a single half-duplex connection using TCP sockets. This fact enables us to easily communicate with the mail server via a simple telnet client that is capable of opening a TCP connection (as we have done already with HTTP, FTP, and NNTP). As in the previous chapters, don't forget to turn on Local Echo in the telnet client if you are following along with our samples.

As with the other protocols we've looked at, our first task is to obtain a list of the commands supported by the IIS mail server, as demonstrated in the following code. User input is shown here in boldface. The server listens on TCP port 25; therefore, connecting to this port with the telnet client allows us to communicate directly with the server.

```
220-leonbr-hm Microsoft SMTP MAIL ready at Tue, 3 Feb 1998 19:31:44 -
0800 Version: 5.5.1774.114.11
220 ESMTP spoken here
HELP
214-This server supports the following commands:
214-HELO EHLO STARTTLS RCPT DATA RSET MAIL VRFY QUIT HELP ETRN
214 End of HELP information
QUIT
221 leonbr-hm Service closing transmission channel
```

This code raises some interesting issues. As soon the connection is established, the server identifies itself by its name and indicates that it is ready to receive further commands. To get the list of supported commands, we send the HELP command to the server. In reply, the server sends three lines with text information. As we've seen earlier, each line starts with a reply status code followed by a text message; the first and second digits of the status code indicate what the status code means. Because more than one line is sent back to the client, the status codes and the text are separated by a hyphen on all lines except the last one.

Extended SMTP

Notice in the preceding code that the server includes the statement "ESMTP spoken here" with its initial response. You might be wondering what this means—after all, we just told you that SMTP is the language used by mail servers. "ESMTP" stands for Extended SMTP. If you think of SMTP as a language, you can think of ESMTP as a dialect.

SMTP adheres to a strict standard to facilitate communication among different machines running different versions of mail software. Servers can't just add new commands to support some sort of extended functionality (such as support for authentication). Even if a server added extra functionality, clients written to conform to SMTP RFC 821 would know nothing about these new capabilities. There is, however, a way of extending SMTP.

RFC 1425, "SMTP Service Extensions," defines how new extensions (such as new commands) can be added to a mail server. Two requirements must be met in order to extend the functionality of SMTP. First the new extensions must be known and correctly implemented by the clients. Of course, this step is necessary only if the server's developers want their extensions to be publicly supported. This task is performed by registering new extensions with the Internet Assigned Numbers

Authority (IANA) and issuing an RFC for the extension. But correct implementation of the extension by the client is only half the job. The second step is to create a mechanism that allows the server to notify clients of the extensions it supports.

To complete this second requirement, clients supporting ESMTP should issue an EHLO command instead of a HELO command upon connecting to the server. Remember that HELO is used to identify the connecting client. If the server does not support ESMTP, it will issue an error reply status code notifying the client that the command is not supported (something like "500 Unrecognized Command"). The client will interpret this reply status code, abort the mail transaction using the RSET command, and then retry using the HELO command. If the server supports ESMTP, the server will reply with a success status code and a list of supported extended commands will follow. The following code illustrates the extensions supported by the Microsoft SMTP mail server:

```
220-leonbr-hm Microsoft SMTP MAIL ready at Sat, 7 Feb 1998 12:12:17 -
0800 Version: 5.5.1774.114.11
220 ESMTP spoken here
EHLO EARTH
250-leonbr-hm Hello [192.155.1.2]
250-AUTH=NTLM LOGIN
250-SIZE 2097152
250-PIPELINING
250-8bitmime
250-TURN
250 TLS
```

In this example, a computer named *EARTH* connects to our server and wants to determine whether ESMTP is supported. *EARTH* issues an EHLO command and gets a list of extension commands. Some of these commands might make sense only for specific clients. For example, this server supports NT LAN Manager (NTLM) authentication, as mentioned on the AUTH line, which is useful only for Microsoft mail clients (or servers) that support the NTLM type of authentication.

Along with proprietary commands, Microsoft mail servers support industry-wide standard extensions. The "SIZE 2097152" text message reply indicates that the server supports RFC 1427, "SMTP Service Extension for Message Size Declaration." This extension enables connecting clients to specify the message size (in bytes) as a parameter of the MAIL FROM command. The message limit set by our server is 2,097,152 bytes, or 2MB. (This value can be changed on the SMTP Messages page of the Site Properties window in the Microsoft Management Console, as we saw in Chapter 11.) If a message size is not specified by the client, the client won't receive an error message until after it has transmitted possibly a large amount of data—the server's message size limit to be exact—thus wasting precious network bandwidth. The following code demonstrates how the SIZE command is used. Notice that the server reports an error before the huge message is actually sent.

```
...
mail from: <leonbr@leonbr-hm> size=999999999
552 Message size exceeds fixed maximum message size
...
```

If you think that an e-mail message can't be as large as 2 MB, think again. These days you can attach almost anything to a mail message—for example, an AVI or a WAV file, picture files in different formats, database files, and so on. All these attachments don't come cheap and can easily grow to even larger than 2 MB.

The "8bitmime" server reply text message indicates that the server supports RFC 1426, "SMTP Service Extension for 8bit-MIMEtransport." Mail attachments are encoded via a specific Multipurpose Internet Mail Extensions (MIME) encoding scheme and inserted directly into the body of the message. When binary data is encoded using the default scheme—7-bit encoding—it is represented as ASCII-only data in which all characters are printable. On the other hand, 8-bit encoded data might contain nonprintable characters. The encoding type is specified by using the BODY keyword in a MAIL FROM command such as the following:

```
mail from: <leonbr@leonbr-hm> body=8bitmime
```

When attachments are included in the body of the message, a message header identifies their type and encoding schemes. We will discuss the details of message headers in the section "Mail Message Format" later in this chapter. We won't go into all the details of the various MIME types and encoding since there is more than one RFC dedicated to this topic. If you are interested in investigating this topic further, you might want to start with RFC 1521, "MIME (Multipurpose Internet Mail Extensions) Part One: Mechanisms for Specifying and Describing the Format of Internet Message Bodies."

Because of the Extended SMTP support, in reply to the HELP command the server might send some commands that are not included in SMTP RFC 821. The ETRN command is an example of such a command. Its usage is explained in RFC 1985, "SMTP Service Extension for Remote Message Queue Starting." The ETRN command is by no means trivial; it can be used to convert the mail-sending peer to the mail-receiving peer. By issuing this command and connecting to an SMTP peer server that would normally be sending new mail to your server, your current server becomes a mail receiver machine, thereby receiving mail from the server it has just connected to. This feature is handy when one of the two mail servers does not have a dedicated network connection and is connected via something like a modem. Say machine A connects to machine B by modem only a few times a day to send all queued e-mail. Machine B receives and accumulates e-mail for the domain served by machine A (while machine A is unreachable in the absence of the modem connection). After machine A initiates a connection to machine B, it can change roles and become a mail receiver as well, receiving any mail that has accumulated for it. In fact, ETRN is a "reincarnation" of the original SMTP command TURN. The ETRN command has a special provision that the original TURN command did not have that prevents bogus clients (such as the telnet client in our earlier examples) from connecting to the server and downloading mail sent to some other domain.

Creating a Mail Transaction

Extended SMTP is a fascinating topic, but let's get back to basics. Remember that five simple commands (HELO, MAIL FROM, RCPT TO, DATA, and QUIT) are sufficient to deliver a mail message. Using our friendly telnet client once again, in this section we'll create a full-fledged SMTP transaction.

First let's review the command sequence used to send mail from one machine to another. The mail sender can be either Outlook Express or another SMTP client. The following code demonstrates a simple mail transaction; user input is shown in boldface:

```
220-leonbr-hm Microsoft SMTP MAIL ready at Tue, 3 Feb 1998 19:58:21 -
0800 Version: 5.5.1774.114.11
220 ESMTP spoken here
HELO EARTH
250 leonbr-hm Hello [192.155.1.2]
MAIL FROM: <joe@cmpny.com>
250 joe@cmpny.com....Sender OK
RCPT TO: <leonbr@leonbr-hm>
250 leonbr@leonbr-hm
DATA
354 Start mail input; end with <CRLF>.<CRLF>
This is a test. This is only a test.
.
250 001b63159030428LEONBR-HM Queued mail for delivery
QUIT
221 leonbr-hm Service closing transmission channel
```

This transaction sends mail from *joe@cmpny.com* to *leonbr@leonbr-hm*. Before we analyze the telnet session, let's verify that our efforts were successful. The READMAIL.ASP sample from Chapter 11 can be used to determine whether *leonbr@leonbr-hm* has indeed received an e-mail message. Figure 26.2 shows that the e-mail message was successfully received by the server. The Subject header is missing because it was never entered in the telnet session as a part of the data.

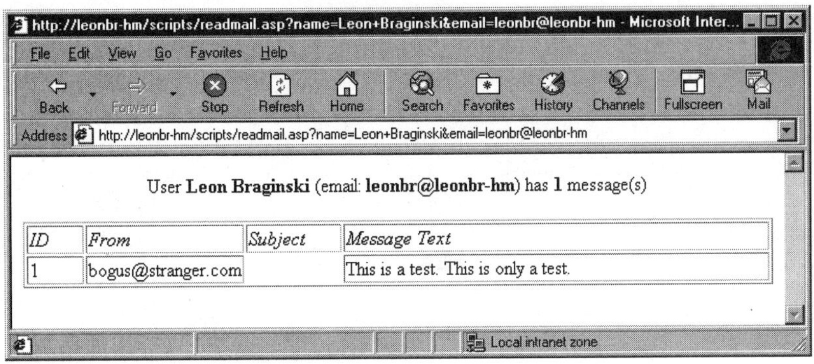

FIGURE 26.2

Using READMAIL.ASP to determine whether an e-mail message was received by the server.

The first step of the mail transaction is to identify the client. The client's machine name is the parameter of the HELO command. Here client identification was successfully accepted by the server, which responded with reply status code 250; this value was then sent back to the client. Remember that a first digit 2 in the status code indicates a positive completion result and a second digit 5 indicates the mail system category.

The next command, MAIL, indicates that the mail message should be mailed (not "sent" and not "sent or mailed") from *joe@cmpny.com*. Notice that the server does not perform any further validation of the sender's address. See how easy it is to fake e-mail from any sender? So don't panic if one day you get e-mail from *auditor@irs.gov* notifying you of problems with your tax return. It could be just a practical joke.

The mail recipient is indicated by the RCPT command. As mentioned, the IIS mail server does not provide individual mailboxes (remember that mail for any and all users is accepted and deposited in the \Mailroot\Drop directory by default); therefore, specifying any mailbox is perfectly all right. Other systems might be pickier, however. If a user does not have a mailbox on the server, the RCPT operation might fail.

One optional command returns a user's full name from the user's mailbox: VRFY. But even though IIS does support the VRFY command, it's not particularly useful because our simple SMTP mail server has no concept of user names and individual mailboxes. Here's how the VRFY command is used:

```
VRFY <leonbr>
250 <leonbr@leonbr-hm>
```

This command didn't return anything we didn't already know. It merely appended *@fully_qualified_domain_name* to the address. Our server's fully qualified domain name is a bit short because our machine is not configured to be part of a Domain Name System (DNS). If our server were part of the *runningiis.com* domain, VRFY would have returned an address such as *leonbr@leonbr-hm.runningiis.com*. Note also that some e-mail systems deliberately disable the VRFY and EXND commands as potential security holes that might infringe on a user's privacy.

Once the sender and recipient names are entered, we can finally get to the most important part of the message: the message data. We start by sending the DATA command. We then enter the text of our message, ending the message with a single period on a separate line. After the message data is entered, the client can safely notify the server that the mail transaction is complete by using the QUIT command.

In our sample, we simply entered some message text. In real life, the message should follow the specific syntax described in RFC 822, "Standard for the Format of ARPA Internet Text Messages." (ARPA stands for Advanced Research Projects Agency, part of the U.S. Department of Defense. ARPA created ARPANET, which was the predecessor of the Internet.) The correct mail message format is the subject of the next section.

Mail Message Format

Before we start examining RFC 822, let's take a look at a real mail message. In the preceding example, we sent a mail message to *leonbr@leonbr-hm* using a telnet connection. The server accepted the message and delivered it to the intended user. In the case of a user in the local domain, the server simply creates a text file in the \Mailroot\Drop directory. Here's how this text file looks:

```
x-sender:joe@cmpny.com
x-receiver: leonbr@leonbr-hm
Received: from EARTH - 192.155.1.2 by leonbr-hm with Microsoft
    SMTPSVC(5.5.1774.114.11);
    Tue, 3 Feb 1998 19:59:31 -0800
From: joe@cmpny.com
Bcc:
```

```
Return-Path: joe@cmpny.com
Message-ID: <001b63159030428LEONBR-HM@leonbr-hm>
Date: 3 Feb 1998 20:00:05 -0800

This is a test. This is only a test.
```

If you refer back to the telnet session, you'll see that the only data entered for the message that we sent was two sentences: *This is a test. This is only a test.* We did not enter any of the information you see here before our two sentences.

As in HTTP and NNTP, an SMTP mail message consists of two parts: the message headers and the message body. All these protocols use headers to transfer auxiliary information. The headers have the following format: *header name: header value*. The individual headers are separated by CR-LF pairs. Headers are separated from the body of the message by a null line (simply a CR-LF with no additional text).

Even when the client does not explicitly supply these headers, the server is smart enough to fill in the blanks. The X-sender, From, and Return-Path headers are derived from the MAIL FROM command that we sent prior to sending our message data. The X-receiver header gets its value from the RCPT TO command. RFC 822 specifies quite a few headers that serve a variety of purposes—for example, the Message-ID header uniquely identifies the message, the Return-Path header indicates where replies should be sent, and so on.

Some of the headers start with an *x-*, which indicates that the header is an extension—that is, it is not a part of the standard SMTP message format specification defined in RFC 822. Clients can use extension headers to pass extended information to the server, or, as in our example, servers can add these headers to the messages themselves. If you look carefully at your own mail messages, you might notice many extension headers.

In addition to the many optional headers described in RFC 822, some headers are mandatory. These mandatory headers specify the date, the source of the message, and the destination. In Outlook Express, we see these headers as the Date and From fields. If a client such as Outlook Express were to read our test message, the To field, denoting the destination, would be absent. If we had properly formatted our message, it would have included a To field before the message text. A number of other informative headers are available, such as the Subject, Carbon Copy (CC), and Blind Carbon Copy (BCC) headers. The CC and BCC headers indicate to whom a message should be copied and are not mandatory. Even though the Subject header can be omitted, just as we did in our example, its presence greatly simplifies the task of reading large quantities of e-mail.

NOTE

To learn more about the specifics of the SMTP message format, refer to RFC 822. A word of caution, however: the Backus-Naur Form (BNF) notation used in the RFC to describe the message format and syntax is not for the fainthearted.

Sending Your Message

At this point, you have the tools necessary to create any kind of elaborate e-mail message. So let's try sending a correctly formatted message via our telnet connection. This process is actually quite simple. The command sequence up to the DATA command is the same as it was in our last session. Only the text entered after the DATA command is changed to reflect the new headers, as shown here:

```
data
354 Start mail input; end with <CRLF>.<CRLF>
To: leonbr@leonbr-hm
Subject: test

Hello
.
250 001d92752010828LEONBR-HM Queued mail for delivery
```

Notice the empty line separating the last header (Subject) from the body of the message. This time we will ensure the proper formatting of the message by using Outlook Express rather than our custom ASP script. Figure 26.3 shows the test message in Outlook Express. As you can see, the To and Subject fields are correctly filled in.

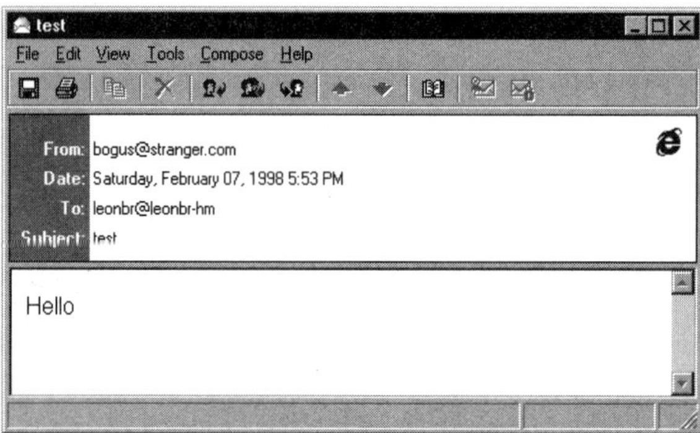

FIGURE 26.3

Using Outlook Express to display the To and Subject headers in the mail message.

NOTE

The IIS mail server stores all incoming mail in files with an .EML extension. When Outlook Express is installed, it associates EML files with Outlook Express. Therefore, by default EML files are opened by the Outlook Express mail program. You can also open EML files using Outlook Express by running MSIMN.EXE at a command line with the EML file's name as a parameter—for instance, D:\Program Files\Outlook Express\msimn.exe /eml:001d92752010828LEONBR-HM.eml.

We've reached the end of our discussion of SMTP, the last protocol covered in this book. Keep in mind that many more protocols are used over the Internet, however. Their complexity varies from a few supported commands to protocols similar to TCP itself. New protocols are constantly being created to accommodate new trends and technologies. Older protocols either are updated or become obsolete. Understanding protocols might not be an easy task (just try to read some of the RFCs and you'll see what we mean), but by having a deeper understanding of the mechanics of network applications such as IIS, you'll be able to take your applications to new heights.

Index

INDEX

Note: Italicized page references indicate figures or tables.

A

A tag, 602–3
Abandon method, 464
acceptPKCS7 method, 367
Access Control Entries (ACEs), 290
Access Control Lists (ACLs), 182, 290
AccessFlags property, 97
AccessFlags value, 99
access permissions, 72–73
AccessPerm property, 95, 97
access tokens, 291
ACEs (Access Control Entries), 290
ACID properties, 488
Ack property, 516
ACLs (Access Control Lists), 182, 290
ACTION attribute, 610
Active Directory Services Interface (ADSI), 101–3
active open, 650
Active Server Pages (ASP). *See also* transactional Active Server Pages (ASP)
- % and % delimiters, 440–41
- application, session, and page scopes, 450–55, *451*, *455*
- *Application* events, 465
- *Application* methods, 465
- *Application* object, 450–55, 456, 464–65
- applications, 76–78, *76*, *78*

Active Server Pages (ASP), *continued*
- calling IIS Admin objects from ASP scripts, 103
- components
  - ActiveX Data Objects (ADO), 469
  - Ad Rotator, 466–68
  - Browser Capabilities, 468–69
  - CDO for NTS, 472
  - Certificate Server request, config, and admin objects, 473
  - COM objects and, 475–80, *479*
  - Content Linking, 469–72, *471*
  - Counters, 472
  - defined, 465
  - IIS Admin objects, 473
  - Index Server query and utility objects, 473
  - introduced, 465
  - Posting Acceptor, 474
  - threading models and, 480–84, *481*, *482–3*
  - Tools, 472
  - transactional objects, 484
- debugging scripts, 484–85, *485*
- GLOBAL.ASA file, 451–55, *455*
- introduced, 5, 439–41, *442*
- manipulating pages
  - include directives, 444–45
  - introduced, 442
  - objects, methods, properties, and collections, 448–50
  - output directives, 443
  - processing directives, 443, *444*
  - writing your own procedures, 445–47

Active Server Pages (ASP), *continued*
  ObjectContext object, 456, 465
  PERMISSIONCHECK.ASP file, 309–10, *310*
  posted data, 646–47
  POSTINFO.ASP file, 203
  reading e-mail with ASP scripts, 262–64
  READMAIL.ASP file, 262–64
  Request collections, 456–58
  Request methods, 458–59
  Request object, 433, 455, 456–59
  Request properties, 456
  Response collections, 461
  Response methods, 461–62
  Response object, 433, 441, 448–50, 456, 459–62
  Response properties, 459–61
  scripts, 432–33
  searches with Index Server
    hit highlighting, 174, *175*, 176
    introduced, 167, *171*
    QUERY.ASP file, 167–74
  SENDMAIL.ASP file, 265–66
  Server methods, 462–63
  Server object, 449, 456, 462–63
  Server properties, 462
  Session collections, 463–64
  Session events, 464
  Session methods, 464
  Session object, 450–55, 456, 463–64
  Session properties, 463
  UPLDSMPL.ASP file, 201
  UPLOADN.ASP file, 203
  UPLOADX.ASP file, 203
Active Template Library (ATL), 105
ActiveX Data Objects (ADO), 469
AddHeader method, 461
add-ons. *See* FrontPage Server Extensions; Site Server Express
addresses
  IP (*see* Internet Protocol (IP) addresses)
  media access control (MAC), 30
  physical, 21
  pools of, 36
Address Resolution Protocol (ARP), 30
administration queues, 403
Admin page, 63, *63*
AdminQueue property, 516
ADO (ActiveX Data Objects), 469
Ad Rotator, 466–68
ADSI (Active Directory Services Interface), 101–3
alerts, sending, 135–37, *136*, *137*
AllocMem function, 577
AllowAnonymous registry key, 202
American Standard Code for Information Interchange (ASCII), 17, 18
annealing merges, 153, 155
anonymous access, 81–83, *82*
anonymous requests, 433
apartment model objects, 294, 482, *482*, 483–84, *483*
apartments and threads, 294
AppCreate method, 100, 102
AppendToLog method, 462
AppFriendlyName property, 99, 100
AppIsolated property, 99, 100
Application collections, 464
Application events, 465
application layer (OSI model), *15*, 18
Application methods, 465
Application object, 450–55, 456, 464–65

application programming interfaces (APIs)
asynchronous API calls in ISAPI extensions, 552–55
CreateProcess, 292
CreateProcessAsUser, 292, 293
CreateService, 300
DebugBreak, 305–6
ISAPI (*see* Internet Server API (ISAPI))
LogonUser, 293, 295
MessageBox, 305
Messaging Application Programming Interface (MAPI), 304
TerminateProcess, 303
application scope, 450, *451*
AppRoot property, 99
AppSpecific property, 515
AppWamClsid GUID, 99
AREA tag, 606–7
ARP (Address Resolution Protocol), 30
ARP utility, 48–49
ArrivedTime property, 517
ASCII (American Standard Code for Information Interchange), 17, 18
ASCII log files, 112, *112*, *113*
ASP. *See* Active Server Pages (ASP)
ASP object, 134
asynchronous requests, 513
ATL (Active Template Library), 105
AtlAdvise function, 107
Atomicity property, 488
attribute flags, 93
auditing, 318–21, *319*, *320*
authentication
Basic, 81–83, *82*, 314–16, *315*
forcing, 311–14, *312*, *313*
authentication, *continued*
introduced, 81–83, *82*, 247–48, 310–11, 433
NT LAN Manager (NTLM), 81–83, *82*, 315–16
schemes for, 314–16, *315*
using public/private key pairs for, 330
Automation, 448

B

Backup Domain Controllers (BDCs), 307
Backup method, 102
Backup/Restore Configuration option, 61
Backup Site Controller (BSC), 400
bandwidth counters, 128, *128*
base 64 encoding, 81
Basic authentication, 81–83, *82*, 314–16, *315*
BDCs (Backup Domain Controllers), 307
BinaryRead method, 458–59
BinaryWrite method, 462
bitmasks, 97
block ciphers, 327
blocking, 550
block mode, 667
Boolean operators, 155–56
Boot Protocol (BOOTP), 35
BORDER attribute, 600
broadcasts, 22, 31
Browser Capabilities component, 468–69
BSC (Backup Site Controller), 400
BSTR strings, 511
Buffer property, 459
buffers, 15
built-in objects, 449
byte-mode protocols, 23

C

cache, 31

CacheControl property, 459

CachedIsapi property, 90–91, *90*

caching counters, 127, *127*

callback functions for the Extension Control Block (ECB), 545–47, 548–49, *548*, *549*

Carrier Sense Multiple Access with Collision Detection (CSMA/CD), 19–20, 27–28, *28*

catalogs, 147, 182

CDO. *See* Collaboration Data Objects (CDO) for NTS Library

CELLPADDING attribute, 600

certificate authorities, 332, 334–35

certificate mapping, 343–47, *344*, *346*, *347*

Certificate Revocation Lists (CRLs), 335, 349

certificates, 332–33, *334*

Certificate Server
- certificate extensions, 373–74
- coordinating front-end and back-end interfaces, 374–78, *375*, *377*
- handling requests, 350–52, *350*
- installing, 352–56, *353*, *354*, *355*, *356*
- introduced, 349
- managing
  - administration, 362–64, *363*, *364*
  - command-line utilities, 364–65
  - installing certificate authority certificates, 359–60, *359*
  - introduced, 356, *357*
  - requesting client authentication certificates, 358, *358*
  - requesting server-side certificates, 360–62, *361*

Certificate Server, *continued*
- programming and scripting interfaces
  - back-end interfaces, 369–73
  - front-end interfaces, 365–69, *368*
  - introduced, 365

Certificate Server objects, 473

CERTREQ.EXE utility, 364–65

CERTUTIL.EXE utility, 364

CGI. *See* Common Gateway Interface (CGI)

CGITimeout property, 90–91, *90*

challenge/response authentication, 81–83, *82*

charting counters, 134–35, *135*

child authorities, 335

CiDaemon process, 152

classes, 99

Clear method, 462

ClientCertificate collection, 458

client scripting
- client-side scripting versus server-side scripting, 446
- introduced, 611–12, *612*
- JavaScript, 612–13
- VBScript, 614–15

client/server architecture
- introduced, 11–12
- three-tiered, 420–22, *421*, *422*
- two-tiered, 419–20, *420*

CloseKey method, 105

CoCreateInstance function, 371

CoCreateInstance method, 104, 107

CodePage property, 463

CoInitialize method, 104

Collaboration Data Objects (CDO) for NTS Library
  as ASP components, 472
  introduced, 262
  reading e-mail with ASP scripts, 262–64
  sending e-mail from Web pages, 264–66
collections
  Application, 464
  ClientCertificate, 458
  Contents, 463–64
  Cookies, 449, 458, 461
  defined, 448, 449, 615
  Form, 457
  forms, 615
  QueryString, 457
  Request, 456–58
  Response, 461
  ServerVariables, 456–57
  Session, 463–64
  StaticObjects, 464
COM (Component Object Model), 294
.com (commercial) domain, 45, *45*
Command object, 177
CommandText property, 177
CommitOrAbort method, 501, 503, 506
Common Gateway Interface (CGI). *See also* Internet Server API (ISAPI)
  applications
    creation, 532–35, *534*
    debugging, 535–36
    introduced, 423–24
    sample, 528–32, *530*, *531*, *532*
  internals, 528
  introduced, 4, 525–26
  invocation, 526
  thread pool configuration and, 527
COM objects, 448
completion ports, 430
Component Object Model (COM), 294
Computer Properties window, 412–13, *412*
condensed hit highlighting, 174, *175*
configuring the Web server. *See also* metabase
  Admin page, 63, *63*
  Backup/Restore Configuration option, 61
  Custom Errors page, 86, *87*, 88
  Default Web Site Properties window, 62, *62*. (*see also specific page name*)
  Directory Security page
    anonymous access and authentication control, 81–83, *82*
    introduced, 80–81, *80*
    IP address and domain name restrictions, 83–86, *83*, *84*, *85*, *87*
    secure communications section, 83
  Documents page, 79–80, *79*
  Home Directory page
    access permissions, 72–73
    application configuration, 74–78, *74*, *75*, *76*, *78*
    application settings, 73–74
    content control, 73
    introduced, 68, *69*
    other options, 78–79
    server variables and wildcards, 71–72, *71*
    share location, 69
    URL redirection, 70–71, *70*
  HTTP Headers page, 84–86, *84*, *85*
  introduced, 59–61, *60*, *61*
  ISAPI Filters page, 67–68, *68*
  Master Properties window, 61, 62, *62*
  Operators page, 65–66, *66*
  Performance page, 66–67, *67*
  Web Site page, 64–65, *64*

connection counters, 131, *131–32*
Connection object, 177
connector servers, 400
Consistency property, 488
Content Analyzer, 186–89, *187*, *188*, *189*
CONTENT attribute, 608
content control, 73
ContentIndexed property, 95
ContentIndex registry key, 148, *149*, 182
Content Linking component, 469–72, *471*
content ratings, 85–86, *85*
Contents collection, 463–64
–contents prefix, 157
ContentType property, 460
conversion log utility, 121
cookies, 638–40
Cookies collection, 449, 458, 461
COORDS attribute, 606–7
corpus, 146
CorrelationId property, 516, 517
counters
  bandwidth, 128, *128*
  caching, 127, *127*
  charting, 134–35, *135*
  connection, 131, *131–32*
  data transmission, 129, *129*
  performance, 125–26
  request, 129, *130–31*
  user logon, 132, *133*
Counters component, 472
Counters object, 453
Count method, *490*, 491
CreateFile function, 584
CreateInstance method, 107, *490*
CreateObject method, 170, 449, 463, 502, 506, 518
CreateProcess API function, 292, 434–35, 532
CreateProcessAsUser API function, 292, 293, 434–35, 532–35
CreateRecordSet method, 170
CreateService API, 300
critical sections, 579
CRLs (Certificate Revocation Lists), 335, 349
CSMA/CD (Carrier Sense Multiple Access with Collision Detection), 19–20, 27–28, *28*
Custom Errors page, 86, *87*, 88
Custom installation, 55, 56–57, *56*, *57*

D

DACLs (Discretionary Access Control Lists), 290
Data Encryption Standard (DES), 327
datagrams, 31
data link layer (OSI model), *15*, 16
data structures
  Extension Control Block (ECB)
    callback functions, 545–47, 548–49, *548–49*
    introduced, 542–45
  HTTP_FILTER_CONTEXT, 569
  METADATA_RECORD, 104, 105
Data Transfer Process (DTP), 653–54, *654*
data transmission counters, 129, *129*
Date function, 441, 442
dead letter queues, 402
DebugBreak API function, 305–6, 536
debugging
  CGI applications, 535–36
  ISAPI extensions, 561–62
  scripts, 484–85, *485*
  Windows NT services, 305–6
DebugOut function, 586–87

Default NNTP Site Properties window, 242, *242. See also specific page name*
default routes, 39
Default Web Site Properties window, 62, *62. See also specific page name*
default Web sites, 57–58, 60, *60*
DELETE method, 631, 645
Delivery property, 515
Delivery property page, 280–83, *282*
DenyRequest method, *368*, 378
DES (Data Encryption Standard), 327
descriptor codes, 667
desktop object, 298–99
desktop security, 298–99
DestinationQueueInfo property, 517
DHCP (Dynamic Host Configuration Protocol), 35–37, *36*, *37*
DHTML (Dynamic HTML), 617–20, *617*, *620*
dial-up connections, 26–27, *26*
digital signatures, 331–35
DirBrowseFlags property, 96, 97
directives
  include, 444–45
  output, 443
  processing, 443, *444*
Directory Security page
  anonymous access and authentication control, 81–83, *82*
  in FTP server, 229, *229*
  introduced, 80–81, *80*
  IP address and domain name restrictions, 83–86, *83*, *84*, *85*, *87*
  in NNTP service, 247–48, *248*
  secure communications section, 83
Directory Security property page, 284, *284*, *285*
DisableCommit method, *490*
Discretionary Access Control Lists (DACLs), 290
DllEntryPoint API function, 539
DllMain function, 539, 568, 593
DNS (Domain Name System), 44–47, *45*
!DOCTYPE declaration, 601
document digests, 331
document object, 615
Documents page, 79–80, *79*
domain accounts, 306–7
domain name restrictions, 83–86, *83*, *84*, *85*, *87*
Domain Name System (DNS), 44–47, *45*
domains, 44–47, *45*. *See also* name resolution
DTP (Data Transfer Process), 653–54, *654*
DUMPBIN.EXE utility, 562
Durability property, 488
Dynamic Host Configuration Protocol (DHCP), 35–37, *36*, *37*
Dynamic HTML (DHTML), 617–20, *617*, *620*
dynamic link libraries (DLLs)
  defined, 5
  DUMPBIN.EXE utility, 562
  filter, 150–52, *152*
  loading ISAPI extension DLLs, 539–41, *541–42*, 542
  MSPROXY.DLL, 438
  sample ISAPI DLL, 556–60, *558*, *559*, *560*
  SSPIFILT.DLL, 438
  word-breaker, 152
dynamic routing tables, 39

E

EBCDIC (Extended Binary Coded Decimal Interchange Code), 17, 18
ECB (Extension Control Block) structure
  callback functions, 545–47, 548–49, *548*, *549*
  introduced, 542–45

- *#echo* command, 426
- .edu (educational) domain, 45, *45*
- e-mail. *See* Simple Mail Transport Protocol (SMTP)
- *EnableCommit* method, *490*
- *EncryptAlgorithm* property, 515–16
- encryption. *See also* security
  - Data Encryption Standard (DES), 327
  - introduced, 323–26
  - Private Communication Technology (PCT), 338–39
  - public key
    - digital signatures, 331–35
    - introduced, 328
    - public key (RSA) algorithm, 330
    - public/private key pair, 328–30, *329*
  - RC2 block cipher, 327
  - RC4 stream cipher, 327
  - Secure Socket Layer (SSL), 335–38, *336*, 342, *343*
  - secure Web communication setup
    - certificate mapping, 343–47, *344*, *346*, *347*
    - introduced, 339
    - Key Manager, 339–42, *340*, *341*
    - SSL configuration options in the Management Console, 342, *343*
  - symmetric, 326–27, *327*
- *End* method, 462
- Enterprise Properties window, 408–10, *408–10*
- entity headers, 637–38
- *EnumNames* method, 510
- ephemeral ports, 655
- ESMTP (Extended SMTP), 697–700
- Ethernet, 19–20, 27–28, *28*
- events
  - Application, 465
  - defined, 448, 615
- events, *continued*
  - OnTransactionAbort, 491, 495, 496
  - OnTransactionCommit, 491, 495, 506
  - Session, 464
- event sinks, 105–8
- Event Viewer, 122–24, *123*, *124*, *125*
- *#exec* command, 426
- executable files, 5
- exit modules, 352
- expanded strings, 93
- expiration policies for NNTP service, 253–54, *254*
- *ExpiresAbsolute* property, 460
- *Expires* property, 460
- Extended Binary Coded Decimal Interchange Code (EBCDIC), 17, 18
- Extended Properties page, 112, *113*
- Extended SMTP (ESMTP), 697–700
- Extension Control Block (ECB) structure
  - callback functions, 545–47, 548–49, *548*, *549*
  - introduced, 542–45
- extension handlers, 351
- extension headers, 638

F

- *FileSystemObject* object, 449–50
- File Transfer Protocol (FTP)
  - connection management
    - active FTP semantics, 654–56
    - benefits of using multiple connections, 657–58, *657*
    - data connection, 653–54, *654*
    - introduced, 651–52, *652*, 653, *653*
    - passive FTP semantics, 656–57

File Transfer Protocol (FTP), *continued*
- data representation
  - file structure, 667
  - introduced, 665
  - transmission mode, 667–68
  - transmission types, 666
- ephemeral ports, 655
- implementation
  - introduced, 650
  - socket interface, 650
- introduced, 649–50
- logs in IIS log file format, 117–18
- properties, 222, *222*, *223*, 224
- service object, 134
- service security, 321
- using the FTP client, 658–62
- using the telnet client, 662–65
- well-known ports, 651

File Transfer Protocol (FTP) server
- configuration options
  - creating new sites, 215–18, *216*, *217*, *218*
  - creating virtual directories, 219–20, *219–20*
  - Directory Security page, 229, *229*
  - FTP Properties window, 220, *221* (*see also specific page name*)
  - FTP Site page, 224–25, *224*, *225*
  - Home Directory page, 228–29, *228*
  - introduced, 214–15, *214*
  - Messages page, 227, *227*
  - properties and inheritance, 222, *222*, *223*, 224
  - Security Accounts page, 225–27, *226*
  - testing configurations, 229–31
- installing, 213, *213*
- introduced, 211–12, *212*

File Transfer Protocol (FTP) server, *continued*
- managing programmatically
  - IIS Admin Base object, 233–36
  - IIS Admin objects, 232–33, *232*

File Upload Control, 199–203, *202*

FilterDirectories registry setting, 151

filter DLL, 150–52, *152*

FilterFilesWithUnknownExtensions registry setting, 151

filtering with Index Server, 150–53, *152*

FilterRetries registry key, 152

firewalls, 27

#flastmod command, 426

Flush method, 462

ForcedNetPathScanInterval registry setting, 150

Form collection, 457

forms collection, 615

FORM tag, 608–11, *609*

frames, 16

free-text queries, 157

free-threaded objects, 294, 482–84, *483*

FrontPage Server Administrator, 207–9, *207*, *208*, *209*

FrontPage Server Extensions. *See also* Site Server Express
- FrontPage Server Administrator, 207–9, *207*, *208*, *209*
- introduced, 204, *205*, 206–7, *206*

FTP. *See* File Transfer Protocol (FTP)

FTP Properties window, 220, *221*. *See also specific page name*

FTP server. *See* File Transfer Protocol (FTP) server

FTP Site page, 224–25, *224*, *225*

full hit highlighting, 174, *175*

full scans, 150

functions and subroutines, 447

G

gateways, 16–17, 37–40, *38, 39, 40*
GenerateCharacterization registry key, 152
GetAdvertisement method, 468
GetCertificate method, 365–67, 376
GetCRL method, *368*
GetDefaultFolder method, 264
GetDescription method, 369
GetExtensionVersion function, 424, 435, 436, 539, 540, 562, 579, 584–87
GetFilterVersion function, 567, 568, 574, 575
GetHeader function, 576
GetHttpExtension function, 595
GetLocation function, 200
GET method, 526, 610–11, *610*, 629, 645
GetObjectContext method, 501
GetObject function, 101, 103
GetProperty method, 510
GetRequestAttribute method, 372
GetRequestId method, 374
GetRevocationReason method, *368*
GetServerVariable function, 576–77
GetUserName API function, 531, 533
GLOBAL.ASA file, 451–55, *455*
global filters, 93, 437
.gov (government organization) domain, 45, *45*
group security identifiers (SIDs), 290
Groups page, 251, *251*

H

hash algorithms, 332
hash functions, 331
hash tables, 239
HEAD method, 629–30, 645
HEAD tag, 613
hit highlighting, 174, *175*, 176
home directories, hierarchy of, 58
Home Directory page
  FTP Server, 228–29, *228*
  NNTP service, 244–46, *245*
  Web server
    access permissions, 72–73
    application configuration, 74–78, *74, 75, 76, 78*
    application settings, 73–74
    content control, 73
    introduced, 68, *69*
    other options, 78–79
    server variables and wildcards, 71–72, *71*
    share location, 69
    URL redirection, 70–71, *70*
HOSTNAME utility, 48
HOSTS files, 41–42
HREF attribute, 602–3
HTML. *See* Hypertext Markup Language (HTML)
HTMLEncode method, 463
HTML tag, 439
HTTP. *See* Hypertext Transfer Protocol (HTTP)
HTTP-EQUIV attribute, 608
HttpExtensionProc function, 424, 425, 429, 430–31, 435, 436, 539, 541, *541*, 550–51, 552, 562, 579, 587–93
HTTP_FILTER_CONTEXT structure, 569
HttpFilterProc function, 567, 569–70, *570–71*, 571, 572–73, *572*, 574–75, 577
HTTP Headers page, 84–86, *84, 85*
HTX files in HTM/IDQ/HTX searches
  introduced, 158, *159, 166*
  QUERY.HTM file, 159–62
  QUERY.HTX file, 164–67
  QUERY.IDQ file, 162–64

hyperlinks, 599, 602–3
Hypertext Markup Language (HTML)
  A tag, 602–3
  ACTION attribute, 610
  administrative interface to Index Server, 179–80, *180*, *181*
  architecture
    embedded images, 602
    FORM tag, 608–11, *609*
    hyperlinks, 599, 602–3
    image maps, 603, 606–8, *606*
    introduced, 599–602, *601*
    META tag, 608
  AREA tag, 606–7
  BORDER attribute, 600
  CELLPADDING attribute, 600
  client scripting
    introduced, 611–12, *612*
    JavaScript, 612–13
    VBScript, 614–15
  CONTENT attribute, 608
  COORDS attribute, 606–7
  !DOCTYPE declaration, 601
  Dynamic HTML (DHTML), 617–20, *617*, *620*
  elements in version 4.0, *604–5*
  file servers, 4
  FORM tag, 608–11, *609*
  HEAD tag, 613
  HREF attribute, 602–3
  HTM/IDQ/HTX searches
    introduced, 158, *159*, *166*
    QUERY.HTM file, 159–62
    QUERY.HTX file, 164–67
    QUERY.IDQ file, 162–64
  HTML tag, 439
  HTTP-EQUIV attribute, 608
Hypertext Markup Language (HTML), *continued*
  IMG tag, 602
  INPUT tag, 609–10, 613
  Internet Service Manager, 56–57, *57*
  introduced, 439–41, *442*
  LANGUAGE attribute, 613
  MAP tag, 606–7
  META tag, 608
  METHOD attribute, 610
  NAME attribute, 608, 609–10
  objects, 615–16, *616*
  POST method, 504, 526, 610–11, *610*
  SCRIPT tag, 446–47, 613, 614
  SHAPE attribute, 606–7
  SPAN tag, 619
  SRC attribute, 602
  TABLE tag, 600
  TD tag, 600–601
  TITLE attribute, 602
  TITLE tag, 439, 600
  TR tag, 600–601
  TYPE attribute, 609–10
  VALUE attribute, 609–10
Hypertext Transfer Protocol (HTTP)
  DELETE method, 645
  details, 640–47, *641*
  GET method, 526, 610–11, *610*, 645
  HEAD method, 645
  introduced, 23–24, 27–28, *28*
  OPTION command, 640–41, 644
  overview
    connection management, 624–25
    credential management, 625–27
    HTTP and TCP/IP, 622–23, *622*
    introduced, 621–22
    request/response format, 623–24

Hypertext Transfer Protocol (HTTP), *continued*
POST method, 645
PUT method, 644–45
requests
DELETE method, 631
GET method, 629
headers, 631–33
HEAD method, 629–30
introduced, 627–28
OPTIONS method, 628–29
POST method, 630
PUT method, 630
TRACE method, 629
responses
cookies, 638–40
entity headers, 637–38
extension headers, 638
headers, 636–37
introduced, 633
status codes, 633, *634–36*, 636
TRACE command, 640–41, 644

I

IAB (Internet Architecture Board), 34
IActiveScript interface, 432
IANA (Internet Address Numbering Authority), 34
ICertAdmin interface, 368–69, *368*
ICertConfig interface, 365
ICertEncodeLongArray interface, 373
ICertExit interface, 352, 373
ICertPolicy interface, 351, 369–71
ICertRequest interface, 350, 352, 365–67
ICertServerExit interface, 373
ICertServerPolicy interface, 371–72
IDA files, 181
IDC (Internet Database Connector) scripts, 427–28, *428*
IDispatch interface, 105, 233
Id property, 517
IDQ. *See* Internet Data Query (IDQ) files
ID ranges in the metabase, 94–95, *94*
IEnumNames interface, 510
IGetContextProperties interface, 510
IIS. *See* Microsoft Internet Information Server (IIS)
IIS Admin Base object, 103–5, 233–36, 257
IIS Admin objects, 101–3, 232–33, *232*, 257, 473
IIsCertMapper interface, 345
IIsComputer object, 101, 102
IIsFtpServer object, 232, *232*
IIsFtpService object, *232*
IIsFtpVirtualDir object, *232*
IIsWebVirtualDir object, 102
image maps, 603, 606–8, *606*
IMapper interface, 200
IMG tag, 602
impersonation
introduced, 291–94, 434
launching CGI applications, 434–35
launching ISAPI applications, 435–36
returning static files, 434
tokens, 293
IMSAdminBase interface, 233
IMSAdminBase object, 107
IMSAdminBaseSink interface, 105–8
include directives, 444–45
incremental scans, 150
indexing with Index Server, 153–55

Index Server
administering
HTML administrative interface, 179–80, *180, 181*
introduced, 177–78
Management Console administrative interface, 178–79, *178*
query logging, 181
ASP searches
hit highlighting, 174, *175*, 176
introduced, 167, *171*
QUERY.ASP file, 167–74
catalogs, 182
configuration, 146
filtering, 150–53, *152*
HTM/IDQ/HTX searches
introduced, 158, *159, 166*
QUERY.HTM file, 159–62
QUERY.HTX file, 164–67
QUERY.IDQ file, 162–64
indexing, 153–55
installation, 147–49, *147, 149*
introduced, 145
memory required, 146
objects, 473
query language, 155–57
remote computers and, 183
resource requirements, 146
scanning, 149–50
security, 181–82
setting up, 146–49, *147, 149*
SQL searches, 176–77, *176*
Index Statistics page, 179, *180*
inheritance in the metabase, 90–91, *90*
Initialize method, 369
in-process applications, 308, 538
INPUT tag, 609–10, 613
installing components
Certificate Server, 352–56, *353, 354, 355, 356*
FTP server, 213, *213*
Index Server, 147–49, *147, 149*
MSMQ, 403–7, *404, 405, 406, 407*
MTS, 381–82, *382*
NNTP service, 238–40, *239, 240*
SMTP, 266–68, *266*
Web server, 55–57, *56, 57*
International Organization for Standardization (ISO) OSI model. *See* Open Systems Interconnection (OSI) reference model
Internet Address Numbering Authority (IANA), 34
Internet Architecture Board (IAB), 34
Internet connections, 52–54, *53*
Internet Database Connector (IDC) scripts, 427–28, *428*
Internet Data Query (IDQ) files in HTM/IDQ/HTX searches
introduced, 158, *159, 166*
QUERY.HTM file, 159–62
QUERY.HTX file, 164–67
QUERY.IDQ file, 162–64
Internet domain names, 44–47, *45*. *See also* name resolution
Internet Explorer objects, *617*
Internet Information Center (InterNIC), 34
Internet Information Server. *See* Microsoft Internet Information Server (IIS)
Internet Information Services Global object, 127–28, *127, 128*
Internet mailing lists, 669

Internet news delivery systems. *See also* NNTP service
- Internet mailing lists, 669
- introduced, 669
- news articles, 672–74, *673*, *674*
- news distribution, 670–72, *671*
- USENET news, 670

Internet Protocol (IP), 21–22
Internet Protocol (IP) addresses. *See also* machine names; name resolution
- classes of, 32–33, *33*
- decoding, 32–33, *33*
- dotted decimal notation, 32–33
- introduced, 21–22
- multiple, 211–12, *212*
- network masks and, 32, 33
- restrictions, 83–86, *83*, *84*, *85*, *87*
- uniqueness of, 34–35

Internet Server API (ISAPI). *See also* Common Gateway Interface (CGI)
- Extension Control Block (ECB) structure
  - callback functions, 545–47, 548–49, *548–49*
  - introduced, 542–45
- extensions
  - architecture, 536–37
  - asynchronous API calls in, 552–55
  - debugging, 561–62
  - introduced, 424
  - loading DLLs, 539–41, *541–42*, 542
  - sample DLL, 556–60, *558*, *559*, *560*
  - threads and, 549–52
- filters
  - advanced tasks, 581–82
  - architecture, 566

Internet Server API (ISAPI), filters, *continued*
  - defined, 565
  - implementation, 566–70, *570–71*, 571, 572–73, *572*
  - introduced, 437–38, 565
  - *SmartRedir* sample, 573–80
- IIS 4.0 and, 537–39
- introduced, 4, 536
- script interpreters
  - introduced, 582–83
  - *SSIDemo* sample, 583–96, *594*, *595*
- thread management
  - introduced, 429
  - I/O thread pool, 429–30
  - Web Application Manager (WAM) objects, 430–32, *431*
  - worker threads, 429

Internet Service Manager, HTML, 56–57, *57*
Internet Service Providers (ISPs), 29–30
InterNIC (Internet Information Center), 34
intranets, 29, 34–35
intrinsic objects, 449
IObjectContext interface, 491, 510
IObjectContext methods, 510
I/O thread pool, 429–30
IP (Internet Protocol), 21–22
IP addresses. *See* Internet Protocol (IP) addresses
ISAPI. *See* Internet Server API (ISAPI)
ISAPI Filters page, 67–68, *68*
IsCallerInRole method, *490*
IsClientConnected property, 459
IsInTransaction method, *490*
Isolation property, 488

ISO (International Organization for Standardization) OSI model. *See* Open Systems Interconnection (OSI) reference model
ISPs (Internet Service Providers), 29–30
IsSecurityEnabled method, *490*
IsValidCertificate method, *368*
isvalidyear function, 613, 614
Item method, *490*, 491
IUSR_*computername* account, 306–14, 317–18, 321, 433, 434, 533, 535, 539
IWAM_*computername* account, 306, 308, 309, 436, 539

J

JavaScript, 612–13
Journal property, 516
journal queues, 402

K

Key Manager, 339–42, *340*, *341*
key managers, defined, 351
keys, 90–91, *90*, 326, 329
KeyType property, 96

L

Label property, 515, 518
LANGUAGE attribute, 613
LANGUAGE property, 447
layered architecture, 12–14, *13*
layers, 11
LCID property, 463
library packages, 389–90
LMHOSTS files, 42–43, *43*
LoadLibrary API function, 536, 537
local accounts, 306–7
LocalAlloc API function, 584
local domains, 272
local filters, 93
Localhost object, 101
locally unique identifiers (LUIDs), 295
Local System account, 301–5, *302*
local systems accounts, defined, 70
Lock method, 465
log files
  ASCII, 112, *112*, *113*
  conversion log utility, 121
  custom logging modules, 121
  formats and naming conventions, 110–12
  FTP logs in IIS log file format, 117–18
  introduced, 109–10, *110*
  National Center for Supercomputing Applications (NCSA) common log file format, 118–19
  ODBC, 113–15, *113*, *114*
  Windows NT event log, 122–24, *123–25*
  World Wide Web Consortium (W3C) extended log file format, 119–21, *119–20*
  WWW logs in IIS log file format, 115–16
logging activity to files, 138, *139*
logging modules, custom, 121
Logging Properties dialog box, 112, *112*
logging queries in Index Server, 181
logon counters, 132, *133*
LogonSMTP method, 264
LogonUser API, 293, 295
LookupQueue method, 518
LUIDs (locally unique identifiers), 295

M

MAC (media access control) addresses, 30
machine names. *See also* name resolution
    HOSTS files, 41–42
    introduced, 40–41
    static mapping, 41
MAIL command, 695–96
mailing lists, 669
Mail Server. *See* Simple Mail Transport Protocol (SMTP)
Management Console interface, 59–60, *60*. *See also* metabase
Management Information Base (MIB) files, 140–43
manual scans, 150
MAPI (Messaging Application Programming Interface), 304
MapPath method, 462–63
mapping modules, 200
MAP tag, 606–7
marshaling, 480
masquerade domains, 281, *282*
master indexes, 153, 154
master merges, 153, 154–55
Master Properties window, 61, 62, *62*
MaxCharacterization registry key, 152
MaxFreshCount registry value, 155
MaxIdealIndexes registry parameter, 155
MaxMergeInterval registry parameter, 155
MaxPoolThreads registry key, 527
MaxShadowFreeForceMerge registry value, 155
MaxShadowIndexSize registry value, 155
MaxTimeToReachQueue property, 516
MaxTimeToReceive property, 516
MaxWordLists registry value, 154
MB_SERVICE_NOTIFICATION flag, 305
media access control (MAC) addresses, 30
merges, 153, 154–55
MessageBox API, 305
message-mode protocols, 23
message numbers, 673
Message Properties window, 414–15, *415*
message queues, 401–3
message queue scripts, 398–99
Message Queue Server. *See* Microsoft Message Queue Server (MSMQ)
Messages page, 227, *227*
Messages property page, 278–80, *279*
Messaging Application Programming Interface (MAPI), 304
metabase
    applications and
        event sinks, 105–8
        IIS Admin Base object, 103–5
        IIS Admin objects, 101–3
        introduced, 100
    defined, 66
    editing, 96–100, *97*, *98*, *99*, *100*
    entries, 93–94
    hierarchy
        introduced, 89–91, *90*
        keys, 90–91, *90*
        objects in, 92–93, *92*
        subkeys, 90–91, *90*
    ID ranges, 94–95, *94*
    inheritance in, 90–91, *90*
    manipulating, 96–100, *97*, *98*, *99*, *100*
    properties, 94–95, *94*
Metabase Editor, 96–100, *97*, *98*, *99*, *100*
Metabase property, 532–33, 535
METADATA_RECORD structure, 104, 105

META tag, 608
METHOD attribute, 610
methods
Abandon, 464
acceptPKCS7, 367
AddHeader, 461
AppCreate, 100, 102
AppendToLog, 462
Application, 465
Backup, 102
BinaryRead, 458–59
BinaryWrite, 462
Clear, 462
CloseKey, 105
CoCreateInstance, 104, 107
CoInitialize, 104
CommitOrAbort, 501, 503, 506
Count, 490, 491
Counters, 472
CreateInstance, 107, 490
CreateObject, 170, 449, 463, 502, 506, 518
CreateRecordSet, 170
defined, 448, 615
DELETE, 631, 645
DenyRequest, 368, 378
DisableCommit, 490
EnableCommit, 490
End, 462
EnumNames, 510
Flush, 462
GET, 526, 610–11, 610, 629, 645
GetAdvertisement, 468
GetCertificate, 365–67, 376
GetCRL, 368
GetDefaultFolder, 264
methods, *continued*
GetDescription, 369
GetObjectContext, 501
GetProperty, 510
GetRequestAttribute, 372
GetRequestId, 374
GetRevocationReason, 368
HEAD, 629–30, 645
HTMLEncode, 463
Initialize, 369
IObjectContext, 510
IsCallerInRole, 490
IsInTransaction, 490
IsSecurityEnabled, 490
IsValidCertificate, 368
Item, 490, 491
Lock, 465
LogonSMTP, 264
LookupQueue, 518
MapPath, 462–63
ObjectContext, 490–91
OpenKey, 105
OPTIONS, 628–29
POST, 504, 526, 610–11, 610, 630, 645
PublishCRL, 368
Put (ADSI), 103
PUT (HTTP), 630, 644–45
Receive, 519, 520
Redirect, 461
Request, 458–59
Response, 461–62
ResubmitRequest, 368, 378
RetrievePending, 376
RevokeCertificate, 368
Security, 490

methods, *continued*
Send, 265, 517, 519, 522
Server, 462–63
Session, 464
SetAbort, 491, 496, 501
SetCertificateExtension, 368, 372
SetComplete, 491, 496, 501
SetData, 105
SetInfo, 103
SetRequestAttributes, 368, 370
Shutdown, 369
ShutdownNotify, 106
SinkNotify, 106
Submit, 365–66, 374
TRACE, 629
Unlock, 465
URLEncode, 463
VerifyRequest, 369–71
Write, 448–50, 462
MIB (Management Information Base) files, 140–43
Microsoft Cluster Server, 393
Microsoft Internet Explorer objects, *617*
Microsoft Internet Information Server (IIS). *See also* networks
add-ons (*see* FrontPage Server Extensions; Site Server Express)
architecture, 423–24
dial-up connections, 26–27, *26*
features in version 4.0, 6
future of, 6–7
hierarchy, 57–59, 60–61
installation, 55–57, *56*, *57*
introduced, 3
OSI model layers and, *24*
setup, 55–57, *56*, *57*
subcomponents, 56–57, *57*
Microsoft Logging Properties dialog box, 112, *112*
Microsoft Management Console interface, 59–60, *60*. *See also* metabase
Microsoft Message Queue Explorer (MSMQ Explorer)
Computer Properties window, 412–13, *412*
Enterprise Properties window, 408–10, *408*, *409*, *410*
introduced, 407–8, *407*
Message Properties window, 414–15, *415*
Queue Properties window, 413–14, *414*
Site Properties window, 411, *411*
Microsoft Message Queue Server (MSMQ)
asynchronous requests and, 513
defined, 6
installing, 403–7, *404*, *405*, *406*, *407*
introduced, 397
managing
Computer Properties window, 412–13, *412*
Enterprise Properties window, 408–10, *408*, *409*, *410*
introduced, 407–8, *407*
Message Properties window, 414–15, *415*
Queue Properties window, 413–14, *414*
Site Properties window, 411, *411*
messages
introduced, 514–15
message properties set by the sender, 515–17
queues, 401–3
queue scripts, 398–99
receiving messages, 518–20, *520*
sending messages, 517–18
server roles, 399–401, *399*
transactional messaging, 520–23, *521*

Microsoft Script Debugger, 484–85, *485*

Microsoft Transaction Server (MTS). *See also* transactional Active Server Pages (ASP)
- defined, 6
- installing, 381–82, *382*
- introduced, 379–81
- ISAPI thread management and, 430–32, *431*
- managing
  - component configuration options, 391–92, *391*
  - computer configuration options, 392–95, *393*
  - introduced, 382, *383*, 384
  - packages, 380–81, 384–91, *384–89*
  - remote components, 395
- monitoring, 395–97, *396*, *397*

Microsoft Visual InterDev, 204

Microsoft Windows NT
- event log, 122–24, *123*, *124*, *125*
- security model, 296–97, *296*, *298*
- services
  - debugging, 305–6
  - introduced, 299, *300*
  - Local System account, 301–5, *302*
  - Service user account, 300, *301*

.mil (military) domain, 45, *45*

Minimal installation, 55

MinMergeIdleTime registry parameter, 155

MinSizeMergeWordLists registry value, 154

moderating newsgroups, 252

modulus, 324

monitoring performance. *See* Performance Monitor; Simple Network Management Protocol (SNMP)

MSMQ. *See* Microsoft Message Queue Server (MSMQ)

MSMQ Information Store, 401

MSMQMessage object, 517, 519, 522

MSMQQuery object, 518

MSMQQueueInfo object, 518

MSMQQueue object, 517, 518, 519

MSPROXY.DLL, 438

MSUSAGE.MDB database, 190–91, *190*

MTS. *See* Microsoft Transaction Server (MTS)

multihomed hosts, 38

multi-threaded apartments, 294

N

NAME attribute, 608, 609–10

named pipes, 292

name resolution. *See also* machine names
- Domain Name System (DNS), 44–47, *45*
- introduced, 30, 42
- LMHOSTS files, 42–43, *43*
- Windows Internet Names Service (WINS), 43–44, *43*

name spaces, 102

National Center for Supercomputing Applications (NCSA) common log file format, 118–19

NBF (NetBIOS Frames Protocol), 42

NCSA. *See* National Center for Supercomputing Applications (NCSA) common log file format

NDIS (Network Driver Interface Specification), 21

NetBIOS Frames Protocol (NBF), 42

.net (network provider) domain, 45, *45*

Network Driver Interface Specification (NDIS), 21

network layer (OSI model), *15*, 16–17
network masks, 32, 33
Network News Transfer Protocol (NNTP). *See also* NNTP service
 commands
  introduced, 675
  navigating through groups and articles, 678–84
  obtaining a list of, 677–78
  posting news, 684–85, *685*
  status response, 675–77, *676*
 control messages, 688–89
 introduced, 675
 news distribution between servers, 685
 receiving news using the *IHAVE* command, 685–86
  sending news to other servers, 686–88
networks. *See also* Microsoft Internet Information Server (IIS); Open Systems Interconnection (OSI) reference model; protocols
 basic truths about, 9–10
 broadcasts, 22, 31
 client/server architecture, 11–12, 19, *20*
 configuring, 47–52, *47*
 connections, 52–54, *53*
 domains, 44–47, *45* (*see also* name resolution)
 Ethernet, 19–20, 27–28, *28*
 gateways, 16–17, 37–40, *38*, *39*, *40*
 Internet Service Providers (ISPs), 29–30
 intranets, 29, 34–35
 layered architecture, 12–14, *13*
 layers, 11
 packets, 11
 routers, 16–17, 37–40, *38*, *39*, *40*
 serial connections, 20–21
networks, *continued*
 subnets, 16–17, 29, 31–32, 34–35
 Token Ring, 19–20, 24–26, *25*, 40, *40*
 zones, 44
NewMail object, 265, 266
news. *See* Internet news delivery systems; NNTP service
news articles, 672–74, *673*, *674*
NewsCrawlerTime registry value, 254
news distribution, 670–72, *671*
news feeds, 237
Newsgroup Properties window, 251–52, *252*
newsgroups, 237, 252
News Site page, 243–44, *244*
NNTP. *See* Network News Transfer Protocol (NNTP)
NNTP service. *See also* Internet news delivery systems; Network News Transfer Protocol (NNTP)
 configuration options
  corruption recovery, 255–56, *256*
  current sessions, 255, *255*
  Default NNTP Site Properties window, 242, *242* (*see also specific page name*)
  Directory Security page, 247–48, *248*
  expiration policies, 253–54, *254*
  Groups page, 251, *251*
  Home directory page, 244–46, *245*
  introduced, 240–41, *242*
  Newsgroup Properties window, 251–52, *252*
  News Site page, 243–44, *244*
  NNTP Settings page, 248–51, *249*
  Rebuild option, 255–56, *256*
  Secure Communications area, 246, *247*
  Security Accounts page, 253, *253*
  Virtual Directory page, 244–46, *245*

NNTP service, *continued*
directory structure, 239–40, *240*
installing, 238–40, *239*, *240*
introduced, 237–38
managing programmatically, 256–57
NNTP Settings page, 248–51, *249*
noise (stop) words, 153
NSLOOKUP utility, 50–52
NT LAN Manager (NTLM) authentication, 81–83, *82*, 315–16
NullSessionPipes registry value, 303, *304*
null sessions, 303
NullSessionShares registry value, 303, *304*
NumExpireThreads registry value, 254

O

object context, 380, 432, 489–91, *489*, *490–91*
ObjectContext methods, 490, *490–91*
Object Identifiers (OIDs), 139–41
object, IIS Admin Base, 103–5, 233–36, 257
objects
apartment model, 294, 482, *482*, 483–84, *483*
Application, 450–55, 456, 464–65
ASP, 134
built-in, 449
Certificate Server, 473
COM, 448
Command, 177
Connection, 177
Counters, 453
desktop, 298–99
document, 615
FileSystemObject, 449–50
free-threaded, 294, 482–84, *483*
objects, *continued*
FTP service, 134
HTML, 615–16, *616*
IIS Admin, 101–3, 232–33, *232*, 257, 473
IIsComputer, 101, 102
IIsFtpServer, 232, *232*
IIsFtpService, *232*
IIsFtpVirtualDir, *232*
IIsWebVirtualDir, 102
IMSAdminBase, 107
Index Server, 473
Internet Explorer, *617*
Internet Information Services Global, 127–28, *127*, *128*
intrinsic, 449
Localhost, 101
metabase hierarchy of, 92–93, *92*
MSMQMessage, 517, 519, 522
MSMQQuery, 518
MSMQQueue, 517, 518, 519
MSMQQueueInfo, 518
NewMail, 265, 266
ObjectContext, 380, 432, 456, 465, 489–91, *489*, *490–91*, 507–9, *509*, 511
presentation, 193–94
Query, 170
Recordset, 177
Request, 433, 455, 456–59
Response, 433, 441, 448–50, 456, 459–62
securable, 289
Server, 449, 456, 462–63
Session, 450–55, 456, 463–64
single-threaded, 480–81, *481*
synchronization, 579
threading models for, 480–84, *481*, *482*, *483*

objects, *continued*
transactional, 380, 484
Utility, 170
Web Application Manager (WAM), 430–32, *431*, 537–39
Web Service, 129, *129*, *130–31*, 131, *131–32*, 132–33, *133*
window station, 298–99
OBJECT tag, 453
octets, 32
ODBC log files, 113–15, *113*, *114*
OIDs (Object Identifiers), 139–41
OnTransactionAbort event, 491, 495, 496
OnTransactionCommit event, 491, 495, 506
OpenKey method, 105
Open Systems Interconnection (OSI) reference model
application layer, *15*, 18
data link layer, *15*, 16
HTTP and, 622
IIS layers and, *24*
introduced, 15, *15*
network layer, *15*, 16–17
physical layer, 15–16, *15*
presentation layer, *15*, 17
session layer, *15*, 17
transport layer, *15*, 17
operators, 155–56
Operators page, 65–66, *66*
Operators property page, 277, *278*
OPTION command, 640–41, 644
OPTIONS method, 628–29
.org (nonprofit organization) domain, 45, *45*
OSI model. *See* Open Systems Interconnection (OSI) reference model
out-of-process applications, 308, 538
OutputDebugString API function, 587
output directives, 443
owner security identifiers (SIDs), 290

P

–P variable, 71–72, *71*
package files, 390–91
packages, 380–81, 384–91, *384*, *385*, *386*, *387*, *388*, *389*, 431
packets, 11
page scope, 450, *451*
page-structured files, 667
passive open, 650
Path property, 96, 103
PCT (Private Communication Technology), 338–39
PDC (Primary Domain Controller), 307
PEC (Primary Enterprise Controller), 400
performance counters, 125–26
Performance Monitor
ASP object, 134
FTP service object, 134
Internet Information Services Global object, 127–28, *127*, *128*
introduced, 125–27, *126*
logging activity to files, 138, *139*
sending alerts, 135–37, *136*, *137*
simple chart reading, 134–35, *135*
viewing reports, 137, *138*
Web Service object, 129, *129–33*, 131–33
Performance page, 66–67, *67*
PERMISSIONCHECK.ASP file, 309–10, *310*

persistent connections, 622
physical addresses, 21
physical layer (OSI model), 15–16, *15*
PICS property, 460–61
PICS ratings, 85–86, *85*
PING utility, 49
pipelining, 622
pipes, named, 292
policy modules, 351
pools of addresses, 36
PoolThreadLimit registry value, 527
POP (Post Office Protocol), 260–61, *261*
ports
  defined, 650
  ephemeral, 655
  well-known, 651
POSTINFO.ASP file, 203
Posting Acceptor, 197–203, *201*, 474
POST method, 504, 526, 610–11, *610*, 630, 645
Post Office Protocol (POP), 260–61, *261*
presentation layer (OSI model), *15*, 17
presentation objects, 193–94
Primary Domain Controller (PDC), 307
Primary Enterprise Controller (PEC), 400
Primary Site Controller (PSC), 400
Priority property, 515
Private Communication Technology (PCT), 338–39
private queues, 401–2
privileges, 295–96, *295*
PrivLevel property, 515
processes, 4
processing directives, 443, *444*
properties
  AccessFlags, 97
  AccessPerm, 95, 97
  ACID, 488
  Ack, 516
  AdminQueue, 516
  AppFriendlyName, 99, 100
  AppIsolated, 99, 100
  AppRoot, 99
  AppSpecific, 515
  ArrivedTime, 517
  Atomicity, 488
  Buffer, 459
  CacheControl, 459
  CachedIsapi, 90–91
  CGITimeout, 90–91
  CodePage, 463
  CommandText, 177
  Consistency, 488
  ContentIndexed, 95
  ContentType, 460
  CorrelationId, 516, 517
  defined, 448, 615
  Delivery, 515
  DestinationQueueInfo, 517
  DirBrowseFlags, 96, 97
  Durability, 488
  EncryptAlgorithm, 515–16
  Expires, 460
  ExpiresAbsolute, 460
  FTP, 222, 223, 224
  Id, 517
  IsClientConnected, 459
  Isolation, 488
  Journal, 516

properties, *continued*
- *KeyType*, 96
- *Label*, 515, 518
- *LANGUAGE*, 447
- *LCID*, 463
- *MaxTimeToReachQueue*, 516
- *MaxTimeToReceive*, 516
- *metabase*, 94–95, 94
- *Metabase*, 532–33, 535
- *Path*, 96, 103
- *PICS*, 460–61
- *Priority*, 515
- *PrivLevel*, 515
- *Request*, 456
- *Response*, 459–61
- *ResponseQueueInfo*, 517
- *RUNAT*, 446
- *ScriptTimeout*, 462
- *SenderId*, 517
- *SenderIdType*, 517
- *SentTime*, 517
- *Server*, 462
- *ServerState*, 90, 91
- *Session*, 463
- *SessionID*, 463
- *SourceMachineGuid*, 517
- *Status*, 448, 459
- *Timeout*, 463
- *TotalBytes*, 456
- *Trace*, 516
- *UploadReadAheadSize*, 544
- *Win32Error*, 96

property value queries, 157

protocols
- Address Resolution Protocol (ARP), 30
- Boot Protocol (BOOTP), 35
- byte-mode, 23
- defined, 12, 621
- Dynamic Host Configuration Protocol (DHCP), 35–37, *36*, *37*
- FTP (*see* File Transfer Protocol (FTP))
- HTTP (*see* Hypertext Transfer Protocol (HTTP))
- Internet Protocol (IP), 21–22
- introduced, 621
- message-mode, 23
- NetBIOS Frames Protocol (NBF), 42
- NNTP (*see* Network News Transfer Protocol (NNTP))
- Post Office Protocol (POP), 260–61, *261*
- Reverse Address Resolution Protocol (RARP), 30
- Simple Network Management Protocol (SNMP), 139–43, *140*, *143*
- SMTP (*see* Simple Mail Transport Protocol (SMTP))
- Transmission Control Protocol (TCP), 22–23
- Transmission Control Protocol/Internet Protocol (TCP/IP), 21, 622–23, *622*
- User Datagram Protocol (UDP), 22

proxies, HTTP, 27–28, *28*

proximity operators, 156

PSC (Primary Site Controller), 400

public key (RSA) algorithm, 330

public key encryption
- digital signatures, 331–35
- introduced, 328
- public key (RSA) algorithm, 330
- public/private key pair, 328–30, *329*

public queues, 401–2
PublishCRL method, *368*
put command (FTP), 199
Put method (ADSI), 103
PUT method (HTTP), 630, 644–45

Q

–*Q* variable, 71–72, *71*
queries, 157
QUERY.ASP file, 167–74
QUERY.HTM file, 159–62
QUERY.HTX file, 164–67
QUERY.IDQ file, 162–64
query language in Index Server, 155–57
query logging in Index Server, 181
Query object, 170
QueryString collection, 457
Queue Properties window, 413–14, *414*

R

RARP (Reverse Address Resolution Protocol), 30
RAS (remote access service), 53
ratings, 85–86, *85*
RC2 block cipher, 327
RC4 stream cipher, 327
read-ahead buffers, 544
ReadClient API function, 546, 555
ReadFile function, 581
READMAIL.ASP file, 262–64
realms, 626
Rebuild option in NNTP service, 255–56, *256*
Receive method, 519, 520
Recordset object, 177
redirection, 70–71, *70*
Redirect method, 461
registry. *See also* metabase
  AllowAnonymous key, 202
  ContentIndex key, 148, 149, 182
  FilterDirectories setting, 151
  FilterFilesWithUnknownExtensions setting, 151
  FilterRetries key, 152
  ForcedNetPathScanInterval setting, 150
  GenerateCharacterization key, 152
  introduced, 89
  MaxCharacterization key, 152
  MaxFreshCount value, 155
  MaxIdealIndexes parameter, 155
  MaxMergeInterval parameter, 155
  MaxPoolThreads key, 527
  MaxShadowFreeForceMerge value, 155
  MaxShadowIndexSize value, 155
  MaxWordLists value, 154
  MinMergeIdleTime parameter, 155
  MinSizeMergeWordLists value, 154
  NewsCrawlerTime value, 254
  NullSessionPipes value, 303, 304
  NullSessionShares value, 303, 304
  NumExpireThreads value, 254
  PoolThreadLimit value, 527
  RestrictNullSessAccess value, 303
  SNMP and, 112
  UsePoolThreadForCGI value, 527
remote access service (RAS), 53
remote domains, 272
report queues, 403
Report Writer, 189–91, *190*, 193–97, *194–96*
request attributes, 370–71

Request collections, 456–58
request counters, 129, *130–31*
Request methods, 458–59
Request object, 433, 455, 456–59
Request properties, 456
Response, collections, 461
Response methods, 461–62
Response object, 433, 441, 448–50, 456, 459–62
Response properties, 459–61
ResponseQueueInfo property, 517
RestrictNullSessAccess registry value, 303
ResubmitRequest method, *368,* 378
RetrievePending method, 376
Reverse Address Resolution Protocol (RARP), 30
RevertToSelf function, 436
RevokeCertificate method, *368*
roles, 380–81
root authorities, 335, 359–60
routers, 16–17, 37–40, *38, 39, 40*
ROUTE utility, 50
routing domains, 285
routing servers, 400
routing tables, 38, 39
RSA (public key) algorithm, 330
RUNAT property, 446

S

–S variable, 71–72, *71*
SACLs (System Access Control Lists), 290
SAML command, 696
scanning with Index Server, 149–50
scheduling with Site Server Express, 196–97
schemas, 92–93
SCM (Service Control Manager), 299
scope, 147, 450, *451*
Script Debugger, 484–85, *485*
script files. *See also* client scripting
  ASP scripts, 432–33
  Internet Database Connector (IDC) scripts, 427–28, *428*
  introduced, 424
  ISAPI thread management
    introduced, 429
    I/O thread pool, 429–30
    MTS and, 430–32, *431*
    Web Application Manager (WAM) objects, 430–32, *431*
    worker threads, 429
  JavaScript, 612–13
  script maps, 425–26, *426*
  Server Side Includes (SSI), 425–26, *426*
  VBScript, 614–15
script interpreters
  introduced, 582–83
  SSIDemo sample, 583–96, *594, 595*
script maps, 425–26, *426*
SCRIPT tag, 446–47, 453, 613, 614
ScriptTimeout property, 62
searching. *See* Index Server
securable objects, 289
Secure Communications area, 246, *247*
Secure Socket Layer (SSL), 335–38, *336,* 342, *343*
secure Web communication setup
  certificate mapping, 343–47, *344, 346, 347*
  introduced, 339
  Key Manager, 339–42, *340, 341*
  SSL configuration options in the Management Console, 342, *343*

security. *See also* encryption
  Access Control List (ACL), 182, 290
  access permissions, 72–73
  access tokens, 291
  applications and, 308–10, *310*
  auditing, 318–21, *319*, *320*
  authentication
    Basic, 81–83, *82*, 314–16, *315*
    forcing, 311–14, *312*, *313*
    introduced, 81–83, *82*, 247–48, 310–11, 433
    NT LAN Manager (NTLM), 81–83, *82*, 315–16
    schemes for, 314–16, *315*
    using public/private key pairs for, 330
  descriptors, 290–91
  desktop, 298–99
  Directory Security page
    anonymous access and authentication control, 81–83, *82*
    in FTP server, 229, *229*
    introduced, 80–81, *80*
    IP address and domain name restrictions, 83–86, *83*, *84*, *85*, *87*
    in NNTP service, 247–48, *248*
    secure communications section, 83
  Directory Security property page, 284, *284*, *285*
  domain accounts and, 306–7
  FTP service, 321
  identifiers (SIDs), 290, 291
  impersonation
    introduced, 291–94, 434
    launching CGI applications, 434–35
    launching ISAPI applications, 435–36
    returning static files, 434
    tokens, 293

security, *continued*
  Index Server, 181–82
  introduced, 289
  local accounts and, 306–7
  logic overview, 317–18, *317*
  Operators property page, 277, *278*
  other access control mechanisms, 316
  privileges, 295–96, *295*
  Secure Communications area, 246, *247*
  Security Accounts page, 225–27, *226*, 253, *253*
  threads and, 294
  Windows NT security model, 296–97, *296*, *298*
  Windows NT services
    debugging, 305–6
    introduced, 299, *300*
    Local System account, 301–5, *302*
    Service user account, 300, *301*
Security Accounts page, 225–27, *226*, 253, *253*
Security method, *490*
SEND command, 695–96
SenderId property, 517
SenderIdType property, 517
sending alerts, 135–37, *136*, *137*
SENDMAIL.ASP file, 265–66
Send method, 265, 517, 519, 522
SentTime property, 517
serial connections, 20–21
Server methods, 462–63
Server object, 449, 456, 462–63
server packages, 389–90
Server properties, 462
server redirection, 70–71, *70*

- Server Side Includes (SSI), 425–26, *426*
- server-side scripting versus client-side scripting, 446
- *ServerState* property, *90*, 91
- *ServerSupportFunction*, 546–47, 548, *548–49*, 549, 551, 552–53, 555, 558, 572, 577
- server variables and wildcards, 71–72, *71*
- *ServerVariables* collection, 456–57
- Service Control Manager (SCM), 299
- services, 55
- Service user account, 300, *301*
- *Session* collections, 463–64
- *Session* events, 464
- *SessionID* property, 463
- session keys, 326, 329
- session layer (OSI model), *15*, 17
- *Session* methods, 464
- *Session* object, 450–55, 456, 463–64
- *Session* properties, 463
- session scope, 450, *451*
- *SetAbort* method, 491, *491*, 496, 501
- *SetCertificateExtension* method, *368*, 372
- *SetComplete* method, 491, *491*, 496, 501
- *SetData* method, 105
- *SetInfo* method, 103
- *SetRequestAttributes* method, *368*, 370
- setting up components
  - Certificate Server, 352–56, *353*, *354*, *355*, *356*
  - FTP server, 213, *213*
  - Index Server, 147–49, *147*, *149*
  - MSMQ, 403–7, *404*, *405*, *406*, *407*
  - MTS, 381–82, *382*
  - NNTP service, 238–40, *239*, *240*
  - SMTP, 266–68, *266*
  - Web server, 55–57, *56*, *57*
- SGML (Standard Generalized Markup Language), 601
- shadow indexes and merges, 153, 154
- *SHAPE* attribute, 606–7
- *Shutdown* method, 369
- *ShutdownNotify* method, 106
- SIDs (security identifiers), 290, 291
- Simple Mail Transport Protocol (SMTP)
  - CDO for NTS Library and
    - introduced, 262
    - reading e-mail with ASP scripts, 262–64
    - sending e-mail from Web pages, 264–66
  - checking the status of the SMTP service, 268–69, *268*
  - commands, 696–97
  - configuring sites
    - Default SMTP Site Properties window, 276 (*see also specific page name*)
    - Delivery property page, 280–83, *282*
    - Directory Security property page, 284, *284*, *285*
    - Messages property page, 278–80, *279*
    - Operators property page, 277, *278*
    - SMTP Site property page, 276–77, *277*
  - creating domains, 285–87, *286*, *287*
  - creating mail transactions
    - introduced, 700–702, *701*
    - mail message format, 702–4
    - sending messages, 704–5, *704*
  - delivering e-mail, 260–61, *261*
  - Extended SMTP (ESMTP), 697–700
  - implementation
    - introduced, 692–93
    - sending or mailing messages, 695–96
    - server command reply status codes, 693, 694, *694*, 695

Simple Mail Transport Protocol (SMTP), *continued*
installing, 266–68, *266*
introduced, 691
MAIL command, 695–96
overview, 691–92, *692*
POP3 and, 260–61, *261*
SAML command, 696
SEND command, 695–96
sending e-mail, 259–60
setting default domain properties
introduced, 271–72, *271, 272*
using smart hosts, 276
using STMP server to process mail, 272–75, *273, 274*
starting the SMTP Service Manager, 269–70, *270*
Simple Network Management Protocol (SNMP), 139–43, *140, 143*
single-threaded apartments, 294
single-threaded objects, 480–81, *481*
SinkNotify method, 106
sinks, 476
site filters, 437
Site Properties window, 411, *411*
Site Server Express. *See also* FrontPage Server Extensions
Content Analyzer, 186–89, *187, 188, 189*
File Upload Control, 199–203, *202*
introduced, 185, *186*
Posting Acceptor, 197–203, *201*
Report Writer, 189–91, *190,* 193–97, *194–96*
scheduling, 196–97
task automation, 196–97
Usage Import, 189–93, *190, 192, 193,* 196–97
WebPost APIs, 198, 199
Web Publishing Wizard, 197–203, *198*
Sleep API function, 535
smart hosts, 276
SmartRedir ISAPI filter sample, 573–80
SMTP. *See* Simple Mail Transport Protocol (SMTP)
SMTP Site property page, 276–77, *277*
SNMP (Simple Network Management Protocol), 139–43, *140, 143*
socket interface, 650
sockets, 65
source journaling, 402
SourceMachineGuid property, 517
source routing, 19
SPAN tag, 619
spiders, 191
SQL searches with Index Server, 176–77, *176*
SQL table definitions, *114*
SRC attribute, 602
SSI (Server Side Includes), 425–26, *426*
SSIDemo sample script interpreter, 583–96, *594, 595*
SSL (Secure Socket Layer), 335–38, *336,* 342, *343*
SSPIFILT.DLL, 438
Standard Generalized Markup Language (SGML), 601
static mapping, 41
StaticObjects collection, 464
static routing tables, 39
Status property, 448, 459
stop (noise) words, 153
stream ciphers, 327
stream mode, 667
strings, expanded, 93
structures. *See* data structures
subcomponents of IIS, 56–57, *57*
subkeys, 90–91, *90*

Submit method, 365–66, 374
subnets, 16–17, 29, 31–32, 34–35
subroutines and functions, 447
symmetric encryption, 326–27, *327*
synchronization objects, 579
System Access Control Lists (SACLs), 290
system queues, 403

T

TABLE tag, 600
target journaling, 402
task automation with Site Server Express, 196–97
TCP (Transmission Control Protocol), 22–23
TCP/IP (Transmission Control Protocol/Internet Protocol), 21, 622–23, *622*
TD tag, 600–601
telnet client, 662–65
TerminateExtension function, 539, 542, 551
TerminateFilter entry point, 567, 573
TerminateProcess API, 303
threading models for objects, 480–84, *481*, *482*, *483*
thread pools
  configuration and CGI, 527
  defined, 528
  I/O, 429–30
threads
  apartments and, 294
  defined, 5
  ISAPI extension behavior and, 549–52
  security and, 294
  WinProc, 481
  worker, 5, 429, 550–51
three-tiered client/server architecture, 420–22, *421*, *422*
Timeout property, 463
TITLE attribute, 602
TITLE tag, 439, 600
Today function, 447
Token Ring, 19–20, 24–26, *25*, 40, *40*
tokens, 20
Tools component, 472
TotalBytes property, 456
TRACE command, 640–41, 644
TRACE method, 629
Trace property, 516
TRACERT utility, 49–50
transactional Active Server Pages (ASP). *See also* Microsoft Transaction Server (MTS)
  C/C++ components, 510
  introduced, 487, 492–93, *494*
  ObjectContext object and, 489–91, *489*, *490–91*
  transacting components called from ASP
    calling transactional components from ASP, 502–7, *507*
    creating transactional components, 500–502, *502*
    introduced, 500
    using built-in ASP objects from *ObjectContext*, 507–9, *509*
  transaction directive attributes, 494, *494*, 495–96, *496*
  transactions using ADO from ASP, 497–500
transactional messaging, 520–23, *521*
transactional objects, 380, 484
@*TRANSACTION* directive, 490, 492, 494, *494*, 495, 499
transaction queues, 402–3

transactions, 487–89
Transaction Server. *See* Microsoft Transaction Server (MTS)
Transmission Control Protocol (TCP), 22–23
Transmission Control Protocol/Internet Protocol (TCP/IP), 21, 622–23, *622*
TransmitFile API, 553–55
transport layer (OSI model), *15*, 17
traps, 139
TR tag, 600–601
two-tiered client/server architecture, 419–20, *420*
TYPE attribute, 609–10
Typical installation, 55, 56

U

UDP (User Datagram Protocol), 22
Unlock method, 465
UPLDSMPL.ASP file, 201
UPLOADN.ASP file, 203
UploadReadAheadSize property, 544
UPLOADX.ASP file, 203
URLEncode method, 463
URL redirection, 70–71, *70*
Usage Import, 189–93, *190*, *192*, *193*, 196–97
USENET news, 670
UsePoolThreadForCGI registry value, 527
User Datagram Protocol (UDP), 22
user logon counters, 132, *133*
user state, 5
user types, 94
Utility object, 170

V

–*V* variable, 71–72, *71*
VALUE attribute, 609–10
VBScript, 614–15
vector space queries, 157
VerifyRequest method, 369–71
viewing reports, 137, *138*
virtual circuits, 651
virtual directories
  creating with FTP server, 219–20, *219*, *220*
  hierarchy, 58–59
Virtual Directory page, 244–46, *245*
Virtual Root Data page, 180, *181*
virtual root (VRoot) properties, 96–100, *97*, *98*, *100*
virtual servers, 93
Visual InterDev, 204
VRoot (virtual root) properties, 96–100, *97*, *98*, *100*

W

W3C (World Wide Web Consortium) extended log file format, 119–21, *119–20*
Web Application Manager (WAM) objects, 430–32, *431*, 537–39
Web farm, 200
WebMap, 186, 187
WebPost APIs, 198, 199
Web Publishing Wizard, 197–203, *198*
Web server
  applications (*see* Common Gateway Interface (CGI); Internet Server API (ISAPI))
  configuration (*see* configuring the Web server)
  hierarchy, 57
  installation, 55–57, *56*, *57*
  setup, 55–57, *56*, *57*

Web Service object, 129, *129*, *130–31*, 131, *131–32*, 132–33, *133*
Web Site page, 64–65, *64*
Web sites
  administration, 57–58, 60, *60*
  default, 57–58, 60, *60*
  hierarchy, 57–58
Weekday function, 441
WeekDayName function, 441
well-known ports, 651
wildcard operators, 156
Win32Error property, 96
Windows Internet Names Service (WINS), 43–44, *43*
Windows NT. *See* Microsoft Windows NT
Windows Scripting Host (WSH), 256
window station object, 298–99
WinProc thread, 481
WINS (Windows Internet Names Service), 43–44, *43*
word-breaker DLL, 152
word lists, 154
worker threads, 5, 429, 550–51
World Wide Web Consortium (W3C) extended log file format, log files, 119–21, *119–20*
WpPost API function, 199
WriteClient function, 546, 552–53, 587–88
WriteFile function, 555
Write method, 448–50, 462
WSH (Windows Scripting Host), 256
WWW logs in IIS log file format, 115–16

X

X.500, 334
Xenroll control, 367

Z

zones, 44

Matthew Powell

Matthew Powell is a support engineer for Microsoft's Developer Support organization in Bellevue, Washington, where he has been helping developers of Microsoft Windows applications with their network and Internet programming questions for the last four years. Before that, he worked in Microsoft's Corporate Network Support group, where he supported early versions of Windows NT and OS/2 LAN Manager. Prior to his career at Microsoft, Powell administered a variety of PC networks while working for Electronic Data Systems in Plano, Texas.

Powell got his M.S. in Theoretical Mathematics from Florida State University in 1988. The four years before his life in Florida were spent in the seemingly contradictory pursuits of a bachelor's degree in Mathematics and a bachelor's degree in English. Whitman College in Walla Walla, Washington, awarded the two degrees in 1986.

Together Powell and Braginski have authored articles for the *Microsoft Systems Journal* and *Microsoft Interactive Developer* magazine. Powell has also written a number of articles for *NT Developer* and is a constant contributor to the Microsoft Knowledge Base.

Matt married his wife, Cindy, six days after they both graduated from Whitman College, and they have since become the proud parents of six beautiful children: Katie, Alyssa, McKenna, Tanner, Nole, and Maylynn.

Leonid Braginski

Leonid Braginski started his programming career in 1989 at the Moscow Institute of Civil Engineering in what was then Moscow, USSR. After his high school graduation, he had no idea what field to study but eventually began learning about computers and realized that they were his future. Braginski's initial understanding of Microsoft was that it was a mysterious word that came up on the screen of his school's PC/XT 8088 every time it was rebooted.

Braginski came to the United States in 1991. Here he discovered that Pascal and Fortran were not particularly popular anymore, and he decided to go back to school. While studying at California State University at Northridge, Braginski did some Unix network programming and network administration for an Internet service provider in the Los Angeles area. This work was his entrance into the world of the Internet.

Braginski joined Microsoft in 1995 and presently works on the Internet Server team in Microsoft's Developer Support group. He has coauthored several articles in various computer magazines and is a frequent contributor to the Microsoft Knowledge Base. He has also authored a number of the samples in the Microsoft Platform SDK, including HTTPDUMP, whose code has been reused in dozens of articles, samples, and other sources of information.

When Braginski isn't working, he spends his time climbing in the Cascade Mountains of Washington. And he is still trying to figure out how the words "a", "an", and "the" are used in English because there is no equivalent in his native Russian.

The manuscript for this book was prepared and submitted to Microsoft Press in electronic form. Text files were prepared using Microsoft Word 7.0 for Windows 95. Pages were composed by Microsoft Press using Adobe PageMaker 6.0 for Windows 95, with text in Palatino and display type in Emigre BaseNine. Composed pages were delivered to the printer as electronic prepress files.

Manuscript Editor
Jennifer Harris

Principal Compositor
Elizabeth Hansford

Principal Proofreader
Pamela Buitrago

Indexer
Hugh Maddocks

Electronic Artist
Travis Beaven

Cover Graphic Designer
Greg Hickman

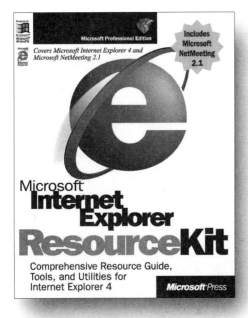

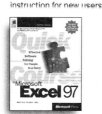

MICROSOFT LICENSE AGREEMENT

(*Running Microsoft® Internet Information Server* – Book Companion CD)

IMPORTANT—READ CAREFULLY: This Microsoft End-User License Agreement ("EULA") is a legal agreement between you (either an individual or an entity) and Microsoft Corporation for the Microsoft product identified above, which includes computer software and may include associated media, printed materials, and "online" or electronic documentation ("SOFTWARE PRODUCT"). Any component included within the SOFTWARE PRODUCT that is accompanied by a separate End-User License Agreement shall be governed by such agreement and not the terms set forth below. By installing, copying or otherwise using the SOFTWARE PRODUCT, you agree to be bound by the terms of this EULA. If you do not agree to the terms of this EULA, you are not authorized to install, copy or otherwise use the SOFTWARE PRODUCT; you may, however, return the SOFTWARE PRODUCT, along with all printed materials and other items that form a part of the Microsoft product that includes the SOFTWARE PRODUCT, to the place you obtained them for a full refund.

The SOFTWARE PRODUCT is protected by United States copyright laws and international copyright treaties, as well as other intellectual property laws and treaties. The SOFTWARE PRODUCT is licensed, not sold.

1. **GRANT OF LICENSE.** This EULA grants you the following rights:

   a. **Software Product.** You may install and use one copy of the SOFTWARE PRODUCT on a single computer. The primary user of the computer on which the SOFTWARE PRODUCT is installed may make a second copy for his or her exclusive use on a portable computer.

   b. **Storage/Network Use.** You may also store or install a copy of the SOFTWARE PRODUCT on a storage device, such as a network server, used only to install or run the SOFTWARE PRODUCT on your other computers over an internal network; however, you must acquire and dedicate a license for each separate computer on which the SOFTWARE PRODUCT is installed or run from the storage device. A license for the SOFTWARE PRODUCT may not be shared or used concurrently on different computers.

   c. **License Pak.** If you have acquired this EULA in a Microsoft License Pak, you may make the number of additional copies of the computer software portion of the SOFTWARE PRODUCT authorized on the printed copy of this EULA, and you may use each copy in the manner specified above. You are also entitled to make a corresponding number of secondary copies for portable computer use as specified above.

   d. **Sample Code.** Solely with respect to portions, if any, of the SOFTWARE PRODUCT that are identified within the SOFTWARE PRODUCT as sample code (the "SAMPLE CODE"):

   i. **Use and Modification.** Microsoft grants you the right to use and modify the source code version of the SAMPLE CODE, *provided* you comply with subsection (d)(iii) below. You may not distribute the SAMPLE CODE, or any modified version of the SAMPLE CODE, in source code form.

   ii. **Redistributable Files.** Provided you comply with subsection (d)(iii) below, Microsoft grants you a nonexclusive, royalty-free right to reproduce and distribute the object code version of the SAMPLE CODE and of any modified SAMPLE CODE, other than SAMPLE CODE, or any modified version thereof, designated as not redistributable in the Readme file that forms a part of the SOFTWARE PRODUCT (the "Non-Redistributable Sample Code"). All SAMPLE CODE other than the Non-Redistributable Sample Code is collectively referred to as the "REDISTRIBUTABLES".

   iii. **Redistribution Requirements.** If you redistribute the REDISTRIBUTABLES, you agree to: (i) distribute the REDISTRIBUTABLES in object code form only in conjunction with and as a part of your software application product; (ii) not use Microsoft's name, logo, or trademarks to market your software application product; (iii) include a valid copyright notice on your software application product; (iv) indemnify, hold harmless, and defend Microsoft from and against any claims or lawsuits, including attorney's fees, that arise or result from the use or distribution of your software application product; and (v) not permit further distribution of the REDISTRIBUTABLES by your end user. Contact Microsoft for the applicable royalties due and other licensing terms for all other uses and/or distribution of the REDISTRIBUTABLES.

2. **DESCRIPTION OF OTHER RIGHTS AND LIMITATIONS.**

   - **Limitations on Reverse Engineering, Decompilation, and Disassembly.** You may not reverse engineer, decompile, or disassemble the SOFTWARE PRODUCT, except and only to the extent that such activity is expressly permitted by applicable law notwithstanding this limitation.
   - **Separation of Components.** The SOFTWARE PRODUCT is licensed as a single product. Its component parts may not be separated for use on more than one computer.
   - **Rental.** You may not rent, lease or lend the SOFTWARE PRODUCT.

- **Support Services.** Microsoft may, but is not obligated to, provide you with support services related to the SOFTWARE PRODUCT ("Support Services"). Use of Support Services is governed by the Microsoft policies and programs described in the user manual, in "on line" documentation and/or other Microsoft-provided materials. Any supplemental software code provided to you as part of the Support Services shall be considered part of the SOFTWARE PRODUCT and subject to the terms and conditions of this EULA. With respect to technical information you provide to Microsoft as part of the Support Services, Microsoft may use such information for its business purposes, including for product support and development. Microsoft will not utilize such technical information in a form that personally identifies you.
- **Software Transfer.** You may permanently transfer all of your rights under this EULA, provided you retain no copies, you transfer all of the SOFTWARE PRODUCT (including all component parts, the media and printed materials, any upgrades, this EULA, and, if applicable, the Certificate of Authenticity), **and** the recipient agrees to the terms of this EULA.
- **Termination.** Without prejudice to any other rights, Microsoft may terminate this EULA if you fail to comply with the terms and conditions of this EULA. In such event, you must destroy all copies of the SOFTWARE PRODUCT and all of its component parts.

3. **COPYRIGHT.** All title and copyrights in and to the SOFTWARE PRODUCT (including but not limited to any images, photographs, animations, video, audio, music, text, SAMPLE CODE, REDISTRIBUTABLES, and "applets" incorporated into the SOFTWARE PRODUCT), and any copies of the SOFTWARE PRODUCT are owned by Microsoft or its suppliers. The SOFTWARE PRODUCT is protected by copyright laws and international treaty provisions. Therefore, you must treat the SOFTWARE PRODUCT like any other copyrighted material **except** that you may install the SOFTWARE PRODUCT on a single computer provided you keep the original solely for backup or archival purposes. You may not copy the printed materials accompanying the SOFTWARE PRODUCT.

4. **U.S. GOVERNMENT RESTRICTED RIGHTS.** The SOFTWARE PRODUCT and documentation are provided with RESTRICTED RIGHTS. Use, duplication, or disclosure by the Government is subject to restrictions as set forth in subparagraph (c)(1)(ii) of the Rights in Technical Data and Computer Software clause at DFARS 252.227-7013 or subparagraphs (c)(1) and (2) of the Commercial Computer Software—Restricted Rights at 48 CFR 52.227-19, as applicable. Manufacturer is Microsoft Corporation/One Microsoft Way/Redmond, WA 98052-6399.

5. **EXPORT RESTRICTIONS.** You agree that you will not export or re-export the SOFTWARE PRODUCT, any part thereof, or any process or service that is the direct product of the SOFTWARE PRODUCT (the foregoing collectively referred to as the "Restricted Components"), to any country, person, entity or end user subject to U.S. export restrictions. You specifically agree not to export or re-export any of the Restricted Components (i) to any country to which the U.S. has embargoed or restricted the export of goods or services, which currently include, but are not necessarily limited to Cuba, Iran, Iraq, Libya, North Korea, Sudan and Syria, or to any national of any such country, wherever located, who intends to transmit or transport the Restricted Components back to such country; (ii) to any end-user who you know or have reason to know will utilize the Restricted Components in the design, development or production of nuclear, chemical or biological weapons; or (iii) to any end-user who has been prohibited from participating in U.S. export transactions by any federal agency of the U.S. government. You warrant and represent that neither the BXA nor any other U.S. federal agency has suspended, revoked or denied your export privileges.

DISCLAIMER OF WARRANTY

NO WARRANTIES OR CONDITIONS. MICROSOFT EXPRESSLY DISCLAIMS ANY WARRANTY OR CONDITION FOR THE SOFTWARE PRODUCT. THE SOFTWARE PRODUCT AND ANY RELATED DOCUMENTATION IS PROVIDED "AS IS" WITHOUT WARRANTY OR CONDITION OF ANY KIND, EITHER EXPRESS OR IMPLIED, INCLUDING, WITHOUT LIMITATION, THE IMPLIED WARRANTIES OF MERCHANTABILITY, FITNESS FOR A PARTICULAR PURPOSE, OR NONINFRINGEMENT. THE ENTIRE RISK ARISING OUT OF USE OR PERFORMANCE OF THE SOFTWARE PRODUCT REMAINS WITH YOU.

LIMITATION OF LIABILITY. TO THE MAXIMUM EXTENT PERMITTED BY APPLICABLE LAW, IN NO EVENT SHALL MICROSOFT OR ITS SUPPLIERS BE LIABLE FOR ANY SPECIAL, INCIDENTAL, INDIRECT, OR CONSEQUENTIAL DAMAGES WHATSOEVER (INCLUDING, WITHOUT LIMITATION, DAMAGES FOR LOSS OF BUSINESS PROFITS, BUSINESS INTERRUPTION, LOSS OF BUSINESS INFORMATION, OR ANY OTHER PECUNIARY LOSS) ARISING OUT OF THE USE OF OR INABILITY TO USE THE SOFTWARE PRODUCT OR THE PROVISION OF OR FAILURE TO PROVIDE SUPPORT SERVICES, EVEN IF MICROSOFT HAS BEEN ADVISED OF THE POSSIBILITY OF SUCH DAMAGES. IN ANY CASE, MICROSOFT'S ENTIRE LIABILITY UNDER ANY PROVISION OF THIS EULA SHALL BE LIMITED TO THE GREATER OF THE AMOUNT ACTUALLY PAID BY YOU FOR THE SOFTWARE PRODUCT OR US$5.00; PROVIDED HOWEVER, IF YOU HAVE ENTERED INTO A MICROSOFT SUPPORT SERVICES AGREEMENT, MICROSOFT'S ENTIRE LIABILITY REGARDING SUPPORT SERVICES SHALL BE GOVERNED BY THE TERMS OF THAT AGREEMENT. BECAUSE SOME STATES AND JURISDICTIONS DO NOT ALLOW THE EXCLUSION OR LIMITATION OF LIABILITY, THE ABOVE LIMITATION MAY NOT APPLY TO YOU.

MISCELLANEOUS

This EULA is governed by the laws of the State of Washington USA, except and only to the extent that applicable law mandates governing law of a different jurisdiction.

Should you have any questions concerning this EULA, or if you desire to contact Microsoft for any reason, please contact the Microsoft subsidiary serving your country, or write: Microsoft Sales Information Center/One Microsoft Way/ Redmond, WA 98052-6399.

Register Today!

SUPER CROWN #786

```
05/23/00   09:30    E         16      23061
   EVERYTHING DISCOUNTED, EVERY DAY
   PUBLISHER                CROWN    CROWN
   PRICE                    SAVINGS  PRICE
CD-OPERA D'ORO
  1@   9.99 1572268379       0%        9.99
CD-OPERA D'ORO
  1@   9.99 1572268379       0%        9.99
CD-OPERA D'ORO
  1@   9.99 1572268379       0%        9.99
CD-OPERA D'ORO
  1@   9.99 1572268379       0%        9.99
CD-OPERA D'ORO
  1@   9.99 1572268379       0%        9.99
CD-OPERA D'ORO
  1@   9.99 1572268379       0%        9.99
RUNNING MS INTERNET INF
  1@  39.99 1572315857      10%       35.99
APACHE DEFINITIVE GD W/
  1@  34.95 1565925289      10%       31.46
SUBTOTAL                         $   127.39
SALES TAX @  8.75%               $    11.15
TOTAL                            $   138.54
TENDERED CHARGE                  $   138.54
4782006001946238   12/00 APPROVAL  938480

   YOUR SAVINGS AT CROWN... $ 7.49
```

Return this

t® *Internet Information Server*

stration card for

osoft Press® catalog

ion below and mail postage-free. Please mail only the bottom half of this page.

NG MICROSOFT® NFORMATION SERVER

Owner Registration Card

NAME

INSTITUTION OR COMPANY NAME

ADDRESS

CITY STATE ZIP

Microsoft® Press

Quality Computer Books

For a free catalog of
Microsoft Press® products, call
1-800-MSPRESS